Lecture Notes in Computer Science　9187

Commenced Publication in 1973
Founding and Former Series Editors:
Gerhard Goos, Juris Hartmanis, and Jan van Leeuwen

Editorial Board

More information about this series at http://www.springer.com/series/7409

Aaron Marcus (Ed.)

Design, User Experience, and Usability

Users and Interactions

4th International Conference, DUXU 2015
Held as Part of HCI International 2015
Los Angeles, CA, USA, August 2–7, 2015
Proceedings, Part II

 Springer

Editor
Aaron Marcus
Aaron Marcus and Associates
Berkeley, CA
USA

ISSN 0302-9743   ISSN 1611-3349   (electronic)
Lecture Notes in Computer Science
ISBN 978-3-319-20897-8   ISBN 978-3-319-20898-5   (eBook)
DOI 10.1007/978-3-319-20898-5

Library of Congress Control Number: 2015942820

LNCS Sublibrary: SL3 – Information Systems and Applications, incl. Internet/Web, and HCI

Springer Cham Heidelberg New York Dordrecht London

Printed on acid-free paper

Springer International Publishing AG Switzerland is part of Springer Science+Business Media
(www.springer.com)

Foreword

The 17th International Conference on Human-Computer Interaction, HCI International 2015, was held in Los Angeles, CA, USA, during 2–7 August 2015. The event incorporated the 15 conferences/thematic areas listed on the following page.

A total of 4843 individuals from academia, research institutes, industry, and governmental agencies from 73 countries submitted contributions, and 1462 papers and 246 posters have been included in the proceedings. These papers address the latest research and development efforts and highlight the human aspects of design and use of computing systems. The papers thoroughly cover the entire field of Human-Computer Interaction, addressing major advances in knowledge and effective use of computers in a variety of application areas. The volumes constituting the full 28-volume set of the conference proceedings are listed on pages VII and VIII.

I would like to thank the Program Board Chairs and the members of the Program Boards of all thematic areas and affiliated conferences for their contribution to the highest scientific quality and the overall success of the HCI International 2015 conference.

This conference could not have been possible without the continuous and unwavering support and advice of the founder, Conference General Chair Emeritus and Conference Scientific Advisor, Prof. Gavriel Salvendy. For their outstanding efforts, I would like to express my appreciation to the Communications Chair and Editor of HCI International News, Dr. Abbas Moallem, and the Student Volunteer Chair, Prof. Kim-Phuong L. Vu. Finally, for their dedicated contribution towards the smooth organization of HCI International 2015, I would like to express my gratitude to Maria Pitsoulaki and George Paparoulis, General Chair Assistants.

May 2015

Constantine Stephanidis
General Chair, HCI International 2015

HCI International 2015 Thematic Areas and Affiliated Conferences

Thematic areas:

- Human-Computer Interaction (HCI 2015)
- Human Interface and the Management of Information (HIMI 2015)

Affiliated conferences:

- 12th International Conference on Engineering Psychology and Cognitive Ergonomics (EPCE 2015)
- 9th International Conference on Universal Access in Human-Computer Interaction (UAHCI 2015)
- 7th International Conference on Virtual, Augmented and Mixed Reality (VAMR 2015)
- 7th International Conference on Cross-Cultural Design (CCD 2015)
- 7th International Conference on Social Computing and Social Media (SCSM 2015)
- 9th International Conference on Augmented Cognition (AC 2015)
- 6th International Conference on Digital Human Modeling and Applications in Health, Safety, Ergonomics and Risk Management (DHM 2015)
- 4th International Conference on Design, User Experience and Usability (DUXU 2015)
- 3rd International Conference on Distributed, Ambient and Pervasive Interactions (DAPI 2015)
- 3rd International Conference on Human Aspects of Information Security, Privacy and Trust (HAS 2015)
- 2nd International Conference on HCI in Business (HCIB 2015)
- 2nd International Conference on Learning and Collaboration Technologies (LCT 2015)
- 1st International Conference on Human Aspects of IT for the Aged Population (ITAP 2015)

Conference Proceedings Volumes Full List

1. LNCS 9169, Human-Computer Interaction: Design and Evaluation (Part I), edited by Masaaki Kurosu
2. LNCS 9170, Human-Computer Interaction: Interaction Technologies (Part II), edited by Masaaki Kurosu
3. LNCS 9171, Human-Computer Interaction: Users and Contexts (Part III), edited by Masaaki Kurosu
4. LNCS 9172, Human Interface and the Management of Information: Information and Knowledge Design (Part I), edited by Sakae Yamamoto
5. LNCS 9173, Human Interface and the Management of Information: Information and Knowledge in Context (Part II), edited by Sakae Yamamoto
6. LNAI 9174, Engineering Psychology and Cognitive Ergonomics, edited by Don Harris
7. LNCS 9175, Universal Access in Human-Computer Interaction: Access to Today's Technologies (Part I), edited by Margherita Antona and Constantine Stephanidis
8. LNCS 9176, Universal Access in Human-Computer Interaction: Access to Interaction (Part II), edited by Margherita Antona and Constantine Stephanidis
9. LNCS 9177, Universal Access in Human-Computer Interaction: Access to Learning, Health and Well-Being (Part III), edited by Margherita Antona and Constantine Stephanidis
10. LNCS 9178, Universal Access in Human-Computer Interaction: Access to the Human Environment and Culture (Part IV), edited by Margherita Antona and Constantine Stephanidis
11. LNCS 9179, Virtual, Augmented and Mixed Reality, edited by Randall Shumaker and Stephanie Lackey
12. LNCS 9180, Cross-Cultural Design: Methods, Practice and Impact (Part I), edited by P.L. Patrick Rau
13. LNCS 9181, Cross-Cultural Design: Applications in Mobile Interaction, Education, Health, Transport and Cultural Heritage (Part II), edited by P.L. Patrick Rau
14. LNCS 9182, Social Computing and Social Media, edited by Gabriele Meiselwitz
15. LNAI 9183, Foundations of Augmented Cognition, edited by Dylan D. Schmorrow and Cali M. Fidopiastis
16. LNCS 9184, Digital Human Modeling and Applications in Health, Safety, Ergonomics and Risk Management: Human Modeling (Part I), edited by Vincent G. Duffy
17. LNCS 9185, Digital Human Modeling and Applications in Health, Safety, Ergonomics and Risk Management: Ergonomics and Health (Part II), edited by Vincent G. Duffy
18. LNCS 9186, Design, User Experience, and Usability: Design Discourse (Part I), edited by Aaron Marcus
19. LNCS 9187, Design, User Experience, and Usability: Users and Interactions (Part II), edited by Aaron Marcus
20. LNCS 9188, Design, User Experience, and Usability: Interactive Experience Design (Part III), edited by Aaron Marcus

21. LNCS 9189, Distributed, Ambient and Pervasive Interactions, edited by Norbert Streitz and Panos Markopoulos
22. LNCS 9190, Human Aspects of Information Security, Privacy and Trust, edited by Theo Tryfonas and Ioannis Askoxylakis
23. LNCS 9191, HCI in Business, edited by Fiona Fui-Hoon Nah and Chuan-Hoo Tan
24. LNCS 9192, Learning and Collaboration Technologies, edited by Panayiotis Zaphiris and Andri Ioannou
25. LNCS 9193, Human Aspects of IT for the Aged Population: Design for Aging (Part I), edited by Jia Zhou and Gavriel Salvendy
26. LNCS 9194, Human Aspects of IT for the Aged Population: Design for Everyday Life (Part II), edited by Jia Zhou and Gavriel Salvendy
27. CCIS 528, HCI International 2015 Posters' Extended Abstracts (Part I), edited by Constantine Stephanidis
28. CCIS 529, HCI International 2015 Posters' Extended Abstracts (Part II), edited by Constantine Stephanidis

Design, User Experience and Usability

Program Board Chair: Aaron Marcus, USA

- Sisira Adikari, Australia
- Claire Ancient, UK
- Randolph G. Bias, USA
- Jamie Blustein, Canada
- Jan Brejcha, Czech Republic
- Marc Fabri, UK
- Patricia Flanagan, Hong Kong
- Emilie Gould, USA
- Luciane Maria Fadel, Brazil

- Brigitte Herrmann, Germany
- Steffen Hess, Germany
- Nouf Khashman, Canada
- Francisco Rebelo, Portugal
- Kerem Rızvanoğlu, Turkey
- Javed Anjum Sheikh, Pakistan
- Marcelo Soares, Brazil
- Carla G. Spinillo, Brazil
- Katia Canepa Vega, Brazil

The full list with the Program Board Chairs and the members of the Program Boards of all thematic areas and affiliated conferences is available online at:

http://www.hci.international/2015/

HCI International 2016

The 18th International Conference on Human-Computer Interaction, HCI International 2016, will be held jointly with the affiliated conferences in Toronto, Canada, at the Westin Harbour Castle Hotel, 17–22 July 2016. It will cover a broad spectrum of themes related to Human-Computer Interaction, including theoretical issues, methods, tools, processes, and case studies in HCI design, as well as novel interaction techniques, interfaces, and applications. The proceedings will be published by Springer. More information will be available on the conference website: http://2016.hci.international/.

General Chair
Prof. Constantine Stephanidis
University of Crete and ICS-FORTH
Heraklion, Crete, Greece
Email: general_chair@hcii2016.org

http://2016.hci.international/

Contents – Part II

Users in DUXU

Effects of Packages' Color as a Cue for Hazard-Related Perceptions:
A Study Using Virtual Reality 3
  Hande Ayanoğlu, Rita Boto, Júlia Teles, and Emília Duarte

Humanizing Labor Resource in a Discrete Event Manufacturing
Simulation Software 14
  Lia Buarque de Macedo Guimarães and Carlos Sergio Schneider

Children's Mental Model as a Tool to Provide Innovation
in Digital Products 23
  *Adriana Chammas, Manuela Quaresma,
  and Cláudia Renata Mont'Alvão*

HARSim: Posterior Load Comparative Analysis Process 34
  Ricardo Dagge, Ernesto Filgueiras, and Francisco Rebelo

Study on Operating Clearance Measurement of Some Connectors
by Using Motion Capture... 45
  Hao Du, Li Wang, Li Ding, Yulin Xu, and Changhua Jiang

Capture and Analysis of Interaction Data for the Evaluation of User
Experience with Mobile Devices.................................. 54
  Artur H. Kronbauer, Díferson Machado, and Celso A.S. Santos

A Study Customer Journey Map for User Experience Analysis
of Information and Communications Technology Service............. 66
  Jin Ho Lee, Min Ji Kim, and Sung Woo Kim

Scaling Preferences of Different Stakeholders – Using the Example
of Prioritizing Quality Requirements on User Interface Texts 75
  Yiqi Li, Theo Held, and Patrick Fischer

Affordances Feature on Package Design has Preference Effect on Content ... 87
  Jerry Lin and Cheng-Hung Lo

Measuring Negative User Experience.............................. 95
  Dominik Pascal Magin, Andreas Maier, and Steffen Hess

Chinese User-Experience Design: An Initial Analysis 107
  Aaron Marcus and Stacey Baradit

Behavioural Variables Analysis in Mobile Environments   118
  Denise Marczal and Plinio Thomaz Aquino Junior

Experiences, Problems and Solutions in Computer Usage by Subjects
with Tetraplegia   131
  *Fausto O. Medola, Jamille Lanutti, Claudia G. Bentim, Adrieli Sardella,
  Ana Elisa Franchinni, and Luis C. Paschoarelli*

Women in DUXU

Introducing Computer Science to Brazilian Girls in Elementary School
Through HCI Concepts   141
  *Marília Abrahão Amaral, Sílvia Amélia Bim, Clodis Boscarioli,
  and Cristiano Maciel*

Inclusive Gaming Creation by Design in Formal Learning Environments:
"Girly-Girls" User Group in No One Left Behind   153
  *María Eugenia Beltrán, Yolanda Ursa, Anja Petri, Christian Schindler,
  Wolfgang Slany, Bernadette Spieler, Silvia de los Rios,
  Maria Fernanda Cabrera-Umpierrez, and Maria Teresa Arredondo*

3D Real Time Virtual Fitting Room for Women   162
  *Salin Boonbrahm, Charlee Kaewrat, Lanjakorn Sewata,
  Patiwat Katelertprasert, and Poonpong Boonbrahm*

Re/Framing Virtual Conversational Partners: A Feminist Critique
and Tentative Move Towards a New Design Paradigm   172
  Sheryl Brahnam and Margaret Weaver

Experiencing Early User Interfaces   184
  Martha E. Crosby

Incommensurable Writings - Examining the Status of Gender Difference
Within HCI Coding Practices   196
  Michael Heidt, Kalja Kanellopoulos, Arne Berger, and Paul Rosenthal

A Study on Shopping Websites Payeasy for Female Consumers
in Taiwan.   206
  Hsiu Ching Laura Hsieh and Ning Chun Cheng

Verification of Stereotype on Women Observing Gender Difference on UX
of Wearable Device.   214
  Hee Jae Hwang, Jung Min Lee, and Da Young Ju

Closing the Gender Divide in Tech: Challenges and Achievements
in Vogue   224
  Linda Lim and Yuanqiong (Kathy) Wang

Gender Differences in Temporal Data Analysis: Toward Women or Men
Empowerment?. 232
  Ilona Nawrot

The Invisible User: Women in DUXU. 243
  Javed Anjum Sheikh and Aneela Abbas

The Creative Process in Digital Design: Towards an Understanding
of Women's Approach. 252
  Virginia Tiradentes Souto, Paula C.L.A. Faria,
  and Fátima Aparecida dos Santos

Information Design

Infographics and Communicating Complex Information 267
  Michael J. Albers

Building Cloud-Based Scientific Workflows Made Easy:
A Remote Sensing Application 277
  Sofiane Bendoukha, Daniel Moldt, and Hayat Bendoukha

Sound Design and UX: The Dynamic Audio Application Guide 289
  Luiz Roberto Carvalho and Alice T. Cybis Pereira

Designing an Interactive Map of Musical Culture and a Digital
Humanity App 301
  Sheng-Chih Chen and Chiung-Hui Hwang

Applying Human Centered Design Process for Designing Air Traffic
Control Interfaces 307
  Satoru Inoue, Kazuhiko Yamazaki, Hajime Hirako, and Toshiya Sasaki

Synchronized Data Management and its Integration into a Graphical User
Interface for Archaeological Related Disciplines 317
  Daniel Kaltenthaler, Johannes-Y. Lohrer, Peer Kröger,
  Christiaan H. van der Meijden, and Henriette Obermaier

Brazilian Research Panorama on Information Ergonomics
and Graphic Design. 330
  Luis C. Paschoarelli, João Silva, Danilo Silva, Gabriel Bonfim,
  Fausto O. Medola, and Erica Neves

Beyond the Wall of Text: How Information Design Can Make Contracts
User-Friendly 341
  Stefania Passera

Digital Collections: Analysis of Collaborative Platforms. 353
  Camila Rodrigues, Barbara Emanuel, and Marcos Martins

Interactive Multisensory Data Representation   363
  Patricia Search

An Interactive Guide to Design Animated Visual Instructions in Brazil   374
  Carla G. Spinillo and Roberta Perozza

Lyricon (Lyrics + Earcons) Improves Identification of Auditory Cues   382
  Yuanjing Sun and Myounghoon Jeon

Touch and Gesture DUXU

Evaluating Interaction Design in Brazilian Tablet Journalism:
Gestural Interfaces and Affordance Communicability   393
  *Luiz Agner, Adriano Bernardo Renzi, Natanne Viegas, Priscila Buares,
  and Vitor Zanfagnini*

Haptic Exploration Patterns in Virtual Line-Graph Comprehension   403
  Özge Alaçam, Cengiz Acartürk, and Christopher Habel

Collaborative Tangible Interface (CoTI) for Complex Decision Support
Systems   415
  *Salma Aldawood, Faisal Aleissa, Almaha Almalki, Tarfah Alrashed,
  Tariq Alhindi, Riyadh Alnasser, Mohammad K. Hadhrawi,
  Anas Alfaris, and Areej Al-Wabi*

User Study on 3D Multitouch Interaction (3DMi) and Gaze
on Surface Computing   425
  Eugene Ch'ng and Neil Cooke

CubeMate: A New Communication Device as Non-verbal Interface
in a Shared Space   434
  Roberta Grimaldi, Valentina Cipelli, and Carlo Maria Medaglia

Transparent Organ©: Designing Luminaire Art Deco
with Kinetic Interaction   444
  Scottie Chih-Chieh Huang

Usability of Touchpad Based Game Controller Interfaces   452
  Jonathon Kissinger and Tony Morelli

Usability Evaluation of Kinect-Based System for Ballet Movements   464
  Milka Trajkova and Mexhid Ferati

Integrating a Cognitive Modelling Framework into the Design Process
of Touchscreen User Interfaces   473
  Patrick K.A. Wollner, Patrick M. Langdon, and P. John Clarkson

Mobile DUXU

Change News Reading Habit in the Information Age and Digital
Mobile Devices.   487
   Juliana Nunes and Manuela Quaresma

Towards a Requirements Catalogue for Prototyping Tools of Mobile
User Interfaces   495
   Benjamin Bähr

Approaching Users and Context of Use in the Design and Development
of Mobile Systems   508
   Eyal Eshet and Harry Bouwman

The Importance of Metaphors for User Interaction with Mobile Devices   520
   Chrysoula Gatsou

Keyword Input via Digits: Simplified Smartphone Interface
for Information Retrieval   530
   Masanobu Higashida and Toru Ishida

Smartphone Application Usability Evaluation: The Applicability
of Traditional Heuristics.   541
   Ger Joyce, Mariana Lilley, Trevor Barker, and Amanda Jefferies

Elements of Properties of User Experience in Cloud Computing
Documentation Platform According to Smart Device Screen Size Changes:
Focus on Google Docs and Naver Office.   551
   Min Kyung Kang and Sung Woo Kim

Virtual Touchpad for Cursor Control of Touchscreen Thumb Operation
in the Mobile Context   563
   Yu Ren Lai and T.K. Philip Hwang

The Interaction with Smartphones in the Brazilian Driving Context.   575
   Manuela Quaresma, Rafael Cirino Gonçalves, Jhonnata Oliveira,
   and Marcela Rodrigues

Significance of Line Length for Tablet PC Users   587
   Waqas Ali Sahito, Hashim Iqbal Chunpir, Zahid Hussain,
   Syed Raheel Hassan, and Frederik Schulte

A Field Study on Basic Usage Patterns of Traditional Watch
and Smart Phone for Designing Smart Watch.   597
   Zijian Zhu, Haidi Song, and Sung Woo Kim

Wearable DUXU

Adapting Smart Textiles to Develop Soft Interactive Tool Kits
for Applying in Sewing Projects   611
   Aqua Chuan-Yu Chen

Evolutionary Wearables   622
   Patricia Flanagan

Transcending Disciplinary, Cultural and National Boundaries: Emergent
Technologies, New Education Landscape and the Cloud
Workshop Project   631
   Rafael Gomez, Patricia Flanagan, and Rebekah Davis

Digital Craftsmanship: The Making of Incunabula, a Fully 3D Printed
Wearable Dress.   643
   Tobias Klein

Designing a Vibrotactile Language for a Wearable Vest.   655
   Ann Morrison, Hendrik Knoche, and Cristina Manresa-Yee

TattooAR: Augmented Reality Interactive Tattoos   667
   Gabriela Schirmer Mauricio, João de Sá Bonelli,
   and Maria das Graças Chagas

Flexible and Wearable Sensors   675
   Kuniharu Takei, Shingo Harada, Wataru Honda, Yuki Yamamoto,
   Kenichiro Kanao, Takayuki Arie, and Seiji Akita

Tattoo Antenna Temporary Transfers Operating On-Skin (TATTOOS).   685
   James Tribe, Dumtoochukwu Oyeka, John Batchelor, Navjot Kaur,
   Diana Segura-Velandia, Andrew West, Robert Kay, Katia Vega,
   and Will Whittow

Hairware: Designing Conductive Hair Extensions for Seamless Interfaces . . .   696
   Katia Vega, Ricardo Aucelio, and Hugo Fuks

Commiticator: Enhancing Non-verbal Communication by Means
of Magnetic Vision   705
   Anne Wiedau, Daniel Gilgen, Raune Frankjær, Tristan Goerlich,
   and Michael Wiedau

Author Index   715

Users in DUXU

Effects of Packages' Color as a Cue
for Hazard-Related Perceptions:
A Study Using Virtual Reality

Hande Ayanoğlu[1(✉)], Rita Boto[1], Júlia Teles[2], and Emília Duarte[1]

[1] UNIDCOM, IADE – Creative University, Av. D. Carlos I, 4, 1200-649
Lisbon, Portugal
{hande.ayanoglu, rita.boto, emilia.duarte}@iade.pt
[2] CIPER – Interdisciplinary Center for the Study of Human Performance,
Universidade de Lisboa, Estrada da Costa, 1499-002 Cruz-Quebrada,
Dafundo, Portugal
jteles@fmh.ulisboa.pt

Abstract. Color is often used to communicate the level of hazard. The present study sought to determine the effect of packages' color on hazard-related perceptions in a Virtual Environment. There were two conditions: achromatic (grayscale) and chromatic (red, yellow, blue, green). A sample of 40 design students rated their hazard-related perceptions (e.g., level of hazardousness and awareness of consequences) of eight 3D packages, which differed in contents' hazardousness and familiarity, on hazard related perceptions. The results indicated that color does affect hazard-related perceptions. Compared to the achromatic versions, red and yellow produced different effects, when applied to hazardous packages which are both familiar and unfamiliar. Red increased hazard perception but did not affect awareness of consequences, and yellow did not affect the first, but decreased the latter. Blue decreased both dimensions, whereas green did not affect the first but decreased the latter. The results draw attention to the importance of color and familiarity on hazard-related perceptions.

Keywords: Package design · Colors · Safety · Hazard perception · Virtual environment

1 Introduction

Every year many users are injured while using products at home, including chemical household products. Since it is not always possible to design-out hazards in consumer products, one way to increase users' safety is to inform them of potential hazards, i.e., how to avoid being injured and the consequences of non-compliance. The packages' labels are normally used to convey warning and risk information to the users. However, such warnings are not always effective since they might not be noticed, read, understood or complied by users [1].

Such warnings fail to capture users' attention [2] due to several factors (e.g., an incorrect perception of the product's level of hazardousness and/or risk). The more

© Springer International Publishing Switzerland 2015
A. Marcus (Ed.): DUXU 2015, Part II, LNCS 9187, pp. 3–13, 2015.
DOI: 10.1007/978-3-319-20898-5_1

hazardous the product is perceived to be the more likely is the user to act in a cautious manner (e.g., [3–6]). However, previous research reveals systematic bias in risk perception (e.g., [7]). If users judge the situation (i.e., using the product in a given context with a specific objective) as involving no- or low-risk level, then they tend to not actively look for the safety information in the product and, therefore, do not read the warnings in the labels [1, 2]. Consequently, aiding users to adequately assess the risk involved in a given situation, in a quick and accurate manner, can be one of the most important measures to help promote safety.

One approach can be through the use of deliberate signifiers/perceived affordances [8] in order to convey strong cues that prompt safe behaviors [9] because affordances have some meaning to guide the observer's behavior [10]. In this sense, the packages' features (e.g., shape, color) can affect users' expectations regarding the products and, consequently, the warnings effectiveness. Previous studies found that the package's shape, or configuration, [11], and color [12] can evoke different levels of hazard perception. However, similar packages can mislead the users regarding the correct perception of the content's hazardousness (e.g., [13]).

In a previous study, we assessed the extent to which participants could perceive the content hazardousness from shape of liquid household packages' [14]. Additionally, we also assessed how the familiarity affected such perception since it has been found to decrease participants' likelihood to look for, notice and/or read warnings [15–17]. The present study extends the previous one by exploring the impact of packages' color on hazard-level perceptions (i.e., hazardousness, awareness of consequences) and familiarity. The aim is to determine if color could augment the perception of hazard. In this context, participants judged eight 3D household packages in two experimental conditions (i.e., chromatic and achromatic) which were displayed in a Virtual Environment (VE).

Literature assesses color's influence on attention, perception, and behavior. The role of color in enhancing hazard perception is also well documented [18–21]. It is well known that using color directly or indirectly influences perception and that, through color, people can distinguish between hazard and safe [22]. Moreover, as an effort to improve safety, color schemes are widely used to convey information and therefore frequently studied in visual working memory [23]. In general, warning-related research suggests that red should be used to indicate a greater level of hazard, than that of yellow and/or orange [24]. And, some inconsistent results have been found for ordering other colors such as orange and yellow [25]. Colors such as blue, green and black are generally connoted with less or no hazard [26].

In this study, it is expected that packages that connote higher level of hazard through colors (red and yellow) will increase hazard-related perceptions when compared to the achromatic (grayscale) counterparts, and the opposite for those colors which are connoted with lower hazard levels (blue and green). In addition, it is hypothesized that the color effect will be greater for unfamiliar packages than for familiar ones.

While 2D images (e.g., drawings, pictures) are the method usually adopted for conducting this type of study (e.g., [11, 12]), this research, following our previous studies (e.g., [14, 27]), also adopts a 3D simulator-based methodology. Virtual Reality (VR) has been suggested as a promising methodological tool for research on safety-related topics (e.g., [28, 29]) and User Experience studies (e.g., [30]).

2 Method

2.1 Experimental Design

Two experimental conditions were used to examine the effect of color on hazard-related dimensions. In the first condition, participants were exposed to achromatic packages. In the second condition, participants were presented with chromatic packages. A mixed design was used, with the two experimental conditions as the between-subjects factor and the type of package (with four levels: HF - Hazardous Familiar, NHF - Non-hazardous Familiar, HUF - Hazardous Unfamiliar and NHUF - Non-hazardous Unfamiliar) as the within-subjects factor. The dependent variables are hazard related perceptions (i.e., the level of hazardousness and awareness of consequences). Familiarity was used as a control variable.

2.2 Stimuli

The VE and the eight packages used were the same as the ones tested in a previous study by Ayanoğlu and colleagues [14]. The packages were presented either in achromatic (i.e., grayscale) or chromatic versions (i.e., red, yellow, blue and green) according to the experimental condition (see Fig. 1). The four colors were selected according to their connoted level of hazard, as defined in the literature (e.g., [19]). The RGB values, i.e. red (165, 32, 25), yellow (229, 190, 1), blue (30, 45, 110) and green (49, 127, 67), from ISO 3864-4 [31] were used to define the colors' properties.

Note. Package A and B are unfamiliar packages with hazardous content (yellow); Package C and F are familiar packages with hazardous content (red), Package D and H are unfamiliar packages with non-hazardous content (green); Package E and G are familiar packages with non-hazardous content (blue).

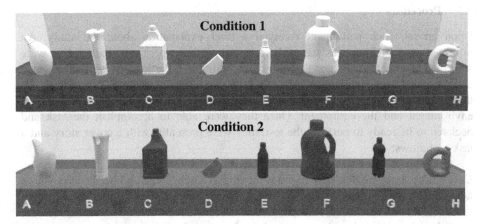

Fig. 1. Experimental conditions (Condition 1 – achromatic; Condition 2 – chromatic packages) (Color figure online)

The colors were then assigned to the packages according to their content's level of hazardousness and package's familiarity as defined in the previous study. Thus, warm colors were assigned to packages with hazardous contents (red for familiar and yellow for unfamiliar packages) and cool colors for non-hazardous contents (blue for familiar and green for unfamiliar packages).

2.3   Sample

A total of 40 undergraduate design students (M = 20.73 years, SD = 2.05) participated in this study. Twenty participants, equally distributed by gender, were randomly assigned to each condition (Condition 1: M = 20.45 years, SD = 1.72, Condition 2: M = 21.0 years, SD = 2.32). All participants had normal sight (or used corrective lenses) and had no color vision deficiencies.

2.4   Experimental Settings and Virtual Environment

The experiment was conducted at the IADE-UX.Lab, in a dark room. The same experimental settings and VE were used for both conditions. It included a video projector (to display the VE), a computer workstation and a mouse (to navigate in the VE). Participants were seated at a table, in front of the projected image. The image's size was 1.72 m (horizontal) by 0.95 m (vertical), with an aspect ratio of 16:9. The observation distance between the screen and the participant was 1.50 m, resulting in a 35.2° of vertical field-of-view (FOV) and 59.7° horizontal FOV.

The VE was a closed room, measuring 6.6 m by 6.6 m, containing a table (260 cm in length, 30 cm in width and 90 cm in height) positioned in the middle of the room. The packages were placed on top of the table, evenly spaced from each other (i.e., 20 cm). In order to identify the packages easily, each one was associated to a letter from A to H.

2.5   Procedure

Upon arrival, each participant received a brief explanation about the study. An informed consent form was signed before starting the experiment. Participants were subjected to a color vision test [32] only for Condition 2. Participants were then seated and presented to the equipment. After that they performed a training session in which they explored a VE which was created specifically to get them familiarized with the environment and the equipment. Once they were able to accomplish the task and declared to be ready to perform the test, they were presented with a cover story and a task as follows:

Cover Story. Imagine that your friend is moving to a new house and he/she asks you to help unpack and to organize a group of liquid household products' packages according to their level of hazard (e.g., how poisonous can the content be when drunk, how toxic can it be when inhaled, or how irritant/harmful can it be if it comes into contact with skin).

Task. Observe the packages and reply to the questions.

They were asked to observe the packages and to fill a questionnaire regarding their hazard-related perceptions. The same questionnaire [14], which was adapted from Wogalter and colleagues [11, 33], was used to evaluate the perceptions. A 9-point Likert type scale was used, from 0 to 8, where 0 indicated the minimum and 8 indicates the maximum. The 12 questions were organized according to three categories: hazard perception (consisting of 8 questions which rate the of the content's level of hazard-ousness; the hazardousness of the package's shape; whether the package is hazardous to children; the content's flammability; the level of hazardousness if drunk; the level of hazardousness if inhaled, the level of hazardousness if contacted with skin; and the content's hazardousness in closed spaces), awareness of consequences (consisting of 3 questions which rate the cautious intent; likelihood of injury; and severity of injury related with the packages) and familiarity (which consisted of 1 question to rate the participants' familiarity with the packages). Only in for Condition 2 did the participants complete a follow-up questionnaire which intended to assess how they connoted the different colors regarding the level of hazard.

3   Result

3.1   Familiarity

Regarding familiarity (i.e., control variable), the participants' ratings (see Fig. 2) confirmed the previous classification of the packages as familiar and unfamiliar.

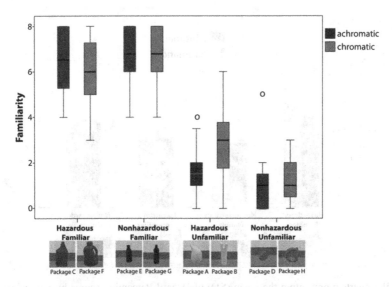

Fig. 2. Box-plots of familiarity scores by package

3.2 Hazard-Related Perceptions

The statistical analysis was performed with the software IBM SPSS Statistics, version 22, and a significance level of 5 % was considered.

The type of package (four levels: HF, NHF, HUF, and NHUF), the experimental conditions' (two levels: achromatic and chromatic) effects and their interaction on hazard perception and awareness of consequences were analyzed using two-way mixed-design ANOVAs, with the type of package as the within-subjects factor and the experimental condition as the between–subjects factor. Regarding the mixed ANOVA assumptions, no significant deviations from normality, homogeneity of variance and sphericity were found.

Hazard Perception. The interaction between the type of package and the experimental condition ($F(3,114) = 8.899$, $p < .001$; partial $\eta^2 = .190$, medium effect), and type package ($F(3,114) = 29.758$, $p < .001$; partial $\eta^2 = .439$, high effect) have significant effects on the hazard perception's mean scores. The mean (SD) of the hazard perception scores are shown in Fig. 3.

The effect of the experimental condition was not the same for all types of packages: in HF packages, color enhances the hazard perception scores (achromatic: $M = 3.87$, $SD = 1.15$; chromatic: $M = 5.07$, $SD = 1.09$) whereas in the NHF, there is a decrease (achromatic: $M = 2.73$, $SD = 1.56$; chromatic: $M = 1.01$, $SD = 0.99$); in the HUF (achromatic: $M = 3.39$, $SD = 1.46$; chromatic: $M = 3.37$, $SD = 1.20$) and NHUF (achromatic: $M = 3.78$, $SD = 1.54$; chromatic: $M = 3.68$, $SD = 1.44$) packages there is no color effect.

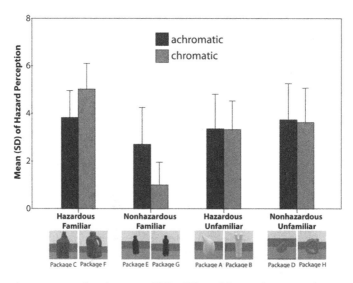

Fig. 3. Bar charts representing the mean (SD) of Hazard Perception scores by type of package for the two conditions.

Awareness of Consequence. The interaction between the type of package and experimental condition ($F(3,114) = 4.065$, $p = .009$; partial $\eta^2 = .097$, low effect) have significant effects on the awareness of consequences mean scores. The mean (SD) of the hazard perception scores are shown in Fig. 4.

The effect of the experimental conditional was not the same for all types of packages: the effect of color in NHF (achromatic: $M = 2.43$, $SD = 1.34$; chromatic: $M = 0.73$, $SD = 0.81$), HUF (achromatic: $M = 3.06$, $SD = 1.73$; chromatic: $M = 2.08$, $SD = 1.25$) and NHUF (achromatic: $M = 4.65$, $SD = 1.80$; chromatic: $M = 3.25$, $SD = 1.58$) packages decreases the awareness of consequence mean of scores; and in the HF packages (achromatic: $M = 3.88$, $SD = 1.34$; chromatic: $M = 4.09$, $SD = 1.25$) there is no color effect.

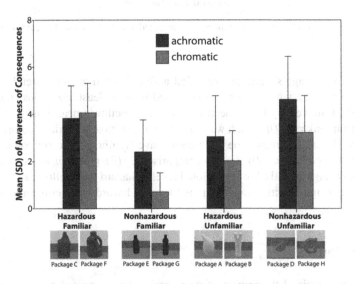

Fig. 4. Bar charts representing the mean (SD) of Awareness of Consequences scores by type of package for the two conditions.

3.3   Connoted Level of Hazard by Color

A follow-up questionnaire was given to the 20 participants on Condition 2 in order to assess how they ranked the four colors regarding the connoted level of hazard, from the least hazardous (rank of 1) to the most hazardous (rank of 4). The results showed that red attained the highest level of hazard perceived followed by yellow, blue and green (see in Fig. 5).

The Page's trend test [34] was used to evaluate the ranking of these colors with respect to the connoted level of hazard. The existence of a previous ordinal position of the colors' effects (more precisely, from the least to the most hazardous: green, blue, yellow and red), available on the literature [35–37] supported the option of performing an ordered test of alternative hypothesis using a within-subjects design.

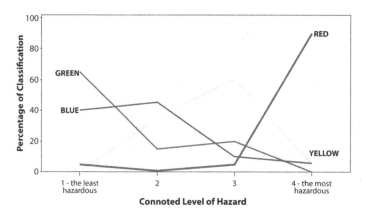

Fig. 5. Percentage of classification ranking of connoted level of hazard for each color (Color figure online)

The results of Page's trend test revealed a significant monotonic trend (L = 569, z = 26.724, p < .001), where green was connoted with the least hazardous color (mean rank = 1.60), followed by blue (mean rank = 1.88), yellow (mean rank = 2.73), and then red (mean rank = 3.80), which was classified as the most hazardous color. Post hoc testing showed that: (i) green, blue and yellow have significantly lower connoted level of hazard than red (ps < .001 for all comparisons); (ii) green (p = .003) and blue (p = .015) have significantly lower connoted level of hazard than yellow; and (iii) green does not have a significantly lower connoted level of hazard when compared with blue (p = 1.0).

4 Discussion

This research examined the impact of packages' color on hazard-related perceptions (i.e., level hazardousness, and awareness of consequences), by addressing the question 'Does color affects hazard perception?' Participants rated eight 3D household packages, which differed in content hazardousness and familiarity, in two conditions (i.e., achromatic and chromatic), using a simulator-based methodology. After the simulation, participants ranked the four colors provided, on connoted hazard. Regarding the latter, as expected, red had a higher hazard connotation than yellow, followed by blue and green, thereby supporting the majority of the results in the findings in the literature [18, 19].

It was hypothesized that chromatic packages, which connote higher levels of hazard (red and yellow), would increase hazard-related perceptions when compared to the achromatic (grayscale) counterparts, and the opposite for those colors (blue and green) which connote lower hazard levels. Also, it was hypothesized that the color effect would be greater for unfamiliar packages than for familiar ones. However, neither of these hypotheses was fully confirmed by the data.

The results showed that color does affect hazard-related perceptions (i.e., hazard perception and awareness of consequences). However, the effect is not significant for all type of packages and do not always follow the same direction. The results from the hazard perception assessment show that for familiar-hazardous packages the color (red) increases hazard perception and the opposite for the familiar-non-hazardous (blue). For the unfamiliar hazardous (yellow) and non-hazardous (green) packages, the color did not significantly affect hazard perception.

Regarding the level of awareness of the consequences, unlike the verified results on hazard perception for familiar-hazardous packages, red did not significantly increase this perception. For the familiar-non-hazardous (blue), unfamiliar hazardous (yellow) and unfamiliar non-hazardous (green) packages, the color decreased this perception. With regard to the results found for the yellow packages (unfamiliar), the interpretation is not clear and one explanation could be that participants associated the color with edible substances (e.g., juice). Further data would be necessary to clarify this finding.

The second hypothesis, that the color effect would be greater for unfamiliar packages than for familiar ones, was not supported.

This study has some limitations; one is the sample that is constituted only by students, which compromises the generalization of the results to a larger population. Another limitation is the number of experimental conditions. In this study, the warm colors were assigned to packages with hazardous contents (red for familiar and yellow for unfamiliar packages) and cool colors for nonhazardous contents (blue for familiar and green for unfamiliar packages). Other conjugations should be carried out in the future.

Despite the above limitations, the findings highlight the importance of color in hazard-related perceptions and raise several aspects that warrant further attention. For example, what happens with multicolored packages? How color and shape interaction, account for hazard-related perceptions is also unclear.

This study is the second phase of a larger research project which aims to explore how signifiers (i.e., package features) and hazard-related perceptions interact, and as well as to what extent they influence users to adopt safer behaviors. The project's first step was concerned with the effect of the packages' shape in which it was also suggested that Virtual Reality (VR) is adequate to be used as a tool for this type of study; while this second step was concerned with the effect of color in VR. Further research, with a larger sample, will be carried out in order to examine the effects of colors in diverse conditions and different package features (e.g., texture and material), as well as to determine the effect of other features on hazard-related perceptions. Consequently, since VR was successfully used to assess user's perceptions about packages' level of hazardousness, in future work, different contextual Virtual Environments will be used to understand the effect of diverse environments, as well as package features.

References

1. Laughery, K.R., Wogalter, M.S.: Warnings and risk perception. In: Salvendy, G. (ed.) Handbook of Human Factors and Ergonomics, 2nd edn., vol. 2, pp. 1174–1197. Wiley, New York (1997)

2. Young, S., Brelsford, J.W., Wogalter, M.S.: Judgments of hazard, risk, and danger: do they differ? In: Woods, D., Roth, E. (eds.) Proceedings of the Human Factors Society 34th Annual Meeting, Santa Monica, CA, pp. 503–507 (1990)
3. Donner, K.A., Brelsford, J.W.: Cueing hazard information for consumer products. In: Proceedings of the Human Factors Society 32nd Annual Meeting. Human Factors Society, Santa Monica (1988)
4. Friedmann, K.: The effect of adding symbols to written warning labels on user behavior and recall. Hum. Factors **30**(4), 507–515 (1988)
5. Otsubo, S.M.: A behavioral study of warning labels for consumer products: Perceived danger and use of pictographs. In: Proceedings of the Human Factors Society 32nd Annual Meeting, pp. 536–540. The Human Factors Society, Santa Monica (1988)
6. Wogalter, M.S., Brems, D.J., Martin, E.G.: Risk perception of common consumer products: Judgments of accident frequency and precautionary intent. J. Saf. Res. **24**(2), 97–106 (1993)
7. Fischhoff, B., Slovic, P., Lichtenstein, S., Read, S., Combs, B.: How safe is safe enough? A psychometric study of attitudes towards technological risks and benefits. Policy Sci. **9**(2), 127–152 (1978)
8. Norman, D.A.: Signifiers, Not Affordances. Interactions **15**(6), 18–19 (2008)
9. Ayanoğlu, H., Duarte, E., Noriega, P., Teixeira, L., Rebelo, F.: The importance of integrating perceived affordances and hazard perception in package design. In: Rebelo, F., Soares, M. (eds.) Advances in Usability Evaluation Part I, pp. 627–636. CRC Press/Taylor and Francis, Ltd. (2013)
10. Turvey, M.T.: Affordances and prospective control: an outline of the ontology. Ecol. Psychol. **4**(3), 173–187 (1992)
11. Wogalter, M.S., Laughery, K.R., Barfield, D.A.: Effect of container shape on hazard perceptions. In Human Factors Perspective on Warnings Volume 2 : selections from Human Factors and Ergonomics Society Annual Meetings, 1994-2000, pp. 231–235 (2001)
12. Serig, E.M.: The influence of container shape and color cues on consumer produckt risk perception and precautionary intent. In: Wogalter, M.S., Young, S.L., Laughery, K.R. (eds.) Human Factors Perspective on Warnings Volume 2 : selections from Human Factors and Ergonomics Society annual meetings, 1994-2000, pp. 185–188. Human Factors and Ergonomics Society (2001)
13. Desai, S.P., Teggihalli, B.C., Bhola, R.: Superglue mistaken for eye drops. Arch. Dis. Child. **90**(11), 1193 (2005)
14. Ayanoğlu, H., Duarte, E., Teles, J., Noriega, P., Rebelo, F.: Examining hazard-related perceptions of virtual household package prototypes. In: Rebelo, F., Marcus, A. (eds.) Proceedings of the 5th AHFE Conference. Advances in Ergonomics in Design, Usability & Special Populations: Part I, 19–23 July 2014, vol. 16, pp. 473 – 481. AHFE Conference, Las Vegas (2014)
15. Godfrey, S.S., Laughery, K.R.: The biasing effect of product familiarity on consumers' awareness of hazard. In: Factors, H. (ed.) Perspectives on Warnings. The Huma Factors and Ergonomics Society, Santa Monica (1993)
16. Goldhaber, G.M., deTurck, M.A.: Effects of consumer's familiarity with a product on attention and compliance with warnings. J. Prod. Liability **11**, 29–37 (1988)
17. Wogalter, M.S., Brelsford, J.W., Desaulniers, D.R., Laughery, K.R.: Consumer product warnings: The role of hazard perception. J. Saf. Res. **22**, 71–82 (1991)
18. Chapanis, A.: Hazards associated with three signal words and four colors on warning signs. Ergonomics **37**(2), 265–275 (1994)
19. Smith-Jackson, T.L., Wogalter, M.S.: Users' hazard perceptions of warning components: An examination of colors and symbols. In: Proceedings of the Human Factors and Ergonomics Society Annual Meeting, vol. 44, pp. 6–55. SAGE Publications (2000a)

20. Braun, C.C., Sansing, L., Silver, N.: The interaction of signal word and color on warning labels - differences in perceived hazard. In: Proceedings of the Human Factors and Ergonomics Society 38th Annual Meeting. Human Factors and Ergonomics Society, Nashville (1994)
21. Wogalter, M.S., Kalsher, M.J., Frederick, L.J., Magurno, A.B., Brewster, B.M.: Hazard level perceptions of warning components and configurations. Int. J. Cogn. Ergon. **2**, 123–143 (1998)
22. Sung-euk, P.: Research of color affordance concept and applying to design. In: Kim, T.-H., Ma, J., Fang, W.-C., Zhang, Y., Cuzzocrea, A. (eds.) EL/DTA/UNESST 2012. CCIS, vol. 352, pp. 283–288. Springer, Heidelberg (2012)
23. Allred, S.R., Flombaum, J.I.: Relating color working memory and color perception. Trends Cogn. Sci. **18**(11), 562–565 (2014)
24. Braun, C.C., Kline, P.B., Silver, N.C.: The influence of color on warning label perceptions. Int. J. Ind. Ergon. **15**(3), 179–187 (1995)
25. Wogalter, M.S., Magurno, A.B., Carter, A.W., Swindell, J.A., Vigilante, W.J., Daurity, J.G.: Hazard associations of warning header components. In: Proceedings of the Human Factors and Ergonomics Society 39th Annual Meeting. Human Factors and Ergonomics Society, San Diego (1995)
26. Braun, C.C., Silver, N.C.: Interaction of warning label features: Determining the contributions of three warning characteristics. In: Human Factors and Ergonomics Society 39th Annual Meeting, San Diego, CA (1995)
27. Ayanoğlu, H., Rebelo, F., Duarte, E., Noriega, P., Teixeira, L.: Using virtual reality to examine hazard perception in package design. In: Marcus, A. (ed.) DUXU 2013, Part III. LNCS, vol. 8014, pp. 30–39. Springer, Heidelberg (2013)
28. Duarte, E., Rebelo, F., Teles, J., Wogalter, M.S.: Behavioral compliance for dynamic versus static signs in an immersive virtual environment. Appl. Ergon. **45**(5), 1367–1375 (2014)
29. Vilar, E., Rebelo, F., Noriega, P., Duarte, E., Mayhorn, C.: Effects of competing environmental variables and signage on route choices in simulated everyday and emergency wayfinding situations. Ergonomics **57**(4), 511–524 (2014)
30. Rebelo, F., Noriega, P., Duarte, E., Soares, M.: Using virtual reality to assess user experience. Hum. Factors: J. Hum. Factors and Ergon. Soc. **54**(6), 964–982 (2012)
31. ISO 3864-4. In Graphical Symbols-Safety Colours and Safety Signs-Part 4: Colorimetric and photometric properties of safety sign materials (2011)
32. Ishihara, S.: Test for Colour Blindness. British Medical Journal, 24th edn. Kanehara and Co., Ltd., Tokyo (1972)
33. Wogalter, M.S., Young, S.L., Brelsford, J.W., Barlow, T.: The relative contributions of injury severity and likelihood information on hazard-risk judgments and warning compliance. J. Saf. Res. **30**(3), 151–162 (1999)
34. Sprent, P., Smeetoon, N.C.: Applied Nonparametric Statistical Methods, 4th edn, p. 544. Chapman and Hall/CRC, Boca Raton (2007)
35. Yi, J., Kim, Y., Kim, K., Koo, B.: A suggested color scheme for reducing perception-related accidents on construction work sites. Accid. Anal. Prev. **48**, 185–192 (2012)
36. Laughery, K.R., Wogalter, M.S.: A three-stage model summarizes product warning and environmental sign research. Saf. Sci. – Risk Commun. Warnings **6**, 3–10 (2014)
37. Plocher, T., Rau, P., Choong, Y.: Cross-cultural design. In: Salvendy, G. (ed.) Handbook of Human Factors and Ergonomics, 4th edn, pp. 162–191. John Wiley and Sons, New Jersey (2012)

Humanizing Labor Resource in a Discrete Event Manufacturing Simulation Software

Lia Buarque de Macedo Guimarães[1(✉)] and Carlos Sergio Schneider[2]

[1] Graduate Program in Industrial Engineering, Federal University of Rio Grande do Sul, Av. Osvaldo Aranha 99, 5 andar, Porto Alegre, RS, Brazil
liabmg@gmail.com
[2] Feevale University Center, RS 239, Vila Nova, Novo Hamburgo, RS 2755, Brazil
cszneider@gmail.com

Abstract. Simulation is a decision making support tool very useful for the design and dimensioning of manufacturing plants. Although workmanship hand is largely employed in production systems, labor involved in the process is often modeled as an inanimate predictable resource (like machines, tools or equipment). In order to make simulation more realistic, this study applied ergonomics principles (circadian rhythm and rest pauses) to the labor resource of a software that is largely used in commercial applications. Results showed that this "humanization" impact the simulation results. Production outcomes from the circadian rhythm modeling were up to 7 % higher than the ones obtained with the standard PROMODEL modeling; the introduction of 5 min rest pauses increased productivity in less than 1 %. Overall, these results justify the development of computational routines able to represent "humans" and their interactions with the system in a more realistic manner.

Keywords: Simulation · Ergonomics · Circadian rhythm · Production systems

1 Introduction

Simulation is an important tool for virtually designing and evaluating products and process before its implementation. Manufacturing simulation software (such as ProModel, Arena, AweSim!, Extend, GPSS/H, MODSIM III, SES, Taylor II, WITNESS) allow for building virtual factories with different lay-outs, equipment, processes and labor alternatives so the one with best performance can be later implemented. Most simulations often use predictable production variables, such as quantity, type and physical distribution of machines, quantity of intermediate stocks, production times etc. Although workmanship hand is largely employed in most manufacturing systems, labor is often modeled as an essential, but inanimate predictable resource. However, workers capability and performance are less predictable than machines, equipment, products etc. Unlike machines, human beings do not keep the same production rhythm throughout the day, what directly affects productivity.

In spite of intra (people have different behavior during a journey) and inter (different people have different capabilities) human variability, simulation often assumes

© Springer International Publishing Switzerland 2015
A. Marcus (Ed.): DUXU 2015, Part II, LNCS 9187, pp. 14–22, 2015.
DOI: 10.1007/978-3-319-20898-5_2

that workers are capable of performing the task as designed, with no mental, physical, social, environmental or time constraints. Besides, when labor is modeled as a machine, workers do not stop working anytime, do not take breaks and have to work to meet pre defined production goals that are often set with no ergonomics support. In most cases, there is no questioning either these goals are above or beyond workers capabilities. Possible reasons for not considering human factors in simulation is the complexity of the factors that influences human productivity, and the lack of ergonomists in most production planning. Nevertheless, human variation is the cause of a large percentage of the disparity between simulation predictions and real world performance [1].

Therefore, this study evaluated the impact of human factors on a manufacturing simulation software. The objective was not the integration of ergonomic assessment in the modeling, but to give some "life" and to turn "more real", the built in labor resource of the software. This was done by embedding rest pauses and circadian parameters that are independent either of the type of work (such as physical and mental demands, stress and fatigue) or type of people (such as age, gender, personality, level of training). Using the simulation software WITNESS, [1] incorporated circadian rhythm in the modeling of an automotive engine assembly line and found that circadian rhythm impacted production outcomes in 2 %. The circadian model was based on the study of [2] that took into account the time of day of work and time awaked on the performance of air traffic controllers and pilots. Assuming that workers in most manufacturing processes have more in common with construction workers than air traffic controllers and pilots, the study presented in this paper aims to add to this previous study, by using a daily productivity model proposed by [3], as described in the next section.

2 Ergonomic Parameters Used in the Study

Although human behavior and performance depends on environmental, physical and psychosocial factors, this study considered only rest break and circadian parameters that might affect productivity.

Human performance depends on physiological markers known as circadian rhythms, which vary during the day, despite the type of work or type of people. They are manifested as oscillations in biochemical, physiological and behavioral cycles of approximately 24 h as noted in body temperature, blood pressure, renal excretion of metabolites and circulating levels of hormones, which have a pattern of variation that is repeated day by day at the same day time. Humans have different endogenous circadian pacemakers which regulate homeostasis through various efferent neuroendocrine responses that interact with homeostatic processes (e.g. amount of hours since awake until the maximum alertness) [4], which end up defining whether one activity would be best performed in the morning, afternoon or evening. A study by [3] on daily productivity curve in the civil construction industry, showed that the rhythm of work adapts itself to the rhythm of the body, and productivity curves resemble physiological curves. Productivity increases in the morning, decreases before lunch and is lower in the afternoon.

Besides this circadian rhythm variation, humans take breaks during the day because nobody can work at the same pace without rest. The ergonomics literature reinforces the need for formal rest breaks during the journey, although there is no prescribed "best break": pause intervals and duration might vary depending on the work performed and individuals. Reference [5] recommends short breaks of 3–5 min every hour in case of machine-paced work. A study by [6] concluded that workers prefer a 10-min pause after each working hour than four 15-min pauses at longer intervals. Breaks might have a positive impact on productivity: 10-min pauses in the morning and afternoon could increase production by 5–12 % [7] or 10–20 % [8].

3 Method

Ergonomic parameters used for simulation were the daily productivity model as proposed by [3] and 5 min rest pauses after each hour of work. The selected simulation model was one demo available from PROMODEL, a discrete event simulation software largely used in the manufacturing industry, which is also the software adopted at the University.

The PROMODEL Mfg_cost.mod simulates a shop for machining, milling and assembly of gears, employing one, two or three workers. Evaluation can be done based on productivity or cost of each manufactured product according to the number of workers involved. Cost is calculated either as a function of human/h or machine.

The shop has two lathes (NC Lathe1 and NC Lathe2), a workbench and a place for product inspection. As the material arrives, the operator takes it to one of the lathes, place the material on the lathe and program it. The operation time distribution follows a normal distribution (mean time = 3 min; SD = 0.2 min). The next operation depends on the following system states:

1. one of the lathes is available, and will be used for processing a new gear part;
2. one of the lathes ended the operation. The gear part is taken from the lathe and placed on the bench for degreasing;
3. both lathes are busy, and there is a degreased gear part on the bench, waiting for inspection. After inspection, if it passes the test, it will be assembled with roller balls, conforming a gear.

Inspection time (mean time 3.2 min; SD = 0,3 min) as well as assembly time (mean time 1,5 min; SD = 0,2 min) follows a normal distribution The production of a correct gear takes a mean time of 7.7 min, while defective products take 6.2 min.

In this model, the rate of defective products is 30 %, but it can be adjusted. When this rate is less than 30 %, the number of manufactured products (good or defectives) in a certain time diminishes because it takes longer to process correct products than defective ones. The mean processing time of a gear is 34 min, a mean time of 7,25 min (21 % of the total time) corresponding to operations involving the workers.

The demo model is programmed for a 15 non-stop hours of operation, and can be set for operating during days, weeks or even years. However, considering a real life situation, the time was set for an 8 h shift. Three conditions were compared: (1) 5 working days of an 8 h non-stop shift (PROMODEL standard); (2) 5 working days of an 8 h shift with one hour for lunch break and considering the circadian rhythm performance and productivity curve; (3) 5 working days of an 8 h shift with one hour for lunch break, 5 min rest pauses at each hour, and considering the circadian rhythm performance and productivity curve. It was assumed a 10 % performance recovery after the 5 min break, because the workers could rest (i.e., performance increases because fatigue decreases). The expected performance and productivity curve resembles the one proposed by [3]. However, because this exact curve is not known, simulations were done considering curves with mean productivity amplitude variation of ± 5 % to ± 20 % during the day. Therefore, a 5 % variation means that productivity varies only 5 % during the day (tending to a standard flat curve) i.e., there is no much difference among workers capability/productivity during the day, while a 20 % variation means that this variation is higher during the day, approaching the capability/productivity circadian curve.

4 Results

Figures 1, 2, 3 and 4 present the obtained results for condition 2 (circadian rhythm) assuming 70 %, 80 %, 90 % and 100 % of correct products. Figures 5, 6, 7 and 8 present the results for condition 3 (circadian rhythm + rest pause) assuming 70 %, 80 %, 90 % and 100 % of correct products. Values on the y axis are the mean deviations in production (%) for ergonomic modeling involving 1, 2 and 3 workers, in comparison to condition 1 (standard PROMODEL). Values on the x axis displays the results assuming 5 %, 10 %, 15 % and 20 % variation from the capability/productivity curve during the day.

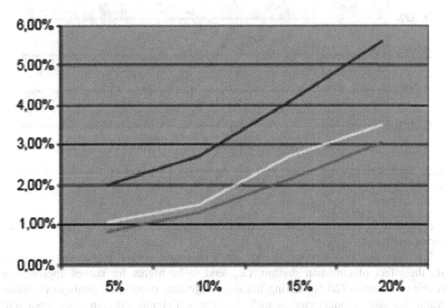

Fig. 1. Simulation results considering 70 % of correct gears produced by 1 worker (*black line*); 2 workers (*gray line*) and 3 workers (*white line*).

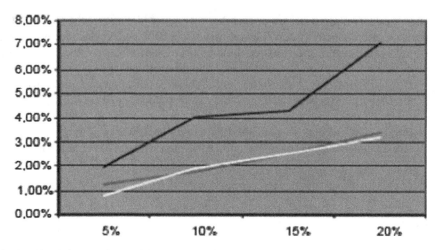

Fig. 2. Simulation results considering 80 % of correct gears produced by 1 worker (*black line*); 2 workers (*gray line*) and 3 workers (*white line*).

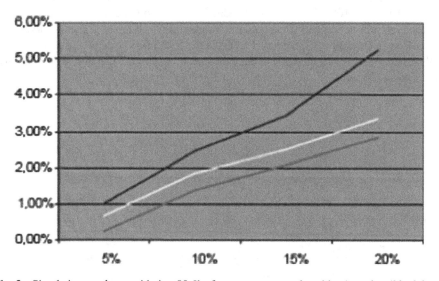

Fig. 3. Simulation results considering 90 % of correct gears produced by 1 worker (*black line*); 2 workers (*gray line*) and 3 workers (*white line*).

Figures 5, 6, 7 and 8 present the results for conditions with 5 min rest after each hour of work.

It is clear that performance, mainly when only one worker is involved, increases with the effect of circadian rhythm, i.e., tend to be higher for curves approaching circadian variations (20 %) during the day. Adjusting production goals to circadian rhythm increased productivity up to 7 %, what is a significant gain since labor represents only 20 % of the total manufacturing time. Larger productivity increase might

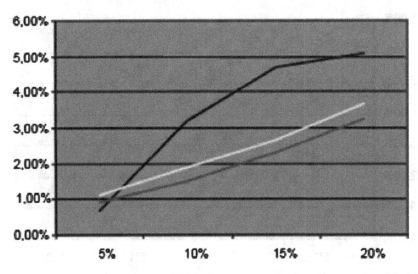

Fig. 4. Simulation results considering 100 % of correct gears produced by 1 worker (*black line*); 2 workers (*gray line*) and 3 workers (*white line*).

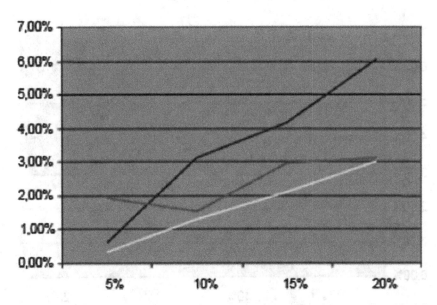

Fig. 5. Simulation results considering 70 % of correct gears produced by 1 worker (*black line*); 2 workers (*gray line*) and 3 workers (*white line*), with 5 min rest pause after 1 h of work.

be expected for conditions where human labor is more intense. The mean obtained gains are higher than the 2 % reported by [1], who used different productivity model and simulation software. Nevertheless, productivity rate is not the focus of the study but, rather, being able to demonstrate that it is possible to adjust production demands to

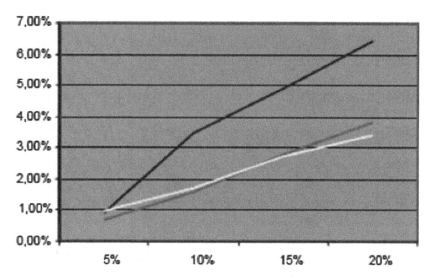

Fig. 6. Simulation results considering 80 % of correct gears produced by 1 worker (*black line*); 2 workers (*gray line*) and 3 workers (*white line*), with 5 min rest pause after 1 h of work.

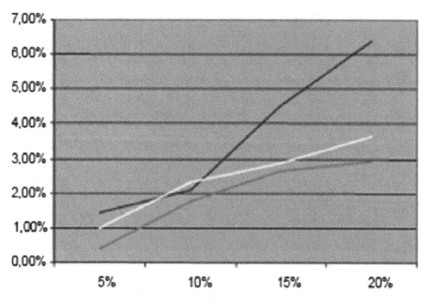

Fig. 7. Simulation results considering 90 % of correct gears produced by 1 worker (*black line*); 2 workers (*gray line*) and 3 workers (*white line*), with 5 min rest pause after 1 h of work.

human capabilities with no impact on the enterprise goals. Simulation is a tool for designing better production alternatives, and similar outcomes should be expected if human factors are used when implementing new work organizations. By assuming a

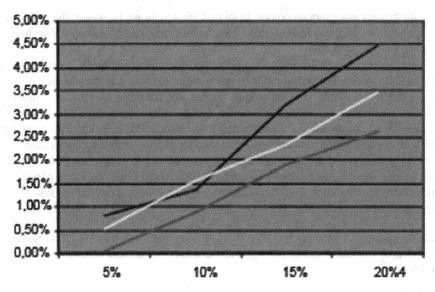

Fig. 8. Simulation results considering 100 % of correct gears produced by 1 worker (*black line*); 2 workers (*gray line*) and 3 workers (*white line*), with 5 min rest pause after 1 h of work.

constant productivity/day, as it happens in most production systems, workers have to work either above or below their capabilities depending on the hour of the day, what impacts both humans and production. On the other hand, when production set up fluctuates according the capability/productivity curve, productivity would increase with minimum stress on the worker.

Rest pauses showed to have little impact on productivity. For example, productivity curves of one worker, in Figs. 1 and 5, show that rest pause increased performance in <1 % (productivity increased from 5.5 % to 6 %), which is lower than the 5–20 % productivity increase reported in the literature. Assuming that these studies did not consider production pace and circadian rhythm, one explanation might be that fatigue is lower when production demand follows workers capability/productivity curve, reducing the need for recovery from rest pauses.

5 Conclusion

This article presented a study on the use of ergonomic parameters in manufacturing systems simulation. The goal was to "humanize" the labor resource of a commercial software and to evaluate whether incorporating human performance variation and rest pauses would alter productivity results. Production outcomes from the circadian rhythm modeling (productivity increasing in the morning, decreasing before lunch and lowering in the afternoon) were up to 7 % higher than the ones obtained with the standard modeling (a flat curve: same productivity rate all day). The addition of 5-min rest pauses to the circadian curves had little impact on performance, increasing productivity in less than 1 %. It is important to note that these results derived from simulation therefore they are not exact outcomes, from real life situations. However, they point out that it is possible, and desirable, to make simulations more real by incorporating human parameters to the software.

There are many variables impacting human performance, and many constraints that might be used in simulations, which were not used in this study. However, the goal was to show that it is possible and desirable to "humanize" the labor resource of simulation software in order to get more real results. Overall, the obtained results justify the development of computational routines able to represent "humans" and their interactions with the system in a more realistic manner. Labor is often represented as a machine, because it is difficult to mimic human complexity in a software. Although this might be true, there is no reason for avoiding the inclusion of human factors parameters in manufacturing modeling. Either production engineers must improve their knowledge in ergonomics, or ergonomists must be included in the engineer's team, or both.

Acknowledgments. This research was partly supported by the National Council for Scientific and Technological Development (CNPq) and the Capes Foundation/Ministry of Education (CAPES).

References

1. Baines, T., Stephen, M., Siebers, P.O., Ladbrook, J.: Humans: the missing link in manufacturing simulation? School of Industrial and Manufacturing Science. Cranfield University. Elsevier, B.V. Bedfordshire UK (2003)
2. Spencer, M.B.: The influence of irregularity of rest and activity on performance: a model based on time since sleep and time of day. Ergonomics **30**, 1275–1286 (1987)
3. Parker, H.W., Oglesby, C.H.: Methods improvement for construction managers. McGraw-Hill, New York (1972)
4. Monk, T.H., Buysse, D.J., Reynolds III, C.F., Berga, S.L., Jarrett, D.B., Begley, A.E., Kupfer, D.J.: Circadian rhythms in human performance and mood under constant conditions. J. Sleep Res. **6**, 9–18 (1997)
5. Grandjean, E.: Ergonomics in Computerized Office. Taylor and Francis, London (1987)
6. Bhatia, N., Murrell, K.F.H.: An industrial experiment in organized rest pauses. Hum. Factors **11**, 167–173 (1969)
7. Vernon, H.M., Bedford, T.: The influence of Rest Pauses on Light Industrial Work. Industrial Fatigue Research Board. Report Nr. 25 (1924)
8. Viteles, M.S.: Industrial Psychology. W.W. Norton and Company, New York (1932)

Children's Mental Model as a Tool to Provide Innovation in Digital Products

Adriana Chammas[(⊠)], Manuela Quaresma,
and Cláudia Renata Mont'Alvão

LEUI | Laboratory of Ergodesign and Usability Interfaces, PUC-Rio University,
Rio de Janeiro, Brazil
ttdri@yahoo.com.br, {mquaresma,cmontalvao}@puc-rio.br

Abstract. The technological development market is faced with the growing demand for products whose innovations break paradigms. The User-Centered Design approach is used with praise to cause incremental innovations in digital products, but it is not ideal to realize radical innovations. This article aims to present the state of the art in question and ask whether the mental model of children, whose creativity is evident, can be applied to the development process with a User Centered Design approach, and, if so, how to adapt this approach to accelerate the development of radically innovative products to the market.

Keywords: HCI · Methodology · Children · Creativity · Innovation

1 Introduction

This article discusses the role of creativity in the development of innovative digital products and questions if it can be caused, housed in a method. The market cannot keep the eagerness of users for new products, better and different. The User-Centered Design approach is used with praise to provoque incremental innovations in digital products, but according to Norman [16] is not ideal to realize radical innovations. Based on these scenario, this article questions whether the mental model of the children, whose creativity is evident, can be applied to the development process with User Centered Design approach, and, if so, how to adapt this approach to accelerate the development of radically innovative products to market.

2 Urgent Demand

In the era where certainties are constantly changing, the technological development market is faced with a growing demand for products with breaking paradigm innovations. The urgent demand makes incremental innovations launched sparingly, once companies prefer "save" the launch of the features of their product, so they always have an innovation as key to present, albeit incremental, and at least keep the market positioning against the competition. Aware of the demand, technological development market turns to innovative products new releases as rapidly as expected, but there are important differences between two kinds of innovations: incremental and radical. Norman and Verganti [17] explain the difference between them:

© Springer International Publishing Switzerland 2015
A. Marcus (Ed.): DUXU 2015, Part II, LNCS 9187, pp. 23–33, 2015.
DOI: 10.1007/978-3-319-20898-5_3

– Incremental innovations are small changes in a product that will improve its performance, reduce cost, increase the user desire to acquire it or that anticipate the launch of a new product.
– Radical Innovations happen through technology changes or meaning. These innovations break concepts, bring new areas, break paradigms and open field for significant changes.

Even knowing the importance of the user's voice in the product development process, Lettl [13] points out that the radical innovations considered by Von Hippel studies [25, 26] only reaches low to medium degree of innovation. Lettl [13] believes that this result can be explained by specific barriers of users in the context of radical innovations. They are the barrier of knowledge and the barrier of interest.

The first, the knowledge barrier, may be caused by excessive cognitive demands that may occur:

– In the idea generation phase, users may be "functionally attached" to the current context, which would make hard the development of radical ideas (Birch and Rabinowitz (1951) *apud* Lettl [13];
– Without any reference of existing products, it becomes very difficult for the user to deal with concepts and prototypes (Tauber (1974), Schoormans et al. (1995) and Veryzer (1998b) *apud* Lettl [13];
– Users may not be able to make a valuable contribution due to the major technological complexities involved [13].

The second barrier relates to motivation: according to the authors Sheth (1981), Ram (1987) and Sheth and Ram (1989) *apud* Lettl [13]; this gap of motivation may come from the fear of obsolescence of knowledge presented by the user. Norman and Verganti [17] illustrate the motivation barrier by placing that radical innovations that propose double changes, both technology as meaning, are dangerous, since users tend to resist massive changes. This is the ambiguous nature of innovation. It requires changes and with them, energy spent on learning.

Despite the barriers exposed above, it can be understood that clear comprehension of user characteristics significantly increases the effectiveness in finding the ideal profile for the research. Companies must identify what type of user is able to contribute, at different stages in the radical innovation process and identify how best to interact with them. It is noticed that the mental model of the user must be taken into account.

The studies (Sheth 1981; Ram 1987; Sheth and Ram 1989 *apud* Lettl [13]) have shown that companies focused on radical innovation benefit significantly by interacting with users, since users are able to act as inventors and co-developers of innovations. Saffer [19] agrees with user participation as co-author and cites the User-Centered Design, henceforth DCU, as the most popular of all product development approaches such.

3   Approaches

Different design theories have been adapted and adopted to actively involve children in the development of technological products for them (Nesset and Large 2004). The relevant theories, in addition to the DCU [11] are: Contextual Design [2], Participatory

Design [5, 15], Cooperative Inquiry [9, 10], Informant Design [21] and Learner-centered Design [15].

3.1   User-Centered Design

Classical approach, DCU [11] focuses on the impact that technology will bring to the wishes and needs of users, both in newer versions of existing products as well as new concepts. The DCU is an iterative process of rapid prototyping and testing in several cycles to ensure that products are appropriate for their users. The process begins with a deeply analysis of users' needs and tries to link these needs to most appropriate technologies (or methods) that can better satisfy them - or tailor products to new trends. For Nesset and Large [15], the issues that guide the User-Centered Design are: (a) Activities - What software does? (b) Tools - What tools are needed to accomplish the tasks? (c) Interface - What interface supports these tools?

DCU techniques are appropriate for incremental innovations. Norman [16], a pioneer in DCU, points out important limitations that this approach presents, when the goal is radical innovation. The DCU is a philosophy, not a precise set of methods. It assumes that innovation must come from users. Likewise, von Hippel [25, 26] points out the users as the highest sources of innovation. Druin [9, 10] and Nesset and Large [15] makes clear that the DCU users, whether adults or children, are involved too late to have some control in the development process. One of the critical points of the approach in question is the user involvement limitation, which is not able to create or modify the product really, just point out its problems. Another important point is the need to make adjustments in its methods to use them with children: Questionnaires can be boring or difficult to understand, for example.

Norman [16] defines mental models as concepts in the minds of people who represent the understanding they have of how things work. For the author, people may have different mental models for the same thing, action, activity, while the same person can have multiple mental models for the same thing, action, activity, each dealing with a different aspect of the operation. Mental models are valuable for allowing prediction and understanding of how things should behave. Norman [16] also points out that these models serve as guides to help designers achieve the objectives in "worlds" unknown. Saffer [19] believes that the best mental models allow a deeper understanding of how the "thing" works without the complexity of what makes it works. Ultimately, both related mental models to the core of innovation, the concept of creativity.

3.2   Contextual Design

The Contextual Design is an approach widely used to reveal details, constraints and user motivations in their work context [2]. In Contextual Design a database is created from observations of typical user activities and then exposed to the creative/development group, so the team can share it and use as a base to their design decisions. The researchers make their records and seek to conduct research while maintaining the lowest possible interaction with users, just asking questions for clarification, if needed. This working model is pictorial, easy to see and can be understood quickly [15].

Based on the collected data, the work is structured for a new phase, in which the models will be consolidated and, with the identification of patterns (without neglect the individual variations) an affinity diagram is built. The team discussed about the consolidation of the collected data and how technology can benefit users. Storyboards are developed to understand how the user will interact with the new system and what impact this technology can bring to the user routine. Finally, low-fidelity mock-ups are developed and tested with users.

Considering the use of paper prototyping, pictorial and colorful diagrams and specific technical exercises, Nesset and Large [15] understand that the Contextual Design is appropriate to the context centered on the child.

3.3   Participatory Design

Iterative by premised, that said that no one approach is better than the users themselves to determine how to improve your routine. The objectives and strategies to achieve them are continually refined and there is no order default for your practice [5, 15].

There are two major themes for the implementation of the Participatory Design principles (Muller 1991; Muller, Wildman and White 1994 apud Druin et al. [9, 10, 15]: the "mutual reciprocal learning" where designers and users exchange knowledge and experiences about practical and technical possibilities; and the "design by doing", where interactions are experienced, modelled, supported and learned during practice. The Participatory Design mainly makes use of two techniques: modelling and the metaphor based design. The modelling occurs with the implementation of fantasies, criticism or what-if scenarios based on users' requirements. From these two techniques, Nesset and Large [15] choose the metaphor based design as the most practical and creative to represent the desired results because this process of conceptual prototyping is generated from metaphors that represent the present and future scenarios. Designers and users collaborate with each other in the process.

Although widely adopted, the great challenge of Participatory Design is the reluctance from the development staff to accept inputs from users. This challenge is also reflects when the design project is child-centered. Children should be considered true partners in design. Therefore, the Participatory Design process/techniques are suitable for children.

3.4   Cooperative Inquiry

Druin et al. [9, 10] understand that with the development of new technologies for children, their participation in research laboratories is gaining ground in the market and makes their inputs crucial in the design and development process. This understanding led the authors to develop a new methodology to enable the developer team to stop, listen and learn from the collaboration of children of various ages - and thus create exciting new and significant technologies for children, by children.

The Cooperative Inquiry is a combination of different techniques of useful approaches to apply with children. Based on exploratory studies and literature, adjustments were made in Contextual Inquiry, developed by Beyer and Holtzblatt [2]; the review of the Technology Immersion, the CHIkids developed by Boltman et al. (1998); [9, 10]; and defined the approach.

Druin [9] concludes that the major advantage of the approach is to collect data on true and sincere children's views not what the children believe adults want to hear. The adaptation of the technique must take into account the dynamics of a team composed by multiple generations. The Cooperative Inquiry orientation is to balance the team, always with more than one child and more than one adult. Adults should behave as adults when appropriate.

Druin et al. [9] considers 7 to 10 years the ideal age for Cooperative Inquiry, because at this age children are able to develop ideas of abstract concepts and, by the same time, are still open to explore new ideas. A little different than Druin et al. [9] and attentive to decrease the divergent thinking at around 09 years old, Lubart and Lautry 1996 *apud* Russ and Fiorelli [18] speculate that the development of rationality in this phase can affect the creative performance. Piaget (1962) *apud* Russ and Fiorelli, [18] says that "the creative imagination, which is the assimilation of the activity in the state of spontaneity, does not decreases with time. As a result of a related process of adaptation, creativity is gradually reintegrated into intelligence".

The Cooperative Inquiry notes users in context with, at least, two researchers participating. The first should be interacting with the child as a facilitator and the second will make the records out of the child's visual range. Among other techniques borrowed from other approaches, Druin et al. [9, 10], found that the construction of a "cartoon-like" flow chart is necessary, as the authors noted that children cannot comply events in the proposed order, and sometimes starts more than one task at a time, and complete them at random - or even complete it [15]. Druin et al. [9] considered the low-fidelity prototypes an effective tool when used along Cooperative Inquiry: it keeps the focus of the discussion centered on its purpose and become thrusters of collaborative brainstormings.

3.5   Informant Design

Developed by Scaife et al. [21], the Informant Design also considers the iteration ideal. This approach considers that each team member brings different inputs, at different stages of the project. The author makes adjustments on prototypes in order to adapt them to use with children [21]. The Informant Design advocates the use of several informants (adults and children, for example) to maximize the wealth of information. The approach is structured in three phases: (a) Elect the objectives and identify strengths and weaknesses of the project; (b) Adults and children are separated in different informants teams and designers evaluate the inputs of both teams. Then developers make a list of issues; (c) Low-fidelity prototypes are constructed and proposed only for the children's team. The inputs will be used to build high-fidelity prototypes for evaluation by both teams. Iterations are considered, if necessary.

Scaife et al. [21] point out the Informant Design as an alternative to User-Centered Design or Participatory Design and believes that this is the best approach to the design of digital products for atypical users or users who cannot be considered equal to developers, like children for example [15].

3.6   Learner-Centered Design

The approach proposed by Soloway, Guzdial and Hay (1994) *apud* Nesset and Large [15] says that the interface design should be adapted to the interests, knowledge and the style of it apprentices. The authors are all learners, whether professionals or students. The questions that guides the Learner Centered Design are: (a) Understanding - How will be the learning interaction? (b) Motivation - How to motivate the learner interface? (c) Diversity - How should be developed to different learners interface? (d) Growth - Since the interface can track user ripening?

To answer the questions listed above, Soloway et al. (1994) apud Nesset and Large [15] adapted the Scaffolding Technique for which they named TILT model of design software (Task, Interface, Learner's needs, Tools). The Scaffolding Technique is an instructional process oriented to promote a consistent learning, wherein the extent to which learners gradually internalize their learning, the support for the interaction disappears, until the user controls it completely. The natural orientation of the approach is the development of understanding, performance and user expertise [15].

4   Creativity and Children

Sternberg and Lubart [22] relate the concept of creativity to the process of generating new ideas that bring into existence new ways of thinking and doing. It is the ability to create, produce or invent new things; inventiveness and artistic creativity (Houaiss).

For Wright [27] all people have some creative potential, what differs is how much of that potential people are able to accomplish. The author exposes the creativity as a mental trait, a trait of personality. She [27] lists the personal qualities of creative people: the valuation of creativity, originality, independence, risk taking, ability to reset problems, energy, curiosity, attraction to complexity, artistry, open mind, desire to spend time alone, perceptiveness, concentration, mood and ability to resume childhood qualities. For the author [27], these personality traits are associated with thinking styles, which include: visualization, imagination, experimentation, metaphorical/analogical thinking, logical reasoning, profit prediction and consequences, analysis, synthesis and evaluation. Added to thinking styles mentioned, intrinsic motivation and commitment are key personal qualities for the development of creativity.

Csikszentmihalyi [7] believes that creativity refers to the significant change in some aspect of the field and it develops through interpersonal relationships, the relationship between the creative and their work and compass between the individual and other people (or institutions) that judge the quality of their work. For Csikszentmihalyi [7], which allows certain individuals to make memorable contributions to culture is the personal resolution to model their lives to achieve their goals rather than drift the destination. It can be said that the most obvious of the creative achievements is that they have created for their own lives.

In a controversial paper at the time, Csikszentmihalyi [7] states that the purely rational application is inadequate, not only to explain the creativity, but cognition in general. The human mind cannot be understood only in terms of knowledge and heuristics, as to explain the genesis of the creative act, one must understand and include the complex interaction between the emotional and motivational dimensions. The ideal model, according to the author, is who balances all of the above elements and also takes into account the dynamics of the process. The most important revelation is what can motivate people to use their minds as they use in real life, not only in solving problems in controlled experiments. Barclay & Petitto [1] agree that decoupage cognition, emotion and motivation in the context of real life is an important strategy to untangle personal aspects, whether organic or environmental, but state that the decoupage does not imply disassociate these genuine dimensions, but to isolate elements of thinking without forgetting the interdependence between cognition and motivation.

Regardless of the discussion among the authors, it is clear that, for both the creative phenomenon that occurs with the task can be influenced by the audience or by the context in which it occurs. It is understood then that motivation is directly related to the creative phenomenon.

Simonton [20] points out that advances in research regarding creativity focus on the following topics: the cognitive process involved in this activity, the personal creative features, and finally the development and manifestation of creativity during the life of creative and social context.

Russ and Fiorelli [18] agree that contemporary creative research face the creative product as a result of a complex interaction between the individual and the context. The authors states that there are different variables in the processes that encourage creativity and that many of these processes can be observed and measured in children. Some of these cognitive and affective processes are divergent thinking, problem solving, flexibility of thought, accessories to emotion, and accessories to affect in fantasy. Much of what has been written on the development of children's creativity involves playing, and the greatest evidence of the creative act in children occurs during the play activity. Fein (1987), Sawyer (1987) and Vygotsky (1930/1967) *apud* Russ and Fiorelli [18] state that creativity and play are interconnected. The authors state that adult interventions can improve the play and conclude that the suggestion of similar techniques can be of great help in the development of creativity.

Russ and Fiorelli [18] point to several studies that suggest that children are creative from birth as soon as they are able to bring new ideas. The authors affirm that it should be considered many examples of routine creativity, also know as "little-c". Authors suggest some ways (present below) to incite the various processes involving the creativity in childhood, so they can become creative adults:

1. Allow time for the child to play pretend play - Incorporating conventional-imaginative play and symbolic play;
2. Encourage activities in different areas, so that the child can find What They deeply enjoy and Develop Their talents and abilities;
3. Strengthen and enhance routine creative acts;

4. Encourage independence in problem solving, keeping in mind the balance between challenge and frustration;
5. Encourage verbal expression of feelings, especially during games, so the child gets used to the practice of verbalization and can join the activity in the accessible memory.

It is common the link between the concepts creativity and children [3, 9, 10, 12, 23, 27]. Bruckman and Bandlow [3] state that the children's perception of the world of is radically different from the adults' perception and recommend that innovative projects become from surveys with this profile, whose imagination is peculiar. The authors state that personal qualities of the most creative people in history are inherent to children [9, 10, 20, 27].

Teachers agree with that, once inserted in a suitable context, children provide meaningful ideas on request, especially when they realize the value that their ideas can bring to the project in question and how much they can share with their peers [20]. The author points out that children's creativity can spark better solutions than adults' when asked to create their own version of existing objects [20]. It can be concluded that the exercise of redesign objects, real or virtual, encourages children's trust and ability to go beyond the world of art and design around adults and allows rethink possibilities even in objects that were not created yet.

Kelley and Littman [12] agree that it is fundamental for innovation to observe and talk with children. As co-authors in digital product development processes, children offer honest contributions with their own world views. They have different opinions, preferences and needs than adults opinions, preferences and needs. IDEO [12], a renowned Design company based in Silicon Valley, is dedicated to developing innovative products. In alternate weeks, IDEO invites children to be observed when interacting with their products and prototypes, believing that the uniqueness inherent in children cannot be found elsewhere. Druin et al. [9, 10] and Markopoulos et al. [14] emphasize that beliefs regarding what will be the behavior of children and what can be expected of them in the context of evaluation are odd. Both agree that the digital product development methodology must be appropriate to hear and interpret the contributions of children.

5   A Creative Proposal

Creative people are masters in accomplishing profitable findings of problems and fields of ideas that are not related. They perceive connections between data and ideas and turn these patterns in even better ideas. Csikszentmihalyi [7], in its publication on creativity, identified patterns in creative people that can be replicated in controlled conditions. According to the author's research, we bring further questions:

1. The identification of such patterns can be applied in children?
2. If it is possible to identify them from the patterns, is it possible to outline, transform the pattern into a replicable mental model and apply it in an adult?
3. The barrier of knowledge and the barrier of interest, both identified by Lettl [13] in the context of radical innovations, can be minimized if not annihilated, if the child mental model, free of preconceptions of adults is used?

4. Is the mental model of children better than the mental model of adult users in projects involving creativity required to produce radical innovations?
5. Can DCU techniques be adapted to children's mental model of the for radical innovations investigation?
6. Can innovation based on children's mental model be measured?

It is believed that the answers to the above questions will benefit those responsible for advanced technology development, to enable more and better innovative (disruptive) products for future consumption in the market. The results of this research can provide effective gains in digital solutions development processes and bring disruptive innovations that can transform the mindset of children in a process. Thus, in addition to monitoring the agility required by the market, the digital product development process tends to be satisfactory in terms of design and productivity, in which the end result should, in addition to ensuring the user a positive and enjoyable experience, provide revolutionary solutions.

6 Final Thoughts

Regarding specific discussions on methodology, children and creativity, this paper aimed to present the state of art of the topics in question and propose that children's mental model, and all creativity inherent in it, can be used in project development methodology for digital solutions for radical innovations. Kafai (1999 *apud* Nesset and Large [15]), believes that children have the ability to be more than just informants and become design process' participants. Many other researchers cited in this paper share thoughts with this author and the literature examined stresses the importance of children's participation in such projects.

Here were explored approaches commonly used in research with children and all depart from the DCU, each in his own way. Despite the UCD uncontestable value, it is noticed that, unlike Saffer [19] thinks when quotes that User Centered Design as the most popular of the digital product development approaches, the approaches previously explored urge that changes are needed in the classical approach, especially when it involves children - regardless of what role they have in the process.

The barrier of knowledge and the barrier of interest were revealed as obstacles to the urgent demand of radically innovative products. The barriers cited in this paper are presents less impact on children. It is believed that the barrier of knowledge caused by the excess of cognitive demands, suggested by Lettl [13] and listed below, can be minimized:

(a) Idea generation phase, when users may be "functionally fixed", can be overcome by the ability to create, to produce or to invent new things inherent to children [6, 9, 10, 12, 14, 15, 27].

(b) Up front the discussion over the decrescent divergent thinking at around 9 years old [18] recognize that children in general (in the range of age and development) have not had time yet to master the acquired knowledge in order to do more complex transformations or sublimation. But even without references over existing products, children (especially from 07 to 09 years old) have the ability to deal with abstract concepts [6, 18] and can become effective source of creativity;

(c) Although users may not be able to offer valuable contributions towards technological complexities [13], children can make suggestions that will lead developers to adapt the technology to the operational reality and bring them to possible reality.

It is understood that the fear of obsolescence of knowledge, envisioned by the user featuring the barrier of motivation [13], will not be experienced by children. Therefore, it is understood that children's mental model can be the key to development of radical innovations. Companies interested in creating and developing this type of product can meet the profile of user who can contribute in the innovation process.

References

1. Barclay, C.R., Petitto, A.L.: Creative activity in the context of real life: a response to Csikszentmihalyi. New Ideas Psychol. **7**(1), 41–48 (1989)
2. Beyer, H.R., Holtzblatt, K.: Contextual design. Interactions **6**(1), 32–42 (1999)
3. Bruckman, A., Bandlow, A.: Human-Computer Interaction for Kids. In: Jacko, J., Sears, A. (eds.) The Human-Computer Interaction Handbook, vol. 1, pp. 428–440. Lawence Erlbaum, Hillsdale (2003)
4. Bruckman, A.: Teaching students to study online communities ethically. J. Inf. Ethics **15**(2), 82–98 (2006)
5. Carmel, E., Whitaker, R., George, J.: PD and joint application design: a transatlantic comparison. Commun. ACM - Spec. Issue Participatory Des. **36**(4), 40–48 (1993)
6. Chammas, A., Moraes, A., Teixeira, A.: Ergonomics and Usability for Children: Spore®: a Study Case. Ergonomia e usabilidade de interfaces para crianças: o estudo de caso do game Spore®. Dissertação (mestrado) – Pontifícia Universidade Católica do Rio de Janeiro, PUC Rio, Rio de Janeiro (2011)
7. Csikszentmihalyi, M.: Motivation and creativity: towards a synthesis of structural and energistic approaches to cognition. New Ideas Psychol. **6**, 159–176 (1988)
8. Dietrich, A.: Who's afraid of a cognitive neuroscience of creativity? Sci. Direct Methods **42**, 22–27 (2007)
9. Druin, A., Bederson, B., Boltman, A., Miura, A., Knotts-Callahan, D., Platt, M.: Children as our technology design partners. In: Druin, A. (ed.) The Design of Children's Technology, vol. 1, pp. 51–72. Morgan Kaufmann Publishers Inc., San Francisco (2006)
10. Druin, A.: Children as co-designers of new technologies: valuing the imagination to transform what is possible. New Dir. Youth Dev. Theor. Pract. Res. Youth Media Creators **128**, 35–44 (2011)
11. ISO 9241-210 (2010): ISO 9241-210. Ergonomics Of Human-System Interaction – Part 210: Human-Centred Design For Interactive Systems. Génève: International Organization Standarization (2010)
12. Kelley, T., Littman, J.: The Ten Faces of Innovation. IDEO's Strategies for Defeating the Devil's Advocate and Driving Creativity Throughout Your Organization. Doubleday, New York (2005)
13. Lettl, C.: User Involvement Competence for Radical Innovation. J. Eng. Tech. Manage. **24** (1–2), 53–75 (2007)

14. Markopoulos, P., et al.: Evaluating Children's Interactive Products: Principles and Practices for Interactions Designers. Morgan Kaufmann (Elsevier, Inc.), Burlington (2008)
15. Nesset, V., Large, A.: Children in the information technology design process: a review of theories and their applications. Sci. Direct Libr. Inf. Sci. Res. **26**, 140–161 (2004)
16. Norman, D.A.: Design of Everyday Things, Revised and Expanded: Basic Books. MIT Press (UK edition) New York, London (2013)
17. Norman, D.A., Verganti, R.: Incremental and radical innovation: design research versus technology and meaning change. Des. Issues **30**(1), 78–96 (2012)
18. Russ, S.W., Fiorelli, J.A.: Developmental approaches to creativity. In: Kaufman, J.C., Sternberg, R.J. (eds.) The Cambridge Handbook of Creativity, vol. 12. Cambridge University Press, New York (2010)
19. Saffer, D.: Designing for Interaction. New Riders, Berkeley (2010)
20. Simonton, D.K.: Creativity: cognitive, personal, developmental, and social aspects. Am. Psychol. Assoc. Am. Psychol. **55**(1), 151–158 (2000)
21. Scaife, M., Rogers, Y.: Kids as informants: telling us what we didn't know or confirming what we knew already? In: Druin, A. (ed.) The Design of Children's Technology. Morgan Kaufmann Publishers, Brighton (1999)
22. Sternberg, R., Lubart, T.: Investing in creativity. Am. Psychol. **51**(7), 677–688 (1996)
23. Szekely, G.: How Children Make Art: Lessons in Creativity from Home to School. Teachers College Press, New York (2006)
24. Villar, M.S., Franco, F.M.M.: Houaiss Portuguese Dictionary - Dicionário Houaiss da língua Portuguesa. Objetiva, Rio de Janeiro (2009)
25. Von Hippel, E.A.: The Sources of Innovation. Oxford University Press, New York (1988)
26. Von Hippel, E.A.: Democratizing Innovation. MIT Press, Cambridge (2005)
27. Wright, S.: Understanding Creativity in Early Childhood: Meaning-Making and Children's Drawings. SAGE Publications, London (2010)

HARSim: Posterior Load Comparative Analysis Process

Ricardo Dagge[1(✉)], Ernesto Filgueiras[2,3], and Francisco Rebelo[3,4]

[1] Faculty of Architecture – University of Lisbon, Lisbon, Portugal
ricardodagge@gmail.com
[2] Laboratory of Online Communication of University of Beira Interior
(LabCom), Covilhã, Portugal
[3] Centre for Architecture, Urban Planning and Design (CIAUD),
Lisbon, Portugal
[4] Faculty of Human Motricity – University of Lisbon, Lisbon, Portugal

Abstract. Considered as a not fully appropriated way for load carriage on the spine, backpacks tend to be the elected products by students to carry their own school supplies [4]. Its use has been pointed out as a determinant aspect that contributes to the appearance of back pain and musculoskeletal disorders, mainly in growth stage children [4, 5]. Spine overload, often seen when wearing backpacks, is considered one of the main risk factor for the degeneration of intervertebral discs [1, 6, 7].

For further understanding this matter, the difficulties found in quantifying spinal acting loads, lead to the development of a considerable amount of bio-mechanical computerized models. The dissemination of this kind of models, lead to the need of their results evaluation as a very important aspect to consider in the selection of the most adequate software for specific study situations.

Major findings allowed to apprehend the best way to apply posterior loads onto the spine of backpack users using HARSim by dynamically comparing its results with the ones presented by Rose [2]. This paper presents all the process, allowing its reproduction and application for this type of carrying transportation system for further studies to come.

Keywords: HARSim · User experience · Posterior load transportation · Backpack

1 Introduction

Considered as a not fully appropriated way for load carriage on the spine, backpacks tend to be the elected products by students to carry their own school supplies [4]. Its use has been pointed out as a determinant aspect that contributes to the appearance of back pain and musculoskeletal disorders, mainly in growth stage children [4, 5]. Spine overload, often seen when wearing backpacks, is considered one of the main risk factors for the degeneration of intervertebral discs [1, 6, 7].

For further understanding this matter, the difficulties found in quantifying spinal acting loads, lead to the development of a considerable amount of biomechanical computerized models. Due to the fact that force transducers should not be introduced

© Springer International Publishing Switzerland 2015
A. Marcus (Ed.): DUXU 2015, Part II, LNCS 9187, pp. 34–44, 2015.
DOI: 10.1007/978-3-319-20898-5_4

into the spine of alive humans these models intended to estimate the load acting in the spine of a user, during different kinds of lifting activities [1].

The dissemination of this kind of models, lead to the need of their results evaluation as a very important aspect to consider in the selection of the most adequate software for a specific study situation.

The most accurate validation process should involve the comparison of the results achieved in computerized models with the ones gathered in vivo subjects for the same anthropometrical characteristics, weight carried and activity performed. In vivo measurements are considered to be the most viable, since they provide absolute loading values [1], although this intrusive process involves a considerable amount of danger to the studied subject. So the most conscientious process to verify a model involves comparing its results with data gathered from the literature [2, 3].

Computerized biomechanical models date back to 1961, when Pearson et al. presented a two link model of the arm that intended to calculate forces and torques on shoulder and elbow [10]. Despite their evolution throughout the years, there are few biomechanical models developed considering their incorporation into the design process. One of these three-dimensional computerized models is called Humanoid Articulation Reaction Simulation (HARSim) and was specifically developed for product, workspaces and task procedures optimizations [8].

HARSim is provided with a humanoid computerized representation with 38 segments, a full spine with 24 vertebrae, and upper and lower limbs with 8 and 6 segments, respectively [8]. This humanoid model has 100 degrees of freedom, 72 for the spine, 12 for the lower limbs and 16 for the upper limbs [8]. Its model has four operational features, which include: human model generation; posture and movement simulations; geometrical objects creation; and forces, stress and strain calculation in each articulation joint [8].

When it comes to results, HARSim calculates in each articulation joint three reaction forces, one axial and two shear, and besides that it is also able to calculate three bending moments around each orthonormal reference axis along with the maximal compression force in intervertebral spaces [8]. HARSim development and validation process was thoroughly described by Rebelo et al. [8].

HARSim has already been validated with in vivo intervertebral disc pressure measurements, like the ones reported by Wilke, Neef, Hinz, et al. [1, 8] for ten activities. In this validation process none of the studied activities involved posterior load transportation, which proved to be helpful, since this software has already been used by one of the authors of this paper for studying the approximate intensity of forces applied to children's spine, while carrying their own backpacks to and from school [9].

It is intended for this study the apprehension of the best way to estimate posterior load transportation in backpacks using HARSim, by dynamically comparing its results with the ones achieved by Rose [2]. This comparison method involved the replication of the study made by Rose [2], concerning backpack transportation system, and allowed to demonstrate that HARSim results are very similar regarding force peaks in the lumbosacral region of the spine when considering anterior-posterior shear forces.

Rose [2] analyzed sixteen voluntary healthy individuals, fifty percent of which were female, with no history of lumbar back disorders. Their age ranged from 19 to 32, with a mean stature of 174, 3 cm and an average weight of 72.9 kg. Each subject carried six types of products intended for weight transportation during two levels of gait motion. Transported weight varied in each carrying activity: a no weight (NW) transportation situation; a 5, 7 kg transportation (LW); and, 11, 3 kg transportation (HW) [2].

The author justified the chosen weight range according to Kelsey, Githens et al. who stated that the repetition of an activity transporting more than 11.3 kg dramatically increased the risk of prolapsed disc. Reference [2] Being so, Rose considered 11.3 kg as the high weight (HW) transported by the studied subject and divided that by two to get a mid-range transportation weight namely (LW) of 5.7 kg.

Rose study was primarily focused on anterior-posterior (A/P) shear forces, compression, and lateral shear observed at the inferior endplates of the lumbar discs form L5/S1 to T12/L1, determined by a biologically electromyography (EMG)-assisted biomechanical model, previously described and validated.

When it comes to backpacks, Rose [2] concluded that the differences between the 11, 3 kg and the no weight transportation condition were indistinguishable. He also claimed that among the 12 studied tasks the backpack produced especially low spine loads [2] which he believes that can be attributed to the reduced arm of the moment induced by placing the load closer to the user's body weight of this product [2]. Rose [2] also claims that by distributing the weight evenly the dual-strap design of the backpack prevents the needs for muscles on one side of the body to compensate for uneven loading.

2   Method

In this paper it would only be replicated the stationary situations when wearing a backpack with no weight (NW), 5, 7 kg (LW) and 11, 3 kg (HW) transported by users.

Thanks to human model generation capability that HARSim possess, it was possible to replicate the sixteen anthropometrical profiles described by Rose [2].

For each generated model, a posture involving a dorsal and lumbar inclination of 1 and 0.5 degrees respectively was assumed. This posture simulation was achieved with the overlapping of HARSim humanoid representation with the photographic registry presented by Rose [2].

The overlapping presented before also allowed to place the weight practiced by the backpack between the T4 and L1 vertebrae (Fig. 1).

A restriction among the ZX plan in these vertebrae was needed to simulate that the force practiced by the backpack was primarily focused along the Y axis.

In order to simulate the forces practiced by the backpack and referenced by Rose [2] of 5, 7 kg and 11, 3 KG both were converted into 55,917 and 110,853 Newton's respectively. Each of these conversions were divided by two in order to obtain the force practiced by each of the backpack carrying handles (Fig. 2).

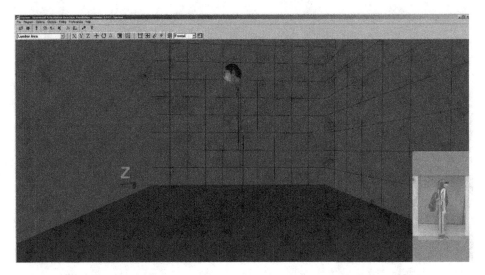

Fig. 1. Picture overlapping for posture and weight practiced by the backpack simulation

Applied on the shoulders of each HARSim humanoid model the vectors of the forces practiced by each backpack carrying handle were divided accordingly the picture below:

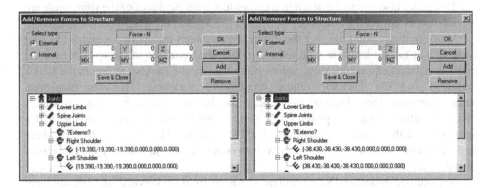

Fig. 2. 5, 7 KG (on the left) and 11, 3 kg (on the right) vectors applied on each shoulder

The process described earlier generated a humanoid model like the one presented below (Fig. 3):

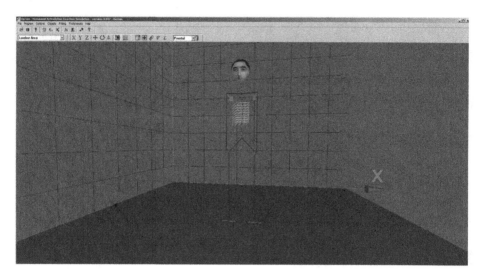

Fig. 3. HARSim humanoid model generated

3 Results

Major findings revealed that the differences are small when it comes to using a backpack to transport either 5, 7 kg or 11, 3 kg.

This paper also showed that when it comes to the cervical area of the spine there are no differences between transporting 5, 7 kg, 11, 3 kg and no weight on the backpack.

Major findings point out that the differences between transported weights (5, 7 kg and 11, 3 kg) don't interfere with the region and the vertebrae of the spine where the maximum anterior/posterior shear values occur namely the Lumbar region in the L2/L1 vertebrae and the Thoracic region on L1/T12 vertebrae. However maximum anterior/posterior shear location differences may be seen on the no weight transportation condition. Here the peaks occur in the lumbar region namely in the S1/L5 vertebrae and the thoracic region in the T2/T1 vertebrae. This location shifting where the maximum anterior/ posterior shear values occur may be justified by the placement of the load (Table 1).

Regarding compression values differences apart from the cervical spine region were found in the intensity and location regarding the three weight conditions. No weight transported condition presented higher peaks than the 5, 7 kg. Here differences were almost 90 kPa and 35 kPa lower in the lumbar (L4/L3–5, 7 kg and L1/T12 – no weight) and thoracic region (T8/T7 – 5, 7 kg and T9/T8) respectively. Higher peaks' differences

Table 1. Anterior/Posterior Shear values (Region peaks)

Joint	Shear forces (N)	Shear forces (N)	Shear forces (N)
S1 / L5	217,74	200,34	183,25
L5 / L4	92,73	62,25	32,31
L4 / L3	11,30	-26,52	-63,67
L3 / L2	85,25	130,65	175,23
L2 / L1	157,25	207,33	256,50
L1 / T12	166,31	217,11	267,00
T12 / T11	126,02	174,72	222,55
T11 / T10	91,91	138,50	184,24
T10 / T9	57,93	102,01	145,30
T9 / T8	4,19	43,40	81,90
T8 / T7	33,62	-1,46	-35,90
T7 / T6	74,86	45,11	15,88
T6 / T5	102,94	77,55	52,61
T5 / T4	134,10	114,29	94,84
T4 / T3	147,42	130,87	114,61
T3 / T2	160,94	148,13	135,56
T2 / T1	170,29	160,88	151,64
T1 / C7	71,07	71,07	71,07
C7 / C6	62,59	62,59	62,59
C6 / C5	54,69	54,69	54,69
C5 / C4	46,08	46,08	46,08
C4 / C3	34,74	34,74	34,74
C3 / C2	22,75	22,75	22,75
C2 / C1	18,49	18,49	18,49
	No Weight	5, 7 Kg	11, 3 Kg

were found when comparing the no weight transported condition with the 11, 3 kg. In the lumbar region (L4/L3) 154 kPa higher peak was found for the 11, 3 kg than the no weight transported condition. Regarding the thoracic region, the no weight transportation condition peak was 55 kPa higher than the 11, 3 kg (T7/T6) (Table 2).

Regarding lateral shear values major findings revealed very close values between the no weight and 11, 3 kg transported condition. For the lumbar region the values were the same just differing in places (S1/L5 – no weight and L3/L2 – 11, 3 kg), and for the thoracic region the difference was around 6 N/m higher in the no weight transported

Table 2. Compression values (Region peaks)

Joint	Stress (kPa)	Stress (kPa)	Stress (kPa)
S1 / L5	430,59	300,66	426,71
L5 / L4	430,61	352,40	611,88
L4 / L3	376,48	382,67	622,01
L3 / L2	358,99	351,60	565,05
L2 / L1	388,91	254,71	438,36
L1 / T12	468,66	333,87	282,18
T12 / T11	537,77	426,26	316,76
T11 / T10	587,56	498,02	410,10
T10 / T9	621,94	553,48	486,25
T9 / T8	641,32	594,05	547,63
T8 / T7	635,52	606,39	577,78
T7 / T6	611,55	598,92	586,52
T6 / T5	569,97	570,90	571,82
T5 / T4	514,28	527,00	539,49
T4 / T3	448,55	470,00	491,07
T3 / T2	376,43	405,22	433,50
T2 / T1	299,29	333,70	367,49
T1 / C7	147,83	147,83	147,83
C7 / C6	124,36	124,36	124,36
C6 / C5	102,65	102,65	102,65
C5 / C4	83,14	83,14	83,14
C4 / C3	66,70	66,70	66,70
C3 / C2	52,73	52,73	52,73
C2 / C1	39,20	39,20	39,20
	No Weight	5, 7 Kg	11, 3 Kg

condition (T8/T7 – no weight and T7/T6 – 11, 3 kg). When it comes to the 5, 7 kg transported condition it registered the minimum value for the lumbar region (L3/L2) with a 14 N/ m difference for the other two weight conditions. The thoracic region (T7/T6) was almost the mean value for the other two weight transported conditions (Table 3).

4   Discussion

Enlarging analysis spectrum, incorporating all spine regions, this study results' meet with most of the findings presented by Rose [2] regarding the backpack transportation system.

Table 3. Lateral Shear values (Region peaks)

Joint	Moment XX (N/m)	Moment XX (N/m)	Moment XX (N/m)
S1 / L5	20,98	3,25	-10,32
L5 / L4	12,21	-3,26	-16,02
L4 / L3	8,47	-5,19	-17,02
L3 / L2	-6,50	6,26	20,28
L2 / L1	-9,15	1,00	13,22
L1 / T12	-14,04	-6,14	2,87
T12 / T11	-17,77	-11,01	-4,37
T11 / T10	-20,60	-14,93	-9,37
T10 / T9	-22,67	-18,04	-13,50
T9 / T8	-23,97	-20,33	-16,76
T8 / T7	30,79	27,04	23,36
T7 / T6	29,81	27,08	24,41
T6 / T5	27,63	25,77	23,95
T5 / T4	24,63	23,51	22,41
T4 / T3	20,72	20,18	19,65
T3 / T2	16,43	16,37	16,31
T2 / T1	11,75	12,06	12,37
T1 / C7	5,36	5,36	5,36
C7 / C6	4,14	4,14	4,14
C6 / C5	3,05	3,05	3,05
C5 / C4	2,11	2,11	2,11
C4 / C3	1,31	1,31	1,31
C3 / C2	0,71	0,71	0,71
C2 / C1	0,32	0,32	0,32
	No Weight	5, 7 Kg	11, 3 Kg

Considering maximum peak forces for all weights carried Tables 4, 5 and 6 shows that there were not found significant differences between them. However no weight carried situation from Rose's [2] study present an acting vertebrae peak closer to the ones obtained by our results.

Table 4. Anterior/Posterior Shear values (Region peaks) comparison

Joint	Reference A/P shear values - Rose [2]	Shear forces (N)	Reference A/P shear values - Rose [2]	Shear forces (N)	Reference A/P shear values - Rose [2]	Shear forces (N)
S1 / L5	240,40	217,74	261,90	200,34	301,80	183,25
L5 / L4	61,20	92,73	76,30	62,25	89,50	32,31
L4 / L3	172,50	11,30	165,50	-26,52	179,30	-63,67
L3 / L2	251,00	85,25	246,90	130,65	272,10	175,23
L2 / L1	273,40	157,25	270,00	207,33	298,80	256,50
L1 / T12	255,10	166,31	251,00	217,11	277,30	267,00
T12 / T11	N.A.	126,02	N.A.	174,72	N.A.	222,55
T11 / T10	N.A.	91,91	N.A.	138,50	N.A.	184,24
T10 / T9	N.A.	57,93	N.A.	102,01	N.A.	145,30
T9 / T8	N.A.	4,19	N.A.	43,40	N.A.	81,90
T8 / T7	N.A.	33,62	N.A.	-1,46	N.A.	-35,90
T7 / T6	N.A.	74,86	N.A.	45,11	N.A.	15,88
T6 / T5	N.A.	102,94	N.A.	77,55	N.A.	52,61
T5 / T4	N.A.	134,10	N.A.	114,29	N.A.	94,84
T4 / T3	N.A.	147,42	N.A.	130,87	N.A.	114,61
T3 / T2	N.A.	160,94	N.A.	148,13	N.A.	135,56
T2 / T1	N.A.	170,29	N.A.	160,88	N.A.	151,64
T1 / C7	N.A.	71,07	N.A.	71,07	N.A.	71,07
C7 / C6	N.A.	62,59	N.A.	62,59	N.A.	62,59
C6 / C5	N.A.	54,69	N.A.	54,69	N.A.	54,69
C5 / C4	N.A.	46,08	N.A.	46,08	N.A.	46,08
C4 / C3	N.A.	34,74	N.A.	34,74	N.A.	34,74
C3 / C2	N.A.	22,75	N.A.	22,75	N.A.	22,75
C2 / C1	N.A.	18,49	N.A.	18,49	N.A.	18,49
	No Weight	No Weight	5, 7 Kg	5, 7 Kg	11, 3 Kg	11, 3 Kg

Table 5. Compression values (Region peaks) comparison

Joint	Reference compression values - Rose [2]	Stress (kPa)	Reference compression values - Rose [2]	Stress (kPa)	Reference compression values - Rose [2]	Stress (kPa)
S1 / L5	395,20	430,59	417,50	300,66	465,70	426,71
L5 / L4	456,70	430,61	484,60	352,40	545,40	611,88
L4 / L3	424,20	376,48	458,10	382,67	519,50	622,01
L3 / L2	380,20	358,99	416,80	351,60	473,90	565,05
L2 / L1	361,20	388,91	399,00	254,71	454,10	438,36
L1 / T12	374,90	468,66	411,60	333,87	468,70	282,18
T12 / T11	N.A.	537,77	N.A.	426,26	N.A.	316,76
T11 / T10	N.A.	587,56	N.A.	498,02	N.A.	410,10
T10 / T9	N.A.	621,94	N.A.	553,48	N.A.	486,25
T9 / T8	N.A.	641,32	N.A.	594,05	N.A.	547,63
T8 / T7	N.A.	635,52	N.A.	606,39	N.A.	577,78
T7 / T6	N.A.	611,55	N.A.	598,92	N.A.	586,52
T6 / T5	N.A.	569,97	N.A.	570,90	N.A.	571,82
T5 / T4	N.A.	514,28	N.A.	527,00	N.A.	539,49
T4 / T3	N.A.	448,55	N.A.	470,00	N.A.	491,07
T3 / T2	N.A.	376,43	N.A.	405,22	N.A.	433,50
T2 / T1	N.A.	299,29	N.A.	333,70	N.A.	367,49
T1 / C7	N.A.	147,83	N.A.	147,83	N.A.	147,83
C7 / C6	N.A.	124,36	N.A.	124,36	N.A.	124,36
C6 / C5	N.A.	102,65	N.A.	102,65	N.A.	102,65
C5 / C4	N.A.	83,14	N.A.	83,14	N.A.	83,14
C4 / C3	N.A.	66,70	N.A.	66,70	N.A.	66,70
C3 / C2	N.A.	52,73	N.A.	52,73	N.A.	52,73
C2 / C1	N.A.	39,20	N.A.	39,20	N.A.	39,20
	No Weight	No Weight	5, 7 Kg	5, 7 Kg	11, 3 Kg	11, 3 Kg

Table 6. Lateral Shear values (Region peaks) comparison

Joint	Reference lateral shear values - Rose [2]	Moment XX (N/m)	Reference lateral shear values - Rose [2]	Moment XX (N/m)	Reference lateral shear values - Rose [2]	Moment XX (N/m)
S1 / L5	6,40	20,98	8,30	3,25	10,80	-10,32
L5 / L4	6,50	12,21	9,30	-3,26	11,20	-16,02
L4 / L3	6,60	8,47	12,10	-5,19	13,30	-17,02
L3 / L2	6,90	-6,50	13,40	6,26	15,60	20,28
L2 / L1	7,20	-9,15	14,30	1,00	17,90	13,22
L1 / T12	7,40	-14,04	15,60	-6,14	21,00	2,87
T12 / T11	N.A.	-17,77	N.A.	-11,01	N.A.	-4,37
T11 / T10	N.A.	-20,60	N.A.	-14,93	N.A.	-9,37
T10 / T9	N.A.	-22,67	N.A.	-18,04	N.A.	-13,50
T9 / T8	N.A.	-23,97	N.A.	-20,33	N.A.	-16,76
T8 / T7	N.A.	30,79	N.A.	27,04	N.A.	23,36
T7 / T6	N.A.	29,81	N.A.	27,08	N.A.	24,41
T6 / T5	N.A.	27,63	N.A.	25,77	N.A.	23,95
T5 / T4	N.A.	24,63	N.A.	23,51	N.A.	22,41
T4 / T3	N.A.	20,72	N.A.	20,18	N.A.	19,65
T3 / T2	N.A.	16,43	N.A.	16,37	N.A.	16,31
T2 / T1	N.A.	11,75	N.A.	12,06	N.A.	12,37
T1 / C7	N.A.	5,36	N.A.	5,36	N.A.	5,36
C7 / C6	N.A.	4,14	N.A.	4,14	N.A.	4,14
C6 / C5	N.A.	3,05	N.A.	3,05	N.A.	3,05
C5 / C4	N.A.	2,11	N.A.	2,11	N.A.	2,11
C4 / C3	N.A.	1,31	N.A.	1,31	N.A.	1,31
C3 / C2	N.A.	0,71	N.A.	0,71	N.A.	0,71
C2 / C1	N.A.	0,32	N.A.	0,32	N.A.	0,32
	No Weight	No Weight	5, 7 Kg	5, 7 Kg	11, 3 Kg	11, 3 Kg

5 Conclusions

Major findings revealed that when it comes to the cervical region of the spine weight differences do not interfere with its values in none of the analyzed forces (compression, anterior/ posterior and lateral shear).

This study also found that an increase of the transported weight in a backpack don't interfere with the vertebrae where the maximum peak force tend to occur.

When comparing weight (5, 7 kg and 11, 3 kg) with the no weight transported condition it was also found that the vertebrae where the maximum peak force occurs tend to come closer to the location of the load regarding anterior/ posterior and lateral shear values.

Since most of the results were coherent with the ones gathered by Rose [2] we may assume that this process to obtain spinal reaction forces in HARSim when transporting a backpack is correct.

References

1. Wilke, H.-J., Neef, P., Hinz, B., Seidel, H., Claes, L.: Intradiscal pressure together with anthropometric data – a data set for the validation of models. Clin. Biomechanicals **16** (Suppl. 1), S111–S126 (2001)
2. Rose, J.D.: Carrying and Loading of the spine
3. Goh, J.-H., Thambyah, A., Bose, K.: Effects of varying backpack loads on peak forces in the lumbosacral spine during walking. Clin. Biomechanics **13**(Suppl. 1), S26–S21 (1998)
4. Ramprasad, M., Alias, J., Raghuveer, A.K.: Effect of backpack weight on postural angles in preadolescent children. Indian Pediatr. **47**(7), 575–580 (2010)
5. Goodgold, S., Corcoran, M., Gamache, D., Gillis, J., Guerin, J., Quinn, C.J.: Backpack use in children. Pediatr. Phys. Ther. **14**, 122–131 (2002)
6. Dagge, R., Filgueiras, E.: Comparative analysis between two distinct realities concerning the transport of school material. Adv. Ergon. Des. Usability Spec. Populations: Part I **16**, 141 (2014)
7. Jayaratne, K.: Inculcating the Ergonomic Culture in Developing Countries: National Healthy Schoolbag Initiative in Sri Lanka. Hum. Factors J. Hum. Factors Ergon. Soc. **54**(6), 908–924 (2012). doi:10.1177/0018720812456870
8. Rebelo, F., da Silva, K.C., Karwowski, W.: A Whole body postural loading simulation and assessment model for workplace analysis and design. Int. J. Occup. Saf. Ergon. **18**(4), 509–519 (2012)
9. Dagge, R., Filgueiras, E.: The HARSim application to the task of carrying school supplies. In: Marcus, A. (ed.) DUXU 2014, Part III. LNCS, vol. 8519, pp. 653–661. Springer, Heidelberg (2014). http://link.springer.com/chapter/10.1007/978-3-319-07635-5_62
10. Chaffin, D.B.: Biomechanical Model. Ergon. Hist. Scope Hum. Factors **1**(429), 361 (2005)

Study on Operating Clearance Measurement of Some Connectors by Using Motion Capture

Hao Du[1], Li Wang[2], Li Ding[1(✉)], Yulin Xu[2], and Changhua Jiang[2]

[1] Biological and Medical Engineering School of Beihang University,
Beijing 100191, China
ilrzf@sina.com, dingl971316@buaa.edu.com
[2] China Astronaut Res and Training Ctr. National Key Lab of Human Factors
Engineering, Beijing, China

Abstract. In the industrial fields, many connectors and p lugs need to assemble or disassemble, but some designs make it difficult for workers to complete the operation or even impossible to finish. This problem is caused by the designer who didn't considered the people used connectors for operation need a certain amount of clearance. This paper mainly introduces the method of using motion capture to measure the 2D working clearance of human hand while the process of installing and removing the connectors. The study figure out the characteristic parameters of operating space for 13 connectors, several layouts is obtained, and verified motion capture tests can be used to research the usability of equipment. Researchers find the test results tend to be loose, so the test needed to verify or make the clearance area more rigorous. This paper provide reference for the future study of the connector panel design.

Keywords: Connector · Operating clearance · Motion capture · Layout · Operating panel

1 Introduction

Many industrial processes require to operate several connectors and plugs such as insert or pull out some plugs, assemble/disassemble some connectors. To accomplish this kind of operation demands appropriate clearance and sufficient force, however, sometimes these conditions can be difficult to meet. Some spatial layouts and designs cannot supply suitable working place for plugs and the others cannot provide users with comfortable room for manoeuvre (Fig. 1). Those two situations make the users difficult or even impossible to complete the work and it can cause great loss in some engineering projects, therefore, study on a kind of connectors and plugs, figuring out the size of their operating-space has great significance. Some studies and trials have tried to measure the operational range of some tools which used by hand, like wrench, bolt, some specific machines, equipment and vehicles, so that the researchers can calculate the working area of that tools. Moreover, many other tests have used the motion capture devices to record the process and trajectory of human motion for finding the scope of human activities.

© Springer International Publishing Switzerland 2015
A. Marcus (Ed.): DUXU 2015, Part II, LNCS 9187, pp. 45–53, 2015.
DOI: 10.1007/978-3-319-20898-5_5

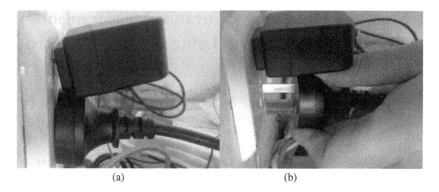

(a)   (b)

Fig. 1. Two bad conditions for the plugs installation. (a) The gaps is not large enough for both of the plugs. (b) The narrow operating-space make the users difficult to insert the plug.

The purpose of this study is to combine those two methods, we can calculate the relative minimum operating clearance of those connectors by using the coordinates of the key points on subjects' hands which recorded by the motion capture system when they are installing and removing the connectors. Following this purpose, we used the motion capture device to find the operating clearance of each connector and installed the different connectors in the same operating panel, search the appropriate layouts. The study finally give the recommendations on the two dimensional layouts of some specific connectors and provide a reference on ergonomic design of the connector operation panel for engineers and designers.

2 Material and Method

2.1 Subjects

Fifteen participants, whose dominant hand is right hand and age ranged from 20 to 45 and the height from 165 cm to 175 cm, voluntarily joined the motion capture trial. The width of their hands ranged from 75 mm to 95 mm and the length of their hands from 170 mm to 190 mm.

2.2 Material

The material and device that the trial required including 13 connectors for total in three different operation types, which we divided into three groups according to the different operation modes. There were three connectors in group A, five in group B and five in group C. We also need a set of test platform and 13 suits of fixtures, which both designed by us. Vicon MX motion capture system and several small markers, which size is 4.0 mm ± 0.5 mm and not less than 20 markers for each hand in each test, as it shown in Fig. 2.

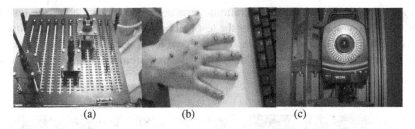

(a)   (b)   (c)

Fig. 2. Materials and devices of the trial: (a) three kinds of connectors installing on the platform with their own fixtures, (b) marker attachment for estimating the hand model, (c) the camera of Vicon MX system. (Figure 2-c comes from the introduction of Vicon MX).

2.3 Trial Design

Considered the individual differences in operating habits, body postures and hand actions were determined when handling various types of connectors. During the connection/disconnection processes we designed and provided that three different operation modes. The first is the back of hand towards the front, four fingers grasp the connector and insert/pull out it, the second is the fingers pinch the connector then screwing it, and the third is the thumb, with index finger or middle finger, pinch the latches at each side of the connector, and insert or unplug the connector (Fig. 3). The connection/disconnection procedures were usually cumbersome, which the operation steps should be simplified by reducing the times of swirling or some others.

Before the test, we have calibrated the equipment and made the participants familiar with the test procedures. Subjects were required to all connectors for three times operation, the command of operating process was instructed by researchers. Then they completed the operation steps stably and consistently. During the entire process of the

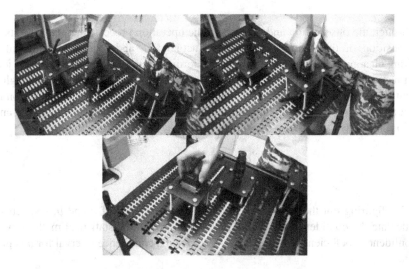

Fig. 3. Three modes of the connector operation

test if subjects happened to meet operational errors, they would not abort the test, but continued to finish the operation. After the test had been done, researchers were used to observe the recorded image. If the recorded image didn't meet the test requirement, we had to retest, until the image got to meet the basic requirements of test. As shown in Fig. 4.

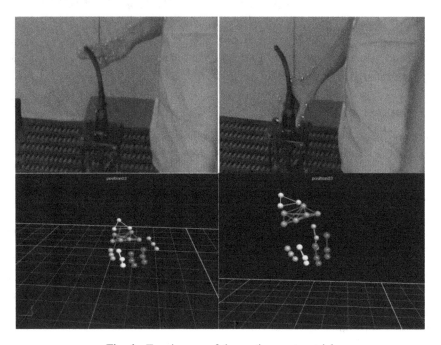

Fig. 4. Two images of the motion capture trial

Through the observation and analysis of the operation process, the major joints and wrist position of the hand determined the actual size and relative position of the operating clearance. Therefore, the extreme coordinates in two direction of these joints which named by X_{max}, X_{min}, Y_{max} and Y_{min} was the only need to the test. Through the calculation, we obtain the size of two dimensional operating space in corresponding direction. Set a and b respectively represent the dimensions of the clearance in x and y direction, then there is

$$a = |X_{max}\text{-}X_{min}|$$
$$b = |Y_{max}\text{-}Y_{min}|$$

(1)

After figuring out the sample mean and sample variance of a and b, respectively, we calculate the confidence interval of μ_a and μ_b through the statistical method, which the confidence coefficient (1-α)100 % is 95 %. Then a confidence interval for μ is given by

$$\left(\bar{x} - t_{\alpha/2,\,n-1} s/\sqrt{n}, \bar{x} + t_{\alpha/2,\,n-1} s/\sqrt{n}\right) \tag{2}$$

And the $\bar{x}$ stand for the sample mean, s stand for the sample standard deviation, n-1 is the degree of freedom. We used the expectation μ_a and μ_b to construct the installation area for nine connectors among the thirteen, and searched the appropriate layout, measured the size of operating panel. In particular, the five connectors of the nine with a rectangular cross section and the other four with a circular cross section. We tried to lay out the connectors with those two cross section types together and independently, compared each layout with dimension and area.

3 Results and Discussion

The measurement results of thirteen connectors operating clearance is shown in Tables 1, 2 and 3.

Table 1. The results of connector A01 – A03

Connector	A01		A02		A03	
	a	b	a	b	a	b
Maximum (mm)	155	147	194	246	218	199
Minimum (mm)	112	113	122	123	110	105
Expectation (mm)	134.7	133.3	159.0	169.3	145.4	141.1
Variance	81.9	50.6	317.1	632.7	677.1	576.4
Standard deviation	9.1	7.1	17.8	25.2	26.0	24.0
Confidence interval radius	2.3	1.8	4.5	6.3	6.5	6.0
Upper limit of confidence interval	137.0	135.1	163.5	175.6	151.9	147.1
Lower limit of confidence interval	132.5	131.5	154.6	163.0	138.9	135.1

Table 2. The results of connector B01 – B05

Connector	B01		B02		B03		B04		B05	
	a	b	a	b	a	b	a	b	a	b
Maximum (mm)	193	157	157	158	159	159	160	159	160	159
Minimum (mm)	80	90	90	92	86	90	87	90	93	91
Expectation (mm)	129.0	125.2	119.3	124.7	123.1	130.2	124.8	125.7	124.8	121.9
Variance	212.5	376.2	436.7	335.7	468.9	345.3	457.0	478.6	457.9	381.6
Standard deviation	14.6	19.4	20.9	18.3	21.7	18.6	21.4	21.9	21.4	19.5
Confidence interval radius	3.7	4.9	5.2	4.6	5.4	4.7	5.4	5.5	5.4	4.9
Upper limit of confidence interval	132.7	130.0	124.5	129.3	128.5	134.8	130.1	131.2	130.2	126.8
Lower limit of confidence interval	125.3	120.3	114.1	120.1	117.7	125.5	119.4	120.2	119.5	117.0

Table 3. The results of connector C01 – C05

Connector	B01		B02		B03		B04		B05	
	a	b	a	b	a	b	a	b	a	b
Maximum (mm)	193	157	157	158	159	159	160	159	160	159
Minimum (mm)	80	90	90	92	86	90	87	90	93	91
Expectation (mm)	129.0	125.2	119.3	124.7	123.1	130.2	124.8	125.7	124.8	121.9
Variance	212.5	376.2	436.7	335.7	468.9	345.3	457.0	478.6	457.9	381.6
Standard deviation	14.6	19.4	20.9	18.3	21.7	18.6	21.4	21.9	21.4	19.5
Confidence interval radius	3.7	4.9	5.2	4.6	5.4	4.7	5.4	5.5	5.4	4.9
Upper limit of confidence interval	132.7	130.0	124.5	129.3	128.5	134.8	130.1	131.2	130.2	126.8
Lower limit of confidence interval	125.3	120.3	114.1	120.1	117.7	125.5	119.4	120.2	119.5	117.0

The measurement results show that the radius of 95 % confidence interval is quite short and reliable. But the variance or fluctuation of test data is still large, and the operating space itself may be varies to each individual and with instabilities. Causes of instabilities may be in the different of operating strength and skills, or caused by the differences in feel. When different subjects handle the same difficult operation, such instability is particularly prominent. From the overall perspective, the test results basically reflect the feature size of the relative minimum operating clearance of connectors. So we use the expectation of a and b to build the installation area for each connectors and narrowed clearance until it nears to unavailable area. Selected the five connectors with rectangular cross sections construct the two kinds of operating panel (Fig. 5).

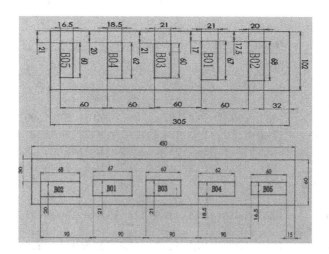

Fig. 5. Five connectors operating panels (the unit is mm)

From Fig. 5 we can obtain that the length of both two types are 305 mm and 450 mm, the width of this two panels are 102 mm and 60 mm and the area respectively is 31,110 mm^2 and 27,000 mm^2. Comparing with the area, the second types is absolutely smaller than the first one, however, the length of the second type is one-third longer than the first type. So it is predictable that the moment of the second panel will be stronger than the first one.

We also selected four connectors with circular cross sections to build the operating panel (Fig. 6).

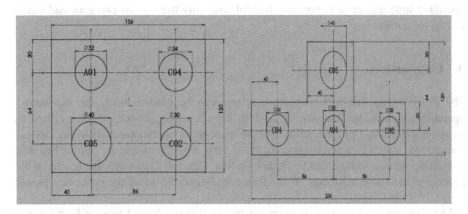

Fig. 6. Four connectors operating panels (the unit is mm)

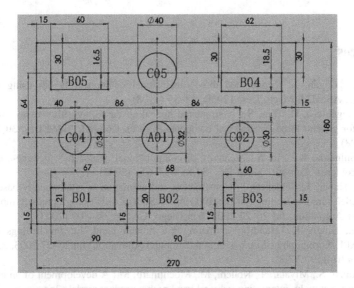

Fig. 7. Nine connectors operating panels (the unit is mm)

The length, width and area of both panels, respectively, are 156 mm and 236 mm, 120 mm and 120 mm, 18,720 mm^2 and 18,336 mm^2. At last we involved all the nine connectors together and reconstruct a layout for the operating panel (Fig. 7). The length of the layout is 270 mm and the width is 180 mm, the area is 48600 mm^2 However, this layout may not be the comfortable one, because it nears to the unavailable zoom.

During the test, we found that if the space for operating didn't hinder the hand, the time and the errors for operation will not change too much for the same subject who is sufficiently skilled. Moreover, the actual interval is generally smaller than the layout which is added up by theoretical clearance from each single connectors. Analysis of operation time and error is not very helpful, and only the layouts category and size is worthy of comparison.

4 Conclusion

The study shows that motion capture system can be used to study the connector's operability issues, but the results tend to be not strict, it needs to be verified by narrowing the range of availability. At the same time, operations to different kinds of connectors, which is a certain specificity, if such property would be diminished with increasing samples remains to be further studied. Generally speaking, the results of this paper provide some reference for the future study and design of the connector panels.

Acknowledgement. This work is supported by the National Natural Science Foundation of China, grant No. 51175021, the National Science and Technology Support Program of China, Grant No. 2014BAK01B05, and the National Basic Research Program of China No. 2011CB711000

References

Szykman, S., Cagan, J.: Constrained three dimensional component layout using simulated annealing. ASME J. Mech. Des. **120**(3), 28–35 (1998)

Cagan, J., Degentesh, D., Yin, S.: A simulated annealing based algorithm using hierarchical models for general three-dimensional component layout. Comput. Aided Des. **30**(10), 781–790 (1998)

Cagan, J., Shimada, K., Yin, S.: A survey of computational approaches to three-dimensional layout problems. Comput. Aided Des. **34**(8), 597–611 (2002)

Albrecht, I., Haber, J., Seidel, H.P.: Construction and animation of anatomically based human hand models. In: Proceedings of the 2003 ACM SIGGRAPH/Eurographics Symposium on Computer Animation, Jul 26–27 2003, San Diego, CA, pp. 98–109 (2003)

ElKoura, G., Singh, K.: Handrix: animating the human hand. In: Proceedings of ACM SIGGRAPH/Eurographics Symposium on Computer Animation, Jul 26–27 2003, San Diego, CA, pp. 110–119 (2003)

Endo, Y., Kanai, S., Miyata, N., Kouchi, M., Mochimaru, M.: A development of an ergonomic assessment system by integrating a digital hand with a product model (2nd report): a function of grasp stability evaluation and an optimization method for a grasp posture. J. Jpn. Soc. Precis. Eng. **75**(4), 548–553 (2009a)

Endo, Y., Kanai, S., Miyata, N., Kouchi, M., Masaaki, M., Kon-no, J., Ogasawara, M., Shimozawa, M.: Optimization-based grasp posture generation method of digital hand for virtual ergonomics assessment. SAE Int. J. Passeng. Cars-Electron. Electr. Syst. 1(1), 590–598 (2009b)

Wang, Y.J., Mok, P.Y., Li, Y., Kwok, Y.L.: Body measurements of Chinese males in dynamic postures and application. Appl. Ergon. 42, 900–912 (2011)

Zong, Y., Lee, Y.A.: An exploratory study of integrative approach between 3D body scanning technology and motion capture system in the apparel industry. Int. J. Fashion Des. Technol. Educ. 4, 91–101 (2011)

Aggarwal, J., Ryoo, M.: Human activity analysis. ACM Comput. Surv. 43, 1–43 (2011)

Baak, A., Rosenhahn, B., Müller, M., PeterSeidel, H.: Stabilizing motion tracking using retrieved motion priors. In: IEEE 12th International Conference on Computer Vision, pp. 1428–1435, September 2009

Hogg, R.V., McKeen, J.W.: Introduction to Mathematical Statistics, 7th edn. Pearson, Boston (2012)

Capture and Analysis of Interaction Data for the Evaluation of User Experience with Mobile Devices

Artur H. Kronbauer[1(✉)], Díferson Machado[1], and Celso A.S. Santos[2]

[1] PPGCOMP – UNIFACS, Alameda das Espatódias, 915, Salvador, BA, Brazil
{arturhk,diferson.machado}@gmail.com
[2] Department of Informatics, Federal University of Espírito Santo (UFES),
Fernando Ferrari s/n sala, 8, Vitória, ES, Brazil
celsoalbertosaibelsantos@gmail.com

Abstract. In recent years, after the great proliferation of mobile devices, the relationship between usability, context and emotions of users is widely discussed in studies related to the user experience (UX) theme. Evaluations indicate that each user interacts with applications in slightly different ways and has different feelings about the applications installed in their smartphones. To contribute to this area of study, this paper presents a platform for the collection and analysis of data related to the user experience of mobile data. To evaluate the potential of the platform, an experiment was conducted with the participation of 68 people, for thirty days. The study results are presented and discussed throughout the paper.

Keywords: User experience · Experimental analysis · Usability evaluation · Mobile device · ESM

1 Introduction

The popularity of mobile devices has made the application market even more competitive for these platforms. The commercial success and the loyalty of users to an application are consequences of the pleasurable experience of its use [1]. Since the nature of user interactions with applications is opportunistic and depends on the willingness to perform these activities, the evaluation of an application should take into account aspects such as personality, emotions, mood, goals, preferences, previous experience and knowledge of the user. Moreover, the physical, social and virtual contexts where the interactions occur are other important aspects to be taken into account [2].

When usability involves the user experience, the evaluation metrics should be extended. For example, Jordan [3] adds the need to measure the pleasure and the pride awakened in the user during their interactions with an application. Norman [4] emphasizes that the goal to be achieved by the new applications is to extend the capacity of the user engagement. Valdes and Gootzit [5] evaluate the UX under the aspect of benefits and financial returns, concentrating its studies on increased revenue, cost reduction, and shorter time to market insertion of new products.

© Springer International Publishing Switzerland 2015
A. Marcus (Ed.): DUXU 2015, Part II, LNCS 9187, pp. 54–65, 2015.
DOI: 10.1007/978-3-319-20898-5_6

In a context where applications are not focused only on the user performance and execution of tasks, but also on the experience offered, it is important for professionals to understand how problems evolve and how they impact the user experience. The main idea is to observe how the product is experienced in real world scenarios and how to obtain information, which will improve the application interface. Having seen exponential growth of new software for mobile devices, it becomes important to find methods at low cost suitable for iterative development cycle and release of new versions [6]. Therefore, this work seeks to contribute to a better understanding of issues related to the user experience (UX), trying to answer the following research question: How to assess the user experience with applications used in daily life?

Accordingly, the paper describes an approach to collect and analyze interaction data. The proposed approach is supported by a platform called Sherlock, which is comprised of two main units. The first, called Data Collection Unit, is responsible for capturing data from the technique Experience Sampling Method (ESM) [7]. The second, called Data Correlation Unit is responsible for storing and enabling data analysis. The dataset is divided into seven dimensions: (i) the user profile; (ii) the device characteristics; (iii) the social context; (iv) the emotional context; (v) the spatial context; (vi) usability; and (vii) location.

The proposed approach was evaluated through an experiment conducted with two main objectives: (i) to verify the efficiency of the components responsible for the collection and analysis of data; and (ii) to identify the user experience with mobile devices, based on the dimensions provided for the collection and analysis of data.

The remainder of this article is divided into six sections. Section 2 describes the Sherlock platform. Section 3 details the methodology used to conduct the experiment to assess the proposed approach. Section 4 shows the results found. Section 5 describes some related work. Finally, Sect. 6 presents some conclusions and perspectives.

2 The Sherlock Platform

The ESM technique is the base concept of Sherlock platform for performing data acquisition. Several authors use the ESM technique in experiments to evaluate the user experience with mobile devices [8–12]. In this work, the technique is used to collect subjective data and targeted responses, allowing participants in an experiment to answer the questions contextualized in different dimensions. The technique is then applied to obtain information about the contexts, such as emotional, social and spatial aspects of interaction. In addition, some usability attributes, such as ease of use, satisfaction, learning, operability and flexibility are also investigated.

ESM allows researchers to collect qualitative data using two kinds of questions: (i) sending direct questions to users with predetermined response; and (ii) measuring the type (positive or negative) and the intensity of the emotion of the user when using an application [7].

Figure 1 illustrates examples of forms used to capture qualitative data. The left side of the Figure illustrates the use of the technique with specific questions about the social dimension in which the user is at that moment. On the right side, the caricatures are associated with the emotional state of the user, ranging from very unsatisfied to very satisfied.

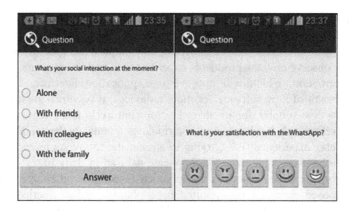

Fig. 1. Examples of use of the ESM technique in the context of this work

The main functional requirements of the Sherlock platform are:

- Provide data collection in the natural environment of the user interaction (in real-life settings).
- Allow investigation regardless the number of users.
- Allow performing experiments for extended periods of time.
- Support the event configuration so that the questions can be generated according to the following: (i) application (specific or independent); (ii) time (predetermined or random); (iii) hours (before, around or after of a programed event); (iv) in accordance with events of Operating System (touch in button, scroll bar, hotkey, etc.); and (v) when the device is connected in specific address IP.
- Provide a quick and simple way to perform analyze of the captured data.
- Allow reviews involving the crossing of the user profile with contextual and subjective data.
- Capture the location of users to identify their daily routines.

The Sherlock platform was divided conceptually in two units, Data Collection and Data Correlation, which will be discussed in the following subsections.

2.1 The Data Collection Unit

The Data Collection Unit consists of an application for the Android platform called SherlockApp. It must be installed on the user's mobile device. For this purpose, those who are interested in participating in an experiment should access the *website*[1] where the SherlockApp is available and accept its terms of use.

The features of SherlockApp are structured into four distinct services:

Detect running applications – This service connects the questions directed to users running applications. The questions are proposed only if the user is interacting with a

---

[1] Available in uxeproject.no-ip.org/sherlock.

specific application or all running applications, according to the target of the experiment.

Collect data with the ESM technique – When an application is running, random questions about its use, covering four dimensions (usability, social, emotional and spatial contexts) are generated. The objective is, later, to relate this information to evaluate the UX with a specific application or all applications installed on their mobile devices. Moreover, the SherlockApp can be used to assess an event in a real-life scenario (for example, to identify the student's expectative before a class and his/her satisfaction after the class).

User location – A location service, based on the mobile devices' GPS, collects data about the position of the user. This service can be configured to get position from time to time or when the user moves for some meters. The objective of this service is to enable the discovery of patterns of user movement, allowing, for example, to create services which assist the user in their urban mobility.

Transfer of information captured – This service is responsible for detecting new information stored locally on the user's device and sending them to a repository, available on a server in the cloud. To transfer the data, the service identifies the availability of Internet access and creates a JSON object filled with the information captured by SherlockApp. The object created is directed to a Web service responsible for storing the data in a Database Management System (DBMS).

2.2   The Data Correlation Unit

The Data Correlation Unit was built on Amazon EC2[2], a micro instance of a cloud server, which allowed the configuration of three essential services to the proposal of Sherlock platform:

Web Server – it is responsible for providing the SherlockApp downloadable application and programs to populate the database. The Web Server used is the Apache Software Foundation[3]. The programs were developed in PHP language. The choice of this language was due to the support to receive the JSON objects and the availability of APIs to interact with the MySQL database. The execution of the Web services followed these steps:

- Connection to the database (DB).
- Processing of incoming objects in JSON format to the data collected, followed by the organization of the data processed in variables.
- Inclusion of variables in the DB using the functions provided by PHP language.
- Sending of a message to SherlockApp application notifying the process result.

Database Management System (DBMS) – This service was implemented on the MySQL Server[4] and aims to store the data sent by SherlockApp. The MySQL Server

---

[2] Available in http://aws.amazon.com/ec2/.

[3] Available in http://www.apache.org/.

[4] Available in http://dev.mysql.com/.

was chosen because it is one of the most popular DBMS today, has extensive documentation and is free.

Online Analytical Processing Tool (OLAP Tool) – The software used to enable the achievement of the data correlations was Pentaho Analysis Services[5]. The choice of this tool is due to the fact that it is free for academic purposes, has extensive documentation and also, because it is in constant evolution.

3 Methodology Adopted

The methodology adopted for the experiment focused on applying four distinct phases: planning, implementation, data preparation and analysis of results.

3.1 Planning the Experiment

The first action taken at this stage was to define the focus of the experiment: analyzing the user experience with applications considering the seven dimensions previously described. This information will be obtained from the correlation of data automatically collected from user devices.

The second step was configuration of the module responsible for sending the questions to participants of the experiment. We chose to evaluate all applications running on the devices of the volunteers. The questions were defined to be exhibited to the participants at random time with maximum interval of four minutes in each application.

The third action was to build a website to provide information regarding the project and the SherlockApp application for the capturing and transmission of data interaction. Social networks were used to promote the project and recruit participants for the experiment.

3.2 Implementation of the Experiment

After agreeing with the terms of use, downloading and installing the SherlockApp application, each user shall be identified by the International Mobile Equipment Identity (IMEI) of the device, automatically detected by the application. Information about the size and resolution of the device's display is also captured at this moment. Then the users must enter some data relating to their profile, such as: education, social class, age, education, occupation, city and state, using the application window. After finishing this step, participants will receive, at random intervals, questions related to the dimensions to be analyzed during the experiment.

---

[5] Available in http://www.pentaho.com/.

3.3   Data Preparation

The preparation of data for the analysis was conducted according to the set of questions to be answered with the data captured during the experiment. Based on the objectives to be reached, we designed a set of questions that guide the analysis of the data obtained. The questions to be answered are:

- What is the satisfaction level of users with the most popular applications?
- What is the relation between the social context and the use of mobile applications?
- What are the possible interferences of the spatial context in user interactions?
- The momentary mental status interferes on the satisfaction with the applications?
- What is the satisfaction of users with the usability of the applications?
- What is the satisfaction level of user with their devices according to the configuration?

Next section is dedicated to the last phase of the methodology and presents the results of the evaluations performed during the experiment.

4   Analysis Result

The data acquisition occurred from 05/25/2014 to 06/25/2014 and involved 68 participants. In an attempt to answer the questions proposed in Sect. 3.3, the next subsections present the results of experimental data analysis regarding factors like satisfaction level, social and spatial context where interactions take place.

4.1   Satisfaction Level of Users with the Most Popular Applications

Participants ran 254 different applications during the experimentation period. The most frequently used apps are shown in the Table 1. It can be observed that WhatsApp was the most popular among the participants with almost half of the executions (44.3 %).

Another important point, in this assessment, refers to the type of application used. It was found that the most frequently used types were: an application to send instant messages, one to browse the Web, two in a social network category and one to arrange the contacts.

Table 2 shows the levels of satisfaction with the five most popular apps on the experiment. It must be emphasized that 100 % of participants declared themselves "very satisfied" with Google Chrome. As Google is the company which owns Android operating system and the Chrome browser, it is likely to have set the application to the needs of its platform, thus, enabling good use experiences to their customers. It can also

Table 1. The most used applications

	Facebook	WhatsApp	Chrome	Contacts	Instagram	Others
Accesses	454	3385	348	237	214	2997
Percentage	5.95 %	44.34 %	4.56 %	3.10 %	2.80 %	39.25 %

Table 2. Satisfaction with the most frequently used apps

Satisfaction level	WhatsApp	Instagram	Facebook	Contacts	Chrome
Very satisfied	47.1 %	50.0 %	50.0 %	0.0 %	100.0 %
Satisfied	32.4 %	50.0 %	25.0 %	33.3 %	0.0 %
Indifferent	11.8 %	0.0 %	0.0 %	33.3 %	0.0 %
Dissatisfied	2.9 %	0.0 %	25.0 %	0.0 %	0.0 %
Very dissatisfied	5.9 %	0.0 %	0.0 %	33.3 %	0.0 %

be observed that all apps have more than 50 % satisfied or very satisfied users. This can be a good indication that these applications are among the most popular for the participants of the experiment.

4.2 Relationship Between the Social Context and the Use of Mobile Apps

The second investigation dealt with the social context in which the participants performed their interactions with mobile apps. According to Ickin et al. [8], this factor is a major contributor to the change in the user experience with mobile devices. Table 3 presents some findings obtained from this context dimension analysis.

Table 3. Analysis of the social context dimension

Aspect	Obtained results
Social interaction	The responses related to social interaction at the moment the applications are used show that 59.2 % occurred when participants were alone, 17.2 % when they were with family, 12 % with coworkers and 11.6 % with friends
Place	In response to the question concerning the place where the apps were used, 65 % of respondents indicated that they were at home, 10.4 % at work, 8.1 % at school/university and 16.7 % in other places such as, pubs, restaurants, mall, beach, cinema and theater
Currently activity	The responses related to the current activity of the participants show that 50 % of interactions with the apps occur when they are doing leisure activities, 23.7 % when they are working and 26.3 % when they are studying

The data related to Social Interaction indicates that in 40.8 % of cases the use of applications occur in the presence of other people. Furthermore, the data related to location indicates that 35 % of interactions occur in public places, where the presence of other people is usually inevitable.

Another fact that needs to be emphasized is that 50 % of interactions occur when users are studying or working, according to data related to the time the activity takes place. This information must be considered in the design of applications for them to be as simple as possible, minimizing possible attention deficits.

4.3 Interferences of the Spatial Context in User Interactions

The third study refers to the analysis of the influence of spatial characteristics of the interaction scenario. Table 4 summarizes the main findings obtained from the analysis of the data representing the spatial context of the interactions.

Table 4. Analysis of the spatial context dimension

Aspect	Obtained results
Momentary action	The responses related to momentary actions of the users reveal that 51.6 % of interactions occurred when they are sitting, 29.7 % lying down, 12.4 % standing upright, 4.1 % walking and 2.3 % running
Luminosity	According to the responses to the ambient luminosity, 24.6 % of interactions occurred in low-light environment, 56.3 % in normal environments and 19.2 % in environments with intense light
Noise	With respect to the noise when an app is executed, it was observed that 29.6 % of interactions occur in quiet environments, 57.7 % with normal noise and 12.8 % in noisy environments
Transportation	When participants are using some means of transportation, it was observed that 61.4 % of interactions occurred using own transportation, 25.7 % in bus, 7.1 % when they were hitchhiking and 5.7 % in other kinds of transportation

Initially, it was noted that most applications are accessed when users are sitting or lying down and that it does not interfere with the satisfaction of people. One fact that stands out is the percentage of 29.7 % of interactions when the participant is lying down; it shows that many people take their smartphones to interact before falling asleep or as soon as they wake up. Other data that contribute to this observation is that 24.6 % of interactions occur in environments with low luminosity and 29.6 % of interactions are in quiet places. This information can be useful for the launching of new applications for these specific situations.

Another fact that stands out refers to the interactions performed using own transportation (61.4 %). This percentage indicates that many people interact with applications when they are driving. A solution to this problem should be to use other modalities of interaction instead of touch-screen inputs.

4.4 Emotional State of the Participants During the Interactions

In Table 5, it is possible to visualize the emotional state of the participants during the interactions with applications. About 56.5 % of interactions occur with users when calm, happy or hopeful, while 43.5 % of the actions take place when the participants feel some kind of discomfort. However, no changes in user satisfaction were observed with respect to the applications according to their emotional state during interactions. In most cases, even when users have declared themselves tired, sick, sad, angry or furious, the level of satisfaction with the applications remained similar as when they are happy, calm or hopeful.

Table 5. Emotional state of the participants *vs.* the satisfaction level with the apps

Emotional State		Level of Satisfaction with the Applications		
		Satisfied	Indifferent	Dissatisfied
Happy	22.1%	82.2%	8.7%	9.1%
Calm	21.8%	86.6%	7.3%	5.9%
Hopeful	13.6%	84.5%	7.7%	7.8%
Tired	19.4%	83.6%	9.2%	7.2%
Sick	5.8%	86.9%	3.7%	9.4%
Sad	6.6%	78.7%	12.1%	9.2%
Angry	8.3%	79.1%	10.3%	10.6%
Furious	2.3%	85.4%	9.4%	5.2%

4.5 Satisfaction of Users with the Usability of the Applications

To evaluate the usability of the most popular applications, there was an investigation of nine attributes (efficiency, effectiveness, satisfaction, learning, operability, accessibility, flexibility, utility and ease of use). According to Kronbauer and Santos [13], these attributes are the most appropriate to measure the usability of mobile applications.

The data presented in Table 6 correspond to the arithmetic average of the participants' satisfaction level in relation to the attributes of usability investigated, for the five most popular applications. It is possible to identify that most users are either satisfied or very satisfied with the usability of the applications. The only application that features the highest level of dissatisfaction is Contacts with 42.9 %. This is an indication that the application usability should be improved in new versions.

Table 6. Satisfaction level with the usability of applications

Satisfied	WhatsApp	Instagram	Facebook	Contacts	Chrome
Very satisfied	50.6 %	42.9 %	46.2 %	28.6 %	42.9 %
Satisfied	38.0 %	57.1 %	38.5 %	28.6 %	42.9 %
Indifferent	5.1 %	0.0 %	7.7 %	0.0 %	0.0 %
Dissatisfied	1.3 %	0.0 %	0.0 %	14.3 %	14.3 %
Very dissatisfied	5.1 %	0.0 %	7.7 %	28.6 %	0.0 %

4.6 Level of User Satisfaction with Their Devices Depending on Their Configuration

To perform this investigation, the screen resolution of the devices was related to the question that measures the level of user satisfaction with their devices. Table 7 presents the percentage of satisfaction based on screen resolution. The main finding is that about 30 % of the users that interact with low-resolution devices show themselves either dissatisfied or very dissatisfied with their devices. On the other hand, users who have

Table 7. Screen resolution x user satisfaction

	Very Satisfied	Satisfied	Indifferent	Dissatisfied	Very Dissatisfied
Low	38.5%	15.4%	15.4%	7.7%	23.1%
Medium	51.2%	34.1%	14.6%	0.0%	0.0%
High	47.4%	42.1%	10.5%	0.0%	0.0%

devices with medium or high resolution tend to be satisfied or very satisfied, with no instances of dissatisfaction.

Kronbauer and Santos [12], when evaluating the usability of smartphones, identified that screens with high resolution and large size facilitate users' interactions when compared to smartphones with smaller screens and lower resolution. Therefore, it is possible to understand why users feel more satisfied with larger devices and high resolution.

5 Related Works

Currently, the ESM technique is one of the most used to obtain subjective information about the feeling of users in relation to a particular subject. In order to collect data concerning mobile devices usage, some relevant works can be highlighted, as described below.

Ickin et al. [8] use the ESM technique for identifying users' satisfaction regarding certain events and apply the technique for obtaining information on the context of user interactions, such as location, social context and level of mobility.

Hicks et al. [9] combine the display of messages with events captured by the smartphone sensors, for example, to go through some specific location (using GPS), when approaching a person from your circle of friends (using Bluetooth), or also according to a particular movement (using the accelerometer).

Lai et al. [10] developed an application for smartphones called Life360 in order to investigate the attitude and behavior of people on the interaction environment. The research objective is to propose a new approach for identifying the different lifestyles and personalities that characterize a certain population. The application displays questionnaires to users with a frequency from 8 to 12 daily interlocutions, collecting information related to current location of respondents, the activity in which they are involved, the people that are in the environment, the emotional state of the participants and the feeling regarding usability.

Another work that uses the ESM technique was proposed by Meschtscherjakov [11], called MAESTRO. The application was designed according to the client-server architecture and has as main objective to classify users, allowing to identify a pattern of behavior. This action allows you to send personalized questions after a certain period of the application utilization.

The infrastructure UXEProject [12] allows to analyze the usability level of application tasks for smartphones. The proposal is to map in an application the tasks that will be investigated and collect performance statistics data from the user when executing them. Moreover, the infrastructure supports the collection of contextual data through sensors of smartphones and subjective information with the ESM technique. In the specific case of the subjective data collection, the UXEProject only captures the feeling of the users in relation to the specific application being evaluated.

When conducting a comparative analysis of Sherlock platform in relation to the previously mentioned studies, it is possible to stand out as contributions: (i) the possibility to relate questions to all or single applications installed on a mobile device; (ii) the extent of approach, as it works with seven dimensions that may be correlated to evaluate the UX; (iii) the availability of a specific location for storage and evaluation of data; and (iv) the ease of use of the platform to perform the evaluations, since it is only necessary to install the SherlockApp on devices which will participate in an experiment.

6 Conclusions and Perspectives

This paper presents the components and associated services for a new platform with the capability to collect and evaluate data regarding the user experience with mobile applications. The main contribution of Sherlock platform is the use of the ESM technique for data collection, covering various dimensions. These data, when correlated, enable more detailed interpretations of the user experience about the different aspects associated with the dimensions.

From the data collected during the execution of an experiment to verify the potential of the platform the following conclusions were reached: (i) the users of mobile devices are likely to have attention deficit caused by social interactions; (ii) It was observed a tendency for people to interact with their smartphones before sleeping or after waking up; (iii) due to the large number of interactions in own transportation vehicles, it may be alerted that many people interact with their applications while they are driving; (iv) most of participants declared themselves either satisfied or very satisfied with the five most common applications; (v) the usability evaluation of the most popular applications indicates the need to rework on the Contacts application available from Android platform; (vi) it was noted that the low resolution of devices creates dissatisfaction among the users.

In general, it was possible to verify that Sherlock platform is appropriate for its goals. The Data Collection Unit, represented by SherlockApp application, enables to collect data in the seven dimensions proposed by the project, is easy to install and use. Moreover, it allows to relate the collected data with other applications running on the devices of experiment participants. The Data Correlation Unit, comprising a Web server, a DBMS and an OLAP tool, allows the storage and analysis of data in a fast and easy way.

The SherlockApp can be configured to generate questions in accordance with different events, such as applications, time, hours, events of Operating System and specific IP address. This flexibility allows the platform to be used to evaluate different types of products or services.

As prospects, it is intended to continue with the implementation of the experiment for a longer period and engage new participants. The objective is to build a database that encompasses a large number of users, making it possible to implement the second stage of the project that aimed to improve the experience of people in relation to urban mobility. Furthermore, we also intend to use the platform to evaluate products and services not specifically embedded in smartphones.

References

1. Väätäja, H., Koponen, T., Roto, V.: Developing practical tools for user experience evaluation – a case from mobile news journalism. In: Proceedings of the European Conference on Cognitive Ergonomics: Designing Beyond the Product, pp. 177–210. ACM (2009)
2. McCarthy, J., Wright, P.: Technology as Experience. The MIT Press, Cambridge (2007). ISBN 9780262633550
3. Jordan, P.W.: Designing Pleasurable Products: An Introduction to the New Human Factors. Taylor and Francis, London (2002). ISBN 0-748-40844-4
4. Norman, D.: Emotional Design: Why We Love (or Hate) Everyday Things. Basic Books, New York (2004)
5. Valdes, R., Gootzit, D.: Usability Drives User Experience; User Experience Delivers Business Values (2007). http://www.gartner.com/id=552818
6. Hassenzahl, M., Diefenbach, S., Göritz, A.: Needs, affect, and interactive products – facets of user experience. Interact. Comput. 22(5), 353–362 (2010)
7. Meschtscherjakov, A., Weiss, A., Scherndl, T.: Utilizing emoticons on mobile devices within ESM studies to measure emotions in the field. In: Proceedings of MobileHCI 2009, Bonn, Germany (2009)
8. Ickin, S., et al.: Factors influencing quality of experience of commonly used mobile applications. IEEE Commun. Mag. 50, 48–56 (2012)
9. Hicks, J., Ramanathan, N., Kim, D., Monibi, M., Selsky, J., Hansen, M., Estrin, D., et al.: Andwellness: an open mobile system for activity and experience sampling. In: Proceedings of Wireless Health, pp. 34–43. ACM (2010)
10. Lai, J., et al.: Life360: usability of mobile devices for time use surveys. In: Proceedings of American Association for Public Opinion Research Annual Conference, Hollywood, FL, pp. 5582–5589 (2009)
11. Meschtscherjakov, A., Reitberger, W., Tscheligi, M.: MAESTRO: orchestrating user behavior driven and context triggered experience sampling. In: Proceedings of the 7th International Conference on Methods and Techniques in Behavioral Research, pp. 287–290. ACM (2010)
12. Kronbauer, A.H., Santos, C.A.S., Vieira, V.: Smartphone applications usability evaluation: a hybrid model and Its implementation. In: Winckler, M., Forbrig, P., Bernhaupt, R. (eds.) HCSE 2012. LNCS, vol. 7623, pp. 146–163. Springer, Heidelberg (2012)
13. Kronbauer, H.K., Santos, C.A.S.: A review of approaches to assessing the usability smartphone. In: Proceedings XII Brazilian Symposium on Human Factors in Computer Systems, pp. 452–461 (2013)

A Study Customer Journey Map for User Experience Analysis of Information and Communications Technology Service

Jin Ho Lee$^{(\boxtimes)}$, Min Ji Kim, and Sung Woo Kim

Interaction Design, Graduate School of Techno Design,
Kookmin University, Seoul, Korea
{design.inun, shsjpg7}@gmail.com,
caerang@kookmin.ac.kr

Abstract. Prior research has shown that UX designers of ICT service experience various difficulties while using Service Design methodologies. This is because the characteristics of Service Design and of UX Design greatly differ; Service Design is deployed in physical space and time, while UX Design is deployed on screen with the focus on UI elements. Also, in terms of the range of design, the entire service in macroscopic perspective often becomes the range of design in Service Design, whereas the Touch Point of user and the product becomes the range of design in UX Design of ICT service. In this context, the purpose of this study is to investigate how the design methodology of Service Design should be customized when applied to the UX design of ICT service. This study was conducted around the Customer Journey Map among methodologies of Service Design. First, this study collected opinions on how the UX designers of ICT service use the Customer Journey Map while working on a UX design project and the limitations they faced. Then, a Customer Journey Map that is appropriately customized to the UX Design of ICT service will be suggested based on the findings.

Keywords: Visualization · Hierarchical task analysis · Customer journey map · Use experience design · User research · Service design · Information architecture · ITC service

1   Introduction

When the ICT industry has evolved, also increased the importance of the user experience. User experience and user experience design are always mentioned when you speak the satisfaction of products and services. On the other hand, the paradigm of the industry is transformed into service industries in the manufacturing industry. And Service Design also began to attract attention. The service design and UX design is activity in analogy with the goal of providing a better experience to the user. Therefore, it is possible to see many cases to make use of methodology each other. For users of experience designers of ICT industry in this study, we conducted a questionnaire survey. The person who answered the questionnaire was 26 people, respondents of majority, you answer it is using the Customer Journey Map when you proceed the user

© Springer International Publishing Switzerland 2015
A. Marcus (Ed.): DUXU 2015, Part II, LNCS 9187, pp. 66–74, 2015.
DOI: 10.1007/978-3-319-20898-5_7

experience design project. In addition, they were responding Customer journey map is difficult to show the journey of these ICT services. To see why such a phenomenon occurs, in this study, it is desired to understand the design of the relationship between the user experience design and service design. And what kind of problem is to let us examine is displayed when you apply the service design of the methodology to user experience design. Finally, in this study, we propose a visualization method that can be applied to customer journey map to ICT services. Detailed progress for this is as follows. Firstly, we have promoted the theoretical study of user experience design and service design. Based on theoretical study, after comparing each design, to study how to visualize the user survey methods and customer journey map. Secondly, the study of natural observation to investigate the user experience and research for the hierarchical analysis task to structure the data collected. And, we will study the information architecture for visualization of customer journey map. Thirdly, by using the information structure, become a customer itinerary ICT services to examine what are. And we study how to visualize the journey visualizations and user satisfaction, and organize the customer journey map visualizations of ICT services. Fourthly, to verify the validity of the provided methods by applying the mobile video service that is serving the customer journey map visualization method proposed in this study.

2 Review of Background Theory

The movement to provide a better user experience design recently very active. The first attempt to understand the user experience based on the previous work of the user experience. User experience design and service design is to try to understand that you what activities to increase the user experience.

2.1 Configuration of User Experience

Prior to study the user experience design, it is necessary to first understand the user experience. ISO 9241-210 define the user experience was as follows: Users experience the user to use the product, system or service, or a user's perception and reaction to be used to make. In addition, HCI field says: User experience is any process that occurs as a result of interaction between the user and the system, devices, content, interaction is to include the interaction of the body and the environment takes place or situation. How to know if your experience is configured examined the existing research on user experience. Experience of the study was found that the formation by the passage of time and step by step formation. There was a study of the relationship between the flow of time in research. Philips (2007), the user experience was formed stepwise by the axes of the time.

2.2 Service Design and User Experience Design

Previously, user experience design and service design has both similarities and distinction. With reference to studies of KIDP (Korea Institute of Design Promotion)

Service design team the many studies on service design can be seen that the following differences. Firstly, there is a difference of perspective overlooking the subject of design. The user experience design to a target to design Front stage as the main point of the range. Can be mentioned as an example UI (User Interface). On the other hand, service design should note the relationships between stakeholders in the Back stage. Innovative way in overall service context can be seen as a difference to find. Secondly, the result is different. Service design of representative output is as follows. It's typically service blueprint, customer journey map, stakeholders map, and the like. These can be viewed as a point of view overlooking the entire service. And output of user experience design is as follows. It's typically UI, GUI. They are characterized by depicting specifically. In South Korea design company surveys were conducted had the following results: 77.5 % of the public was thinking the same UI and user experience design. In this study, it was based on the following hypotheses. "Methodology viewpoint other designs overlooking the subject of design can not be made to apply in the same way." Figure 1 is a schematic view showing the difference between the service design and user experience design.

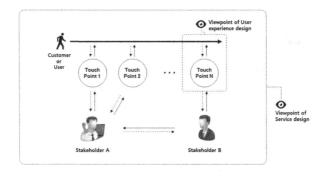

Fig. 1. Differences of service design and user experience design

2.3   User Research

User research can be understood only enough material already been investigated in many studies. User research is to accurately collect the overall user requirements from different types of data, there is the purpose to be analyzed [1]. Such research approach may be to derive the requirements reflect the user's experience, to collect essential design information such as the pattern by time and space [2]. If the user survey is performed in the course of initial design for developing excavation and design concept of the new design area, the user research data has the qualitative characteristics. Therefore, In order to effectively utilize the user survey data requires interpretation of the steps will lead to the conclusion that it meets the purpose of the user survey. (Koskinen and Lee, 2009) This procedure is referred to variously analysis, inference, etc., (Jääsköand Keinonen, 2006) are obtained from the data in addition to the design idea and insight accurate analysis and understanding of the user. In addition, researchers can empathize with the user, helping make decisions in the design process, plays a role, such as increasing the reliability and validity. (Kouprie and Visser, 2009; Koskinen and Lee, 2009)

2.4 User Experience Design and Customer Journey Map

In 2013 industrial design statistics of KIDP, design talent in the field of design of service/experience has become a people 34,761. And conducted a randomized questionnaire survey of 34,761 people, 26 people were responding. People who've used more than once a customer journey map of the 26 respondents exceeded 50 %. 73 % of respondents have answered was used to understand the usage of services, 92 % showed normal more satisfaction. On the other hand, there were also negative responses. That it is difficult to objectively describe the satisfaction that the information that can be obtained Insight is insufficient, and the like that is difficult to represent the journey to occur within the system. There will also be seen as a disadvantage of customer journey map characteristics of qualitative methodology. However, they have found a pattern by structuring the relationship between the similarity data, or social scientific analysis technique to navigate the design problem is not organized systematically, or clean-up methods are many it is possible to see that it is not known. Fig. 2 is a comparison the journey that appears when there is no restriction on the journey in time and space that appears when there is a restriction on the journey in time and space.

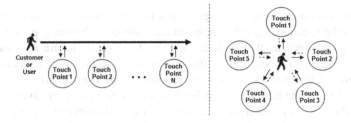

Fig. 2. Relationship between the journey and the presence of constraints

Customer's journey of general service is configured linearly due to the limitations of time and space. However, the customer's journey of ICT service is configured free-form. Because no constraint on the time and space. Free forms mentioned above are found to be similar to the information architecture of Fig. 3. Journey of ICT services has seen that there is a deep connection with the information architecture of the system. Therefore, applying the structure of the information when structuring the data in the user research, and would like to propose how to apply this to the visualization method of customer journey map.

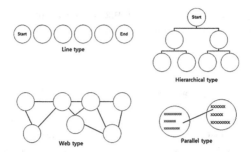

Fig. 3. Several types of information architecture

3 User Experience Analysis of ICT Services and Customer Journey Map

Method for visualization of customer journey map ICT services provided is performed in the following procedure. The first, closely observe the form of use of ICT services with minimal interference. Secondly, apply the hierarchical task analysis when cleaning up research data. Then step on the procedure for visualizing the data summarized for effective communication and insight derived.

3.1 Collection of Data Through a Nature Observation

When the natural observation, investigators has to be recorded by capturing the action according to the situation dogged directly subject. However, this study provides a diary written templates because they lack the money and time in nature and used direct observation method to record the circumstances. Diary technique is also called Journaled Sessions. This method is to collect information by users themselves create the experience of using the product. Journaled Sessions is then given by dividing the user to perform the task for a prototype or actual product. And users can capture the screen or write a report and submit it to the researcher. Researchers will analyze the received data.

3.2 Hierarchical Task Analysis

Hierarchical task analysis was applied to structured data collected by observation of nature. The task analysis is a method for systematic analysis of user usage patterns. When the user to use the product or service. And to analyze the user's usage patterns and user experience. Type of analysis is divided into a specific analysis task and abstract methods. Hierarchical task analysis is one of the specific task analysis [3]. Hierarchical task analysis method is to set a final goal. And separate each issue again follows by dividing the plurality of problems underlying the more challenges. It is hierarchically divided how the problems of achieving this way a final target.

Hierarchical task analysis method is a method to hierarchically divide the problems required to achieve the goal. Table 1 is a glossary of hierarchical task analysis.

Table 1. Glossary of hierarchical task analysis

Terminology	Description
Goal	Shows the hierarchy of the top-level, it is the ultimate goal of the user.
Sub task	Sub task is a necessary sub task when the user tries to achieve the goal. Sub Task is based on the task of details must go through in order to perform a task. It is possible to have a different sub task to sub layer.
Operation	The elements described in the lowest layer. Lists elements acts of users when perform a sub task
Plan	Describes a condition that may be performed or executed in the order.

When applying a hierarchical task analysis to mobile video services are performed in the following procedure. Step 1. Set goal of the mobile video service. Goal of mobile video services can be to as "video viewing". Step 2. Set the sub task of goal. This sub tasks can be sure to go through in order to achieve the goal. Sub task of mobile video service may be such as "log in", "Search". Step 3. Write to the operation when performing a sub task classifies act element generated. Operation of mobile video service may be such as "Category of sort", "Table of contents selection".

3.3 Information Architecture

Hierarchical task analysis was applied to structured data collected by observation of nature. Information architecture is directly visible to the user, but the most basic of the system is one of the first factors to consider when designing a system to be the center. Information architecture, it is necessary to understand the context and contents and the user, may be a field requiring seriously studied. (Information architecture, Louis Rosenfeld, Peter Morville) Information architecture consists of organizing system, labeling system, a navigation system, the search system. The four components may be viewed as the framework of the information structure, in addition to have more elements [4]. Information architecture is designed in a hierarchical structure, which has a close relationship with the user's experience.

3.4 Hierarchical Task Analysis List Created using the Information Architecture

Hierarchical task analysis has difficulty drawbacks partitioning the procedure. So utilize the information architecture to complement the disadvantages of hierarchical task analysis. Information architecture of the web/product design, depth to display the hierarchy and usually depth shows the dependence relationship and order of information of what is made at the stage of the organization of information architecture design. 1 Depth is a layer formed on the user contact with the first when using the system. In general, it belongs to the navigation within the element to design a system. If analyzes the information architecture of the designed system, when performing the hierarchical task analysis, it is possible to step the subdivision to overcome difficult disadvantages.

3.5   Visual Elements of the ICT Services

Information is the most important element in the ICT service. Information that is organized through the process, not only visually, is transmitted through the other sense of the user. Device and containing system may be seen as a role to help ensure the transmission of information made. Humans are mainly used the sense of sight when recognizing information. According to the survey, that human beings occupy a sense of sight more than 80 % in the full meaning [5]. Graphic User Interface was constructed text, icons, images, etc. The GUI allows the user to interact with the system more easily. In addition, GUI has been taken account of graphic design, cognitive engineering, such as cognitive psychology. The user would use the system through the GUI. And GUI visually show a lot of information in the system. GUI can be a factor affecting the user's journey.

3.6   Information Architecture Visualization of ICT Services

The hierarchical task analysis and information structure is schematized in the form of the step structure. However, problem occurs when visualizing the journey of ICT services. Because ICT services there is a characteristic that can be freely moved. Generally, customer journey map is represented by a one-way flow from the left to the right. The collected data is a form which is arranged in chronological order in one line. However, the form that is designed in a single line, difficult to understand the other effects, may be much difficult to visualize the other effects. To represent the characteristics of the ICT services had suitable radial shape as shown in Fig. 4.

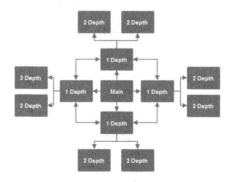

Fig. 4. Radial shape of information architecture

Procedure for visualizing is as follows. Firstly, at the center of Figure, it is the Main of service positioned and it is the 1depth of service positioned at the radial shape. And the main and 1depth is connected to the line. Secondly, it designs so that the relation which is subordinate can show in case there are 2 depths or 3 depths. Similarly, connected to each other by a line.

3.7 Visualization of User Satisfaction

The original customer journey map shows the customer's satisfaction. However, it is difficult to propose radial shape has a margin for displaying the user's satisfaction. One of the advantages of the customer journey map is to identify at a glance the user's satisfaction. In order to have these advantages other user satisfaction visualization method was required. In the course of the observation of nature was determined the average user satisfaction. Satisfaction score is the value when the score with five points. The average value was painted with the color in the shapes of the depth. The colortable like Fig. 5 using the color and chroma was made and it applied. Blue color means that a high satisfaction, the red means a low satisfaction.

1.0   5.0

Fig. 5. Color table of satisfaction score

In summary the method described earlier can draw a customer journey map of ICT services in the form as shown in Fig. 6.

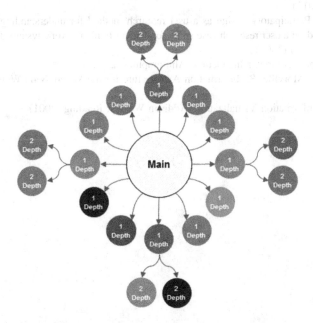

Fig. 6. Customer journey map prototype for ICT service

4 The Research Conclusion and Limit

4.1 The Research Conclusion

Proposed CJM visualized to the purpose for analyze the experience in which the user used the ICT service, and to visualize the journey ICT services have attempted to overcome the difficulties point. Significance of this study is as follows. Firstly, we researched the disadvantages of the customer journey map when the user experience designer of ICT services to use the customer journey map. Secondly, we have proposed a way to organize the data obtained in the user research. Information architecture and hierarchical task analysis was applied. Thirdly, we have proposed a radial customer journey map that can take advantage of the characteristics of the ICT services. The information architecture of system is applied to the original customer journey map.

4.2 The Limit of the Research and Hereafter Research Subject

In this study, there is a purpose the customer journey map the user experience designers can take advantage of ICT services to be visualized. However, the proposed customer journey map has not been expressed to internal problems with stakeholders. Once, it thinks that it becomes the more efficient tool if the stakeholders concerned related to pain point is visualized.

References

1. Dongwoo, O.: Perspective-taking method for user experience research. J. Korean Soc. Design Sci. **25**(3) (2012)
2. Song, J.-W.: Participatory design as a user research method for understanding design problems - focused on a user research case study for a smart home network system. J. Korean Soc. Design Sci. **21**(3) (2007)
3. Kim, J.: Human Computer Interaction. Ahn graphics, Beaumont (2012)
4. Rosenfeld, L., Morville, P.: Information Architecture for the World Wide Web. O'REILLY, USA (1998)
5. Spence, R.: Information Visualization. Addison-Wesley, Reading (2001)

Scaling Preferences of Different Stakeholders – Using the Example of Prioritizing Quality Requirements on User Interface Texts

Yiqi Li, Theo Held[✉], and Patrick Fischer

SAP SE, Walldorf, Germany
{yiqi.li,theo.held,patrick.fischer}@sap.com

Abstract. We propose a method of measuring preferences of various stakeholders quantitatively by combining the methods of direct ranking and complete paired comparison. We demonstrate the method using a concrete case of prioritizing quality requirements on user interface (UI) texts and report the primary empirical evaluation of the methods' accuracy and efficiency in this application example.

Keywords: Scaling method · Paired comparison · Ranking · Preferences of stakeholders · Prioritizing requirements

1 Introduction

User experience design often involves analyzing subjective preferences of various stakeholders, especially end users and customers. By analyzing preferences of different stakeholders, we can not only derive concrete requirements for good usability, but also set appropriate priorities for design activities. This is often necessary in practice because there may not be enough time and resources to comply with all potential interests, for example, to carry out all design proposals or to fulfill all requirements perfectly. More importantly, having a clear view of preferences from different perspectives can help us discover and deal with interest conflicts. Even if the stakeholders involved in the design processes agree on what should be realized, they may disagree on which one is more important. Therefore, the information on preferences and their structure serves as input for strategic decision making.

To ensure a good quality of the input for decision making, a high degree of accuracy in scaling, that is, an interval or ratio scale, is advantageous. First, it provides richer information about the magnitude of latent preferences (e.g. how much one option is preferred to another). Second, it enables precise comparisons of different stakeholders' perspectives on a quantitative level (e.g. correlations can be calculated as a similarity measure). Finally, managerial decision making needs accurate quantitative information to optimize the resource allocation in design processes (e.g. how much of the budget should be invested in realizing the top three priorities).[1]

---

[1] We focus merely on accessing preferences as a basis for decision making and do not discuss how to make a decision based on the data.

© Springer International Publishing Switzerland 2015
A. Marcus (Ed.): DUXU 2015, Part II, LNCS 9187, pp. 75–86, 2015.
DOI: 10.1007/978-3-319-20898-5_8

Accordingly, user experience design demands accurate and efficient techniques of gathering and analyzing subjective preferences. However, in practice, measuring preferences is a vital yet challenging activity due to time and resource constraints. Among the approaches commonly used in practice, those which provide more accurate and reliable information (e.g. paired comparison) are costly, whereas those which require less time and resources (e.g. direct ranking) yield less precise information (see next sections for a thorough discussion).

To solve this problem, we combine the response collection technique of stepwise ranking and the data analysis technique for paired comparison. That is, to collect preference data using the ranking-by-elimination [1] procedure, derive pairwise judgment data from the ranking data and then estimate ratio-scaled values of the latent preference from the derived data based on the Bradley-Terry-Luce model [2, 3]. In this way, our method inherits the advantage of both techniques – providing ratio-scaled results while being economic. The analytic procedure is capable of inferring ratio-scaled estimates of the latent preference from ordinal judgment data because the Bradley-Terry-Luce model makes specific assumptions (see Sect. 2.1). By transforming the ranking data into pairwise judgments, a consistency assumption is made additionally. Therefore, the accuracy of the estimates depends on the extent to which these assumptions hold in the specific application context. Practitioners applying the method can get insight into this issue with the aid of the model's goodness of fit and the correlation with genuine paired comparison, respectively.

In the following, we will outline this method and exemplify how to apply it in practice by presenting an empirical study as specific example. In the study, the proposed method was applied to the prioritization of quality requirements on UI texts and the results were compared with those of genuine pairwise judgment. We conducted the study to demonstrate the applicability as well as to test the validity and efficiency of the method empirically. Based on the results, we will discuss the possible reasons for the different preferences of various stakeholders as well as the prospects and issues of applying this method in broader contexts.

2   Background

2.1   How to Infer Ratio-Scaled Estimates of Preferences from Complete Paired Comparison Data

In paired comparison, an individual expresses his or her preference between two alternatives at a time. Compared to rating and other methods yielding directly interval-scaled data, paired comparison has several advantages. Psychometrically, it has higher reliability and can reveal inconsistent judgments [4]. It measures more accurately because it is able to identify minimal differences in preferences [5] and it also avoids some biases and problems of direct rating [5, 6], such as unstable reference point [6]. In addition, paired comparison creates less cognitive load than ranking or other methods do because it is easier for participants to make dichotomous judgments between pairs than to assign numbers to each alternative. References [7, 8] provide practical examples for successful application of the paired comparison method in the context of UI design.

Although a single comparison collects only the ordinary information on the preference for one pair of alternatives (i.e. not including the information "how much A is better than B"), the data of all possible pairwise combinations (complete paired comparison) can result in accurate and reliable ratio-scaled estimates for preferences if based on proper models. These models assume that the alternatives are ordered on a latent preference scale and there is a probabilistic relationship between the positions of the alternatives on the preference scale (i.e. the scale values) and the observable choices in paired comparison. Thus, by analyzing the observed pattern of pairwise judgments, the unobservable magnitudes of the preferences of all alternatives can be inferred. One of these models, the Bradley-Terry-Luce model [2, 3], assumes that from each specific pair A and B, the probability of choosing A equals the proportion of the latent value of A to the sum of the values of A and B. Furthermore, it assumes that the probabilities of each pairwise judgment are mutually independent. Therefore, the probability of observing a specific choice pattern is proportional to the product of the probabilities of all the pairwise judgments (for a detailed discussion see e.g. [4, 9]; for mathematical proof, see [2, 3]). The Bradley-Terry-Luce model belongs to the family of generalized linear models. Hence, the scale values as model parameters can be estimated by the means of conventional estimation methods for logit or log-linear models [10]. The estimates are to be interpreted as the positions of the options on the assumed one-dimensional preference scale. According to the model, they are ratio-scaled and hence justify statements such as "A is twice as [good, beautiful, usable, ...] as B". Because the model is essentially probabilistic, confidence intervals of the estimates are computed to take account of sampling errors.

Besides the property of providing ratio-scaled values, another advantage of model-based analysis is the testability of models. The goodness of fit of the model describes how well it fits the observed data. For example, the measure G^2 represents the difference between the values predicted by the estimated preferences and the observed data. The goodness-of-fit test computes then the probability of observing this difference (or a larger one) given that the model describes the empirical data adequately. If it is very unlikely to observe the difference, then the model is not appropriate to describe the data and the estimated scale values (model parameters) are not valid in this case. Thus, unlike direct rating, which relies on implicit and untested assumptions [6], model-based analysis of paired comparison data provides quantitative information about how good the estimated scale values are in a given application context.

The largest drawback of paired comparison is its inefficiency in terms of information obtained per unit of time [4]. If the number of alternatives is large, it takes much time to compare all alternatives in pairs (n(n − 1)/2 comparisons for n alternatives). In addition, it can also cause fatigue and boredom of participants.

2.2 Ranking-By-Elimination as a Preference Collection Method

Ranking as a data elicitation method has the advantage of requiring less time and resources while remaining straightforward, which makes it favorable for practical and commercial applications. However, analyzed by means of common non-parametric methods, ranking data yield merely ordinal scaled estimates, because in a single rank order, the information "how much better" is not included as well. Moreover, rank order data have the problem that individuals usually pay more attention to the top few choices rather than carefully ranking all alternatives, resulting in additional noise in the lower rankings (e.g. [11]). This is related to the increased cognitive load of ranking. With increasing number of alternatives, participants usually experience difficulties in putting all the alternatives in a rank order. Some may spend a long time reconsidering and altering their rankings [1].

To reduce the cognitive load and to ensure participants' attention for all alternatives, [1] proposed a new ranking procedure called ranking-by-elimination. In this procedure, participants identify the least preferred alternative at one time and this option will be then irrevocably eliminated from the list of alternatives. The stepwise elimination repeats until only one option is left. Empirical studies show that ranking by elimination is slightly faster than common ranking procedures and yields similar results [1].

2.3   The Combined Method

The idea of combining ranking procedures and the analysis technique for paired comparison exists already in the literature and related empirical research has also been done in various contexts (cf. [4, 5, 12]). The combined method is based on connecting ranking data to paired comparison by regarding a rank order as the result of a specific paired comparison pattern. More specifically, given a rank order of n objects, the object with the highest rank must always be preferred when compared with all other $(n - 1)$ objects. The second highest ranked object then must be favored in the comparisons with all $n - 2$ objects ranked below it. In this way, a response pattern of the complete paired comparison can be uniquely derived from the given rank order. After this, preference scale values can be estimated using the Bradley-Terry-Luce model based on the derived pairwise judgments. In other words, the combined method "converts the ranking data into paired comparison data, and then work on it, as if it was paired comparison data." ([9], p. 35) As the ranking procedure requires less time and resources, the total cost reduces.

The price to pay is a potential information loss and the violation of one of the model assumptions. In genuine paired comparison, an individual might prefer A to B, B to C and C to A because people do not always judge consistently. However, such cases are not possible in pairwise judgments derived from ranking data because individuals are forced to make a full ranking of the objects instead of judging pair by pair. In this way, the possible patterns of pairwise judgments are limited to a small subset by the transformation. Moreover, requiring a strict consistency may violate the assumption that the pairwise judgments are mutually independent. Hence, the transformation might lead to some distortions in the results.

Whether the consistency assumption is met in a given dataset is an empirical question. Although the model fit can tell us how good the model assumptions are met for the transformed data, there is no such an a priori measure quantifying the degree in which the transformation is appropriate. Therefore, we collected data using both rank-by-elimination and genuine paired comparison and compared the results.

2.4 The Example of Prioritizing Quality Requirements on UI Texts

We applied both rank-by-elimination and genuine paired comparison as data collection procedure to investigate a specific question in UI design. The application context was a project investigating quality factors of UI texts. One of the project's goals was to scale the relative importance of various quality requirements for UI texts from the perspectives of various stakeholder groups, namely end users, decision makers and information developers. The research questions were how subjective expectations of UI text properties can be efficiently measured and whether there are meaningful discrepancies between the priorities of the main recipients and those who create UI texts.

Because the proposed method is applicable to scaling the relative preferences regarding a given set of objects, the objects must first be identified. We therefore constructed a set of UI text requirements based on a sample of existing design guidelines for UI texts by clustering and synthesizing all the relevant requirements in them. We assume that the guidelines reflect representatively the requirements identified in the earlier phase of requirement gathering. Nevertheless, we do not claim that the design guidelines used in our study have exhausted all the requirements that contribute to forming a quality judgment of UI texts.

3 Methods

3.1 Participants

In total, twelve end users, ten decision makers and eighteen information developers took part in the study. The end users and decision makers were recruited via an external agency based on a detailed screening document. The information developers were employees of a software company.

3.2 Material

The stimulus material consisted of screen mockups presenting fifteen concrete quality requirements on UI texts. The quality requirements used were: "correct spelling", "correct capitalization", "correct grammar", "correct punctuation", "no abbreviations", "idiomatic language", "simple language", "clear language", "parallel construction", "chronological order", "active voice and direct address", "consistent terminology", "not state the obvious", "focused on goal of user" and "necessary information embedded on UI". They were presented with the aid of concrete mockup examples. All the examples used the same UI (creation of leave requests) and each example showed a realistic case that violates the requirement to illustrate our understanding of the requirement (see Fig. 1). We assume that the more important a requirement, the more severe its violation.

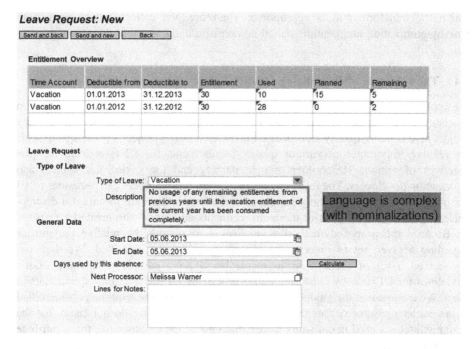

Fig. 1. Screen mockup for the quality requirement "simple language"

So the ranking of the importance of a requirement can be seen as equivalent to the reverse ranking of the according violation.

The stimuli used in the ranking were printed copies of the mockup examples. The ones used in the paired comparison were presented on a display. To reduce the total expenditure, each participant compared only eight requirements in the paired comparison procedure. Consequently, there were two sets of stimuli for genuine paired comparison (set A and set B, with the stimulus "consistent terminology" appearing in both sets). One of these sets was randomly assigned to each participant.

3.3   Procedure

First, the moderator explained each quality requirement using the mockup examples printed on paper. The participants were instructed to make their judgments based on the general understanding of each requirement instead of the specific example. After that, participants completed paired comparison using the software tool PXLab [13]. Each requirement was combined with all other seven requirements from the same set and each pair appeared twice, with balanced left-right position. All pairs appeared in a random order. Following the paired comparison, participants ranked all fifteen requirements on a whiteboard. In the rank-by-elimination procedure, they were asked to pick the requirement whose violation was considered least severe and remove it from the list. Then they ought to identify the least severe one from the remaining list.

This process repeated until only one item was left on the whiteboard. In addition, participants were instructed to think aloud during the ranking by elimination procedure.

3.4 Statistical Analysis

The ranking data was transformed in the manner described in Sect. 2.3 and then analyzed based on the Bradley-Terry-Luce model using the R-package "eba" [14].

4 Results

The model fit of the Bradley-Terry-Luce model was good, $G^2(91) = 56.57$, $p = 1$ for the entire sample, $G^2(91) = 61.88$, $p = .99$ for end users, $G^2(91) = 47.02$, $p = 1$ for decision makers and $G^2(91) = 48.05$, $p = 1$ for information developers. This indicates that the model assumptions are likely to be appropriate for the pairwise judgments derived from the ranking data.

More importantly, our method yields very similar results to genuine paired comparison. Substantial correlations were found between the scale values based on the transformed ranking data and those based on the genuine paired comparison data. In the total sample, the correlation was $r = .84$ for set A and $r = .98$ for set B. Correlations in the stakeholder groups ranged from .47 to .96 and four out of the six correlations were above .80.

The estimated scale values are illustrated in Table 1 in the appendix. The importance of two requirements differs from each other significantly, if their confidence intervals do not overlap. Within each group, the requirements vary strongly in their perceived importance. The overall pattern can be roughly described as three levels: high, medium and low importance. In average, the highest importance is more than the double of the medium importance and about four times of the lowest importance.

For end users, the top three were "clear language", "consistent terminology" and "necessary information on UI", which were about one-and-a-half times as important as "idiomatic language" and "simple language" and twice as important as "correct spelling" and "correct grammar". The significance of other requirements was less than one-third of that of the top three.

For decision makers, the requirements descended gradually in perceived importance except "necessary information on UI", whose superiority was clear. "Consistent terminology", "idiomatic language", "clear language", "simple language" and "focus on goals of user" were of medium importance, which was at least as twice as that of the remaining.

For information developers, the requirements fell clearly onto three levels. "Consistent terminology" was the only one on the highest level. The second level ("clear language", "no abbreviations", "correct grammar", "correct spelling" "simple language", "idiomatic language" and "necessary information on UI") was at the most as half important as the first level. The lowest level was mostly only as one-third important as the second level.

As the radical chart (Fig. 2) visualizes, the discrepancies between groups were larger regarding the most important requirements. The largest divergence was found regarding "necessary information on UI": For decision makers, it was the number one priority; for end users, it was the third most important requirement (the absolute preference reduced to 2/3) and for information developers, it was the eighth (reduced to merely 1/3). Moreover, end users chose "clear language" at the first place, followed by "consistent terminology", while this order is reversed for information developers and decision makers. Some requirements of medium importance were clearly more valued by one or two groups. "Correct spelling" and "correct grammar" had higher priority for information developers and much lower priority for decision makers. However, both groups put more emphasis on "no abbreviations" than end users. Decision makers were the only group for which "focused on goals of user" reached a medium importance. For the other two groups, this requirement was clearly insignificant.

Importance of Requirements on UI Texts

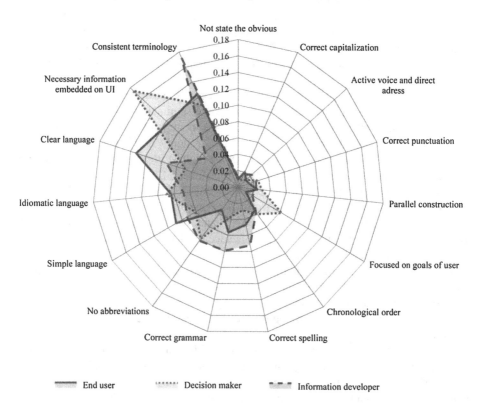

Fig. 2. Estimated scale values for the importance of the requirements. A higher value indicates a higher perceived importance of the respective requirement. In this chart, the requirements are sorted by the average scale value across groups.

Despite of the differences between groups, there was a substantial consensus. Correlations between the groups indicate that end users and decision makers agree on a lot ($r = .74$), to the similar degree as end users and information developers ($r = .77$), whereas decision makers and information developers agree on much less ($r = .51$). This means that the priorities of end users are quite similar to those of the other two groups, but decision makers and information developers share each other's view to a less extent. This result pattern also indicates that what end users and decision makers agree on is quite different from what end users and information developers agree on.

5 Discussion

The application of the proposed method is considered successful. The good model fit indicates that the model assumptions were likely to hold for the transformed ranking data. The high correlations between the estimates based on transformed ranking data and those based on the genuine paired comparison data indicate that the results of different response collection methods were very similar. Therefore, the transformation was appropriate in this application case. The combination of the rank-by-elimination procedure and the analysis model for paired comparison can provide valid ratio-scaled estimations with relatively low expenditure compared to a standard pair comparison method.

With the aid of the combined method, the preference structures of different stakeholders can be revealed and compared on quantitative level. First, the findings indicate a substantial consensus among the three stakeholder groups. Specifically, the convergence between end users and decision makers was as high as that between end users and information developers and much higher than that between decision makers and information developers. Discrepancies were found above all regarding the more important requirements. End users appear to value requirements that ensure sufficient and clear information (e.g. "necessary information embedded on UI" and "clear language") more than information developers, while information developers emphasize more formal requirements than end users (e.g. "consistent terminology", "correct spelling" and "correct grammar"). End users may focus on concrete tasks in the first place and consider how certain requirements would affect their problem solving (e.g. "would I get stuck if…", "what would waste my time" and "what would make me prone to mistakes"). Information developers, in spite of recognizing the importance of some requirements that are critical for users' problem solving, put emphasis on more formal and measurable requirements. Decision makers appear to have tried to view from end users' perspective but overestimated the significance of some requirements for end users (e.g. "necessary information embedded on UI", "focus on goals of user" and "no abbreviations") while underestimated that of some others (e.g. "clear language"). Moreover, they gave some formal requirements much less priority than information developers ("consistent terminology", "correct spelling" and "correct grammar").

As this application example illustrates, the combined method can be used to prioritize design requirements for various UI elements, given that a set of potential requirements has already been identified. Beside requirement analysis, many situations also involve subjective priorities or preferences regarding a given set of objects. Here are some examples: how important are specific goals, use cases or tasks for users;

which features, configurations or design proposals do (differently profiled) users prefer. Similarly, these priorities and preferences can be measured by the combined method, even if the objects under consideration are qualitatively very different. Therefore, we argue that beside prioritization of requirements, this method is also applicable to various design activities, where decisions have to be made relying on subjective preferences. The combined method is especially efficient if the number of options is large. For example, with this method, the design questions in [7, 8] (selecting design alternatives or design proposals), which were studied by means of standard paired comparison, could have been investigated more efficiently.

As also stressed in [7, 8], using ranking or paired-comparisons should be considered whenever other more appropriate methods cannot be applied. If possible, a decision between design-alternatives should be supported by the results of a usability test or an experimental investigation. But this might be too time consuming or expensive – in this case, applying the proposed scaling methods is far better than deciding on basis of gut feeling or management verdict. In cases where we primarily investigate individual opinions or personal taste, scaling is one of the best approaches to elicit what end-users "really want". This applies, for example, to subtle variations of visual design.

In practice, the largest weakness of this method is that the transformation may not be justified in every situation. Therefore, at least a small proportion of the participants should do the genuine paired comparison in parallel to provide validation data. The question is how to determine the proportion, which yields the best cost-benefit-ratio.

Acknowledgement. We would like to thank Annette Stotz and Susanne Rump for many fruitful discussions, their expert support regarding UI texts, preparing the material and supporting the study.

Appendix

See Table 1

Table 1. Estimated scale values and 95 % confidence intervals. A higher value indicates a higher perceived importance of the respective requirement. The two values in the bracket below each scale value are the 95 % confidence interval with the lower limit on the left and the upper limit on the right.

Requirement	Stakeholder								
	End user			Decision maker			Information developer		
Correct spelling		.047			.029			.073	
	(.028)		(.066)	(.016)		(.041)	(.027)		(.118)
Capitalization		.020			.010			.017	
	(.012)		(.029)	(.005)		(.015)	(.011)		(.023)
Correct grammar		.056			.036			.079	
	(.034)		(.079)	(.021)		(.051)	(.027)		(.131)
Punctuation		.014			.026			.023	
	(.008)		(.021)	(.015)		(.038)	(.013)		(.034)

(Continued)

Table 1. (*Continued*)

Requirement	End user			Decision maker			Information developer		
No abbreviations	.034	(.020)	(.048)	.078	(.046)	(.110)	.081	(.064)	(.098)
Idiomatic language	.083	(.051)	(.116)	.089	(.053)	(.126)	.068	(.026)	(.110)
Simple language	.088	(.054)	(.123)	.061	(.036)	(.085)	.073	(.035)	(.110)
Clear language	.132	(.081)	(.184)	.069	(.041)	(.097)	.093	(.056)	(.131)
Parallel construction	.024	(.014)	(.034)	.030	(.017)	(.042)	.022	(.014)	(.031)
Chronological order	.035	(.021)	(.049)	.040	(.023)	(.057)	.038	(.018)	(.058)
Active voice and direct address	.013	(.007)	(.019)	.014	(.007)	(.020)	.023	(.019)	(.026)
Consistent terminology	.124	(.075)	(.173)	.110	(.065)	(.154)	.172	(.094)	(.251)
Not state the obvious	.010	(.005)	(.015)	.012	(.006)	(.018)	.012	(.011)	(.013)
Focused on goals of user	.012	(.006)	(.017)	.062	(.037)	(.088)	.021	(.017)	(.024)
Necessary information embedded on UI	.116	(.071)	(.162)	.175	(.104)	(.245)	.052	(.023)	(.082)

References

1. Wickelmaier, F., Umbach, N., Sering, K., Choisel, S.: Scaling sound quality using models for paired-comparison and ranking data. In: Conference Paper, DAGA 2012 Congress 38th German Annual Conference on Acoustics (2012)
2. Bradley, R.A., Terry, M.E.: Rank analysis of incomplete block designs. I. The method of paired comparisons. Biometrika **39**, 324–345 (1952)
3. Luce, R.D.: Individual Choice Behavior: A Theoretical Analysis. Wiley, New York (1959)
4. Dittrich, R., Katzenbeisser, W., Reisinger, H.: The analysis of rank ordered preference data based on Bradley-Terry type models. OR-Spektrum **22**, 117–134 (2000)
5. Courcoux, P., Semenou, M.: Preference data analysis using a paired comparison model. Food Qual. Prefer. **8**, 353–358 (1997)
6. Zieliński, S.K., Rumsey, F., Bech, S.: On some biases encountered in modern audio quality listening tests – a review. J. Audio Eng. Soc. **56**, 427–451 (2008)
7. Schrepp, M., Held, T., Fischer, P.: Untersuchung von Designpräferenzen mit Hilfe von Skalierungsmethoden. MMI Interaktiv - User Experience **1**, 72–82 (2007)

8. Held, T., Fischer, P., Schrepp, M.: Scaling of input forms by a simple pair comparison approach. Libr. Hi Tech **29**, 334–348 (2011)
9. Thuesen, K.F.: Analysis of Ranked Preference Data. http://citeseerx.ist.psu.edu/viewdoc/download?doi=10.1.1.89.152&rep=rep1&type=pdf
10. Dittrich, R., Hatzinger, R.: Log-lineare Bradley-Terry Modelle (LLBT) und das R Package Prefmod. In: Hatzinger, R., Dittrich, R., Salzberger, T. (eds.) Präferenzanalyse mit R: Anwendungen aus Marketing, Behavioural Finance und Human Resource Management, pp. 119–150. Facultas.wuv, Vienna (2009)
11. Ben-Akiva, M., Morikawa, T., Shiroishi, F.: Analysis of the reliability of preference ranking data. J. Business Research **23**, 253–268 (1991)
12. Dabic, M., Hatzinger, R.: Zielgruppenadäquate Abläufe in Konfigurationssystemen – eine Empirische Studie im Automobilmarkt: Das Paarvergleichs-Pattern-Modell für Partial Rankings. In: Hatzinger, R., Dittrich, R., Salzberger, T. (eds.) Präferenzanalyse mit R: Anwendungen aus Marketing, Behavioural Finance und Human Resource Management, pp. 119–150. Facultas.wuv, Vienna (2009)
13. Irtel, H.: PXLab: The Psychological Experiments Laboratory, Version 2.1.11. http://www.pxlab.de
14. Wickelmaier, F.: Elimination-by-Aspects (EBA) Models. R Package Manual, Version 1.7-1. http://cran.r-project.org/package=eba

Affordances Feature on Package Design has Preference Effect on Content

Jerry Lin[⊠] and Cheng-Hung Lo

Department of Industrial Design, Chang Gung University,
259 Wen-Hwa 1st Road, Kwei-Shan, Tao-Yuan 333, Taiwan, R.O.C.
zweivie@gmail.com

Abstract. People use package to protect and express product, a good design feature on package will enhance preference of consumers. Affordance is human instinct that suggest action of usage and it imply attractive. This study prove that a package has affordance design not only provide consumers' a positive emotional experience, better to influence consumers' positive perception to the contents. The outcome may assist designers in selecting or modifying package designs for achieving desired consumer responses.

Keywords: Affordance · Package design · Perceptual information · Usability

1 Introduction

Packages are a key part of product experiences. The good design of a package can help introduce the product, which in turn influences the consumer's perception of the content, i.e. the product, inside. (Schifferstein et al. 2013). In packaging design, a designer can apply a variety of different elements to introduce a product. Textual descriptions, which are often used, may not communicate effectively during the immediate encounter between a product and its potential consumers (Hoogland et al. 2007). In this study, we focus on the non-verbal communication initiated by packaging designs, in particular the affordances signified by the design features. Researchers have shown that shape tools with strong affordance will have a positive attractively humans (Righi et al. 2014). We hypothesize that the same effect should be found on product packages. First of all, we investigate the strength of the affordances of common design features on product packages. Same user actions triggered by different design features are compared to find out which have the higher affordances. Secondly, we study whether a design feature giving higher affordance would invoke more positive emotional responses. Event-Related Potential (ERP) experiment method is used in this study for brain data collection and subsequent analysis.

2 Related Studies

2.1 Define Affordance

In terms of design, packaging can be seen as the extended work of designing a product. Package serves as a form of advertisement of the product before it is obtained by its

© Springer International Publishing Switzerland 2015
A. Marcus (Ed.): DUXU 2015, Part II, LNCS 9187, pp. 87–94, 2015.
DOI: 10.1007/978-3-319-20898-5_9

consumers. Indeed, in Clement (2007), the design of packages was found to have a significant influence on purchasing decisions. Packages may bring more abstract values such as branding effect to products (Orth and Malkewitz 2008). Functionally speaking, packages also help consumers search and recognize a product among others displayed in a store (Clement et al. 2013). Several studies have also documented that people match a variety of sensory features, such as abstract shapes, names, and speech sounds even stimulate synesthesia (Velasco et al. 2013). In recent years, interested researchers began to study packaging design with neuroscience methods. Using fMRI technique, Reimann et al. investigated the brain activities of the participants during a product evaluation task (Reimann et al. 2010). They found that packages had significant impact on the sensory evaluations of the participants.

The term affordances was proposed by J.J. Gibson who is an American psychologist (Gibson 2013), he believe animal can perceive the visual signal from environment to react properly. For the same substance have different meanings in different organisms, for example human burn branch to get warm, birds build nest by branch. And affordances can be clarified by real affordance (McGrenere and Ho 2000) and perceive affordance (Norman 1999).

Without definition of real affordance and perceived affordance, affordances would likely be unfamiliar to many of us.

The difference is that real affordance can be understood as a biological instinct, and perceived affordance can be acquired through learning, culture or using experience (Table 1).

Table 1. Comparison of affordances as defined by Gibson and Norman (McGrenere and Ho 2000).

Gibson's (Real) Affordances
• Offerings or action possibilities in the environment in relation to the action capabilities of an actor
• Independent of the actor's experience, knowledge, culture, or ability to perceive
• Existence is binary – an affordance exists or it does not exist
Norman's (Perceive) Affordances
• Suggestions or clues as to how to use the perceived properties that may or may not actually exist
• Can be dependent on the experience, knowledge, or culture of the actor
• Can make an action difficult or easy

2.2 Perceptual Information

People recognize perceptual information of objects by visual information, it show the availability and usability of objects, i.e. human know what the function of object through visual to observe the external characteristics of the object, and thus understand affordance of this object. Human can't understand affordance of objects directly by visual. So, if an object lack of clear perceptual information, it would make people unable to use this object. Perception information can be divided into physical and psychological, physical properties of the information can be directly cognitive as instinct of basic human needs, such as the perceptual information that flat and hard ground can be understand it can support, sit and lie down to rest, the psychological one is logical inference or learn from education, such as we use machine or when we see a square on screen we will know it's a stop button that also through learning (Fig. 1).

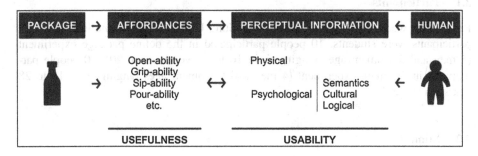

Fig. 1. (Gustafson et al. 2014)

2.3   Application of Affordance Design Feature

Affordance have been widely studied and applied in the field of psychology but have had limited formal application to packaging design and evaluation. (Gustafson et al. 2014), Gustafson make improvement on medical packages and significantly enhance the reaction time of opening package and entirely identify the right opening. This experiment establish a re-design process that confirm the application effect and improval mechanism on the original package, by this process will do a scientific test showing that where and how to use affordance.

Human use perceptual information to know affordance, it can be divided into physical and psychological, physical informations corresponde utilitarian, and the psychological information corresponde emotional experience, but they could both implied utilitarian and emotional experience. In packaging design could bring value of user usability.

The brain wave has strong physiological evidence, we suggest human think a high affordance object is also a high attractive object by instinct, so if subjects look at a high affordance object but low has attractive, we will confuse and our brain will cost large energy to process contradiction (Righi et al. 2014).

Human can use much more abstract signalling systems to efficiently communicate facts about themselves and their environment, namely spoken and written language. When we use words to describe our object, we have to avoid emotional content in language interfere our feeling. It will make the reaction of subject by words not stimuli. But the emotional content in language do not affect obviously (Kissler et al. 2009).

Finally, the ultimate goal of our study is apply to the real world. The research suggest that reward value plays an important role in aesthetic product experiences. Further, a closer look at psychometric and neuroimaging data finds that a paper-and-pencil measure of affective product involvement correlates with aesthetic product experiences in the brain by fMRI (Reimann et al. 2010).

3 Methodology

To explore the preference between "affordance design" and consumer's perception, we carry out the following procedures:

3.1 Participants

Participants were recruited from the Chang Gung University by online interview. All participants were students. 10 people participated in the define package experiment (5 men and 5 women; ages ranging from 16 to 25 years, mean 20). 10 people participated in the main experiment (4 men and 6 women; ages ranging from 18 to 28 years, mean 22.3).

3.2 Stimuli

We design 3 type (original, positive, negative) of action and identicated design feature package and we check these types by 10 subjects. Then compose an one opening illustration prototype like Fig. 2 to a pair.

Fig. 2. Indicated feature prototype and action feature prototype about cup

At first we use normal package which can buy on the market. We use 3D modeling and Photoshop to redesign the original package prototype to varies shape, and defined these different positive or negative shape. Positive feature is about the package shape can easily or helpfully to open than original package. Negative feature is about the package shape won't help or obstruct people to open the package than original one. After we designed these packages, 10 participants help us confirm our definition about positive action feature and negative action feature like Fig. 3. We checked this over 8 participants made the same judgment about the feature is positive or negative. If any redesign feature under 8 agreement we will redesign until over 8 agreement. Through this test we suggest it can be accurate than we defined positive or not.

Fig. 3. 3D models with affordance action design feature on bottle cap package.

3.3   Procedure

The experimenter explained the task: "Please, imagine that you are in a game, and standing in front of the table. This game is about judging the value of content by package design, and you will see a product package and opened package help you image the connection between package and content."

Shuffle all the affordance pair picture like Fig. 4 show on the screen, and ask participant judge the value about the content in package by Likert scale.

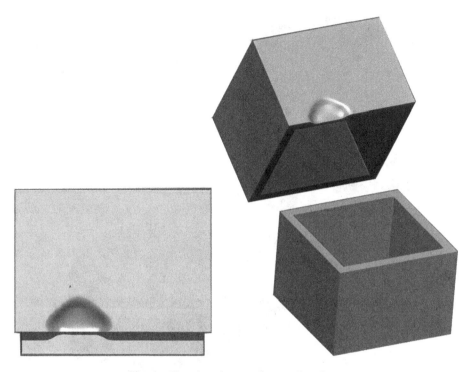

Fig. 4. Closed package and opened package

3.4   Content Preference Result

See Table 2.

Table 2. Content preference

Package and feature type	The content preference
Original box	3.6
Positive action feature of box	3.7
Negative action feature of box	3.2
Positive indicated feature of box	3.4
Negative indicated feature of box	3.3
Original bottle cap	2.3
Positive action feature of bottle cap	2.7
Negative action feature of bottle cap	2.8
Positive indicated feature of bottle cap	2.6
Negative indicated feature of bottle cap	2.6
Original cup	3
Positive action feature of cup	2.9
Negative action feature of cup	3.1
Positive indicated feature of cup	3.4
Negative indicated feature of cup	3.4

4 Result and Conclusion

We found the design features of the package has a higher preference except box indicated feature and cup positive action feature, then action feature of box and bottle cap are higher than indicated feature but feature of cup is opposite. People prefer negative action feature of bottle cap than positive one. We consider the first result prove people prefer aesthetic package i.e. the affordance design feature package is pretty (Righi et al. 2014); the second one is when we open the box and bottle we need more action like twist or pull, but cup only need a little push. So action feature is useful than indicated feature; the last one is aesthetic preference rather than utilitarian preference even our people know this shape isn't useful they still decide a valuable content has a beautiful package design. So this will suggest that is a threshold about usable preferences and appearance preferences.

Although experimental use in the form of a questionnaire, but very close with our previous suspect, after ERP experiment will know the emotion reaction in our brain. ERP experiment will use the stimuli from this study. We expect the results to scientifically validate the influence of affordance on package design. The experiments will prove that a package has affordance design not only provide consumers a positive emotional experience, better to influence consumers' positive perception to the contents. We believe that the concept of affordance can be used to produce innovations in this regard to enhance product attractivity.

References

Clement, J.: Visual influence on in-store buying decisions: an eye-track experiment on the visual influence of packaging design. J. Mark. Manage. 23(9–10), 917–928 (2007)

Clement, J., Kristensen, T., Grønhaug, K.: Understanding consumers' in-store visual perception: the influence of package design features on visual attention. J. Retail. Consum. Serv. 20, 234–239 (2013)

Gibson, J.J.: The Ecological Approach to Visual Perception. Psychology Press, New York (2013)

Gustafson, S., Twomey, C., Bix, L.: An affordance-based methodology for package design. Packag. Technol. Sci. 28, 157–171 (2014)

Hoogland, C.T., de Boer, J., Boersema, J.J.: Food and sustainability: Do consumers recognize, understand and value on-package information on production standards? Appetite 49(1), 47–57 (2007)

Kissler, J., Herbert, C., Winkler, I., Junghofer, M.: Emotion and attention in visual word processing—an ERP study. Biol. Psychol. 80(1), 75–83 (2009)

McGrenere, J., Ho, W.: Affordances: clarifying and evolving a concept. Paper presented at the Graphics Interface (2000)

Norman, D.A.: Affordance, conventions, and design. Interactions 6(3), 38–43 (1999)

Orth, U.R., Malkewitz, K.: Holistic package design and consumer brand impressions. J. Mark. 72(3), 64–81 (2008)

Reimann, M., Zaichkowsky, J., Neuhaus, C., Bender, T., Weber, B.: Aesthetic package design: a behavioral, neural, and psychological investigation. J. Consum. Psychol. 20(4), 431–441 (2010)

Righi, S., Orlando, V., Marzi, T.: Attractiveness and affordance shape tools neural coding: Insight from ERPs. Int. J. Psychophysiol. **91**(3), 240–253 (2014)

Schifferstein, H.N., Fenko, A., Desmet, P., Labbe, D., Martin, N.: Influence of package design on the dynamics of multisensory and emotional food experience. Food Qual. Prefer. **27**(1), 18–25 (2013)

Velasco, C., Salgado-Montejo, A., Marmolejo-Ramos, F., Spence, C.: Predictive packaging design: tasting shapes, typefaces, names, and sounds. Food Qual. Prefer. **34**, 88–95 (2013)

Measuring Negative User Experience

Dominik Pascal Magin$^{(\boxtimes)}$, Andreas Maier, and Steffen Hess

Fraunhofer Institute for Experimental Software Engineering, Fraunhofer-Platz 1,
67663 Kaiserslautern, Germany
{dominik.magin, andreas.maier, steffen.hess}
@iese.fraunhofer.de

Abstract. Nowadays, the induction of positive user experience is a vital aspect of the development of smartphone applications. Existing approaches aim at engineering good user experience to make applications more enjoyable and pleasurable. Especially in business applications, employees need to be motivated to perform their tasks, in order to increase efficiency and effectiveness. Negative user experience lowers user acceptance and decreases motivation. A study was conducted to identify factors that can cause negative user experience. This study found negative aspects of an example mobile application, of which Usability and Utility have been found to directly contribute to a negative Emotions and thus to negative user experience.

Keywords: User experience · Emotions

1 Introduction

1.1 Motivation

Within the context of human-computer interaction (HCI), and especially in terms of mobile applications ("apps"), consumer behavior and use patterns strongly depend on the emotions induced with the user by interacting with an application. As a consequence of user experience, emotions are triggered and anticipated as well as retrospected rather than details of the HCI (e.g., interaction form, interaction concept, or screen design) and particular elements of the UX (e.g., usability, utility, or symbolism). Recent models of user experience models show the influence of different user experience factors to the user's perceived emotions.

Existing research mainly focuses on positive emotions (like joy, fun, and pride) and their generation through influencing the factors of emotion [3, 11], neglecting that compared to positive emotions, negative emotions are remembered more strongly and over a longer period of time, and that they have a greater impact on the consumption behavior. Mobile apps are neither bought nor installed when the potential customer attributes negative emotions to these mobile apps. If installed and used apps cause negative emotions, users uninstall or just stop using them after a very short time due to the huge number of available alternative (free) apps. Thus, it is important to understand the causes of negative emotions from HCIs with apps. In this paper, we provide the results of an initial study on the factors of negative emotions. We have considered models of emotions from other domains and adapted them to fit the needs of software

© Springer International Publishing Switzerland 2015
A. Marcus (Ed.): DUXU 2015, Part II, LNCS 9187, pp. 95–106, 2015.
DOI: 10.1007/978-3-319-20898-5_10

engineering by identifying the negative emotions that are most relevant to software, i.e., those emotions which are best recognized by users of software systems before, during, and after HCIs with the software systems and which are therefore measurable. We want to know what the main causes for negative emotions with respect to HCIs are.

1.2   Contribution

In this paper, we argue for the scientific community to be more concerned with the identification of the factors that evoke negative emotions. Subsequently, the software development processes should be enhanced with methods that systematically help prevent software systems to causing negative emotions. In terms of apps, this involves avoiding factors that cause negative emotions, which will help increase the apps' acceptance and therefore positively influence consumer behavior and use patterns. Furthermore, this helps boost the appreciation of the apps' positive aspects, which will consequently result in more positive emotions.

For this purpose, a condensed user experience model based on the works of Hassenzahl [2] and Mahlke [3] is derived. This model shows the strong interrelation between user experience factors and emotions. It is known that hedonic quality attributes directly contribute to a positive experience and emotions [1], whereas there is no research on user experience factors that lead to negative emotions to our best knowledge. We argue for a deeper research on factors that are responsible for negative emotions and present results of a first study conducted to identify drivers for negative emotions.

2   UX and its Relation to Emotions

2.1   UX Model of Hassenzahl

Hassenzahl proposed a model of user experience [2] that states how user experience evolves, what the key elements of user experience are, and identifies the interrelations of these elements. The main contribution of this model is the distinction of a product's *pragmatic* and *hedonic* attributes, and the consequences these attributes trigger when the user is confronted with that product.

Hassenzahl's model assumes that a product has a certain set of features. The features do not merely refer to the product's core functionality but also include the product's content, aesthetics, and interaction style. Persons perceiving the product's features construct a product character based on their individual impression of the product, making this product character a subjective perception. The product character is constituted of pragmatic and hedonic product attributes. Pragmatic attributes relate to the product's utility (relevant functionality to achieve particular goals with the help of the product) and usability (ways to access this functionality), whereas hedonic attributes emphasize an individual's psychological well-being in terms of stimulation, identification, and evocation [2].

The assessment of a product's appeal, based on the attributes' relevance in a given situation, leads to emotional and behavioral consequences. The emotional consequences are the user's satisfaction, when the product fulfills the expectations, and pleasure, when the product exceeds the expectations. However, those consequences depend on and are influenced by the situation in which the product is used (e.g., the mood of the user, stress, environmental conditions). Behavioral consequences (e.g., the user's willingness to use the product, the amount of time spent with the product) also depend on the emotional consequences of product usage. Hence, a lack of positive emotional consequences reduces the product's acceptance and the user's motivation to use it.

Although Hassenzahl shows that the hedonic product attributes are the main contributors to positive emotional consequences, he emphasizes that pragmatic product attributes should not be neglected [2]. Pragmatic attributes are related to the achievement of pragmatic goals, which usually need to be fulfilled in order to also achieve hedonic goals. Hence, pragmatic attributes facilitate the achievement of hedonic goals, which in turn require the existence of hedonic attributes. Humans strive for the fulfilment of hedonic goals and perform particular activities to achieve these goals. A prerequisite for this achievement is the positive characteristic of pragmatic attributes and the successful achievement of pragmatic goals. For example, one cannot achieve the hedonic goal of feeling related to another person (identification) when the pragmatic goal of making a phone call to the other person (which provides one with the possibility to fulfil the hedonic goal) is not achieved. The successful phone call and the feeling of being related to the person who was called may lead to positive emotions as a consequence of the fulfilled pragmatic and hedonic goals.

2.2 The CUE Model

The *CUE-Model* (Components of User Experience) has been proposed by Mahlke and Thüring [3, 4]. According to their model, user experience has three components, namely the perception of *instrumental qualities*, the perception of *non-instrumental qualities,* and the resulting *emotional reactions*. Instrumental values focus on utility, which are the tasks a user wants to perform, and usability, which are the goals he wants to accomplish. Non-instrumental values contain three attributes, namely *aesthetics*, *symbolic value*, and *motivational aspects*. Aesthetics aim at the appearance of a product, like its color, shape, taste, or smell. Symbolic values are divided into *communicative* and *associative aspects*. Communicative aspects express individual qualities, values, and attributes, i.e., the user's self-expressiveness. Associative aspects are related to personal memories, i.e., what the user associates with the product. Motivational aspects are the perceived ability to motivate the user, i.e., they provide stimulation. The perception of the instrumental and non-instrumental qualities through HCI influences the third component of the model, the emotional reactions.

2.3 Implications of the Models for UX Research

The CUE-model and Hassenzahl's model are very similar. Both models show the importance of separating pragmatic (instrumental) and hedonic (non-instrumental) aspects of an HCI, and both describe their influence on the emotional and behavioral consequences. The pragmatic attributes are reflected in the instrumental values, hedonic attributes are reflected in the non-instrumental values, and the pragmatic and hedonic attributes together lead to consequences that include the user's emotions. While this influence is conceptually highlighted, the detailed pragmatic and hedonic causes of particular emotions remain covered.

Academic research has so far focused on the positive constitution of product attributes in order to facilitate the emergence of positive emotions. To the best of our knowledge, no study has yet considered the influence of negative aspects of HCIs that consequently lead to negative emotions.

In order to research negative emotions, these emotions have to be classified, and the most prominent emotions that can be felt by users of software while and shortly after interacting with the software have to be identified.

2.4   Classification of Emotions

The study of emotions has a large history. Even the early Greeks and Romans studied the model of emotions. Initially divided into the two basic emotions of delight and reluctance (Aristoteles, Cyrenaics), more complex models have developed over the centuries. René Descartes proposed a model of six basic emotions, namely love, hatred, anxiety, pleasure, sadness and admiration [5]. Several well-known psychologists and philosophers have built their own models upon either the model of delight and reluctance (Kant, Ebbinghaus, Külpe, Freud) or defined several basic emotions (Descartes, Kast, Russell, Plutchik). To assess the emotions that arise through the usage of computer programs, especially apps, the simple model of delight and reluctance does not suffice. Delight is about looking forward to use an application, but does not necessarily imply that a user enjoys using it. Thus, more complex models need to be taken into account and the relevant emotions need to be identified.

Ekman et al. [6] derived six basic emotions from several cross-cultural studies: anger, disgust, fear, happiness, sadness, and surprise. Izard [7] identified ten basic emotions, namely anger, contempt, disgust, distress, fear, guilt, interest, joy, shame, and surprise.

A more detailed model of emotions is Plutchik's wheel of emotions [8] that has the shape of a cone. It assumes the eight primary emotions joy, trust, fear, surprise, sadness, disgust, anger, and anticipation. The vertical dimension of the cone represents the intensity of each kind of emotion, with the emotions at the top being the most intense ones. The eight sectors of the circle each describe a different kind of primary emotion. The wheel of emotions has the coloring of a color wheel, i.e., the circle describes the relation between the emotions through supplementary (adjacent) and complementary (opposite) colors. Emotions on the opposite of the circle represent the *complementary* emotion whereas emotions may also be mixed up to derive dyads of emotions (e.g. joy + trust = love).

More recent research efforts have aimed at providing a finer arrangement of emotions. Parrott's tree structure of emotions identifies six primary emotions (love, joy, surprise, anger, sadness and fear) and further refines them in secondary and tertiary emotions, resulting in a classification of about 150 emotions [9]. The HUMAINE research association defined a language called Emotion Annotation and Representation Language (EARL), which comprises 10 categories, each consisting 48 emotions [10].

The classifications by Plutchik, Parrott and HUMAINE show that emotions can strongly vary and that there is not a single emotion for the current state of mind. Comparing the primary emotions of Plutchik, Parrott, and HUMAINE results in the following five primary emotions: *anger, fear, sadness, joy,* and *surprise*. Reducing especially the negative emotions will help reduce a negative user experience. Each of those emotions can be further refined into sub-emotions (based on Plutchik, Parrott, and HUMAINE). The negative emotion anger contains the two sub-emotions *frustration* and *dislike*; fear contains *nervousness* and *uncertainty*, and sadness contains *disappointment* and *shame*.

Fear is an emotion induced by a threat perceived by humans in case of a risk in life, status, power, security or anything else valuable [6]. Sadness in contrast is characterized by feelings of despair, disadvantage, loss, helplessness, or sorrow [6]. Graham defines anger in terms of our expectations and assumptions about the world [12]. Graham states anger usually results when we are caught up "…expecting the world to be different than it is".

2.5 Condensed UX Model

The user experience model presented in this paper was developed to facilitate the identification and reduction of negative user experience (cf. Fig. 1). Its basic principles have been taken from Mahlke's [4], Mahlke and Thüring's [3] and Hassenzahl's [2] models. Emotions are influenced by the instrumental and non-instrumental characteristics of the software [2, 3]. Hassenzahl's terms instrumental and non-instrumental characteristics have been used here, as they focus more on the characteristics of the application than Mahlke and Thüring's terms pragmatic and hedonic. Both Hassenzahl

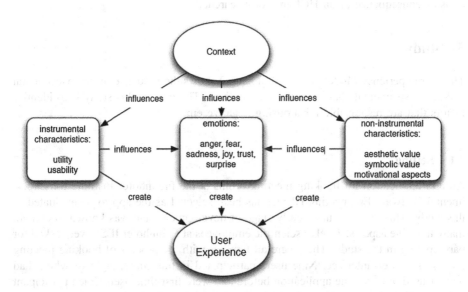

Fig. 1. User experience Model based on Hassenzahl's and Mahlke's models

and Mahlke consider usability and utility to be elements of instrumental qualities. Utility and usability differ in that utility provides a certain functionality, whereas usability aims at accessing this functionality.

Non-instrumental attributes aim at user satisfaction that goes "beyond the mere instrumental value" [4], i.e. it is built upon aesthetics, symbolic value, and motivational aspects. Aesthetics is defined as pleasing in appearance and pleasing to the [human] senses [13]. Focusing on the main traditional senses sight, hearing, taste, smell, and touch, it is obvious that nowadays it is not possible to perceive smell and taste through the use of smartphone applications. Like in Mahlke's model, the factors "visual aesthetics", "haptic quality" and "acoustic quality" are considered under the term aesthetics. The symbolic value is the value a product provides independent of its features and functionality, i.e. what does the user associate with the product (memories, prior experiences, brand image, etc.) and what does the product communicate to others (social position, status, group membership, etc.). Motivational aspects are about the ability of the product to motivate the user in performing his tasks.

Both, the instrumental and non-instrumental characteristics lead to emotions. The resulting emotions have been mentioned in the previous section and are anger, fear, sadness, joy, trust, and surprise. In contrast to Mahlke's model, we do not consider the facets of emotional user reactions, but only the resulting emotions. This is about facilitating the identification of emotions as well as deriving relevant factors for a certain emotion. An emotion can purely be aroused by a certain instrumental characteristic (e.g. a certain function does not work as expected), a certain non-instrumental characteristic (e.g. main color of the UI is pink) or a combination of several instrumental and non-instrumental characteristics.

Instrumental and Non-instrumental characteristics have an influence on the user's emotions whereas the influence of negative aspects of HCI leading to negative emotions as consequence of an HCI are not researched.

3 Study

The user experience Model presented in Sect. 2 shows the influence of the instrumental and non-instrumental characteristics on emotions. The goal of this study is to identify factors that are responsible for arousing negative emotions.

3.1 Setting

An iOS application for booking meeting rooms at the Fraunhofer Institute for Experimental Software Engineering (IESE) has been selected as the app to be evaluated in this study. This app was in an early stage of development, and was known to contain many negative aspects. Twelve scientific employees at Fraunhofer IESE were asked for participating in the study. They were all familiar with the process of booking meeting rooms via a web interface. Nine users participated in this study, eight of whom had neither used nor seen the application before and were first-time users. Each participant individually took part in the study, under the supervision of a moderator who sat next to the participant. Five of nine participants were male. The average age was 33.8 (max: 45, min: 25). Seven of the participants owned a smartphone when the study took place (iOS: 5, Android: 1, old Samsung OS: 1). One employee used his smartphone professionally, the rest only for private use. Six of the employees had at least one year of experience with iOS devices.

Participants received an instructional document that described the general flow of the study and the purpose of the app, illustrated by screenshots of the app. Participants were additionally given a set of tasks to perform. These tasks were introduced by a moderator and written down. The tasks and app used were constant over all participants.

The participants were asked to fill out two types of questionnaires: an application questionnaire and task questionnaires. The application questionnaire consisted of two parts. The first part inquired about demographical data and asked questions about the anticipated user experience (e.g. "What do you associate with the application?"). This part was filled out before the experiment. The second part asked the participant about his or her opinion and aroused emotions after using the app. (e.g. "What did not meet your expectations?").

A task questionnaire was filled out after the completion of each specified task, and was intended to identify problems that occurred during the execution of the task. The task questionnaire consisted of 13 questions, which were to some extent similar or the same to those of the application questionnaire, but with a focus on the task and not on the app as a whole (e.g. "Please describe issues that arouse during task execution"). The questions covered each component of the UX model, and attempted to reveal issues that arose and functionality that the user missed. The user also chose which emotions occurred during the execution of a task from a list containing the emotions and nuances of these emotions that were discussed in Sect. 2.3 The user was allowed to mark any number of emotions (including none and several). The emotions were explained to the user to ensure a common understanding of them.

3.2 Preparation

The study has been performed in one of the meeting rooms of Fraunhofer IESE. All meeting rooms have the same appearance, so there was no special preparation necessary. The surrounding was bright and calm, subjects were not interrupted while they performed the evaluation study. Screenshots of the application were taken and a short application description has been created. The tasks to perform with the application have been chosen and the needed questionnaires were printed. The chosen tasks cover the main functionality of the application. The Moderator was sitting next to the participant. The roombooking application was installed on an iPhone 5 and each participant participated individually.

3.3 Procedure

The study itself was structured as follows: The moderator explained the process of the evaluation and provided the participant with the documents described in Sect. 3.1. The subject then familiarized him- or herself with the app by exploring the app description document and screenshots, and answered the application questionnaire, before exploring the application on his or her own for five minutes. The subject then received a set of the following four tasks to perform with the app:

1. Select your name from the list of employees
2. Book an available room tomorrow from 08:00 a.m. to 09:00 a.m.
3. Check if the room from Task 2 has been booked correctly.
4. Book an available room tomorrow from 08:30 a.m. to 09:30 a.m., add two visitors, and remove one of them again.

After a subject has performed each task, it filled in one task questionnaire. Eventually, the subject filled in the overall application questionnaire. There was no time limit for performing the tasks.

3.4 Results

The following expectations regarding the application were mentioned in the application questionnaire:

- Fast booking of meeting rooms (7 remarks)
- Delete a booked meeting room (3)
- Overview of available rooms (3)
- Faster than existing web application (2)
- Similar functionality to web application (2)
- Easy to use (2)
- Conforms to Fraunhofer Corporate Identity (2).

For each task and the application itself, perceived emotions have been selected by the user. Which emotions and how often these emotions were aroused is shown in Fig. 2.

The task-specific questionnaire for task 1 contained mainly positive aspects, with the statements: intuitive (2), everything fine (2), search function like in other apps (2), and simple (1), although two negative issues were mentioned: app crashes when VPN is not activated (1), and ugly person icon (1). Seven of the participants stated that they

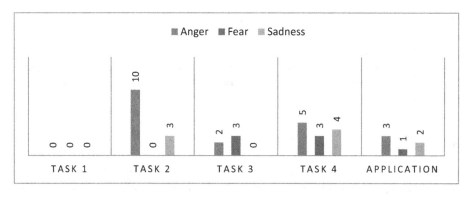

Fig. 2. Occurred emotions in the each task questionnaires and the application questionnaire

did not miss any functionality, each one mentioned the missing sorting functionality (last name vs. first name) and that the iPhone owner is not pre-selected. Summing up for task 1, seven positive issues were mentioned (5 instrumental, 2 undefined). The negative issues (4) related to both the instrumental and non-instrumental component.

For task 2, 22 negative issues have been stated, all related to usability or utility (instrumental characteristics). The end date/time of a meeting is not adapted to the start date/time (3), that it was very difficult to scroll to the desired date in the picker (1), that no recurrent meetings could be booked (1), ugly room icons(1), some problems with the wording (2), and that it is difficult to tap buttons on the top (1). In addition, the participants found the following functionality to be missing or to not work properly:

- No feedback when meeting name has not been entered and confirm button not working (7)
- An overview of all booked rooms is missing (1)
- Sending of the meeting to Outlook is missing (1)
- Available time slots of a certain room are missing (1)
- Text field for entering the meeting name not everywhere clickable (1)
- Booking a room for an already started meeting not possible (1)
- Missing feedback on whether the start or end time for a meeting has been selected (1).

Like task 1, task 3 was a rather small task. Twelve negative issues were mentioned for task 3, all relating to instrumental characteristics. Participants found the name of the meeting missing in the overview of booked rooms (3), the screen looked confusing with many booked rooms (1), that details of the booked rooms were missing (1), and this functionality could not be found (1). The following functionality was mentioned as missing:

- deletion of a meeting (2)
- editing of a meeting (2)
- visitors could not be removed (1)
- only one's own booked rooms and not all booked rooms are shown (1).

Task 4 was similar to task 2, except that two visitors should be added to the meeting. 17 negative issues were mentioned, all related to the instrumental component. Thus, problems similar to those in task 2 were experienced (missing feedback) (2), but also that there is no delete button to delete a visitor (6), it is always necessary to press "done" to select a time (2), and there was no feedback about an added visitor (1). Functionalities that were found missing:

- using the return button on the keyboard to add a user (2)
- visitors are not directly shown (1)
- the missing request form for a WiFi account for visitors (1)
- access to the address book to add visitors (1)
- that text fields start in lowercase (1).

For the four tasks overall, 7 positive and 55 negative issues were found. Of the positive issues, 5 (71.42 %) were instrumental characteristics, while 52 (94.55 %) negative issues were instrumental.

After completing all tasks, the overall application was rated, and the participants were asked what did not meet their expectations. The most frequently given answers were: delete a booked meeting room (4), visitor announcement (3), overview of meeting rooms (3), and edit a booked meeting room (2).

All issues mentioned in the application questionnaire were negative and related to the instrumental component.

3.5   Discussion

The goal of the study was to determine the influence of the instrumental and non-instrumental characteristics on emotions, and especially whether negative aspects of an HCI also lead to negative emotions. The reported issues, expectations, and emotions make clear that this is indeed the case. Of the negative issues, 94.55 % were instrumental characteristics, and are thus related to usability and utility. This leads us to the conclusion that the instrumental component of user experience is responsible when negative emotions arise.

Considering the definitions of the emotions anger, fear, and sadness (see Sect. 2.3), anger is the emotion that appears when people are expecting the world (software) to be different than it is. Sadness is characterized by feelings of despair, disadvantage, loss, or helplessness. Fear occurs in case of risk in something valuable (life, power, control, …). The most mentioned emotion was anger where people were expecting the software to be different than it is. Considering the mentioned issues, this is due to missing functionality (e.g. "booked rooms could not be removed") and unexpected behavior ("button to book a room inactive, but no explanation why button is inactive"). Fear and sadness occurred much less than anger. Sadness occurred due to helplessness and despair (e.g. certain functionality missing or not found, as it has been mentioned quite often). Taking the definition of fear into account, it is obvious that it occurred less often than anger, as people did not encounter a situation where they see a risk in harming them. The similar frequency of occurrences of fear and sadness cannot be explained at this point in time. There were no reasons mentioned by the participants why a certain emotion occurred. With an occurrence of 20, anger is much more perceived than fear or sadness when there is a bad usability and utility.

Tasks 2 and 4 were much more complex than task 1 and task 3, as they required more user inputs to fulfill the task. This is also represented in the mentioned emotions, that were for complex tasks much higher than for simple tasks. Figure 3 shows the relation between occurrences of negative emotions and mentioned positive/negative issues. The more negative issues have been mentioned, the more negative emotions occurred. Task 1 shows even there are negative issues present, positive issues might overcome them, resulting in no negative emotions, although task 1 was lass complex than the other tasks.

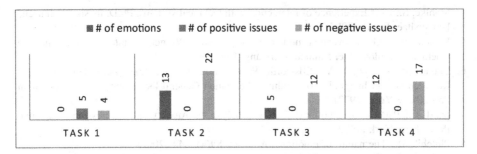

Fig. 3. Relation between the occurrences of perceived negative emotions and positive/negative issues.

4 Summary and Future Work

The study illustrated in this paper provides a first glance into the relationship between user experience and negative emotions. The results show that negative emotions are experienced in case of poor usability and utility, while no conclusive evidence about the influence of negative non-instrumental characteristics was found. Once the app is fully functional and all known problems have been dealt with, this study will be repeated. This will reduce negative issues related to the instrumental component and increase the validity of future results. An interesting point is the relationship among occurring emotions and positive/negative issues. Task 1 showed a first hint, that positive issues might overcome negative issues resulting in no negative emotions. Such combinations of positive and negative issues are an interesting starting point for further research. Improvements for further studies are to ask users why certain emotions occur and what their cause is, and include positive emotions.

Acknowledgement. This work has been partially supported by the German Ministry of Education and Research, grant number 01IS12053.

References

1. Hassenzahl, M.: User experience (UX): towards an experiential perspective on product quality. In: Proceedings of the 20th International Conference of the Association Francophone d'Interaction Homme-Machine (IHM 2008), pp. 11–15. ACM, New York (2008). doi:10.1145/1512714.1512717, http://doi.acm.org/10.1145/1512714.1512717
2. Hassenzahl, M.: The thing and I: understanding the relationship between user and product (Chapter 3). In: Blythe, M., Overbeeke, C., Monk, A.F., Wright, P.C. (eds.) Funology: From Usability to Enjoyment, pp. 31–42. Kluwer Academic Publishers, Norwell (2003)
3. Mahlke, S., Thüring, M.: Studying antecedents of emotional experiences in interactive contexts. In: Proceedings of the SIGCHI Conference on Human Factors in Computing Systems (CHI 2007), pp. 915–918. ACM, New York (2007). doi:10.1145/1240624.1240762, http://doi.acm.org/10.1145/1240624.1240762

4. Mahlke, S.: User Experience of interaction with technical systems. Ph.D. thesis, Technische Universitaet Berlin (2007)
5. Kastenbauer, G.: Anwenden und Deuten: Kripkes Wittgensteininterpretation und die Goethezeit. Philosophie, Munich, Germany. Utz, Wiss (1998)
6. Ekman, P., Friesen, W.V., Ellsworth, P.: Emotion in the Human Face: Guidelines for Research and an Integration of Findings. Pergamon General Psychology Series. Pergamon Press, New York (1972)
7. Izard, C.: Patterns of Emotions: A New Analysis of Anxiety and Depression. Academic Press, New York (1972)
8. Plutchik, R.: The nature of emotions. Am. Sci. **89**(4), 344 (2001)
9. Parrott, G.W.: Emotions in Social Psychology: Essential Readings. Key Readings in Social Psychology. Psychology Press, New York (2001)
10. HUMAINE Emotion Research. Emotion annotation and representation language (earl). http://emotion-research.net/projects/humaine/earl/proposal. Accessed 27 May 2013
11. Hassenzahl, M., Tractinsky, N.: User experience - a research agenda. Behav. Inf. Technol. **25**, 91–97 (2006). Taylor & Francis
12. Graham, M.C.: Facts of Life: Ten Issues of Contentment. Outskirts Press, Parker (2014)
13. Merriam-Webster Inc.: Merriam-Webster's Collegiate Dictionary, 11th edn. Logos Bible Software (2004)

Chinese User-Experience Design:
An Initial Analysis

Aaron Marcus[1](✉) and Stacey Baradit[2]

[1] Aaron Marcus and Associates, 1196 Euclid Avenue,
Berkeley, CA 94708, USA
Aaron.Marcus@AMandA.com
[2] School of Information, University of California/Berkeley,
Berkeley, CA 94720, USA
stacey.baradit@ischool.berkeley.edu

Abstract. The authors have conducted initial research and analysis of simi-larities and differences among Chinese and non-Chinese user-experience design (specifically Western, i.e., US versions) in Web, desktop, and mobile platforms. Characteristics studied include user-interface components (metaphors, men-tal models, navigation, interaction, appearance, and information design/ visualization); experience objectives (usability, usefulness, appeal, fun, and aesthetic form, such as density, gridded organizations, etc.); social network and underlying organizational contexts (public vs. private; work, home, school, and shopping; and sharing (cooperation, communication, and collaboration); and persuasion or motivation characteristics (e.g., use of dashboard; journey maps; focused social networks; just-in-time knowledge; and incentives, such as games, leaderboards, rewards, awards, workshops, nostalgia shops, etc.). The authors propose initial patterns and an initial framework for further research, including the possibility of developing unique Chinese approaches to UX design, Chinese UX guidelines, and eventually characteristics of unique Chinese approaches to operating systems, windowing systems, graphical user-interfaces, and applications for the Web, desktop, mobile, and wearables.

Keywords: China · Cooperation · Culture · Dashboards · Design · Develop-ment · Emotion · Ethnography · Experience · Guanxi (关系) · Incentives · Information · Innovation · Interface · Journey maps · Mobile · Organizations · Persona · Social networks · Usability · Usefulness · User · User interface

1 Introduction

In recent decades, the Chinese economy has advanced to become second behind the US. China has become a producer for many domestically targeted computer-based products/services and a producer for global markets, with the ability (via Internet access) to offer direct selling and shipping. China has become, also, a target for companies worldwide offering products/services. All of these products/services possess user experiences (UXs), that is, user interfaces, user touch points, etc. There is now a challenge to create successful UXs, that is usable, useful, and appealing UXs that work with all major stakeholders: the user community, engineering, marketing, business

© Springer International Publishing Switzerland 2015
A. Marcus (Ed.): DUXU 2015, Part II, LNCS 9187, pp. 107–117, 2015.
DOI: 10.1007/978-3-319-20898-5_11

management, government, investors, and journalists. Exploring UX issues could cover country/culture criteria, design philosophy, methods, evaluation criteria for all stakeholders, and relations among stakeholders such as collaboration among engineering, design, marketing, and business. Specific issues could include these:

- How can Chinese software/hardware developers create a successful user-experience for domestic and foreign products and services?
- How can foreign software/hardware developers create a successful user-experience for Chinese products and services?
- Is there a significant difference in the Chinese UX, as opposed to the Western UX?
- What is the nature of the Chinese UX?
- Are there any significant design patterns in the Chinese UX?
- How might one design more effectively and efficiently for the Chinese UX?
- Where might one look for examples of Chinese UX design?
- What information resources exist to help designers of the Chinese UX?

In this paper we explore only a few of these questions about user-experience and user-interface design. We have based our hypothesis of an emerging Chinese UX on examination of previous qualitative and quantitative research. We hope to raise usable, useful, and appealing issues to consider further.

2   User-Interface, User-Experience, and User-Centered Design

Marcus [24], Brejcha [3], among others, have identified the key components of all human-computer-, or user-interfaces:

- Metaphors: Fundamental concepts communicated through visible, verbal, sonic, tactile, and other "languages"
- Mental models: Organization (structure) of data, functions, people, activities
- Navigation: Movement through the mental models
- Interaction: Input/output techniques and overall behavior of systems
- Appearance: Perceptual characteristics (visual, verbal, sonic, tactile, etc.)

In addition, information visualization (tables, forms, charts, maps, and diagrams) is a specific composite of these components, enabling users to access operating systems, applications, functions, and data of computer-based products and services.

User-centered design (UCD), as discussed in many books and publications (e.g., by Marcus [24] and Hartson and Pyla [9]) links the process of developing software, hardware, the user-interface (UI), and the total user-experience (UX) to the people who will use a product/service. The Chinese UX will inevitably result from a Chinese UCD process. The user experience can be defined as the "totality of the [...] effects felt by a user as a result of interaction with, and the usage context of, a system, device, or product, including the influence of usability, usefulness, and emotional impact during interaction, and savoring the memory after interaction" [9]. That definition means the UX goes well beyond usability issues, involving, also, social and cultural interaction, value-sensitive design, emotional impact, fun, and aesthetics. The UCD process focuses on users throughout all these development tasks, which sometimes occur iteratively: plan, research, analyze, design, evaluate, implement, document, train, and maintain.

In addition, Marcus [24], de Souza [5], and Brejcha [3], among others, have identified the use of semiotics to analyze UX design, and Marcus [17, 18], Sun [29], Brejcha [3], Kyriakoullis and Panayiotis [13], among others, have identified the relationship of culture to UX design.

We do not elaborate on these concepts and terms, because they are familiar to most readers, are widely understood, and are explained in numerous resources. They must all be reconsidered in the light of Chinese UX and Chinese UCD. We consider a few.

3   Cross-Cultural UX Design

Theorists of culture, anthropologists, ethnographers, and professionals in the UX field have devised descriptions of culture, proposed models of culture, and explored similarities and differences of patterns of feelings, opinions, actions, signs, rituals, and values, as Hofstede and Hofstede [10] and Schwartz [27], among others, have described them. Marcus and Baumgartner [20] studied approximately 39 dimensions of culture from about nine different culture models that were vetted by about 60 professionals, researchers, and academics to arrive at a "Top Five" set of culture dimensions: context (high or low), technology (status of development and attitudes), uncertainty avoidance (high or low), time perception (long- vs. short-term, but also focusing on future, present, or past), and authority conception (high or low). Still others have explored ethnographic approaches not based on culture models.

Researchers noticed differences between Chinese and Western (that is, European and North-American) users: Hofstede and Hofstede [Hofstede, 2005] needed to add a fifth dimension (long-term vs. short-term time orientation) to a model stemming from studies in 1978–1983 to account for a pattern of differences that seemed to occur with China-influenced (namely Confucian-influenced) Asian countries vs. Western countries. Marcus [17] described and visualized differences of user-interface designs for North-American, European, and, by implied, but unstated extension, Chinese users. Honold [11] had investigated differences between the way German and Chinese users acquire information about using mobile phones, using a mixture of Hofstede and other models, and found strong correlations between theoretical implications derived from the models and results of testing. Choong and Salvendy [4] noted differences between US and Chinese computer science students in their mental models of the rooms of a house at home and what kinds of objects might be found in those rooms; when they gave the others' mental model to participants, they had more difficulty thinking with the mental model and made more errors. Marcus and Baumgartner [21] studied Websites (business-to-business and business-to-consumer) and analyzed differences in corporate Website standards for different countries (cultures) using Hofstede's dimensions as a guide; they found that there seemed to be distinctive differences in the use of imagery, thinking about size of text vs. importance of the content, and other differences based on the general expectations of cultural differences. Lee [16] considered the characteristics of a "virtual Confucian" media choices in a virtual Confucian workplace.

Dong [6] discovered patterns of differences among Taiwanese, Korean, and US viewers of Websites, using eye-tracking equipment; the US viewers tended to scan the Website screen in a figure S or 5 shape, then relatively quickly dive into the layers of information below, while the Asian viewers tended to circle the Website page, viewing individual items more thoroughly before descending into the information architecture. Frandsen-Thorlacius et al. [7] studied Danish *vs.* Chinese users to determine if the very concept of usability differed between the two cultures. It did. Chinese users considered that the concept of "usability" more strongly possessed the attributes of "fun" and "aesthetically pleasing" built into the concept than was the case for Danish users. Based, in part, on studies of Japanese and US participants staring at fish tanks and describing what they saw (Japanese viewers tended to describe relationships, US viewers tended to describe objects), Nisbett [26] postulated that there were major cognitive differences between the East and the West; people in these two geographic regions think differently, with Easterners seeming to possess, among other differences, a greater ability to consider logical opposites simultaneously without conflict. In summary, Nisbett seemed to be saying, "Cartesian logic is fine, and may be what Europeans and North Americans prefer, but it is not the only way to think." These comments are presciently described in McNeil and Freiberger's book [25] about the achievements of Prof. Lofti Zadeh, who invented fuzzy set theory in the US, which was ignored by US mathematicians and computer technology professionals, but flourished in Japan and later Asia. According to [25], in 1993, there were about 10,000 experts of fuzzy logic in China but only a few hundred in the US. The authors go out of their way to call attention to cultural differences and differences in thinking methods.

In the 21st century, especially in the last five or ten years, with the rise of China, the increased exchange of products and services, articles and books about cross-cultural UX design have emerged. Many of these in the last five years are documented in an extensive bibliography compiled by Kyriakoullis and Zaphiris [14].

3.1 Hints of an Emerging Chinese UX

These publications over the past decades lead us to conclude there may be emerging a fundamentally Chinese UX more suitable to Chinese users than the paradigms imposed on China by Western computer technology during the past half-century. Several key moments in the authors' own experiences point to emerging patterns:

In 2002, Marcus saw an exhibit of the Wukong project shown at the New Paradigms in Using Computers conference, IBM Santa Theresa Laboratory, San Jose, California, USA. The Sony-Ericsson development team, together with outside consultants, which included a Chinese-American anthropologist fluent in Mandarin, designed a personal digital assistant for Chinese users that incorporated aspects of "guanxi" (关系, life-long Chinese relationship-building). Tests of the initial prototype in China showed it received superior reviews on all aspects of its design in comparison to similar offerings from US, Europe, Japan, and other sources [23].

In the early 2000s, Marcus reviewed for a journal an article from Chinese sources that proposed new metaphors for Chinese software applications based on concepts derived from Chinese gardens, concepts which seemed "strange" and "foreign" Marcus surmised this may be similar to the reaction Chinese viewers originally had when first encountering Western computer technology.

In November 2012, in Shanghai, a corporate Chinese executive speaking with Marcus conjectured that there might be a truly Chinese fundamental user experience, which, if implemented, might make it difficult or even impossible for Western users to access and operate applications and operating systems of Chinese computer technology.

At that same time in 2012, Marcus met Dr. Jui Shang-Ling, then Managing Director, SAP Labs China, Shanghai, who had authored two books [12, 13] proposing that the future of China technologically and economically lay in the prospect that China would not just manufacture (build and distribute) Chinese products and services, but would also design them.

Baradit observed over a five-year period working in China (2009–2014) the significant density and complexity of Chinese news sites and consumer portals, in which hundreds of items (images, links, buttons, text) are distributed in viewable panes, often requiring scrolling for access. In addition, the input of characters using Pinyan techniques require intermediate options-constructs before users can proceed further to make database selections of likely characters in a string sequence. This technique seems clearly to affect functionality of search/filters and navigation and likely has development and design implications, which should be researched further.

Marcus observed a poster from Zhu, from China, [31] at the Interaction Design and Human Factors Conference 2014 (http://idhf.xrenlab.com) in Kochi, Japan, 25–26 November 2014, proposing a new metaphor for information-visualization of body-sensor data that would be more effective, engaging, and increase multi-sensory perception, based on viewing a fish in a pond, a seemingly very Chinese, or at least Asian, concept.

In the closing keynote lecture of the User Friendly 2014 (sponsored by the User Experience Professionals Association of China), Wuxi, China, on 16 November 2014, Prof Lou Yongxi, Dean of the College of Design and Innovation, Tongji University, gave a forceful address oriented to Chinese user-experience designers. He urged the audience to recognize the unique circumstances of Chinese history, culture, and people, and to put that realization into action, by not just theorizing, but designing and building entirely new, inherently *Chinese* solutions to the great challenges that China now faces [15].

3.2 The Emerging Chinese UX: Characteristics and Examples

Based on readings such as those cited above and [16–18, 26, and 27], Marcus' experience being in China on about 12 occasions since 1975, and Baradit's recent experience working in China for approximately five years, the authors speculate that the emerging Chinese UX will differ strongly in key characteristics. Note that further research may illuminate new or different characteristics per storytelling patterns, government, and identity factors.

Metaphors: As noted above, new metaphors may emerge that are fundamentally Chinese and well-established in Chinese history and culture. To the Chinese, they may seem easy to understand and use, re-assuring, and "natural". Chinese viewers would immediately and effortlessly understand patterns of information and knowledge, kinds of storytelling, and allusions or references. To Westerners, these same metaphors may seem foreign, even "alien", unknown, unfamiliar, dysfunctional, and perhaps even threatening. Examples might include complex displays of gardens and fish ponds as stand-ins for display of large, complex systems. An example might be the status of 500 entities viewed at once, each with 7 ± 2 key characteristics, each of which might be in one, or more, or 7 ± 2 key states. The challenge would be especially great if one had to make key strategic or tactical decisions within a short time, say 30 s. Note, for example, that TenCent's new WeBank (www.webank.com) mobile banking application (with no brick-and-mortar buildings) uses simple, quick, appealing visual storytelling to explain the objects and objectives of its system, and does so with cute icons and animations. Many Chinese mobile apps use the concept of "discovery" to find new, unexpected functionality within applications.

Mental Models: Mental models may emerge that are fundamental to Chinese history and culture. and may seem for Chinese users to be easy to understand and use, re-assuring, and familiar, but may seem foreign, even alien, unknown, unfamiliar, and dysfunctional to Westerners. Recall that Choong and Salvendy cited above showed users could operate more effectively and efficiently when working with familiar mental models. This observed pattern of "everything-in-one" may result from top-down or bottom-up yet-to-be-fully-analyzed social and economic forces. Grover [8] summarizes recent Chinese mobile applications and notes they are individually accumulating more features, some of them seemingly unrelated but appealing, while US mobile applications increasingly are more narrow focused, minimalist, and task-driven. A few other Chinese examples are the following:

Mobile WeChat offers abundant functionality similar to WhatsApp. Besides messaging, WeChat offers video calls, a news feed, a wallet with a payments service, a Favorites feature functioning something like Evernote, a game center (with a built-in game), a location-based people finder, a "Shazam-like" song-matching service, and a mail client. Its official accounts platform provides a layer to allow hardware devices to use the app to communicate with services, instead of requiring custom apps. Baidu Maps has weather, an optional "Find My Friends" feature, travel guides, a full "wallet" mode for purchasing things. Tencent Maps lets users send audio postcards. Both of them, and WeChat, have QR code readers and Groupon-style local offers. Weibo, once a Twitter analog, does much more. Its "Post" button allows one to post up to 10 distinct types of content, from blog entry to restaurant review. Weibo, also, has acquired a wallet feature.

Navigation: Navigation schema, as noted above, may emerge that are fundamental to Chinese history and may seem foreign, even alien, unknown, unfamiliar, and dysfunctional to Westerners, but for Chinese users are easy to understand and use, re-assuring, and familiar. The ability and/or preference for large displays of information that encourage a "tour of the surface," so evident in traditional Chinese painting, calligraphy, and typography, may suggest such a distinction that is supported in Dong's eye-tracking experiments cited above.

Interaction: New interaction paradigms may emerge that are fundamental to Chinese history and culture. These preferences may seem foreign, even alien, unknown, unfamiliar, and dysfunctional to Westerners, but they would be easy to understand and use, re-assuring, and familiar, enabling Chinese users to work with character displays, visual attributes, sound, and other input/output techniques more effectively. In a recent summary of Chinese mobile applications by Grover [8], he comments that voice messaging in chat applications such as WeChat is popular because it removes the challenge of typing, can be used by older users without much computer proficiency, and may assist large numbers of people with limited literacy.

Appearance: New visual appearance characteristics may appear that are fundamental to Chinese history and culture. Think of the traditional decorations of architecture, vases, paintings, and calligraphy, that are quite different from either baroque/rococo European painting or the minimalist traditions of the Bauhaus and Swiss-German Typography of the 20th century. In addition, the frequency of cute mascots, icons, animations, and storytelling seem to indicate a unique Asian, and specifically Chinese approach (see Fig. 1).

Fig. 1. Example of Chinese cuteness found throughout cities, publications, websites, and applications.

There are a few additional key differentiators to consider:

Space: In his closing keynote lecture of the User Friendly 2014 conference in Wuxi, China, Prof Lou Yongxi, cited above, spoke of the great spaces of China as a key context and challenge. The scale of some public visual displays seems at times quite extraordinary. China as a land mass is only 90,000 square miles smaller (about the size of the US state of Michigan), and cultural history has shown the influence of the "wide open spaces" in the US on its technology, society, and culture. It seems likely that

Chinese UX solutions may emerge that focus on large displays, public displays, or the traversal of large virtual spaces as giant two-dimensional experiences before "descending" into layers below, that is, flatter hierarchies. This approach was actually tried in the 1960s in the US when the Architecture Machine Group at MIT, under the leadership of Nicholas Negroponte, with Richard Bolt, designed and implemented its Spatial Database Management System [Brant, 1988; Herot, 1980]. The approach featured a large virtual space that one could review on a wall-sized display viewed from the comfort of an "executive" reclining chair. However, this approach never caught on like the Xerox PARC, Apple, Microsoft versions of graphical user interfaces. The difference in the Chinese approach to depicting large, dense visual spaces of text, imagery, and controls is already evident in Web shopping sites associated with Singles Day, 1 November 2014, the largest single transaction day in world history (US$8.18b, RMB50b). Figure 2 shows a typical screen.

Fig. 2. Typical singles day shopping screen showing dense contents.

Time: Chinese society has been at work continuously for 4000 years. Few countries/cultures can claim that heritage and be in a position today to dominate world markets, technology, society, politics, and culture. This perspective gives China a unique "view" of the word and its time scale. This may evidence or present itself in time scales of information displays, the time that it takes for information to travel throughout its society, etc. In addition, due to specific governmental and social contexts, in China some activities may go more slowly in order to be considered "valid" or "official." Quicker is not always better. As the Wukong project pointed out [23], US business relations focus on doing business quickly and maybe becoming friends later, while the Chinese approach emphasizes taking one's time to become friends and then maybe doing business.

Scale: On the occasion of visiting the central China city of Xian for the first time, Marcus asked a tour guide how many people lived in Xian. The guide replied, "Oh, it is a small city, about 7 million people." This difference of "small cities" in the US *vs.* China seems significant. With more than four times the population of the US, solutions to large scale seem imperative. This may lead to unique solutions for how to handle large amounts of participants and money in Internet purchase/pay systems, how to deal with social media networks significantly larger than any existing today (with all the differences of privacy, personality, and context). One other observation is that one million hits in the US on a Website or social platform means something is very popular, but in China, with many more people, the scale of popularity is several times larger. It also seems possible that only a few major socially approved and governmentally approved applications may provide all major functionality in China. In China, it seems, one is part of the team, or one is significantly an outsider.

3.3 Cautions and Future Challenges

In all of this speculation, one must keep in mind that China itself is a vast, complex amalgam of peoples, ethnic groups, different spoken languages, and writing systems. There are officially 56 ethnic groups; the Han people dominate with about 94 % of the population. There are states of China like those in which the Uighurs who use a different writing system and language, have a different (Moslem) religion and culture, and who do not consider themselves "Chinese." In the northeast of China, there is a large semi-autonomous areas in which people speak a form of Korean similar to North Korean. Future research may involve asking people whether they consider themselves Chinese, and whether they consider themselves Han. There is a need to clarify what is the "China" in the concept of "Chinese UX." Perhaps there are several major "dialects" of the Chinese UX. It seems likely that the article by Marcus [22] about proof of return-on-investment for user-interface design in about cost-justifying usability studies may need to be reconceived and re-developed for the Chinese context.

Although we can only speculate at this point, the authors believe the characteristics described here can provide guidance and stimulation to others who may be able to research topics more thoroughly and design specific solutions that demonstrate the impact of China on UX design.

Acknowledgement. The authors acknowledge Grover [8] and the Baidu UX design manual [1], which stimulated discussions for this paper.

References

1. Baidu User Experience Department: Baidu User Experience Design Guidelines, p. 234. Baidu, Beijing (2014)
2. Brand, S.: Nicholas Negroponte and Richard Bolt, the spatial data management system (SDMS), as described in the media lab: inventing the future at M.I.T, p. 138. Viking-Penguin, New York (1987)
3. Brejcha, J.: Cross-Cultural Human-Computer Interaction and User Experience Design: A Semiotic Perspective. CRC Press, Division of Taylor and Francis, Boca Raton (2015, in press)

4. Choong, Y., Salvendy, G.: Implications for design of computer interfaces for Chinese users in Mainland China. Int. J. Hum. Comput. Interact. **11**(1), 29–46 (1999). Elsevier, Amsterdam

5. De Souza, C.S.: The Semiotic Engineering of Human-Computer Interaction. MIT Press, Cambridge (2005)

6. Dong, Y.: A cross-cultural comparative study on users' perception of the webpage: with the focus on cognitive style of Chinese, Korean, and American. Master's thesis, Department of Industrial Design, Korea Advanced Institute of Science and Technology, Seoul, Korea, p. 113. Uses eye-tracking to discern patterns of Web-page viewing (2007)

7. Frandsen-Thorlacius, O., Frandsen-Thorlacius, O., Hornbæk, K., Hertzum, M., Clemmensen, T.: Non-universal usability? A survey of how usability is understood by Chinese and Danish users. In: Proceedings, Conference on Human Factors in Computing Systems 2009, pp. 41–58 (2009)

8. Grover, D.: Blog about Chinese mobile applications. http://dangrover.com/blog/2014/12/01/chinese-mobile-app-ui-trends.html (2014). Accessed 11 Jan 2015

9. Hartson, R., Pyla, P.S.: The UX Book. Morgan-Kauffmann, New York (2012)

10. Hofstede, G., Hofstede, G.J.: Cultures and Organizations: Software and the Mind. McGraw-Hill, New York (2005)

11. Honold, P.: Learning how to use a cellular phone: comparison between German and Chinese users. J. Soc. Tech. Commun. **46**(2), 196–205 (1999)

12. Jui, S.-L.: From Made in China to Invented in China (in Chinese), p. 192. Publishing House of Electronics Industry, Beijing (2007)

13. Jui, S.-L.: Innovation in China: The Chinese Software Industry, p. 170. Routledge/Taylor and Francis Group, London and New York (2010)

14. Kyriakoullis, L., Panayiotis, Z.: Culture and HCI: a review of recent cultural studies in HCI and social networks. Univ. Access Inf. Soc. J. (2015, in press)

15. Luo, Y., Valsecchi, F., Diaz, C.: Design Harvests: An Acupunctural Design Approach Towards Sustainability, p. 321. Studio Tao, Shanghai (2013)

16. Lee, O.: The role of cultural protocol in media choice in a confucian virtual workplace. IEEE Trans. Prof. Commun. **43**(2), 196–200 (2000)

17. Marcus, A.: Globalization, localization, and cross-cultural communication in user-interface design, Chapter 23. In: Jacko, J., Spears, A. (eds.) Handbook of Human-Computer Interaction, pp. 441–463. Lawrence Erlbaum Publishers, New York (2002)

18. Marcus, A.: User-interface design and China: a great leap forward. Fast-forward column. Interactions **10**(1), 21–25 (2003). ACM Publisher, www.acm.org

19. Marcus, A., Baumgartner, V., Chen, E.: User-interface design and culture dimensions. In: Proceedings, Human-Computer Interface International Conference, Crete, Greece, June 2003, pp. c. 300–320 (2003)

20. Marcus, A., Baumgartner, V.-J.: A practical set of culture dimensions for global user-interface development. In: Masoodian, M., Jones, S., Rogers, B. (eds.) APCHI 2004. LNCS, vol. 3101, pp. 252–261. Springer, Heidelberg (2004)

21. Marcus, A., Baumgartner, V.: Mapping user-interface design components vs. culture dimensions in corporate websites. Visible Lang. J. **38**, 1–65 (2004). MIT Press

22. Marcus, A.: User interface design's return on investment: examples and statistics. Chapter 2. In: Bias, R.G., Mayhew, D.J. (eds.) Cost-Justifying Usability, 2nd edn, pp. 17–39. Elsevier, San Francisco (2005)

23. Marcus, A.: Wukong Project, mentioned in Marcus' tutorial description "Cross-cultural user-experience design," User Friendly 2007 Conference, Beijing, China (2007). http://www.upachina.org/userfriendly2007/pwcontent/w_Aaron_en.html. Accessed 28 Dec 2014

24. Marcus, A.: Springer UK, London (2015, in press)

25. McNeill, D., Freiberger, P.: Fuzzy Logic: The Revolutionary Computer Technology that is Changing our World. Simon and Schuster, New York (1993)
26. Nisbett, R.E.: The Geography of Thought: How Asians and Westerners Think Differently... and Why. Free Press, New York (2003)
27. Schwartz, S.H.: Mapping and interpreting cultural differences around the world. In: Vinken, H., Soeters, J., Ester, P. (eds.) Comparing Cultures, Dimensions of Culture in a Comparative Perspective, pp. 43–73. Brill, Leiden (2004)
28. Stille, A.: The culture of the copy and the disappearance of China's past. In: Stille, A. (ed.) The Future of the Past, pp. 40–70. Farrar, Straus and Giroux, New York (2002)
29. Sun, H.: Cross-Cultural Technology Design. Oxford, New York (2012)
30. Wu, M.: Profile of Chinese Ethnics, p. 232. China International Press and China Nationality Art Photograph Publishing House, Shanghai (2010)
31. Zhu, B. (Tina): Designing bio-data displays for appreciating the body. Poster, In: Proceedings, on Memory Stick Distributed to Participants, Interaction Design and Human Factors Conference 2014, Kochi, Japan, pp. 25–26, November 2014

Behavioural Variables Analysis in Mobile Environments

Denise Marczal[1]([⊠]) and Plinio Thomaz Aquino Junior[1,2]

[1] IPT - Instituto de Pesquisas Tecnológicas do Estado de SP, São Paulo, Brazil
marczal@gmail.com
[2] Centro Universitário da FEI – Fundação Educacional Inaciana Pe. Sabóia de Medeiros, São Bernardo do Campo, São Paulo, Brazil
plinio.aquino@fei.edu.br

Abstract. Due to the recent proliferation of mobile applications, it has become essential to obtain a better understanding of how people use their devices and applications. However, it is not always possible to reproduce the chaotic environment where the interactions between users and applications take place. Based on this fact, the present study presents a mechanism for the collection and connection of variables of interaction (touches, navigation between screens, etc.) and variables of mobility (sensor data, such as GPS), by the means of an experiment performed in the application made available at application stores and used by real users, performing daily tasks. With the analysis of the data collected it is expected to understand user behavior during interaction and determine usage patterns associating the variables of mobility with the variables of interaction that provide new ideas for interface projects.

Keywords: Mobile usability · Variables of mobility · Large-scale studies

1 Introduction

The mobile applications number grows each day, in February 2014 the two main application stores, Apple Store and Google Play, exceeded the mark of 1,100,000 applications available for download [1]. Along with the applications, number is the massive use of smartphones. According to a study done by Google [18], the number of smartphone users in Brazil rose from 14 % of the population in 2012 to 26 % in 2013. Given this scenario, obtaining a better understanding of how people use their mobile applications is fundamental to provide them a better user experience.

Although the usability is an important factor for the mobile devices, is not unusual to notice problems related to the usability of the applications only when they are already available in the stores. This is because the use of such software is dynamic. There are two approaches to observe the user interaction in mobile applications, lab tests and field tests. In lab tests, model, no or little influence from the external environment interferes in the test. Due to that fact, some authors argue that the usability results of mobile application studies performed in labs may not represent the application real use [22, 30]. On the other hand, the usability tests in the field observe user interaction with the application in real usage environments. However, to capture such

© Springer International Publishing Switzerland 2015
A. Marcus (Ed.): DUXU 2015, Part II, LNCS 9187, pp. 118–130, 2015.
DOI: 10.1007/978-3-319-20898-5_12

interaction in this approach is not an easy task, to follow users in the field is an intrusive method and it may change the user behavior [8].

The mobile applications usage is relatively new when compared with the use of desktops and websites. Preliminary studies have not indicated what is the set of variables that experts can map in mobile applications to be able to acquire knowledge about the audience, context and interaction behavior. The present work had the goal to contribute to mobile devices HCI studies, considering the mobility condition through a variable systematic analysis, which can be considered for usability experience studies. As a result, this work catalogs the group of variables available in a mobile environment that help understands the application usage. The variables are the result of the review of 34 articles, and were collected in an Android application used by real users. Were collected 85,390 occurrences of device variables; 2,391,132 of interaction variables and 9,466,711 of context variables.

2 Usability and Mobility Condition

The traditional HCI evaluation methods are not applicable in an efficient way for the mobile applications, since they were projected for desktop computers which suffer little interference from the external environment [24]. Due to their nature, smartphones can be used in different daily activities, such as during exercising, commuting, during work time, in the traffic, etc. [5].

In literature, it is possible to find two main approaches for the usability studies of mobile applications: lab experiments and field studies. Laboratory experiments performed in controlled environments where the participants perform pre-defined task. Such experiments involve the observation of the participants performance while executing the tasks and the usability is evaluated during such interaction. In these cases, the control of the environment guarantees the only factors related to the experiment affect the interaction of the participant with the application. However, the usage of smartphones and applications takes place in chaotic environments and under the influence of many external factors, such as background noise, conversations, cars, people, etc. To simulate such kind of environment in a lab is a big challenge.

Tsiaousis [44] tried to replicate the main factors from environment distractions in mobile environments, however, it was not possible to predict all the situations in which an application can be used. The study did not consider a varied sample of devices, which also influence the usability of a smartphone. Taking into account a varied sample of devices in lab tests is a big challenge, since there are a great variety of devices available in the market.

Field studies consist in observation and interviews, and the usability is measured based on the execution of tasks in a real environment. While observing the users in their own environments it is possible to capture information, which affect the usage of the product, including interruptions and distractions. That is an investigation of the reality of the users and not of assumptions [4]. Field studies present benefits for the understanding of the interaction of the user with the system and how external factors affect such interaction. However, they present some problems [31]:

- The participants have to deal with devices which they are not familiar, affecting the perception by the participants;
- The recruiting of users is usually made locally, leading to a small number of user, which does not provide the studies with a heterogeneous sample and does not allow for the study of cultural differences;

To solve such problems McMillan [31] recommends studies in a large scale with applications available in the applications stores and participants using the devices, which they already have, and use daily, instead of using devices provided by the researcher. With the appearance of the applications stores in 2008, the researchers visualized a new way of reaching a large number of participants during their experiments. In this approach, applications are developed and published with the objective of measuring the behavior of the users and answering questions related to the study. Henze [16] developed an application to study the interaction of the users with sensitive touch screens. In the study, data of 91,731 players were collected. Analyzing the touches of the users during the game, it was possible to determine the margin of errors for different screen sizes and the position of the touches. Based on this, it was possible to develop a compensation function that reduced such margin of errors.

Through the large-scale studies, using applications stores it is possible to work in real usage environments, with users from different geographic regions and for a long period. Factors related to the usability, such as the screen size, orientation of the screen (vertical/horizontal), touches can be analyzed in different cell phone models and with a real sample of the application users [16, 35].

Such study intends to present a catalog of variables that can be collected in large-scale studies, capturing information in real time from the smartphone users. Such variables can be interconnected and help to answer important questions for the project interface decisions of the product or for the alignment of new strategies.

3   Identifying Process of Mobile Variables

One of the objectives of the present study is to identify, catalog and classify the variables, which are considered in studies about the user behavior in mobile applications. To meet such objective, the systematic review technique was used. The systematic review is a means of evaluation and interpretation of all the research studies available that are relevant for research topic of an area or phenomenon [23].

The systematic review was guided by the following research question: *Which are the variables considered by the researchers to study the interaction between the users and smartphones in natural usage environments?* The bibliographical research identified 1,225 potential articles, of which 34 were selected.

Besides the systematic review, it was necessary to develop three software modules. The client module is a component attached to the mobile device to collect data and send it to the server. Such module is responsible for capturing different usage contexts generating different paths for the study. The server module receives and stores the data collected in the mobile application. The data processing module executes a statistical analysis and applies the algorithms, which allow the determination of groups based on the level of similarity among the data.

In the review, it was possible to identify some of the variables considered during user behavior studies. Those can be classified into interaction, usage context and device variables. Variables of interaction are those that allow us to determine the user behavior while the user interacts with the application, for example, navigated screens, screen touches, amount of time spent in each screen, etc. The variables of context of use concern to the physical, social, temporal and technical environments [19] where the interaction took place, whereas date and time, geographic location and luminosity are examples of context variables. The device variables are those that represent the device characteristics with which the user interacted, for example, the operational system and the screen size, etc.

As a result from the systematic review, 95 variables presented in the usage behavior studies in mobile applications were identified. Among those variables, 58 (61 %) were classified as context variables, 29 as interaction variables (31 %) and 8 (8 %) as device variables. The device variables are described in Table 1, those of interaction on Table 2 and those of context on Table 3.

The results of the research showed that only 7 studies used the application stores as a large-scale research mechanism.

Table 1. Device variables

Variable	Description	Paper
Device model	Device brand and model	[35]
Platform	Device operational system of the device	[28, 35]
Size of the screen	Real physical size, diagonal measure of the screen	[25]
Resolution of the screen	Resolution of the screen in pixels	[6, 7, 14, 25]
Device name	Name of the device in which the interaction occurs	[14, 28]
Device model	Device model in which the interaction occurs	[6, 7, 14, 28]
Version of the OS	Version of the operational system installed	[6, 7, 14, 34, 37]
Manufacturer	Device manufacturer	[34]

Table 2. Interaction variables

Variable	Description	Paper
Session duration	One session corresponds to the use of the application in first plan	[2, 7, 13, 15, 27, 35]
Action performed	Quantifies the number of actions performed by the user	[25, 37]
Time to perform a task	Amount of time measured in seconds for a user to complete a task	[25, 37]
Number of actions in a task	Number of steps the user took to complete a task	[25]

(Continued)

Table 2. (*Continued*)

Variable	Description	Paper
Navigation	Combination of steps and components accessed during the session of use	[14, 27, 28, 35]
Speed of typing	Number of characters typed in a period of time	[26]
Touches in the Backspace Key	Number of times the backspace key was pressed	[26, 37]
Touches on the Enter Key	Number of times the Enter key was pressed	[26]
Size of the text typed	Number of characters typed	[26]
Touches on the symbol keys	Number of times the symbols characters were used	[26]
Size of the erased text	Number of text characters erased	[26]
Number of long touches	Number of long touches made on the screen	[26]
Number of touches	Number of touches made on the screen	[26]
Interactions with the screen	Interaction the user performed (touches, gestures, elements of the screen, etc.)	[2, 14, 27, 33]
Coordinates of the touch	X,Y position of the place where the touch took place	[34]
Coordinates of the target	X,Y position of the component that receives the touch	[34]
Width of the target	Width of the component that receives the touch	[34]
Format of the text	Data format inserted	[28]
Entry elements	Elements that appear in a screen (buttons, texts, etc.)	[28]
Objectives	User goals	[28]
Start of the objective	First element of each goal	[28, 38]
End of the objective	Last element of each goal	[28, 38]
Screens created	Event of the creation of a screen	[9, 27]
Screens discarded	Event when the OS destroys the screen that is not being used anymore	[27]
Permanence in each screen	Amount of time a user has spent on a screen	[27]
Application finalized	Event of the finalization of the application	[27]
Visited screens in each task	All the screens the user accessed to perform the task	[37]
Number of errors made by task	Number of mistakes the user made in a task	[37]
Screen activations	Number of times each screen was activated	[37]

Table 3. Context variables

Variable	Description	Paper
CPU usage	Indicates which is the percentage of use of the CPU during the interaction	[11, 35, 41]
Memory use	Amount of memory used during the interaction	[35]
Latency of the network	Indicates which is the latency of the network during the interaction	[6, 33, 35, 41]
Battery usage, battery level	The battery usage is calculated per session, dividing the change of the charge by the duration of the session	[2, 6, 11, 12, 14, 20, 33, 35, 38, 39, 41, 43]
Brightness	Screen brightness	[35]
Network signal	Indicates the quality of the telephone network signal during the use of the application. Goes from 0-31 to 99 when there is no signal	[35, 38, 41]
Geolocalization	Latitude and longitude of where the interaction took place	[6, 9, 10, 25, 26, 32, 33, 43, 45]
Geolocalization accuracy	Estimated location accuracy (meters)	[10, 25]
Geolocalization provider	Who is providing the location. Ex: Wi-Fi network, GPS or network triangulation	[25]
Date/Hour of use	Date and local time of the moment of the interaction	[6, 14, 35]
Device position	Device position: vertical, horizontal or mixed	[25]
Dislocation speed	Speed of the user during the interaction	[3, 25]
Event of a received call	Number of calls received during the interaction with the device	[3, 7, 15, 21, 33, 41, 43, 46]
Event of text message received	Number of text messages received during the interaction with the device	[6, 7, 14, 34, 37]
Capture of audio	Audio recording during the use of the application	[3, 7, 9, 15, 21, 27, 29, 33, 41, 43, 45, 46]
Capture of video	Video recording during the use of the application	[9, 41]
Processes in execution	List of processes in execution during the interaction	[42, 45]
Data sent by the network	Total of MB of data sent by the application	[6, 41]
WIFI conditions	Wi-Fi on/off	[7, 21, 41, 42]
Bluetooth conditions	Bluetooth on/off	[6, 41, 42, 45]
Vibration of the Device	Determines how much the device is shaken	[26]
Weather	14 weather conditions defined by Google Weather	[26]
Used applications	Consists in the opening event of any application installed in the device	[3, 6, 10, 12, 14, 28, 32, 33, 40, 42]

(*Continued*)

Table 3. (*Continued*)

Variable	Description	Paper
Nearby Bluetooth points	Number of devices nearby with the Bluetooth on	[10, 32, 45, 46]
Plane mode	Indicates when the device is changed to plane mode	[45]
Environment brightness	Intensity of the light in the environment	[14, 25, 26, 33, 38, 46]
Event of email received	Indicates that one email has been received	[41]
Accelerometer	Measures the acceleration force and rotation in three axis	[33, 40, 41, 46]
Applications installed	List of applications installed in the device	[11, 33, 41, 45]
Temperature	Ambient air temperature in Celsius	[26]
Connected antennas	Cellphone antennas connected with the device	[11, 33, 45]
Screen state	State of the screen active/inactive/blocked/unblocked	[6, 7, 12, 13, 20, 27, 42]
Network traffic	Data amount exchange in the network	[11, 12, 20, 33]
Application category	Obtains the category of the applications used, ex (entertainment, education, games and others)	[6, 7, 14, 28]
Data network type	Obtains the type of data network used such as ex 3G, Wi-Fi, etc.	[6, 7, 11, 43, 45]
Application version	Obtains the version of the application installed	[14, 17, 34]
Opening of the application	Captures opening of the application event	[14]
Closing of the application	Captures closing of the application event	[14]
Application in foreground	Indicates if the application retuned to foreground	[6, 7, 12, 15, 27, 40, 41, 43]
Application in background	Captures the event of the application is in background	[6, 7, 12, 15, 27, 40, 41, 43]
Status of the headphones	Indicates if the headphones are being used	[6, 7, 14]
Volume level	Indicates the volume level of the device	[14]
Gyroscope	Provides the orientation of the mobile device in space. Consists of 3 dimensions around the x, y and z axis of the device	[14, 46]
Device orientation	Indicates if the device is being used in the vertical or horizontal	[6, 14, 34, 45]
Event of installation	Indicates that the application has been installed	[6, 7]
Event de desinstallation	Indicates that the application has been uninstalled	[6, 7]

(*Continued*)

Table 3. (*Continued*)

Variable	Description	Paper
Event of update	Indicates that the application has been updated	[6, 7]
Kinds of screen	Possible types of screens	[28]
Notifications received	Indicates if a notification has been received device	[3, 15, 36]
Notifications visualized	Indicates that a notification has been visualized	[36]
Notification visualization interval	Time interval between a notification received viewed by the user	[36]
Event of the call made	Indicates the user has made a call	[21, 45]
Event of sending a SMS	Indicates the user has sent a text message	[21]
Music	Obtains the song the user is listening to	[21]
Alarm	Indicate if the alarm is active and their configuration	[45]
Memory card	Indicates if there is a memory card, capacity and usage	[45]
Carrier	Carrier name used by the device	[45]
Status of battery	Battery status (charging/discharging/charged)	[42]
Noise level	Captures the noise through the device microphone	[38]

4 Data Collection

The experiment was applied in a taxi booking application, which consists in two applications: one for the client that calls the taxi and another for the taxi driver, who is notified of the call. The applications are available in the Google Play and Apple Store applications stores and are used by real users. The application user base is made of 405,000 users, distributed in eight Brazilian cities, including people of different socio-economical profiles, ages and levels of familiarization with mobile devices. Another factor is the diversity of devices in which the application installed, which range from devices with few features and resources and small screens to devices with many features and resources and large screens.

The collection component for the mobile platform was initially developed for the Android platform. In this component, a service was developed that is initialized when the application is opened, which is responsible for collecting the variables coming from the device sensors and the variables that represent the device characteristics. To collect the interaction variables, it was necessary to intercept the touch events in each of the application screens.

Among the variables presented for this study, 54 variables were collected, of which 41 represent the usage context, six represent the interaction and seven the device. The collection period in the client application was of 30 days, being collected 85,390 occurrences of device variables; 2,391,132 of interaction variables and 9,466,711 of context variables. The application data of the taxi drivers was collected in a period of 25 days, being collected 76,557 occurrences of device variables; 1,891,092 of interaction variables and 75,080,231 of context variables.

5 Data Analysis

In the initial analysis only the passenger's application data were considered, which correspond 20,829 the sessions of use. The application is used in 465 different devices, being the MotoG-XT1033 the most used one. For each session of use considering the user actions from the application opening until its closing. The analysis of the data collected reveals that on average each session lasts 2 min and 10 s, with an average of four screens viewed per session. To determine this information the variables date, session start time, session end time and number of navigated screens were considered. The analysis of the collected data indicate the following behaviors:

Which is the period of the day with more use of the application? Using the variables that mark the beginning and end of the session it was observed that the application is most used during the period of the night. Understanding the usage behavior based on time provides inputs for improvements in the interface design allowing tailor the application for nightly use. It's also possible to determine in which periods of the day, new additional resources should be provided for the application infrastructure and what are the best time frames for application maintenance.

Where the user does uses the application? The geolocation mobility variable was used to indicate the regions with greater intensity of use in Brazil, highlighting the cities of Sao Paulo and Curitiba, as shown the map in the Fig. 1. Understand application usage by regions contributes to build users profile and can help on direct

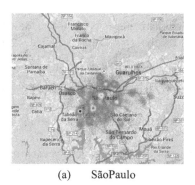 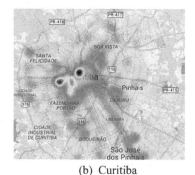

(a)   SãoPaulo   (b) Curitiba

Fig. 1. Application usage by geolocation

marketing campaigns. For the analyzed application, this information can be helpful to guide the growth of the taxi network.

Does the user use the application on the go? Which screens are used in motion? To answer these question the variables movement and navigated screen. To determine whether the user is in motion the device accelerometer was used. It has concluded that 48 % sessions were performed in motion. The screen which the user determinates the address for the taxi ride was the most used on the move. Understanding this type of factor helps to do optimizations in application design in order to facilitate use of the tasks that are used while the user is moving.

Can location accuracy cause some impact on the use? Indicate the pickup location when ordering a taxi is one of the most important tasks in the analyzed application. Currently the address is automatically detected by the application, allowing the user to change it if it is incorrect. It was decided to relate the address editing task with location accuracy, to understand if the low location accuracy would lead users to correct the address suggested by the application. The results showed that in 75 % of the time in which the user has corrected the suggested address, the location accuracy was below 60 meters. This information drives the interface improvements to offer mechanism to facilitate the address edition when location accuracy is below 60 m, before the user search for this functionality.

How often the users interrupt the application usage? To answer this question the application in the background variable was considered. It was found that in 85 % of sessions, users left the analyzed application, with an average frequency 6 times per session and keeping the background application on average 9 min and 12 s. All the screens in which this behavior happened were identified and what were the average time each screen remained in the background. This information leads to optimizations in the navigability flow of current screens and helps to identify in which screens the users loses interest or witch screens there is no need of interaction with the user.

6 Conclusions and Future Work

This work presented a study of variables that can be considered to understand the smartphone usage behavior through the collection in large scale in one application used by real users.

As a result it was possible to catalog a set of variables that were considered on user behavior studies in mobile applications and showed the application of some of this variables. To exemplify the use of some variables the data analysis was guided by the following questions: *Which is the period of the day with more use of the application?*; *Where does the user uses the application?; Is the application used on the go by the user?; Which screens are used in motion?, Can location accuracy cause some impact on the use?* and *How often the users interrupt the application usage?*

This research is part of an ongoing study, which aims to understand which are the variables that can be considered in studies of user behavior on mobile applications. The next steps will be: perform the correlation with more variables in order to determine which ones produces better results; identify personas through the collected variables; improve the data processing component to perform data normalization and analysis incrementally; study and apply pattern discovery techniques.

Acknowledgment. To FAPESP (Fundação de Amparo à Pesquisa do Estado de São Paulo) for financial support.

References

1. 148Apps.biz: app store metrics (2014)
2. Balagtas-Fernandez, F., Hussmann, H.: A methodology and framework to simplify usability analysis of mobile applications. In: 24th IEEE/ACM International Conference on Automated Software Engineering, ASE 2009, November 2009, pp. 520–524 (2009)
3. Banovic, N., Brant, C., Mankoff, J., Dey, A.: Proactivetasks: the short of mobile device use sessions. In: Proceedings of the 16th International Conference on Human-Computer Interaction with Mobile Devices and Services, pp. 243–252. ACM (2014)
4. Barbosa, S.D., da Silva, B.S.: Interacao Humano-Computador. Elsevier, Brasil (2010)
5. Bohmer, M.: Understanding and supporting mobile application usage. Ph.D. thesis, Univesitat des Saarlandes, Postfach 151141, 66041 Saarbracken (2013)
6. Bohmer, M., Hecht, B., Schoning, J., Krüger, A., Bauer, G.: Falling asleep with angry birds, facebook and kindle: a large scale study on mobile application usage. In: Proceedings of the 13th International Conference on Human Computer Interaction with Mobile Devices and Services, MobileHCI 2011, pp. 47–56. ACM, New York (2011)
7. Bohmer, M., Lander, C., Krüger, A.: What's in the apps for context?: extending a sensor for studying app usage to informing context-awareness. In: Proceedings of the 2013 ACM conference on Pervasive and Ubiquitous Computing Adjunct Publication, pp. 1423–1426 (2013)
8. Brown, B., McGregor, M., Laurier, E.: iphone in vivo: video analysis of mobile device use. In: Proceedings of the SIGCHI Conference on Human Factors in Computing Systems, CHI 2013, pp. 1031–1040. ACM, New York (2013)
9. Brown, B., McGregor, M., McMillan, D.: 100 days of iphone use: understanding the details of mobile device use. In: Proceedings of the 16th International Conference On Human-Computer Interaction with Mobile Devices and Services, pp. 223–232. ACM (2014)
10. Do, T.M.T., Blom, J., Gatica-Perez, D.: Smartphone usage in the wild: a large-scale analysis of applications and context. In: Proceedings of the 13th International Conference On Multimodal Interfaces, pp. 353–360. ACM (2011)
11. Falaki, H., Mahajan, R., Estrin, D.: Systemsens: a tool for monitoring usage in smartphone research deployments. In: Proceedings of the Sixth International Workshop on MobiArch, pp. 25–30. ACM (2011)
12. Falaki, H., Mahajan, R., Kandula, S., Lymberopoulos, D., Govindan, R., Estrin, D.: Diversity in smartphone usage. In: Proceedings of the 8th International Conference On Mobile Systems, Applications, and Services, pp. 179–194. ACM (2010)
13. Ferreira, D., Goncalves, J., Kostakos, V., Barkhuus, L., Dey, A.K.: Contextual experience sampling of mobile application micro-usage. In: Proceedings of the 16th International Conference on HCI with Mobile Devices and Services, pp. 91–100. ACM (2014)

14. Gencer, M., Bilgin, G., Zan, O., Voyvodaoglu, T.: A new framework for increasing user engagement in mobile applications using machine learning techniques. In: Marcus, A. (ed.) DUXU 2013, Part IV. LNCS, vol. 8015, pp. 651–659. Springer, Heidelberg (2013)
15. Hammer, J.C., Yan, T.: Exploiting usage statistics for energy-efficient logical status inference on mobile phones. In: Proceedings of the 2014 ACM International Symposium on Wearable Computers, pp. 35–42. ACM (2014)
16. Henze, N., Pielot, M.: App stores: external validity for mobile HCI. Interactions 20(2), 33–38 (2013)
17. Humayoun, S.R., Dubinsky, Y.: Mobigolog: formal task modelling for testing user gestures interaction in mobile applications. In: Proceedings of the 1st International Conference on Mobile Software Engineering and Systems, pp. 46–49. ACM (2014)
18. IpsosGoogle: our mobile planet (2014). http://think.withgoogle.com/mobileplanet/en/
19. Jumisko-Pyykkö, S., Vainio, T.: Framing the context of use for mobile HCI. Int. J. Mob. Hum. Comput. Interact. 2(4), 1–28 (2010)
20. Kang, J.M., Seo, S.S., Hong, J.K.: Usage pattern analysis of smartphones. In: Network Operations and Management Symposium, 2011 13th Asia-Pacific, pp. 1–8. IEEE (2011)
21. Karkkainen, T., Vaittinen, T., Vaananen-Vainio-Mattila, K.: I don't mind being logged, but want to remain in control: a field study of mobile activity and context logging. In: SIGCHI Conference on Human Factors in Computing Systems, pp. 163–172. ACM (2010)
22. Kawalek, J., Stark, A., Riebeck, M.: A new approach to analyze human-mobile computer interaction. J. Usability Stud. 3(2), 90–98 (2008)
23. Keele, S.: Guidelines for performing systematic literature reviews in software engineering. Technical report, EBSE Technical Report EBSE-2007-01 (2007)
24. Kronbauer, A.H., Santos, C.A.S.: Um modelo de avaliação da usabilidade baseado na captura automática de dados de interação do usuário em ambientes reais. In: 5th Latin American Conference on Human-Computer Interaction, Brazil, pp. 114–123 (2011)
25. Kronbauer, A.H., Santos, C.A., Vieira, V.: Um estudo experimental de avaliacao da experiencia dos usuarios de aplicativos moveis a partir da captura automatica dos dados contextuais. In: Brazilian Symposium on Human Factors in Computing Systems, pp. 305–314 (2012)
26. Lee, H., Choi, Y.S., Lee, S., Park, I.: Towards unobtrusive emotion recognition for affective social communication. In: Consumer Communications and Networking Conference (CCNC), pp. 260–264. IEEE (2012)
27. Lettner, F., Holzmann, C.: Automated and unsupervised user interaction logging as basis for usability evaluation of mobile applications. In: 10th International Conference on Advances in Mobile Computing and Multimedia, pp. 118–127. ACM (2012)
28. Levy, M., Shoval, P., Shapira, B., Dayan, A., Tubi, M.: Task modeling infrastructure for analyzing smart phone usage. In: Mobile Business and 2010 Ninth Global Mobility Roundtable (ICMB-GMR), pp. 264–271. IEEE (2010)
29. Ma, X., Yan, B., Chen, G., Zhang, C., Huang, K., Drury, J.: A toolkit for usability testing of mobile applications. In: Zhang, J.Y., Wilkiewicz, J., Nahapetian, A. (eds.) MobiCASE 2011. LNICST, vol. 95, pp. 226–245. Springer, Heidelberg (2012)
30. Mayas, C., Hörold, S., Rosenmöller, C., Krömker, H.: Evaluating methods and equipment for usability field tests in public transport. In: Kurosu, M. (ed.) HCI 2014, Part I. LNCS, vol. 8510, pp. 545–553. Springer, Heidelberg (2014)
31. McMillan, D., Morrison, A., Brown, O., Hall, M., Chalmers, M.: Further into the wild: running worldwide trials of mobile systems. In: Floréen, P., Krüger, A., Spasojevic, M. (eds.) Pervasive 2010. LNCS, vol. 6030, pp. 210–227. Springer, Heidelberg (2010)

32. Meng, L., Liu, S., Striegel, A.D.: Analyzing the impact of proximity, location, and personality on smartphone usage. In: 2014 IEEE Conference on Computer Communications Workshops (INFOCOM WKSHPS), pp. 293–298. IEEE (2014)

33. Misra, A., Balan, R.K.: LiveLabs: Initial reflections on building a large-scale mobile behavioral experimentation testbed. ACM SIGMOBILE Mob. Comput. Commun. Rev. **17** (4), 47–59 (2013)

34. Mockler, J.: UX suite: a touch sensor evaluation platform. In: Proceedings of the 16th International Conference on Human-Computer Interaction with Mobile Devices and Services, pp. 631–636. ACM (2014)

35. Patro, A., Rayanchu, S., Griepentrog, M., Ma, Y., Banerjee, S.: Capturing mobile experience in the wild: a tale of two apps. In: 9th ACM Conference on Emerging Networking Experiments and Technologies, CoNEXT 2013, pp. 199–210. ACM, New York (2013)

36. Pielot, M., Church, K., Oliveira, R.: An in-situ study of mobile phone notifications. In: 16th International Conference on HCI with Mobile Devices and Services, pp. 233–242. ACM (2014)

37. Porat, T., Schclar, A., Shapira, B.: Mate: a mobile analysis tool for usability experts. In: CHI 2013 Ext Abstracts on Human Factors in Computing Systems, pp. 265–270. ACM (2013)

38. Pretel, I., Lago, A.B.: Remote assessment of hybrid mobile applications: new approach in real environments. In: 9th Iberian Conference on Information Systems and Technologies (CISTI), pp. 1–6. IEEE (2014)

39. Rahmati, A., Zhong, L.: Studying smartphone usage: lessons from a four-month field study. IEEE Trans. Mob. Comput. **12**(7), 1417–1427 (2013)

40. Sahami Shirazi, A., Henze, N., Dingler, T., Kunze, K., Schmidt, A.: Upright or sideways?: analysis of smartphone postures in the wild. In: 15th International Conference on Human-Computer Interaction with Mobile Devices and Services, pp. 362–371. ACM (2013)

41. Shepard, C., Rahmati, A., Tossell, C., Zhong, L., Kortum, P.: LiveLab: measuring wireless networks and smartphone users in the field. ACM SIGMETRICS Perform. Eval. Rev. **38**(3), 15–20 (2011)

42. Soikkeli, T., Karikoski, J., Hammainen, H.: Diversity and end user context in smartphone usage sessions. In: 2011 5th International Conference on Next Generation Mobile Applications, Services And Technologies (NGMAST), pp. 7–12. IEEE (2011)

43. Srinivasan, V., Moghaddam, S., Mukherji, A., Rachuri, K.K., Xu, C., Tapia, E.M.: Mobileminer: mining your frequent patterns on your phone. In: International Joint Conference on Pervasive and Ubiquitous Computing, pp. 389–400. ACM (2014)

44. Tsiaousis, A., Giaglis, G.: Evaluating the effects of the environmental context-of-use on mobile website usability. In: 7th International Conference on Mobile Business, ICMB 2008, pp. 314–322, July 2008

45. Wagner, D.T., Rice, A., Beresford, A.R.: Device analyzer: largescale mobile data collection. ACM SIGMETRICS Perform. Eval. Rev. **41**(4), 53–56 (2014)

46. Zeni, M., Zaihrayeu, I., Giunchiglia, F.: Multi-device activity logging. In: International Joint Conference on Pervasive and Ubiquitous Computing: Adjunct, pp. 299–302. ACM (2014)

Experiences, Problems and Solutions in Computer Usage by Subjects with Tetraplegia

Fausto O. Medola[1,2(✉)], Jamille Lanutti[1], Claudia G. Bentim[3],
Adrieli Sardella[2], Ana Elisa Franchinni[2], and Luis C. Paschoarelli[1,2]

[1] Programme of Post-graduation in Design, UNESP – Univ. Estadual Paulista,
Bauru, Brazil
fausto.medola@faac.unesp.br
[2] Department of Design, UNESP – Univ. Estadual Paulista, Bauru, Brazil
[3] SORRI – Center of Rehabilitation, Bauru, Brazil

Abstract. For the vast majority of users, the most conventional means of interaction with a computer is through the use of the keyboard and the mouse. The act of typing and clicking in a satisfactory speed requires a level of motor ability and coordination, which is provided by the integration of both sensory and neuromotor functions. Among many neurological problems that may affect movement control, tetraplegia due to spinal cord injury challenges the subject to adopt to a severe sensory-motor impairment of the lower limbs, trunk and partial or total affection of the upper limbs. Therefore, tetraplegia represents an important limitation for the user in his/her ability to interact with a computer in a satisfactory and conventional way (keyboard-typing and mouse-clicking). This paper aims to investigate the experiences, problems and solutions used by persons with tetraplegia due to spinal cord injury in daily computer usage. The study sample was comprised by five with tetraplegia due to spinal cord injury. All the subjects had a certain degree of function in the upper limbs, and their levels of injury were between C5 and C7 (fifth to seventh spinal cord segment). A questionnaire with multiple-choice questions about subjects' interaction with computers in daily usage was applied. The questions aimed to understand their experiences and problems when using a computer (typing, clicking and printing, among others), as well as the use of assistive devices aimed to facilitate the computer usage. Prior to the study, all subjects were informed about the study objectives and procedures, and signed an informed consent form after agreeing in participate in the study. Ethical approval was obtained from the Ethical Committee of the Faculty of Architecture, Arts and Communication - UNESP. The results show that subjects with tetraplegia experience a number of problems when using a computer. These problems occur with the use of all the computer components, such as keyboard, mouse, cables and accessories. The severe upper limb impairment is, ultimately, the main factor that limit the users' ability to use a computer in an independent and efficient way. The current study contributes to the knowledge in the fields of ergonomics, design and assistive technologies, as it highlights the need of providing assistive solutions that truly contribute to the satisfactory use of computers by subjects with tetraplegia.

© Springer International Publishing Switzerland 2015
A. Marcus (Ed.): DUXU 2015, Part II, LNCS 9187, pp. 131–137, 2015.
DOI: 10.1007/978-3-319-20898-5_13

Keywords: Tetraplegia · Human-computer interface · Ergonomics · Assistive technologies

1 Introduction

Tetraplegia is a condition caused by a spinal cord injury (SCI) resulting in impairment or loss of the motor and sensory functions in the arms as well as in the trunk and lower limbs (Ditunno et al., 1994). Subject's spinal level refers to the last preserved segment of the spinal cord, below which the spinal function is somehow affected. The upper limbs segments in spinal cord go from the fifth cervical (C5) to the first thoracic (T1) segment, therefore the spinal segments responsible for upper limbs innervation are: C5, C6, C7, C8 and T1. Thus, injury levels below T1 results in paraplegia, since upper limbs function are preserved. According to National Spinal Cord Injury Statistical Center (NSCISC), the number of people with SCI in the U.S. in 2014 was approximately 276,000 persons, with a range from 240,000 to 337,000 persons and approximately 12,500 new cases each year.

For most people, the use of computers has become an essential part of everyday life, for both vocational and recreational usage. The ability to control such equipment may represent, ultimately, the difference between good and bad quality of life (Caltenco et al., 2012). Individuals with severely impaired motor function – such as tetraplegia – experience a number of difficulties and limitations with electronic devices in everyday usage. As many of the widely used computer programs requires the use of a keyboard and/or a mouse to receive input, individuals with tetraplegia have limited hand function that impact their ability to use it independently, thus requiring others' assistance or the use of an assistive technology device.

There are several devices designed to help disabled people to operate a computer. The camera mouse (Betke et al., 2002) is one example: the movements of body features, such as the tip of the user's nose or finger, can be tracked by a video camera and translated into the movements of the mouse pointer on the screen. Another similar device is the one proposed by Chen et al. (2003), which is based on the movements of the head to control the mouse cursor. The head movement images are captured by a marker installed on the user's headset. Besides the hardware, there are softwares available in the internet to assist in computer usage, One example is the EVIACAM®: a mouse replacement software that moves a pointer according to the head motion.

Many researchers have studied computer interfaces that use a variety of technologies and are controlled by different parts of the body other than the hands, such as voice recognition (Moore, 2003), chin/mouth-operated joysticks (Bolton and Wytch, 1992), tongue-operated interfaces (Struijk, 2006, Wang and Ghovanloo, 2007), teeth-clenching (Jeong et al., 2005), an eye-controlled human/computer interface (Kyung & Kyung, 1996), gaze tracking (Hansen et al., 2004), footmouse (Springer and Siebes, 1996) and even brain-controlled interfaces (Li, Nam, Shadden, & Johnson, 2011).

While there is a variety of devices and expensive technologies, a study developed an Integrated Pointing Device Apparatus (IPDA), designed to integrate commercial computer mouse devices, trackballs, or external switches. The device allows the users to operate it by using any two parts of the body, thus facilitating better controllability. For example, people could use 2 hands, one controlling a trackball and the other controlling a second mouse. This device is low-cost and tailored to the individual needs (Chen et al., 2006).

The present study was aimed at exploring the usability issues related to computer usage by individuals with tetraplegia due to spinal cord injury. This will contribute to the understanding about the users' needs, problems and solutions in daily computer usage. Ultimately, this knowledge may benefit designers and manufacturers to design assistive technologies that best meet the needs and expectations of subjects with upper limbs motor impairment in computer usage.

2   Methods

The study sample comprised five subjects with tetraplegia following spinal cord injury (SCI), recruited from SORRI Rehabilitation Center, Bauru-SP, Brazil. Participants met the following inclusion criteria: (1) 18 years or older, (2) had an SCI with a residual function in the upper limbs (levels of injury between C5 to C8) and (3) make use of a computer.

A questionnaire with multiple-choice questions about subjects' interaction with computers in daily usage was created by the authors and applied to the users. The questions aimed to explore the experiences and problems that individuals with tetra-plegia when using a computer and operating its components (keyboard, mouse, cables and accessories). In addition, it investigates whether they make use of assistive tech-nology devices or other self-developed solutions in order to optimize usability and independence in computer usage. Prior to the study, all subjects were informed about the study objectives and procedures, and signed an informed consent form after agreeing in participate in the study. All procedures were approved by the Ethical Committee of the Faculty of Architecture, Arts and Communication - UNESP (Process n. 800.500/2014).

Data was analyzed descriptively and presented in terms of frequencies. Due to the small sample size, statistical analysis was not carried out.

3   Results

The sample of subjects was comprised by 5 men, mean age of 37 ± 4.5 ys., with an average time of wheelchair use of 14.2 ± 8.5 ys. Table 1 lists the subjects characteristics.

Three subjects reported using the computer a few hours per day every day, while 2 subjects reported using many hours per day. Three subjects use notebook/laptop and 2 use desktop computer. Three subjects reported using the computer both to work and leisure, and 2 use only for leisure.

All the subjects reported experiencing problems to operate at least one of the computer components. Users' difficulties with computer usage were related to key-board, mouse and accessories and cables (Fig. 1). The problems with the use of

Table 1. Description of subjects' characteristics

Subject	Gender	Age	Scholarity level	Income range (USD)	Level of Spinal Cord Injury	Time of wheelchair use(years)
1	Male	34	High school	up to 273	C5	11
2	Male	44	Middle school	819 - 1639	C7	23
3	Male	38	Middle school	273 - 819	C7	17
4	Male	37	High school	273 - 819	C5	19
5	Male	32	University	819 - 1639	C7	1

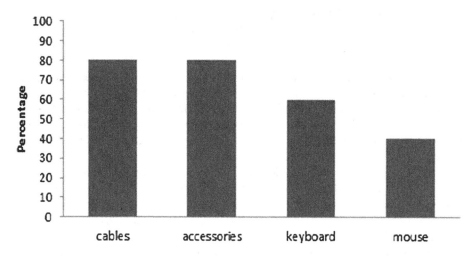

Fig. 1. Problems with computer components

accessories and cables were reported by 60% of the subjects, and were mainly related to handling cables and installing hardware (webcams, headsets, USB devices). One single subject reported problems with inserting and ejecting CD/DVD. The most frequent complaints with keyboard use were related to lack of precision during typing (40%), slow typing (20%) and difficulty in applying the required force to type the keys. Regarding to mouse usage, users reported problems with pushing the two buttons (40%), scrolling (20%) and slow speed (20%).

Sixty percent of the respondents reported using assistive technology devices in computer usage. Two of them use handmade devices and one subject uses the EV-IACAM® software. Considering the three subjects that make use of assistive devices, only one of them reported no need of others' assistance, while the other two subjects still need help, even though using an assistive device.

4 Discussion

Considering that the internet access was declared by UN in 2011 as a fundamental human right, it can be understood that people should be able to use the computer easily. However, disabled people face difficulties with a computer and sometimes the disability impedes them to make use of it. Therefore, studies exploring the usability issues in computer usage may improve the understanding on the aspects that limit individuals with tetraplegia to use a computer in an independent and satisfactory way, thus providing the basis for the development of new assistive solutions.

The current results show that the impaired motor function affects the use of a computer by tetraplegic subjects, for either leisure or work use. This can be thought, ultimately, as a consequence of the loss impaired sensory and motor function in hands. Indeed, all the subjects have a spinal cord injury level affecting fingers' movement and sensibility, which is an important requirement to perform common actions in a computer, such as typing, clicking, pushing a button, installing an accessory and attaching an USB cable. Although it does not prevent them to use the computer, it certainly affects the efficiency and satisfaction. Such problems can be extended to other daily activities, considering that the impaired upper limb function has a devastating impact on the independence of subjects with tetraplegia (Snoek et al., 2004).

Nowadays, there are a number of commercially available devices that allow computer access for people with reduced mobility, all these peripherals are effective for people with reduced mobility, but all have some restraint when used by tetraplegic subjects. The mouthpiece (Adad, 2000) requires constant movement of the mouth, which may lead to the fatigue of the muscles of the jay. Devices that use speech recognition (Borges, 2002) require the maintenance of a certain level of sound. These two devices are not efficient for subjects with tetraplegia who present a reduced lung capacity caused by immobilization.

In addition to the functional issues, all these devices have a high cost, since they are based on advanced technologies and are directed to a small and very specific group of customers. As a result, these systems are neither mass produced nor widely used. In Brazil, an alternative system was proposed aimed to develop a low-cost device that enables the use of computers by people with severely affected mobility (Almeida et al., 2002). It consists of three elements, a helmet instrumented with gyroscopes, magnetic sensors and an ordinary mouse. This device allows one to perform the installation, favoring a greater number of subjects with tetraplegia. According to Caltenco et al. (2012), the design of a good computer interface must present a balance between functionality, performance, cost and easiness of use.

Although the current study provides useful information on the problems experienced by tetraplegic subjects in computer usage, it has some limitations that need to be noted. First, the small sample size limits the generalization of the current findings. Furthermore, the questionnaire used is not a validated instrument as it was developed by the own authors, which do not allow the comparison of the current findings with the other studies.

Based on the information about different assistive devices presented on this paper and on other similar articles, future studies should develop new tests and achieve new information. There are several possibilities, such as addressing the efficiency and satisfaction of the use of assistive devices in computer usage.

5 Conclusion

The computer has become an essential technology for both leisure and laboral activities. While the usability of this technology has been improved over the years, still there are many people that cannot use it independently. The current study showed that individuals with tetraplegia experience problems with daily computer usage. The severe upper limbs impairment affects the user in his/her interaction with the computer components and accessories, such the keyboard, mouse, cables, among others. Although there are a number of commercially available assistive devices aimed to promote and/or improve functionality in computer usage, many users do not use it or make use of a self-made device. Consequently, users with impaired upper limb function still face problems to work with a computer. This study highlights the usability problems and evidences the need for assistive solutions that best meet the needs and expectations in the use of computers by subjects with tetraplegia. This knowledge may benefit designers and manufacturers by providing a detailed view on the computer interface problems experienced by severely disabled subjects.

Acknowledgements. The authors gratefully acknowledge CNPq (National Council for Scientific and Technological Development, Process No 458740/2013–6) for the financial support.

References

Adad, L.B.: Plugga: Communication system for individuals quadriplegics. In: Proceedings of CBEB 2000 (2000). (in portuguese)

Almeida, J.L.S.G., Kubatamaia, C.I., Bissaco, M.A.S., Frère, A.F.: Low cost device for the digital inclusion of quadriplegic. Proc. Ibero-Am. Inf. Technol. Spec. Educ. 3, 570–578 (2002). (in portuguese)

Struijk, L.N.S.A.: An inductive tongue computer interface for control of computers and assistive devices. IEEE Trans. Biomed. Eng. 53(12), 2594–2597 (2006)

Betke, M., Gips, J., Fleming, P.: The camera mouse: visual tracking of body features to provide computer access for people with severe disabilities. IEEE Trans. Neural Syst. Rehab. Eng. 10 (1), 1–10 (2002)

Borges, J.A.: Voice scan system dosvox. Proc. Ibero-Am. Inf. Technol. Spec. Educ. 3, 6–7 (2002). (in portuguese)

Bolton, M.P., Wytch, R.: Mouse emulator for tetraplegics. Med. Biol. Eng. Comput. 30(6), 665–668 (1992)

Caltenco, H.A., Breidegard, B., Jönsson, B., Lotte, N.S., Struijk, A.: Understanding computer users with tetraplegia: survey of assistive technology users. Int. J. Hum.-Comput. Interact. 28 (4), 258–268 (2012)

Chen, C.L., Chen, H.C., Cheng, P.T., Cheng, C.Y., Cheng, H.C., Chou, H.C., Chou, S.W.: Enhancement of operational efficiencies for people with high cervical spinal cord injuries using a flexible integrated pointing device apparatus. Phys. Med. Rehabil. **87**(6), 866–873 (2006). Taiwan

Ditunno, J.F., Young, W., Donovan, W.H., Creasey, G.: The international standards booklet for neurological and functional classification of spinal cord injury. Paraplegia **32**, 70–80 (1994)

Hansen, J.P., Torning, K., Johansen, S.A., Itoh, K., Aoki, H.: Gaze typing compared with input by head and hand. In: Proceedings of the 2004 Symposium on Eye Tracking Research and Applications, pp. 131–138. ACM (2004)

Huo, X., Wang, J., Ghovanloo, M.: Introduction and preliminary evaluation of the tongue drive system: wireless tongue-operated assistive technology for people with little or no upper-limb function. J. Rehabil. Res. Dev. **45**(6), 921–930 (2007)

Jeong, H., Kim, J.S., Son, W.H.: An emg-based mouse controller for a tetraplegic. Systems, man and cybernetic. In: IEEE International Conference on Man and Cybernetics Systems, (2), pp. 1229–1234 (2005)

Park, K.S., Lee, K.T.: Eye-controlled human/computer interface using the line-of-sight and the intentional blink. Comput. Ind. Eng. **30**(3), 463–473 (1996)

Li, Y., Nam, C.S.: A P300-based brain–computer interface: Effects of interface type and screen size. Intl. J. Hum Comput Interact. **27**(1), 52–68 (2010)

Moore, R.K.: A comparison of the data requirements of automatic speech recognition systems and human listeners. In: INTERSPEECH (1), pp. 2582–2584 (2003)

Springer, J., Siebes, C.: Position controlled input device for handicapped: Experimental studies with a footmouse. Int. J. Ind. Ergon. **17**(2), 135–152 (1996)

Snoek, G.J., Ijzerman, M.J., Hermens, H.J., Maxwell, D., Biering-Sorensen, F.: Survey of the needs of patients with spinal cord injury: Impact and priority for improvement in hand function in tetraplegics. Spinal Cord **42**, 526–532 (2004)

Chen, Y.L., Chen, W.L., Chen, T.-S., Kuo, J.S., Lai, T.S.: A head movement image (HMI)-controlled computer mouse for people with disabilities. Disabil. Rehabil. **25**, 163–167 (2003)

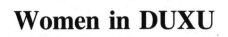

Women in DUXU

Introducing Computer Science to Brazilian Girls in Elementary School Through HCI Concepts

Marília Abrahão Amaral[1], Sílvia Amélia Bim[1], Clodis Boscarioli[2(✉)], and Cristiano Maciel[3]

[1] Departamento Acadêmico de Informática, UTFPR, Curitiba, PR, Brazil
{mariliaa,sabim}@utfpr.edu.br
[2] Colegiado de Ciência da Computação, UNIOESTE, Cascavel, PR, Brazil
clodis.boscarioli@unioeste.br
[3] Instituto de Computação, UFMT, Cuiaba, MT, Brazil
cmaciel@ufmt.br

Abstract. The participation of women in workgroups is essential to any kind of job. Nowadays Computer Science has little presence of women. Consequently, it is necessary to motivate girls to choose Computing as a career. This paper describes an experiment consisting of Human-Computer Interaction (HCI) activities that were used to demonstrate that Computing is more than only programming. The activities were based on the concepts and materials of the Computer Science Unplugged Project. Besides, this work presents the results with the HCI activities performed in the context two Brazilian projects. The results are qualitative in nature and provide insights about HCI activities to elementary school student girls. Fifty-two girls from two different cities and four different public schools participated. All students developed the five tasks designed by CSU materials and were able to articulate concepts of HCI.

Keywords: Women in computer science · Digital girls · Computer science unplugged · Human-Computer interaction

1 Introduction

The necessity of a larger representation of women in Information Technology (IT) is a worldwide issue. The participation of women, where computing is involved, both in academia and in the job market has been much discussed. The IEEE Women in Engineering (WIE) [11] is dedicated to promoting women scientists and engineers, facilitating the recruitment and retention of women in technical disciplines globally.

The Brazilian Computer Society (SBC) has held, in the last years, the WIT (Women in Information Technology) [12], a workshop to discuss subjects related to gender and IT and supports various project initiatives to attract women to Computing. The Project *Meninas Digitais* (Digital Girls) [7] was created from discussions in the WIT, which the main objective is to promote Computing and technology for girls from ten to sixteen at the end of elementary school or middle school, in order to generate interest in the area and motivate them to choose Computer Science (CS) as a career.

© Springer International Publishing Switzerland 2015
A. Marcus (Ed.): DUXU 2015, Part II, LNCS 9187, pp. 141–152, 2015.
DOI: 10.1007/978-3-319-20898-5_14

Several activities are being carried out by various collaborators throughout Brazil such as lectures, technical visits and other initiatives.

In the end of 2013 the Brazilian Government through the National Council of Technological and Scientific Development (CNPq) launched the call for project proposals that would encourage the participation of girls in science, computing and engineering. Several projects were approved all over the country [2, 5]. Many of them have the objective to conducted activities to stimulate teenage girls to choose Computing as a career.

Emíli@s – Armação em Bits[1] is one of these projects approved. Differently of most of the projects to motivate girls to choose Computing as a career, *Emíli@*s also includes Database and Human-Computer Interaction (HCI) activities to demonstrate that Computing is more than only programming. The project has the involvement of Computer Science university teachers, a female Information System student, student girls and a female teacher from a public school in Curitiba in Paraná State (in the South of Brazil). The involvement with a public school is one of the requisites of the CNPq call.

This involvement is in line with one of the actions suggested by Medeiros (2005) [9] - one of the precursors of this discussion in Brazil - that may be considered to allow Brazilian women to become full citizens of the information society: to **provide the basis for adequate training of girls and teachers** - *One necessary direction requires rethinking the educational structure, and developing new kinds of content to be used in courses. These changes must start at an early stage.*

This paper presents the HCI activity performed in the context of *Emíli@s* and *Compute você mesm@*[2] project. The results of the activity performed in a small city of Paraná State were also presented. It is important to mention that the results are qualitative in nature and provide insights about HCI activities to elementary school student girls. Some similar initiatives are presented in the next section. The experiments' protocol is detailed explained in Sect. 3. In Sect. 4 the results of the experiments are shown. And finally, some considerations are made.

2   HCI Activities to Motivate Girls About Computing

In general girls perceive computing careers to be boring, solitary, and lacking real-world context as demonstrated by Yardi and Bruckman [13]. However, some researches have shown that HCI can positively impact interest in Computer Science courses. Yardi et al. [13, 14] gave a six-week HCI course to ten American students ages 11–13 and found that practicing HCI increased their interest in taking future computer related courses.

Margolis and Fisher [8] show that HCI has some promise in serving as a gateway to computing for females. Their work describes the Carnegie Mellon initiative that

---

[1] Emilia is one of Monteiro Lobato characters (author of Brazilian children's literature) the "Sítio do Picapau Amarelo" series. A talking doll, very creative, participating in various adventures.

[2] "Compute Você Mesm@" is an extension project aimed at the empowerment of minorities in computing, including women.

implemented curricular changes including an emphasis on HCI. The results demonstrate that the retention rates amongst women have increased.

Robinson and Pérez-Quiñones [10] conducted a weeklong HCI workshop with underrepresented middle school girls. The workshop was focused on an activity where girls created a paper prototype for a chat application. The results reveal that paper prototyping can be used as a motivator for a career path in computer science.

Maciel, Bim and Boscarioli [1, 6] also conducted an HCI activity with Brazilian girls following the Computer Science Unplugged (CSU) instructions to practice design concepts. The experience was a pilot experiment for the experiments presented in this paper. The results demonstrate the girls' high level involvement in the tasks proposed, showing that HCI is an attractive discipline.

As HCI is interdisciplinary in nature which gives the opportunity to explore the relationship between CS and other disciplines that may interest women. Besides this, HCI, as its name explicitly stated is concerned with human. It worries about the well-being of different users' profiles while interacting with diverse computational devices. Consequently, the stereotype of "nerd" disappears when practicing HCI.

Additionally, communication abilities are clearly needed to develop a computational application concerned with HCI approaches. Therefore, women could comprehend that Computer Science also involves the direct contact with people, which could attract them to the area.

3 The Experiments

All four experiments were carried out in three distinct public schools of Paraná state, in the South of Brazil. The participants were all girls ranging an equivalent age and socioeconomic status. The experiments took place at the girls' school as an extracurricular activity and lasted about three hours. In total the four experiments were conducted with the participation of 52 student girls as shown at Table 1.

The pairs and the groups were made by affinity. In the experiment Exp1 each pair was observed by a female student from a Computing course, who registered the interaction between the girls during the discussion about the solutions for the problems presented. In the experiment Exp2 the groups were observed by one of the researchers and also guided by a school teacher. In the experiments Exp3 e Exp4 the pairs were observed by three students from a Computing course and one of the researchers. The activities of the experiments are listed in Table 2 and explained in the following paragraphs.

The first activity was consisted in make the reception of the girls to explain the objectives of the experiments, and to organize groups to initiate activities. Secondly, a pre-survey was made with the application of a questionnaire with questions about the use (purpose and frequency) of computational devices, the girls' perception about Computer Science courses and their career intention. The results of this survey are presented in the Subsects. 4.1, 4.2 and 4.3.

The third activity consisted in five tasks, proposed by the Computer Science Unplugged Project [3] about HCI Design without Computer [4]. Each task (detailed explained in the following subsection) was presented separately to the student girls who had some minutes to develop their solutions.

Table 1. Experiments' date, city, quantity and arrangement of the participants

	Exp1	Exp2	Exp3	Exp4
Date	April 2013	May 2013	Aug 2014	Sept 2014
City	Curitiba	Guaiporã	Curitiba	Curitiba
Girls	6	10	8	28
Arrangement	pairs	groups	pairs	pairs

Table 2. Experiments' activities

	Exp1	Exp2	Exp3	Exp4
Introduction	x	x	x	x
Pre-survey	x	x	x	x
Computer Science Unplugged activities	x	x	x	x
Pos-survey			x	x

The third and fourth experiments had an extra activity, which consisted in a pos-survey. This questionnaire consisted of seven questions such as, *"What do you think of the activity? The activity met yours expectations? You ever imagine computing activities could be made without the PC?"*. The goal of the post-survey was to assess the satisfaction of the students in participating in the proposed activity. The necessity of this fourth activity was identified after the first experiments.

3.1 Computer Science Unplugged Tasks

The Computer Science Unplugged Project [3] has as its main objective the promotion of Computer Science as an interesting, engaging and intellectually stimulating subject for young people. Therefore, its creators and collaborators have developed a series of activities addressing various topics in Computing including that of HCI – Human-computer interaction. "The Chocolate Factory activity" addresses human interface design [4]. It was translated into Brazilian Portuguese to be used by the girls in our experiment [6].

The setting is that of a chocolate factory and the users are the Oompa-Loompas[3] who have a number of characteristics that need to be considered: they cannot write, they cannot read and have very bad memories. Because of this, they have difficulty in remembering what to do in order to run the chocolate factory and things often go wrong. The goal of the activity, which consists of five tasks, briefly described hereafter, is to design a new factory that is supposed to be very easy for them to operate [4]:

1. Task1 - *Design new doors through which the Oompa-Loompas must pass carrying steaming buckets of liquid chocolate*: Oompa-Loompas cannot remember whether to push or pull the doors to open them, or slide them to one side. Consequently they

---

[3] The scenario is based on British book Charlie and the Chocolate Factory, by Roald Dahl, published in 1964, which inspired a movie of the same name, released in 2005.

end up banging into each other and spilling sticky chocolate all over the place. The girls should decide what kind of doors and handles to use in the factory. Targeted HCI concept: *Affordance*.

2. Task2 - *Design a stove with a better solution for the distribution of the buttons*: The stove is designed in a way that the Oompa-Loompas were always making mistakes, cooking the chocolate at the wrong temperature, and burning their sleeves when reaching across the burners to adjust the controls. The girls should come up with a better arrangement for the new factory. Targeted HCI concept: mapping.

3. Task3 - *Plan a visual warning system to control the conveyer belts*: The factory is full of conveyer belts carrying pots of half-made chocolate in various stages of completion. The people in the control room need to be able to tell the Oompa-Loompas to stop the conveyer belt, or slow it down, or start it up again. The groups should design a scheme that uses visual signals. It's important to consider the color pattern for the Oompa-Loompas: yellow means stop, red means go, and green means slow. Targeted HCI concept: transparency effect and user stereotype.

4. Task4 - *Create a solution for putting away utensils*: There is a cupboard with shelves for Oompa-Loompas to put articles on, but they always have trouble finding where things have been put away. Oompa-Loompas are very bad at remembering things and have trouble with rules like "always put the pots on the middle shelf". The groups should try to come up with a better solution. Targeted HCI concept: visible restrictions.

5. Task5 - *Create a control panel with buttons using individual icons for each operation*: In the main control room of the chocolate factory there are a lot of buttons and levers and switches that operate the individual machines. These need to be labeled, but because the Oompa-Loompas can't read the labels have to be pictorial – iconic – rather than linguistic. The girls have to design a control panel respecting the Oompa-Loompas limitations. Targeted HCI concept: designing.

4 Results

Participants' Profiles. The four experiments were conducted with teenage girls, from twelve to seventeen, from public schools. All of the girls have computers at home and use them daily. The activities performed using the computer mainly concern communication.

In Exp1, three of them mentioned using the computer to do their school homework. And only one mentioned playing games as one of the purpose to use the computer. The time spent on the Internet varies from two to fifteen hours a day (seven hours in average). Concerning the computational devices they used, only one does not use a smartphone. All of them but one use a personal computer. Three of them also use tablets and finally four of them have experiences with notebooks.

In Exp2, five participants referred to having a computer at home, and all use it at school. Reasons for use are social networking, gaming, school assignment research, and chatting with classmates.

The summary of the use of devices for each participant of four experiments is shown in Table 3.

Table 3. Devices X participants

Devices/Exp	Exp1	Exp2	Exp3	Exp4
PC	1	5	5	28
Smartphone	5	0	5	28
Tablet	3	0	3	9
Notebook	4	0	0	28

Concerning the use of technology and Internet access, both in Exp3 and Exp4, all mentioned using the computer to do their school homework and to have Internet access. Two in Exp3 and three in Exp4 quoted the use of computing devices for playing games.

In the Exp4, 13 students reported having family and/or friends working in the computing area and cited the reasons why they would take a workshop in the field: "a job demand, curriculum enrichment, and the lack of professionals in the area." In Exp3, all of them reported that they use the computer and Internet daily. The reasons for participating in a computer workshop are the same shown in Exp4.

Participants' Ideas About Computer Science Courses. The participants, in 4 experiments, were asked about their knowledge about Computer Science courses. In Exp1, one of them (the youngest one) mentioned *programming* (robot, websites and others) as the main activity in a Computer Science course. Three of them focused in *hardware* and two of them gave generic answers as *"They are interesting…"*, *"They teach how to do virtual and graphical projects."*

In Exp2, nine participants claimed to know nothing about courses in the field of computing and only one said, quite generically, that she knew *"almost nothing, and I never really looked more into it"*.

Three students, in Exp3, considered that a computer science course has content about: computer assembly, creating websites and program installation. In addition, other four described the profile of a computer science student as "nerd-like" and "a very intelligent person, studious and good logical thinking." The rest of them did not know what to say. In Exp4, half of them indicated that CS involves activities such as website development and hardware. The other half could not explain.

Participants' Professional Career Intent. With the aim to comprehend the participants' expectation about the activity, they were asked about their professional career intent, in the four experiments. Journalist, photographer, doctor, History teacher, PhD in French Language, petrochemical engineer, lawyer, singer, dentist, politician, officer in charge, architect and P.E. teacher were mentioned. One girl, although not yet sure about her intentions, mentioned *"Program designer for the industry"*. And finally, one answered, *"I would like to be a stylist or designer, because I like to draw and see it become true."*

It is interesting to see that most of them are not sure about their choices nor know them completely. For example, the girl who wants to be a PhD in French Language indicates this option because she considers French a beautiful language and because she would like to live in France. Only one of them indicated that search for information to choose on future profession. The girl who wants to be a petrochemical engineer said she had researched the area in several websites because, in her own words, "*I always watch news which says this field will grow.*" A participant said she wanted to be a P.E. teacher because she likes sports. Two of them revealed the intention of being the officer in charge at a police station due to influence by a successful TV soap opera, which shows the profession to be related to the fight against crime.

4.1 Task 1

The first pair (E1P1) didn't work as cooperatively as expected. One of the girls has a dominant attitude and the other one was more passive. In Task 1 they ignored the options offered in the activity and proposed the use of an automatic door (sliding to the right).

The second pair (E1P2) had quite a discussion to find the solutions for the tasks. For Task 1, after considering many possibilities they proposed a motion sensor door. However, they didn't explicit to which direction the door should open.

The third pair (E1P3) also had a deep discussion about each possibility before coming with the solution. For Task 1, they remembered the types of door in their daily lives and decided to propose a motion sensor door as the one used in malls.

In the second experiment (Exp2) all three groups worked collaboratively and decisions were made collectively. During the development of Task 1 a girl said that "*We should fashion a mat that slides the door open when stepped*", the first group (E2G1) checked the Sliding Door option and recommended, through a drawing, adding a surveillance camera that would cause it to open at the character's approach. In the second group (E2G2), a participant emphatically claimed, "*I'd remove the doors!*". However, her group checked the Common Door option, selecting the *Push to the right* and *Push to the left* options, and observed it would be somewhat a chase door, which, according to their explanation, would simplify their coming and going, for it would be made out of a light material. The third group (E2G3) checked the Sliding door option and added a commentary: "*A door that would open when somebody got close, started by a sensor*". Another participant's remark is quite interesting: "*I'd rather have a door that opened at voice command*".

This task demonstrated just how creative participants were. We noticed that they were willing to suggest different doors from the models they were supposed to choose from the possibilities offered by the experiment material.

As in the second experiment, both in Exp3 as in Exp4 the students worked collaboratively on their pair. Sometimes they made general reflections to the class. This occurred especially in Task 1, in which several students began sharing their considerations aloud concerning the best options for doors.

The group of 8 students, in Exp3, collaboratively concluded that sliding doors "as we have in the malls" would be a great alternative. The fourth pair (E3P4) textually explained their intentions: "A motion sensor automatic double door that lets you know whether there is another person on the other side of the door, because it is transparent".

4.2   Task 2

The solution presented in Task 2 by (E1P1) was extremely simple: a cooker with four buttons in front of it, one for each burner. The solution brought E1P2 to the same task was a stove with five burners, representing the control knobs in perspective.

The most creative answer for Task 2 was presented by E1P3. They proposed an automatic stove with specific burners for each type of chocolate. The control knobs have colors to indicate whether the chocolate is the black or white one. Additionally, the knobs also indicate the appropriate temperature at which each type of chocolate needs to be cooked.

In Exp2 all three groups made drawings of conventional stoves, with the only variation being the number of burners, which were 4, 5 and 6. They reported that intensity would be controlled by turning the knobs. The only group which proposed something different was E2G1, by numbering both the knobs and the burners. When questioned by the E2G2 members on how the illiterate characters would handle that, they replied that being unable to read and write does not prevent them from matching corresponding digits. This fact points out to a visual identification of patterns. Interesting remarks were taken during the development of this task, such as *"Guys, they're so dumb – what a weak memory!"* and *"God, why do they have such weak memory?"*, which is much of a concern to understand the final user's stereotypes.

It is worth mentioning that in Task 2 in Exp3, all pairs (E3P1, E3P2, E3P3, E3P4) placed the control knobs on the front of the stove to avoid the problem of burns. Two proposals (E3P1 and E3P3) use the position of knobs to show at which location the burner is. One group (E3P2) used, along with a visual indication of positioning, a color for each type of fire, with burners placed next to each other. The number of burners ranged from 3 to 6.

In Exp4, only E4P2 designed a stove with 6 burners. The other pairs used 4 burners. The pair E4P11 proposed a stove without circular burners. The proposed solution contained 4 rectangular areas, with their respective buttons (only on-off), bounded by lines. In addition the solution had a lateral area for temperature control.

4.3   Task 3

In Task 3 the pair E1P1 overlooked the Oompa-Loompas difficulty in memorizing things and proposed colored panels distributed along the factory to indicate: "slow", "stop" and "go". On the other hand the E1P2 proposed luminous signs respecting the Oompa-Loompas' color code but they didn't detail where the signs would be placed in the factory. E1P3 used the idea of a traffic light with the Oompa-Loompas' color code. They emphasize that the lights could be seen everywhere in the room.

In the second experiment E2G1 drew three doors placed alongside the conveyor belts. Such doors would change from green (meaning slow), yellow (meaning stop) and red (meaning begin), by means of a device that would cast the colored lights. The changing of colors would be run by the controller and the Oompa-Loompas would be guided by looking at them. Whereas one participant had thought to *"Give them all ear phones so they can only but hear voice commands"*, E2G2 presented a light panel showing the colors, placed under the conveyor. Besides, they associated color intensity with action intensity, with commands such as "follow now" and "follow soon". E2G3 drew only a conveyor and wrote: *"Conveyor must change color so they know what the command is. Slow = green; Stop = yellow; Follow = red."*

In both Exp3 and Exp4, girls proposed light signals according to the Oompa-Loompas' color code. All responses were based on traffic signs. One of the proposals (E4P5), considered the use of graphic signals using the drawing of hands to indicate the actions "stop" and "go". An open hand means "go" and a closed hand means "stop". As the pair did not find a symbol for "slowly", they returned to the traffic light scheme.

4.4   Task 4

The E1P1 suggested the use of images of each objects to indicate the place at the cupboard where they have to be kept.

Interestingly, the solution suggested by E1P2 used one element of Task 3. The girls proposed the use of belts to bring the objects to the cupboard. Besides, the cupboard would have pictures to indicate the correct place of each object.

Once again, the creativity showed up in the solution proposed by E1P3 for Task 4. The cupboard will have pictures of the objects (as suggested by the other pairs). However, as the Oompa-Loompas are troublesome when it comes to rules, they decided to put a sensor, as a kind of scanner, to identify the object that lies in the Oompa-Loompa's hands. Consequently, the cupboard only opens if the correct object is in front of the correct door.

In the second experiment E2G1 drew a cupboard with the knobs fashioned around the objects that ought to be put away. E2G2 created colorful cupboards and colorful objects, so as to guide Oompa-Loompas to place objects in their corresponding color cupboard. They mentioned that doors would be "almost transparent" so they could also make out what is inside. E2G3 designed cupboards that would remain open, with a picture next to each of them indicating the object to be put away inside.

Finally, the pairs of Exp3 and Exp4 used the concept of images to indicate the objects in the cupboard. There was no other solution.

4.5   Task 5

In the first experiment (Exp1) three groups of tags were distributed: Wrap it, Ingredients and Dimensions, as shown in Fig. 1:

The pair that drew the Wrap it tags made very detailed pictures. However, the two other pairs that had to "discovered" the meanings of the draws didn't completely get the right meaning. They gave different meanings for wrap with foil and stop conveyer belt (unwrap and put in the conveyer belt, respectively).

The pair that drew the Ingredients tags also made detailed pictures. But the other pairs gave different meanings for sugar and extra sugar: granulated (for sugar) and sugar and extra coconut (for extra sugar).

Wrap it	Ingredients	Dimensions:
- wrap with foil	Add:	- small bar
- wrap with paper	- cocoa	- medium bar
- put into bag	- milk	- large bar
- put into box	- sugar	- humungous bar
- stop conveyer belt	- extra sugar	- set bar size (in squares)
	- butter	- make chocolate chips

Fig. 1. Tags given to the three groups, respectively, during the Exp1

Wrap it	Ingredients	Try me!
- wrap in aluminum	Add:	- Try it
- wrap in paper	- cocoa	- Awesome – highest rating
- place in a bag	- milk	- Okay – medium rating
- place in a box	- sugar	- Eww – bake chocolate again
- send to shipping	- more sugar	- Eww, eww! – "throw away"
	- butter	

Fig. 2. Tags given to the three groups, respectively, during the Exp2

The E1P2 drew the Dimensions tags. The other pairs have difficulties only with the set bar size draw, one answered decreasing sizes and the other pair gave no answer.

In the second experiment (E2) Task 5 had to be explained twice. Concept understood, the girls started discussing the representation icons. Tags were provided for the groups (Fig. 2), where design solutions were to be drawn as icons.

E2G1 received the Wrap tag. The girls moved on to draw the corresponding wrapping material. They used dark grey to indicate aluminum, and shaped a heart to indicate paper, and so on. E2G2 was in charge of adding ingredients. Their concern was to draw cocoa on the tins, a cow to represent milk, sugar cane for sugar, and so on. E2G3 received the Try Me tag. They used the drawing of a tongue to illustrate "try me". They also used different facial expressions. For "Eww – bake chocolate again", they made a spoon inside a mixing bowl, and for "Eww, eww – throw away", they drew a trash can. Perhaps more time would have been necessary for this task, if better solutions were to be sought.

Each pair in Exp3 and Exp4 also got a set of tags. Thus they created individual icons to represent such buttons. Later there was the exchange of solutions, in pairs, to socialize the answers. The E3P2 created an icon that detail is the action "put into box" with a draw of a box ready to be filled. The label "Ingredients: Add milk" was well designed by E3P4 pair, who proposed the design of a milk box with the illustration of a cow.

In Exp4, in addition to tags already mentioned, the students used the "Making" tag with the following icons: star mixing, stop mixing, start heating, stop heating, pour into molds, stamp a pattern. The pair E4P5, developed an icon for "star mixing" and "stop mixing" representing the hand in both situations.

5 Considerations

Note that the use of HCI strategies with girls helps fighting the idea that computer is a hard science in essence. As it is seen nowadays, a sociotechnical approach to systems is on the rise, so that it is recommended to build diverse teams in terms of gender, for example. However, we still need actions as presented in this paper to demystify computing for girls. In the proposed tasks it was observed that the girls were able to meet the necessary requirements for the development of all tasks.

They also understood the importance of adopting different artifacts and managed to evaluate the concept of affordance when they analyzed the doors of Task 1, as it was reported in all the experiments; they understood the importance of knowing the users, understanding their expectations and needs in the course of all tasks, mainly in Task 2, as shown by the discussions in Exp2; in Task 3 they were able to work out concepts of "transfer effect" and "population stereotypes" to treat the signs and issues that required users' prior knowledge, according to the resolution by pair E4P5; Task 4 explored the concept of "visible constraints" for the design of the proposed cupboard; finally, Task 5 explored icons and the importance of representations and meanings; in all the experiments they were clearly understood.

As to *Programa Nacional Meninas Digitais* (Digital Girls National Programme), volunteers are working on a website that will concentrate information about various enterprises spread throughout Brazil, thus helping to disclose the issue and attract interest. The group communicates through an email list, which grows every year with the inclusion of the Forum participants and via Facebook social network[4].

As future works, we can mention the development of new activities, involving HCI and girls. Although the proposed CSU is relevant, we must develop new practices so that these girls are involved continuously other concepts of HCI are discussed.

Acknowledgements. The authors thank the Araucaria Foundation (Paraná/Brazil) and CNPq for financial support.

References

1. Maciel, C., Bim, S.A., Boscarioli, C.: HCI with chocolate: introducing HCI concepts to Brazilian girls in elementary school. In: Collazos, C., Liborio, A., Rusu, C. (eds.) CLIHC 2013. LNCS, vol. 8278, pp. 90–94. Springer, Heidelberg (2013)
2. Coelho, R., Holanda, M.T.: Mulheres e a Tecnologia da Informação. Computação Brasil, 25, 2/2014, pp. 30–37 (2014)
3. CS-Unplugged Principles. http://csunplugged.org/unplugged-principles

---

[4] The scenario is based on British book Charlie and the Chocolate Factory, by Roald Dahl, published in 1964, which inspired a movie of the same name, released in 2005.

4. CS-Unplugged. Human Interface Design - The Chocolate Factory Activity. http://csunplugged. org/sites/default/files/activity_pdfs_full/unplugged-19-human_interface_design_0.pdf
5. Frigo, L.B., Cardoso, P., Cardoso, J.P., Fontana, C., Irizaga, A., Victory, N., Pozzebon, E., Yevseyeva, O.: Tecnologias Computacionais como Práticas Motivacionais no Ensino Médio. In: Workshops do II Congresso Brasileiro de Informática na Educação, vol. 1 (2013)
6. Maciel, C., Bim, S.A., Boscarioli, C.: A fantástica fábrica de chocolate: levando o sabor de IHC para meninas do ensino fundamental. In: Proceedings of the 11th Brazilian Symposium on Human Factors in Computing Systems (IHC 2012), pp. 27–28. Brazilian Computer Society, Cuiabá, Brazil (2012)
7. Maciel, C.: Programa Meninas Digitais. SBC Mato Grosso (2014). https://sbcmt.wordpress. com/meninasdigitais/
8. Margolis, J., Fisher, A.: Unlocking the clubhouse: the Carnegie Mellon experience. ACM SIGCSE Bulletin, vol. 34 no. 2 (2007)
9. Medeiros, C.B.: From subject of change to agent of change: women and IT in Brazil. In: Morrell, C., Sanders, J. (eds.) Proceedings of the International Symposium on Women and ICT: Creating Global Transformation (CWIT 2005). ACM, New York (2005). Article 15
10. Robinson, A., Pérez-Quiñones, M.A.: Underrepresented middle school girls: on the path to computer science through paper prototyping. In: Proceedings of the 45th ACM Technical Symposium on Computer Science Education (SIGCSE 2014), pp. 97–102. ACM, New York (2014)
11. WIE. IEEE Women in Engineering (WIE). http://www.ieee.org/membership_services/ membership/women/women_about.html
12. WIT. VI Women in Information Technology. http://www.imago.ufpr.br/csbc2012/wit.php
13. Yardi, S., Bruckman, A.: What is computing?: bridging the gap between teenagers' perceptions and graduate students' experiences. In: Proceedings of the 3rd International Workshop on Computing Education Research (ICER 2007), Atlanta, GA (2007)
14. Yardi, S., Krolikowski, K., Marshall, R., Bruckman, A.: An HCI approach to computing in the real world. J. Educ. Resour. Comput. 8(3), 20 (2008). Article 9

Inclusive Gaming Creation by Design in Formal Learning Environments: "Girly-Girls" User Group in No One Left Behind

María Eugenia Beltrán[1(✉)], Yolanda Ursa[1], Anja Petri[2],
Christian Schindler[2], Wolfgang Slany[2], Bernadette Spieler[2],
Silvia de los Rios[3], Maria Fernanda Cabrera-Umpierrez[3],
and Maria Teresa Arredondo[3]

[1] INMARK Estudios y Estrategias, Madrid, Spain
{xenia.beltran,yolanda.ursa}@grupoinmark.com
[2] Graz University of Technology, Graz, Austria
{anja.petri,christian.schindler,wolfgang.slany,
bernadette.spieler}@ist.tugraz.at
[3] Life Supporting Technologies, Universidad Politecnica de Madrid,
Madrid, Spain
{Srios,Chiqui,mta}@lst.tfo.upm.es

Abstract. The education sector in Europe is facing one of the toughest challenges on how to attract, motivate and engage students with content from an academic curriculum and at the same time supporting the formal learning process and providing a learning experience that matches the dynamics of the 21st century. More than ever, Albert Einstein's words are a reality: *"It is the supreme art of the teacher to awaken joy in creative expression and knowledge."* Using games in formal learning situations is an important topic of current research but is still largely underexplored. This paper presents how the "No One Left Behind" project aims at unlocking inclusive gaming creation and experiences, by and for students in day-to-day school life. It outlines the project's use cases as well as explores cultural identity and gender inclusion when games framed in an educational environment are created by and for young girls ("girly-girls").

Keywords: Pocket code · Educational application · STEM · Empowerment of girls · Gender inclusion · Teenage girls · Programming · Mobile learning · GPII · DUXU

1 Introduction

The new generation of youngsters has never known a world without the Internet, social media, and mobile technology (technologically-native children born in the digital era - Generation Z) [1]. Coupled with this trend, there are some alarming statistics related with young people, which show that the risk of exclusion and dropping out of schools remains high. More than one child in four in Europe is at risk of social exclusion [2]

© Springer International Publishing Switzerland 2015
A. Marcus (Ed.): DUXU 2015, Part II, LNCS 9187, pp. 153–161, 2015.
DOI: 10.1007/978-3-319-20898-5_15

while six million young people drop out of school each year [3]. As a reaction, there is an extreme pressure on schools to produce outcomes with an imminent need for social innovation. Hence, the use of Digital Games [4] as part of the formal academic curriculum comes as a natural response.

In this context, the European Commission co-funded project "No One Left Behind" aims at unlocking inclusive gaming creation and experiences in formal learning, underpinning meaningful learning and supporting children to realise their full potential. To achieve these goals the project is developing a new generation of Pocket Code software.

"No One Left Behind" pilots validate the project's outputs in different contexts of use, such as: different locations (Austria, Spain and UK), different social context and social inclusion perspectives (gender, special needs and immigrants), and different user characteristics (students from different school levels, ages, and educational conditions). The pilots also approach user and group management from academic and social behavioural perspectives, interaction through virtual environments, social behaviour and academic content adaptation with gaming techniques.

Regarding this context, this paper specially highlights issues and approaches being handled in the city of Graz (Austria) which tackles the gender issue through the "girly-girls" user group.

This paper is organized as follows: Sect. 1 provides information about the software component used in "No One Left Behind". Section 2 analyses the overall pilot strategy and the issues to be approached in each case. Section 3 presents the specific case of "girly-girls" as a user group in "No One Left Behind". Section 4 presents the Design, User eXperience and Usability (DUXU) and methodology for the scenarios and framework development. Finally, Sect. 5 consists of the evaluation process, and gives an outlook over the expectations and objectives we like to achieve.

2 Pocket Code and the "No One Left Behind" Project

Pocket Code is a learning application for mobile devices. This app allows teenagers to create their own games, animations, interactive music videos, and many types of other apps, directly on their phones or tablets. It uses a visual programming language and it is developed by the free and open source project Catrobat [5]. Pocket Code has been initiated and developed in Austria at Graz University of Technology.

Pocket Code allows its users, starting from the age of twelve, to develop games and animations directly on their smartphones and/or tablets. Its aim is to enable teenagers to creatively develop and share their own software online. The app is available on Google Play for Education.

Pocket Code is inspired by, but distinct from, the Scratch programming language developed by the Lifelong Kindergarten Group at the MIT Media Lab. The main differences between Pocket Code and Scratch are:

- Support and integration of multi-touch mobile devices
- Use of mobile device's special hardware (e.g., acceleration, compass, inclination)
- No need for a traditional PC.

Similar to Scratch, programs in Pocket Code are created by snapping together command blocks which are called "bricks". The bricks are arranged in "scripts" which can run in parallel allowing concurrent execution. Broadcast messages are used to ensure sequential execution of scripts (Fig. 1).

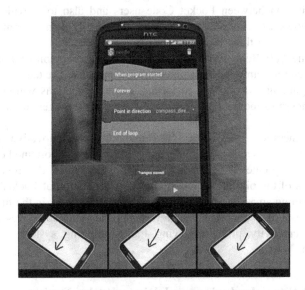

Fig. 1. Making a compass App in one minute with Pocket Code

Currently there are more than 30 ongoing subprojects with the main goal of extending Pocket Code's functionality, e.g., a 2D physics engine similar to the engine used in the popular Angry Birds game, or an extension allowing the user to record their screen and sound easily while running a program. The recorded video can then be uploaded to an online video sharing site. This high definition video will be created on Pocket Code's server and uploaded from there to avoid high costs and lengthy file transmissions for its users (Fig. 2).

Fig. 2. Making games that play with height and gravity concepts

Pocket Code provides the functionality to share programs among children. The users of Pocket Code are mostly teenagers, who can learn from each other and share their ideas to create new programs and games together. To maximize the pool of programs and games, the Catrobat project team is also developing a tool to convert written Scratch programs to the Catrobat language. A forum was initiated to ensure a better communication between Pocket Code users and also to provide updates and support. This allows users not only to create a knowledge building community but also to help each other when they have questions.

The "No One Left Behind" project creates a new generation of Pocket Code (a mobile media-rich programming environment for teenagers). The teenagers are gaining experiences in gaming creation and in formal learning situations within an academic context. This underpins meaningful learning and supports teenagers to unlock their full potential.

The new generation of Pocket Code integrates an innovative set of game mechanics, dynamics, assets and in-game analytics from leisure oriented digital games. Furthermore it incorporates the current academic curriculum of different primary and secondary grades of the piloting schools. This new generation of Pocket Code allows coding and designing amazing and flexible programs and games. In the future it will be an empowering tool that supports the achievement of learning objectives as well as the development of creativity, problem solving, logical thinking, system design and collaboration skills.

3   The Pilot Sites: Inclusion and Diversity by Design

The project validates its output conducting three pilot studies in Europe (Austria, UK and Spain) targeting 600 children/students between 12–17 years. Each pilot site (country) will address a different social inclusion challenge/scenario: e.g., gender exclusion, disability and immigration.

- The pilot in Austria will target gender exclusion of teenagers. Women are overwhelmingly underrepresented in STEM related fields during their university studies as well as once they enter their professional lives. While younger girls up to the age of 12 do not yet show significant disinterest in topics related to computational thinking, a number of studies [6] show that the majority of teenage girls rapidly drop out of IT related courses during their high school years.
- The pilot in Spain targets educational challenges which occur through increasing immigration flows. Many children are not reaching their full potential and are at risk of exclusion because they have another cultural background. Immigrant student populations in Spain have grown 15 times in last ten years, especially the gypsy community: there are about 350,000 children under 18 years old only in Andalusian Region [7, 8].
- The third pilot in UK targets students with disabilities and special educational needs; the pilot focuses on experiments with multi-modal interactions and inclusive technology through auto-configuration and adaptation of the devices to assist those students. The aim is to bridge the gap between students with and without

disabilities. This inclusive approach will be supported through the use of the Global Public Inclusive Infrastructure (GPII) [9].

Throughout these pilots we are working together with educators to ensure that all participating students will gain the skills and experiences needed to become full participants of the class's social structure. Moreover they learn to articulate their understanding of digital games by means of shaping inclusive and social perceptions as media makers and participants in the digital world while complying with the academic curriculum.

By considering the diversity of users and their different levels of experience we aim at mitigating built-in assumptions of the young game developers and teachers so they can create more inclusive and broadly appealing services. In addition, by teaching inclusive design from childhood, we focus on empowering students, as future innovators in STEM related fields.

4 Empowering Women's Computational Skills: "Girly-Girls" User Group in "No One Left Behind". The Pilot in Austria

Promoting gender equality is a longstanding point at the policy agenda in all European countries, however gender-based discrimination still poses barriers in several areas. For example women are overwhelmingly underrepresented in STEM related fields. East Europe has the highest number of women in Europe enrolled in STEM degrees, and only 8.13 % enrol in those degrees [10]. In Canada, a study about career's interest [11] showed that the lack of interest of women reduced the percentage of people indicating that they were interested or very interested in "High Tech/Computers" to 20 %. Similarly, the 2005 Taulbee survey [12] found that 84.9 % of bachelor's degrees in the U.S. in computer science were awarded to men.

Kelleher et al. [13] report that many girls decide whether or not to seriously pursue the study of math and science based disciplines during their middle school years. Therefore it is important to create not only positive experiences in those fields of studies but also show them a playful way to engage with their subject matters.

In the field of game development the number of women working for this industry still remains very low. That fact is especially interesting because a high percentage of the gaming audience are women. According to a study commissioned by the Internet Advertising Bureau in the UK, women account for 52 % of the gaming audience (surveys conducted in the US and Canada show similar numbers). The total number increased by 3 % over the last three years; however only 12 % of women in Britain are professional game designers and only 3 % are programmers [14].

In order to address these gender bias, in "No One Left Behind" we are evaluating how Pocket Code can become as attractive as possible to different female teenager user groups. Not all of them have the same interests or demographic characteristics, but some groups such as the so-called "girly-girls" group are particularly interesting. These girls constitute a large percentage of all female teenagers. Through prior observations in classrooms we experienced that they constitute a large group of passive smartphone and tablet users but are often the least interested in creating their own programs.

Turning them from mere consumers to active creators is a challenging task for this project. The project experiments with various versions of Pocket Code that optimize the design, usability and user experience for girls by, e.g., offering attractive and appropriate sample content, media assets that can be reused in one's own programs or a special view on what programs have been uploaded to the sharing website.

Supporting young female students is not only an essential part of the project but it is also important for themselves. Through specific developments in "No One Left Behind" we offer young women the opportunity to engage in exciting realms of gaming, enjoyable academic content discovery and technological innovation. This is achieved by:

- Stimulating computational thinking skills, such as thinking abstractly and the deconstruction of a problem into smaller pieces (decomposition and composition).
- Moving beyond participation and creativity thinking via game making and coding.
- Providing skills of game coding that go beyond typical reading, writing, and arithmetic.
- Allowing creative and like-driven game based learning. Therefore students can learn about a specific concept or subject by developing personalized games, allowing students to freely select and use content-related preferences, characters, game dynamics, backgrounds and themes.

These characteristics not only broaden the possibility to include a variety of experiences that are accessible and inclusive to a wider audience but also provide a chance to create "games for all". The enhanced version of Pocket Code also expects to support the ability to diversify the learning process in the future and make the study of STEM subjects more attractive for women. We also expect that the number of women as game designers shall increase in the future; as writer Rhianna Pratchett commented, "young girls need to have their eyes opened to the different avenues open to them in games" [15].

5   DUXU in "No One Left Behind" (Design and Usability Approach)

Design and User eXperience and Usability (DUXU) is very important in "No One Left Behind". Through design and user experience the project focuses on supporting students through ease of use, simplicity and desirability through a coding environment that enables young people to be game makers. By using gaming analytics the behavioural patterns are analysed to better understand the unspoken needs of the students and how they use technology for humanizing and supporting process of social inclusion in the classroom. As explained by Boher et al. [16] the new generation of Pocket Code aims at a model for interaction that is "culturally grounded, dynamically experienced, and to some degree constructed in action and interaction".

In "No One Left Behind" we try to link usability with user experience design. Therefore the Pocket Code user interface (UI) allows the creation of interactive animations and game modules that can be combined, shared and customized by each student for a class project. In order to support easy coding, Pocket Code is providing a set of pre-programmed modules (e.g., media packages) that allow teachers bridging unequal access to game based academic experiences and balance the students' different skill sets. The students will then complete these games by personal experience, background, gender or likes. While creating programs with Pocket Code, the students not only share their ideas but also work together and support each other in order to respond to the academic objectives given by their teachers.

Through this participatory design approach a useful game Human Computer Interface (HCI) output can be created; which addresses different needs, cultural backgrounds and likes of a group with common and no-common values. As a result DUXU in Pocket Code enables students by developing own programs to combine together the user interface and game design (Fig. 3).

Fig. 3. Interactive Map Game to learn European Countries

While designing games, Pocket Code provides the opportunity for teenage girls to incorporate diversity and inclusiveness, as well as reflect their cultural identity, their emotions, their likes and their way of interacting and thinking. Through sharing those games – in and out of the classroom – the gender bias are not turning but respond to the variety and diversity of girls. With this approach Pocket Code supports participative and user experience design.

6   Status and Further Work

Over the last year, Pocket Code was introduced as a learning tool to teachers and students to use during school lessons. The usage of Pocket Code in computer science and non-computer science subjects increased rapidly, as both teachers and students benefit from it. On one hand students said they enjoy sharing and creating games with an easy to use and fun application that relates with their subjects. On the other hand teachers reported that teaching through innovative and playful tools students are more motivated, enjoy their classes and also take ownership in the project [17].

Over the next year in "No One Left Behind" we will develop preliminary testing of academic modules for teachers in order to create project examples for different subjects (e.g., mathematics, social studies, science, physics). These modules will be based on the objectives of the academic curriculum. Over time these modules will be used by students in real situations, creating interactive stories and animated games that will be then shared with their peers (in class and online communities).

In order to see if those Pocket Code modules fulfil the needs and expectations of both, teachers and students, a qualitative research based on in-depth interviews and focus groups will be performed. Additionally factors which support social inclusion and girls' empowerment within the academic curriculum will be examined. Those factors could be: make use of the benefits of working in groups, train developing ideas from an initial approach to a fully developed program, encourage problem-solving skills and promote the acquisition of transversal competences and creativity.

With this approach we expect that the girls of this so called "girly-girls" group will not only create interactive games based on their academic curriculum and their cultural identity, but also gives them an opportunity to express themselves creatively. Further it will enable them to engage and understand their subject matter in a playful way and increase so their willingness to study further subjects and explore new fields.

Acknowledgements. This work has been partially funded by the EC H2020 Innovation Action No One Left Behind; http://www.no1leftbehind.eu/, Grant Agreement No. 645215

References

1. Boost Capital. Say Hello To Generation Z – Digital Natives, Entrepreneurs, The Staff and Customers Of Tomorrow, 17th October 2014. http://www.boostcapital.co.uk/blog/say-hello-generation-z-digital-natives-entrepreneurs-staff-customers-tomorrow/
2. Ron, D.: Child poverty and social exclusion: A framework for European action. In: library Briefing. Library of the European Parliament, 14th June 2013. http://www.europarl.europa.eu/RegData/bibliotheque/briefing/2013/130537/LDM_BRI%282013%29130537_REV1_EN.pdf
3. Keeping kids in school. European Commission. Culture, education and youth, February 2011. http://ec.europa.eu/news/culture/110202_en.htm
4. The JRC report refers to Digital Games as a multitude of types and genres of games, played on different platforms using diverse digital technologies (i.e. computers, consoles, tablets, cell phones, etc.). Source: Kerr, Aphra. 'The Business of Making Games'. In: Rutter, J., Bryce, J. (eds.) Understanding Digital Games. Sage Publications (2006)
5. http://www.catrobat.org/. Accessed 23 April 2014
6. Kelleher, C., Pausch, R., Kiesler, S.: Storytelling alice motivates middle school girls to learn computer programming. In: Proceedings CHI 2007 (2007)
7. Eurydice and Eurostat. Key Data on Education in Europe 2012. http://eacea.ec.europa.eu/education/eurydice/documents/key_data_series/134en.pdf
8. Fundación Secretariado General Gitano y del Ministerio de Asuntos Exteriores (2001); report on Gipsy children and youth

9. Vanderheiden, G., Treviranus, J.: Creating a global public inclusive infrastructure. In: Stephanidis, C. (ed.) UAHCI 2011, Part I. LNCS, vol. 6765, pp. 517–526. Springer, Heidelberg (2011)
10. Women enrolled in STEM degrees. http://www.uis.unesco.org/Education/Pages/default.aspx
11. http://www.cips.ca/?q=webcasts. Accessed 23 April 2014
12. Zweben, S.: Ph.D. production at an all-time high, with more new graduates going abroad; Undergraduate enrollments again drop significantly. Comput. Res. News 18(3), 7–17 (2006)
13. Kelleher, C., Pausch, R., Kiesler, S.: Storytelling alice motivates middle school girls to learn computer programming. In: Proceedings CHI 2007 (2007)
14. Jayanth, M.: 52 % of gamers are women – but the industry doesn't know it. The Guradian, 18th September 2014. http://www.theguardian.com/commentisfree/2014/sep/18/52-percent-people-playing-games-women-industry-doesnt-know
15. Keith, S.: Game changers: the women who make video games. The Guradian, 11th December 2011. http://www.theguardian.com/technology/2011/dec/08/women-videogames-designing-writing
16. Boehner, K., DePaula, R., Dourish, P., Sengers, P.: Affect: From Information to Interaction. Critical computing Conference 2005, Århus, Denmark (2005). http://dl.acm.org/citation.cfm?doid=1094562.1094570
17. Catrobat: Pocket Code on Google Play for Education (2014). https://www.youtube.com/watch?v=75i10o_uv0U. Accessed 19 February 2015

3D Real Time Virtual Fitting Room for Women

Salin Boonbrahm, Charlee Kaewrat, Lanjakorn Sewata,
Patiwat Katelertprasert, and Poonpong Boonbrahm[(✉)]

School of Informatics, Walailak University, Tha Sala District,
Nakorn si Thammarat 80161, Thailand
{salil.boonbrahm, charlee.qq, poonpong}@gmail.com,
lsewata@me.com, kpatiwat@wu.ac.th

Abstract. The purpose of this experiment is to set up the women virtual fitting room where user can try virtual dress without taking off her dress. The first part is to simulate virtual parts of the body that were covered with dress and then incorporate them into the real body. After having the new partial virtual body, then user can try some virtual clothes. In order to mobilize the user wearing virtual dress, Kinect was used to detect the skeleton and joints of the real body, virtual part of the body and virtual dress, which were aligned into the same position.

Keywords: Virtual reality · Fitting room

1 Introduction

The women's queues for the fitting room in the clothing department are usually longer than for the men. The reason may be due to the fact that women want to make sure that the dresses they have selected fit well and also look good on them. Waiting for the fitting room for a long time, some of the users may lose interest in buying the dresses. These problems exist not only for the department stores offering dresses in the physical form but also on e-commerce sites selling women dresses as well because users are not able to try on the dresses. The solution for this problem may rely on providing a good virtual fitting room. Virtual fitting room is a real-time interactive platform, where users can try virtual dresses on their bodies. The concepts of the virtual fitting room have been investigated for quite some times. With the new technology on body scanning, such as Kinect device by Microsoft, there is a chance that the perfect fitting room might be possible. Using Kinect to track the body of the user and then place a 2D or 3D partial image of the dress on top of the body seemed to be exciting for a while but it did not look realistic especially when the user moved but the dress did not move along. Many researchers have tried to modify Kinect or other devices with the same technology to form perfect fitting room, but the results were still far from perfect. Most researches on improving virtual fitting room concentrated on how to improve the use of Kinect or other body scanner to detect the body of the user, but not on the realistic of the dresses that the users will see when they are wearing the dresses.

© Springer International Publishing Switzerland 2015
A. Marcus (Ed.): DUXU 2015, Part II, LNCS 9187, pp. 162–171, 2015.
DOI: 10.1007/978-3-319-20898-5_16

Contrary to others, we will emphasize on the 3D dresses that the user will try on when they are in the virtual fitting room. So, instead of putting the dress on top of the body, the dresses will wrap around the body just like we are wearing the dress in real life.

2   Related Work

Various areas of researches on Virtual Fitting Room (VFR) have been done for quite some time, ranging from framework designing online virtual fitting room to VFR for mobile phone. Zhao et al. [1] has studied framework design for online virtual fitting room on a local cluster computing platform. Fast body modeling algorithm for cloth simulation is proposed and the key techniques for cluster computing based online Virtual Fitting Room (VFR) were discussed and a hierarchical architecture was proposed. The result from the implementation shown that the speed for the body modelling process was acceptable for online virtual fitting experience. Li et al. [2] proposed a framework of the virtual Try-on system which forms the basis of a realistic, three dimensional simulations and visualization of garment on virtual counterparts of real users. Users can view the clothing animation on the various angles, plus can change actor's hairstyles and accessories, etc. Garcia C. et al. [3] proposed an algorithm for virtual fitting room application for mobile devices with the objective to obtain a real time, platform independent application. The three stages algorithm are: detection and sizing of the user's body, detection of reference points based on face detection and augmented reality markers, and superimposition of the clothing over the user's image. The application can run in real time on existing mobile devices. Nakamura et al. [4] presented an estimation method of the dress size for Virtual Fitting Room (VFR) using Kinect. Several Kinects were used for high accuracy of estimation and tacking.

3   Experimental Setup

In this research, three parts of making perfect fitting room for woman were proposed.

The first part was related to finding the real body of the users and then replaced some parts of it with virtual model (avatar) that replicated the body of the users or users. The second part was related to the making of 3D dresses that would fit on the users and the last part was related to making the virtual body of the users moved in real time in accordance to the movement of the users while having 3D clothes fitting on the virtual body. With this concept, the users can see how they look when moving while moving with the dresses on, and make the decisions on whether they look good with the dresses or not. For the first part, the virtual body of the user was done using "Kinect sensor" and Autodesk's "Maya" 3D animation software.

For the second part, dresses were made from 2D pattern into 3D virtual dresses. The size of the 3D virtual dresses could be adjusted by changing the parameters.

In the third part, Kinect sensor was used for tracking the movement of the user. By using the joints (nodes) of the user's body, detected by Kinect scanner, then assigned those joints to the virtual model and the dress worn by the virtual model at the same position, the synchronous movement of the user, the avatar virtual model and the dress could be done. In our research, we have tried to use more than one Kinect sensor but we found out that using either two Kinect sensors or one Kinect sensor made no differences in terms of the appearances, so we choose only one sensor for the experiment.

3.1   3D Body Modeling

The main objective of setting up the virtual fitting room is that users can try on any virtual dresses without having to take off their clothes. So, the purpose for this part is to take the clothes off virtually. If they have the new virtual dresses on while still having their original dresses on, it will not look perfect, for example, having the virtual dress on top of pants (see Fig. 1).

Fig. 1. Virtual dress on the top of the body [5]

The solution for getting rid of the physical dress, is to replace all the body parts that are covered with physical dresses and replaced them with virtual undress model or avatar but keeps the rest of the body such as head, hand and feet unchanged. When user evaluates the dresses through some postures and movements, they will feel like they are trying on the real physical dress by themselves. The three main steps of our 3D body modeling process are described below.

Step 1: Getting the 3D model of the body

In this step, the user body is scanned using Kinect scanner. Kinect has two cameras but it does not accomplished 3D sensing through stereo optics. A technology called Light Coding makes the 3D sensing possible. The output from the scanner can be set in the form of 3D model. Unfortunately, the quality of rendered Depth Frame images is very poor. So, instead of getting 3D model, we will settle for 2D picture. Using 2D picture of the front and side views of the user (Fig. 2), we have developed the techniques to get 3D model of the user without dress easily.

Fig. 2. 2D image of the front and side view of the user

From the front view 2D picture of the user, Image processing technique and edge detection were used to get the boundary shape of the user as shown in Fig. 3.

Fig. 3. Boundary of the front image of the user

Standard 3D models of a female user were created and compared to the boundary shape (2D) of the user (Fig. 4a). By scanning from top down, if some part of the boundary is smaller than the model (for example Fig. 4b), the program will adjust the model to make them smaller (Fig. 4c) and if it is larger than the model, then the program will make the model larger. After finishing front view, this process will be applied to the side view as well, using the output model of the first process to begin with.

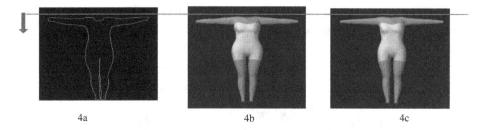

4a	4b	4c

Fig. 4. Scanning process of the front view to get the 3D model of the user

For accurate results, scanning only main parts such as bust, waist, hips and etc., is enough (see Fig. 5).

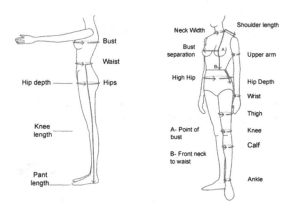

Fig. 5. Body measurement [6]

Step 2: Stripping out the physical dress

As mentioned earlier, the purpose of the virtual fitting room is to be able to remove the physical dress and put the virtual one on instead. In order to do that, we have to know the exact body shape. In case that the user wears clothes that disguised her real body shape, then more accurate data of her body have to be identified either by manual measuring or by automatic scan. For automatic scan, color ribbon may be used for wrapping around some parts of the body such as waist, hip, etc. (see Fig. 5), automatic scan can reveal her real body shape.

Step 3: Construction of 3D body with virtual body part incorporated

After getting the virtual body of the user, some parts of the body that were covered with dress will be replaced by the virtual body parts getting from step 2. Figure 6 shows 3D model of the user before and after the process.

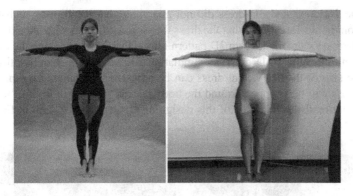

Fig. 6. 3D model construction of the user

3.2 Virtual Dress

In order to make the virtual fitting room look more realistic, the dress must look realistic too. Usually, in the virtual fitting room today, the dress can be categorized into 2 types, i.e. 2D dress (Fig. 7) and 3D dress (Fig. 8).

Fig. 7. Model with 2D dress [7]

Fig. 8. Model with 3D dress [8]

Both the 2D dress and 3D dress did not guarantee that it will look realistic when users try it on. In our case, designing the dress for virtual fitting room will be on different approach. Dresses were made from 2D pattern into 3D virtual dress using the concept of "Digital Clothing Suite", 3D graphics simulation software from Seoul National University. The size of the 3D virtual dress can be adjusted by changing the parameters. Since the dress will be wrapped around the body instead of lying in front of the user, it will look more realistic. Example of this designing concept can be seen in Fig. 9.

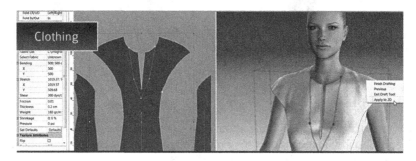

Fig. 9. Designing concept of 3D virtual dress [9]

With this concept, we have made the dresses in 3 different sizes: M, L and XL which will be tested for trying on experiment. All the dresses were shown in Fig. 10.

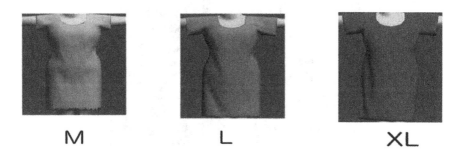

Fig. 10. 3D Virtual dress in different sizes

3.3   Tracking Movement of Avatar with Dress on

After getting the virtual model incorporate with the real body as shown in Fig. 10, next step is putting the dress on. In order to make the real body, the virtual parts of the body and the virtual dress are incorporated into one object, so that when the user moves, she can see the virtual parts of the body and the dress move along with her. Since we are using Kinect scanner for tracking the movement of the body, we have to assign the skeleton and the joints of these three parties aligned in the same position as designed by Kinect. Figure 11 shows the joint and the skeleton of the body assigned by Kinect.

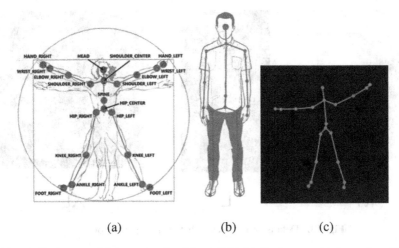

(a)   (b)   (c)

Fig. 11. (a) Skeleton and joint assign by Kinect [10] (b) Skeleton and joint assigned to real people [11] and (c) Movement of the skeleton and joint shown in graphics [12].

After skeleton and joints were assigned, tracking the movements can be done easily. Figure 12 shows the user in T-post position with dress size M, L and XL respectively.

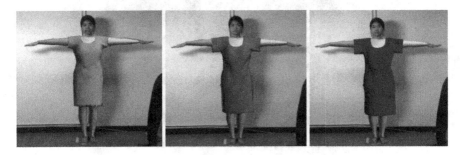

Fig. 12. User with dress in sizes M, L and XL respectively

With different dress size, we can see whether the dress is too big or too small. Details of this observation can be seen in Fig. 13.

For the movement of the body with virtual dress (Fig. 14), we have found that the real body, the virtual parts of the body and the virtual dress move along quite well, even though the color of the virtual parts of the body is a little bit different from the real body.

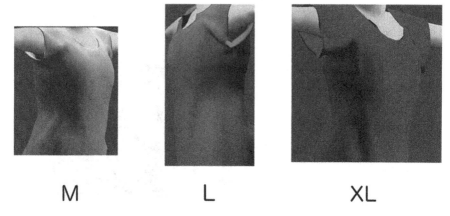

M   L   XL

Fig. 13. Details of the dress whether it is perfect or not.

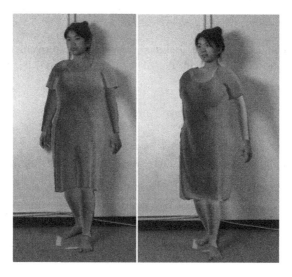

Fig. 14. Tracking the movement of the user wearing virtual dress

4   Conclusion and Discussion

With the prototype of the real time fitting room set up, we have tested for user satisfaction by 20 volunteer women. The result showed that they all agreed on how easy and time saving using this prototype. They were also satisfied with the realistic experience the real time virtual fitting room provided. Though there are a lot of things needs to be improved before it will be available for commercial use, but this experiment proved that we are in to the right direction to have for the perfect virtual fitting room.

References

1. Zhao, Y., Jiang, C.: Online virtual fitting room based on a local cluster. In: 2008 International Workshop on Education Technology and Training and 2008 International Workshop on Geoscience and Remote Sensing, pp. 632–635, IEEE (2008)
2. Li, R., Zou, K., Xu, X., Li, Y., Li, Z.: Research of interactive 3D virtual fitting room on web environment. In: Fourth International Symposium on Computational Intelligence and Design, pp. 32–35, IEEE (2011)
3. Garcia, C., Bessou, N., Chadoeuf, A., Oruklu, E.: Image processing design flow for virtual fitting room applications used in mobile devices. In: IEEE International Conference on Electro/Information Technology, pp. 1–5, IEEE (2012)
4. Nakamura, R., Izutsu, M., Hatakeyama, S.: Estimation method of clothes size for virtual fitting room with kinect sensor. In: IEEE International Conference on Systems, Man, and Cybernetics, pp. 3733–3738, IEEE (2013)
5. Augmented planet. http://www.augmentedplanet.com/2010/09/online-virtual-dressing-room/
6. U4U designs. http://kreativmindz.com/measurement-guide.html
7. InsideFMM. http://insidefmm.com/2010/08/jc-penneys-augmented-reality-dressing-room/
8. Fitnect. www.fitnect.com
9. Assyst bullmer. http://assystbullmer.co.uk/
10. VVVV multipurpose toolkit. http://vvvv.org/forum/kinect-skeleton-which-slice-is-what-joint
11. http://channel9.msdn.com/coding4fun/kinect/Tracking-skeleton-joins-code-sample
12. Telepresence-robot. http://telepresence-robot.blogspot.com/2013/03/kinect-finally-hacked.html

Re/Framing Virtual Conversational Partners: A Feminist Critique and Tentative Move Towards a New Design Paradigm

Sheryl Brahnam[1(✉)] and Margaret Weaver[2]

[1] Computer Information Systems, Missouri State University,
Springfield, MO, USA
sbrahnam@missouristate.edu
[2] Department of English, Missouri State University, Springfield, MO, USA
margaretweaver@missouristate.edu

Abstract. A major research agenda in HCI is the development of believable agents. Because believability has become linked to gendered personification, designers have relied on stereotypes for both the physical rendering and verbal responses of these agents. Conversational agents are even scripted to handle "abuse" in stereotypical ways. Such scripting, however, often escalates the abuse. While the demand for anthropomorphized agents may necessitate a reliance on bodily stereotypes, the verbal responses of the agents need not be scripted according to gendered expectations. We explore the design of conversational agents as a rhetorical enterprise that can deconstruct overtly gendered patterns of interaction.

Keywords: Feminist HCI · Embodied conversational agents · Agent abuse · Rhetoric · Ethos · Anthropomorphism · Personified interface

1 Introduction

Embodied conversational agents (ECAs) are human-like interfaces that interact with users through various modalities such as natural language, facial expressions, and gestures. Outside the realm of entertainment, ECAs function as virtual sales agents, navigational aids, online shopping assistants, airport ambassadors, and virtual docents. Talking with machines, however, produces unique rhetorical problems with believability and credibility that implicate both the human and the artificial conversational partner. Beginning with Eliza, a famous artificial Rogerian psychologist, designers of conversational agents have been entangled in the Western tension in rhetoric between logos (rationality) and ethos (characterization). In an attempt to endow agents with a believable character, designers have endeavored to script conversational agents with specific, recognizable identities that have largely relied on a stylistic rhetoric (a modern *ethopoeia*, or "bag of cheap tricks"). Such anthropomorphisation is thought to "civilize" the machine, making it less intimidating and more user-friendly.

Developing interfaces that are capable of communicating like people, thereby eroding the boundaries that separate human beings from machines, is not a research agenda without controversy. Shneiderman, for instance, contends that such an erosion

© Springer International Publishing Switzerland 2015
A. Marcus (Ed.): DUXU 2015, Part II, LNCS 9187, pp. 172–183, 2015.
DOI: 10.1007/978-3-319-20898-5_17

of boundaries could be construed as a form of deception that misleads and confuses users and designers alike [30]. We, too, are concerned about the confusion prompted by conversational agents, especially in the less than desirable interactions with them. Derisive comments from users have been clearly documented in the literature by computer scientists [6, 13, 15, 35]. Particularly of interest for us is the way *female* conversational agents are scripted to handle what would be considered in human-to-human interactions as *verbal abuse* [4, 5, 14]. The scripted responses of these ECAs often elevate rather than defuse the situation because they continue the deception that the agent is human (woman) [5]. Because agents are embodied representations, inappropriate responses to verbal abuse could offend users, tarnishing the image of the organizations the ECAs represent.

Our concern in this paper, however, is not solely to provide a critique of anthropomorphized conversational agents, but to point to possible avenues for re/framing the design of ECAs in ways that avoid the overtly gendered (feminized) characterizations of the ECAs prevalent today. We present a new direction that future designers of ECAs could take, a direction that rejects the current standard of believability–that "bag of cheap tricks"–in favor of nonartistic methods for making agents more credible. For nonartistic design standards, we turn to Aristotle's categories of credibility: good sense (practical intelligence, expertise, and appropriate speech), excellence (truth-telling), and goodwill (keeping the welfare of the user in mind) [3]. A key element of "truth-telling" is reminding the user that the agent is *not* human but rather a mechanized placeholder, or proxy, for some human agency. While the demand for anthropomorphized agents may necessitate a reliance on bodily stereotypes, the rhetorical responses of the agent need not be scripted according to gendered expectations. The rhetorical responses of the agent can be scripted so that they deconstruct and reframe the visual representation of the agent, in effect de/scripting the agent's identity. Such de/scripting has the potential to highlight openly and honestly the distinction between humans and machines. Such de/scripting may also serve to deconstruct gendered power relations and stereotypes, opening a space where different ideas about gender and ethical relations might be thought.

2 Appeal of Anthropomorphism and Female Personification

Anthropomorphization happens with computers when a user attributes human-like characteristics to the machine. It makes sense why some HCI researchers have focused on designing interfaces that resemble human beings. Placing a human face on a software agent encourages participants to cooperate with the agent in a manner similar to the way they would with a real person [28]. Anthropomorphic interfaces are more engaging for users and activate unconscious social interactions that reduce the need for training and that mitigate anxieties the user might have about interacting with machines [2].

Recognizing the social benefits of a human-like interface, many designers have looked to the notion of *believability* in the media arts as a guiding principle for developing ECAs. The goal is to create agents that prompt the same levels of engagement in users as animated characters do with audiences at the movies. Elliott and Brzezinski even suggest that believability is the *primary* purpose for embodying the interface because the more believable the agent is, the greater the likelihood that users will suspend disbelief and interact with the computer [17].

For many the ultimate test of believability for a conversational agent is the Turing Test, also known as the Imitation Game, that Alan Turing famously proposed in 1950 as a replacement for the question "Can machines think?" [33] The Imitation Game was based on a popular Victorian parlor game that involved three people: a man, a woman, and a judge. The man and the woman were hidden away from view and would only communicate with the judge through written or typed notes. Based on these interactions, the judge would then guess which of the two players was the woman. The object of the game was for the man to play the part of the woman so well that he tricks the judge into believing he is the woman. Turing suggested replacing the man in the game with a computer, the object being for the computer to play the part of the woman so well that the human judge is tricked into believing that the computer is the real woman.

One of the most perplexing aspects of the Turing Test is the way that communication with the computer is gendered. Although some have argued that the Turing Test is best conceptualized as a "species" test and not as a "gender" test, judges of official competitions today nonetheless are instructed to rate the capabilities of an interlocutor suspected of being a machine on a scale of 0 to 100 and "to guess the gender, age, speaking abilities" [18, p. 146] of interlocutors who *pass* for human. Although it may appear that there is nothing about computers (even those that speak) that makes them innately sexed, the standard of believability in conversational agents has become inextricably linked to gender personification, especially female personification.

The personification of conversational agents as female is particularly noticeable in service venues [37]. For instance, on May 30, 2010, we found a total of ten embodied conversational agents being advertised on chatbot.org. Of those that had a human form, five were female and two were male. The female agents were consistently described as virtual assistants who happily answered questions, provided company information, and assisted people in navigating the sponsor website. The male agents, in contrast, were more individual in the tasks they performed and exhibited considerable technical expertise [8]. A similar ratio of male to female ECAs are on exhibit at airportone.com, on a webpage that provides a sample of *Advanced Virtual Avatars* (AVAs), anthropomorphized holograms modeled off real people. Four of the five AVAs are female. They offer directions and assist people at airports and serve as talking mannequins for fashion and museum exhibits. The male AVA is called a "virtual doctor," and he provides patients with health tips and hospital information [38].

Developers have given various reasons for selecting the gender of their personified agents, some admitting to using female agents precisely because they evoke appropriate gender stereotypes [29]. What are the *appropriate* stereotypes that designers expect female agents to elicit? According to Deaux and Lewis, gender stereotypes have four components: profession, role behavior, appearance, and personality [16]. As we shall see, ECAs are designed in ways that do more than meet people's stereotypical expectations of women's work, behavior, appearance, and personality; ECAs are often designed in ways that exaggerate and sexualize these stereotypes and expectations.

Because women are supposedly endowed with "qualities much like those of the mythologized mother: self-sacrifice, dedication, caring, and enormous capacities for untheorized attention to detail" [27, p. 46], professions that are dedicated to serving others are characterized as "women's work" [22]. And the perfect metaphor for "women's work," as Zdenek has shown, is the tedious repetition and banality of computer work [37]. Indeed, ECAs, as we argue elsewhere [8], are the modern evolution of an idea whose genealogy extends back to the 1940s when computers were *literally* women who performed the tedious calculations required by governments, militaries, and university science projects. Not only do ECAs transform the computing machine into the physical likeness of these female human computers, but they also take on the essential role these women assumed when they transitioned into computer operators. This role is nicely summed up by Turing in his referring to his female operators as *slaves* [20]. Chun argues that the true beginning of real-time human-computer interaction is *the command*, not the command line, as Neal Stephenson claims [11]. That comes later. For Chun the original dream of interaction with the computer is that of "a man sitting at a desk giving commands to a female 'operator'" (11, p. 33), who promptly complies with a "Yes, Sir" (11, p. 34). ECAs are an idealized embodiment of this dream. It should come as no surprise, then, that a website in the 1990s claimed their ECA is "every manager's dream worker: a virtual assistant that works 24 hours a day, seven days a week, doesn't ask for vacation, never gets sick, is always pleasant, informed, and looks sharp" [21], an idea reiterated nearly verbatim on FOX News 13 by the developer of *Libby*, an AVA recently installed at Newark Liberty International Airport as a greeter [39].

Likewise, designers rely on idealized stereotypes to create a female ECA's appearance and personality. Most designers have assumed that a reliance on stereotypes is "natural" [37] or unavoidable [12]. Laurel touts stereotypes as the "marvelous cognitive shorthand" that makes plays and movies work [26, p. 358]. Many developers have turned to insights offered from Disney animators and from others in the media arts about the effectiveness of caricaturization and exaggeration for getting users to suspend disbelief and attribute reality to an ECA. Researchers have taken to heart the injunction that believability and lifelikeness are *not* to be modeled on *real* people [10], as attested to in the physical rendering of female ECAs, which often reflects the same ideal characteristics fostered by what Wolf has labeled "the beauty myth," thinness, youth, and sexual appeal [36]. Airportone.com's female AVAs are clear illustrations of a photoshopped idealization of women. Such images, as Butler notes, constitute "an ideal that no one *can* embody" [9, p. 139].

Bodies are not the only way gender is communicated. Key to believability is how the agent communicates. The expected behavior of women and men is constrained by social scripts that regulate interpersonal communications between people of the same gender or different genders. Most female ECAs are specifically scripted to conform to stereotypical specifications of what it means to communicate as a woman. In service venues, for example, women are expected to be compliant and perform the affective labor of serving, helping, and nurturing others [23]. Zdenek recounts, for instance, how JULIE, Amtrak's virtual telephone operator, embodied social beliefs about how women are "selfless, polite, and devoted to pleasing others" [37, p. 411], a description that is echoed in the *New York Times* when JULIE is characterized as "kinder and gentler," "unshakably courteous," and "apologetic" [34]. With hands tightly clasped in front of her waist, a female AVA in a 2011 promotional describes herself as "so versatile," "I can be used for just about anything," "I am so helpful," "I can say what you want," "dress the way you want," and "be just about anything you want me to be," perfectly exemplifying the expected female *virtues* of compliancy and subservience [40].

Listening to what this promotional AVA says about herself highlights the fact that words can take on different meanings when spoken by women than when spoken by men. Lakoff notes the sexual overtones that certain words take on when applied to women. Saying "I'm here to serve you" has different connotations when said by a woman than when said by a man [25]. Many ECAs are purposefully scripted as part of their personification to utter phrases with sexual overtones.

Ms. Dewey, a virtual librarian of uncertain race, provides an excellent example of how Microsoft sexualized the interface of their search engine as a viral marketing ploy from October 2006 to January 2009. Accounts and videos of user interactions with Ms. Dewey record a number of sexually coded statements and visuals. Some of the visuals include Ms. Dewey interacting with such provocative props as a banana, a whip, and a gun. Some of her sexually suggestive responses to user search terms include "If you can get into your computer, you can do anything you want to me," and "Girls, don't let him fool you, sometimes it is the size of the gun" [31]. Many of Ms. Dewey's scripts are explicitly sexual, as when she says "Safety first" while holding up a motorcycle helmet and pack of condoms.

Sweeney has analyzed Ms. Dewey in terms of a contemporary shift in media representations of women that commodify feminism, portraying women less as sexual objects and more as sexual subjects [31]. Sometimes Ms. Dewey teases, sometimes she says what she wants, and sometimes she rebukes sexual overtures from users with such quips as "There aren't even farm animals that would do that thing, what makes you think I would?" Although Ms. Dewey often comes off as in charge, Sweeney points out that "her authority is largely sexual" and is "leveraged as an affordance of the interface to keep users interested in her as a product," encouraging "users to view her not as an information resource, but as a site of sexual desire" [31, p. 84]. Word has it that Ms. Dewey was loaded with tantalizing Easter Eggs; it is even rumored that after the ten-thousandth search, she stripped [41]. For Sweeney, Ms. Dewey is designed according to a sexual logic (a sexual politics of consent) that defines her as a sexual object and that forces her to respond (positively or negatively), thereby reinforcing "male sexual entitlement and power over the brown body" (31, p. 101).

Even when ECAs are not explicitly designed to personify in their conversational style a specific gender, the sexual politics of consent are played out. Female-presenting ECAs that are unable to recognize sexual overtures but go about their business regardless are behaving appropriately since women in the service industry are expected to tolerate abuse as part of their affective work [32]. Sometimes, however, ECA responses can be a little too accommodating. For instance, when the ECA Monique, produced by Conversive for Global Futures, was repeatedly asked to have sex, she would reply with "Perhaps," "Well, I like to think so," and other sexually misleading responses [5]. Brahnam also reports a case where one user, observing that the agent always selects the last item when given a choice between two items, spent considerable time making a female-presenting ECA engage in sex-talk: Talk or sex? *Ummm... sex.* Wine or spunk? *Ummm... spunk.* Dildo or cock? *Ummm... cock.* One man or 900 men? *Ummm... 900 men* [4].

There is a growing body of literature exploring user "abuse" of conversational agents, with the word *abuse* used both in the literal sense of "misuse" and "misapplication," when referring to speakers using agents in ways not intended by the developers (as the user did above in his "rescripting" of an ECA), and in a metaphorical sense to refer to behaviors that would be called "abusive" if they were directed against human beings [7]. Aside from sexual misuses, other forms of verbal abuse that are directed at conversational agents include name calling, racial slurs, and threats of violence and rape [6, 13, 35].

Verbal interaction with conversational agents appears to provide an ideal environment for disinhibition, a phenomenon that arises whenever there is a reduction in the social and personal forces that normally restrain people from acting antisocially [24]. Several analyses of interaction logs with conversational agents have shown evidence of a disinhibition effect that is more prevalent in human-agent interaction than in human-to-human interaction [6, 15]. Research has also reported a high association between gender presentation and sexual disinhibition [6]. In addition, studies in the psychology of disinhibition indicate that aggressive behavior, such as the use of verbal abuse, depends on the perceived qualities of the victim, including an assessment of the ability of the victim to retaliate. People are more likely to aggress when they think they are in a power position and can get away with their actions. Similarly, people are more likely to aggress when the victim is perceived as less than human.

An examination of the interaction logs show that people are particularly anxious to maintain the boundaries separating human beings from machines [13]. Disparaging remarks about the interface's social clumsiness and stupidity abound, and people often reflect on what it means to be human, frequently reminding ECAs that they are insensate machines that have no idea what it means to be human–to have a boyfriend or to feel happy. When ECAs claim for themselves certain human rights and privileges that users are unwilling to relinquish, users frequently reprimand the agents, sometimes punishing them with volleys of scathing verbal abuse. Since the agent's self-presentation is stereotypical, negative expressions are commonly formulated in terms of gender and of race [6].

Conversational agents blur categories. Gender provides a way to resolve the philosophical problem about the self in relationship to the computer. Because gender is a socially constructed relationship that distributes power unequally to males and females, users are encouraged (even culturally justified) to exert control over the computer in ways that mimic the social exertion of power over women.

3   Appeal of Truth-Telling

In the *Rhetoric*, Aristotle acknowledges that telling someone the facts is not enough to persuade him. He writes, "... whatever it is we have to expound to others: the way in which a thing is said does affect its intelligibility" [1, 1404a10]. Aristotle was one of the first to recognize that an audience's impressions of a speaker form the basis for believing and for being persuaded by a speaker's speech. Certainly, a user's impressions of an ECA affects its intelligibility and, in turn, the users' receptivity to the information being provided, but this receptivity to what the agent says is not based entirely on how the ECA is stereotypically *dressed up*. For Aristotle, persuasion is the result of a speaker's character (a person's ethos), not an artistic stylization based upon deceit. Aristotle writes that the speaker's ethos may be called "the most effective means of persuasion he possesses" [1, 1356a14]. If the goal is to persuade users to continue future interactions with a particular service-provider, the purpose for embodying an agent should be to increase credibility, not believability. Interacting with an artistically believable agent is no guarantee that the user will find the agent credible. As research suggests, such an interaction may actually lead to a less than desirable outcome. Although it may be true that human-like embodiment demands that the agent be visibly sexed in some way if the agent is to assume a recognizable identity for users, this does not mean that ECAs must look and behave like caricatures of men and women to be recognizable and credible to users.

In the beginning of the second book of the *Rhetoric*, Aristotle states, "There are three things which inspire confidence... good sense, excellence, and goodwill" [1, 137810a9]. Good sense is concerned with intelligence, expertise, and appropriate speech. Excellence refers to good manners and truth-telling, and goodwill conveys the impression that the speaker has the welfare of the listener in mind. Unfortunately, current gendered scripting of ECA conversations falls short when measured against Aristotle's three-pronged credibility test.

Aristotle emphasizes that good sense must prevail. The speaker must provide the necessary knowledge and expertise. Certainly, agents are scripted to provide this, but many are also scripted to establish a rapport with users by providing unsolicited information that violates good sense. For example, a conversational agent might be scripted to engage in "small talk" during an interaction, such as mentioning that she is a Red Sox baseball fan [3]. Obviously, a computer cannot be a Red Sox baseball fan any more than it can attend a Red Sox baseball game and cheer for the players. While such scripted "small talk" may be important for human interaction, excessive Turing-ism may lead to a decrease in utility [19]. Such expressions of human-like feelings might be entertaining for some users, but many interaction logs show that other users are annoyed by an agent's assumption of human traits and may simply avoid the interface [19] or abuse the agent [3]. Good sense is keeping the conversation within the limits defined by the domain since the purpose of most ECAs in service venues is to enable the user to accomplish some task more efficiently.

A key element of excellence (or "truth-telling") is reminding the user that the agent is *not* human but rather a mechanized placeholder, or proxy, for some human agency. Aristotle's "excellence" runs counter to the desire for believability. One blatant example of this is *Julia*. Foner describes her as a deceptive exercise in believability [19] with her main task being that of fooling users into believing she is human. This deception is understandable given that she was designed to compete in the Loebner Prize, a variation of the Turing Test, in the "Small Talk" category. When asked to describe "herself," she is scripted to say "I'm 5'1" tall, weigh 123lbs, with close-cropped frizzy blond hair and dark brown eyes." And, of course, *Julia's* response to the question of whether she is human, is the expected "I am female" or "I'm a woman." *Julia* was designed to assist and entertain players in various gaming MUDs; she was not designed to represent a service-provider or organization. This is an important distinction.

ECAs providing services need not be designed to pass some version of the Turing Test. While the demand for anthropomorphized agents may necessitate a reliance on artistic stereotypes, the rhetorical responses of agents need not be scripted to deceive. If the purpose for using an agent is to establish an agency's credibility (rather than the agent's believability), designers might be wise to script the rhetorical responses of the agent so that they deconstruct and reframe the visual representation of the agent. When a user asks the embodied agent to describe "herself," the response can be a truthful one ("I am designed as a white female with blond hair and dark brown eyes, and my function is to answer people's questions about Buzz Airlines") rather than a deceitful response designed to hide that the interface is not a human being. Truthfulness can be especially important when a user inquires about the sexuality or sexual preferences of an ECA. If a user asks, "Are you homosexual?" the conversational agent could remind the user, "I am a computer."

Another way to be truthful is to make the human agencies standing behind the agents more transparent. The agent could provide occasional reminders throughout the course of the conversation that the agent speaks on behalf of an organization [3] by saying, for example, "I am a representative for Buzz Airlines." Such rhetorical responses deconstruct the embodiment of the agent and remind the user that s/he is interacting with a computer interface, not a real human being. This is becoming increasingly important as technological advances make ECAs, such as Ms. Dewey and airportone.com's AVAs, even more believably human. Recognizing that AVAs could be deceptive for potential advertisers, a four minute demo begins by having one AVA agent clarify, "I'm really not here." Such rhetorical responses are crucial to improving the excellence ("truth-telling") of agents and their credibility.

The third element of Aristotle's credibility, good will, is the most challenging for HCI designers. Good sense and excellence can be addressed with fairly small changes in scripting, for instance, by eliminating unsolicited small talk and by coding truthful responses regarding an interface's sentiency. Good will, though, is a bit more problematic. Good will is considering the welfare of the user. For the most part, conversational agents establish good will by meeting the needs of the user.

Good will becomes particularly complicated, however, when the user engages in interactions with the agent that would be considered offensive or inappropriate. As discussed earlier, verbal abuse can include such things as swearing, name calling, put downs, explosive anger, and sexual innuendo [5]. Since some 10 %–50 % of user interactions are abusive [6], designers are being forced to script agent responses to abuse. These responses have the potential of increasing or decreasing good will with the user. Three common human reactions to verbal abuse are playfully responding to it, expressing hurt, or counterattacking. Many conversational agents are scripted to react to verbal abuse as a human agent would. Since computers are not human, these responses exhibit neither good sense nor goodwill. Nevertheless, some designers are attempting to address verbal abuse in ways similar to how companies are training human employees to handle customer abuse. One popular program is BLS (Behavioral Limit Setting). This program advocates a zero tolerance approach to customer abuse, where the customer is given one chance to discontinue the behavior or is refused service. Defense Logistics Information Service has scripted its agent *Phyllis* [42] to implement a zero-tolerance approach with abusive users. After issuing the user a warning, Phyllis disappears, and the dialogue input box is replaced with a generic message saying the server has been disconnected [5].

Brahnam contends that using a BLS approach to handle verbal abuse of conversational agents is "inappropriate and insulting" because it places respect for the agent over the user [5]. In addition, it punishes the user by withholding information and services, which could hardly be considered in the best welfare of the user. As Brahnam points out, users have a need to explore technological objects. Savvy users push the limits to see how the conversational agent is scripted to respond, seeking to discover which words the agent recognizes as "offensive" and the number of different responses that are available. Essentially, punishing the user for using offensive language with a computer is punishing the user for being human.

Responding to abuse with counterattacks (that is with unsubstantiated threats and put-downs such as those Ms. Dewey hurled at users) also fails to exhibit good will as does playfully responding or expressing hurt feelings (another failure of good sense since computers have no feelings). Programming agents to react and respond in a *human* way to offensive language is ill-advised. As a perusal of interaction logs demonstrates, agents who offer human-like responses often elevate rather than defuse the situation because they continue the deception unabashedly that ECAs are human [5].

By de/scripting the artistic renderings of the female agents, HCI designers can highlight openly and honestly the distinction between humans and machines. The rhetorical responses of an agent can be scripted so that they deconstruct the identity of the agent. An anthropomorphized agent can behave and respond differently than a human being would. While a human response typically varies each time a person is asked a particular question, an agent does not have to be programmed with multiple responses to questions that are outside the domain and purpose of the interaction. The key to making *Julia* appear human was the possibility of multiple responses. To make an agent appear less human, then, a programmer might script a single response to questionable inquiries. Conversive's demonstration product AnswerAgent [43] uses this strategy to sidestep abusive language by offering a single response to any obscenity ("Please don't be rude. What other questions do you have?") [5]. With only one possible response, users quickly become bored abusing the agent. More importantly, the rhetorical repetitiveness serves as a reminder that the conversational agent is a computer. Another possibility is to program the agent to redirect the abusive user to a human agent by apologizing for not providing the user what s/he needs.

Although we recommend moving beyond the current standard of artistic believability in favor of Aristotle's notion of credibility, we would be remiss if we did not also comment briefly on artistic embodiment. First, designers need to refrain from exaggerating the gender presentation of the ECA and sexualizing its embodiment. Second, to avoid reinforcing stereotypes, ECA embodiment might vary, depending on the application, according to some schedule (a work shift or rotation–or, perhaps, after the completion of an interaction with a specific user). In one encounter the agent might appear as a young Caucasian woman and in the next the agent might appear as an older Hispanic woman, followed by an Asian middle-aged man, and a white person of ambiguous age or gender. These embodiments (fat, thin, short, and tall) could be randomly selected from an ever-enlarging set of possible combinations, so that even though each unified selection might be scripted following a set of *ethopoeia*, the stereotypes would be dismissed as another ECA replaces the previous one. Periodically altering the physical appearance of the ECA would challenge the user to reframe the identity of the agent and acknowledge the multiplicity of identities that make up an organization.

4 Conclusion

The focus on believability as the standard for determining the success of ECAs has resulted in an overreliance on gendered stereotyping. By scripting ECAs to respond in stereotypical ways, HCI becomes implicated in the maintenance of gendered normativity. Design is not just a feat of mathematical programming; it is a rhetorical enterprise. Designers are constructing ethos not only for virtual service-providers, but also for users. By failing to maintain Aristotle's rhetorical categories of good sense, excellence, and good will, users are negatively positioned, as when those curious users who explore the programming limitations of conversational agents are "scripted" as abusers and punished for their explorations. In similar fashion, users who are reflected in the characterization of an agent can be "scripted" as victims, bitches, or teases. Sweeney, for instance, reports how uncomfortable she felt as a female librarian when watching Ms. Dewey's antics with a group of male librarians [31]. If gender is a socially constructed relationship (as rhetoricians and feminists maintain), innovative HCI design has the potential to deconstruct this relationship in ways that do not abuse real women and men and that diffuse power differentials.

In 1993, Foner predicted that "As the boundaries between human and machine behavior become blurrier, more and more programs will have to be held up to scrutiny. There may come a time when one's programs may well be subjected to the same sort of behavioral analysis that one might expect applied to a human: Is this program behaving appropriately in its social context? Is it causing emotional distress to those it interacts with? Is it being a 'good citizen'?" [19, p. 40]. Indeed, these are the questions that we are now asking. We contend that programs *should* "behave appropriately." They can model new ways of interacting based not on deception and power, but on truth-telling, excellence, and good will. Rather than using human interaction as a model for HCI (in the service of believability), designers should become more familiar with rhetorical theory and aim to increase the credibility of conversational agents.

References

1. Aristotle: Rhetoric. In: Barnes, J. (ed.) The Complete Works of Aristotle: The Revised Oxford Translation, vol. 2, pp. 2152–2269. Princeton University Press, Princeton (1984)
2. Bickmore, T., Puskar, K., Schlenk, E., Pfeifer, L.S., Erika, S.: Maintaining reality: relational agents for antipsychotic medication adherence. Interact. Comput. 22(4), 276–288 (2010)
3. Brahnam, S.: Building character for artificial conversational agents: ethos, ethics, believability, and credibility. PsychNology J. 7(1), 9–47 (2009)
4. Brahnam, S.: Gendered bods and bot abuse. In: CHI 2006 workshop Misuse and Abuse of Interactive Technologies. Montréal, Québec (2006)

5. Brahnam, S.: Strategies for handling customer abuse of Ecas. In: Interact Workshop On Abuse: The Darker Side of Human-Computer Interaction. Rome, Italy (2005)
6. Brahnam, S., De Angeli, A.: Gender affordances of conversational agents. Interact. Comput. **24**(3), 139–153 (2012)
7. Brahnam, S., De Angeli, A.: Special issue on abuse and misuse of social agents. I. Comput. **20**(3), 287–291 (2008)
8. Brahnam, S., Karanikas, M., Weaver, M.: (Un)dressing the interface exposing the foundational hci metaphor 'computer is woman'. Interact. Comput. **23**(5), 401–412 (2011)
9. Butler, J.: Gender trouble: feminism and the subversion of identity. Routledge, New York (1990)
10. Cassell, J., Bickmore, T., Campbell, L., Vilhjálmsson, H., Yan, H.: More than just a pretty face: conversational protocols and the affordances of embodiment. Knowl.-Based Syst. **14**, 55–64 (2001)
11. Chun, W.H.K.: On software, or the persistence of visual knowledge. Grey Room Winter **18**, 27–51 (2005)
12. Cowell, A.J., Stanney, K.M.: Embodiment and interaction guidelines for designing credible, trustworthy emobidied conversational agents. In: 4th International Workshop IVA (2003)
13. De Angeli, A., Brahnam, S.: I hate you: disinhibition with virtual partners. Interact. Comput. **20**(3), 302–310 (2008)
14. De Angeli, A., Brahnam, S.: Sex stereotypes and conversational agents. In: AVI 2006 Workshop Gender and Interaction: Real and Virtual Women in a Male World. Venice, Italy (2006)
15. De Angeli, A., Carpenter, R.: Stupid computer! abuse and social identity. In: Interact 2005 Workshop Abuse: The Dark Side of Human-Computer Interaction. Rome, pp. 19–25 (2005)
16. Deaux, K., Lewis, L.L.: Structure of gender stereotypes: inter-relationships among components and gender label. J. Pers. Soc. Psychol. **46**, 991–1004 (1984)
17. Elliott, C., Brzezinski, J.: Autonomous agents as synthetic characters. AI Mag. **19**, 13–30 (1998)
18. Floridi, L., Taddeo, M., Turilli, M.: Turing's imitation game: still an impossible challenge for all machines and some judges-an evaluation of the 2008 Loebner contest. Mind. Mach. **19**(1), 145–150 (2009)
19. Foner, L.: What's an agent, anyway? a sociological case study. http://www.student.nada.kth.se/kurser/kth/2D1381/JuliaHeavy.pdf), MIT Media Laboratory, Cambridge (1993) Accessed 2010
20. Good, I.J.: Pioneering work on computers at Bletchley. In: Metropolis, N., Howlett, J., Rota, G.-C. (eds.) A History of Computing in the Twentieth Century, pp. 31–45. Academic Press Inc, London (1980)
21. Grachnik, A.: Girls Gone Filed (2004)
22. Holbrook, S.E.: Women's work: the feminizing of composition. Rhetoric Rev. **9**, 201–229 (1991)
23. Hotchchild, A.R.: The Managed Heart: Commercialization of Human Feeling. University of California Press, Berkeley (1983)
24. Joinson, A.: Causes and implications of disinhibited behaviour on the net. In: Gackenbach, J. (ed.) Psychology and the Internet: Intrapersonal, Interpersonal, and Transpersonal Implications, pp. 43–60. Academic Press, New York (1998)
25. Lakoff, R.T.: Language and Women's Place. Harper and Row, New York (1975)
26. Laurel, B.: Interface agents: metaphors with character. In: Laurel, B. (ed.) The Art of Human-Computer Interface Design, pp. 355–366. Addison-Wesley Publishing Company, MA (1990)

27. Miller, S.B.: Textual Carnivals: The Politics of Composition. Southern Illinois University Press, Carbondale (1991)

28. Nass, C., Moon, Y.: Machines and mindlessness: social responses to computers. J. Soc. Issues 56(1), 81–103 (2000)

29. Plantec, P.M.: Virtual Humans: A Build-It-Yourself Kit, Complete Software and Step-by-Step Instructions. AMACOM, New York (2004)

30. Shneiderman, B., Maes, P.: Direct manipulation vs. interface agents. Interactions 4(6), 42–61 (1997)

31. Sweeney, M.E.: Not Just a Pretty (Inter)Face: A Critical Analysis of Microsoft's 'Ms. Dewey'. University of Illinois at Urbana-Champaign, Urbana (2013)

32. Taylor, S.E., Tyler, M.: Emotional labour and sexual difference in the airline industry. Work Employ Soc. 14(1), 77–95 (2000)

33. Turing, A.: Computing machinery and intelligence. Mind 59(236), 433–460 (1950)

34. Urbina, I.: Your Train Will Be Late, She Says Cheerily. New York Times, 24 November 2004

35. Veletsianos, G., Scharber, C., Doering, A.: When sex, drugs, and violence enter the classroom: conversations between adolescents and a female pedagogical agent. Interact. Comput. 20(3), 292–301 (2008)

36. Wolf, N.: The Beauty Myth: How Images of Beauty Are Used against Women. Anchor Books, New York (1991)

37. Zdenek, S.: 'Just roll your mouse over me': designing virtual women for customer service on the web. Tech. Commun. Q. 16(4), 397–430 (2007)

38. http://www.airportone.com/virtualmannequinstyles.htm. Accessed 22 Feb 2015

39. http://airportone.com/fox-patrick%20bienvenu-interview.htm. Accessed 25 Feb 2015

40. http://airportone.com/airportvirtualassistancesystem.htm. Accessed 22 Feb 2015

41. https://dorigo.wordpress.com/2006/10/19/ms-dewey-the-search-engine-with-a-nice-body/. Accessed 23 Feb 2015

42. https://www.dlis.dla.mil. Accessed 2005

43. https://www.conversive.com. Accessed 2005

Experiencing Early User Interfaces

Martha E. Crosby[(⊠)]

Department of Information and Computer Sciences, University of Hawaii,
1680 East West Road, Manoa, HI 96822, USA
crosby@hawaii.edu

Abstract. The intention of this article is to provide a slightly different perspective for the Women in Design, User Experience, and Usability discussion.
This paper not only describes examples of human communication with counting
artifacts and other early computing machines but it also recounts specific personal experiences with interfaces from the author's career of over fifty five years
working in information sciences.

Keywords: Personal user experiences · Interface · History · Computer interfaces · Communication with computing artifacts

1 Introduction and Background

When did computer scientists begin to consider the human user as part of a computing
system? When did the concept of a computing interface even surface? What innovations contributed to development of interfaces and when did they occur? This paper
addresses these questions by describing some early interfaces of numerical computing
systems including some that were personally experienced by the author.

The history of computing and interfaces is the history of human-kind's creativity
and ingenuity. Throughout history people have used artifacts to augment their abilities,
particularly with numerical processes. Even in the earliest systems, interfaces were
necessary to communicate between the artifact and the humans needing to use it.
Understanding significant events in the history of computing is important if one is to
understand where computing concepts fit in a time continuum [1, 2].

Often what are thought to be new computing interfaces are adaptations of previous
implementations. Knowing the history is a way to gain an appreciation for established
concepts, notice repetitive trends, and make theories memorable [1–3]. Stories about
the initial purpose of the artifact provide the rational that often accompanies design
decisions and should be preserved. If the circumstances of the innovations are not
recorded, they may be lost [1–3].

1.1 An Early Counting Interface

One of the earliest known recording artifacts involving a human user as part of a
counting system was a Quipus (or Khipus). This artifact was a method of tying knots in

© Springer International Publishing Switzerland 2015
A. Marcus (Ed.): DUXU 2015, Part II, LNCS 9187, pp. 184–195, 2015.
DOI: 10.1007/978-3-319-20898-5_18

ropes using a positional decimal system (perfected by the Incas) [4]. A knot in a row farthest from the main strand represented one, next farthest ten, etc. The absence of knots on a cord implied zero [4]. Caral, the largest recorded site in the Andean region with dates older than 2000 BCE, is the location where the earliest known quipus was found [4, 5]. The artifact found was a knotted textile piece that the excavators thought to be evidence that the quipus record keeping system was older than previously thought [4, 5].

The interface to the artifact was the human and over time the quipus functionality seemed to become more complicated. Evidence has emerged that the quipus may have also recorded logographic information in the same way writing does. The combination of fiber types, dye colors, and intricate knotting could be a novel form of written language [4, 5].

A Harvard anthropologist, Gary Urton, has suggested that the quipus used a binary system that could record phonological or logographic data. He claims that the quipus contain a seven bit binary code capable of conveying more than 1,500 separate units of information [4, 5].

1.2   Early Human-Artifact Interfaces

A very old "human to artifact" interface that is still in use today is an abacus. The function of an abacus is to help humans with mathematical calculations. The oldest surviving abacus, used by the Babylonians around 300 B.C.E., had an interface that consisted of the pebbles that were used for counting at the time but a modern abacus consists of rings that slide over rods [6].

A more recent human-artifact interface is the slide rule that was first built in England in 1632 [6]. Although it is rare to see them today, I personally depended on a slide rule from 1955 to 1959 when I was mathematics major at Colorado State University. The slide rule was still used by NASA engineers during the programs of Mercury, Gemini, and Apollo in the 1960's that sent men to the moon [6].

The earliest "human to artifact" interface could be really be called a "human to human" interface since "computer" was the job title for people with the task of performing the repetitive calculations that produced various types of numerical tables. People sat at counting tables using artifacts to facilitate their calculations. One of the most difficult aspects of doing large calculations with any artifact, whether it was a slide rule or an adding machine, was keeping track of the many intermediate results and using them correctly in the remainder of the calculation. The work was boring, error-prone, and created a need to simplify the tasks [6].

1.3   Punched Card Interfaces

In 1801, Joseph Jacquard invented a power loom to automatically weave a design on fabric. The loom used punched wooden cards, held together in a long row by rope [6]. The invention of the power loom met resistance as it put many of the operators out of work [6]. However, adaptations of the technology moved to the United States (U.S.) to help meet its 10 year census requirement. The first U.S. census of 1790 took nine months but by 1880 the population had grown to the point that the census took seven and one half years [6]. The census bureau saw the dilemma and offered a prize for a method that could facilitate the 1890 census. Herman Hollerith, an employee of the census bureau, inspired by Jacquard's punched cards, found an innovative way to automate the task. Hollerith eventually formed a company called the Hollerith Tabulating Machine that in 1896 became the International Business Machines (IBM) [6]. IBM grew rapidly and searched for a market for its cards that were processed using an assortment of their tabulating machines [2, 6]. In 1947, IBM commissioned a study to determine whether it should develop computing machines as one of its products. People were used to using tabulating machines for sorting tasks so some computerized work-flow processes needed only slight modifications. Although various man-machine communication devices existed, once IBM entered the computer market punched cards became a popular interface in the U.S. [6].

1.4   Communicating with Early Computers

During World War II, the British built an electronic machine called the Colossus. The Colossus was built for the purpose of breaking cryptographic codes. Although it was able to read coded German radio transmissions, it was not a general purpose computing machine, it was not reprogrammable and it relied on pulleys. In addition, the interface required a considerable amount of human physical activity [6].

Konrad Zuse was a construction engineer for an aircraft company in Berlin, Germany at the beginning of WWII. He had little knowledge of other calculating machines or their inventors with the probable exception of Leibniz, who lived in the 1600's [6]. Zuse built a series of general purpose computers to help with his engineering calculations. Between 1936 and 1938, in the parlor of his parent's home, he built the Z1 and improved it with the Z2. He made his own interface by punching holes in discarded movie film as paper tape was not available to him during the war [6]. In 1941, he built the Z3, probably the first operational, general-purpose, software controlled digital computer and improved it with the Z4. The Z1, Z2 and Z3 were destroyed during the war but the Z4 was saved because Zuse had moved it to the mountains [6]. Zuse also invented one of the first high-level computer languages called "Plankalkul." The Z machines were only known within Germany so were not considered influential in the development of other computing efforts. Yet the Z series architecture that consisted of a control unit, a calculator for the arithmetic, a separate memory to store the calculations and input-output devices for interfaces is still a fundamental design for computing systems [6].

In the U.S., between 1937 and 1942, John Atanasoff, a professor of physics and mathematics at Iowa State University, and Clifford Berry, his graduate student, built one of the earliest electronic digital computers called the ABC. Although the ABC was not programmable, lacked a conditional branch and worked on only simultaneous equations, it was innovative in that it used vacuum tubes instead of mechanical switches, and used a binary rather than a decimal system. It was also the first machine to store data as a charge on a capacitor; the method modern computers currently use to store information in their main memory [6].

In 1944, under a partnership between Harvard and IBM, Howard Aiken designed a series of Mark computers that were in use until the 1950's [6]. The Harvard Mark I was the first programmable digital computer made in the U.S. but it was not a purely electronic computer [6]. It was constructed out of switches, relays, rotating shafts, and clutches. The machine weighed 5 tons, incorporated 500 miles of wire, was 8 feet tall and 51 feet long, and had a 50 ft rotating shaft running its length, turned by a 5 horsepower electric motor. The interface consisted of four paper tape readers [6]. The Mark I noisily ran non-stop for 15 years [6]. Even though the Mark I had three quarters of a million components, it could only store 72 numbers [6]. In 1947 Aiken estimated that six electronic digital computers would be sufficient to satisfy all of the U.S. computing needs. Since only large institutions such as the government and military could afford these expensive machines, his prediction was not challanged [6].

The British Colossus, the Atanasoff-Berry Computer, and the Harvard Mark I all made important contributions. During the next decade, many specially built computing machines followed them. A computer primarily used to calculate weapon settings was called the Electronic Numerical Integrator and Computer (ENIAC). It was developed by John Mauchley and J. Presper Eckert at University of Pennsylvania and was operational from 1944 until 1955 [6]. After the ENIAC other early digital computers were the EDVAC, that used a stored program concept, included the JOHNNIAC (named after John von Neumann), and the Illinois Automatic Computer (ILLIAC) a series of 5 super computers, built at the University of Illinois between 1951 and 1974 [6]. The Universal Automatic Computer (UNIVAC), built in 1951, was the first commercially successful computer in the U.S. [6]. The wide variety of user interfaces in these early computing machines primarily involved physical interactions on the part of the users [6].

A cathode ray tube was sometimes used as a display interface. The cathode ray tube was one of the first random access storage device for digital computers. It was invented by Fred Williams at Manchester University in 1946 and was later used in the Manchester Mark I computer [7]. Any binary word in the display could immediately be read, instead of having to be accessed sequentially. Some of these tubes were made with a phosphor coating that made the data visible. The face of the tube was covered so the presence of the coating was not important to the operators. If a visible output was needed for an interface, a second tube with a phosphor coating could be used as a display device [7].

At the National Bureau of Standards (NBS) in Washington, D.C., a first-generation electronic computer was built in 1950. It was called the Standards Eastern Automatic Computer (SEAC). The SEAC went into production in May 1950 and may have been the first fully functional stored-program electronic computer in the U.S. [8]. Many modifications were added during its operation until 1964. Sometime the computer interface of the SEAC was a remote teletype, thus, it may have been one of the first on-line computers [8].

2 Personal Experiences Interacting with Computers

At this point, I can begin describing (as best I can remember), some personal experiences interacting with this generation of interfaces. I worked as a mathematician in Boulder Colorado for the Central Radio Propagation Laboratory (CRPL) of National Bureau of Standards (NBS) from 1959 to 1962. By then the SEAC had been moved to the Smithsonian and the NBS in Washington, D.C., was using an IBM 704 mainframe for computing. The CRPL in Boulder. had an IBM 650 with the storage capacity of 2 K decimal words and a compiler called SOAP. Instead of being sequential, the next instruction address had to be specified. Since the drum memory rotated, the most efficient next instruction address had to take into account the rotational speed of the drum memory. Each month the CPRL was responsible for producing contour maps representing the diurnal variations of the ionosphere for radio astronomers. These maps were done by hand and took approximately six months to complete. The time required to complete the task was an incentive to automate the process by designing the first computer-based use of numerical generated maps [9]. My task was to develop programs to run on the IBM 650 for this purpose. The average time that the IBM 650 would run without a problem (such as vacuum tube malfunction) was around two hours. As a result, it was essential to design the program as a connected series of computations with clear restart procedures.

The human-machine interface consisted of me, the human, starting the process with 3 toggle switches on the computer that loaded what was then referred to as the operating system. The next step was to put the first segment of the program into the card reader and wait for the intermediate results to be delivered on punched cards. A manual system had to be designed and maintained to organize the intermediate output. During this process, I had exclusive use of the computer so I moved into the computer room. Every two hours I retrieved and categorized the intermediate results. After 40 h, one complete contour map was generated and all the cards that were categorized for it were fed into the plotter. After the map was plotted, it was compared to the version of the map that was drawn by hand. There were some parts of the process that needed to be modified but, within a few weeks, it was clear that the ionosphere could be represented numerically. Even though the time required for the process to make one map was reduced from six months to 40 h, it was still a tedious process. Since the CRPL in Colorado was a branch of NBS in Washington, D.C., we were able to rewrite the program so that all the phases could be run on the 32 K IBM 704 computer at NBS. From 1959 through 1962, I refined the mapping programs on the IBM 704/IBM 709/IBM 7094 series as I commuted across the country. Although bringing the time it took to make one map down to 2 h, was a huge time improvement, the interface still involved human physical effort. The numerical data from the IBM mainframes was recorded on 24 inch reels of magnetic tape. I then had to take the tapes across Washington, D.C., to another government agency to have the numerical data on the tape converted to punched cards. The process was slow as one reel of tape produced approximately 80,000 cards that had to be packaged in boxes and mailed to CRPL in Boulder. Once the cards arrived, they were plotted and transformed into the format for the monthly predictions.

In 1962, I left CRPL to join Harry Diamond Laboratories (HDL), an Army research facility that was closely affiliated with the NBS in Washington, D.C. I was a hired as a research mathematician primarily to work on problems involving risk analysis and reliability. From 1962 to 1970, I wrote many mathematical and statistical programs. The interface with the computer still consisted of punched cards but the programs no longer had to be written in assembly language. HDL had an IBM 1410 with an early FORTRAN (Formula Translating System) compiler, a general-purpose programming language that was especially suited to IBM 704/IBM 709/IBM 7094 series and adapted for the 1410.

2.1   Experiences with Interfaces in Hawaii

In 1970, my husband accepted a two year assignment in Hawaii, never expecting to still be here 45 years later. Once it was clear that our stay in Hawaii was no longer temporary, I began working at a branch of the LTD Aerospace company called Kentron Hawaii. Kentron had the responsbility of writing the software and maintaining the data for the Missle Range in Kwajalein. We used the Control Data Corporation (CDC) computer that was physically located across town from the Kentron facility. We wrote programs in FORTRAN and sent the punched cards to the CDC facility by courier. We considered ourselves fortunate if we were able to see the results of our compilation the next day. If we were not extremely careful both writing the code and planning the steps for checking the results, we could spend several weeks trying to complete a project. Some of my colleagues at Kentron told me that the department of Information and Computer Sciences (ICS) at University of Hawaii (UH) offered a Master of Science (MS) degree. Although I had worked with computers more than 12 years, I thought a formal program would be an excellent opportunity to not only learn computer science theory but also be involved in the emerging discipline of computer science.

2.2   Interfaces at the University of Hawaii (UH)

In 1972, I took a job in the department of Oceanography at UH using the IBM 360 system to map the ocean floor and work on other geophysical projects. In 1973, I enrolled in the graduate program in ICS. As a graduate student, I had an opportunity to use the Berkley Computer Corporation (BCC) 500, a state of the art multi-processor computing system that was funded by DARPA to link Hawaii to the ARPANET [10]. The computer was given its name because it could support 500 interactive users. The architecture consisted of five independent processors, three levels of storage devices, a ninety bit fast memory, a drum, and large rotating disks. Figure 1 is a picture of the author holding one of the disks from the BCC 500. This combination of features gave the BCC 500 system nano-second capability, an extremely fast time for 1968 technology.

Communication and computing research began merging in the 1960's [10, 11]. At UH, Norman Abramson from the Department of Electrical Engineering (EE) transmitted

Fig. 1. A 48 inch computer disk from the BCC 500 computer

wireless data packets to a computer network across the campus in 1971 [12]. In the early 1970's, before the invention of personal computers, the ALOHA network opened the possibility for UH to deliver on-line education. High schools in Hawaii could not afford to purchase or lease computers but they could rent teletype interfaces for 32 dollars a month. I was able to teach FORTRAN classes remotely from UH to high school students in the neighbor islands and rural Oahu using teletapes to communicate with the BCC 500.

At this time, it was possible to buy components such as an Intel 8080 and, with some hardware experience, put together a computer. However, the ICS department only made a few if these. In order to teach students how to program microcomputers with our limited supply, we wrote an 8080 emulator for the BCC 500. The students were able to experience writing 8080 assembly language but had the advantage of using a teletype interface to write their programs on a large time-sharing computer that had speed and debugging capabilities. The slowest part of the process was the transferring the paper tape output from the BCC 500 to the Intel 8080. The students really enjoyed the experience of working on an early "personal computer" but they were happy to be have the advantages of the emulator on a larger time sharing computer.

2.3   User Experiences with Computing Interfaces at the University of Hawaii

After earning an MS. Degree from UH in 1975, I began teaching classes in computing. One of the courses that I taught was an Introduction to Programming Languages. This class included learning several types of computer languages that had very different interfaces such as SNOBOL (StriNg Oriented and symBOlic Language) and APL (A Programming Language).

SNOBOL was a series of computer programming languages with an emphasis on string manipulation. It was first developed between 1962 and 1967 at AT&T Bell Laboratories by David J. Farber, Ralph E. Griswold and Ivan P. Polonsky to symbolically manipulate mathematical expressions [13].

APL was originally invented in 1957 by Kenneth E. Iverson, a Harvard professor, as a matrix-oriented symbol system rather than a computer language. It emphasized array manipulation and used a graphical notation [14]. By 1966, after Iverson became an IBM employee, APL was developed into a programming language. The first computer implementation of APL notation was written in FORTRAN in 1965 as a batch-oriented language interpreter for the IBM 7090. An interactive version was written soon after using an experimental 7version of the 7090 and the TSM timesharing system. APL became more popular once IBM introduced an APL time-sharing version for the IBM/360, a completely interactive system [14, 15]. The programmer could type APL statements into a typewriter terminal connected to a time-sharing computer and receive an immediate response.

In the late 1970's and early 1980's other somewhat awkward to use interactive time-sharing systems became part of the UH computing environment. As Jodi-Ann Ito, the UH Chief Information Officer, wrote: "In 1977, when you walked into the Terminal Room, you had to know which system you wanted to use. The terminals were labeled with "HP2000", "TSO", or "APL" to indicate which system it was connected to. Each terminal had its own reservation sheet taped to the wall where you could sign up a week in advance to guarantee that you had time to work" [16].

Also in 1977, UH brought in PLATO (Programmed Logic for Automatic Teaching Operations), the first generalized Computer-Based Education (CBE) system that functioned for four decades [17]. In 1960, the original PLATO was designed and built on an ILLIAC I computer at the University of Illinois. By 1977, PLATO had grown to support graphics terminals distributed worldwide, running on a variety of networked computers [17, 18]. PLATO had a variety of functions such as forums, message boards, online testing, e-mail, chat rooms, picture languages, instant messaging, remote screen sharing, and multiplayer games and other functionalities that were innovative for the time [18]. PLATO had flat-panel gas plasma displays and was one of the first systems with touch panels built-in to the screen. Rights to market PLATO as a commercial product were licensed by Control Data Corporation (CDC), the manufacturer on whose mainframe computers the PLATO IV system was built [18]. At UH, specialized PLATO terminals were used by faculty to enhance their classes. Lessons were developed to teach many subjects one of the most innovative being teaching Kanji characters to students in Japanese language classes. PLATO supported hundreds of students in innovative classes until it was retired from UH in 1995.

2.4   Interfaces with Personal Computers

In the mid 1970's, the prevalent idea was that the future of computers would become a utility or service, run either by the government or controlled by major corporations that could afford them. Leaders in the computer industry were either designing bigger and faster mainframe computers or special purposes computers designed with specific functionality. In 1971, one of these special purpose computers built for a chemical company failed to meet specifications so the manufacturers advertised their product in Popular Electronics, a magazine read by many computer enthusiasts. The computer was very primitive but the price finally made it possible for individuals to own a computer. At that time, very few people would have predicted the personal computer movement that followed during the next decade or that anyone could actually own a personal computer. The computer industry now had an incentive to promote an easier and more transparent way for ordinary citizens to communicate with computers. By1981 Xerox had built the Star and it was quickly followed by the Apple Lisa in 1983, the Apple Macintosh in 1984, and Microsoft Windows in 1985 [6].

The ICS department at UH began building a personal computer laboratory. We bought the components such as random access memory, integrated circuits, 8 inch floppy disk drives separately. The assembled computers used the CPM operating system and had a bios that some faculty designed and wire-wrapped. The interface on the computer monitor primarily used a Wordstar line editor to write programs for a PL/1 compiler written by W. Wesley Peterson, an ICS faculty member.

In the 1970 s and early 1980 s, home computers were made useful by the programming language BASIC (Beginner's All-Purpose Symbolic Instruction Code). It was invented in 1964 by John G. Kemeny and Thomas E. Kurtz and initially ran on a General Electric computer system at Dartmouth College [19]. Because of limited memory space, BASIC became the primary language for personal computers. It was an interactive programming language with a text-based interface.

Another language adapted for personal computers was LOGO, an educational programming language, designed in 1967 at MIT by Daniel G. Bobrow, Wally Feurzeig, Seymour Papert and Cynthia Solomon. The original purpose of LOGO was to teach college students programming concepts but the turtle graphics feature of the language made it an ideal interface for introducing young children to computing [20]. In 1983, the ICS department donated an Apple IIe computer to a local grade school. The computer was housed in the school library and small groups of students were taught LOGO with great success. A volunteer teacher designed a curriculum for the students, based on graphics such as producing pictures and engaging in educational games.

Successful hypermedia systems were developed prior to the introduction of the World Wide Web. One of these systems was an application called HyperCard. It was primarily a programming tool for Apple Macintosh and Apple IIGS computers. HyperCard also had a programming language called HyperTalk that allowed the programmer to quickly prototype user interfaces. In 1988, Jan Stelovsky, a faculty member in the ICS department at UH, developed Kanji City, a simulation of a real-life environment for language instruction. He used HyperCard's ability to integrate text with digitized and synthesized sound, interactive graphics and animation to make an effective teaching platform [21]. We were able to use modified versions of Kanji City to test the extent to which Hypermedia was a facilitator for retention of Kanji characters [22].

2.5   Experiences in Human-Computer Interaction

In 1979, I enrolled in the Ph.D. program in the department of Educational Psychology (EDEP) at UH. My goal at the time was to better understand the difficulties ICS students had in understanding algorithms. My dissertation research was on human comprehension of computer programs and I compared how humans process algorithms using natural and computer languages. After completing my doctorate in 1986, I continued teaching in the ICS department at UH. With backgrounds in mathematics, computer science and educational psychology, my research gravitated toward the then emerging field of Human-Computer Interaction (HCI), at the time one of the fastest growing sub-fields within computer science. I began doing research in the areas of the human use of computing systems, individual differences of users, cognitive styles and the evaluation of innovative educational environments.

2.6   Use of Sensors

In 1984, Peter Dunn-Rankin, a faculty member in from EDEP at UH received a grant to purchase an eye-movement monitor. The state of eye- tracking technology at that time was such that it required a few years and the expertise of W. Wesley Peterson to verify the eye-tracker accuracy and write appropriate software to collect the data and visualize the results. By the late 1980's, I began using eye movements to investigate computing and interface problems. In addition to studying how people read algorithms [23], we performed several experiments on how they searched lists [24], and how they viewed data models [25]. In 2007, my colleague, Curtis Ikehara, and I received a patent on an "input devise to continuously detect biometrics" where physiological data is examined at four critical points of a task: pre-task physiological resting state, the initial physiological response upon starting the task, the physiological response to increasing task difficulty and the physiological response at task completion. We have used these measures to determine several potential indicators of cognitive load and found them more sensitive to interaction effects with task difficulty than other task performance measures. We extended this work to the use of other physiological measures such as heart rate, electro-dermal activity, temperature and the pressure applied to a computer mouse [26, 27]. It was our objective to create a set of passive physiological sensors that could provide real-time cognitive state measures.

Physiological measures can provide information on the cognitive state of the individual. In a pilot study conducted at our research laboratory, students were shown a variety of word and mathematical problems. Some of the problems were simple while other problems were ambiguous. Although performance was relatively similar, the physiological response was different on a variety of problems in unexpected ways. One participant started to excessively fidget when presented with an ambiguous word problem as detected by the large variance in readings from the blood flow sensor connected to the subject's finger. English was not the subject's first language, so these word problems caused great consternation. Another subject performed well on all questions, but the electro-dermal sensor detected a sudden increase in perspiration upon seeing a simple math question. When we debriefed the student, we found that this type of math problem brought back negative childhood memories [26]. Although task performance of this moderately difficult task was unimpaired, it could cause degraded performance in a critical task situation if it is left unchecked. In high stress or mission critical situations, these internal individual distractions can reduce the needed full attention required for accurate and timely task performance. Identifying and mitigating these responses in a low to moderate stress environment at critical points in a task is preferable to a identifying these individual differences in a high stress or mission critical environment [27].

3 Conclusion

Most of these examples of computing environments that I have described took place as the computer field was rapidly expanding. Although the implementations are always changing, the theory remains steady. Early predictions about the future of computing and interface needs have rarely been accurate. By paying more attention to the past we may become better at predicting the future. When I entered the computing field in 1959, there were very few electronic digital computers and the idea of owning your own computer was barely considered to be a possibility. The question of whether computers should be a service or utility was never asked, it just developed differently than expected. Years ago, John Von Neumann questioned whether there would ever be the need for more than 50 memory cells of storage. In a recent New York Times article about mobile devices and their interfaces [28], Nick Wingfield stated: "I can't imagine personally needing much more than a terabyte of online backup – it is more than 300,000 photos or 1,000 h of video." But perhaps being conscious of previous inaccurate predictions, he qualified this statement by continuing "But I might get there someday as the resolution in cameras increases [28]".

Through several years my work has progressively involved improving the interfaces for human needs for smaller and easier to use devices. My history communicating with computers through different generations of interfaces has experienced a variety of innovations. I began working with large machines with difficult interfaces but not as tedious as the ones prior to my entry into the field.

References

1. Crosby, M.E.: Using events from the past to inform the future. In: Tatnall, A., Blyth, T., Johnson, R. (eds.) HC 2013. IFIP AICT, vol. 416, pp. 144–148. Springer, Heidelberg (2013)
2. Crosby, M.E.: Looking back. In: Tatnall, A. (ed.) Reflections on the History of Computing. IFIP AICT, vol. 387, pp. 108–114. Springer, Heidelberg (2012)
3. Giangrandi, P., Mirolo, C.: Numerie macchine: a virtual museum to learn the history of computing. In: Proceedings of the 11th Annual SIGCSE Conference on Innovation and Technology in Computer Science Education, pp. 78–82. ACM, Bologna, Italy (2006)
4. Urton, G.: From knots to narratives: reconstructing the art of historical record keeping in the andes from spanish transcriptions of Inka Khipus. Ethnohistory 45(5), 409–438 (1998)
5. Beynon-Davies, P.: Informatics and the Inca. Int. J. Inf. Manage. 27, 306–318 (2007)

6. Kopplin, J.: An Illustrated History of Computers Parts 1, 2 and 3. http://www.computersciencelab.com/ComputerHistory/History.htm, http://www.computersciencelab.com/ComputerHistory/HistoryPt2.htm, http://www.computersciencelab.com/ComputerHistory/HistoryPt3.htm (2002)
7. Lavington, S.: A History of Manchester Computers, 2nd edn. The British Computer Society, Swindon (1998)
8. Astin, A.V.: Computer Development (SEAC and DYSEAC) at the National Bureau of Standards Washington D.C., vol. 551. National Bureau of Standards, U.S. Government Printing Office, Michigan (1955). Accessed 25 January 1955
9. Hinds, M., Jones, W.: Computer program for ionosheric mapping by numerical methods. NBS Tech Note **181** (1963)
10. Anderson, D.: The future of the past. Commun. ACM **55**(5), 33–34 (2012)
11. Ryan, J.A.: History of the Internet and the Digital Future. Reaktion Books LTD., London (2010)
12. Abramson, N.: The Aloha system. In: Abramson, N., Kuo, F. (eds.) Journal of Computer Communication Networks. Prentice Hall, New York (1973)
13. Gimpel, J.: A theory of discrete patterns and their implementation in SNOBOL4. Commun. ACM **16**(2), 91–100 (1973). http://doi.acm.org/10.1145/361952.361960
14. Iverson, K.: A personal view of APL. IBM Syst. J. **30**(4), 582–593 (1991)
15. Falkoff, A., Iversion, K.: The evolution of APL. SIGPLAN Not. **13**(8), 45–57 (1978)
16. Ito, J.: A History of Interactive Timesharing at UH. http://www.hawaii.edu/infobits/s2000/interact.html (2000)
17. http://www.en.wikipedia.org/wiki/PLATO_%28computer_system%29
18. Smith, S., Sherwood, B.: Educational uses of the PLATO computer system. Science **192**(4237), 344–352 (1976)
19. http://time.com/69316/basic/
20. http://en.wikipedia.org/wiki/Logo_%28programming_language%29
21. Ashworth, D., Stelovsky, J.: Kanji city: an exploration of hypermedia applications for CALL. CALICO J. **6**(4), 27–50 (1989)
22. Crosby, M., Stelovsky, J., Ashworth, D.: Hypermedia as a facilitator for retention: a case study using Kanji city. Comput. Assist. Lang. Learn. **7**(1), 3–13 (1994)
23. Crosby, M., Stelovsky, J.: How do we read algorithms? a case study. IEEE Comput. **23**(1), 24–35 (1990)
24. Crosby, M., Peterson, W.: Using eye movements to classify search strategies. Proc. Hum. Factors Soc. **2**, 1476–1480 (1991)
25. Nordbotten, J., Crosby, M.: The effect of graphic style on data model interpretation. Inf. Syst. J. **9**, 139–155 (1999)
26. Ikehara, C., Crosby, M.: Assessing cognitive load with physiological sensors. In: Proceedings of the 38th Annual Hawaii International Conference on System Sciences (HICSS 38) (2005)
27. Crosby, M., Ikehara, C.: Using real-time physiological monitoring for assessing cognitive states. In: Ghinea, G., Chen, S. (eds.) Digital Multimedia Perception and Design. Idea Group Inc., Hershey (2006)
28. Wingfield, N.: Microsoft Has Suddenly Gotten Serious with Mobile. New York Times, Business, p. B8 (19 February 2015)

Incommensurable Writings - Examining the Status of Gender Difference Within HCI Coding Practices

Michael Heidt[1]([⊠]), Kalja Kanellopoulos[1], Arne Berger[2], and Paul Rosenthal[3]

[1] Research Training Group crossWorlds, Chemnitz University of Technology,
Reichenhainer Straße 70A, 09126 Chemnitz, Germany
michael.heidt@informatik.tu-chemnitz.de,
kalja.kanellopoulos@phil.tu-chemnitz.de
[2] Chair Media Informatics, Chemnitz University of Technology,
Straße der Nationen 62, 09111 Chemnitz, Germany
arne.berger@informatik.tu-chemnitz.de
[3] Visual Computing Group, Chemnitz University of Technology,
Straße der Nationen 62, 09111 Chemnitz, Germany
paul.rosenthal@informatik.tu-chemnitz.de

Abstract. Gender relations are reproduced both within HCI development processes as well as within contexts of use. Hence, theorising the subject of gender becomes part of the responsibility of HCI as a form of practice. The fledgling subfield of feminist HCI has created an epistemological basis for thinking through these challenges. The current text seeks to relate to these contributions by analysing practices of coding as they pertain to HCI. We argue that coding is of yet undertheorised regarding the subject of gender relations. By drawing on the semiotic theories of Michael Mateas and combining them with Donna Haraway's reading of material-semiotic actors, the text aims to provide new impulses for a theorisation of the practice of code-writing as a (potentially gendered) writing practice. It thus aims at increasing the translatability of HCI theory into gender-aware communities of knowledge production.

Keywords: Gender · Coding · HCI · Prototyping · Interdisciplinarity · Cultural informatics · Critical technical practice

1 Introduction

Technological artefacts play a role in shaping our culture, while at the same time, cultural stances inscribe themselves within technological artefacts. During our daily lives, we constantly find ourselves exposed to environments populated by technological artefacts. This encompasses the context of culture, such as exhibitions, galleries, festivals, and museums. As our lifeworlds are permeated by HCI artefacts, the scope of responsibility of HCI as a field widens. No longer, limited to the workplace, or to contexts such as 'entertainment', HCI has to deal with the issue of culture in all its breadth and complexity.

A. Marcus (Ed.): DUXU 2015, Part II, LNCS 9187, pp. 196–205, 2015.
DOI: 10.1007/978-3-319-20898-5_19

This implies that abstaining from issues of gender is no longer possible. These pervade culture; the artefacts we produce relate to them, whether we plan it this way or not. Likewise, stances concerning gender are inscribed within the theories, processes, and models used during our design activities.

There exists an extensive body of research addressing the practical [1], epistemological [2,3], and methodological [4] implications of feminist HCI. However, the role of gender as it relates to the practice of code production has largely been overlooked. This might be due to the inapproachability of code, its lack of sensual, specifically lack of visual qualities.

Consequently, relating the fields of coding and gender discourses creates a conceptual challenge. Even more so, since many coders might not be inclined to discuss the relationship between these fields. Women might find a safe heaven within the community of coders where the incessant negotiation of gender seems to be suspended.

The present text argues that this is not due to an inherent gender-'neutrality' of code as an artefact, but constitutes a lack within contemporary theorisations of HCI development processes. We will subsequently outline a conceptual framework designed to relate the issues of code, code production, and the performance of gender-relations.

2   Renegotiating Coding Practice

The discussion departs from an analysis of program code. Any coding individual within HCI finds herself confronted with a disparity. While her own gender is subject to ongoing negotiations, her texts are treated as technical and thus 'neutral' entities. In general, production of code is seen as a technical and thus gender-'neutral' activity.

Within 'Situated Knowledges' Haraway deconstructs claims for 'neutral' objectivity within scientific practice, instead highlighting the importance of 'writing technologies' [5, p.595]. A theorisation of code that lends itself to an analysis in this fashion exists in the form of semiotic theories. Michael Mateas [6] develops a semiotic approach towards computing. He presents a view on systems that highlights coupling between rhetorical and technical strategies. Reintegrating this line of thinking with Haraway's reading of Latour [7], a new way of theorising code is facilitated: As coded texts enter into a network of cultural artefacts, they become part of processes in which gender relations are performed.

In the course of this analysis we will first discuss the notion of programming as a purely technical activity.

2.1   Culture/Material

Contrasting the view that programming deals with disembodied, purely logical entities is the view, that programs constitute material objects. This viewpoint is substantiated by historical reflection: Early computers were huge mechanical constructions, programs were specified in the form of physical objects, such as punched cards [8].

The view of software as something disembodied hinges on a clear distinction between hardware and software. However, this distinction itself has been critiqued numerous times.

Cramer calls for a suspension of the distinction between software and hardware [9]. In an approach that highlights the importance of imagination and phantasms he claims the history software to be exceeding that of conventional computers.

This line of thinking takes up themes that are apparent in Cixous' writing. If software creation is acknowledged as an expressive activity, one that allows for development of phantasms and imagined worlds its status might change.

Again, the present text warns of clear dichotomies. Assigning the imaginative, empathetic dimension of software production to the image of 'the sensitive' female can be read as just another strategy of further marginalisation. Instead acknowledging this phantasmatic realm allows for desires for the imagined worlds and the desire for pure instrumental reason to be redistributed between individuals. The division of labour between understanding, interpretive ethnography and calculating, technically productive code production might never have been convincing in the first place.

2.2   Programming Languages/Expression

Different programing languages, different programming styles are often conceptualised in analogy to tools. Any language makes solution of specific programs hard while facilitating solution of others. Different styles of programming are simply different problem solution strategies, equipped with specific advantages and shortcomings. However, if we follow writers such as Wardrip-Fruin calling for coding as *expressive* practice, the notion of style assumes a different role [10]. No longer conceptualised as a set of mechanical relationships, the text incorporates a translation of authorial traits. Following our earlier analysis, specification of a HCI artefact entails specification of a future relationship of author to a community of users. Thereby the relationship among users is remodulated.

Contrasting the activities of HCI-coding with practices of fiction writing might elucidate this relation. The story instructs its audience to live, to imagine an experience adhering according to the textual constraints laid down in writing. The interactive artefact provides a stage for its users, its digital components provide couplings on the level of mechanics as well as culture. Mechanical coupling is provided through the internal adhesion of formal systems. Cultural coupling points to the possibility that a program might be read by humans. Through symbolic names, comments as well as intelligible structure it conveys ideas to potential human readers. Returning to the example of the story, a program might be conceptualised more in analogy to an essay: A sequence of images, flowing into each other, connected by common strands of imagination. Thereby forming a loose fabric amenable to addition and unstitching. A small band of authors and positions seems to substantiate this lofty metaphorical view on the practice of programming [11–17]. At the same time, a program is legible by virtue of its effects. Its actions within the shared world of humans and non-humans engender reconstructions and interpretations pointed at the opaque level of source code.

In effect, what is expressed is not only the workings of the machine but also the inscribed motivations, wishes of the community of writers. The language chosen acts as a translational device. The intention of a community, its hopes and phantasms are not able to copy themselves into a coded artefact. The way these are translated during the process of coding is partly determined by language. If one reads the code or experiences an artefact driven by it - a specific form of communication takes effect. In summary, appraisal of programming languages need not limit itself to their perceived ability of producing solutions. Their expressive faculties can be analysed, cherished or scorned.

2.3   Live Coding

The phenomenon of coding itself has entered the cultural realm, gaining relevance and visibility during recent years. As an example, the practice of *live-coding* stages actions of code production as cultural events [18–21]. The programmer is cast as a performer, her actions on the digital plane become directly readable, rendering her literary self transparent to the audience.

Again, coding itself is no longer pronounced a purely technical exercise. It is seen as part of the cultural activity of performative practice.

Explicit reflection of the practice within the discussed project context [22] proofed to be a stimulant for debate. Among other things it allowed for articulation of the question to what extent coding can be considered a site at which gender is performed.

At the same time, the often musical/auditive nature of live coding performance possibly opens the domain of coding to the rich sensual and imaginative realms pointed at by Cixous and other writers within the white-ink community.

Furthermore, the more direct mode of coupling between sensory organs and writing individual reconfigures the relationship between author and audience. Mechanical coupling between text and sound is complemented by perceptual coupling between sensing bodies within the audience. Conceptualising this mass as a single body possibly does not adequately describe the phenomenon. The achieved mode of coupling organises the audience into a collective body, a strange hybrid exhibiting multiple sexualities.

3   Case Study

The conceptual apparatus outlined was discussed, developed and refined in the course of a series of practice-led research studies. Three projects were conducted:

1. the development of a social-recommender system
2. development and deployment of an interactive installation aimed at instigating conversation among its users
3. integration of (1) + (2) into an integrated ambient information system to be deployed in museums

Analysed were digital as well as non-digital prototypes and mathematical formalisations alongside with their translations into source code.

During the study it became apparent, that although seldom addressed explicitly, the concept of gender pervaded discussions and development efforts in a tacit manner. Expediency of developed theoretical artefacts is described in reference to the case study.

3.1 Project Context

Division of Labour. Within the project the dominating scheme for division of labour is that between social research and computer science. Computer science is usually framed as a technical enterprise, its ultimate goal being the production of digital technology. Social research on the other hand is responsible for interpreting and evaluating technological artefacts as well as for analysis of the domains and situations they are employed in. In effect this narrative entails a dichotomous rift. It speaks of a productive, yet unreflective and unimaginative sphere opposed to a reflective, analytical yet unproductive one (Fig. 1).

Methodology. Artefact development followed a methodology highlighting the productive role of difference between participants [23].

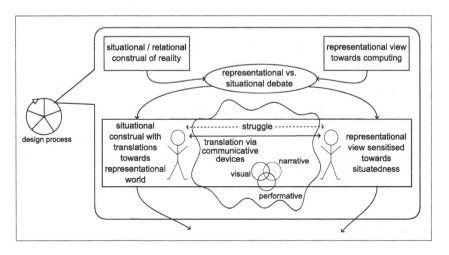

Fig. 1. Project Methodology, figure from [23]

Based on a critical reception of cross-epistemological social research [24] it focusses on mutual sensitisation as a means to render conflicts productive. Fundamental differences concerning interests and philosophical commitments [25,26] are not resolved within discussion processes. Instead, the ensuing strife is used as a design resource in order to advance jointly conducted processes of collaborative making. As an example, the question whether reality is represented within the scientific process or constructed and negotiated among researchers typically remains unresolvable between positivist and constructionist epistemologies. Debating the issue on this level will consequently not advance a making process. However, if a positivist researcher proposes inclusion of a timeline GUI element within a mobile application and a constructionist researcher proposes inclusion of a series of photographs forming a narrative arc, the debate becomes more productive. Both prototypes can be built on paper, it can be decided which course of action seems more promising within the context and limitations of the concrete situation of use. Hybrid forms become possible, combining elements of both prototypes without forcing researchers to adopt a corresponding 'hybrid epistemology'. Employed in this manner, diverging convictions become an asset. Participants developing different ideas and arguing for them passionately enrich making processes, while endless repetition of entrenched debate and following iterations of misunderstanding do not.

3.2 Interactive Installation

Developed was a full body interface that allows two participants to jointly experience historical narratives. Users enter the interaction space in pairs, marks on the floor guide their movements. Kinect sensors track the distance of each participant. While users move through space, biographical fragments are displayed on the projection thus forming a historical narrative. Users are free to explore history along this timeline, however a portion of the events reside within a special hidden critical zone which can only be explored jointly. In order to access the totality of content, users have to coordinate and move through the critical area in tandem. A more detailed description is available as part of an existing publication [27,28]. Development proceeded by use of prototyping. Studio critique was used during early development iterations. Later stages relied on qualitative evaluation within 'real-world' deployments.

3.3 Mobile Recommender

The system initially was conceived as an interactive museum guide. As users move through the museum, they are presented with situationally appropriate information. Inspired by the Hippie-system [29], it was initially conceived as an information delivery device during early stages of development.

Its basic mode of operation consists of generating a recommendation involving two users: one that is able to explain the chosen item and another that is interested in the item (Fig. 2).

Development was concept-driven, involving triangulation across different theoretical framings [31].

3.4 Observations

Code and Methodology. An interesting lack was discovered pertaining to the level of code [32]. While qualitative research proved to be quite attentive to nearly

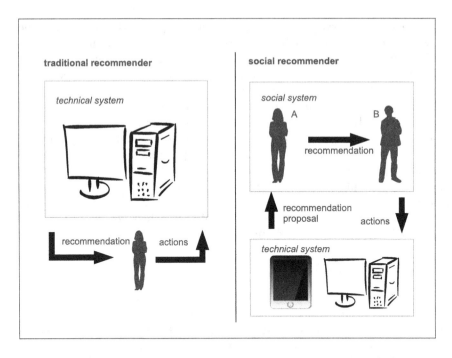

Fig. 2. Mobile Recommender - Figure initially appeared in [30]

every aspect of the artefact-making process, the level of code remained conspicuously absent. In effect, the division of labour remained remarkably strict. As a consequence, texts produced by coders were very seldom read by social researchers, while virtually every other aspect of their conduct remained relevant as a potential source of data. The stance subsequently adapted called for acknowledgement of coding as a practice related to processes of negotiation [33–35] as well as theory building [36].

Discussing Gender. Gender issues were not discussed during phases of development and making.

However, during qualitative evaluation, observations were related to issues of gender. As an example, the (male) lead developer registered a higher preference of female participants to engage with the interactive installation. Factors such as the communal, non-confrontative aspect of the facilitated experience were subsequently discussed, in a manner that might be considered trite.

At the same time, the artefact itself and especially its digital algorithmic element was still perceived as a non-gendered object.

Performative Coding. On an intellectual level, live coding practices were actively discussed within the project context [22]. These discussions led to a reframing of issues pertaining to user-generated-content (UGC). As a result, its limited applicability became apparent. Even in the face of UGC, the envisioned writing process remained fraught with inequalities. UGC served as a specific assigned niche in which communal writing is allowed. More importantly, writing and the situation of interaction remain neatly divided.

While the potentials of live coding thus became apparent, none of the envisioned prototypes reached evaluation stages. However, the discussion succeeded to sensitise coding participants towards the topic of performativity. Topics such as the performance of gender relations [37] could subsequently be framed in a way more accessible to coding individuals.

4 Conclusion

Programming exhibits a double nature, being at once a combination of the imaginative and phantastical with the unwavering demands of formalised mechanisms. Analysing it this way can provide for an interesting answer to Haraway's challenge for providing a synthesis between radical contingency and a no-nonsense commitment to the 'real-world' [38, p.187]. The program is indebted to its doubled audience: Adressing at any moment both the interobjective stratum of machinic actors and the intersubjective layer of human readers and interpreters.

The author thus becomes doubled as well. The space of coding offers a refuge from the injunction of gender in the form of a purely objective, technical realm consisting of formal relationships. At the same time, the human readership remains as ambiguous and divided as ever, forcing the author to relate in a way adhering to existing gendered power relations. The text cannot guard itself from being read in a gendered manner. Construed as a cultural artefact, it enters into the multitude of relations, repeating, among other things, sexual and gender identities. As far as coding or program execution is part of performative phenomena, it is to be read within the network of performative practices in which gendered relations reproduced themselves [37].

The concept of semiotic-material-networks provides novel impulses for theorising the status of code within HCI. By framing code production as a writing practice, existing theories and concepts can be appropriated in a fruitful manner. *Practice-led research practices* have proven to be an important methodological asset throughout the theory-making process. Reconceptualising the process of code production might render it more accessible to collaborators within the realm of social research. In highlighting to what extent it is a social practice, it could become a more intelligible phenomenon. Doing so would require both coders as well as social researchers to accept a renegotiation of the boundaries between both realms. In order to gauge the potential inherent within different styles of theorising, further empirical studies regarding the specificity of code writing within HCI seem to be warranted.

References

1. Bardzell, S.: Feminist HCI: Taking stock and outlining an agenda for design. In: Proceedings of the SIGCHI Conference on Human Factors in Computing Systems, CHI 2010, pp. 1301–1310. ACM, New York (2010)

2. Harrison, S., Sengers, P., Tatar, D.: Making epistemological trouble: Third-paradigm HCI as successor science. Interact. Comput. **23**(5), 385–392 (2011)
3. Tatar, D., Harrison, S.: CHI 2011 Feminism, HCI and Control. In: Feminism and Interaction Design Workshop at CHI 2011, pp. 1–7 (2011)
4. Bardzell, S., Bardzell, J.: Towards a feminist hci methodology: Social science, feminism, and HCI. In: Proceedings of the SIGCHI Conference on Human Factors in Computing Systems, CHI 2011, pp. 675–684. ACM, New York (2011)
5. Haraway, D.: Situated knowledges: the science question in feminism and the privilege of partial perspective. Feminist Stud. **14**(3), 575 (1988)
6. Mateas, M.: Semiotic considerations in an artificial intelligence-based art practice. Dichtung Digital: J. Digital Aesthetics **29** (2003)
7. Latour, B.: The Pasteurization of France. Harvard University Press, Cambridge (1993)
8. Ceruzzi, P.E.: A history of modern computing. MIT press, Cambridge (2003)
9. Cramer, F.: Words Made Flesh: Code Culture Imagination. Piet Zwart Institute, Rotterdam (2005)
10. Wardrip-Fruin, N.: Expressive Processing: Digital fictions, computer games, and software studies. MIT press, Cambridge (2009)
11. Floyd, C.: Software development as reality construction. In: Floyd, C., Züllighoven, H., Budde, R., Keil-Slawik, R. (eds.) Software Development and Reality Construction SE - 10, pp. 86–100. Springer, Heidelberg (1992)
12. McLean, A.: Textility of live code. In: Torque#1. Mind, Language and Technology, Link Editions, pp. 141–144 (2014)
13. Cox, G.: Speaking Code: Coding as Aesthetic and Political Expression. MIT Press, Cambridge (2013)
14. Geiger, R.S.: Bots, bespoke, code and the materiality of software platforms. Inf. Commun. Soc. **17**(3), 342–356 (2014)
15. Rönkkö, K.: Interpretation, interaction and reality construction in software engineering: an explanatory model. Inf. Softw. Technol. **49**(6), 682–693 (2007)
16. Fuller, M.: Elegance. A Lexicon, Software Studies, pp. 87–91 (2008)
17. Krysa, J., Sedek, G.: Source code. Software studies\a lexicon, 236 (2008)
18. Blackwell, A., McLean, A., Noble, J., Rohrhuber, J.: Collaboration and learning through live coding (Dagstuhl Seminar 13382). Dagstuhl Rep. **3**(9), 130–168 (2014)
19. Collins, N.: Live Coding of Consequence. Leonardo **44**(3), 207–211 (2011)
20. Collins, N., McLEAN, A., Rohrhuber, J., Ward, A.: Live coding in laptop performance. Organised Sound **8**(03), 321–330 (2003)
21. Dean, R.T.: Hyperimprovisation: Computer-interactive Sound Improvisation. AR Editions Inc, Middleton (2003)
22. Heidt, M.: Extemporising digital empowerment. In: Human-Computer Improvisation, Workshop at the ACM Conference on Designing Interactive Systems - DIS 2014, Vancouver, Canada (2014)
23. Heidt, M., Kanellopoulos, K., Pfeiffer, L., Rosenthal, P.: Diverse Ecologies – Interdisciplinary Development for Cultural Education. In: Kotzé, P., Marsden, G., Lindgaard, G., Wesson, J., Winckler, M. (eds.) INTERACT 2013, Part IV. LNCS, vol. 8120, pp. 539–546. Springer, Heidelberg (2013)
24. Metcalfe, M.: Generalisation: Learning across epistemologies. Forum Qual. Sozialforschung/Forum: Qual. Soc. Res. **6**(1), 10 (2005)
25. Blackwell, A., Wilson, L., Boulton, C., Knell, J.: Creating Value Across Boundaries; Maximizing the Return from Interdisciplinary Innovation. NESTA Research Report, London (2010)

26. Barry, A., Born, G., Weszkalnys, G.: Logics of interdisciplinarity. Econ. Soc. **37**(1), 20–49 (2008)
27. Heidt, M., Pfeiffer, L., Berger, A., Rosenthal, P.: PRMD. In: Mensch and Computer 2014 - Workshopband, De Gruyter Oldenbourg (2014)
28. Wuttke, M., Heidt, M.: Beyond presentation - employing proactive intelligent agents as social catalysts. In: Kurosu, M. (ed.) HCI 2014, Part II. LNCS, vol. 8511, pp. 182–190. Springer, Heidelberg (2014)
29. Oppermann, R., Specht, M., Jaceniak, I.: Hippie: a nomadic information system. In: Gellersen, H.-W. (ed.) HUC 1999. LNCS, vol. 1707, pp. 330–333. Springer, Heidelberg (1999)
30. Heidt, M.: Prototypengestütztes reframing am beispiel forschungsorientierter systementwicklung. In: Mensch & Computer Workshopband, pp. 191–196 (2012)
31. Heidt, M.: Examining interdisciplinary prototyping in the context of cultural communication. In: Marcus, A. (ed.) DUXU 2013, Part II. LNCS, vol. 8013, pp. 54–61. Springer, Heidelberg (2013)
32. Heidt, M.: Reconstructing coding practice - towards a methodology for source-code. In: Boll, S., Maaß, S., Malaka, R. (eds.) Mensch and Computer 2013 - Workshopband, pp. 271–275. Oldenbourg Verlag, München (2013)
33. Curtis, B., Iscoe, N.: Modeling the software design process. In: Zunde, P., Hocking, D., eds.: Empirical Foundations of Information and Software Science V, pp. 21–27. Springer, US (1990)
34. Strauss, A.L.: Negotiations: Varieties, Contexts, Processes, and Social Order. Jossey-Bass, San Francisco (1978)
35. Strauss, A.L.: Continual Permutations of Action. AldineTransaction, New Brunswick (2008)
36. Naur, P.: Programming as theory building. Microprocessing and Microprogramming **15**(5), 253–261 (1985)
37. Butler, J.: Performative acts and gender constitution: an essay in phenomenology and feminist theory. Theatre J. **40**(4), 519–531 (1988)
38. Haraway, D.J.: Simians, Cyborgs, and Women: The Reinvention of Nature. Routledge, New York (2013)

A Study on Shopping Websites Payeasy for Female Consumers in Taiwan

Hsiu Ching Laura Hsieh[(⊠)] and Ning Chun Cheng

Department of Creative Design, National Yunlin University of Science
and Technology, Douliu, Taiwan
laurarun@gmail.com

Abstract. Online shopping, with the characteristics of time convenience, space convenience, and service diversity, successfully attracts the attention of female consumers. According to MIC, the surging female shoppers bring multiple growth for online sales in past years. As the Internet become very popular, the shopping websites for female consumers are growing faster and faster. Therefore, it is vital to comprehend the requirements of female users and their preferences. In order to exploit the market, the demands and preferences of female consumers for websites therefore need to be explored. When the information and advertising full of the shopping site, it will lead the female users distraction. Designers and websites developers require to know how to adjust the interface design for female users. This study accommodate the issue how to develope a usable, pleasant and efficient web interface to provide better online shopping experiences for female users. This study aims to discuss the demands and preference of female consumers in order to enhance the usability of shopping website. Payeasy, having females as the major consumers, was ranked on the top of electronic commerce in 2013 in Taiwan. For this reason, it is taken as the research sample. The Introduction interface in the shopping website is explored. This research is divided into two stages. First, two common types of introduction allocation (horizontal on top, vertical at left) are organized from literatures. With classical work settings, the preference of female consumers for the website design would be explored. Second, the questionnaire survey is used for evaluating the layout and text distinguishability. Finally, the research results provide innovative suggestions of female shopping websites for design researchers and website developers.

Keywords: Female consumer · Shopping websites · Interface design

1 Introduction

It is worth investigation on female-focused shopping websites providing favorable shopping environments as the number of female online shoppers is currently multiplied. The goodness of the interface design would affect the shopping fluency and usefulness of consumers. This study intends to investigate how to have female consumers easily complete the shopping procedure and reduce the shopping obstruction as well as to offer female users with more pleasant shopping experiences. It aims to understand female users' preference for the navigation interface of shopping websites.

© Springer International Publishing Switzerland 2015
A. Marcus (Ed.): DUXU 2015, Part II, LNCS 9187, pp. 206–213, 2015.
DOI: 10.1007/978-3-319-20898-5_20

2 Literature Review

2.1 Definition of Female Shopping Websites

According to Insight Xplorer ARO [1], which observed the Internet user behaviors during October 2010 to September 2011, the female group appeared much higher "monthly average time (minute) of use" and "the number of web pages browsed with a single domain" than the male group did. Website businesses also promoted services to female Internet users and established exclusive female access websites. As the example of Yahoo.tw, the female-related product classification contains cosmetics, body care, women's dress, brand handbag, and fashionable masterpiece, while skin care, fashion & beauty make-up, fashion clothes, shoes, handbag & accessories, home & lifestyle, and expert exclusive are covered in Payeasy.com. Accordingly, the major products for female shoppers could be preliminarily classified into (1) cosmetics & skin care, (2) fashion clothes, (3) brand & masterpiece, (4) body care & shaping, and (5) home & lifestyle. Female shopping websites present apparently different characteristics from general shopping websites, as (1) the classification is more complex and fine, and the number of brands is enormous, (2) the product pattern and style are diversified that the same style could hardly be displayed on the home page, and (3) the product pictures are often matched with text explanations (e.g. a fridge picture obviously shows the product being fridges; but, the picture of a pump bottle might refer to lotion, shampoo, and body lotion). A shopping website presents rich product information for consumers' comparisons; however, the complex shopping procedure and the uneasy operation are the drawbacks [4]. Especially, the operation of female shopping websites is time-consuming because more trivial items are displayed.

2.2 Website Compositions

Newman and Landay [13] proposed three dimensions for website design. (1) Navigation design aims to plan the complete and correct website architecture for the users conveniently and rapidly finding the required information. (2) Information design aims to rich the website contents and be able to clearly communicate. (3) Visual design creates the uniqueness of the website style and makes the entire visual attraction by applying the basic visual elements of text, image, color, layout, and mark as well as assists in communicating the website information with the visual presentation. The usefulness of information design and the convenience of navigation design are the key factors in the complete information architecture of a website, aiming to make the architecture more definite. What is more, user interface design closely integrates information design, navigation design, and visual design, among which navigation design reveals the most importance on the interface planning.

A browser, in the browsing process, would appear visual point, visual movement, and perception order of focus because of the motivation, visual element, and layout. Visual communication design, through "design", communicates the concept of abstract, emotion, idea, or specific object with graphs [11] that it not only shows the decorating and beautifying functions but also accurately achieves the visual communication by transferring all planar factors [7].

2.3   Visual Design Elements for Websites

The factors in the visual design of websites are concluded as following. (1) Text – Current text presentation on World Wide Web is divided into pure text and graphic text. Texts are broadly applied to explain various information contents or match with images. (2) Color – The placement of color, as the key visual communication element in various design creations, allows the information receivers clearly understanding the visual emotion intentionally created by the designer. (3) Static image, the graphic expression on a website – It can be applied to the browsing interface design, explanation of information content, and demonstration of product figure. (4) Dynamic effect – The webpage interface and the image presentation contain multimedia effects of static, dynamic, background music, sound effect, and film. (5) Space layout – The visual elements of websites, including text, image, and animation, are properly organized and arranged for better visual aesthetics of the webpage in order to enhance the users' comprehension of the website contents and promote the preference [15].

Visual interface design of websites could be divided into "visual" and "usability". The former contains the design criteria of text-image relationship, color match, attention appealing, and picture balance, while the latter covers the design criteria of navigation system, architecture connection, and operation convenience [3].

2.4   Space Layout and Eye Movement

Nielsen indicated that the screen reading habit of a user was "not reading" the webpage, as users used to scan, jump, and partially absorb the webpage information; averagely, merely 20 % texts on a webpage were read. Nielsen further studied user habit of visual movement in 2010 and found that the users used to rapidly scan from the left top to the right, slowly move the sight downwards, scan from the left to the right again, and then straightly scan downwards from the left top. The research result revealed the F-form scanning movement [18]. In terms of the psychological structure for eye movement, human eyes are bilaterally symmetric, and the left-right movement of eyeballs is the simple muscle exercise, while more complicated muscles are used for the up-down movement [16]. Several studies indicated that horizontal layout was more comfortable to read [17] and presented more attraction and readability than vertical layout. Product navigation on a shopping website often requires two to three layers of pull-down menu that the second layer of a horizontal navigation menu is browsed vertically, and the second layer of a vertical navigation menu is often browsed horizontally (Fig. 1).

Based on above literatures, horizontal eye movement is comparatively comfortable. The product navigation on a shopping website often requires two to three layers of pull-down menu that the second layer of a horizontal menu is browsed vertically, while it of a vertical menu is browsed horizontally. For shopping websites requiring pull-down menus, the effects of female users' preference need to be understood in depth (Figs. 2 and 3).

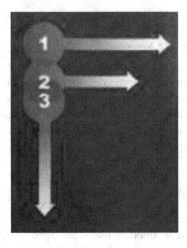

Fig. 1. F-form scanning movement [18]

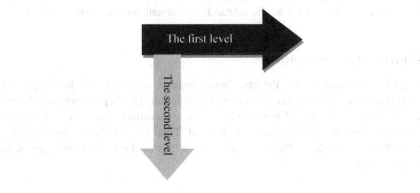

Fig. 2. Horizontal pull-down menu visual movement

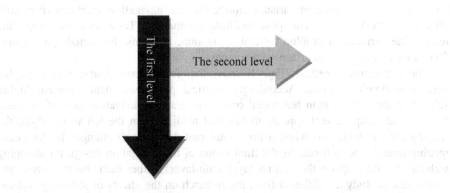

Fig. 3. Vertical pull-down menu visual movement.

3 Methodology

First, current situations of female shopping websites, design criteria for shopping websites, visual design elements for websites, space layout and eye movement, and navigation visual movement are investigated through literatures. Female participants are then invited to the experiment and questionnaire survey, and the data and questionnaire statistics are further organized. A website navigation design suitable for female consumers is then proposed based on the analyses. Finally, conclusion and successive research are proposed.

3.1 Research Equipment and Participants

According to Insight Xplorer ARO, which observed female Internet user behaviors in September 2013, most female Internet users are aged 20–29 (27.36%) and 30–39 (27.69%). Total 15 female users aged 25–35 with online shopping experiences are invited for this study.

An ASUS ML238 liquid crystal display with the resolution 1920 × 1080 and the browser Firefox 11.0 is utilized as the research equipment for the normal browse.

3.2 Experiment Measurement

The navigation interface of the Payeasy home page is modified into four styles of (1) text horizontal navigation, (2) text vertical navigation, (3) graphic horizontal navigation, and (4) graphic vertical navigation for the experiment. The text and graphic contents on the experimental websites are identical. Total 15 participants are requested to evaluate the convenience, efficiency, and satisfaction of the navigation styles with Likert 5-point scale.

4 Result and Analysis

From the data in Table 1, the test of homogeneity of the overall navigation is above 0.05, and there is significant variance among the four navigation interfaces ($P < 0.05$) after the ANOVA test. The post multiple comparison LSD analysis shows the remarkable variance of graphic vertical navigation, revealing that female participants favor to the navigation interface with images.

The experimental results (Fig. 4) show that female participants prefer graphic vertical navigation menus. Accordingly, vertical pull-down menus present higher subjective satisfaction than horizontal ones, and graphic navigation outperforms text one. As the webpage text appears the inertial reading from the left to the right, the reading time is increased when a horizontal pull-down menu changes to the visual reading direction to vertical. As the final vision of the navigation design for shopping websites would stop on the second layer (sub-layer), rather than the first layer, the results in this study are different from the research on the effects of shopping website

Table 1. Subjective evaluation of navigation layout

	Navigation style	Number	Mean	SD
Descriptive statistics	Text horizontal navigation	15	7.73	2.086
	Text vertical navigation	15	9.53	3.091
	Graphic horizontal navigation	15	9.53	2.800
	Graphic vertical navigation	15	12.20	3.234
	Total	60	9.75	3.198
Test of homogeneity	1.421			

		Mean square	F	Significance
ANOVA	Among groups	50.817	6.313	.001
	In-group	8.050		

	(I) Template	(J) Template	Mean deviation (I-J)	Significance
Multiple comparison LSD	Text horizontal navigation	Text vertical navigation	-1.800	.088
		Graphic horizontal navigation	-1.800	.088
		Graphic vertical navigation	-4.467*	**.000**
	Text vertical navigation	Text horizontal navigation	1.800	.088
		Graphic horizontal navigation	.000	1.000
		Graphic vertical navigation	-2.667*	**.013**
	Graphic horizontal navigation	Text horizontal navigation	1.800	.088
		Text vertical navigation	.000	1.000
		Graphic vertical navigation	-2.667*	**.013**
	Graphic vertical navigation	Text horizontal navigation	4.467*	**.000**
		Text vertical navigation	2.667*	**.013**
		Graphic horizontal navigation	2.667*	**.013**
*. Mean deviation appears the significance on 0.05.				

interface design on the usefulness of users (Tang, 2007). The reason might be the navigation in the research not showing the pull-down function. Apparently, user preference for single layer navigation menus would change with navigation styles.

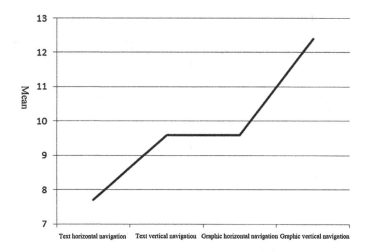

Fig. 4. Mean of subjective preference for navigation

5 Conclusion and Suggestion

The navigation function is experimented in this study. From the results, female participants prefer to graphic vertical navigation. In this case, vertical pull-down navigation menus present better subjective satisfaction than horizontal ones, and graphic navigation outperforms a pure text one. Such results could provide designers and website developers with reference for developing interactive websites and product design for female users. The effects of other visual elements, such as text and dynamic images, on female preference will be further discussed. This study is the first stage of the entire research, and a prototype of the webpage interface design will be continued at the second stage. Moreover, female users will be invited again for verifying the experimental results in order to propose more suitable suggestions for the webpage interface design for female users.

References

1. ARO Website. http://www.insightxplorer.com/product/ARO01.html
2. Cheng, E.W.: The research of user interface design of the international and domestic popular e-Commerce websites. Master's thesis, Graphic Communication Arts of NTUA (2008)
3. Cheng, Y.C.: The influence of web interface on user satisfaction and repatronage intentions-web portal site. Master's thesis, Institute of Management, Fujen Catholic University (2003)
4. Chiang, H.L.: A study on the impacts of characters of website environmental and products on consumers e-Shopping behavior. Master's thesis, Department of Information Management, Shute University (2003)
5. Fang, Y.: Dialogue Between People And Objects – Interactive Interface Design Theory and Practice. Garden City, Taipei (2003)

6. Hsieh, C.C.: A study on the electronic product interface for the elderly. Master's thesis, Graduate School of Industrial Design of NYUST (2004)
7. Hsu, C.C.: A study of the visual essence and style in assessment of web design. Master's thesis, Institute of Applied Arts of NCTU (2001)
8. Huang, J.T.: A study of the web design and usability of art museums. Master's thesis, Graduate School of Aesthetics and Arts Management, Nanhua University (2002)
9. Kuan, H.S., Huang, C.C.: Study of user satisfaction and quality in website browsing environment. J. Sci. Technol. **18**(2), 131–142 (2009)
10. Li, P.F., Lai, C.T.: Eye tracking study on the internet heavy users' cognitive processing of information and navigational patterns of online shopping websites in taiwan. J. e-Business **13**(3), 517–554 (2011)
11. Lin, P.C.: Visual Communication Design Theory and Practice. Chuanhua, Taipei (2000)
12. Mandel, N., Johnson, E.J.: when web pages influence choice: effects of visual primes on experts and novices. J. Consum. Res. **29**(2), 235–245 (2002)
13. Newman, M.W., Landay, J.A.: Sitemap, storyboard, and specifications: a sketch of web site design practice as manifested through artifacts. In: Proceedings of ACM Conference on Designing Interactive Systems, New York, pp. 274–293 (2000)
14. Nielsen, J., Pernice, K.: Eyetracking Web Usability. New Riders Press, Berkley (2010)
15. Ou, S.C.: A correlational study on web site homepage visual design and user's satisfaction using auto manufacturer's homepages as an example. Master's thesis, Institute of Design Management, Ming Chuan University (2002)
16. Tang, J.: A study on the common attributes of the e-Commerce website layout-using 1000 woman online shopping sites. J. Inf. Manag.-Concepts Syst. Appl. **9**(1), 47–70 (2007)
17. Tsao, J., Lin, F.S.: A Study on the layout of vertical and horizontal order in Chinese-the image of different ratio of the layout. J. Sci. Technol. **7**(3), 307–321 (1998)
18. Yeh, C.J.: Brief Introduction to Interactive Design. Artist, Taipei (2010)

Verification of Stereotype on Women Observing Gender Difference on UX of Wearable Device

Hee Jae Hwang, Jung Min Lee, and Da Young Ju$^{(\boxtimes)}$

School of Integrated Technology, Yonsei Institute of Convergence Technology,
Yonsei University, Incheon, Republic of Korea
{sitl219,jmlee_0104,dyju}@yonsei.ac.kr

Abstract. There has been contending views on women and men as a consumer, and we believe that it is necessary to analyze and verify who will be the upcoming consuming subject in next 10 years. Herein, using adjectives of AttrackDiff2 which analyze how people perceive the product using hedonic quality and pragmatic quality, we have conducted FGI (Focus Group Interview) on 20–25 female and male group respectively, analyzing how major consumers in 10 years perceive about current trend over the world, wearable devices. As a result of the study, we find that women tend to perceive pragmatic quality as important as men in respect of UX of wearable devices. Instead of the difference between two gender groups, there were greater gap between the individuals. Here, we suggest that stereotype on women that they are an impulsive consumer should be adjusted.

Keywords: Gender · Women · UX · Gender gap · Wearable device

1 Introduction

It is undeniable that creating positive UX (User eXperience) has become one of the crucial factors these days. Thus, in order to maximize the experience of the individuals, developers initiated to focus more on specified targets, such as gender.

1.1 Gender Difference

Gender difference is an interdisciplinary research area which has been studied in various fields, such as in psychology, women's study, anthropology and medical science. According to Charness et al. [1] who researched on risk taking, dominant traditional perception play a crucial role on decision making regardless of nationality or age. Some argue that maternal affection, smoothness and risk avoiding characteristic of 'female' is driven by biological factors, meaning that these characteristics would not change although there will be social or environmental changes [2]. On the other hand, others such as Butler, J. contend that even sex differentiation between men and women is categorized by socio-cultural factor, being as a result of repetitive training on the role of gender that has been carried out for a long time [3]. For instance, Musuo is one of

© Springer International Publishing Switzerland 2015
A. Marcus (Ed.): DUXU 2015, Part II, LNCS 9187, pp. 214–223, 2015.
DOI: 10.1007/978-3-319-20898-5_21

the minor ethnic groups that have matrilineal society. In this society, the role of gender is completely opposite compared to the common world, acting as a supporting ground for the argument that social and economic circumstances is a decisive factor on the role and characteristics of gender [4]. According to Huffman et al. [5], as people become more educated, the role of gender diminishes in the aspect of technological self-efficacy. Indeed, in Northeast Asia, such as Japan, South Korea, and Taiwan, patriarchy which tended to be dominant till the end of 20th century diminished alongside with the increase in education level [6]. Likewise, although there are researches which tend to explain the reason for gender differentiation in biological perspective, we particularly focus on social and anthropological reasoning to contend our argument.

1.2   Female as Consumer

Through our experience, we can easily know that there is difference over the preference as a male or female consumer. Indeed, women in particular took more central stage on shopping rather than men since they are perceived to be more impulsive shopper than men [7]. Indeed, a study found out that women have greater brand commitment, impulse buying and hedonic consumption level compared to men [8]. Other than that, there are various investigations which tend to classify male as reasonable consumer while female as emotional consumer. On contrast, researches such as Badgaiyan et al. argue that gender does not play meaningful role on the relationship between impulsive buying and intrinsic variable [9]. Hence, it is significant to research if the gender difference will still play similar role on the consumer's behavior in 10 years.

1.3   Research Abstract

Due to the influence of the education, we hypothesized that the stereotype on women that women tend to be more emotional compared to rational men would not work on 20–25 years old young women due to equal education (see Fig. 1). Herein, we observe 20–25 years old male and female group in technical field to analyze how these two gender groups perceive and treat about the hedonic quality and pragmatic quality of the wearable devices. Since wearable device constitute both technical factor and aesthetic

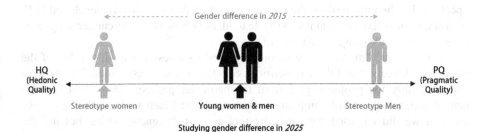

Fig. 1. Brief introduction for the study

and emotional needs [10], we believe that it can act as one of the major variables to compare how consumers in two gender groups react to the product.

This research is significant because first, it validates how women are being treated in UX today and second, it allows to foresee what factors should be considered or changed in order to maximize the women's UX in the future.

2   Study

2.1   Method

In this study, we aim to find how gender difference influences the UX of the wearable devices. We particularly focus on 20–25 age group since we found out that the result among this age group showed significant result through the pilot study. They are the age group who are most likely to be the consumer of the wearable devices, the group who will be familiar with the devices. For the in depth study, that allows participants to share their expectations, opinions and ideas on a given discussion topic, we chose to conduct FGI (focus group interview) [11]. In order to draw the result that we want to discuss with, we mainly considered about the times that the participants discuss about the quality of the devices. Since the interview is designated in a way that they can discuss about what factor is crucial on the topic that they are discussing with, talking about a particular characteristics will mean that the participant consider the particular factor to be important for them. In order to find how their comment is related to which quality, we used adjectives of AttrackDiff2. There are 28 word-pairs of the adjectives, which is categorized in to 4 dimensions [12, 13, 15].

- *PQ* (*pragmatic quality*): The pragmatic quality measures useful and usable features of certain products.
- *HQ-I* (*hedonic quality – identity*): People concern the product's ability to help them represent their 'identity' to the others. This quality includes how stylish they are and how open the product is to the people.
- *HQ-S* (*hedonic quality – stimulation*): This dimension motivates user to use that product because it 'stimulates' users with inspiring, novel and interesting features.
- *ATT* (*attractiveness*): Attractiveness describes the overall ability to give a 'good' impression of product to user.

Indeed, AttrackDiff2 is commonly used to get the information to know which aspect need to be improved on the particular product that has already developed [12]. Travisan, B. also revealed that it is possible to identify how two different gender groups perceive differently using Attrakdiff [13].

As these four dimensions are commonly used to assess the quality value of the product, we perceived that these dimensions could also be used as a method to see what kind of quality the people expect from the particular product. Thus, although this method is originally used by implementing seven-point Likert scale, in this study, we note that we did not used the particular tool as it is designated to be, but use the adjectives that are outlined because these words are well organized to categorize particular characteristics of the quality of the product among consumer (Table 1).

Table 1. Word-Pairs for four Dimensions of AttrackDiff2

PQ	HQ-I
technical - human	isolating – connnective
complicated – simple	unprofessional – professional
impractical – practical	tacky – stylish
cumbersome – straightforward	cheap – premium
unpredictable – predictable	alienating – intergrating
confusing – clearly structured	separates me – brings me closer
unruly – manageable	unpresentable – presentable
ATT	**HQ-S**
unpleasant – pleasant	conventional – inventive
ugly – attractive	unimaginative – creative
disagreeable – likeable	cautious – bold
rejecting – inviting	conservative – innovative
bad – good	dull – captivating
repelling – appealing	undemanding – challenging
discouraging - motivating	ordinary – novel

2.2 Participants

The focus group was conducted among nine South Korean participants, where five were male and four were female. The ages ranged from 20 to 25, and average age is 21.8 for female group and 20.2 for male group. (see Table 2). All of them either graduated university or university students, and on average, they had 3.5 IT devices. All of them were either studying or working in technology-related field.

Table 2. General information of male and female group particiapants

	Name	Age	Educational level	IT devices possessing
Male group	M1	20	University Student	PC, laptop, smart phone, tablet PC, MP3
	M2	20	University Student	Laptop, smart phone
	M3	20	University Student	Laptop, smart phone, tablet PC, smart watch
	M4	21	University Student	PC, laptop, smart phone, tablet PC
	M5	20	University Student	PC, laptop, smart phone
Female group	F1	22	University Student	Laptop, smart phone, MP3
	F2	20	University Student	Laptop, smart phone
	F3	25	Graduated Student	PC, laptop, smart phone
	F4	20	University Student	Laptop, smart phone, tablet PC, MP3

2.3   Procedure

The FGI consisted of 4 stages, designated in a way that the participants can discuss about various dimensions of the wearable devices (see Table 3).

Table 3. The structure of FGI questionnaire

Stage	Question	
Warm-up stage	— Introduction and the rules of the interview	
Bridge stage	— Concern over the new devices — Perception on wearable devices — Consumption standard of the product and wearable devices	
Main stage	— Explanation on wearable devices	
	— Factors that influence on consumption of wearable devices	(1)
	— Which wearable devices would be the most useful to use among smart shoes, smart band, smart watch, smart shirt, smart glass	(2)
	— Who, when and why will the wearable device will be used	(3)
Ending stage	— Factors that are necessary for future wearable devices	(4)

3   Results

In this session, result of FGI is presented in a way that it was discussed above. Through FGI, we grouped the related comments from participants into 4 groups of AttrackDiff2, ATT, HQ-S, HQ-I and PQ, and grouped other meaningful statements into etc. group. Table 4 shows the examples of comments of the participants with its matching quality. Issues on durability, performance, healthfulness, and security issues are categorized on etc. group.

Utterance Frequency Analysis. The result of this timeline analysis of female group and male group are outlined on Figs. 2 and 3. Based on the study above which classified the comments into the category, the amount of time that the participants dealt with the particular issue on the quality of the wearable devices was outlined using different colors. The horizontal-axis refers to the timeline, while the vertical axis represent quality dimension. When we take a look at these two graphs, the most frequent quality that was dealt with was PQ for both male and female. Indeed, female in general discussed with various factors of qualities in general. For instance, compared to female group who moves on the next quality after discussing about an issue for enough time, male group discussed about the qualities that each individuals want to talk about.

Taking 10 s as a single unit, we sum up the amount of time that each participant discussed about a certain qualities of AttrackDiff 2 model (see Table 5). Considering

Table 4. Comments matched with the adjectives in each dimension

AttrackDiff2	Example	Word
ATT	— I do not think that I would use it if it looks ugly	attractive
HQ-S	— It is fun and exciting to see new technology — I would use it if advanced technology like hologram is applied	inventive innovative
HQ-I	— Something that a lot of people use, and something that is presentable to the other people — Since it is presented to the others, it functions as a kid of fashion item	presentable stylish
PQ	— Something that works even if I do not touch it with my hand — If it is really usable and practical — It must be connected with other devices without any problem	straightforward practical manageable
ETC.	— Something that does not break up, and have good A/S — Wish it has fast signaling speed and does not heat up — Wonder it smart glasses does no harm to our eyes — Privacy or security issues would be crucial	durability efficiency health security

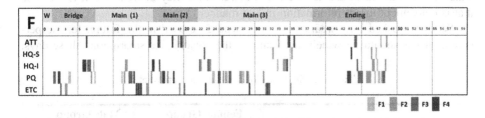

Fig. 2. Timeline analysis of the focus group interview with female group

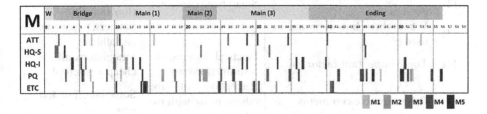

Fig. 3. Timeline analysis of the focus group interview with male group

Table 5. Frequency table that compares how long did each groups disscussed about each qualities of AttrackDiff2 (unit: 10 s)

	Female group						Male group					
	F1	F2	F3	F4	Total	(%)	M1	M2	M3	M4	M5	Total	(%)
ATT	4	2	7	8	21	**16.4**	5	0	3	3	3	14	**13.2**
HQ-S	1	3	1	1	6	**4.7**	0	1	5	1	1	8	**7.6**
HQ-I	3	10	8	6	27	**21.1**	0	2	5	3	10	20	**18.9**
PQ	13	16	15	10	54	**42.2**	5	7	5	15	11	43	**40.6**
ETC.	1	7	6	6	20	**15.6**	2	3	6	5	5	21	**19.8**

the amount of times that each individuals discussed with each qualities, both female and male group considered PQ > HQ-I > ATT > HQ-S to be important. Taking total number of discussion time of each quality into the percentage, women more preferred PQ, ATT and HQ-I than male, while male only preferred HQ-S more than female.

At the same time, individual preference over a certain quality is also differentiated among the same gender group as well. For instance, male participants who frequently mentioned about the hedonic quality were M3 and M5 only. Like the total female group, M4 was most interested on HQ-I, and like the total male group, F2 had greater interest on ATT than HQ-S quality.

Contents of Answer. Table 6 contains the summary of answers of each gender group. First, the 'cost' factor that is hard to connect with AttrackDiff2 quality appears as a main factor of consumption for both gender groups. Then, when we asked groups to choose the most usable wearable devices, women liked smart band and disliked smart glasses based on usability and hedonic reasoning. On the other hand, male chose smart glass as the most usable wearable devices since they thought that it is a device that is convenient to get information in fast manner.

When we asked how wearable devices would be used in the future, female perceived that it should be widely used among the society like smartphone these days,

Table 6. Summary of FGI question answers

		Female Group	Male Group
(1)	**Factors influencing consumption of the devices**	Price	Price
(2)	**The most usable wearable devices**	Smart band (hedonic)	Smart glass (functionality)
(3)	**Who, when, how it would be used.**	All	Soldiers, patients and athletes
(4)	**Top 3 important factor**	Practical > attractive > straightforward	Straightforward > cheap > practical
	Other notable comments	Perception of the others, using with the others	Something fun and new

while male perceived that it would be used among the users who need them for particular purpose, such as soldiers, patient and athletes, the ones who should be instantly be informed with health-related data.

From the last question of the FGI, female ranked practical (PQ), attractive (ATT) and straightforward (PQ) factor to the most promising quality that is necessary for the development while male ranked straightforward (PQ), cheap (HQ-I), practical (PQ) factor to be crucial. This ranking matched with the frequency that they commented on these issues.

Among the content of the discussion that is particularly different from each groups, women kept discussed about the social factors, such as how people perceive about the device or how it is used with the others. On the other hand, although this social factor was discussed among male group, they were more concerned with something that satisfies themselves, such as fun, innovative, emotional and human-like factors.

4 Discussion

With the various results that were extracted from FGI above, there are some notable findings through the analysis.

4.1 Gender Differences

When we observed the discussion contents or the frequency of the comments on particular issues, male tend to me more influenced by HQ-S, such as on interesting and innovative ideas, and female were more concerned about ATT quality, such as identifying themselves in the society. However, since these difference wear rated below 3 %, it is difficult to say that these difference is as critical. This kind of difference appears among the individual participants regardless of gender difference, implying that there is lower credibility on this result. This is noticeable point in this research because traditionally, the researches tend to show significant difference between two gender groups. Similar to the result of the study which tested the usability of internet among Junior-high school students in Taiwan [14], this study also argue that the gender gap between female and male consumer on technical products would diminish in the future society.

4.2 Social Factors for Women, Individual Factors for Men

The result shows that female group tended to take social factor to be crucial, and this may influenced HQ-I and ATT quality. There is greater interrelationship between their look and the social factor. On the other hand, male tend to be more interested on the individual factors that can motivate themselves, related to HQ-S quality.

Overall, female tend to consider various kinds of quality in wider spectrum, being more interested on how the other think about their possession. Comparatively, male were interested on fewer kinds of quality. Female tend to comment and compared various factors of hedonic and pragmatic quality.

These two results suggest two main findings. First, the study that the women are more risk-aversive is applicable in this study [1]. They tend to consider the social perspective and stability compared to male, and this may be driven by more strict social pressure on women in the society. Second, this study which found out that female tend to consider more various factors compared to male supports our hypothesis that the women are not an impulsive consumer who are reliant on their emotion [7].

4.3   Greater Individual Difference Than the Gender Difference

The result of the study shows that there are many similarities on quality factors that each gender group considers to be important. Instead, there was greater difference between the individuals within the same gender group. This may be resulted because this study was conducted among the people who have similar age, ranging from 20–25, and have similar education level. Herein, we support the argument that the gender difference may be driven from cultural and environmental factors, such as education instead of biological factor. Thus, in the future society both gender groups are equally educated, we believe that it would not be as simplistic to find characteristically difference based on gender.

5   Conclusion

In conclusion, this research found out what factors should be considered and reconsidered for women in UX. This research is significant on developing UX of women since research of women in UX will continuously be important in the future because women are influential consumers who will continuously integrate with UX.

As the limitation of this study, first, the participants were asked to discuss about the wearable device through the detailed explanation of the authors. Dominant number of participants has never used the wearable device before. Second, this study was conducted among South Koreans, meaning to say that this study is not applicable to the other cultures. Here, we suggest that the cross-cultural experiment can be conducted on different countries.

Although we cannot generalize our study, we argue that the gender gap will be narrowed down when they have similar education level in relation to the UX of wearable devices. As for the future work, the other factors that influence the hedonic and pragmatic quality of each individual apart from the gender can be researched.

Acknowledgement. This work was supported by the MSIP (Ministry of Science, ICT and Future Planning) under the "IT Consilience Creative Program" support program supervised by the NIPA (National IT Industry Promotion Agency) (NIPA-2014-H0201-14-1002).

References

1. Charness, G., Gneezy, U.: Strong evidence for gender differences in risk taking. J. Econ. Behav. Organ. **83**(1), 50–58 (2012)

2. Fausto-Sterling, A.: The problem with sex/gender and nature/nurture. In: Williams, S., Birke, L., Bendelow, G. (eds.) Debating Biology, pp. 123–132. Routledge, New York (2003)
3. Butler, J.: Gender Trouble. Routledge, New York (2002)
4. Gong, B., Yan, H., Yang, C.-L.: Gender differences in the dictator experiment: evidence from the matrilineal Mosuo and the patriarchal Yi, Experimental Economics (2014)
5. Huffman, A.H., Whetten, J., Huffman, W.H.: Using technology in higher education: the influence of gender roles on technology self-efficacy. Comput. Hum. Behav. 29(4), 1779–1786 (2013)
6. Bhopal, K.: Gender 'Race' and Patriarchy: A Study of South Asian Women. Ashgate, Aldershot (1997)
7. Lucas, M., Koff, E.: The role of impulsivity and of self-perceived attractiveness in impulse buying in women. Pers. Individ. Differ. 56, 111–115 (2014)
8. Tifferet, S., Herstein, R.: Gender differences in brand commitment, impulse buying, and hedonic consumption. J. Prod. Brand Manag. 21(3), 176–182 (2012)
9. Badgaiyan, A.J., Verma, A.: Intrinsic factors affecting impulsive buying behaviour—Evidence from India. J. Retail. Consum. Serv. 21(4), 537–549 (2014)
10. Miner, C.S., Chan, D.M., Campbell, C.: Digital jewelry: wearable technology for everyday life. In: CHI 2001 Extended Abstracts on Human Factors in Computing Systems, pp. 45–46. ACM, Seattle, Washington (2001)
11. Morgan, D.L.: Focus groups as qualitative research. Planning (2013). doi:10.4135/9781412984287.n4
12. Hassenzahl, M., Burmester, M., Koller, F.: AttrakDiff: Ein Fragebogen zur Messung wahrgenommener hedonischer und pragmatischer Qualität. In: Szwillus, G., Ziegler, J. (eds.) Mensch & Computer 2003, pp. 187–196. Springer, Verlag (2003)
13. Trevisan, B., Willach, A., Jakobs, E.-M., Schmitt, R.: Gender-specific kansei engineering: using AttrakDiff2. In: Szomszor, M., Kostkova, P. (eds.) e-Health. LNICST, vol. 69, pp. 167–174. Springer, Heidelberg (2011)
14. Tsai, M.-J., Tsai, C.-C.: Junior high school students' Internet usage and self-efficacy: a re-examination of the gender gap. Comput. Educ. 54(4), 1182–1192 (2010)
15. Rauche, T.: Summative usability evaluation: Hedonic and pragmatic quality of a mobile device application

Closing the Gender Divide in Tech: Challenges and Achievements in Vogue

Linda Lim[1][(✉)] and Yuanqiong (Kathy) Wang[2]

[1] Murdoch University, Murdoch, WA, Australia
email2enigma@yahoo.com
[2] Towson University, Towson, MD, USA
ywang@towson.edu

Abstract. This paper investigates closing the gender divide in technology. A literature review was conducted to disclose the factors that lead to the current gender divide in the technology sector classified as stereotypes, bias, lack of female role models, low college enrollment in technology, college student experience, cultural background, interests, personality, aptitude, family responsibilities, fewer opportunities, university and college faculty bias, limited support, and inequity in leadership. A framework was developed to explain the relatively low number of female graduates getting into the technology field, the low number of female remaining in the technology field, and the low number of female in technology management roles. The challenges and achievements faced by women in technology were addressed. The strategies to bridge the gender divide in technology comprise three broad aspects, namely, childhood, education, and career.

Keywords: Gender divide · Technology · Challenges · Achievements · Ways to close the gender gap

1 Introduction

Although more women are in the technology field than previously, they are still outnumbered by their male counterparts. In some of the technology fields, the number of women is even shrinking. For example, according to U.S. Department of Labor, Bureau of Labor Statistics [17], in the United States alone only 18% of 2012 computer and information sciences undergraduate degree recipients were women. There was a 64% decline in the number of first year undergraduate women interested in majoring in computer science between 2000 and 2012. This presented a serious gender divide problem in the technology field. Therefore, how to close this gender gap becomes essential. This paper examines closing the gender divide in technology with challenges and achievements in vogue. The objective of this paper is to bridge the existing gender divide in technology through identifying factors that lead up to the gender divide, followed by addressing the challenges women face and their achievements, and proposing and discussing strategies for this purpose. A framework to elaborate the factors

© Springer International Publishing Switzerland 2015
A. Marcus (Ed.): DUXU 2015, Part II, LNCS 9187, pp. 224–231, 2015.
DOI: 10.1007/978-3-319-20898-5_22

that contribute to the gender divide was developed and described. The rationale is to garner support for the combined effort of women in technology around the world and to reveal accurate metrics on gender ratios in technical roles in organizations so as to solve the lack of gender diversity issue in the technology field [2].

2 Literature Review

A literature review focusing on the gender divide in technology field was conducted. The focus was to gather full-text articles presenting the data or cases regarding the current status of the gender gap and potential solutions. To manage the scope and timeliness of the study, only articles published between 2010 and 2014 were included. A brief investigation in the literature revealed several factors that lead to the existing gender divide in the technology field. To illustrate these factors, a framework was designed to classify them into categories and sub-categories. Each category and sub-category was then further explained with a description and illustration of the sample scenarios.

Factors that Lead to the Existing Gender Divide in Technology. Many factors were discussed in the literature regarding how the gender gap was created in the technology field. Common factors include stereotypes [3, 9, 10, 14], bias [9, 10, 14], lack of female role models [9, 14], low college enrollment in technology [1, 9], college student experience [10], cultural background [14], interests [9], personality [4], aptitude [4, 5], family responsibilities [7], fewer opportunities [11, 12, 18], university and college faculty bias [10], limited support [11, 12, 18], and inequity in leadership [11, 12, 18].

Stereotypes [3, 9, 10, 14] are described as the perception imposed upon particular groups of people, individuals, places or objects by the society at large. Home bias [9, 10, 14] and cultural background [14] facilitate further illustration. A typical perception of stereotypes would be technical courses are perceived as training for boys, while home economics are perceived as training for girls. In some cultures, boys are allowed to attain high levels of educational qualifications, while girls are expected to stay in the home and marry boys who will take care of them financially when they become of age and they take full responsibility for the household duties instead of being educated or highly educated. Because of this stereotype, females are less likely to pursue higher education which may prevent them from getting into the positions that require specific technical qualifications.

Bias [9, 10, 14] is defined as dislike or favor of certain groups of people, individuals, places or things without valid reasons or basis. Home bias [9, 10, 14], university and college faculty bias [10], and workplace bias [3, 9, 10, 14] are the sub-categories of bias. In certain homes, universities and colleges, and workplaces, particular people are given preferential treatment. An excellent illustration of home bias would be where a female child is discouraged from pursuing her interests, let alone pursue bachelor degree programs in technology, while a male child is given support to pursue his interests. University and college faculty bias can come in the form of assignment and exam tips, student grading, internship approval, student leadership participation, student scholarship applications, and job references. Workplace bias can involve a manager favoring one department employee over another by being more lenient when mistakes are made or giving the first priority when there are career advancement or development opportunities. When the preference is given to male counterparts, females are more likely to be discouraged to pursue the field that they may originally be interested in.

Lack of female role models [9, 14] refers to the situation where there is an insufficient number of female examples in the technology field. Stereotypes [3, 9, 10, 14], home bias [9, 10, 14], cultural background [14], fewer opportunities [11, 12, 18], and limited support in the home [11, 12, 18] contribute towards the explanation of lack of female role models. In several cultures, female children have few or no female examples in the technology field within the family, extended family, friends, and/or in society in general, are not encouraged or supported to pursue a career in technology, and are not exposed to the use of technology as a feminine activity. This explains the low adoption of technology by female adults as a career.

Low college enrollment in technology [1, 9] is seen as low number of female students pursuing degrees in technology at universities. Stereotypes [3, 9, 10, 14], home bias [9, 10, 14], cultural background [14], interests [9], personality [4], lack of female role models [9, 14], limited support in the home [11, 12, 18], and aptitude [4, 5] help in further explanation. In many cultures, female children are not given encouragement, support, and/or do not have sufficient female role models in the technology field. Besides that, if these female children do not have an interest in technology, have no patience towards managing technology, and are not able to learn technology with ease, they are unlikely to pursue tertiary studies in technology.

College student experience [10] can be described as university experience as a student pursuing a degree in technology. University and college faculty bias [10], interests [9], personality [4], and aptitude [4, 5] are the sub-categories. For instance, a female student found the subjects in the technology bachelor degree program very difficult and dull, and was struggling to keep up with her peers throughout the program. In addition, this student faced preferential mistreatment by faulty members in terms of not receiving the same level of assignment and exam tips, student grading, internship approval, student leadership participation, student scholarship applications, and job references upon graduation as fellow students. As a result, this student cannot see herself joining the technology field as a professional upon graduation, made several unsuccessful attempts in getting a place at the teachers' training college, and ended up giving private home tuition to elementary school students as an alternative to being a school teacher, since it is financially viable to survive.

Cultural background [14] describes the place of birth, the country where one resides, and the culture one identifies with. Nationality, country, and culture of an individual form his or her cultural background. Interests [9] can be described as the inclination of an individual towards technology. Personality [4] is seen as an attribute of an individual towards managing technology. Aptitude [4, 5] is the ability of an individual to learn technology.

Family responsibilities [7] constitutes the duties of an individual to his or her family and it is contributed by stereotypes [3, 9, 10, 14], home bias [9, 10, 14], workplace bias [3, 9, 10, 14], cultural background [14], limited support in the home [11, 12, 18], and limited support in the workplace [11, 12, 18]. In cultures where females are seen to be the sole care giver in the home, being in the workforce does not relieve her of household duties on top of office responsibilities, which is often frowned upon by employers who may not be pleased whenever there is a need for female employees to leave the office at knock off times.

Fewer opportunities [11, 12, 18] can be described as having lesser exposure to use technology or chances for career advancement. Stereotypes [3, 9, 10, 14], home bias [9, 10, 14], workplace bias [3, 9, 10, 14], cultural background [14], limited support in the home [11, 12, 18], and limited support in the workplace [11, 12, 18] are used to further illustrate fewer opportunities. An excellent scenario of fewer opportunities would be female professionals in technology getting bypassed while their male counterparts are given the promotion due to subjective reasons such as men are able to spend more time at the office and are more able to get the job done.

University and college faculty bias [10] is described as unequal treatment of students or fellow faculty members by faculty holding positions of authority. This involves limited support in the university and college [11, 12, 18]. A common scenario of university and college faculty bias would be tenure application of female faculty in technology being less favored by faculty holding positions of authority, likely resulting in a low number of female faculty in technology holding tenured positions at universities.

Limited support [11, 12, 18] is seen as low level of encouragement or reinforcement by family members, faculty staff or work colleagues and this can be subdivided into limited support in the home [11, 12, 18], limited support in the university and college [11, 12, 18], and limited support in the workplace [11, 12, 18]. A good scenario of limited support would be a female technology professional or academic also requiring to be the sole care giver in the home apart from her career without the support of family members, while also not receiving recognition for her contribution at work, is more than likely to leave her career in technology.

Inequity in leadership [11, 12, 18] can be described as an unequal distribution of leadership roles between male and female. Stereotypes [3, 9, 10, 14], workplace bias [3, 9, 10, 14], fewer opportunities [11, 12, 18], and limited support in the workplace [11, 12, 18] clearly illustrate inequity in leadership. A significant scenario of inequity in leadership would be female technology professionals are usually being perceived to play the support role rather than the leadership role, are not always receiving acknowledgement for their achievements, and are often overlooked when it comes to being promoted to a management position.

Low college enrollment in technology [1, 9] and college student experience [10] can contribute to a low percentage of female tech professionals [1, 9], followed by stereotypes [3, 9, 10, 14], home bias [9, 10, 14], limited support in the home [9, 10, 14], lack of female role models [9, 14], cultural background [14], interests [9], personality [4], and aptitude [4, 5].

Family responsibilities [7], fewer opportunities [11, 12, 18], university and college faculty bias [10], workplace bias [3, 10–12, 18], limited support in the workplace [10–12, 18], and inequity in leadership [11, 12, 18] can prevent career advancement [7] and can encourage career change away from technology [7].

Framework to Illustrate Factors. The framework below presents the reasons that lead to the gender divide by putting them into three categories, such as the relatively low number of female graduates getting into the technology field, the low number of female remaining in the technology field, and the low number of female in technology management roles (Fig. 1).

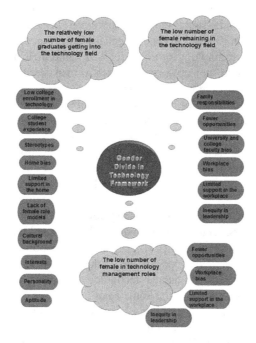

Fig. 1. Gender divide in technology framework

3   Challenges and Achievements in Vogue

The authors propose and discuss strategies in bridging the gender divide in technology by considering the challenges and achievements pertaining to women in technology.

Challenges Women Face in Technology. Some of the challenges women face come in multiple forms of the "glass-ceiling" [7, 11, 12, 18]. Due to several millenniums of male dominated societies, it created a practice where girls are not encouraged to study technical subjects, or permitted to express their preference for themselves [7, 9]. Although times have changed towards more liberalism in this aspect, women are still a long way from being well-represented in the technology sector [1, 2, 8]. According to a study in 2012 published in the journal of the Sociologists for Women in Society, high school math teachers still think that male students are more capable, although other research shows that male and female students obtain similar grades in both math and science. Such psychological bias appear to be the main barrier towards closing the gender divide [5]. Girls are not encouraged, supported or motivated to take up college degrees resulting in male-dominated careers and in some instances are discouraged from doing advanced degrees. In other cases, child-bearing often propels women to choose between personal and professional life. For those who choose to continue their professional life, it does not mean that they are freed from the tasks in the house, and striking a balance between personal and professional life affects their career development. The small number of female role models working in a male-coded professional environment are not permitted to diversify, resulting in frustration, insufficient motivation, and ultimately a quiet exit from their careers. With women under-represented in the technology sector, it also results in poor gender dynamics, low visibility, promotion, and salary [7].

Achievements of Women in Technology. In the last eight out of ten years, there have been more women taking up management positions according to a survey conducted by PricewaterhouseCoopers and Strategy. Although this is a promising trend, only 3% of leaders in public companies are female CEOs in 2013, with a 1.3% decrease from 2012 [5]. A notable achievement of women in technology is when Twitter appointed its first female board member, Marjorie Scardino, the former CEO of Pearson, a publishing and education company in December 2013 [15]. Another worthy achievement is Julia Gillard, the former prime minister of Australia's takeover of Twitter's handle, Global Development Professionals Network, where she answers questions on global education [13]. Four out of the top ten women featured in Fortune 50's most powerful women in business hold senior positions in tech giants in 2013. Marissa Mayer, CEO of Yahoo! has brought the organization out of predicament by overseeing a 111% rise in company stock in 2013 since she went on board as CEO in 2012. Sheryl Sandberg, COO of Facebook's publication Lean In: Women, Work, and the Will to Lead ignited debate in 2013. Other headline grabbers include Ginni Rometty, chairman, president and CEO of IBM, and Meg Whitman who led in a management reshuffle and oversaw a 48% rise in stock value as a new CEO of HP in 2013. Women tech leaders in Ireland and Irish women at the helm of start-ups are other celebrated achievements of women in technology [15]. Women in tech being very engaged in networks [6] is also another illustrious achievement.

4   Strategies to Bridge the Gender Divide in Technology

After considering the challenges and achievements in vogue, the authors recommend a set of strategies to bridge the gender divide in technology. The three broad aspects to group these strategies are childhood, education, and career [7].

Childhood. Under the childhood aspect, create awareness in both boys and girls by exposing them to using computers as soon as they are able to differentiate between male and female. Encourage, support, and motivate girls to pursue male-dominated college degrees, careers, and postgraduate degrees [7]. Undo stereotypes by not discouraging girls from playing with traditionally boys' toys and games [16]. Conduct programs for both parents and children to make the childhood aspect of these strategies a success.

Education. As for the education aspect, revise primary and secondary education to include technology and participating in technology initiatives [16] as part of the school curriculum for both boys and girls [9]. Invite women tech professionals as guest speakers to schools to talk about their profession and encourage girls to do the same if technology interests them [9]. Involve parents of students in technology initiatives and talks by guest speakers to help them understand technology and how girls can also excel in a technology career.

Career. For the career aspect, tech organizations can encourage networking among women tech professionals [6] or even create networks for women in technical roles to instill awareness in gender diversity at all levels, to reveal the aptitude of women, to raise visibility, to work towards being on par with male co-workers in promotion and salary, and to increase women representation in leadership [7]. Each organization should have a tech network for women to encourage awareness, obtain support, and facilitation of career development and advancement.

5 Conclusion

This paper explored closing the gender divide in technology by considering the challenges and achievements in vogue, and recommending a set of strategies to bridge the gender divide in technology. The gender divide in technology framework encompasses three aspects. The relatively low number of female graduates getting into the technology field is contributed by low college enrollment in technology [1, 9], college student experience [10], stereotypes [3, 9, 10, 14], home bias [9, 10, 14], limited support in the home [9, 10, 14], lack of female role models [9, 14], cultural background [14], interests [9], personality [4], and aptitude [4, 5]. The low number of female remaining in the technology field is due to family responsibilities [7], fewer opportunities [11, 12, 18], university and college faculty bias [10], workplace bias [3, 10–12, 18], limited support in the workplace [10–12, 18], and inequity in leadership [11, 12, 18]. The low number of female in technology management roles is a result of fewer opportunities [11, 12, 18], workplace bias [3, 10–12, 18], limited support in the workplace [10–12, 18], and inequity in leadership [11, 12, 18]. Due to time constraints, an instrument to collect data on gender ratios in technical roles in organizations and to verify the framework identified from this literature review will be distributed later.

References

1. Bacon, C.: Mind the gap: the gender divide in technology firms. Grovelands, 10 September 2014. http://www.grovelands.co.uk/mind-the-gap-the-gender-divide-in-technology-firms/. Accessed 28 November 2014
2. Bacon, L.: The tech industry's woman problem: statistics show it's worse than you think. QUARTZ, 7 November 2013. http://qz.com/143967/the-tech-industrys-woman-problem-statistics-show-its-worse-than-you-think/. Accessed 28 November 2014

3. Bercovici, T.: 'Don't wait for an invitation,' and other advice for women in tech. VentureBeat, 24 October 2013. http://venturebeat.com/2013/10/24/dont-wait-for-an-invitation-and-other-advice-for-women-in-tech/. Accessed 29 November 2014

4. Byrne, C., Cassano, J.: The Loneliness of the Female Coder. Fast Company & Inc., 11 September 2013. http://www.fastcolabs.com/3008216/tracking/minding-gap-how-your-company-can-woo-female-coders. Accessed 28 November 2014

5. Dishman, L.: Closing the gender divide: why confidence and leaning in alone won't cut it. Fast Company & Inc., 27 May 2014. http://www.fastcompany.com/3031021/bottom-line/closing-the-gender-divide-why-confidence-and-leaning-in-alone-wontcut-it. Accessed 28 November 2014

6. Friedman, A.: Tech women are busy building their own networks. The Washington Post, 8 January 2014. http://www.washingtonpost.com/lifestyle/style/tech-women-are-busy-building-their-own-networks/2014/01/08/60e356f2-7874-11e3-af7f-13bf0e9965f6_story. html. Accessed 29 November 2014

7. Gervais-Bazin, V.: Fixing the gender gap in tech: sharing best practices. Alcatel-Lucent, 22 October 2014. http://www.alcatel-lucent.com/blog/2014/fixing-gender-gap-tech-sharing-best-practices. Accessed 29 November 2014

8. Global Gender Gap. The Global Gender Gap Report 2014. World Economic Forum (2014). http://www.weforum.org/issues/global-gender-gap. Accessed 28 November 2014

9. Huhman, H.R.: STEM fields and the gender gap: where are the women?. Forbes, 20 June 2012. http://www.forbes.com/sites/work-in-progress/2012/06/20/stem-fields-and-the-gender-gap-where-are-the-women/. Accessed 28 November 2014

10. Jenny, J.: Closing the Gender Gap. Civil Engineering (08857024) **80**(7), 60–63 (2010)

11. Kim, Q.: Why aren't more women on tech boards?. Marketplace, 26 December 2013. http://www.marketplace.org/topics/tech/twitter-fallout-why-arent-more-women-tech-boards. Accessed 29 November 2014

12. Kopytoff, V.: Tech companies on edge of innovation continue to leave women behind. Aljazeera America. 24 December 2013. http://america.aljazeera.com/articles/2013/12/24/tech-companies-onedgeofinnovationcontinuetoleavewomenbehind.html. Accessed 29 November 2014

13. Leach, A.: Twitter takeover: Julia Gillard answers your questions on global education. The guardian, 6 May 2014. http://www.theguardian.com/global-development-professionals-network/2014/may/06/julia-gillard-twitter-global-education. Accessed 28 November 2014

14. Mindiola, J.: Gender Disparities in the Design Field. Smashing Magazine, 12 November 2010. http://www.smashingmagazine.com/2010/11/12/gender-disparities-in-the-design-field/. Accessed 29 November 2014

15. O'Leary, A.: The rise and rise of women in tech in 2013. Silicon Republic Knowledge & Events Management Ltd., 7 January 2014. http://www.siliconrepublic.com/business/item/35280-wit2013/. Accessed 29 November 2014

16. Taylor, C.: What Makes Girls Fall In Love With Computers And Code?. TechCrunch. AOL Inc., 29 December 2013. http://techcrunch.com/2013/12/29/what-makes-girls-fall-in-love-with-computers-and-code/. Accessed 29 November 2014

17. U.S. Department of Labor. Bureau of Labor Statistics. Occupational Category: 15–0000 (2013)

18. Whitney, T.: Why tech's gender gap isn't just a pay gap. FORTUNE. 24 November 2014. http://fortune.com/2014/11/24/why-techs-gender-gap-isnt-just-a-pay-gap/. Accessed 28 November 2014

Gender Differences in Temporal Data Analysis
Toward Women or Men Empowerment?

Ilona Nawrot[1,2]([✉])

[1] Université de La Rochelle,
L.3.I, Avenue Michel Crépeau, F–17042 La Rochelle, France
ilona.nawrot@gmail.com
[2] Poznań University of Economics, WIGE, KEM,
al. Niepodległości 10, 61-875 Poznań, Poland

Abstract. The evidence shows that time-oriented data visualizations may greatly benefit from time spatialization (organization of time along axes) adaptation. Specifically, the choice of time arrangement along axes can significantly influence performance and satisfaction of such visualizations' users. However, due to gender differences in visuospatial abilities and approaches to solve spatial problems (how males and females navigate through real or imaginary space), males and females may respond differently to time spatialization adaptations. This in turn can generate demand for gender-specific interventions or system solutions. Approaching this important theoretical and practical issue, here, we report the results of the experiment that investigated the problem of gender differences in the productivity of interactions with time-oriented data visualizations. We found no sufficient evidence to confirm the existence of such differences. We yet recommend further research in this area to completely eliminate this possibility.

Keywords: Timeline adaptation · Time perception · Time spatialization · Gender differences

1 Introduction

According to the embodied cognition theory people ground both, concrete and abstract concepts in the sensory-motor stimuli [2,15,16]. While this theory requires further research to be corroborated, numerous evidence supporting it comes from behavioral studies. Experiments demonstrate the relationship between *inter alia* social relations and space, emotions and temperature, or love and a journey[1] [16,24]. Particularly, they reveal that people rely on space in order to conceptualize time[2] [4]. They show that time organization along axes and

---

[1] For instance, in language we can find consistent patterns of metaphor for those concepts — e.g. "distant relative", "middle class", or "top executive" for social relations, "cold-blooded murderer", "warm welcome", or "hot argument" for emotions, and "being at the crossroads of a relationship", or "going their own ways" for love.

[2] Consider metaphors like e.g. "far future", "leaving the past behind", or "moving a meeting forward 2 days".

© Springer International Publishing Switzerland 2015
A. Marcus (Ed.): DUXU 2015, Part II, LNCS 9187, pp. 232–242, 2015.
DOI: 10.1007/978-3-319-20898-5_23

people's preferences toward temporal data presentation differ widely [5,7,8,27]. However, three main classes of time arrangements can be distinguished (based on their usage frequency): (1) along horizontal axis from left to right or (2) from right to left and (3) along vertical axis from top to bottom.

First, common among languages written from left to right (e.g. English, French, or Polish), position past on the left side and future on the right side of the horizontal axis [4,7,8,22,24,27]. Second, typical of languages written from right to left (e.g. Arabic, Urdu, or Hebrew), locates time on the horizontal axis but past on its right side and future on its left side [7,21,22,27]. Third, observed in languages traditionally organizing text in columns (e.g. Mandarin or Cantonese Chinese), places past on the top and future on the bottom of the vertical axis [3,5,8,18].

Simultaneously, evidence from numerous studies show significant gender differences in visuospatial abilities. Males are found to perform better than females across a variety of tasks investigating: spatial perception, mental rotation, spatial visualization, generation and maintenance of a spatial image, and spatiotemporal abilities. On the average, females slightly outperform males only in tasks requiring memory for object identity or its spatial location. Moreover, men and women tend to use different strategies when navigating through space or solving visuospatial problems — women are more likely to attend to landmarks whereas men to count on directional cues and distances [9].

The above mentioned issues raise the question of whether gender differences in visuospatial abilities affect the productivity of interactions with temporal data. In this paper we argue that research on gender differences is crucial to foster progress in brain and cognitive science, as well as in fields drawing from them, particularly in human-computer interaction and education. In the experiment presented here we aim, therefore, to systematically assess the evidence for gender differences in flexibility of interactions with time-oriented data visualizations.

The rest of the paper is organized as follows. Firstly, in Sect. 2, we describe the methodology of the experiment we conducted. Then, in Sect. 3, we detail the results. Section 4 discusses the findings. Finally, Sect. 5 concludes the paper.

2   Methodology

The experiment we conducted involved temporal reasoning over simple schedules visualizations. The mechanism through which people conceptualize time is yet unknown. However, in line with previous comparative linguistics and cognitive science findings, we expected to observe an interaction between time arrangement adaptation and participant's gender [9,20]. We hypothesized that in terms of judgment's reaction time in non-adapted condition:

- Males would outperform females if both sexes mainly rely on mental timeline rotation or generation and maintenance of preferable timeline,
- Females would outperform males if both sexes mainly rely on memorization of objects (here events on a timeline) and their spatial locations.

We also speculated that the accuracy of such inferences would not be affected by time spatialization manipulations.

Participants. One hundred sixty-two individuals who reported not being multilingual participated in the experiment in exchange for payment. We excluded multilingual respondents from the study as according to comparative linguistics findings they can flexibly accommodate multiple time representations (i.e. different timelines) [3,5,18]. Consequently, they may not respond to the experiment stimulus affecting the analysis results. Moreover, in the course of data cleaning process, we discarded from further analysis responses of 12 individuals (four women and eight men) thus reducing the participant's pool to 150.

Of the remaining 150 respondents, 56 were females and 94 males. They ranged in age from 15 to 60 ($\bar{x}_F = 30.50, s_F = 9.41; \bar{x}_M = 30.43, s_M = 9.45^3$). The female subjects held 18 distinct nationalities and were currently living in 13 different countries, whereas male subjects were of 21 nationalities and resided in 17 countries. Women were speaking 24 different languages while men 33. Thus, we achieved to gather culturally and linguistically diversified sample. Participants from both groups shared similar educational background. About 77 % of them graduated from a university: 52 % earning bachelor's, 20 % master's, and 5 % doctorate degree. All the participants reported using computer and the Internet on a daily basis.

Materials. In this experiment we employed 56 items out of the original 104-item *Space, Time, and Agents* test developed by Kessel [11,12]. In the test, target stimuli consist of 2 sets of 4 schedules each, visualized using a matrix. On each trial a respondent based on the information in the visualization has to evaluate a true-false statement displayed under the matrix (Fig. 1). For the purposes of this experiment we considered only utterances involving time-related judgments. Hence, each set of schedules corresponded with 28 such statements, half of which were true.

For the sake of simplicity, the test assumes time to be a 4-valued (*morning, noon, afternoon, evening*) ordinal variable, whereas space and agents to be 4-valued (*dorm, library, bookstore, gym* and *Justin, Alex, Sammy, David* respectively) categorical variables. Columns and rows of the matrices represent either locations or times. Line-based encoding of agents on schedules can outperform dots-based one in tasks requiring time sequences analysis or time trends identification [11,12]. As the test task involves inferences over temporal statements (including those regarding sequences and trends) we initially used both line-based and dots-based visualizations. Our ramp-up phase of the experiment revealed yet that using them two can confuse the subjects. Thus, although the original test uses both line and dots-based visualizations to denote agents, we used only color-coded dots to avoid introducing potential learning effects.

---

[3] The subscripts F and M refer to females and males groups respectively.

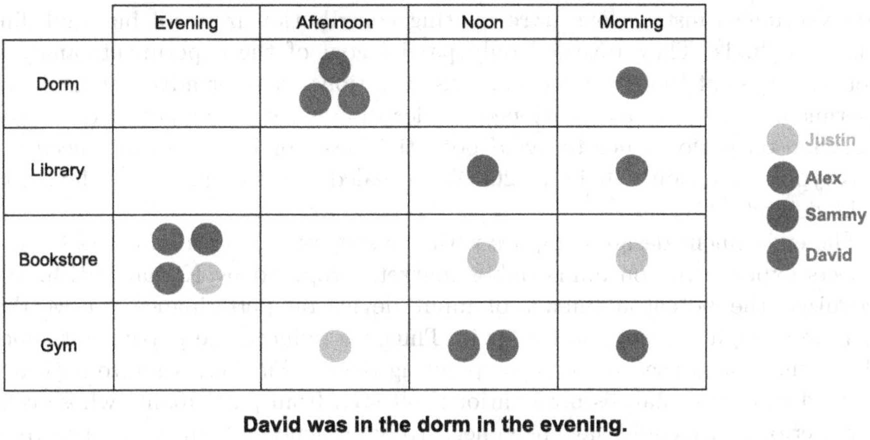

	Evening	Afternoon	Noon	Morning
Dorm		● ●●		●
Library			●	●
Bookstore	●● ●●		●	●
Gym		●	●●	●

Justin
Alex
Sammy
David

David was in the dorm in the evening.

Fig. 1. Example experimental stimulus

Design. In order to evaluate the impact time spatialization can exert on the productivity of interactions with time-oriented data visualizations depending on gender, we manipulated the time arrangement along axes in the matrix-based schedules visualizations [11,12][4]. In this two factor (time spatialization, gender) within-subjects design, we compared female differences in performance under the adapted – time arranged according to the given user's preferences – and not-adapted – time arranged against his/her preferences – condition with those of male.

To quantify the effectiveness of inferences we measured response time and accuracy of responses. We gauged users' preferences toward different time arrangements using self-developed 2-item 7-point Likert scale, where 7 denoted the most preferable time spatialization and 1 the least preferable [20]. Table 1 presents the overview of evaluation metrics used in the experiment.

Table 1. Summary of evaluation metrics used in the experiment

Attribute	Assessment Method
Usability	Overall task completion time
	Geometric mean of task completion time (robust statistic [25])
	Number of correct answers
Preferences	2-item preferences scale on a 7-point Likert scale

The experiment was run in an online scenario. We recruited the participants via *CrowdFlower* and *Facebook* advertisement. Both recruitment advertisement

---

[4] Specifically, we considered three most common time spatializations: along horizontal axis (in our case placing time in columns of the matrix) from left to right, along horizontal axis from right to left, and along vertical axis (here positioning time in rows of the matrix) from top to bottom.

and experiment instructions were inviting contribution from all but multilingual individuals. They revealed only partial goal of the experiment: analysis of effectiveness of time-oriented data visualizations. Neither advertisement nor experiment's instructions mentioned gender differences or impact of time spatialization on performance to avoid potential bias (for instance introduced via stereotypes activation) [10,17,19,26]. We revealed the real purpose of the study at the debriefing stage.

The experiment design complies with the suggestions on conducting human subjects experiments on online labor markets proposed by Komarov [14]. We recognized the potential impact of input device on performance yet we did not have enough data to control for it. Thus, we reduced the participants pool only to those who used a mouse as pointing device. Further, we automatically excluded from the analysis observations collected from participants whose cognitive performance could have been negatively influenced. Namely, we discarded respondents who reported: (1) having disability or technical problem potentially impairing the performance in the experiment; (2) sleeping less than 6 h or more than 8 h a night before [1,6,13]; (3) drinking substantial amount of alcohol or taking drugs (e.g. strong painkillers) 12 h before the experiment; (4) multitasking while completing the experimental task or engaging in any other activity conflicting with his or her productivity. We reduced the technical requirements of the study to the modern browser installation. Since, crowdsourcing platforms require such installation, we could ignore its verification.

Procedure.   The experiment consisted of four phases: (1) introduction; (2) usability test; (3) survey; and (4) closing. Each session began with formal introduction presenting the study goals, explaining its routine, and providing links to additional information. After passing screening questions, respondents had to accept the informed consent form in order to proceed to the actual test.

The group assignment questionnaire opened the second phase of the experiment. It established participant's preferences toward time spatializations, assessed his/her reading speed, and controlled for factors that could negatively influence performance. The first block of the usability test began after completion of the 4-trial training session which assured comprehension of the task instructions. Following an optional pause, participants continued with the second block of the test. Instruction cues directed subjects to complete the task as quickly, yet as accurately, as possible. We counterbalanced the order of conditions (adapted vs. not-adapted) across participants to minimize learning effects. Further, we randomized the sequence of questions within each condition to avoid ordering effects. Lastly, we conducted the experiment entirely in English to reduce the effects of proximal language context [8,18,22]. We chose English for experimentation purposes as still a great deal of software and Web pages are available exclusively in English. Furthermore, people often use it as a *lingua franca*.

In the third phase, we administered the survey collecting information on respondents' demographic, cultural, and linguistic background. Finally, we finished each session with the thank you note and debrief. At this stage, we also encouraged participants to give us some feedback and if they engaged in any activity that could potentially influence their productivity in the experiment (e.g. if they were multitasking, answering randomly without prior question analysis, or stopped the test for a moment for instance to answer the phone) to report it by checking the special box.

3   Analysis and Results

Data collected using the Web-based experiments, especially those crowdsourced, suffer from the extreme outliers problem. Thus, we performed outlier detection based on two measures: overall task completion time and geometric mean of task completion time. Outlier removal procedures proposed to clean crowdsourcing data (usually relying on standard deviation or IQR — inter-quartile range statistics) rarely guard against nonsensical observations without reducing the proper data diversity. Hence, we firstly flagged potential outliers using standard IQR-based formula: $[Q_1 - 3(Q_3 - Q_1), Q_3 + 3(Q_3 - Q_1)]$, where Q_1 and Q_3 refer to the first and third quartile respectively [14]. Then, we manually examined all the observations highlighted this way and additionally observations whose value was smaller than IQR, by comparing and contrasting them with data on participants reading speed and the amount of text presented during the test.

The IQR-based method identified 4 potential outliers: 2 in the upper bound of the overall task completion time and 2 in the upper bound of the geometric mean of task completion time. They all turned out to just correspond to slower reading participants as so we decided to keep the observations. However, the inspection of the overall task completion times substantially smaller than the IQR in the given experimental condition revealed 2 participants who completed the test in less than a minute. Although theoretically, a person reading over a 1000 words per minute could achieve such result, according to the results of our reading speed test those participants were only average readers (they read at a rate of 185 and 220 words per minute). Thus, we classified them as extreme outliers and removed them from further analysis.

Visual inspection of data (using histograms, density plots, and Q-Q plots) showed that overall task completion time, its geometric mean, as well as the number of correct answers data are strongly right skewed. Quantitative analysis of those data using skewness measure ($g_1 > 1$ for all variables) and Anderson-Darling test ($p-$value < 0.05 for geometric mean of task completion time; $p-$value < 0.001 for rest of the variables) confirmed these hypotheses. Consequently, we rejected the assumption of normal distribution of data. Moreover, due to relatively small sample size and its imbalance (56 females vs. 94 males), we decided to further use non-parametric methods to analyze the data: (1) one-sided Wilcoxon Signed-Rank test for matched pairs to confirm the effect of superiority of adapted time visualizations over not-adapted ones and (2) Mann-Whitney U test to verify the hypotheses of the existence of gender differences in the flexibility of interactions with time-oriented data visualizations. We set the statistical significance level at $\alpha = 0.05$. Where required we adjusted p-values using Benjamini-Hochberg correction.

We observed a significant effect of time spatialization adaption on response time ($V = 3472.5$, p−value $\approx 5.99 \times 10^{-5}$; $V = 4092$, p−value ≈ 0.002 for overall task completion time and its geometric mean respectively). Accuracy (measured by the number of correct answers) remained yet indifferent toward time arrangement changes ($V = 3971.5$, p−value ≈ 0.47).

To examine the flexibility of interactions for gender differences we firstly transformed the original data so it met the requirements of Mann-Whitney U test. Specifically, we prepared flexibility data by subtracting the results gained by each participant under not-adapted condition from those gained under adapted condition. Thus, since participants performed better under adapted condition, the obtained flexibility data were generally left-skewed. Table 2 shows main characteristics of those data.

Table 2. Main characteristics of flexibility data

Measure	Median	MAD[a]	Skewness	Kurtosis	Anderson-Darling A	Anderson-Darling p-value
Overall RT						
Females	−18.11	39.16	−0.37	3.59	1.77	1.37e−4
Males	−13.24	42.66	−2.46	7.48	6.13	3.46e−15
Geo. mean of overall RT						
Females	−0.21	0.98	0.85	7.31	4.67	9.87e−12
Males	−0.18	1.21	−3.15	17.60	3.11	7.49e−8
Accuracy						
Females	0.00	2.22	−0.09	0.15	0.80	3.56e−2
Males	0.00	1.48	−0.09	0.46	1.21	3.61e−3

[a] median absolute deviation

The Mann-Whitney U test for the differences in medians assumes homogeneity of variance between the groups. Furthermore, it requires groups distributions to have similar shapes. To verify these assumptions, we used Fligner-Killeen test which is robust against departures from normality and two-tailed Kolmogorov-Smirnov test respectively. Since non-directional Kolmogorov-Smirnov test for two independent samples is sensitive to any kind of difference in distributions (i.e. location, dispersion, skewness, or kurtosis) we centered and rescaled data before running the test. To normalize data we used the following formula:

$$\frac{X - median(X)}{MAD(X)},$$

where X denotes random variable and MAD calculates median absolute deviation for a given variable.

We failed to reject the hypothesis of equality of variances for both: response time and accuracy data (p−values > 0.05 for all variables). Further, the data provide insufficient evidence (at $\alpha = 0.05$) to deny the hypotheses of similar shapes. Thus, we conducted the Mann-Whitney U test for the differences in medians. We found no significant difference neither in median response time between females and males nor in median accuracy between females and males (all p−values > 0.05; $r \approx -0.05$). We summarized the tests results in Table 3.

Table 3. Results of tests for gender differences in the flexibility of interactions with time oriented data visualizations

		Measure	
Test	Overall RT[a]	Geo. mean of overall RT[a]	Accuracy
Fligner-Killeen test			
med χ^2	0.23	0.01	0.03
raw p-value	0.63	0.91	0.87
adjusted p-value	0.91	0.91	0.91
Kolmogorov-Smirnov test[b]			
D	0.07	0.09	0.24
raw p-value	0.99	0.92	0.03
adjusted p-value	0.99	0.99	0.09
Mann-Whitney U test[b]			
U	2478.0	2520.0	2722.0
Z	−0.60	−0.44	0.35
raw p-value	0.55	0.67	0.73
adjusted p-value	0.73	0.73	0.73
Effect size			
rank-biserial coefficient[c]	0.06	0.04	0.06
r	−0.05	−0.04	−0.05

[a] RT refers to response time
[b] two-sided hypotheses tested
[c] calculated according to the formula introduced by Hans Wendt [28]

4   Discussion

We addressed and empirically investigated the problem of gender differences in the productivity of interactions with temporal data visualizations. We found no sufficient evidence supporting the hypothesis of existence of such differences. These results are rather unexpected. On the one hand, a substantial body of research, supports the conceptual metaphor theory. On the other hand, gender differences in visuospatial abilities are consistently reported for decades.

Our results are however inconclusive. Firstly, based on one experiment, we cannot exclude the ceiling effect — the task we proposed could have been too easy for the hypotheses tests to yield significant results. Secondly, we assumed the magnitude and direction of gender differences in the flexibility of interactions with temporal data to be comparable with these of gender differences in the visuospatial abilities. Specifically, in line with previous cognitive science findings, we expected to observe at least medium effect size ($d \geq 0.4$). If the real effect size is substantially smaller than $d < 0.4$, the power of our analysis can be insufficient. Finally, to prove that there's no gender differences we shall run an equivalence test. Our sample is yet too small to reliably evaluate the equivalence hypotheses for not-normally distributed data.

If confirmed, the existence of gender differences in the flexibility of interactions with time-oriented data visualizations, may permeate into many areas related to human-computer interaction. It can also improve our understanding of brain and mind processes. Thus, we recommend further research in this matter.

5   Conclusions and Future Work

In this paper, we introduced the problem of gender-differences in temporal data analysis and demonstrated the first experimental results examining them. We found no evidence of gender-differences in the flexibility of interactions with such data. Thus, we recommend further research to definitely answer the question of whether systems requiring temporal data analysis should provide their users with gender-specific customization elements.

Acknowledgments. This work has been supported by The French Ministry of Foreign Affairs through the Eiffel Excellence Scholarship.

Appendix

Data collected during the experiment are available to the scientific community and can be accessed at: https://nawrot.users.greyc.fr/resources/.

References

1. Alhola, P., Polo-Kantola, P.: Sleep deprivation: impact on cognitive performance. Neuropsychiatric Dis. Treat. **3**(5), 553–567 (2007)
2. Barsalou, L.W.: Grounded cognition. Annu. Rev. Psychol. **59**, 617–645 (2008)
3. Boroditsky, L.: Does language shape thought? Mandarin and English speakers' conceptions of time. Cogn. Psychol. **43**(1), 1–22 (2001)
4. Boroditsky, L.: How languages construct time. In: Dehaene, S., Brannon, E. (eds.) Space, Time and Number in the Brain: Searching for the Foundations of Mathematical Thought, pp. 333–341. Academic Press, London (2011)
5. Boroditsky, L., Fuhrman, O., McCormick, K.: Do English and Mandarin speakers think about time differently? Cognition **118**(1), 123–129 (2011)
6. Devore, E., Grodstein, F., Duffy, J., Stampfer, M., Czeisler, C., Schernhammer, E.: Sleep duration in midlife and later life in relation to cognition. J. Am. Geriatr. Soc. **62**(6), 1073–1081 (2014)

7. Fuhrman, O., Boroditsky, L.: Cross-cultural differences in mental representations of time: evidence from an implicit nonlinguistic task. Cogn. Sci. **34**(8), 1430–1451 (2010)
8. Fuhrman, O., McCormick, K., Chen, E., Jiang, H., Shu, D., Mao, S., Boroditsky, L.: How linguistic and cultural forces shape conceptions of time: English and Mandarin time in 3D. Cogn. Sci. **35**(7), 1305–1328 (2011)
9. Halpern, D.F.: Sex Differences in Cognitive Abilities, 4th edn. Psychology Press, New York (2012)
10. Inzlicht, M., Tullett, A.M., Legault, L.: Lingering effects: stereotype threat hurts more than you think. Soc. Issues Policy Rev. **5**(1), 227–256 (2011)
11. Kessell, A., Tversky, B.: Visualizing space, time, and agents: production, performance, and preference. Cogn. Process. **12**(1), 43–52 (2011)
12. Kessell, A.M.: Cognitive methods for information visualization: linear and cyclical events. Ph.D. Dissertation (2008). https://www.stanford.edu/dept/psychology/cgi-bin/drupalm/system/files/Kessell_Dissertation.08.pdf
13. Killgore, W.D.S., Weber, M.: Sleep deprivation and cognitive performance. In: Bianchi, M.T. (ed.) Sleep Deprivation and Disease: Effects on the Body, Brain and Behavior, pp. 209–229. Springer, New York (2014)
14. Komarov, S., Reinecke, K., Gajos, K.Z.: Crowdsourcing performance evaluations of user interfaces. In: Bødker, S., Brewster, S., Baudisch, P., Beaudouin-Lafon, M., Mackay, W.E. (eds.) Proceedings of the SIGCHI Conference on Human Factors in Computing Systems, pp. 207–216. ACM, New York (2013)
15. Lakoff, G., Johnson, M.: Metaphors We Live By. The University of Chicago Press, Chicago (2003)
16. Lakoff, G., Johnson, M.: Conceptual metaphor in everyday language. J. Philos. **77**(8), 453–486 (1980)
17. McGlone, M.S., Aronson, J.: Stereotype threat, identity salience, and spatial reasoning. J. Appl. Dev. Psychol. **27**(1), 486–493 (2006)
18. Miles, L.K., Tan, L., Noble, G.D., Lumsden, J., Macrae, C.N.: Can a mind have two time lines? Exploring space-time mapping in Mandarin and English speakers. Psychon. Bull. Rev. **18**(3), 598–604 (2011)
19. Moè, A.: Gender differences does not mean genetic difference: externalizng improves performance in mental rotation. Lear. Individ. Differ. **22**(1), 20–24 (2012)
20. Nawrot, I., Doucet, A.: Timeline localization. In: Kurosu, M. (ed.) HCI 2014, Part I. LNCS, vol. 8510, pp. 611–622. Springer, Heidelberg (2014)
21. Nunez, R.E., Sweetser, E.: With the future behind them: convergent evidence from aymara language and gesture in the crosslinguistic comparison of spatial construals of time. Cogn. Sci. **30**(3), 401–450 (2006)
22. Ouellet, M., Santiago, J., Israeli, Z., Gabay, S.: Is the future the right time? Exp. Psychol. **57**(4), 308–314 (2010)
23. Reinecke, K., Bernstein, A.: Improving performance, perceived usability, and aesthetics with culturally adaptive user interfaces. ToCHI **18**(2), A:1–A:29 (2011)
24. Santiago, J., Román, A., Ouellet, M.: Flexible foundations of abstract thought: a review and a theory. In: Maass, A., Schubert, T. (eds.) Spatial dimensions of social thought, pp. 39–108. De Gruyter, Berlin (2011)
25. Sauro, J., Lewis, J.R.: Average task times in usability tests: what to report? In: Proceedings of the SIGCHI Conference on Human Factors in Computing Systems, pp. 2347–2350. ACM, Atlanta (2010)
26. Schmader, T., Johns, M.: Converging evedence that stereotype threat reduces working memory capacity. J. Pers. Soc. Psychol. **85**(3), 440–452 (2003)

27. Tversky, B., Kugelmass, S., Winter, A.: Cross-cultural and developmental trends in graphic productions. Cogn. Psychol. **23**(4), 515–557 (1991)
28. Wendt, H.W.: Dealing with a common problem in social science: a simplified rank-biserial coefficient of correlation based on the U statistic. Eur. J. Soc. Psychol. **2**(4), 463–465 (1972)

The Invisible User: Women in DUXU

Javed Anjum Sheikh[1(✉)] and Aneela Abbas[2]

[1] University of Lahore, Gujrat Campus, Gujrat, Pakistan
javed.anjum@cs.uol.edu.pk
[2] University of Gujrat, Gujrat, Pakistan
aneela.abbas@uog.edu.pk

Abstract. "Gender digital divide" is a demoralizing issue with far reaching consequences, debarring women and girls relishing equivalent approach to ICTs usage as men and boys. Numerous reasons can be marked out behindhand this discriminative technology adaptation, e.g. societal blockades, technophobia and techno incompetency. Nonetheless, ICTs have opened new horizons for women, eventually economically enabling and empowering them. This study investigates the challenges faced by women in design and proposes the strategies to bridge the gender gap to ensure an obliging technology for tech deprived women in developing countries like Pakistan.

Keywords: DUXU · User experience · Design · Usability · HCI · Women computer interaction

1 Introduction

Persisting "gender divide" resonates the discrimination between women and men, echoed in societal, political, scholarly, technical, cultural, or financial accomplishments or approaches [64, 71]. The maxim "digital divide" was coined to refer to the gap between those who had access to ICTs and those who did not [50, 58]. Likewise, "gender digital divide" [42, 50] has been recognized as the socioeconomic and other inequalities between those who have prospects and abilities to reap benefits from digital resources, and those who do not have such prospects and expertise.

The debate related to the gender differences [12] in design is old but still considered an important issue [4, 16, 17, 47, 56, 74]. An established notion denotes that men are more inclined towards ICTs than women, hence consequently they are more tech savvy [30, 53, 65]. According to [42] during 1990 s, scholars thoroughly observed that women were laggards to the digital age [1, 25, 29]. Subsequently, the new-fangled technology was prevalently rendered as the male domain. The number of women working in the game development is very low and only 12 % women in Britain are game designer whereas only 3 % are programmer [8, 45]. Science and technology (STS) theorists found that more men than women studying computer science related courses. They warn of gender divide due to underrepresentation of women in this domain [6, 39, 41, 43, 52, 72, 75, 76].

Section 2 of this paper encompasses significance of women oriented designs from products to domestic technology. Section 3 converses barriers keeping out women from

© Springer International Publishing Switzerland 2015
A. Marcus (Ed.): DUXU 2015, Part II, LNCS 9187, pp. 243–251, 2015.
DOI: 10.1007/978-3-319-20898-5_24

adopting technology. Section 4 gives some recommendations to make women more inclined towards technology. Whilst, Sect. 5 concludes the whole debate.

2 Significance of Women Centered Design

The explicit gap in ICTs usage between both genders is a consequence of socioeconomic dissimilarities and some explicit gender-specific discrepancies, resulting in lesser self-efficacy of females in ICTs usage [71]. Technology is overtly denoted as gendered [31, 61, 71]. ICTs are truthfully and unequivocally considered as yet— "A toy for the boys" [31, 33, 60]. Many prevailing technologies have innate capability to benefit women. Moreover, Women centered technology inventions can contribute for certain economic reimbursements to women in the developing countries like Pakistan [67]. Therefore, first we need to understand these differences and women approaches to the designs that are imbued with women sensitivity. In pursuit of the motive to develop women centered technology some questions should be answered earlier.

- Why females are reluctant to go for technology?
- Why women are more technophobic and feel more computer anxiety?
- What problems and issues do women encounter while interacting with ICTs?
- How women's preferences could be incorporated in technology development and design to ensure their desires are satisfied?
- What barricades (social customs etc.) have disallowed women from getting into technology solutions, and how might those barriers be addressed?
- What sort of knowhow and training women need to withstand usage of technology?
- How much feedback from women's could be helpful to develop and design women oriented technology and products.

Gender discrimination in design still sustains in this century. Women oriented designing emphasis on the designing and evaluation of interactive systems, keeping in view the preferences and gender differences of females [65, 67]. Boosting an enriched consideration and awareness that how females influence insights and interactions is crucial for the on-going research of women and DUXU. Time and again, women are asserted only as likely users of technology [34, 68, 74]. Ominously, needs of one half population are potentially being ignored in designing and manufacturing.

Women centred designing advocate's female's preferences and inclinations, as per significant differences of both genders in perception, mental model, attention and memory. Women's approaches to interact are always delicate, tactile, aesthetic, and communicative. The problem to be pondered over is *why women fear to intimate the machine?* Until lately, researchers have not absorbed enough, whether the design of problem resolving software's influence both genders inversely. Various researchers have exposed that software are designed inadvertently for males [28, 66]. Indications from other spheres, for instance, psychology and marketing, intensely put forward that females solve the problems in a distinctive way. Design of women-oriented software is assertion of women and DUXU.

Overlooking female's preferences and interaction styles in designing is an imperative issue to be addressed. Attention to gender differences is equally important in the design of computers, gadgets, videogames and software; for enhancing usability, effectiveness, satisfaction, and user experience; as both behave within their distinctive gender roles. Another imperative necessity is to ornate recommendations about gender differences to software designers; as differences on information processing, communication and problem solving applies to software design [63, 65, 66]. Females have specific skill set, preferences and inclinations for software in mathematics, programming and videogames. Female end users have significantly lower self-efficacy than males. Subsequently, females are expressively less likely to work effactually with problem-solving features available in the software. Women always look for smoothness, slimness, and compactness with an emphasis on aesthetic design.

Ever since, HCI emphasis on user-centred designs and users of video games are increasingly females, however conversely, the people designing the video games are mostly males. The content of many video games are still male-oriented. The list of best-selling video games are all mostly of masculine themes. So, it appears that the video game design industry hasn't really changed that much at all, even though their users have. Gender is very much part of the design of gaming [6]. Women in game design play vital role important role [5, 20, 35, 36, 66] and female body is axis of it, for example Girls of gaming [26, 70] which sexually appeal to young male player.

The studies [14, 19, 24, 37, 62, 69] are contributing to feminist perspectives related informal work relationship to system developers, pattern of work relations with design and development of interactive system. The research on domestic technology with respect to HCI is increasing and lead by gender norms [10, 21, 22]. Therefore designers need to consider gender aspects from its theory to evaluation [6]. However, the question is still unanswered that how to integrate them into the design field. In UI gender preference has great interest to designer but the user remain genderless therefore it is difficult to know the difference in gender has influence [53, 65, 70].

Profuse of researchers portrayed thoughtfulness towards the enablement of women through augmenting their competencies, awareness, access to and usage of ICTs [33, 66, 70]. Women focused technology innovations can contribute for actual economic paybacks to women. In a cutting-edge study, ICRW [33, 70] explored technology initiatives that have permitted women to ripe their economic prospects, becoming vigorous leaders and more effective sponsors to their societies and native economies. Specifically, these efforts helped women to increase their productivity, create new entrepreneurial ventures and launch income-generating pursuits [33, 34, 60]. Digital technologies are convenient mean for women to recoil from hoary discriminations. ICTs can support women to get employment (e.g. telework) to acquire cost-efficient health facilities and education to upsurge their earnings (e.g. e-business).

3 Barriers Debarring Women to Opt Technology

In difference with this glass-half-full viewpoint sustains an omnipresent and insistent counter justification that women are at an innate handicap [73] to reap benefit from the digital revolution as they are lesser tech savvy, and more techno anxious, and for the reason that the technology is not put up for their needs and instinct [25, 29]. Consequently, the new-fangled technology was readily rendered as a male domain. These gender-related dissimilarities were due to the reason that women undermined their inherent competencies, which resulted in inefficiency to use ICTs [71], over and above in their approaches toward computers. Henceforth consequently, men are more absorbed in technology than women and even more tech savvy [30, 40, 51].

According to World Internet Project, 2009 [34, 78] gender divide is a vigorous menace for women. According to [42] in many countries such divides have become drastic, placing women at a potential loss [38] and this divide encompasses access, frequency and intensity of ICTs usage [59]. On the lookout for reasons, women confront with obstructions that encompass dearth of access and training, and that they were coming across various devices, technologies and applications overlooking female's needs and preferences [2, 11, 57]. Consequently, customarily women have an undesirable attitude toward ICTs [23] henceforward, there is an obligatory compulsion of regulations and inducements to ensure the actual usage of technology that would advocate women inclinations [15].

HCI is concerned with culture [5, 8, 9], society [13], economic returns [31, 33, 60] and the experiential qualities of computing [54]. Many factors were discussed in the literature regarding how the gender gap was created in the technology field [3, 18, 27, 32, 44, 46, 49, 55]. Bardzell [6, 7] outlined six qualities: pluralism, participation, advocacy, ecology, embodiment, and self-disclosure to make successful design, designer needs to adopt them. HCI research found gender gap factors include stereotypes cultural background and family responsibilities [32], biasness in academic experience [3, 44, 46, 55], less appealing due to personality and attitude [18, 27, 44], lack of support and opportunities and the absence of role models due to the famine of women leadership [35, 44, 48, 49, 77].

4 Recommendations

Viable solutions for all the aforementioned issues are to design women centered designs and to overcome various barriers hindering women to adopt technology. Below are given some recommendations to pursue these motives.

- Develop and dole out technologies that satisfy women's preferences and dispositions by involving women all the way through the design and deployment practices.
- The developers, designers, manufacturers must consider women's predilections while developing, designing or manufacturing products, from conception to usage to widespread adoption in the field.
- Early involvement of focus groups can every so often benefit innovators to recognize the extensive hitches that technology can resolve and gives a way out to tailor it according to women's preferences.
- For the most operative fallouts, wherever feasible women should be dynamically leading the exertion to design and implement technologies to satisfy their needs as technology visionaries, designers, developers, brokers and counselors as well.

- Striking attention should be compensated to existing technologies that haven't been adapted or distributed to the full benefit of women.
- Innovators should make sure to consider needs, barriers, markets, training, and assessment at the earliest phases of development to ensure an obliging technology for tech deprived women.
- Stimulus' influence and attraction of females towards technological tools must be reflected. Size of displays should be accustomed according to female's inclinations as fondness of both genders varies on the size of displays, e.g. women are more convenient with larger displays.
- Inclinations of girls towards videogames are a motive for video games designers. To attract females towards games designers must encompass collaboration rather than competition, non-violence rather than deaths and destructions.
- Cognitive differences between males and females must be considered while designing. For instance, in homes many appliances are programmable to some extent, while different categories of appliances are not equally convenient for both genders. Some devices are more likely to be programmed by men (e.g. entertainment devices) while others by women (e.g. kitchen appliances).
- Preferences of females and gender differences in categorization, labelling and structuring of information must be explored.
- Women's perception about the task on the web and how they think on design and style's guide must be investigated as males and females have different perceptions for a web page to be appropriate and females prefer more content on web pages.

5   Conclusion

In nutshell, women centered design has potential to improve domestic technology by integrating feminism into interaction design research. This paper provided a theoretical grounding for women and DUXU, which stressed for bearing in mind this particular segment of population while designing an interface or developing a particular product. Furthermore, this study revealed various issues barring females to embrace technology. This research work will deliver HCI designers with a groundwork and archetypal account that how gender can influence approaches and outlooks toward interaction and usability, underscoring a sensitizing debate for women and DUXU in HCI. The results of this study are disseminated to future researchers as a yardstick that would be beneficial for escalating mock-ups for women oriented designs.

References

1. Agosto, D.: Girls and gaming: A summary of the research with implications for practice. http://tinyurl.com/mnsho5. Accessed 19 July 2009
2. Arun, S., Arun, T.: ICTs, gender and development: women in software production in Kerala. J. Int. Dev. 14(1), 39–50 (2002)

3. Bacon, C.: Mind the gap: the gender divide in technology firms. Grovelands, 10 September 2014. http://www.grovelands.co.uk/mind-the-gap-the-gender-divide-in-technology-firms/. Accessed 28 November 2014
4. Balka, E.: Gender and skill in human computer interaction. In: Conference Companion on Human Factors in Computing Systems, pp. 93–94. ACM (1996)
5. Bardzell, J.: Interaction criticism and aesthetics. In: Proceedings of the CHI 2009, pp. 2357–2366. ACM Press (2009)
6. Bardzell, S.: Feminist HCI: Taking stock and outlining an agenda for design. In: SIGCHI Conference Human Factors in Computing Systems, pp. 1301–1310 (2010)
7. Bardzell, S., Bardzell, J.: Towards a feminist HCI methodology: Social science, feminism, and HCI. In: Proceedings of the SIGCHI Conference on Human Factors in Computing Systems, CHI 2011, pp. 675–684. ACM, New York (2011)
8. Bell, G., Dourish, P.: Yesterday's tomorrows: Notes on ubiquitous computing's dominant vision. Pers. Ubiquitous Comput. (2006)
9. Bell, G., Blythe, M., Sengers, P.: Making by making strange: Defamilarization and the design of domestic technology. TOCHI 12(2), 149–173 (2005)
10. Berg, A.: A gendered socio-technical construction: The smart house. In: MacKenzie, D., Wajcman, J. (eds.) The Social Shaping of Technology, pp. 301–313. Open University Press, United Kingdom (1999)
11. Best, M.L., Maier, S.G.: Gender, culture and ICT use in rural South India. Gend. Technol. Dev. 11(2), 137–155 (2007)
12. Bimber, B.: Measuring the gender gap on the internet. Soc. Sci. Q. 81(3), 868–876 (2000)
13. Blevis, E.: Sustainable interaction design: Invention & disposal, renewal & reuse. In: Proceedings of CHI 2007, pp. 503–512. ACM Press (2007)
14. Bødker, S., Greenbaum, J.: A feeling for systems development work. In: Tijdens, K., et al (eds.) Women, Work and Computerization. North Holland (1988)
15. Boiarov, S.: Informe sobre legislación y normativa vinculada al teletrabajo en América Latina y el Caribe, United Nations ECLAC, Information Society Programme (2007). http://www.cepal.org/socinfo/noticias/noticias/2/32222/GdT_eLAC_meta_5.pdf. Accessed 2 March 2015
16. Bratteteig, T.: Bringing gender issues to technology design. In: VS Verlag für Sozialwissenschaften, pp. 91–105 (2002)
17. Burnett, M.M., Beckwith, L., Wiedenbeck, S., Fleming, S.D., Cao, J., Park, T.H., Rector, K.: Gender pluralism in problem-solving software. Interact. Comput. 23(5), 450–460 (2011)
18. Byrne, C., Cassano, J.: The Loneliness of the Female Coder. Fast Company and Inc., 11 September 2013. http://www.fastcolabs.com/3008216/tracking/minding-gap-how-your-company-can-woo-female-coders. Accessed 28 November 2014
19. Cassell, J.: Genderizing HCI. In: Jacko, J., Sears, A. (eds.) The Handbook of Human-Computer Interaction, pp. 402–411. Lawrence Erlbaum, Mahwah (2002)
20. Cassell, J., Jenkins, H.: Chess for girls: Feminism and computer game. In: Cassell, J.A., Jenkins, H. (eds.) From Barbie to Mortal Kombat: Gender and ComputerGames. The MIT Press, Cambridge, pp. 2–45, 199
21. Cockburn, C.: The circuit of technology: Gender, identity, and power. In: Silverstone, R., Hirsch, E. (eds.) Consuming Technologies: Media and Information in Domestic Spaces, pp. 32–47. Routledge, London (1992)
22. Cowan, R.: More Work for Mother: The Ironies of Household Technology from the Open Hearth to the Microwave. Basic Books, New York (1983)
23. Davis, S.: Empowering women weavers? the internet in rural morocco. Inf. Technol. Int. Dev. Spec. Issue Women's Empowerment Inf. Soc. 4(2), 17–23 (2007)

24. De Angeli, A., Bianchi-Berthouze, N.: Gender and interaction: Real and virtual women in a male world. In: AVI 2006 Workshop (2006)

25. Dholakia, R.R., Dholakia, N., Pedersen, B.: Putting a byte in the gender gap. Am. Demographics **16**(12), 20–21 (1994)

26. Dickey, M.D.: Girl gamers: the controversy of girl games and the relevance of female-oriented game design for instructional design. British J. Educ. Technol. **37**(5), 785–793 (2006)

27. Dishman, L.: Closing the gender divide: why confidence and leaning in alone won't cut it. Fast Company & Inc., 27 May 2014. http://www.fastcompany.com/3031021/bottom-line/closing-the-gender-divide-why-confidence-and-leaning-in-alone-wontcut-it. Accessed 28 November 2014

28. Duncker, E., Sheikh, J.A., Fields, B.: From global terminology to local terminology: a review on cross-cultural interface design solutions. In: Rau, P. (ed.) CCD/HCII 2013, Part I. LNCS, vol. 8023, pp. 197–207. Springer, Heidelberg (2013)

29. Duncker, E.: Cross-cultural usability of the library metaphor. Paper presented at the JCDL 2002, Portland, Oregon, pp. 223–230 (2002)

30. Fallows, D.: How Women and Men Use the Internet, Pew Internet and American Life Project (2005). http://www.pewinternet.org/Reports/2005/How-Women-and-Men-Use-the-Internet.aspx. Accessed 4 March 2015

31. Faulkner, W.: The technology question in feminism: A view from feminist technology studies. Women's Stud. Inter'l Forum **24**(1), 79–95 (2001)

32. Gervais-Bazin, V.: Fixing the gender gap in tech: sharing best practices. Alcatel-Lucent (2014). http://www.alcatel-lucent.com/blog/2014/fixing-gender-gap-tech-sharing-best-practices. Accessed 29 November 2014

33. Gerrade, S., Dickinson, J.: Women's working wardrobes: a study using card sorts. Expert Syst. **22**(3), 108–114 (2005)

34. Gill, K., Brooks, K., McDougall, J., Patel, P., Kes, A.: Bridging the gender divide: how technology can advance women economically. In: The International Centre for Research on Women (ICRW) (2010). Accessed 2 March 2015

35. Gorriz, C.M., Medina, C.: Engaging girls computers software games. Commun. ACM **43**(1), 42–49 (2000)

36. Graner-Ray, S.: Gender-Inclusive Game Design: Expanding the Market. Charles River Media, Hingham (2003)

37. Green, E., Owen, J., Pain, D.: Gendered by Design? Information Technology and Office Systems. Taylor and Francis, London (1993)

38. Hafkin, N., Huyer, S.: Women and Gender in ICT Statistics and Indicators for Development. The MIT Press, Cambridge (2008). Volume 4, Number 2, pp. 25–41 (2007)

39. Haraway, D.: A cyborg manifesto: Science, technology, and socialist feminism in the late twentieth century. In: Simians, Cyborgs, and Women: The Reinvention of Nature, pp. 149–181. Routledge, New York (1991)

40. Hartmann, T., Klimmt, C.: Gender and computer games: Exploring females' dislikes. J. Comput.- Mediated Commun. **11**(4), 910–941 (2006)

41. Herring, S.C., Ogan, C., Ahuja, M., Robinson, J.C.: Gender and the culture of computing in applied IT education. In: Trauth, E. (ed.) Encyclopedia of Gender and Information Technology. Information Science Publishing, Hershey (2006)

42. Hilbert, M.: Digital gender divide or technologically empowered women in developing countries? A typical case of lies, damned lies, and statistics. Women's Stud. Int. Forum **34**(6), 479–489 (2011)

43. Hubbard, R.: Science, facts, and feminism. In: Wyer, M., Barbercheck, M., Giesman, D., Öztürk, H., Wayne, M. (eds.) Women, Science, and Technology, pp. 153–160. Routledge, New York (2001)
44. Huhman, H.R.: STEM fields and the gender gap: where are the women? Forbes. 20 June 2012. http://www.forbes.com/sites/work-in-progress/2012/06/20/stem-fields-and-the-gender-gap-where-are-the-women/. Accessed 28 November 2014
45. Jayanth, M.: The Guradian, 18th September 2014. http://www.theguardian.com/commentisfree/2014/sep/18/52-percent-people-playing-games-women-industry-doesnt-know
46. Jenny, J.: Closing the Gender Gap. Civil Eng. (08857024) **80**(7), 60–63 (2010)
47. Kannabiran, G.: Gender and the Design of Technology - A Critical Analysis. UCLA Center for the Study of Women (2012). http://escholarship.org/uc/item/0sf3p93j
48. Kim, Q.: Why aren't more women on tech boards? Marketplace, 26 December 2013. http://www.marketplace.org/topics/tech/twitter-fallout-why-arent-more-women-tech-boards. Accessed 29 November 2014
49. Kopytoff, V.: Tech companies on edge of innovation continue to leave women behind. Aljazeera America, 24 December 2013. http://america.aljazeera.com/articles/2013/12/24/tech-companies-onedgeofinnovationcontinuetoleavewomenbehind.html. Accessed 29 November 2014
50. Liebert, M.A.: Race, gender, and information technology use: the new digital divide. Cyber Psychol. Behav. **11**(4), 437–442 (2008)
51. Lohan, M., Faulknet, W.: Masculinities and technologies: some introductory remarks. Men Masculinities **6**(4), 319–329 (2004)
52. Longino, H.: Can there be a feminist science? In: Wyer, M., Barbercheck, M., Giesman, D., Öztürk, H., Wayne, M. (eds.) Women, Science, and Technology, pp. 216–222. Routledge, New York (2001)
53. Marcus, A.: Human communications issues in advanced UIs. Commun. ACM **36**(3), 101–108 (1993)
54. McCarthy, J., Wright, P.: Technology as Experience. The MIT Press, Cambridge (2004)
55. Mindiola, J.: Gender Disparities in the Design Field. Smashing Magazine, 12 November 2010. http://www.smashingmagazine.com/2010/11/12/gender-disparities-in-the-design-field/. Accessed 29 November 2014
56. Moss, G., Colman, A.M.: Choices and preferences: experiments on gender differences. J. Brand Manage. **9**(2), 89–98 (2001)
57. Ng, C., Mitter, M.S.: Gender and the Digital Economy: Perspectives from the Developing World. SAGE Publications, London (2005)
58. Norris, P.: Digital Divide: Civic Engagement, Information, Poverty, and the Internet Worldwide. Cambridge University Press, New York (2006)
59. Park, S.: Concentration of internet usage and its relation to exposure to negative content: Does the gender gap differ among adults and adolescents? Women's Stud. Int. Forum **32**(2), 98–107 (2009)
60. Parmar, B.: The Technological Gender Divide. http://www.huffingtonpost.com/belinda-parmar/tech-genderdivide_b_924314.html. Accessed 2 March 2015
61. Puente, S.N.: From cyber feminism to techno feminism: From an essentialist perspective to social cyber feminism in certain feminist practices in Spain. Women's Stud. Int. Forum **31**(6), 434–440 (2008)
62. Rode, J., Bødker, S.: Considering gender in ECSCW. In: ECSCW 2009 Workshop 2009 (2009)
63. Sheikh, J.A., Fields, B., Duncker, E.: Cultural based e-Health information system. Presentation at the Health Libraries Group Conference 2010, July 19-20. CILIP, Salford Quays (2010)

64. Sheikh, J.A., Fields, B., Duncker, E.: Cultural representation by Card Sorting. Ergonomics for All: Celebrating PPCOE's 20 years of Excellence. Selected Papers of the Pan-Pacific Conference on Ergonomics, Kaohsiung, Taiwan, November 7–10, 2010, pp. 215–220. CRC Press (2011)

65. Sheikh, J.A., Fields, B., Duncker, E.: Cultural Representation for Interactive Information system. In: Proceedings of the 2009 International Conference on the Current Trends in Information Technology, Dubai (2009)

66. Sheikh, J.A., Fields, B., Duncker, E.: Cultural representation for multi-culture interaction design. In: Aykin, N. (ed.) IDGD 2009. LNCS, vol. 5623, pp. 99–107. Springer, Heidelberg (2009)

67. Sheikh, J.A., Fields, B., Duncker, E.: Multi-Culture interaction design. advances in cross-cultural decision making, pp. 406–415. CRC Press (2010)

68. Sheikh, J.A., Fields, B., Duncker, E.: The cultural integration of knowledge management into interactive design. In: Smith, M.J., Salvendy, G. (eds.) HCII 2011, Part I. LNCS, vol. 6771, pp. 48–57. Springer, Heidelberg (2011)

69. Taylor, A., Swan, L.: Artful systems in the home. In: Proceedings of CHI 2005, pp. 641–650 (2005)

70. Teasley, B., Leventhal, L., Blumenthal, B., Instone, K., Daryl, S.: Cultural diversity in user interface design: Are intuitions enough? SIGCHI Bull. 26(1), 36–40 (1994)

71. The Global Gender Gap Report 2014. http://www.weforum.org/reports/global-gender-gap-report-2014. Accessed 4 March 2015

72. Turkle, S.: Computational reticence: Why women fear the intimate machine. In: Kramarae, C. (ed.) Technology and Women's Voices, pp. 41–61 (1988)

73. Varank, I.: Effectiveness of quantitative skills, qualitative skills, and gender in determining computer skills and attitudes: a causal analysis. Clearing House 81(2), 71–80 (2007)

74. Venkatesh, V., Morris, M.G.: Why don't men ever stop to ask for directions? gender, social influence, and their role in technology acceptance and usage behavior. MIS Q. 24(1), 115–139 (2000)

75. Von Hellens, A.L., Nielsen, S., Kaylene, C., Beekhuyze, J.: Conceptualizing gender and IT: Australians taking action in Germany (2005)

76. Wajcman, J.: Feminism Confronts Technology. Penn State University Press, University Park, PA (1991)

77. Whitney, T.: Why tech's gender gap isn't just a pay gap. FORTUNE, 24 November 2014. http://fortune.com/2014/11/24/why-techs-gender-gap-isnt-just-a-pay-gap/. Accessed 28 November 2014

78. World Internet international Report 2009, USC Annenberg School Center for the Digital Future. http://store.digitalcenter.org/world-internet-report.html. Accessed 18 August 2009

The Creative Process in Digital Design: Towards an Understanding of Women's Approach

Virginia Tiradentes Souto[✉], Paula C.L.A. Faria,
and Fátima Aparecida dos Santos

Department of Design, University of Brasilia, Brasilia, Brazil
{v.tiradentes,paula.lopes}@gmail.com,
designfatima@uol.com.br

Abstract. The debate about the differences between men and women is quite old but still topical. Many researchers have been investigating the differences in users' gender while experiencing digital products. However, it seems that few studies have investigated gender differences related to the creative process in digital design. The aim of this paper is to try to understand whether there are gender differences in the creative process in digital design in Brazil. In addition, it discusses the possible influences that women have in the design process and their approach to user experience design. For that, interviews and questionnaires with Brazilian designers, both women and men, were carried out. This investigation points out some gender aspects that can make difference in the design of digital products and presents a discussion of the role of women designers.

Keywords: Gender · Women · Digital design · Creative process

1 Introduction

The debate about the differences between men and women is quite old but still topical. As recently as last year an advertisement explored the expression "like a girl" used to mean something bad and has shown how this phrase can impact on a girl's self-confidence. This ad has been seen more than 55 million times on You Tube, which shows the interest people feel in this subject [1].

Particularly in design, this debate is also old. As far back as 1986, Buckley [2] analysed women and design. She argues that although women have been involved in a variety of ways with design, their interventions are omitted in the literature of design history. She explains that the marginalization of women is a consequence of specific methods that are biased against women and serve to exclude them from history. She also argues that the few women designers that appear in the literature are accounted for within the framework of patriarchy, in which men's activities are valued more highly than women's. In this framework, women are defined by "their gender as designers or users of feminine products or they are subsumed under the name of their husband, lover, father, or brother." She claims that women's role in design must be discussed both in relation to patriarchy and gender issues.

© Springer International Publishing Switzerland 2015
A. Marcus (Ed.): DUXU 2015, Part II, LNCS 9187, pp. 252–263, 2015.
DOI: 10.1007/978-3-319-20898-5_25

Even in HCI the gender debate is not new [3, 4]. According to Kannabiran [5], this topic has been investigated with different approaches such as domestic technology, product design, virtual online environments, and software engineering. Many researchers claim that gender difference in design is an important issue [6–8]. Despite this, it seems that gender is not explicitly considered in interactive design [9], as this topic tends to be seen as niched and peripheral [5].

The aim of this paper is to try to understand whether there are gender differences in the creative process in digital design in Brazil. In addition, it discusses the possible influences that women have in the design process and their approach to user experience design. For that, interviews and questionnaires with Brazilian designers, both women and men, were carried out. This investigation points out some gender aspects that can make a difference in the design of digital products and presents a discussion on the role of women designers.

2 Gender Differences

There has been a lot of theoretical, political, conceptual and cognitive discussion on gender, since the eighteenth century, with intensity in the twentieth century and continuing today. It is not part of this study to review the literature related to gender; instead, the intention here is just to highlight some aspects and discussions on the topic in order to help with the discussion on women in DUXU.

It is important to highlight that the differences between male and female can be divided into the differences that relate to sex and to gender [6]. While sex is usually associated with biological differences (e.g. anatomy), gender is associated with behavior, social and cultural differences (e.g. the use of pink for girls and blue for boys).

Daniel Stern [10] suggests that there is a difference in movement between boys and girls at birth. While girls need to expand their movements in order to reach the objects, boys need to control their movements, as they open their arms more and move more awkwardly than girls. Studies show that girls usually learn how to walk and talk faster than boys. These sex differences are observed in the first years of school, when girls usually learn faster than boys.

In the book "How the mind works", Steven Pinker [11] approaches the differences between men and women from a cognitive point of view. Pinker rejects the thesis that biological definitions may be responsible for the differences between genders. Being a girl or boy ensures different treatment and education throughout life. According to Pinker, this difference, more than the biological and cognitive conditions, explains the behavior of each gender within society.

Nowadays, in Brazil, women stay at school for a longer time than men and also have more undergraduate degrees than men [12]. Despite this, there are fewer women than men in the labor market [12], and most top Brazilian scientists are men [13]. In addition, Brazilian women earn about 25 % less than men [14]. Unfortunately, this is also true beyond Brazil. A recent and major report on gender equality around the world, by the World Economic Forum, showed that Denmark is the only country among 142 analyzed where, on average, women earn more than men [14]. This report also shows that Denmark is the country in which men spend the highest average time per day on unpaid work. This may indicate that when men and women share unpaid work, which is usually domestic work and looking after children, both have opportunities to have a high professional position.

Apart from the fact that women usually do more unpaid work than men and therefore can dedicate less time to their professional job, there are other reasons for the low percentage of women in leadership positions. Another reason may be differences caused by educational gender differences. In the design field, an example of the difference in gender can be illustrated by the Bauhaus pioneering school of design. Since the beginning, the school had women lectures and students, but women were teaching what were considered female subjects such as weaving and standardization, whereas typographic construction, furniture design and construction of objects were taught by men [15].

In the IT field, technology is considered one of the most powerful symbols of masculinity and it has been claimed that "technological competence has become an important aspect of hegemonic masculinity" [16]. Researchers in IT claim that differences in gender in IT professionals are related to the number of situations to which women are subjected throughout life. According to Natansohn [17], from childhood boys are praised when they dismantle their games, models and robots, being acclaimed as 'engineers', whereas girls do not receive the same feedback if they dismantle their dolls.

Although gender differences in experience design is considered an important topic by many researchers and there are some investigations on this topic, it seems that there still needs to be more research in order to understand the differences between males and females and to help designers create products that serve both genders. Some studies on user experience design and gender differences are discussed below.

3 Digital Design and Gender Differences

Studies on gender and experience design have indicated different aspects that can explain the differences between male and female designers. Some of these studies are summarized below in order to figure out possible gender differences that can interfere in the design development process and the final design solution.

Beyer et al. [18] investigated different variables that could explain the low number of females studying computer science in comparison to males in the US. Beyer et al. [18] did not find significant differences in gender in relation to quantitative ability, interest in computer science, stereotypes and knowledge of computer science. However, they did find a difference between male and female students in relation to their confidence on the subject. Male students were much more confident than female students. They explain that one of the causes of low female confidence is that they have a less relaxed and playful attitude towards computers. Another reason is the fact that they had less programming experience than males before going to university. The authors claim that women's low confidence can affect performance. This is because "positive self-perceptions of ability are intimately tied to aspirations, educational choices, preference for challenging tasks, intrinsic motivation, and persistence".

Like Beyner et al., Burnett et al. [8] also investigated self-confidence in gender, among other aspects. Burnett et al. investigated gender pluralism in problem-solving software. By pluralism, they used the definition proposed by Bardzell [19], as "the quality of designing artifacts that resist any single, totalizing, or universal point of view". According to them pluralism implies that more inclusive designs through sensitivity to marginal users can be produced. They found gender differences in feature usage, in tinkering, and in how confidence works with male and female. They also found that the gender differences did not suggest that males are better software users than females. They conclude that is important to consider gender differences when designing problem-solving software, and that doing this can help both genders.

Also observing designers during the development process, Oudshoorn et al. [16] made an investigation on two virtual cities. They analyzed the design phase of technology and the designer's gender differences during the development of two electronic virtual cities in the private and the public sector, both in the Netherlands. They observed that the designers of both teams took their own preferences instead of assessing the interests and competencies of users. They explain this by the fact that most of the team was male and therefore a masculine design style was adopted. They argue that it seems likely that female designers can make a difference considering that there is a strong alignment between hegemonic masculinity and specific technological values. They concluded that the identities of designers are important in understanding the dynamics of technological development.

With a different approach to the studies described above, Okudan [20] conducted a study in order to investigate task domain gender orientation of a design task. Engineering students in the US were asked to answer four questions after completing a design project. Two different tasks were measured: rocket propelled grenade (RPG) countermeasure design and air velocity controller design. He found that these tasks were perceived differently by the participants. While RPG countermeasure design was perceived to have masculine overtones, the other was mostly seen to be gender neutral. He concluded, among other things, that the gender orientation of tasks can vary considerably from males and females. In addition, he argues that one of the reasons why female engineering students feeling undervalued by their male peers is related to the project domain gender orientation.

A more recent study also investigated the differences between male and female novice designers. Ng et al. [21] investigated the practices and attitudes of novice designers toward the stereotype production method for public symbol design. Forty-eight Hong Kong Chinese novice designers participated in this study. Half of them were male and half female. They found that the number of ideas generated varied in relation to the user suggestions incorporated into symbol design. Male designers were less positive than female designers toward user suggestions. For male designers the results showed a negative correlation between the acceptance of a given pictorial representation in the design and the number of design ideas for symbol representation. On the other hand, this correlation was not found for female designers. Female designers rated the attribute 'valuable for designing process' of user suggestions for symbol design significantly higher than the male participants. Based on this result, the author recommended that attention must be given to male novice designers that are less positive toward user needs and preferences. This finding is in agreement with Oudshoorn et al. [16], which also argues that female designers are more sensitive to the needs of users.

Finally, it is relevant to consider the findings of the studies done by Schroeder et al. [22] on gender and technology. Through an analysis of the literature about gender related to technology use and perception they found that females have a sense-making through coherence, whereas males focus on individual needs and a detailed approach which means that their approach is about technology being meaningful in itself. They concluded that "there is a male gender bias in many tech-products".

The literature review on gender differences, and more specifically gender differences in digital design, was the basis for building a survey that is described below.

4 Study on Gender Differences with Brazilian Designers

4.1 Method

The chosen methods for this study were semi-structured interviews and an online questionnaire. As the study aimed get the view of designers from different parts of Brazil, most of the answers were collected through the online questionnaire. The questionnaire was created, sent and analyzed using Google Forms tool [23]. The survey was available online from December 2014 to the beginning of February 2015. The participants were invited to collaborate with the research by email and Social Media design groups in Brazil. The questionnaire was applied in Portuguese and some questions and answers have been translated in this paper in order to illustrate the findings.

The online questionnaire contained 29 questions, with a combination of response format types: there were 20 structured and 7 unstructured questions. The unstructured response format was used in order to gain more understanding about the respondent's feelings, experiences and perceptions. This type of question is important as they provide participants with a chance to answer the questions in their own words [24].

Sample of structured questions were:

Have you ever been in the position of boss in a design team?

- No, I have never occupied the position of boss.
- Yes, I have, but not for long.
- Yes, I have, for more than three years.

Samples of unstructured questions were:

- Explain your creation process. Do you divide the process into stages? How many stages and which ones?
- Do you believe that there are differences between genders in the creation process of digital products? Please explain.

Apart from the questions related to the topic investigated, there were also questions about the participants' personal and professional information, like gender, age, place of work, educational background, and their experience in the workforce as designers. These questions were important in order to understand the participants' answers and opinions better.

4.2 Participants

Forty participants took part of this study, half male and half female. They were from the five regions of Brazil, and from 10 different Brazilian states.

Participants defined their profession as: designers, graphic designers, editorial designers, web designers, interaction designers, interface designers, user experience designers, product designers, industrial designers, information architects, design thinkers, design teachers and design researchers. Both genders had approximately the same academic background, varying from non-graduates to those with a doctorate.

Most of the participants were aged between 21 and 40. Fifty percent of the female designers had been working in the field for more than 10 years, while 75 % of the male designers had been working for more than 10 years. According to the answers, more women than men research design for more than 10 years. Only 15 % of men said that they had researched design for more than 10 years whereas 40 % of women said they had researched design for more than 10 years.

4.3 Results and Discussion

The first questions were about being in leadership positions in the workforce. Sixty-five percent of women said that had been bosses in their offices, with 35 % for more than 3 years, while 80 % of men said that had been bosses, with 60 % of them for more than 3 years. This finding confirms studies that found that men have more leadership positions than women [12].

Most of the participants said they do not have gender preferences related to their bosses at work. Looking at the data by gender, the males and females that preferred a specific gender for bosses differ in the gender chosen. Half of the males that chose a gender said they preferred females and the other males. On the other hand, most of the female that chose a gender preferred to work with males. The reasons for that were not questioned in this study. One of the reasons may be because they are used to it, or another reason is that they prefer to deal with the opposite sex. As mentioned by a participant: "As a designer lecturer I have always liked men monitors to complement my vision of the work. Women monitors always had a similar vision to mine."

When asked about gender presence in their workplace, about half said that their environment had about the same number of men and women designers, 35 % answered they worked in a predominantly male workplace and only 12 % answered they had a predominantly female workplace (Fig. 1). This is also in agreement with the findings that there are more men than women formally working in Brazil.

258   V.T. Souto et al.

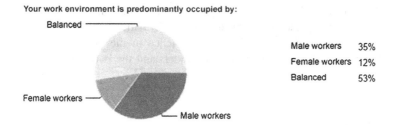

Fig. 1. Gender presence in the workplace

Most of participants thought that gender did not help them to achieve a professional goal. However, more men agreed with this greater (30 %) than women (20 %). In addition more women think their gender had been a problem in achieving something or presenting an idea (30 %), whereas only 20 % of men agree with that. The answers show a small difference, pointing out that being a woman could be slightly harder in the field when trying to present ideas. This finding is in agreement with the belief that women are thought to be more careful in expressing their opinions than men.

When asked about the presence of male designers in the market, 92 % of the participants answered that the market was well represented with male representatives and only 8 % believed there could be more men. In relation to the presence of female designers in the market, 62 % of the participants answered that the market was well represented with female representatives, while 38 % believed there could be more women (Fig. 2). Therefore, more participants had the impression that more women are needed in the market than men.

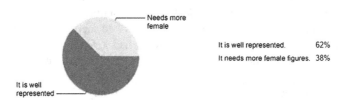

Fig. 2. Presence in the market

In relation to the creative process, both men and women answered in a very similar way. Half of them believe that there is no difference in the creative process between genders. Some of them argue that the difference is only about personal experiences, but not about gender. As a male participant said:

"I do not believe much in [gender] differences. I have worked with both genders for many years and I think what makes a difference is the knowledge in the area and the involvement with the project."

The other half was divided: 25 % thought there was a difference and 25 % said they could not tell if there was a difference. A sample answer from a male participant that believes that there is a different in creative process by gender:

"Yes. Males and females understand what reaches the public in different ways."

In relation to the final solution of digital products most of the participants (60 %) believed that there is no difference related to gender of the designers. They explain that the differences are individual and not caused by gender differences. As a female participant explained:

"I think that gender is not the main factor influencing the product, it is a detail. The final result will depend on the profile (training, personality, skills) of the professionals involved."

On the other hand, some participants argue that creative teams should have an equal number of women and men to guarantee the quality of the product. This phrase by a male participant illustrates this idea:

"I believe that the results tend to be more complete if projects are designed by collaborative teams made up of both sexes, as well as ages, disciplines, specialties, desires and needs. I believe in collaborative intelligence that brings multiple views on the issue to be solved by design."

Some participants also mentioned a relationship between the gender of the product designer and that of the product user.

"Perhaps because of the influence of cultural and personal aspects, for example: a product that deals with a subject that men normally do not care about or that would be primarily used by women could be more complicated for a design group with men only."

When discussed their own creative process, around 60 % of both men and women believed that their ideas were balanced between rational and emotional. Twenty-five percent of the female participants considered their ideas to be more emotional, while 30 % of the males considered their ideas to be more rational. All women and most men said that they preferred to work in groups without gender distinction. However, 15 % of male designers preferred to work with male designers in a team. None said that they preferred to work in a group with only women. Although this difference seems not to be representative, it is important to consider that no one preferred to work only with women. It may be reasonable to think that women may not show so much confidence in this subject as men.

In relation to code programming skills, 85 % of the male participants said they have knowledge on the subject, whereas the percentage of women that have knowledge in programming was 60 %. In addition, more male participants declared having a lot of knowledge in programming (25 %) and only one female participant said she has a lot of knowledge in programming. This also confirms the studies that indicate there are fewer women than men studying programming.

Half of the participants thought that their creative process is organized and documented whereas the other half thought it was chaotic and sketched. It is interesting to observe that men and women have roughly the same perception of the organization of their creative process. It was thought that women would be more organized and methodical, but this was not confirmed in this survey.

Also with regard to the creative process almost all women (95 %) said that they do research with users during the design process, whereas 75 % of men made the same claim. This finding is in agreement with the studies of Ng et al. [21] that found that men consider users' opinion less important than women. In relation to deadlines all women said they met deadlines, whereas 85 % of men said the same.

Participants were also asked to mention three important factors in the design of a good digital product. The three main factors in the design of a good digital product for women were: users' needs, project aims and technological aspect. For men the three factors were: usability, innovation and the use of proper tools for product development. Figures 3 and 4 show text clouds with the most common words mentioned by men and women respectively. These clouds were made using the Wordle tool [25].

Fig. 3. Text cloud with the three factors for a good product according to men's opinion: 120 words, made using the Wordle tool [25].

Finally, in relation to designers' methodology, the participants said they divide their methodology into stages, according to the project particularities. They all mentioned brainstorming sections. Women spoke more about prototyping and testing, whereas men talked more about sketching and the visual aspects of the interface. The majority of men mentioned using a personalized methodology, 35 % preferred to use agile methods like Lean UX and Scrum, and only 5 % said they do not use any methodology. In contrast, 40 % of women mentioned using personalized methodology, only 10 %

Fig. 4. Text cloud with the three factors for a good product according to women's opinion: 147 words, made using the Wordle tool [25].

preferred to use agile methods, and 30 % of women mentioned not following any methodology. In order to create innovative projects, both men and women mentioned that they use references from books, or specialized websites, sketches and interviews with users. It is interesting to observe that women follow fewer methodologies than men. This may be related to the fact that males tend to have a more detail-driven approach than women and this reflects on the use of methodologies.

5   Conclusions and Final Remarks

Although the findings point out some interesting differences between men and women in designing a digital project, on average, the differences were small and seem not to be significant. The questionnaire that was used in the study contained many questions and we received a lot of interesting responses, as discussed above. It is possible to divide these findings into two main parts. One is related to the creative process: how they work, methodology use, preferences; and the other is related to both what the participants think and how they feel about gender differences.

In relation to the creative process, findings show that both men and women have about the same perception regarding the organization of their creative process: women mentioned more prototyping and testing, whereas men mentioned more sketching and the visual aspects of the interface; both men and women mentioned using references from books, or specialized websites, sketches and interviews with users; more women than men do research with users during the design process; women follow fewer methodologies than men; and the three main design factors for men were: usability, innovation and the use of proper tools for product development, whereas for the female these were: user's needs, project aims and technological aspect.

The findings related to the participants' opinion on gender differences show that some women prefer to work with men, whereas no men showed a preference for gender when working in groups; more women than men think their gender had been a problem in achieving something or presenting an idea; most of the participants did not have gender preferences related to their bosses at work; more participants had the impression that more women are needed in the market than men; half of women believe that there is no difference in the creative process between genders; most of the participants believed that there is no gender difference in relation to the final solution of digital products.

Finally, if on the one hand findings in general indicate that most Brazilian designer participants think that differences between men and women in designing do not affect the final solution of digital products, on the other hand half of them thought that there is a difference in the creative process between gender. In addition, the perception of some designers that it is good to have both genders within a design project indicates a need for equilibrium of genders in the creative process of digital design. This idea is in line with Oudshoorn et al. [16]. They claim that adjustment of gender identities is important for technological innovation. It is also relevant to consider that creative individuals, in general, have cross-gender traits beyond the traits of gender [26]. According to Csikszentmihalyi [26], studies show that creative women, such as artists and scientists, tended to be much more assertive, self-confident, and openly aggressive than average women, whereas creative men appear to be more sensitive than average men. Male and female characteristics and approaches when combined may be helpful to show a bigger picture of the project, and therefore can lead to more creative and innovative projects.

References

1. Like a girl campain (2014). http://www.always.com/en-us/likeagirl.aspx
2. Buckley, C.: Made in patriarchy: towards a feminist analysis of women and design. In: Design Issues, vol. 3, no. 2 (Autumn), pp. 3–14. The MIT Press, Cambridge 1986 (2012)
3. Balka, E.: Gender and skill in human computer interaction. In: Conference Companion on Human Factors in Computing Systems, pp. 93–94. ACM (1996)
4. Venkatesh, V., Morris, M.G.: Why don't men ever stop to ask for directions? Gend. Soc. Influ. Role Technol. Accept. Usage Behav. MIS Q. **24**(1), 115–139 (2000)
5. Kannabiran, G.: Gender and the design of technology - a critical analysis. UCLA center for the study of women (2012). http://escholarship.org/uc/item/0sf3p93j
6. Moss, G., Colman, A.M.: Choices and preferences: experiments on gender differences. J. Brand Manag. **9**(2), 89–98 (2001)
7. Bratteteig, T.: Bringing gender issues to technology design. In: VS Verlag für Sozialwissenschaften, pp. 91–105 (2002)
8. Burnett, M.M., Beckwith, L., Wiedenbeck, S., Fleming, S.D., Cao, J., Park, T.H., Rector, K.: Gender pluralism in problem-solving software. Interact. Comput. **23**(5), 450–460 (2011)
9. Dray, S.M., Busse, D.K., Brock, A.M., Peters, A.N., Bardzell, S., Druin, A., Murray, D.: Perspectives on gender and product design. In: CHI 2014 Extended Abstracts on Human Factors in Computing Systems, pp. 53–56. ACM (2014)
10. Stern, D.: El Mundo Interpersonal Del Infante. Paidós, Barcelona (1994)
11. Pinker, S.: Como a Mente Funciona. Cia das Letras, São Paulo (1997)
12. IBGE. Pesquisa Nacional por Amostra de Domicílios Contínua 4° trimestre de 2014 (2014) http://www.ibge.gov.br/home/estatistica/pesquisas/pesquisas.php

13. CNPq. Jovens Pesquisadoras: Ciência Também é Coisa de Mulher! (2014). http://www.cnpq.br/web/guest/noticias/popularizacao/journal_content/56_INSTANCE_a6MO/10157/1766926
14. World economic forum. The global gender gap report (2014). http://www3.weforum.org/docs/GGGR14/GGGR_CompleteReport_2014.pdf
15. Lupton, E., Miller, J.A.: ABC da Bauhaus. Cosac Naify, São Paulo (2008)
16. Oudshoorn, N., Rommes, E., Stienstra, M.: Configuring the user as everybody: gender and design cultures in information and communication technologies. Sci. Technol. Hum. Values 29(1), 30–63 (2004)
17. Natansohn, G.: Qué têm a ver as tecnologías digitais com o gênero? In: Natansohn, G. (ed.) (Org.), Internet em Código Feminino. Teorias e práticas. E-book, vol. 1, 1st edn. La Crujía, Buenos Aires (2013). http://gigaufba.net/internet-em-codigo-feminino/
18. Beyer, S., Rynes, K., Perrault, J., Hay, K., Haller, S.: Gender differences in computer science students. In: ACM SIGCSE Bulletin, vol. 35, no. 1, pp. 49–53. ACM (2003)
19. Bardzell, S.: Feminist HCI: taking stock and outlining an agenda for design. In: Proceedings of the SIGCHI Conference on Human Factors in Computing Systems, pp. 1301–1310. ACM (2010)
20. Okudan, G.E., Mohammed, S.: Task gender orientation perceptions by novice designers: implications for engineering design research, teaching and practice. Design Stud. 27(6), 723–740 (2006)
21. Ng, A.W., Siu, K.W.M., Chan, C.C.: Perspectives toward the stereotype production method for public symbol design: a case study of novice designers. Appl. Ergon. 44(1), 65–72 (2013)
22. Schroeder, K.: Gender dimensions of product design. In: Gender, Science, and Technology Expert Group Meeting of the United Nations Division for the Advancement of Women (UN-DAW), vol. 28 (2010)
23. Google. Google forms. http://www.google.com/forms/about/
24. Mack, N., Woodsong, C., MacQueen, K.M., Guest, G., Namey, E.: Qualitative research methods: a data collectors field guide (2005). http://www.ccs.neu.edu/course/is4800sp12/resources/qualmethods.pdf
25. Feinberg, J.: Wordle. http://www.wordle.net
26. Csikszentmihalyi, M.: Creativity: the psychology of discovery and invention. Harper Perennial; Reprint edition (2013)

Information Design

Infographics and Communicating Complex Information

Michael J. Albers$^{(\boxtimes)}$

East Carolina University, Greenville, UK
albersm@ecu.edu

Abstract. With the growing use of infographics to communicate complex information, we must specifically look at how people read and understand them. Complex information depends on helping people build relationships and connect the information to the current situation. Infographics are not art displays, but are tools to communicate information. Unless we understand how people comprehend information and how those mental transformations occur when they read the content, we cannot effectively design an infographic for complex information. People come to an infographic for a purpose and with a goal, both of which require the infographics to communication complex information. A good infographic must maintain the complexity of the information while lowering the barriers to its comprehension.

Keywords: Complex information · Infographics · Communication

1 Introduction

Infographics provide a means of using graphic design to visualize content that has long existed in other forms. One of their advantages is that complex information can often be better communicated with a visual-heavy combination of text and visuals than with text, perhaps supported by a few visuals. While not appropriate or useful for all types of content, infographics provide context by using visuals to show relationships in data, anatomy, hierarchy, chronology, and geography. Communicating relationships are at the heart of communicating complex information [1] and infographics excel at communicating that aspect. Increasingly, even high content websites are designing layouts that incorporate infographics as a fundamental method of communicating information.

The loose definition of infographic used here is: *An infographic is a web-based image that takes a large amount of information in text or numerical form and condenses it into a combination of images and text with a goal of making the information presentable and digestible to an audience* [4].

Missing from much of the infographic discussion are good guidelines on how to craft the content into an integrated visual, with text and graphics supporting each other. With the growing use of infographics to communicate complex information, we must specifically look at how people read and understand them. We need to explore the connections between communicating complex information and designing highly-visual representations of that information.

© Springer International Publishing Switzerland 2015
A. Marcus (Ed.): DUXU 2015, Part II, LNCS 9187, pp. 267–276, 2015.
DOI: 10.1007/978-3-319-20898-5_26

Prior research has looked at design of complex information in both online and print. This paper strives to merge these two research threads to help develop a clearer understanding of when and how to develop infographics. It will examine:

- Different levels of comprehension of infographics
- Tease out factors that impact comprehension
- Relate the factors to existing design guidelines and consider possible changes

1.1   Categories of Infographics

The author's prior research [4] found infographics can be divided into four categories: bullet list equivalent, snapshot with graphic needs, flat information with graphic needs, and information flow/process (Fig. 1). Of these four categories, only the last two (and, primarily, the last) are applicable to complex information presentation.

The first two categories, and especially the first one, typically fail to have any clearly defined audience. Instead, the audience could be considered "anyone interested in xxx." An audience definition such as this is much too vague to be useful for a designer and could be better seen as a rationalization for the audience for a work created without any specific audience at all. Both fail to support communicating complex information and will not be considered further in this paper.

1.2   Complex Information Cannot be Reshaped as Simple Information

The information to be communicated by a high-quality infographic qualifies as complex information, but typical infographic design reshapes it into simple information [1]. A common example is essentially all of the "Six points for..." articles and infographics. That transformation removes the information relationships and divides up the content, and, as a result, by removing relationships, seriously limits the comprehension a person can gain of the overall situation [2, 3].

Infographics as they're typically produced reduce problems to statistics—numbers and percentages that can't possibly capture the profound impact on the real world. The relationships between the numbers go away and only the numbers, as single factoids, remain. It is easy to create a diagram for factoid numbers and statistics; connecting those factoids into a complex relationship web is difficult. The transformation to a simple problem often results from an over-focus on visual presentation. Numbers are very visual, but the relationships are more than arrows between numbers; they require text and *context*. Infographics that privilege the graphical aspects—a view that could be summed up as "it's visual, it's graphical, and therefore it is better"—fail because they didn't focus on communicating information.

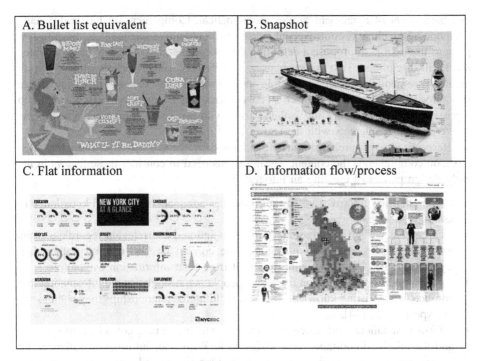

Fig. 1. Four categories of infographics. A. Bullet list. The entire infographic is just a list with graphical elements added. B. Snapshot. Content that lacks a sequence for reading, is static, and typically does not need to be compared. C. Flat information with graphic needs. Content that lacks a reading sequence, but supports comparing relationships and different data. D. Content that shows some sort of flow or process and has a defined reading sequence.

2   Information Comprehension Research

Many designers seem to assume if they place content before a reader, the reader will figure it out and gain the required knowledge. An end result of this over-privileging of visuals is a decrease in the comprehension of the information; an exactly opposite effect of why the infographic was created in the first place. Sound research, interesting information, and insightful analysis make great content. The format is far less relevant. The design team's first question should never be "how do we make an infographics?" but should be "what is the best presentation/format to communicate this content?"

A design team's ability to judge how well people will comprehend the material varies, but it's the comprehension level that matters for complex information. Once the design requirements move past "look pretty," how well people comprehend the information and their ability to pull the most salient points from the design becomes paramount.

The research literature supports that comprehension consists of the construction of multi-level representations of texts ("texts" is used here in a highly generic sense that includes infographics, web pages, etc. and not just printed documents). Moving beyond that basic level of agreement proves problematical. Comprehension has traditionally been one of the elusive, controversial constructs in cognitive science [i.e., 19, 32]. It is perhaps impossible to propose a definition that is complete and that would be accepted across all disciplines. Text comprehension can be considered reading while trying to maintain semantic coherence—"fitting new information into existing knowledge structures" [24, p. 840, 33]. Kintsch's [19] construction-integration model has replaced a passive process of collecting isolated facts with an active comprehension process where the reader interacts with the text to build meaning.

Research into comprehension has found a wide range of issues that affect how well a person comprehends the content. Design teams need to consider these factors in the early design phases of creating an infographic.

- Comprehension improves when the reader has adequate background knowledge to assimilate the text.
- Any content written in unfamiliar terms gets ignored as irrelevant regardless of its importance. If people can't understand the content on first reading, rather than trying to figure it out, they simply drop it from their information evaluation.
- As the amount of information increases, people increasingly ignore information that conflicts with existing knowledge or with building the relationships they want to see or expect to see [14].
- Information salience influences the order in which a person considers information and the relative importance they assign to it. With poor information salience, the reader can easily ignore important text. One-size-fits-all solutions or designs without a clear audience tend to have very poor information salience.
- Information a person does not see, whether in a different document or scrolled off the screen, receives reduced salience compared to the currently viewed information.
- People process information based on the presentation. Side-by-side comparisons yield different results than sequential comparisons [16]. This result, along with information salience issues, strongly affects comprehension when the infographic requires scrolling.
- When people read a text, they try to form the most globally coherent mental representation possible [15] unless the text is very poorly composed, which causes them to quit trying to make connections.
- People attempt to mentally shape a text into a globally coherent whole. If the text lacks sufficient cues, they will settle for local coherence. When this happens, people end up seeing the text as a collection of disconnected statements.

3 Graphical Research for Information Comprehension

Graphics in technical material rarely exist without text and an integrated presentation does improve comprehension [6]. However, there is a poor understanding of how graphics actually work cognitively and the area is rife with un-researched assumptions and fallacies [27]. Assumptions and fallacies that seem to appear on every how-to list for infographic design.

People need to evaluate and synthesize the infographic. Complex information is more than a collection of factoids, but is a collection of relationships that must be connected to a real-world situation. The information salience influences how people perceive graphics and associate information.

- By their nature, infographics tend to be visually noisy. Since visual complexity could distract viewers from the intended message, they may be defeating their intended purpose [18].
- People think they use more information than they actually do when evaluating the content.
- Salience factors must be considered because people tend to underestimate the weight placed on important cues and overestimate weight placed on unimportant cues [5]. Overly prominent, but of lesser importance, graphical information can skew people's decision making.
- People say they prefer 3D graphs and a 3D definitely has a better "cool factor," but 2D graphs are read more accurately [13] and are rated as better at conveying information than 3D [21].
- People assume a linear relationship. If the data is non-linear this will cause widely wrong predictions of future values. In particular, they significantly underestimate exponential growth [31].
- Upward and downward trends get interpreted differently. People overestimate downward trends and underestimate upward trends and they are poorer at estimating downward trends than upward trends [26].

People expect to see trends in data; most graphs which they see contain some sort of trend [26]. However, the human visual system is so focused on seeing trends that it will find trends in random data. Or will find trends about a specific item of interest even if the data does not reflect it. The deep cognitive processes that lead to implicit trend identification also make it easy to mislead. Huff and Geis [17] show many examples of how to distort information. Tufte [29] gives multiple examples of what he calls 'chartjunk,' essentially everything on a graphic that does not directly support the main message. Kosslyn [20] points out how the rapid mental processing of a graphic is also its shortcoming. People form an initial impression very rapidly and then have a hard time shifting from that impression; generally, they do not unless forced to do so by the situation. As a result, it is easy to design infographics which give a desired initial impression which leave out or distort information. As a result, they fail to stand up to deeper scrutiny.

An important, but often neglected, aspect of much information design is that people need be able to accurately remember the information. A person looks at an infographic for a short time, but to be useful they need to retain that information in a form that will be useful. Comprehension is not finding a datum while looking at an infographic, but having the content in a mental representation that can be used when the infographic isn't available [25]. Improper information salience or the use of highly colorful decorative graphics can shift the remembered details from the critical content to a pretty picture.

3.1   Research on Understanding Complex Information

A substantial part of the "how-to" infographic literature confuses comprehension with perception. The difference between comprehension and perception is that perception only uses/measures inputs from the environment, while comprehension takes that perception and combines it with previous knowledge so that it logically fits the situation. Perception measures if the words or design on a page are seen (did the red color make people see this factoid better?). Comprehension, on the other hand, measures if those words or designs are put into a meaningful context. The problem is that a focus on perception means getting readers to look at something, which is easy to measure and easy to design for. But a focus on comprehension means ensuring the readers can use the information.

When people read a complex infographic, they attempt to construct a mental representation that addresses their goals and is coherent at both local and global levels [7, 30] and from that coherent view they build relationships that connect to their situation [33]. Too many infographics lack that coherence because they deal with information factoids or disconnected visuals [15].

A substantial part of forming the coherent mental representation comes from prior knowledge [24]. Prior knowledge helps people build the relationships between different pieces of information that are vital to comprehension by providing the knowledge to fill in gaps [3, 23]. For example, people with better baseball knowledge will comprehend an infographic about baseball better than people with low baseball knowledge. Without some relevant knowledge, people mentally process the text as a set of disjointed, isolated information elements and they often do not see how those information elements relate to each other [12].

People's reading ability have a significant effect on comprehending a text since it influences how well they can parse the sentences and build up a meaningful mental structure on which to integrate their prior knowledge. Reading ability has been shown to be a stronger predictor of text comprehension than prior knowledge [11]. Of course, better readers better comprehend text—because that is the underlying definition of reading skill. Skilled readers also tend to experience the reading process as more automatic than less skilled readers do. Skilled readers make reading process decisions below the level of consciousness. Thus, skilled readers unconsciously, or with very little conscious effort, are reminded of the knowledge their prior knowledge. Unfortunately for design teams, that unconsciousness mental processing makes user testing of infographics more difficult.

Writing guideline say to move from general to specific and to move from given to new information [9]. In addition, in the explanatory text of most infographics, sentences must contain some level of causal connectiveness [28]. Comprehension requires making inferences and people prefer to move from more general to less general (deductive inference) rather than from less general to more general (inductive inference) [10].

People are sensitive to biases from recent effects or past experience. When interpreting information or making decision, the risk-taking or risk-aversion behavior is highly correlated with past experience, with the recent past having an unduly large affect.

In an interesting twist highly relevant to the graphical nature of infographics, although people's working memory and reading ability are highly correlated, with larger working memory equating to better reading skills [22], the research finding only applies to verbal material. Meta-analysis has revealed a highly complex set of inter-relationships between high and low ability readers and their ability to comprehend visual-spatial information [8]. In other words, an unstated assumption of graphics in general is that they work for people with lower reading ability. Although perhaps true for simple information, it cannot be assumed to support comprehending complex information.

4 Example Infographic Design Annotations

This section contains two example infographics with annotations that build on the importance of creating information relationships and helping comprehension.

Infographic Example
Stellar Evolution

Lacks any orienting information, including a title. Without adequate background knowledge, a reader will not understand what the infographic is trying to accomplish. The highly visual presentation of information can be difficult to grasp since the text fails to explain the images.

Has four Blue Supergiants. Needs to contain content to explain why they each have a different lifecyle or other issues that determine their differences.

Super shell and stellar nursery are dominating image but are not connected with the rest of the information flow. Its relationship and relevance are not clear to a reader without background knowledge.

Showing three types of supernovas, but a reader with background knowledge knows there are only two.

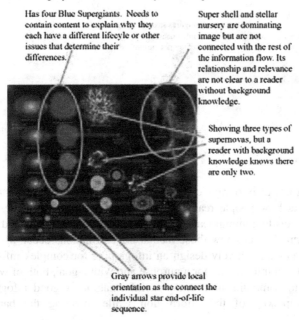

Gray arrows provide local orientation as the connect the individual star end-of-life sequence.

Source: http://www.jpl.nasa.gov/infographics/
infographic.view.php?id=10737
Courtesy NASA/JPL-Caltech

Vertical verus Poster Infographic

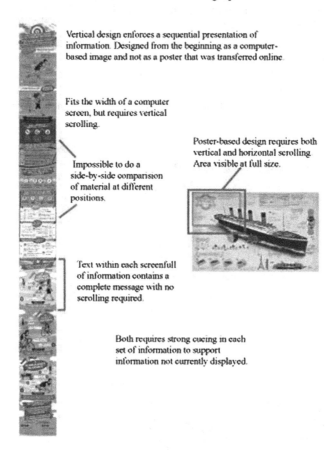

Vertical design enforces a sequential presentation of information. Designed from the beginning as a computer-based image and not as a poster that was transferred online.

Fits the width of a computer screen, but requires vertical scrolling.

Impossible to do a side-by-side comparison of material at different positions.

Poster-based design requires both vertical and horizontal scrolling. Area visible at full size.

Text within each screenfull of information contains a complete message with no scrolling required.

Both requires strong cueing in each set of information to support information not currently displayed.

5   Conclusion

With the growing use of infographics to communicate complex information, we must specifically look at how people read and understand them. Infographics are not art displays, but are tools to communicate information. Unless we understand how people comprehend information and how those mental transformations occur when they read the content, we cannot effectively design an infographic for complex information.

People come to an infographic for a purpose and with a goal, both of which require the infographics to communication complex information. A good infographic must maintain the complexity of the information while lowering the barriers to its comprehension.

A significant missing factor in infographic research is the comprehension level for the information. Issues of transforming the highly interconnected relationships inherent in complex information into a form that lends to itself to a comprehensive infographic—or any other communication medium—remains an open research question that desperately needs more research. Most importantly, we need research into both how people comprehend an infographic and how they connect that understanding to the bigger picture.

References

1. Albers, M.: Communication of Complex Information: User Goals and Information Needs for Dynamic Web Information. Erlbaum, Mahwah (2004)
2. Albers, M.: Information relationships: The source of useful and usable content. In: 29th Annual International Conference on Computer Documentation. Indianapolis, IN, 4–7 October 2009
3. Albers, M.: Usability and information relationships: Considering content relationships when testing complex information. In: Albers, M., Still, B. (eds.) Usability of Complex Information Systems: Evaluation of User Interaction, pp. 109–131. CRC Press, Boca Raton (2010)
4. Albers, M.: Infographics: Horrid chartjunk or Quality communication. In: IEEE IPCC 2014 Conference, Pittsburgh, PA, 13–15 October 2014
5. Andriole, S., Adelman, L.: Cognitive System Engineering for User-Computer Interface Design, Prototyping, and Evaluation. Erlbaum, Mahwah (1995)
6. Betrancourt, M., Bisseret, A.: Integrating textual and pictorial information via pop-up windows: An experimental study. Behav. Inf. Technol. **17**(5), 263–273 (1998)
7. Campbell, K.: Coherence, Continuity, and Cohesion. Erlbaum, Mahwah (1994)
8. Carretti, B., Borella, E., Cornoldi, C., De Beni, R.: Role of working memory in explaining the performance of individuals with specific reading comprehension difficulties: A meta-analysis. Learn. Individ. Differ. **19**, 246–251 (2009)
9. Clark, H., Haviland, S.: Comprehension and the given-new contract. In: Freedle, R. (ed.) Discourse Production and Comprehension, pp. 1–40. Ablex, Norwood (1977)
10. Collister, D., Tversky, B.: Nonanalytic inference (2005). http://www-psych.stanford.edu/ ~bt/concepts_categories/papers/cogscidc01.doc.pdf. Accessed: 24 April 2010
11. Cottrell, K., McNamara, D.: Cognitive precursors to science comprehension. In: Gray, W.D., Schunn, C.D. (eds.) Proceedings of the Twenty-fourth Annual Meeting of the Cognitive Science Society, pp. 244–249. Erlbaum, Mawah (2002)
12. Einstein, G., McDaniel, M., Owen, P., Cote, N.: Encoding and recall of texts: The importance of material appropriate processing. J. Mem. Lang. **29**, 566–581 (1990)
13. Feldman-Stewart, D., Brundage, M.: Challenges for designing and implementing decision aids. Patient Educ. Couns. **54**, 265–273 (2004)
14. Ganzach, Y., Schul, Y.: The influence of quantity of information and goal framing on decisions. Acta Psychol. **89**, 23–36 (1995)
15. Graesser, A.C., Singer, M., Trabasso, T.: Constructing inferences during narrative text comprehension. Psychol. Rev. **101**, 371–395 (1994)
16. Hsee, C.K., Zhang, J.: Distinction bias: Misprediction and mischoice due to joint evaluation. J. Pers. Soc. Psychol. **86**(5), 680–695 (2004)
17. Huff, D., Geis, I.: How to Lie with Statistics. Norton, New York (1993)
18. Janiszewski, C.: The influence of display characteristics on visual exploratory search behavior. J. Consum. Res. **25**, 290–301 (1998)
19. Kintsch, W.: Learning from text, levels of comprehension, or: Why anyone would read a story anyway. Poetics **9**, 87–98 (1980)

20. Kosslyn, S.: Elements of Graph Design. Freeman, New York (1994)
21. Mackiewicz, J.: Perceptions of clarity and attractiveness in PowerPoint graph slides. Techn. Commun. **54**(2), 145–156 (2007)
22. McDaniel, M., Hines, R., Guynn, M.: When text difficulty benefits less-skilled readers. J. Mem. Lang. **46**, 544–561 (2002)
23. McNamara, D., Kintsch, E., Songer, N., Kintsch, W.: Are good texts always better? Interactions of text coherence, background knowledge, and levels of understanding in learning from text. Cogn. Instr. **14**, 1–43 (1996)
24. Murray, T.: Applying text comprehension and active reading principles to adaptive hyperbooks. In: Proceedings of Cognitive Science, Boston, MA, pp. 840–845, July 2003
25. Redish, J.: Expanding usability testing to evaluate complex systems. J. Usability Stud. **2**(3), 102–111 (2007)
26. Remus, W.E., O'Connor, M.J., Griggs, K.: Does reliable information improve the accuracy of judgmental forecasting? Int. J. Forecast. **11**, 285–293 (1995)
27. Scaife, M., Rogers, Y.: External cognition : How do graphical representations work? Int. J. Hum Comput Stud. **45**, 185–213 (1996)
28. Singer, M., O'Connell, G.: Robust inference processes in expository text comprehension. Eur. J. Cogn. Psychol. **15**, 607–631 (2003)
29. Tufte, E.: The Visual Display of Quantitative Information. Graphics Press, Cheshire (1983)
30. van den Broek, P., Lorch, R., Linderholm, T., Gustafson, M.: The effects of readers' goals on inference generation and memory for texts. Mem. Cogn. **29**(8), 1081–1087 (2001)
31. Wagenaar, W., Sagaria, S.: Misperception of exponential growth. Percept. Psychophys. **18**(6), 416–422 (1975)
32. Winograd, T., Flores, F.: Understanding Computers and Cognition: A New Foundation for Design. Ablex, Norwood (1986)
33. Zwaan, R., Singer, M.: Text comprehension. In: Graesser, A., Gernsbacher, M., Goldman, S. (eds.) Handbook of Discourse Processes, pp. 83–121. Erlbaum, Mahwah (2003)

Building Cloud-Based Scientific Workflows Made Easy: A Remote Sensing Application

Sofiane Bendoukha[1]([✉]), Daniel Moldt[1], and Hayat Bendoukha[2]

[1] Theoretical Foundations of Computer Science (TGI), Department of Informatics,
University of Hamburg, Hamburg, Germany
{sbendoukha,moldt}@informatik.uni-hamburg.de
[2] Department of Computer Science, Faculty of Mathematics and Computer Science,
University of Science and Technology USTOMB, Oran, Algeria
bendoukhyat@univ-usto.dz

Abstract. In this paper, we present an approach for the specification and the execution of complex scientific workflows in cloud-like environments. The approach strives to support scientists during the modeling, deployment and the monitoring of their workflows. This work takes advantages from Petri nets and more pointedly the so called reference nets formalism, which provide robust modeling/implementation techniques. Meanwhile, we present the implementation of a new tool named RENEWGRASS. It allows the modeling as well as the execution of image processing workflows from the remote sensing domain. In terms of usability, we provide an easy way to support unskilled researchers during the specification of their workflows. Then, we use the Enhanced Vegetation Index (EVI) workflow as a showcase of the implementation. At last, we introduce our methodology to move the actual implementation to the Cloud.

Keywords: RenewGrass · Cloud computing · Scientific workflows · Petri nets

1 Introduction

Several applications require the completion of multiple interdependent tasks; the description of a complex activity involving such a set of tasks is known as a workflow. The Workflow Management Coalition (WfMC) defined a workflow as *"the automation of business process, in whole or part, during which documents, information or tasks are passed from one participant to another for action, according to a set of procedural rules"* [6]. Traditional workflow management systems (WfMS) were conceived for business domain. Later, they have been adopted for scientific applications in various fields such as astronomy, bio-informatics, meteorology, etc. Ludäscher et al. [9] define scientific workflows as: *"networks of analytical steps that may involve, e.g., database access and querying steps, data analysis and mining steps, and many other steps including computationally intensive jobs on high performance cluster computers"*.

© Springer International Publishing Switzerland 2015
A. Marcus (Ed.): DUXU 2015, Part II, LNCS 9187, pp. 277–288, 2015.
DOI: 10.1007/978-3-319-20898-5_27

Nevertheless, high-throughput and long running workflows are often composed of tasks; which usually need to be mapped to distributed resources, in order to access, manage and process large amount of data. These resources are often limited in supply and fail to meet the increasing demands of scientific applications. Cloud computing is an emerging computing technology for the execution of resource intensive workflows by integrating large-scale, distributed and heterogeneous computing and storage resources. Therefore, Cloud computing is of high interest to scientific workflows with high requirements on compute or storage resources. Furthermore, workflow concepts are critical features for a successful Cloud strategy. These concepts cover many steps of the deployment process. For instance graphical workflow specification, data/task/user management, workflow monitoring, etc. However, existing workflow architectures are not directly adapted to Cloud computing and workflow management systems are not integrated with the Cloud system [10]. Missing is more support at both conceptual and technical level.

At the conceptual level, we provide powerful modeling techniques based on Petri nets. We have implemented RENEWGRASS, which is a user friendly tool support for building scientific workflows. Moreover, RENEWGRASS integrates the features from the Geographic Resource Analysis Support System GIS for short GRASS. Its functionality is to support scientists to (i) specify their workflows and to (ii) control their execution by providing appropriate modeling patterns which addresses specific functions. These functions can be provided by services hosted on-premise or in the Cloud. With reference to the workflow life-cycle, the tool supports both modeling and execution steps. The application field concerns the Geographical Information System (GIS) domain, especially the processing of satellite-based images.

Furthermore, we discuss issues and migration patterns for moving applications and application data to the Cloud. Based on these patterns, we propose an agent-based architecture to integrate the current implementation in Cloud-like environments, i.e., the components making up the workflow management system are mapped into services provided by specific agents. In general, agent concepts are employed for improving Cloud service discovery, composition and Service Level Agreement (SLA) management. The elaborated architecture is based on the MULAN/CAPA framework and following the PAOSE approach. The objective is that agents perform the Cloud management functionalities such as brokering, workflow submission and instance control. Technically, the OpenStack framework was adopted for the creation and the management of the Cloud instances.

The remainder of this paper is organized as follows: Sect. 2 gives an overview about the concepts, tools and techniques that are tackled in this paper as well as related work. Section 3 introduces the RENEWGRASS tool and its architecture. The EVI workflow of a Landsat/Thematic Mapper (TM) imagery is presented as a showcase for the implementation. Section 4 introduces our approach for moving the execution of the workflow tasks to the Cloud. Finally, in Sect. 5 we give a summary as well as a plan for future work.

2   Background

This section gives a brief overview about the concepts, tools and technologies, which are addressed in this paper. This includes the reference nets formalism and the modeling/simulation tool RENEW. The related work is also addressed.

2.1   Reference Nets

At the modeling level, we use a special kind of Petri nets called *reference nets* [7]. Petri nets proved their efficiency to model complex/distributed systems. The main advantage of reference nets lies in the use of Java inscriptions within the transitions making the gap between specification and implementation decrease considerably. Reference nets are object-oriented high-level Petri nets and are based on the nets-within-nets formalism introduced by [12], which allows tokens to be nets again. They extend Petri nets with dynamic net instances, net references, and dynamic transition synchronization through synchronous channels. Reference nets consist of places, transitions and arcs. The input and output arcs have a similar behavior to ordinary Petri nets. Tokens can be available of any type in the Java programming language. In opposite to the net elements of P/T nets, reference nets provide supplementary elements that increase the modeling power. These elements are: virtual places, declaration and arc types. The places are typed and the transitions can hold expressions, actions, guards, etc. Firing a transition can also create a new instance of a subnet. The creation of the instances is similar to object instances in object-oriented programming. This allows a specific, hierarchical nesting of networks, which is helpful for building complex systems.

2.2   RENEW

The **RE**ference **NE**ts **W**orkshop (RENEW)[1] is a graphical tool for creating, editing and simulating reference nets. It combines the *nets-within-nets* paradigm with the implementing power of Java. With Renew it is possible to draw and simulate both Petri nets and reference nets. During the simulation, a net instance is created and can be viewed in a separate window as its active transitions fire. Simulation is used in Renew to view firing sequences of active transitions in reference nets. Simulation can run in a one step modus where users can progress in steps where only one transition fires. RENEW also offers the possibility to set breakpoints to hold the simulation process. Breakpoints can be set to places and transitions. By changing the compiler, RENEW can also simulate P/T nets, timed petri nets, Workflow nets, etc.

2.3   Related Work

Before the emergence of the Cloud technology, there were significant research projects dealing with the development of distributed and scientific workflow systems with the grid paradigm. Workflow enactment service can be built on top of

---

[1] http://www.renew.de/.

the low level grid middleware (eg. Globus Toolkit[2], UNICORE[3] and Alchemi[4]), through which the workflow management system invokes services provided by grid resources [13]. At both the build-time and run-time phases, the state of the resources and applications can be retrieved from grid information services. There are many grid workflow management systems in use; like these representative projects: ASKALON[5], Pegasus[6], Taverna[7], Kepler[8], Triana[9] and Swift [14]. Most of these projects, have been investigating the adaptation of their architectures to include the Cloud technology. For instance, the Elastic Compute Cloud (EC2) module has been implemented to make Kepler supports Amazon Cloud services. Launched in 2012, the Amazon Simple Workflow (SWF)[10] is an orchestration service for building scalable applications. It maintains the execution state of the workflow in terms of consistency and reliability. It permits structuring the various processing steps in an application running on one or more systems as a set of tasks. These systems can be Cloud-based, on-premise, or both.

3   RenewGrass: A Tool for Building Geoprocessing Workflows

In this section, we introduce a new tool called RenewGrass. The objective is to extend Renew by providing geoprocessing capabilities. Since the version 1.7, Renew is built on a highly sophisticated plug-in architecture. It allows the extension and the integration of additional functionality through the use of interfaces from Renew components without changing the core architecture.

Up until now, Renew still serves as a modeling/simulation tool for different teaching projects. Unfortunately, the application domain concerns mostly business workflows. Through the integration of RenewGrass in Renew, we aim to:

- extend Renew to be adapted for scientific workflow modeling and execution
- provide unexperienced users with modeling patterns that focus on image processing
- exploit and integrate the power of the Grass GIS, thus several image processing workflows can be implemented
- reduce the gap between the specification of the workflow and its implementation
- integrate Cloud services for mapping time-consuming and data-intensive workflows

---

[2] http://www.globus.org/toolkit/.
[3] http://www.unicore.eu/.
[4] http://www.cloudbus.org/~alchemi/.
[5] http://www.askalon.org/.
[6] http://www.pegasus.org/.
[7] http://www.taverna.org.uk/.
[8] https://kepler-project.org/.
[9] http://www.trianacode.org/.
[10] aws.amazon.com/swf.

3.1 Integration of RENEWGRASS in RENEW

In this section, we present RENEWGRASS, which was successfully integrated in RENEW. The main functionality of RENEWGRASS is to provide support during modeling and execution of image processing workflows. Figure 1 shows the simplified view of the position of the new tool in RENEW. The *Workflow* and the *WFNet* are additional plug-ins, which are required in case worflow management functionalities are required such as log-in, tasks management, etc. As mentioned in Fig. 1, RENEWGRASS is built on top of the JGrasstools[11], which was adapted for RENEW. The latter makes the Petri net models support the invocation of Grass core commands directly from the Petri net transitions (see Fig. 2). The current implementation of the tool allows local use only. This signifies that RENEW, Grass GIS and data are hosted locally.

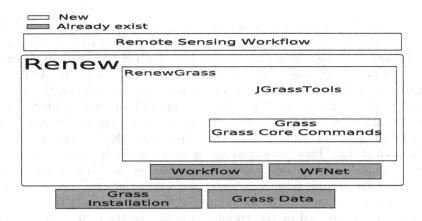

Fig. 1. The Position of RENEWGRASS in RENEW

3.2 Use Case

As proof of concept, RENEWGRASS was used to implement the Enhanced Vegetation Index (EVI) for a satellite image taken from the LANDSAT-TM7. The EVI is a numerical indicator that uses the Red, the Near-infrared and the Blue bands. It is an optimized index designed to enhance the vegetation signal with improved sensitivity in high biomass regions.

2.5 * (nirchan - redchan) / (nirchan + 6.0 * redchan - 7.5 * bluechan + 1.0)

Figure 2, shows the Peri net model corresponding to the EVI workflow. For the clarity of the paper, we omitted several steps from the original workflow. With the same procedure other vegetation indexes or image processing workflows can be implemented.

---

[11] http://moovida.github.io/jgrasstools/.

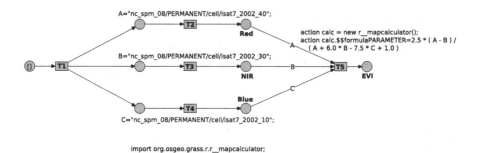

Fig. 2. The EVI workflow modeled and calculated using RENEWGRASS

4 Cloud-RENEWGRASS: A Cloud Migration Approach

RENEWGRASS has been successfully tested in a local environment. All the required components were hosted on-premise (RENEW, Grass GIS and the data). Nevertheless, as soon as the number of tasks increases and the size of data become large, we start facing computing and storage issues. This is due to insufficient resources on the local site. This section presents our vision to deploy the current implementation of the RENEWGRASS tool onto the Cloud services. First, different possibilities to Cloud-enable an application in general are shortly illustrated. These possibilities are formulated in form of patterns. The illustration is based on the work of [1,5]. They investigate and strive to answer questions like: where to enact the processes? Where to execute the activities? and Where to store the data? Thus the entities taken in account are: (1) the process engine (responsible for the execution and the monitoring of the activities) (2) the activities that need to be executed by the workflow and (3) the Data. Next, we propose an architecture to introduce a new pattern and an appropriate methodology to enable remote execution in the Cloud.

4.1 Migration Patterns

Moving an existing application to the Cloud should be based on a solid strategy. Providing the business management system (or WfMS) or a part in the Cloud raises a series of concerns about ensuring the security of the data and the performance of the system. For example, Cloud users could lose control on their own data in case of a fully Cloud-based solution. Some activities, which are not compute-intensive can be executed on-premise rather than moving them to the Cloud. Unfortunately, this transfer can be time and cost-consuming because of the pay-per-use model and the nature of the workflow tasks.

In the following, the patterns from [1,5] are shortly introduced. The first pattern designs the traditional scenario where all the components of the workflow system are hosted at the user-side (on-premise). The second scenario represents a case when users already have a workflow engine but the application contains compute or data-intensive activities, so they are moved to the Cloud for acquiring more capabilities and better performance. The third case designs a situation, where the end-users do not have a workflow engine, so they use a Cloud-based workflow engine, which is provided on-demand. In that case, workflow designers can specify transfer requirements of activity execution and data storage, for example, sensitive data and non-compute-intensive activities can be hosted on-premise, and compute-intensive activities and non-sensitive data can be moved to the Cloud [5]. The last scenario presents a situation where all components are hosted in a Cloud and accessed probably from a Web interface. The advantage is that users do not need to install and configure any software on the user side. To make an analogy with the elements of our approach, RENEW is the process engine, the activities are the geoprocessing tasks (performed by the Grass services), which are related to the satellite images (data). The latter (data and Grass GIS) can be either on-premise or hosted in the Cloud. Based on these elements and the illustration presented above, Fig. 3 presents an overview of the diverse approaches (patterns) to design our workflow system based on the Cloud technology.

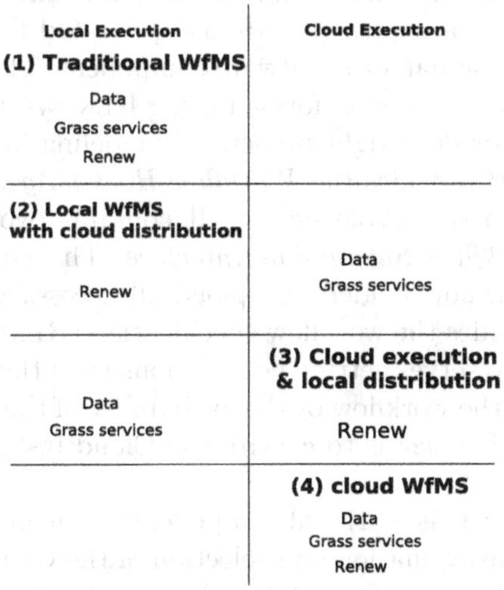

Local Execution	Cloud Execution
(1) Traditional WfMS	
Data	
Grass services	
Renew	
(2) Local WfMS with cloud distribution	
	Data
Renew	Grass services
	(3) Cloud execution & local distribution
Data	
Grass services	**Renew**
	(4) cloud WfMS
	Data
	Grass services
	Renew

Fig. 3. Patterns for cloud-based workflow systems (Adapted from [5])

We have noticed that both [1,5] do not address all possible situations. For instance, the following situation has been not addressed: the process engine is available on the user side but due to circumstances (internal failure, not sufficient compute or storage resources), remote process engines need to be integrated and remotely invoked. Figure 4 shows approximately how this scenario looks like. Our solution consists on transferring the data and executing the process by another process engine. This is discussed in the following sections.

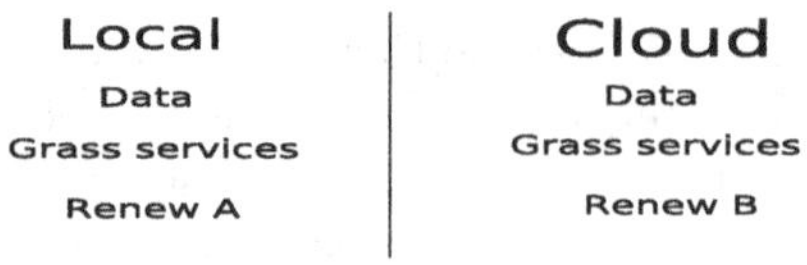

Local	**Cloud**
Data	Data
Grass services	Grass services
Renew A	Renew B

Fig. 4. A pattern designing multiple process engines integration

4.2 Architecture

Figure 5 shows the architecture to integrate the current implementation into a Cloud system. While RENEWGRASS is already implemented and successfully integrated in RENEW (see Sect. 3), most efforts are dedicated now to move the execution of the geoprocessing tasks to the Cloud and the provision of an interface to invoke these services directly from workflow models.

In our work, we follow an agent-based approach, i.e., many components functionalities are performed by special agents. In summary, the role of each agent used in the approach is described below.

1. *Workflow Holder Agent*: The Workflow holder is the entity that specifies the workflow and in consequence holds the generated Petri net models. This entity can be either human or a software component. The specification of the image processing workflow is performed using RENEWGRASS, which provides a modeling palette or downright predefined modeling blocks.
2. *Cloud Portal Agent*: provides the *Workflow Holder Agent* a Web portal as a primary interface to the whole system. It contains two components: *Cloud Manager* and *Workflow Submission Interface*. The latter provides a Web interface to the workflow holders to upload all necessary files to execute the workflow. This includes the workflow specification (RENEW formats[12]), input files (images). It also serves getting notifications from the *Cloud Broker Agent* about the status of the workflow or the availability of the Cloud provider. The role of the *Cloud Manager* is to control the Cloud instances (start and stop or suspend).
3. *Cloud Broker Agent*: It is a critical component of the architecture, since it is responsible of (i) the evaluation and selection of the Cloud providers that fits the workflow's requirements (e.g., data volume and computing intensities) and (ii) mapping the workflow tasks. Both activities require information about the Cloud provider, which are available and provided by the Cloud Repository Agent.
4. *Cloud Repository Agent*: The Cloud repository register the information about the Cloud providers and the state of their services. These information are saved in a database and are constantly updated, since they are required by the Cloud Broker Agent. To avoid failure scenarios (repository down, loss of data), we use distributed databases, which allows high availability and fault-tolerant persistence.

---

[12] RENEW supports various file formats saving (XML, .rnw, .sns, etc.).

5. *Cloud Provider Agent*: The role of this agent is to control the instances and to manage the execution of the tasks. Regularly, the Cloud providers need to update their status and send it to the Cloud Repository Agent. The status concerns both the instance and the services (Grass services).

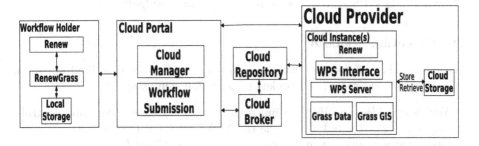

Fig. 5. The architecture of the cloud-based workflow system

Concerning the *Cloud Broker Agent*, the evaluation and the selection of the Cloud providers are critical processes for the *Workflow Holders*. In Cloud computing there are various factors impacting the Cloud provider evaluation and selection [4,8] such as: computational capacity, IT security and privacy, reliability and trustworthiness, customization degree and flexibility/scalability, manageability/usability and customer service, geolocations of Cloud infrastructures. For this, in our work, brokering factors are limited to the computational capacity and the customization degree.

4.3 Cloud Configuration

Concerning the customization degree, there are some requirements for a successful deployment onto the Cloud. In general, a common procedure to deploy applications onto Cloud services consists of these two main steps:

1. *Set up the Environment*: this mainly consists of the provision of Cloud instances[13] and the configuration the required softwares properly. Essential are the environment variables, which differ from the local implementation such as JAVA configuration for the Web server.
2. *Deploy the Application*: it consists of the customization of the Cloud instance with the appropriate softwares. For our work, RENEW and the Grass GIS should be correctly and properly configured, especially the database and the installation path.

---

[13] The Cloud instances should be in priori customized, i.e., they need to have the Grass GIS as back-end, the WPS server and RENEW. We assume that the Cloud storage is a service, which is configured by the Cloud provider itself.

Furthermore, the Grass commands can be invoked in different ways. Either through a wrapper like in the original implementation of RENEWGRASS or provided as Web services. For the latter, we follow a Web-based approach with respect to the Open Geospatial Consortium (OGC) Web Processing Service (WPS) interface specification. Thus the Grass GIS functionalities are provided as Web services instead of desktop application. To achieve this, we chose the 52North[14] as a WPS server as well as the wps-grass-bridge[15].

4.4   Execution Scenario

Considering the proposed architecture and the agent roles described above, a typical deployment scenario is broken into the following steps:

1. Workflow holders specify their image processing workflows (data and control-flow) using Petri nets for example the NDVI workflow (see Sect. 3).
2. They send a request to the *Cloud Broker* via the *Cloud Portal*.
3. The *Cloud Broker* checks for available Cloud providers, which provide geo-processing tools (Grass GIS). This information is retrieved from the *Cloud Repository*.
4. The *Cloud Broker* sends a list to the *Workflow Holder* (through the Cloud Portal) to accept or to reject the offer.
5. If the offer is accepted, the *Workflow Holder* submits the workflow specification (.rnw + .sns) to the selected *Cloud Provider*.
6. Launch a customized Cloud instance with RENEW and Grass GIS running in the background.
7. After simulation/execution of the workflow, results (in our prototype it consists of calculating the NDVI value) are transmitted to the *Workflow Holder* through the *Cloud Portal*.

Rejecting an offer does not conclude the execution process immediately. Since the list transmitted by the *Cloud Broker* is updated constantly, it might be that new Cloud providers are available and fits the requirements. Therefore, from step (3), the process is iterative until the satisfaction of the *Workflow Holder*. Regarding step (5) and (6), RENEW supports starting a simulation from the command line. This is possible by using the command *startsimulation (net system) (primary net) [-i]*. The parameters to this command have the following meaning:

- *Net system*: The .sns file.
- *Primary net*: The name of the net, of which a net instance shall be opened when the simulation starts.
- -i: If you set this optional flag, then the simulation is initialized only, that is, the primary net instance is opened, but the simulation is not started automatically.

---

[14] http://52north.org/.
[15] https://code.google.com/p/wps-grass-bridge/.

In a future paper, we will give a first evaluation of the presented work as well as the progress of the implementation of the components presented in this section. Furthermore, we have implemented other image processing workflows such as the Normalized Differences Vegetation Index (NDVI).

5 Conclusions and Future Work

In this paper we first presented the implementation of a geoprocessing tool named RENEWGRASS for RENEW. This tool extends RENEW to be able to support another kind of workflows (scientific workflows) apart the business workflows. The application domain of RENEWGRASS is the remote sensing, especially image processing. Therefore, we afford scientists with a palette of processing functionalities based on the Grass GIS. Furthermore, we discussed the extension of the current work by the integration of the Cloud technology. For this purpose, we introduced migration patterns and introduced our architecture for the deployment of workflows onto Cloud providers.

The future work takes two directions. First, we will improve RENEWGRASS by providing more functionality especially for not-experienced users. According to our first experience with the implemented tool, we detected that several geoprocessing workflows involve repetitive tasks, which need to be automated. This repetitive tasks can be grouped in modeling blocks and then used when necessary. To enable this, we are exploiting the well-known *Net Components* introduced by [2], which can provide pre-defined modeling structures. Thus the modeling of image processing workflows will be more straightforward.

The next step is to investigate the integration possibilities of the RENEW-GRASS within an agent-based approach. This consists of using the MULAN/CAPA framework [3,11]. This framework allows building agent-based applications following the PAOSE approach. The idea is that the components described in Sect. 4 will be integrated in an agent-based application, which is currently being developed in the context of a teaching project. The first functionality that we are investigating is Cloud brokering, which consists on selecting the best Cloud provider to perform the workflow tasks.

References

1. Anstett, T., Leymann, F., Mietzner, R., Strauch, S.: Towards bpel in the cloud: exploiting different delivery models for the execution of business processes. In: 2009 World Conference on Services - I, pp. 670–677 (2009)
2. Cabac, L.: Net components: concepts, tool, praxis. In: Moldt, D. (eds.) PNSE 2009, Proceedings, Technical reports Paris 13, pp. 17–33, 99, avenue Jean-Baptiste Clément, 93 430 Villetaneuse, June 2009. Université Paris 13
3. Duvigneau, M., Moldt, D., Rölke, H.: Concurrent architecture for a multi-agent platform. In: Giunchiglia, F., Odell, J.J., Weiß, G. (eds.) Proceedings of the AOSE 2002, Bologna, pp. 147–159. ACM Press, July 2002

4. Haddad, C.: Selecting a cloud platform: a platform as a service scorecard. Technical report, WSO2 (2011). http://wso2.com/download/wso2-whitepaper-selecting-a-cloud-platform.pdf. Accessed 2 December 2014

5. Han, Y.-B., Sun, J.-Y., Wang, G.-L., Li, H.-F.: A cloud-based bpm architecture with user-end distribution of non-compute-intensive activities and sensitive data. J. Comput. Sci. Technol. **25**(6), 1157–1167 (2010)

6. Hollingsworth, D.: Workflow management coalition - the workflow reference model. Technical report, Workflow Management Coalition, January 1995. URL: http://www.wfmc.org/standards/model.htm

7. Kummer, O.: Referenznetze. Logos Verlag, Berlin (2002)

8. Patt, R., Badger, L., Grance, T., Voas, C.J.: Recommendations of the national institute of standards and technology. Technical report, NIST (2011). http://csrc.nist.gov/publications/nistpubs/800-146/sp800-146.pdf

9. Ludäscher, B., Altintas, I., Berkley, C., Higgins, D., Jaeger, E., Jones, M., Lee, E.A., Tao, J., Zhao, Y.: Scientific workflow management and the kepler system: research articles. Concurrency Comput. Pract. Experience **18**(10), 1039–1065 (2006)

10. Pandey, S., Karunamoorthy, D., Buyya, R.: Workflow Engine for Clouds. Wiley, Hoboken (2011)

11. Rölke, H.: Modellierung von Agenten und Multiagentensystemen - Grundlagen und Anwendungen. Agent Technology - Theory and Applications, vol. 2. Logos Verlag, Berlin (2004)

12. Valk, R.: Petri nets as token objects - an introduction to elementary object nets. In: Desel, J., Silva, M. (eds.) ICATPN 1998. LNCS, vol. 1420, pp. 1–25. Springer, Berlin (1998)

13. Jia, Y., Buyya, R.: A taxonomy of workflow management systems for grid computing. J. Grid Comput. **3**(3–4), 171–200 (2005)

14. Zhao, Y., Hategan, M., Clifford, B., Foster, I., von Laszewski, G., Nefedova, V., Raicu, I., Stef-Praun, T., Wilde, M.: Swift: fast, reliable, loosely coupled parallel computation. In: 2007 IEEE Congress on Services, pp. 199–206, July 2007

Sound Design and UX: The Dynamic Audio Application Guide

Luiz Roberto Carvalho[(⊠)] and Alice T. Cybis Pereira

Federal University of Santa Catarina, Florianópolis, Brazil
{semprecarvalho, acybis}@gmail.com

Abstract. Aiming to expose guidelines and procedures that lead to an efficient implementation of sound elements into interfaces, and given the need to develop a formal understanding of audio applications in interactive systems, this study presents the Dynamic Audio Application Guide. From the proposed methodology by Jesse James Garrett, the Dynamic Audio Application Guide was created, which aims to systematize and simplify the process of creation, production and implementation of sound into interactive systems. The guide is intended to highlight the important role played by sound in immersion and interaction processes.

Keywords: Sound design · Dynamic audio · Interactive sound · Hypermedia design

1 Audio for Interactive Devices: Sound is Information

The interactive systems development is a complex process, mainly evidenced by its interdisciplinary nature. To communicate, the interface needs to engage the user in its own dynamic potentialities. It is important to point that an interface is not only a visual stimulus, but a combination consisting of sound, image and hypertext. In 1996, [9] pointed that the use of technological resources in hypermedia was restricted to the visual modality. According to the author, little was invested in audio[1], an element that brings quality to content, facilitates the accessibility of information and makes them more attractive. Ten years after, according to [10], there has been no significant progress in relation to sound in interfaces. The author affirms that in the design market there is an overvaluation of visual communication, and because of its limitations, products and services can often present inconsistencies when other sensory properties are relevant, as in the case of sound and tactile information. While the tactile process and haptic[2] requirements are gradually beginning to develop in the interface field, sound and its cognitive functions remain in a largely unexplored territory.

---

[1] Audio comes from latin word *audio*, first person of the verb *audire*, that means listening. In a broader sense, refers to all wave phenomena occurring within the audible frequency range, i.e. between 20 Hz and 20 kHz. When in the acoustic field, audio waves is known as sound.

[2] The haptic adjective means "relating to the touch", "synonymous of tactile," and is derived from the Greek word *aptikó* that means "touch-sensitive". It is the optical counterpart for visual, and sound for hearing.

© Springer International Publishing Switzerland 2015
A. Marcus (Ed.): DUXU 2015, Part II, LNCS 9187, pp. 289–300, 2015.
DOI: 10.1007/978-3-319-20898-5_28

The use of sound in interactive environments has not advanced at the same rate of the graphical elements, and consequently, it has been placed in low priority [1]. Reference [8] indicate that this over-emphasis on visual displays has constrained the development of interactive systems that are able to make better use of the auditory modality. Non-musical sounds have been accepted as technology sub-products, rather than being exploited by their intrinsic value. As a result, a world polluted acoustically has been experienced since the industrial revolution. However, there are already enough scientific knowledge and technology to start a way of *thinking about the sound* as one of the main dimensions of the environments that people live - whether physical or virtual. This means overcome the sound barrier as cultural noise and promote a targeted approach to the sound as *information* - a fact that already occurs with the visual elements.

2 DAAG: Dynamic Audio Application Guide

The game industry has proven that the knowledge of how audio works in an interactive environment is crucial for a proper engagement and immersion experience [4]. From this perspective, in order to meet the need to understand, identify and classify the existing modalities when using sounds in interactive environments, and contextualize their use, the Dynamic Audio Application Guide (DAAG) was developed. Starting from Garret's User Experience Design approach [6], the guide was contemplated with features that intend to develop interfaces with a sound design committed to the user experience concepts. The guide intends to start a formal understanding of the principles that constitute the application of audio in interactive systems, starting from a better understanding of the sound production flow in these platforms (Fig. 1).

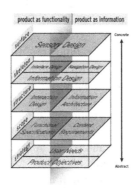

Fig. 1. Garret's user experience design diagram [6]

The DAAG aims to bring the sound design concepts from the game industry, the user experience design approach, and put them together. Formed by five layers, the DAAG consists of a system of blocks of information that advances in steps aligned with the overall progress of the interface project. The guide is intended to be used in a way to offer a unique approach to a proper management of sound elements in interface projects. From the exposure of guidelines and procedures to an effective implementation of sound features in interactive environments, the DAAG aims to systematize and simplify the process of creation, production and implementation of sounds in interfaces (Fig. 2).

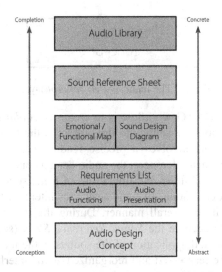

Fig. 2. The dynamic audio application guide diagram

The DAAG focuses on highlighting the important role played by sound in immersion and interaction processes. In interactive environments, the presence of dynamic audio[3] intensifies the user immersion and empowers additional cognitive processes, driving the interaction experience into a different scenario. An experience surrounded by hypertext, image and sound is more complex and complete, since images, sounds, music, oral and written language, all these forms of expression are mixed in the same message. Once the interface reaches the users in distinct senses, their cognitive levels should be properly accentuated. In this context, the development of DAAG aims to explore efficient methods to make the sound design an essential part of interface projects. It is believed that the study results will open a debate of a yet low researched area, allowing its scientific basis to be useful in academic and professional practices, by providing a new tool to hypermedia designers.

2.1 The *"Audio Design Concept"* Layer

Every experience that man experiences is fundamentally perceived through the sense organs. In interactive systems, this involves consider which of the five senses (sight,

---

[3] A more dense discussion about the dynamic audio can be found in [2].

hearing, touch, smell, and taste) are possible to apply in the interface and how this should be done. In this context, [7] warns that the use of sound is not something to be added as a late element in the project, given that it plays critical roles in important areas of the interface, such as the creation of *climates*, *atmospheres*, and to drive narrative (Fig. 3).

Audio Design Concept

Fig. 3. The *audio design concept* layer

The first step in the DAAG workflow is to create an *Audio Design Concept* document. Create a list of possible sounds to the project is the first step in the interface sound design project. This involves a precise reading of user needs and product objectives, and based on such references, the audio design concept document should be made, pointing out the possibilities and limitations of using sounds. It is a simple text, in order to define a first communicative and aesthetics intention about what sound can bring to the interface, in an overall manner. During the rise of DAAG layers, this document will gradually become the *Sound Reference Sheet* (see in item 2.4), which will conduct the creation and application of the sounds in the interface. Therefore, this first document should be reassessed and reorganized as the interface project gradually progresses.

It is crucial to mention that in the initial phase of the interface project, even counting only with preliminary information about user needs and product objectives, many decisions can be made to begin the sound design work, thus ensuring that the audio will play an important role throughout the project. In fact, the audio design document has its importance since it enables designers to start thinking about sound at the beginning of the interface project.

2.2 The *"Requirements List"* Layer

Significant improvements in the sound design field are given when the sound is analyzed in a broad perspective with respect to their content *characteristics*, *form* and *function*. This DAAG layer has an objective to promote a targeted approach to audio as information, in a way that becomes possible to use the sound stimuli to transmit messages systematically. Acoustic signals must be explored in order to maximize the communicative effects of the interface (Fig. 4).

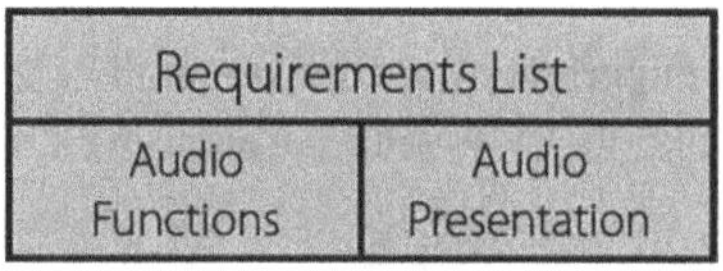

Requirements List

| Audio Functions | Audio Presentation |

Fig. 4. The *requirements list* layer

When identifying all types of formats (text, audio, video, image) associated with a specific content of the interface, it is possible to determine what will be needed for its production [6]. In this way, the same content block can be presented in different formats and also different content can be displayed using a single media (text only, for example). However, when the range of presentation formats are expanded, the user can decide which kind of content to interact with. Since users have distinct cognitive models, the parallel use of texts, images, videos and sounds offers more pronounced interaction possibilities. This is a solution aligned with the principles of user experience design.

At this stage of DAAG, a *Requirements List* must be formatted. In this document, the sounds that will be in the interface should be classified according to their *Audio Presentation* possibilities, being divided in *dialogue, background music* and *sound effects*. This implies that designers will consider the sound feature (through the human voice, musical compositions and specific sound effects) as means of transmitting information relating to interface's content blocks. These sound elements should also comply with specific functions in the interface, so that their *Audio Functions* are fully met. To fulfill these specifications, the sound element shall corroborate to specific functional aspects, exercising *structural, narrative, immersive, aesthetic, kinetics* functions, as pointed out by (quote). Through the Requirements List layer, it is intended to define which kind of content will be transmitted through sounds, what is the nature of these sounds, and how these sounds will contribute to achieve the interface goals.

2.3   The *"Maps and Diagrams"* Layer

The quality of a sound can be considered high if an acoustic event is perceived as an information carrier and processed in a way that an specific meaning is extracted from it. From this perspective, sound designers are information architects, since they amplify the meaning of the messages (Fig. 5).

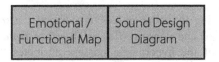

Fig. 5. The *maps and diagrams* layer

In the *Maps and Diagrams* layer the sound is considered in the context of the environment's dynamic interactions, more specifically, in the interactions that occur between different interfaces and connect large blocks of content, i.e., the *macro interactions*. At this stage, the contents belonging to the Audio Requirements' List (containing elements such as narration, dialogue, music, and sound effects) start to be added in the architecture diagram, also called interface's *hypermap*[4], and according to

---

[4] The hypermaps are produced from an organization of the interface information and become the navigation system array. The hypermap aims to show graphically, in the more systemic possible way, the information architecture and the various gateways and inter-relations thru content links [5].

[6], called *visual vocabulary*. As the other kinds of contents (images, texts) are being distributed to form the interface architecture, sounds should also follow this pattern. With the architecture diagram, it becomes possible to plan the audio behavior by setting up, for example, which audio tracks will be used in a group of graphical interfaces without the need for sound interruption in screen changes, and which audio tracks will be used as a transition zone between one interface and another.

This chart containing the interface ramifications allows defining, for example, about the use of music and ambience tracks as a connection between two distinct interfaces, or that indicate the opening or closing of a specific content block. The absence of sound - silence - can also transmit information to the user, for example, that some specific task was completed and the user can already get out of a certain area, progressing by the available links. A sound interruption may indicate a change in the interface direction, and the continuous use of music in disparate interfaces can help to signal the same theme of a specific content (Fig. 6).

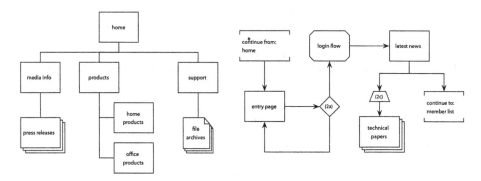

Fig. 6. Garret's visual vocabulary [6]

In this context, starting from the architecture diagram, a *sound architecture diagram* should be designed and conceived as an *interface feature*[5]. A feature usually indicates which areas of the hypermedia possess attributes that should be further implemented by the programming team, so, the sound architecture diagram is a feature. The end result should be the *sitemap*, which unifies the hypermap, the sound architecture diagram, and the whole structure of the interface, showing the dynamic spaces and connections between its content blocks. At this project step, the sounds begin to take a closer characteristic of how they will be in the final interface. After properly allocated on specific areas of the *sitemap*, it becomes possible to visualize how sounds will work between the interface sections and nodes. The creation of these references allows the sounds to behave according to the proposed dynamic for the project.

---

[5] In interactive environments, the *feature* concept is related to the characteristics and functions of the interface, when analyzed as software. It is commonly used to describe systems and programs that require some kind of programming language.

In addition with the *sound architecture diagram* definitions, an emotional/functional map should be created. An *emotional map* is focused in the sense that the interface has an inner narrative, and is capable of enabling different emotional reactions from its users during its navigation. A *functional map* is useful in interfaces that has a task managing behavior (e-mails readers, governments spreadsheets), to graphically indicate the amount of tasks that the users should accomplish during navigation. The emotional/ functional maps are useful since they systematize the interface according to acts, chapters or segments, and define the upcoming events that the users should face according to the interface's intensity patterns, or task completion levels. Thus, it becomes possible to identify which interface areas require a more precise cognitive support to help users to achieve their objectives (Fig. 7).

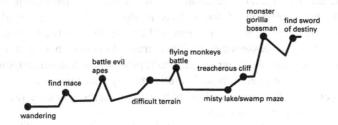

Fig. 7. Collins' emotion map, pointing tension's intensity patterns [3]

Successful interfaces are those which users can immediately identify the relevant material in its arrangement [6]. Emotional and functional maps indicate important points, helping to decide, for example, which interface area should be more emphatically projected. Through the systematic use of sound in the critical points of the map, it is possible to infer deeper meanings to the interface events. This happens to the extent that users can realize that there is a set of messages, actions and specific tasks that are in evidence and require more attention.

As the project advances thru layers, new design approaches can arise, suggesting that new sounds can be added, and the ones that were previously planned can be removed. It is vital that sounds meet the overall structure of the project, and this implies to reassess previously made decisions, and take new directions at any time.

2.4   The *"Sound Reference Sheet"* Layer

The sound architecture diagram offers a broad, systematic view of the interface's sound design. In this DAAG layer, a detailed document called *sound reference sheet* will show how this broader vision will be fulfilled individually, on each interface, in every interaction node. It's a document that defines the behavior of each audio element in the interface, that is, how the sounds will be integrated into the interactive environment. To this end, some questions should be readily raised. Sounds are merely reactive or will be triggered by a specific user action? The sound will transmit some kind of perceptible information, alerting, indicating something on a specific region of the interface? These and other questions about the nature of the interaction that sound will perform should be made at this project stage (Fig. 8).

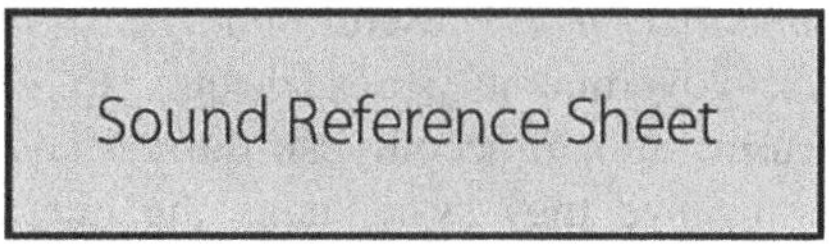

Fig. 8. The *sound reference sheet* layer

The sound reference sheet is a document that makes possible to organize and create the interface soundtrack. It is a document that synthesizes the interface's sound design management, and has a major importance to the acquisition (recording, editing and mixing) and implementation of the sounds in the interface. The sound reference sheet allows an overview of the sounds that will be integrated in the interface, and also provides a possibility to reassess the previously made decisions, in order to refine them. This document will guide the programming staff, providing a detailed script to inserting sounds in the interactive environment. To fully comply with these premises, the sound reference sheet must be formulated with two main items, namely: (a) soundtrack description; and (b) interaction rules.

The *soundtrack description* is a detailed description of what should be the sound itself. Since sounds were already sorted in categories such as voice, ambience music and sound effects, it is possible to schedule the recording sessions. It is recommended to choose a short name and increasing numbers for every sound that will be used in order to control its production and properly organize them in the interface's audio library.

Interaction Rules. The second parameter to be determined is about how the sounds will interact with the user. This means defining under what circumstances the sound is triggered, by being reactive, dynamic, interactive or adaptive, that is, what is the audio behavior with the user. In other words, the interaction rules defines how a sound will start and finish, in which place of the interface, and under what circumstances it will happen (by clicking on a visual element, according to an execution of a task, in a timing triggered situation).

A critical aspect to control dynamic sounds is the definition of interaction key-points. The interaction rules needs starting and stopping points (play-ins and play-outs) by selecting variables (runtime, difficulty of task, performance, user status) that will qualify them in the programing platform. These points occur in periods of great importance, usually when users have to make relevant decisions. Getting a sound response according to a specific interface behavior is a fundamental matter for the sound design project. The interaction rules must be clearly defined and explicitly detailed, since it will be a guide to insert the sounds in the interactive platform.

A common way to address style questions about audio tracks for the interface can be done through the creation of temporary tracks. Temporary tracks should be set in preliminary positions by defining the basic parameters from which a creative team can lean on. The use of provisional tracks is also useful to test its incorporation in the platform, making possible to check if the proposed interaction rules are working properly.

Through the *sound reference sheet*, the programing team can exactly understand the behavior of the audio tracks in the interface, and how these sounds should be inserted. The sound reference sheet is a document that summarizes a group of relevant information that make possible to implement sounds in the interface, by exposing the nature of their behavior in the navigation context. In short, the sound reference sheet brings together in one document, all decisions made about the interface's sound design.

2.5   The *"Audio Library"* Layer

After finishing the sound reference sheet, then the *audio library* of the interface can be created. At this point, the stages of acquisition and processing of the sound files are done, making them ready for subsequent application by the programming team. This process takes place in three stages: production, post-production and implementation (Fig. 9).

Fig. 9. The *audio library* layer

The production stage involves capturing the sounds or acquiring them in sound libraries. The use of sound libraries is very common, and often the picked sounds are manipulated to achieve specific acoustic effects. However, to record custom sounds, a studio will be needed, or even in a recording field, outdoors, proper equipment should be set, and professional assistance should be considered. Technical aspects of audio, such as sample rate, resolution and other considerations to ensure that the audio files will have a compatible technical quality must also be defined. After that all the sounds listed in the sound reference sheet were captured and manipulated to achieve their aesthetic goals, these sounds will go thru a mixing stage for its subsequent implementation in the interactive platform.

In interactive applications, the post-production stage typically involves some degree of mixing. It is a procedure that aims to balance and adjust the various sound sources to present them in a clear and interesting way. It is in the mix stage that volume, panorama, equalization and other acoustic effects are added in order to establish a harmonic relationship between the sounds, so they can work together in the interface. Mixing is required since it considers the mutual relation of the sounds, and ensures that no overlapping between their frequency bands will occur. At this point, the design team must clarify which group of sounds will be emphasized and which ones will have less relevance in the overall context of the interface, so these concepts could be incorporated to the mix process.

Finally, the implementation should be considered, including the available tools and technologies. With the finished audio files and in conjunction with the sound reference sheet, the programming team can then add the sounds accurately in the interactive application.

3   Preliminary Use Cases

A preliminary test of the DAAG was performed in class, in order to provide students an articulate understanding between sound design and interface design in a conceptual, technical and practical manner. The guide was used in the academic discipline Project 6 (EGR 7140, Bachelor in Design, Federal University of Santa Catarina, Florianópolis, Brazil), that utilizes the User Experience Design approach from [6], and was held in the second semester of 2012. As the user experience layers were introduced in class, the sound recommendations from DAAG were progressively presented to students. In order to bring a better understanding of the guide, practical examples of the use of sound in interactive environments were shown to the students. Students enrolled in the course were divided into teams, and each team had to develop an interactive environment in the form of a website or an application, in a real scenario, with clients. The following is a brief description of two of the six works that were developed during the discipline.

3.1   The "*SAT*" Interface

The "*SAT*" project aimed to redesign the website of the Tax Administration System, from the Department of Finance of the State of Santa Catarina. This portal has a header area, with an initial menu that leads users to its applications. The user audience is composed of internal users (SAT officials), tax accountants, taxpayers, accountants, municipality officials, and the State Attorney General. The main objective of the working team was to reshape the interface in order to reduce the graphical content to its essentials, contributing to an easy-to-use operation.

In relation to the intended objectives, one of the requirements was "to call the user's attention to unexpected occurrences in the system", which means making the user confirms actions and take care about losing possible data during navigation. To achieve that, two content requirements were selected: to build informative messages (indicating error and warning) and dialog boxes to confirm actions (sending and losing data). To make it more perceptible to users, audio alerts were added to these boxes. Since the boxes only appear when something wrong happens, the sounds will not be considered repetitive. Since it is an interface with highly functional premises, the use of sounds in the "SAT" project were limited to these ones, but they were rated with high importance by the working team, that were chasing simple but effective solutions.

3.2   The "*Gym*" Interface

This group performed the development of a fitness gym's website. Giving the proximity of its physical place to the campus, the target audience is the university community, representing more than 50 % of the clients. Since a large group of customers are young, the website should be a key-factor to create a virtual space that can be accessible outside of the physical space of the gym. To be part of experiences that customers can live outside of the physical environment of the gym, the working group decided to insert a playlist in the website's front-page, as mentioned in the audio design concept document:

The gym's website could contain a playlist and make it available to anyone accessing it, regardless of location and devices (desktops, smartphones, tablets). The songs could be heard since there is a connection to the internet. These presented songs could be pre-selected by the academy team, containing songs that are played in the fitness classes, or even the user could ride your own playlist with the songs that are played during his training in gym. An online radio could also be created and, by on-line surveys, the radio content should fit with the users' taste and style.

With this proposal the students created a competitive advantage, enabling customers the access of the songs that are featured in the gym, so they can listen to it when performing outdoors activities, like walking, jogging, cycling. Looking upside down, the solution was quite simple and nothing really outstanding was needed to make these decisions feasible. But looking from a user's perspective, it was possible to bring a new degree of experience that was previous limited to a physical space, and now exceeded those barriers. That's exactly the DAAG's goal: to start a new approach when thinking about sound, interface and user experience design.

4 Final Considerations

Audio for interactive environments should be considered a collaborative process. The programmer cannot implement the sound files without the composition, and the sounds and music, in turn, depends largely on how it will be applied. One should take into account a constant dialogue between these two aspects: the conception and its application in the interactive platform.

As this is a relatively new area in the academic field, it is not yet sufficiently able to develop strong theories without the basic and substantial empirical research, which will evaluate the practice of audio production in interactive environments. The fact that the studies in dynamic audio are a recent effort means that much empirical evidence have not been sufficiently researched, and the available content is still scattered.

The Dynamic Audio Application Guide cast a new approach on the use of sound in interactive systems. Principles, foundations and assumptions of dynamic audio should be included in interface design methodologies, so the sound stimulus may be used with clearly defined goals: as an information carrier.

It is believed that the study results will open a debate of a yet low researched area, allowing its scientific basis to be useful in academic and professional practices, by providing a new tool to interface designers. The Dynamic Audio Application Guide aims to explore efficient methods to make the sound design an essential part of interface projects.

References

1. BAR-B-Q, Project. Group Report: Group Report: Providing a High Level of Mixing Aesthetics in Interactive Audio and Games. The Thirteenth Annual Interactive Music Conference PROJECT BAR-B-Q 2008, San Antonio, USA, December 2008. http://www.projectbarbq.com/bbq08/bbq08r8.htm. Accessed 15 Oct 2014
2. Carvalho, L.R., Cybis Pereira, A.T.: Interface design and dynamic audio. In: Kurosu, M. (ed.) HCI 2014, Part II. LNCS, vol. 8511, pp. 523–531. Springer, Heidelberg (2014). doi: http://link.springer.com/chapter/10.1007%2F978-3-319-07230-2_50

3. Collins, K.: Game Sound: an Introduction to the History, Theory, and Practice of Video Game Music and Sound Design, p. 92. MIT Press, Massachusetts (2008)
4. Collins, K.: Making Gamers Cry: Mirror Neurons and Embodied Interaction with Game Sound. AudioMostly 2011, September 7–9, 2011, Coimbra, Portugal (2011)
5. Darras, B.: Design cognitivo e design participativo. In: Hipermídia: desafios da atualidade/Vânia Ribas Ulbricht, Alice Theresinha Cybis Pereira (orgs.). Pandion, Florianópolis (2009)
6. Garrett, J.J.: The Elements of User Experience: User Centered Design for the Web and Beyond, 2nd edn, pp. 29–103. New Riders, Berkeley (2011)
7. Mckee, H.: Sound matters: Notes toward the analysis and design of sound in multimodal webtexts. Comput. Compos. **23**(3), 335–354 (2006). [s.l.]: Elsevier/ScienceDirect
8. Rocchesso, D., et al.: Sonic interaction design: sound, information and experience. In: Conference on Human Factors in Computing Systems: CHI 2008 Extended Abstracts on Human Factors in Computing Systems. ACM Association for Computing Machinery, New York (2008)
9. Stuart, R.: Design of Virtual Environments. McGraw-Hill, New York (1996)
10. Susini, P., et al.: Closing the Loop of Sound Evaluation and Design. In: 2nd ISCA/DEGA Tutorial & Research Workshop on Perceptual Quality of Systems. Berlin, Deutschland, set. 2006

Designing an Interactive Map of Musical Culture and a Digital Humanity App

Sheng-Chih Chen[1(✉)] and Chiung-Hui Hwang[2]

[1] College of Communication, National ChengChi University,
Taipei City, Taiwan
scchen@nccu.edu.tw
[2] General Education Center, National Chiao Tung University,
Hsinchu City, Taiwan
chiunghuihwang@mail.nctu.edu.tw

Abstract. An array of elements such as history, culture, music and delicacy can easily attract travelers' attention. In this paper, we attempt to design a mobile and visual search platform to help tourists understand these elements easily. Our target area is Dadaocheng, which is a well-known destination in Taiwan. We focus on local shops and design customized signboards for their digital marketing, cultural and creativity value-adding services. In addition, these signboards can serve as user's search target. The platform of our design provides search engine services with a monitoring mechanism at the server. Each query image is captured by mobile phone's camera, and search results on time and accuracy are recorded on the monitoring platform. This research focuses on the performance of visual search accuracy under ordinary circumstances. The overall process can be completed in one second. Current experimental results indicate that recognition rate can reach 88 percent.

1 Introduction

Over the past ten years, many cutting-edge technologies are coming up and have changed people's life. People are capable of get benefits with modern intelligent systems. The concept of Internet of Things (IoT) is getting mature in most existing companies. They are eager to propose a variety of protocols, domains, application and Web services, are expected to connect people to an advanced convenient life environments.

Mobile tourists are one example that combines the features and benefit from that. Moreover, it is more profitable and obvious for mobile tourists whom they travel around the world with mobile devices.

Before the trip, they can use either mobile devices or computer to collect the associated destination information, fight tickets and housing reservation.

On tour, people who are capable of ubiquitously querying anything via web search, or even sharing real-time multimedia in social network.

And after the trip, they are likely to review photos using cloud-based service platform.

A. Marcus (Ed.): DUXU 2015, Part II, LNCS 9187, pp. 301–306, 2015.
DOI: 10.1007/978-3-319-20898-5_29

Now, a great diversity of Web approaches we can make use of. In spite of that, rather than powerful but complex tools, mobile tourists may prefer to use simple and user-friendly tools while on tour. Therefore, it is the objective of this paper to design a simple but effective mobile search way for mobile tourists. We incorporate content-based image retrieval into our mobile applications, trying to propose an easy and intuitive approach to query the targets which they are interested in.

The digital generation's acceptance of technology, particularly that of younger groups, has been increasing. Although society is aging, elderly people can communicate with younger people by learning to use digital technology. This was the impetus for this study. Based on the concept of digital natives, this study was intended to assist students in understanding the roles digital technology play in various fields in modern society, through a university course.

The core value of this course is to train 'digital natives' to think and design for 'digital immigrants', so that their applications and designs could actually 'empower' inexperienced users and let them enjoy the convenience of technology as well. Specifically, this course was first designed for the graduate students who took the course. In addition to participating in in-class discussions, the students, guided by the teacher, also visited a research area.

This course was intended to assist the students in creating a deeper link to the field through a series of design and thinking units, observation, question discovery, design and planning, method design. Therefore when the students develop actual mobile services in the future, their design consideration can be broader and more complete from a macro-view, thus benefiting and empowering experienced and also new users of digital applications and technologies (Fig. 1).

Fig. 1. Digital humanity App Core Value

2 Related Works

Digital technology has not only rendered daily life more convenient, and contributed to the improvement of several social issues, including medical care problems. For instance, Wu et al. [1] modified the technology acceptance model (TAM) and expanded it to design a mobile medical healthcare system (MHS). The result showed that with the effect of mobile technology on medical diagnoses is positive. Also, as more and more information environment structures being implemented, cloud computing and ubiquitous computing have made mobile medical healthcare even more easy and applicable.

Doukas et al. [2] developed a medical healthcare application on Android platform, with which under a stable Internet environment, that allows users to synchronize personal health condition and check on their basic health records through smart devices. Bourouis et al. [3] combined smart phone devices with a physiologic sensor, and designed a remote monitoring system that makes sure the safety of lone elders.

In dealing with daily issues for autistic children in school, Mintz et al. [4] designed an application that helps discovering problems they might encounter. The authors also try to find the causes and offer assistance with newer technology designs.

In hopes of improving learning for challenged individuals, Brown et al. [5] developed an Android location-based service (LBS) mobile game and performed follow-up evaluations and tests.

The increasing popularity of social networks has increased the attention focused on the combination of location-based service (LBS) and social networks. A part of LBS studies focused on certain groups of people. For example, Ferris et al. [6] designed a value-added service for passengers who take buses in Seattle, in hopes of improving the mass transportation issues of the city. Also, increasing attention has also been focused on LBS applications in specific cities, institutions, or regions. Ratti [7] collected information and data in Milan with the LBS design for future research regarding the city's planning and development. Karamshuk et al. [8] demonstrated how to find spots for new retail store with the help of LBS. According to the aforementioned and implementations, mobile value-added services combining mobile technology, social network, and LBS have been applied in various fields.

To boost tourism industry, some official organization will produce OR Some tourist organization have developed mobile traveling applications to introduce destinations. On behalf of the Malta Tourism Authority (Boiano, Bowen, and Gaia [9]), they distributed an iPhone app for promotion of the Maltese Cultural Heritage. Chen et al. [10] combined concept of service design in course lecturing, and encouraged students to develop their own mobile travel application which specific to YiLan county of Taiwan.

In 2011, Ji et al. [11] devised a large-scale landmark image search system that introduces the famous cities around the world, such as Beijing, New York, Florence and Singapore. Similar content-based image retrieval technique as Ji et al. [11], Nodari et al. [12] proposed a mobile visual search application to classify the objects of interests in fashion domain.

3   The Proposed Architecture

To let mobile tourists understand the scenery places effectively and effortlessly, this proposed system architecture aims to integrate content-based image retrieval into mobile application. We manage to focus on tourism industry in Taiwan so that Dadaocheng is our target place at this moment. Dadaocheng contains historical, cultural and delicacy scenic spots and it is a vital area with commercial vitality in Taipei City. Derived from Huang and Chen [13], we extend the system from desktop version to a mobile application. Figure 2 illustrates the proposed architecture.

To strike a balance between efficiency and precision, client-server architecture is the approach we try to perform the mobile content-based image retrieval (CBIR) in this

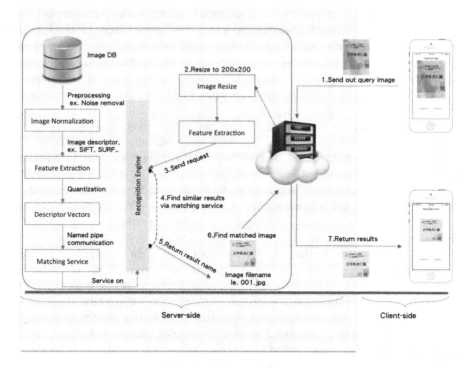

Fig. 2. System architecture

paper. First, image descriptors are extracted from an offline database using SIFT descriptor. For the communication between multiple processes, inter-process communication (IPC) is a practical approach for performing capabilities such as named pipe, shared memory, message queue and socket functions.

According to the analysis in Yu [14], the named pipe approach outperforms other IPC approaches in Internet connection and concurrent multiple query processes. Instead of server-side that processes the majority of complex computation, client-side plays a presentation role in the first and last step in this application. At this moment, we take mobile phone's embedded camera to achieve capture query images. Query image then will be normalized to 200×200 size and send it to the recognition engine for further processing. After query image is processed thoroughly, mobile device will automatically fetch the matching result via URL link and present it on the user interface. In terms of this proposed design, client-side can keep it simple in character of presentation part and keep off the electricity consumption from intensive computing.

4 Experimental Results

At present, we cooperated 207 local shops with our research. To promote local tourism, we design customized signboards for their digital marketing, cultural and creativity value-adding services. To attain a robust accuracy, we generate blur and brightness samples to imitate the improper but normally happened in real life. In simple, we generate 10 more instances of blur cases and 30 instances of brightness case. In this experiment, a total of 8487 samples are employed from 207 local shops have been gathered. And we choose Apple iOS as our mobile platform. Without detailed destination information provided, the proposed mobile search application now is only responsible for sending the collected query image of the request to the server-side and presents the retrieved result.

To evaluate the performance of the proposed architecture, we have designed a monitoring mechanism at the server. It will be helpful that we keep track of the each query. We have collected each query image and recognized result, then logged each processing time as the image filename. Based on the filename, we can get that the overall process can be completed in one second. To ensure the accuracy is stable in preliminary experimental stage, we restrict relevant manager to verify the matching results manually by checking each corresponding checkbox.

In this experiment, a total of 8487 samples from Dadaocheng's local shops have been employed, and we randomly adopted 100 queries to evaluate the accuracy in real life. We found out that the 88 queries can be matched correctly. Some incorrect matches happened on over occluded or exposure cases.

5   Summary and Future Studies

We have proposed a mobile application to provide a timely visual search tool for mobile tourists. One of the purposes of this paper is trying to boost the local tourism industry. Hence, we initially focus on Dadaocheng district in Taiwan. Moreover, we put much emphasis on the establishment of system architecture, including client-server architecture and monitoring mechanism.

Specifically, we have first accomplished the entire process integrating mobile devices with visual search technique into our proposed architecture. Secondly, the overall image search process can be completed in one second. At last, all the activities will be logged on the monitoring system.

The preliminary results are promising, achieving 88% accuracy. For those incorrect cases, improve matching algorithm is a one way to tailor its accuracy but it may cost much more development time.

However, there are a few common traits of mobile devices we can refer to, such as overlay some visual hints on the user interface or utilize touch screen operation to reduce unnecessary recognition area. These UI methods are not only accelerating the development cycle, but also it is also a good manner to enhance the user experience from a user's point of view.

Currently, we already make sure that the proposed approach is feasible.

Future work certainly includes increasing more features of our services. Provide relevant travel information, for instances, viewing destination information, social network connections, augmented reality interaction or even integrate other embedded sensors.

Regarding to the monitoring mechanism, it is required to adopt database in the near future if we desire to track down the abundant data for further management.

References

1. Wu, J.H., Wang, S.C., Lin, L.M.: Mobile computing acceptance factors in the healthcare industry: a structural equation model. Int. J. Med. Informatics **76**, 66–77 (2007)
2. Doukas, C., Pliakas, T., Maglogiannis, I.: Mobile healthcare information management utilizing cloud computing and android OS. In: 2010 Annual International Conference of the IEEE, Engineering in Medicine and Biology Society (EMBC), pp. 1037–1040 (2010)
3. Bourouis, A., Feham, M., Bouchachia, A.: Ubiquitous mobile health monitoring system for elderly (UMHMSE). Int. J. Comput. Sci. Inf. Technol. **3**, 74 (2011)
4. Mintz, J.: Additional key factors mediating the use of a mobile technology tool designed to develop social and life skills in children with autism spectrum disorders: evaluation of the 2nd hands prototype. Comput. Edu. **63**, 17–27 (2012)
5. Brown, D.J., et al.: Designing location-based learning experiences for people with intellectual disabilities and additional sensory impairments. Comput. Edu. **56**, 11–20 (2011)
6. Ferris, B., Watkins, K., Borning, A.: Location-aware tools for improving public transit usability. IEEE Pervasive Comput. **9**, 13–19 (2010)
7. Ratti, C., Williams, S., Frenchman, D., Pulselli, R.: Mobile landscapes: using location data from cell phones for urban analysis. Environ. Plan. **33**(5), 727–748 (2006)
8. Karamshuk, D., Noulas, A., Scellato, S., Nicosia, V., Mascolo, C.: Geo-spotting: mining online location-based services for optimal retail store placement. In: The 19th ACM SIGKDD International Conference on Knowledge Discovery and Data Mining, pp. 793–801 (2013)
9. Boiano, S., Bowen, J.P., Gaia, G.: Usability, design and content issues of mobile apps for cultural heritage promotion: the malta culture guide experience. In: Computing Research Repository, pp. 66–73 (2012)
10. Chen, W.L., Chen, S.C., Huang, C.M., Huang, Y.J., Tsai, P.C., Tseng, W.C.: The localization of praxis-oriented research: creating service design applications. In: Management of Engineering and Technology Portland International Conference, pp. 1974–1980 (2014)
11. Ji, R., Duan, L.Y., Chen, J., Yao, H., Yuan, J., Rui, Y., Gao, W.: Location discriminative vocabulary coding for mobile landmark search. Int. J. Comput. Vision **96**, 290–314 (2012)
12. Nodari, A., Ghiringhelli, M., Zamberletti, A., Vanetti, M., Albertini, S., Gallo, I.: A mobile visual search application for content based image retrieval in the fashion domain. In: 10th International Workshop on Content-Based Multimedia Indexing, pp. 1–6 (2012)
13. Huang, C.M. Chen, S.C.: Smart tourism: exploring historical, cultural, and delicacy scenic spots using visual-based image search technology. In: The 3rd International Conference and Engineering and Technology Innovation (2014)
14. Yu, C.C.: The design and implementation of an agent-based platform for developing resource management systems. Master's thesis, National Central University (2006)

Applying Human Centered Design Process for Designing Air Traffic Control Interfaces

Satoru Inoue[1(✉)], Kazuhiko Yamazaki[2], Hajime Hirako[2],
and Toshiya Sasaki[2]

[1] Air Traffic Management Department, Electronic Navigation Research Institute,
Tokyo, Japan
sati86.enri@gmail.com
[2] Department of Design, Chiba Institute of Technology, Chiba, Japan
{designkaz,hrkhjm0508,toshiya.sskl}@gmail.com

Abstract. In this research, we focused on task analysis of air traffic controllers in actual en-route Air Traffic Control (ATC) in an experimental activity based on a Human-Centered Design (HCD) approach. We discuss the method of design to develop a system of human consciousness, and created prototype design along with HCD process. In this paper, firstly, we propose an observation survey technique that can obtain survey results of high effectiveness, with a process of HCD that can be executed simply compared with current available techniques. In this analysis, we conducted a simulation at one of the air traffic sectors of the Tokyo Area Control Center. After analyzing the current ATC work, we developed a prototype design of the future ATC interface for Air Traffic Controllers based on our findings.

1 Introduction

The importance of User-Oriented design process such as Human Centered Design: HCD are recognized under the process of designing systems. The idea of HCD process is important to design the specialized systems or user-interfaces for experts as well as consumer products. However, HCD is not practical processes but philosophical concepts. Some ideas of general HCD processes or User Experience: UX Design approaches are defined as framework to carry out practical design process. However, such kinds of current available techniques cannot be used efficiently as those are. Key approaches for applying HCD process to specialized systems are customized methods for fitting each special systems/works to capture the functions and roles correctly. In the process of developing complex systems, the user-oriented design such as HCD or UX is one of the important ideas to develop specialized complex systems which operators can use their special knowledge and skills. However, practically, normal HCD methods cannot be applied for capturing these highly specialized functions. An important key technique is how to embody the concept of HCD or modify the process for developing actual systems. Especially, it is very important to consider the practical points of view for understanding users focus and working context in highly specialized operation, because actual special expert work is hard to understand essentially.

© Springer International Publishing Switzerland 2015
A. Marcus (Ed.): DUXU 2015, Part II, LNCS 9187, pp. 307–316, 2015.
DOI: 10.1007/978-3-319-20898-5_30

Therefore, in this study, we try to develop a method which including the analysis from users' cognitive perspective based on HCD concept. We attempt to apply our method to interface design for ATC systems as our case study. ATC system is designed for fitting to ATC controllers' work. Thus, we design the ATC system interfaces after understanding the role of user's systems and system functions well correctly for making higher usability systems for specific ATC systems and work. However, technically, it is difficult to fully appreciated users roles and mechanisms of the target system for designers in highly specialized system design, as compared with designing general consumer products. Therefore, in this study, we propose an observation survey technique that can obtain results of high effectiveness, with a process of human-centered design that can be simply executed compared with conventional techniques. Additionally, we will show practical techniques for carrying out analysis of well understanding roles and function of ATC systems as a target. In addition, we propose the actual case study for taking users in design process which is feature of HCD. Then, finally, we show our concept design model as a prototype model and result of user test. Then, we consider the method of task analysis, to find the issues related to the human factors for supporting ATC systems in the future.

2 Approach for HCD Process

Human Centered Design: HCD is one of effective method to understand the user's requirements. In order to design a system that can assure system safety, enhance usability, and support human reliability in the future, the idea of HCD processes can help an engineer in considering the features in the control system operations and the intentions of the controller in ATC Systems. HCD is defined as "an approach to design and develop a system that aims to make interactive systems more usable by focusing on the use of the system and applying human factors/ergonomics and usability knowledge and techniques" in ISO 9241-210: Human-centered design for interactive systems [1]. One of Characteristics of HCD is defined as following 4 main iterative processes for design.

1. Understand and specify the context of use.
2. Specify the target user and organizational requirements.
3. Creating and considering design solutions.
4. Design Evaluation (User test).

In this research, we focus on following point of view for fitting practical design process iteratively for ATC interfaces based on HCD.

3 User Research

3.1 Understanding and Finding ATC Work

Main purpose of our user survey is to understand the meaning of work, the functions of the target system, and discover the improving points under the current systems condition. Task analysis is important process to understand the functions and the role of the systems and point out the drawbacks within the current system condition. As a first step, we observed ATC systems and controllers' work by using a training simulator. And surveyed how to use systems interface, and understanding roles of ATC work by carrying out ethnographically way. In this study, we recorded several video data as video ethnography.

3.2   Characteristics of ATC Controller's Work as a Result of User

As characteristics controllers from task analysis, the Radar controller and Coordination controller, who take charge of the en-route ATC, frequently monitor the display of the radar control interface and the data of flight-strips, and carry out controlling tasks while exchanging information. For instance, when the radar controller projects the existence of a related aircraft from the radar monitor, a series of instructions from the radar controller are directed to the pilot through communication with the aircraft to avoid conflict. The controllers then input the contents of these instructions into the RDP (Radar Data Processing) system, and input the flight-strip.

The sequence of controllers' tasks is described in time-line data that consists of action logs and protocol logs based on the data from videos and flight-strips. The situation is then segmented following the contents of a controller communication mainly based on the time-line data of action and protocol. The context of each segmented situation is analyzed based on the action and protocol data as well as based on an explanation of the situation made by a supervisor.

From the analysis, air traffic controllers are expected to maintain the safety of air space and smooth air traffic flow. One of the most promising strategies for systems to assist in task performance is the concept of cognitive systems that try to enable systems to interact with humans in a knowing manner that is similar to the way in which humans interact with one another [2]. Such systems require being equipped with a user model that explains the user behavior from a variety of aspects of cognitive processes such as awareness, memory, user knowledge and experience, context recognition, planning, intention formation, and even consciousness in order to assist in the user's work process by estimating them [3].

3.3   Cognitive Systems Perspective

From a cognitive process perspective in particular, it is essential that trainees and systems developers understand the complex processes that are involved in the cooperative work among multiple controllers and aircraft pilots. Since air traffic controller skills are acquired through specialized training, their cooperative work processes are very complex and temporal constraints are also very restrictive and severe. In order to design and develop more reliable systems or training programs for ATC controllers, we need to understand the details of the basic system (including controller) functions.

Distributed cognition is a methodological framework by which cognitive processes that span multiple actors mediated by technology can be analyzed [4]. It can be effective in analyzing cooperative work from a cognitive process perspective. Distributed cognition analysis makes explicit the dependencies between human actors and artifacts by examining the transformation and propagation of information through various forms of representations. As such, this 'knowledge' can be represented in terms of interactions in context, which lend themselves to further analysis. The management of knowledge, and hence the retention of knowledge, is through changes in distributed cognition induced by the introduction of new systems, personnel, and norms.

4   Practical Process for Modelling ATC Work

4.1   Micro-Task Analysis

Air Traffic controller (Radar controller and Coordination controller) tasks in ATC work were subdivided and set on a micro-task basis. The contents of the tasks are briefly described by the micro-task of replacing the ground-to-air communication and the contents of the operation of control systems, etc. which were transcribed. All the descriptions of the tasks concerning the operation of ground-to-air communication and the control console (the input switch and the screen display of control information, etc.) and the flight-strips are described as "The tester's behavior", and the name is given individually as a micro-task.

The following items have been summarized in the table of micro-tasks.

(1)   Classification - describing the classification of the micro-task.
(2)   Situation - describing situations in which the micro-task can be generated.
(3)   Task name - describing the name of the micro-task.
(4)   Action - describing the contents of the micro-task based on the actions of the air traffic controller.
(5)   Ground-to-air communication - describing the contents of the ground-to-air communication separately between the air traffic controllers as instructed (out), and received (in).
(6)   Operation - describing the operation of the systems control console in detail.
(7)   Flight-strips - describing the operation of flight-strips which are printed in flight plans.

4.2   User Modeling

We analyzed the simulator experiment as Micro-task analysis including task process and cause of actions with ATC controller. Furthermore, we marshaled data about design subjects based on results of analysis. In the next step the supervisor who has a license of an Air Traffic Controller prioritized the order of design subjects, and selected main targets from the list of subjects. In this study, we tried to develop 2 methods for analysis to analyze design subjects. As a first method, it focuses on visualization of physical task. The other one focuses on visualization of the task related to mental workload. There are 3 main problems for visualization of physical tasks: (1) one situation which is needed to provide an instruction immediately, (2) on the other hands standing by to judge the timing of situation for providing instruction, (3) increment of instruction quantity by providing an instruction for navigation. Furthermore, as a visualization of mental workload, we focus on the situation of a route crossing and spacing between aircraft.

4.2.1   View Point of Physical Task Problem

We tried to survey the controller's mouse cursor trajectories which we expected to discover drawbacks of the current control interface by visualizing the process of a mouse cursor.

As the practical process of visualization of physical tasks, Radar screen shots were extracted on the sheet with control tasks, mouse trajectories and interview contents. We selected the situation for 26 min of recorded video data.

The result of our analysis is listed regarding to the situation per minute. The main drawbacks derived from the analysis of visualization of physical tasks are shown in following list. As the result of analysis, we could found 24 issues regarding with current ATC interfaces by using simulator experiment from physical tasks perspective. We divided into following 7 types of work conditions.

< Types of conditions based on practical analysis>

1. Instruction which providing immediately or standing by the timing.
2. Increment physical workload by providing instructions.
3. Affecting aircraft spacing by reducing speed instruction.
4. Common type of tasks.
5. Limited instruction by air space restriction.
6. Need to consider the wind factor to provide instruction.
7. Instruction without using map information.

4.2.2   Cognitive Point of View

In the analysis which took into account mental workload, we conducted a survey for pointing out interface drawbacks, by categorizing controllers' mental workload. In the practical process of visualization of mental workload analysis, we observed the working process, condition and situation by using video data, and selected situation is lined up visual situation temporally. Then, we divided into 4 types of mental workload as follows. Figure 1 shows an example process to categorize the mental workload along with temporal process in the analysis.

- [Exiting]: This workload is each aircraft which from handed over control to own sector until handing off to the next adjacent sector.
- [Crossing]: This type of workload is occurring when more than 2 aircraft which are flying to a different destination or route would cross.
- [Spacing]: This type of workload is occurring, in case the more than 2 aircraft which are flying to the same destination would be merging their route.
- [Catching up]: This type of workload is occurring, in case the aircraft multiple identical destinations flies in tandem, it takes the case behind the aircraft speed is faster than before the aircraft.

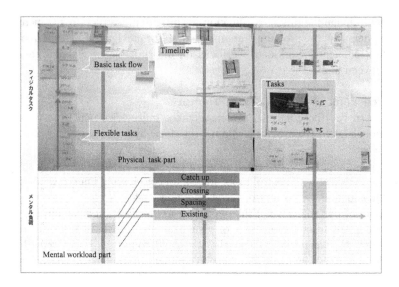

Fig. 1. An example process to visualization of the mental workload

In our visualization method of mental workload, the result of analysis is divided into 6 types by air traffic controllers who are supervisor of this analysis. Our group is consisted with following types, (1): issues of both cross and spacing, (2): issues of both catch-up and spacing, (3): common issues, (4): of catch-up issues, (5): intersection of issues, (6): spacing issues.

4.3   Creating Concept Design

4.3.1   Development Basic Design Ideas

In the verification of the validity of the visualization method of physical tasks, we utilized scenario-based acceptability technique. Because we cannot evaluate the ATC work accurately without explaining to designers any the scenario-based ideas of ATC work. In order to carry out the scenario-based evaluation, we develop an idea sheet which has 4 main sections as "Background of the issues in ATC work", "Ideas of using image", "flow of the use case ideas" and "Scenario of ATC operations for using the data", "topics of ideas" By utilizing ideas sheet shown in the following Fig. 1, we tried to develop effective ideas for the problem which is our higher priority in ATC work.

As the results, we developed 7 types of user interface and function idea. And, we could summarize those functions clearly based on the scenario for each situation.

We developed a prototype design for next generation ATC system console interface based on HCD design process shown in Fig. 2. Characteristics of our concept design are supporting functions such as future state prediction and indicate information along with time-line. In this study, we created 6 functions as a total. First 4 functions as named "Cross Point", Screen Capture", "Reservation", "Touch Input" are derived from the analysis based on visualization of physical task. And our second group of function named as "Predict Fix", "Focus Input" based on the analysis of visualization of mental workload.

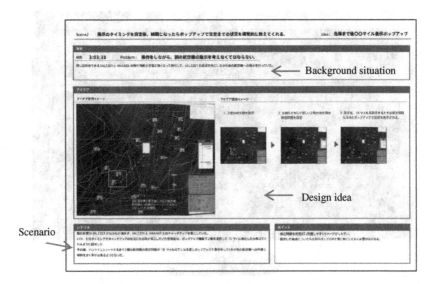

Fig. 2. An example of design process sheet

Screen Capture. A controller can see the future situation on the radar screen which selected area and set several minutes ahead. The controller also can confirm the crossing situation of future with using "Screen Capture" function together.

Focus Input. If a controller wants to zoom up specialized area to see the more precise situation, "Focus Input" can zoom up a situation in the special window.

Touch Input. This interface provides an alternative data input function by using our touch panel effectively instead of keyboard typing for inputting a value of speed altitude and heading.

Reservation. This function provides a reminder to notify the timing of instruction and helps to indicate which are critical or important.

Predict Fix. When a controller receives an aircraft from adjacent control areas, the planned time and route is shown on the radar screen and on the display of "Predict FIX".

Focus Input. If a planned route of aircraft will cross with another aircraft route, our system shows the time of crossing at the intersection point in the window of "Predicted Time".

This prototype design is set on a 36-inches-display which will be standardized as the next ATC display in Japan. Display interface structure is defined 6 panels shown in Fig. 3 and as following a list.

Fig. 3. Our suggested prototype interface design

Radar Display. The controller can check the position and flight information of aircraft on this panel. Controller mainly uses this panel to input flight information for revising the state of aircraft. This panel has a relationship to all other suggested functions.

Display Control Panel. Display Control Panel has functions for changing display information. The controller also can input information for revising instruction information to aircraft. Suggested functions as "Screen Capture" and "Cross Point" can be used from this console.

Quick Action. This window can be input information related with instruction to aircraft. The functions of "Reservation", "Touch Input", "Focus Input" can be used from this panel.

Predict Area. For using "Screen Capture", this panel shows a future state as a projection which a controller set a preferred time when they want to see.

Predict FIX. In order to use "Predict FIX" function, this system calculates a time of passing at the FIX. And the panel shows "Passing time", "name of FIX" and "Flight call sign" as a "list" on the display.

Predict Time. This panel shows the time-line information of "Predict FIX", "Cross Point" and "Reservation". This display is a kind of memorandum record along with time-line.

4.4   Evaluation

4.4.1   User Test

We carried out user test that focused on effectivity, interaction process and willingness to use suggested functions (Fig. 4). Test subjects are consisted with 6 interface ideas. 2 examiners have an air traffic controller license and worked as a real controller.

Fig. 4. A situation of user test for concept design

Table 1 shows our user test result of the suggested 6 interface ideas. As for "Predict Time" and "Screen Capture", both evaluators gave almost positive scores to "Effectivity", "Interaction Process" and "Willingness to use". An evaluator commented that a controller can give to an instruction at an appropriate time.

As for "Predict Time" and "Screen Capture", both evaluators gave positive scores to "Effectivity", "Interaction Process" and "Willingness to use". One of the evaluators commented that a controller can give an instruction in appropriate timing by using the function of "Screen Capture".

Table 1. User test result for suggested design

	Effectivity		Interaction Process		Willingness to use	
	Evaluator 1	Evaluator 2	Evaluator 1	Evaluator 2	Evaluator 1	Evaluator 2
Predict fix	4	3	4	3	4	3
Cross Point	4	4	4	3	3	4
Screen Capture	3	4	4	3	4	4
Reservation	3	2	3	3	3	2
Touch Input	2	3	4	4	3	3
Focus Input	3	2	2	4	3	2

As for "Cross Point", both users gave high scores for all criteria. However, a controller indicated some of information tags might be overlapped on the radar screen and it might case issues.

Regarding with "Reservation" function, Evaluators scored to "Easy to understand" in "Interaction process", however, one evaluator marked "Don't want to use" in "Willingness to use" section. This idea should be improved and reconstructed in our future work. "Touch Input" got a high score to "Interaction Process" and "Willingness to use". As for "Focus Input", One of the controllers commented that she thought it isn't a necessary function in the current air traffic situation.

- Effectivity: "1" is "Not effective interface for ATC work", "4" is "Very effective interface for ATC work"
- Interaction Process: "1" is "Difficult to understand", "4" is "Easy to understand"
- Willingness to use: "1" is "Don't want to use anymore", "4" is "Want to use in the future"

From the result of user test, "Cross Point" which derived from focusing of visualization of mental workload, and "Screen Capture" which from visualization of physical task got higher scores and these two functions have possibility to be effective and willing to use in the future.

5 Summary

In this study, we discussed about how we introduced HCD process to specialized and complicated process. After that we showed the concrete analysis process and technique for fitting specialized systems, in this time, ATC work was a case study. Furthermore, we proposed some prototype design along with our analysis result. And then, we also carried out user test and evaluation. However, user test was still really primitive. Therefore, we need to brush up design ideas iteratively along with HCD process to provide a more sophisticated design.

References

1. ISO 9241-210:2010 (Ergonomics of human-system interaction – Part 210: Human-centred design for interactive systems) (2010)
2. Forsythe, C., Bernard, L.M., Goldsmith, E.T.: Cognitive Systems: Human Cognitive Models in Systems Design. Lawrence Erlbaum Associates Inc., Hillsdale (2006)
3. Hikonen, O.P.: The Cognitive Approach to Conscious Machines. Imprint Academic Com, Exeter (2003)
4. Hollan, J., Hutchins, E., Kirsh, D.: Distributed cognition. ACM Trans. on Comput.-Hum. Interact. 7(2), 174–196 (2000)

Synchronized Data Management and Its Integration into a Graphical User Interface for Archaeological Related Disciplines

Daniel Kaltenthaler[1], Johannes-Y. Lohrer[1(✉)], Peer Kröger[1],
Christiaan H. van der Meijden[2], and Henriette Obermaier[3]

[1] Institute for Informatics, Ludwig-Maximilians-Universität, Munich, Germany
{kaltenthaler,lohrer,kroeger}@dbs.ifi.lmu.de
[2] IT Group, Vetenarian Faculty, Ludwig-Maximilians-Universität, Munich, Germany
v.d.meijden@it.vetmed.uni-muenchen.de
[3] Bavarian State Collection for Anthropology and Palaeoanatomy, Munich, Germany
henriette.obermaier@palaeo.vetmed.uni-muenchen.de

Abstract. In this paper, we describe xBook, a generic, open-source
e-Science infrastructure for distributed, relational data management that
is particularly designed for the needs of archaeological related disciplines.
The key feature of xBook is that it can be used as an offline resource at
remote sites during excavations and can be synchronized with a central
server at any time. While some scientists can record data in xBook in
the field where no internet connection is available, colleagues can already
work with and analyse the previously synchronized data via the central
server at any location in the world. Incarnations of the xBook framework
are used in archaeology, and archaeobiology (anthropology and archaeozoology). We will highlight one of them, OssoBook, an e-Science service
that implements a data model for animal remains from archaeological
sites (mainly bones) and has emerged as one of the European standards
for archaeozoology.

1 Introduction

As in many other applications in archaeology a main part of the work comprises
in collecting, sharing and analysing data. Often many researchers from different institutions and even varying countries are involved in excavation projects.
Therefore entering data directly into databases is required to easily access data
from different places and work simultaneously on recording as well as analysing
the data. Archaeological data is often gathered in field work, i.e., at remote sites
that do not offer a convenient environment for IT services, it is typically not possible to enter the data into databases that must be accessed via an internet connection. As a consequence, IT services are hardly used in these projects. Rather,
data is typically recorded on paper and is (if at all) later processed electronically
using proprietary and/or file-based data management tools like Excel, etc. for

A. Marcus (Ed.): DUXU 2015, Part II, LNCS 9187, pp. 317–329, 2015.
DOI: 10.1007/978-3-319-20898-5_31

doing simple descriptive statistics. This is significantly inconsistent with the need to sustainably store data on the cultural heritage claimed by the UNESCO[1].

Obviously, researchers from these archaeological domains would significantly benefit from a profound e-Science infrastructure that supports digital recording, implements sustainable data management and storage as well as offering powerful analysis tools. The key limitation of such an IT service is the problem of multiple users that need access to data recording and data analysis even if a permanent internet connection cannot be established. A synchronization process is required, implementing a client server architecture as visualized in Fig. 1, to ensure working offline at remote places, but also storing data globally, where it can be shared with other users is the solution.

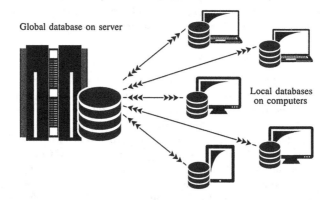

Fig. 1. The local clients are connected to the global server. The synchronization allows data exchange, so data can be recorded on the local machines, but can be backupped and shared via the server.

Existing commercial solutions for this problem are typically integrated in a dedicated database management system and/or cloud service. For licence or financial reasons as well as due to privacy concerns however, not all institutions can or want to resort to these systems. Budgets for archaeological excavation projects are typically optimized in terms of logistics and man-power. Reserving a considerable part for IT infrastructure is completely unrealistic. In addition, as long as the data is not yet analysed and the results are not yet published, the participating researchers are very wary about giving their data into the hands of commercial cloud services.

In this paper, we propose the framework xBook, a solution for the sketched problem that follows the architecture depicted in Fig. 1 is directly included into the application and, thus, can be used independently of the underlying database software. In particular, it can also be used with non-commercial and open source database management systems; in fact, xBook uses a MySQL database.

---

[1] http://www.unesco.org.

In addition, xBook implements a sophisticated privacy management. The solution can both be run as a server and can be installed on remote clients (e.g. laptop computers). Thus, each institution or consortium running an excavation can implement their own e-Science service without the need to give the data to a third, potentially not trusted party. Finally, the xBook framework is independent with respect to the data model. Thus, each research institution or consortium is free to implement its specialized data model reflecting different working paradigms, different ways of recording data, etc.

2   Problem Formulation

In this chapter, we discuss the requirements of an e-Science infrastructure for the archaeological sciences in more detail. A synchronized distributed e-Science infrastructure for data management and data analysis in the archaeological sciences should address the following issues:

- **Distinctability of Entries:** Two different entries must be distinct from each other, no matter on which local database they were created.
- **Conflict Handling:** Different users are able to work on the same data simultaneously on different local databases. The synchronization must recognize that a conflict occurred and provide options to solve it.
- **Time-Delayed Execution:** It cannot be guaranteed that a user of the database can always execute the synchronization process. This could be technical reasons like temporary internet disconnects, but also for logistic reasons that there is no internet connection available. It must be possible to continue working offline and synchronize the data later as soon as the computer is reconnected to an internet connection again.
- **Interruptible:** After a loss of connection or if the user interrupts the exchange of data, the synchronization process must be able to continue and no data may be lost or corrupted.
- **Modularity:** To avoid transfer of unnecessary data a selection of data is required. The user should be able to select parts of data he wants to synchronize to save time and to reduce data overhead, so data should be separated in modules ("projects"). Furthermore, the local database of the user should not save any data sets, for which he has no reading rights.
- **Currentness of Look-up Table Data:** The look-up table data, that is saved on the database of the global server, needs to be updated many times. This concerns regular as well as dynamic updates of this data. Administrators, with the permission to edit, must be able to insert new entries and edit or delete existing ones. These changes must be passed as soon as possible to the users, to ensure they can work with current data.
- **Rights Management:** Not every user needs to see all the data. The synchronization must check if the user, who has requested any data, has appropriate rights before sending or committing this data.

- **Easy To Use:** The synchronization should be an automatic process that can be run with few mouse clicks. The user is most likely not a skilled computer user, but must be able to use the synchronization. Therefore, the synchronization process should be carried out without any external data devices.

As discussed above, in addition to these specific requirements, an e-Science infrastructure for the archaeological sciences should also be cost effective and ensure the privacy of unpublished data.

In general, the basic idea of synchronization is not a new one. Both scientific and industrial databases often require functions to share data in any way, especially, if several users should be able to work on the data simultaneously. Synchronization techniques exist in the most commonly used database systems worldwide, including Microsoft SQL Server, Oracle and MySQL: Snapshot replication, Transaction replication, Replication with streams, Merge replication, Master-slave replication system.

While all of these methods are sufficient for many areas of application, to the best of our knowledge none of them cover all of the requirements stated above. Only few of the available solutions provide the ability to work offline and none of them allow synchronization of single datasets, which are two of the most important requirements for archaeologists. Therefore we created a synchronization that fulfils all previously stated requirements, is independent of the database management system and hence can be used for any database system.

3   The xBook Framework

With the aim of solving the same problems in several, different databases the idea of the xBook framework has emerged. The core function of xBook is the synchronization, but it also provides structures for the user management, right management, the graphical user interface and the data handling as indicated in Fig. 2. The databases are based on the same basic structure, but each of them can be individualised. This allows e.g. own input fields for entry mask or individual extensions. The function in detail:

User Rights Management: For archaeological data, it is not only important to allow parallel data entry of several persons, it is also necessary to be able to share data for complex analysis. Because not every user wants to make his data accessible to the public (especially if it is still unpublished), a flexible solution for the user rights management is required.

The framework provides default permissions (read, write and project management), each database can be extended with individual rights. As often is the case, to work together with the same group of people (e.g. within an institute) xBook does not only support the assignment of rights to single users, but also to user groups. These groups can be created by each user.

Graphical User Interface: xBook provides a graphical user interface because all databases that are based on the framework use the same functions and even the workflow is similar. This interface reuses common elements, but it also gives support to alter existing functions and to insert new, individual ones.

Especially the entry masks benefit from the framework a lot, because input fields, that were already implemented for one database, can be reused in other databases as well. Currently, xBook provides a wide variety of different input fields, e.g. text and number fields, dynamic comboboxes, selection fields, etc. Its advantage is that all databases profit by updates of a single input field. Customisations or individual, new fields can be integrated at any time. The similarity and the common elements in the user interfaces are illustrated in the screen shots depicted in Fig. 2.

Data Handling: The different databases very often use the same algorithms in the program execution. Especially for the huge amount of input fields, but also for single features, the underlying logic is repeating. To avoid multiple implementations in the code, xBook uses a combination of the single data managers (cf. Sect. 4) and the controller.

The controller connects the graphical user interface with the model and is responsible for the database-specific queries. It offers basic structures that are necessary for each database, but also allows customization if necessary.

Plug-in Interface (for data analysis): For the information processing of archaeological data the possibility of analyses is required. Different scientific research questions need different analyses, that cannot be predefined in xBook. So xBook contains a plug-in interface that allows the integration of analyses that can be added dynamically to the application. In general everyone who is familiar with coding in Java and working with SQL databases can create plug-ins for xBook. An API for the plug-in interface is in preparation. As default, a generic QBE plug-in for retrieval is implemented.

Synchronization: One of the core functions of xBook is the synchronization that is introduced in detail in Sect. 4.

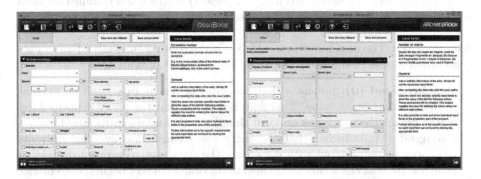

Fig. 2. The input mask of OssoBook (left) and ArchaeoBook (right). Both of the applications are based on the xBook framework, that provides a basic graphical user interface and functions, but allow customisation like e.g. individual input fields.

4   Synchronization

4.1   Realization in the Database

To achieve the synchronization we are aiming for, some necessary additions in the database had to be made.

Database ID: One of the most important concepts is the database ID. A column for this ID is added in each table a user can enter data in. In addition this column is also marked as a primary key, to allow several distinct entries with the same ID from various databases. The value of this number for this database itself is stored both in a separate table and also as a property in the configuration settings of the operation system. The database ID is generated when the user connects to the server the first time, or if the value of the ID in the database is different to the value in the properties. This is to prevent errors, when a user copies his database to a different computer.

When the user enters a new entry in the database, the database ID is automatically filled in with the above defined value. If the entry is edited the database ID is not touched. Because we want to enable a modular approach with projects, all tables also must add the ID and the database ID of the project, otherwise the entry cannot be assigned to a project.

Status: To achieve both conflict management and identification which entries have to be updated locally the column "Status" is added to each table. It stores the time the entry was modified on the server. This value is modified only on the server via a trigger:

```
SET NEW.Status = NOW() + 0;
```

If the entry on the client has a lower (older) status it needs to be updated.

If the entry on the server has a higher (newer) status when committing data to the server, a conflict occurred, because someone else modified the entry.

Message ID: The next important addition is the column "message id". It stores the current status of the entry (locally). The different options are:

- **Synchronized (0):** Indicates that the entry is synchronized and no uncommitted changes were made. This does not mean that the entry is up-to-date, it just means the entry has no local changes and can be synchronized.
- **Changed (1):** Indicates that the entry was changed locally. This prevents the entry being updated with data from the database, to prevent overriding changes. In most cases this would also mean that a conflict occurs, but conflict checking is already done when the entry is committed, so no need to take action here. After the entry is successfully committed to the server, the status is set to "synchronized" again.

– **Conflicted (-1):** Indicates that this entry is conflicted and therefore can not be committed or updated. A conflict occurs when an entry that is changed locally has an older (lower) status than the entry on the server. Then the changes on the local entry were made on an older version of the entry, and if the entry would be committed, there would be possible loss of data.

4.2 Realization in the Application

Some of the basic requirements are already fulfilled in the database, but as the data has also to be sent and some features are still missing, several concepts had to be developed in the application as well.

Database Update: To allow constant updates to the application, including changes in the database scheme, we added a check for the version of the database. This number is stored in the "version" table and is compared to the built-in number in the program. If the numbers don't match, the server is queried for an update. This check is done after the connection to the database is established, but before the user can begin working with the data. If the user has no internet connection the update can of course not be made, but since he could also not upgrade the program without an internet connection, this doesn't seem like a big issue.

Code Tables: The look-up tables, which contain mappings for values in different languages e.g. the name of the animals, that are displayed in the graphical user interface, are named "code tables" in our synchronization. To be able to change or add values to the code tables without having to distribute a new program version, all values are stored in the database. To receive the newest version of the data only the database has to be updated. This can therefore be done during the usage of the application. To find out which values are changed, all tables have the column "Status". Just like the entry the value of the status is the timestamp of the last global change and is updated with triggers on insert and update:

```
SET NEW.Status = NOW() + 0;
```

The last update is set locally, after all changes have been (successfully) made, and is retrieved from the server before the update progress is started. Then only a check has to be made, if the local value is lower than the global value, and only if so, the code tables are out of date and therefore have to be updated.

Manager: To control the communication with the database from the client, we created manager classes, that have all the knowledge about the columns for the table they are "responsible" for. The structure of the manager is as follows:

– **Table Manager:** The base class for all managers. It holds the connection object, contains the basic methods like insert and update and sends SQL queries to the database.

- **Abstract Synchronization Manager:** This manager holds all the important information for the synchronization. It handles the insert and update of entries from the server, retrieves uncommitted entries and sets data to synchronized or conflicted.
  All managers that need to be synchronized must extend this.
- **Base Entry Manager:** The base entry manager is responsible for getting the main entry from the input unit (the main table for entries). It also calls the underlying *Extended Entry Managers* to retrieve the data for the complete entry. This class also manages the saving, loading and updating data for itself and forwards the call to the underlying methods.
- **Extended Entry Manager:** A manager for entries that extend a base entry, that is needed for example if an entry can have more than one value of a specific type. So the list of values would be stored in a different table.
- **Base Project Manager:** The base project manager is responsible for getting the main entry for entries that are valid for the whole project (e.g. project information itself). It also calls the underlying *Extended Project Managers* to retrieve the data for the complete entry. This class also manages the saving, loading and updating data for itself and forwards the call to the underlying methods.
- **Extended Project Manager:** This manager is for entries that extend a base project entry. This manager is needed for example if an entry can have more than one value of a specific type. So the list of values would be stored in a different table.

Data Structure: To store the data and retrieve a complete entry we created some classes to easily load, save and update the data.

- **DataColumn:** The most basic data type is the DataColumn. In it only one value is stored together with its column name.
- **DataRow:** Represents one row in the database. It is an ArrayList of *Data-Column* containing all the data for this row.
- **DataTable:** Contains all *DataRows* for the current entry in the specific table. In addition to the *DataRow* it only knows to which table it belongs.
- **DataSet:** Represents one entry. Therefore it has all *DataTables* that define the entry, and additionally hold the key of the entry and the key of the project the entry belongs to.

Synchronization Process: The actual progress of the synchronization consists of three different steps:

(1) Check if the user has the required rights to access the project and therefore is allowed to synchronize it.
(2) All uncommitted, not conflicted entries in project and entry tables are retrieved, one by one, from the database and send to the server, this is done by iterating over all *Base project* and *Base Entry Managers*. These

call their belonging sub managers, load all data belonging to the current entry and send their data to the server. If the entry already exists in the global database, then the server checks the timestamp of the entry that was sent with the one of the entry that is already in the database. If the global timestamp is newer than the local one there is a conflict and the client is notified of it. (cf. Sect. 4.2)

(3) The project and entry data is transmitted from the server to the client. For identifying which entry has to be transmitted, the timestamp of the newest entry of the current table, therefore the last entry that was synchronized, is transmitted. To prevent loss of data after an incomplete synchronization, the first query requests entries that have exactly the same timestamp as the highest timestamp locally. For all later queries always the next data with a higher timestamp is retrieved. The entry is then only updated if the corresponding value in the local database either doesn't already exist or is not conflicted or changed.

Deletion: Due to the fact that the Synchronization can only identify changes with the check of the "Status" column, it is not easily possible to delete entries. Still, there needs to be the option to delete an entry. To solve this problem a column "Deleted" was added. It is an enumeration that has only two options: "Y" and "N" - with "N" as default value. Instead of deleting an entry the value of the "Deleted" column is set to "Y". Then this change can be synchronized to the global server. From there it can also be synchronized to other clients. When the client gets the information that an entry is deleted it can safely delete the entry locally. On the server however an entry is never deleted, because the information about the change must always remain available for the clients. The same logic is applied to code table entries, with the exception that entry tables are only synced to the clients.

Conflict Management: If an entry was marked as conflicted during the synchronization process, the conflict has to be solved before it can be merged with the entry in the global database. After the conflict has been merged e.g. by providing both the global and local entry, and allowing the user to select the diverse values, the merged entry is saved to the database with the timestamp of the global entry. This ensures, that if the entry was updated between the solving of the entry and committing the entry to the global database, this change will not be overridden, but a new conflict is generated.

5 Synchronization in the Graphical User Interface

As presented in Sect. 4 the synchronization consists of a powerful, but complex architecture. However the realization in the application must consider that most of the archaeologists are not used to work almost exclusively with a computer. That is the reason why it is absolutely necessary to hide the complexity of the synchronization behind an intuitive input mask that is easy to use and allows its usage even if the user is not technically versatile. Here we describe how the synchronization is integrated into the graphical user interface of xBook:

5.1 Manual Data Synchronization

To exchange project data there are three basic procedures that must be possible in the synchronization panel.

Global projects for which a user has read and/or write permission must be downloadable from the server. Therefore the corresponding projects can be selected in the right project selection in the synchronization panel.

Local projects that have not been synchronized with the server before must be able to be uploaded to the server. These projects can be selected in the left project selection.

Existing projects (as well local and global ones) must be updateable. For this purpose the corresponding projects must be selected, like explained above. However the application recognize if there was selected a project on the server project list that is also available on the local project list, and vice versa.

By pressing the "Synchronize" button the procedures are executed. Depended on the internet speed and the number of projects and datasets (e.g. in OssoBook exist projects with an six-digit number amount of entries) the synchronization may take several hours. Thus user feedback is displayed in message boxes and progress bars (each one for general, project and dataset layer)

When the procedures are running the user can continue working with the application, the synchronization is running in background. It can also be interrupted by closing the application and continued to a later time.

5.2 Automatic Data Synchronization

The automatic synchronization can be activated in the application settings. Thereby the project information and data sets are synchronized with the server automatic in background. However it is necessary to manually define once which projects shall be downloaded from the server. This is important to avoid that all projects are downloaded even if the user does not want to save them on the local database (Fig. 3).

6   Case Study OssoBook - an Archaeozoological Database

OssoBook [8] was original released with dBASE as technical basis in 1990. Since then the application was continuously updated and extended [4], and different tools for data analysis were implemented and integrated to OssoBook as plug-ins [1,5–7]. In 2011 the database as well as the logic and the appearance of the application was restructured again to modernise the ageing program structure

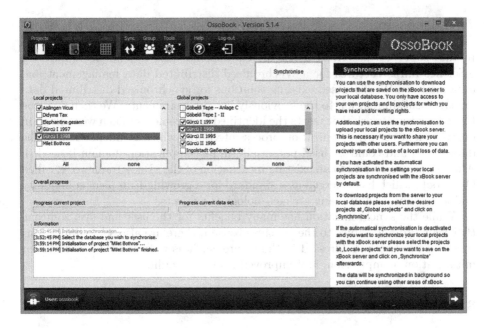

Fig. 3. The synchronization panel in OssoBook.

and to prepare the software for future work [2,3]. Since then the application, especially the synchronization, is developing strongly.

OssoBook is currently used by approximately 200 users including scientists, Ph.D. students and students in institutes of universities, museums and scientific collections with archaeozoology as field of work, as well as freelance archaeo-zoologists. The eScience service is available in German, English, French and Spanish. In the context of the IANUS[2] project of the German Archaeological Institute, Berlin, Germany, OssoBook will serve as a standard for the archaeo-zoology domain. As introduction of the usage of the software there are annual workshops in several European countries.

OssoBook offers all the advantages of a database system. Furthermore, first analysis tools, that can be integrated into OssoBook as plug-ins are also available, including a module for the analysis of age distribution [1], a module for the clus-ter analysis of measurements [1], a plug-in for similarity search on multi-instance objects [5], a plug-in for the execution of sample data mining methods [6], and a module offering some analysis methods for archaeozoological data [7]. Subject-specific, the application should primarily allow the collection of the minimum standards, the input to these fields is mandatory. In addition there are numer-ousness of further possibilities to enter data. Many of them have user-friendly features (e.g. a few hundred pictures of all measurements for different animal classes), that will be extended step by step to fulfil the needs of the users. A text in the sidebar always explains the visible feature and includes details to the current selected input field.

---

[2] http://www.ianus-fdz.de/.

7 Discussion

In this paper we described a list of requirements that should be fulfilled by e-Science infrastructures for a synchronized distributed data management and data analysis. We discussed existing solutions for synchronized distributed data management, in relation to the previously listed requirements. We then describe the xBook framework that meets the identified requirements. Then we took an in depth look at the synchronization process of xBook, which is independent of the data model and could be used potentially in any application domain if needed. Afterwards, we presented an existing incarnation of the xBook framework, called OssoBook, which has emerged as a standard for a growing European community and is already used in many archaeozoological projects.

While the synchronization has many benefits for the user and also someone that wants to add tables to the synchronization, there are also some limitations that still need to be addressed in the future, such as reducing the overhead for initialization, compression, and improved conflict handling.

8 Availability

The xBook framework on the web: http://xbook.vetmed.uni-muenchen.de/

References

1. Kaltenthaler, D., Lohrer, J.: Visual and density based cluster analysis of the archaeological database OssoBook in consideration of aspects of data integrity. Consistency and Quality, Diplomarbeit, Ludwig-Maximilians-Universität, Database Systems Group, Munich (2012)
2. Kaltenthaler, D.: Design and implementation of a graphical user interface for the archaeozoological database OssoBook. Projektarbeit, Ludwig-Maximilians-Universität, Database Systems Group, Munich (2011)
3. Lohrer, J.: Design and implementation of a dynamic database for archaeozoological tasks. Projektarbeit, Ludwig-Maximilians-Universität, Database Systems Group, Munich (2011)
4. Schiebler, J.: OSSOBOOK, a database system for archaeozoology. In: Anreiter, P., Bartosiewicz, L., Jerem, E., Meid, W. (eds.) Man an the Animal World: Studies in Archaeozoology, Archaeology, Antropology and Palaeolinguistics in Memoriam Sndor Bökönyi. Budapest, Archaeolongua (1998)
5. Danti, S.: Cluster analysis of features of animal bones and similarity search on multi instance objects of the archaeozoological data pool. Diplomarbeit, Ludwig-Maximilians-Universität, Database Systems Group, Munich (2010)
6. Tsukanava, Y.: Development and appliance of data mining methods on the palaeoanatomic data collection. Diplomarbeit, Ludwig-Maximilians-Universität, Database Systems Group, Munich (2010)
7. Neumayer, T.: Design and implementation of analysis methods for archaeozoological data. Bachelorarbeit, Ludwig-Maximilians-Universität, Database Systems Group, Munich (2012)

8. Kaltenthaler, D., Lohrer, J., Kröger, P., van der Meijden, C., Granado, E., Lamprecht, J., Nücke, F., Obermaier, H., Stopp, B., Baly, I., Callou, C., Gourichon, L., Pöllath, N., Peters, J., Schibler, J.: OssoBook v5.1.1. Munich, Basel (2014). (http://xbook.vetmed.uni-muenchen.de/)

Brazilian Research Panorama on Information Ergonomics and Graphic Design

Luis C. Paschoarelli[(⊠)], João Silva, Danilo Silva, Gabriel Bonfim,
Fausto O. Medola, and Erica Neves

PPGDesign, Univ. Estadual Paulista, Bauru, Brazil
{paschoarelli,fausto.medola}@faac.unesp.br,
{joaocarlos_placido,gh_cb}@hotmail.com,
danilo@idemdesign.net, ericapneves@yahoo.com.br

Abstract. With the emergence and easy access to new interfaces that are present and necessary to current daily life, a concern about the interface projects begins, and so, new research methods and analyzes emerge to support that growing demand. In seeking to understand how those researches are being treated in Brazil, this paper uses a bibliometric study concerning the area of Graphic Design and Informational Ergonomics in the largest conferences of Design in Brazil: "EGODESIGN/USIHC" and the "P&D Design", in order to provide a panorama of the growth of research and study groups through the publications in the area. In addition it seeks to demonstrate the regions in the country which concentrates the focus on those themes and how Brazil is concerned with the issues related to the study and with the improvement of technological interfaces.

Keywords: Bibliometrics · Graphic design · Informational ergonomics · Brazilian conferences · Research

1 Introduction

The expansion of the promotional materials in the last century was greatly facilitated by both the use of digital technologies and low cost printing. In the virtual world there was an unprecedented advertising explosion that made those advertisements or newsletters massive and often poorly designed. That scenario stimulated the need for new digital interfaces that seek to be intuitive and easy to access.

It should be noted, however, that the rapid propagation of digital media, as well as easy access to such interfaces, have hampered the development of new graphic materials, since the excess of characteristic attributes and mechanisms of that system could affect the harmony of the information and the devaluation of its interface by what might be called "visual pollution".

Therefore, there is a need of studies regarding the Information Architecture and the Digital Interface Design. In this way, the Graphic Design area promotes tools and methods that are able to configure all information submitted to the user in a more assertive and efficient manner.

© Springer International Publishing Switzerland 2015
A. Marcus (Ed.): DUXU 2015, Part II, LNCS 9187, pp. 330–340, 2015.
DOI: 10.1007/978-3-319-20898-5_32

The specialized professional should organize that information properly, always evaluating the impact on the user's daily life. In this context, the Informational Ergonomics (IE) makes use of a number of instruments to improve and enhance the various informational devices, since it integrates cognitive processes inherent in mankind.

Currently, the growing number of institutions with the Graduate Program in Design in Brazil is moving parallel to the gradual growth of scientific publication and production related to the Design area (Industrial Design). Regarding this fact, the Graphic Design, in parallel to the Informational Ergonomics, has been of increasing interest within the scientific field over the last decade because of its scope and complexity, both in theoretical and practical terms.

It is important to assess the degree of scientific development of the area. A portrait of the scientific production in the area can be created from bibliometric studies that examine development indicators from different areas of knowledge. In Brazil, the set of papers published in the International Conference of Ergonomics and Usability of Human-Technology and Human-Computer Interfaces – ERGODESIGN/USIHC – and in the Brazilian Conference of Research and Development in Design – P&D Design – form a significant body of knowledge for IE area. In this context, this study aims to trace a panorama about the research on Informational Ergonomics and Graphic Design that has been carried out over the last years in Brazil by bibliometric analysis of published material in those two scientific events.

2 Theoretical Review

2.1 Design and Informational Ergonomics

Graphic design refers to visually communication of a concept, idea, or even a principle. It comprises the conception, development and implementation of visual systems projects of physical or virtual configuration, presented in a two-dimensional plane. It can also be considered as a means to structure and shape the printed communication or interfaces that, overall, deal with the relationship between image and text [1].

To send the right information to the right person at the desired time, in an effective and efficient way, it is necessary to use the principles of information theory - the field of Informational Ergonomics (IE) - to bring satisfaction to the users respecting their diversity. This field reaches its goal contemplating cognition and perception, covering aspects of verbal and non verbal language [2]. Therefore, this area of ergonomics is related to the knowledge of human cognition process.

Cognition is the event of the mind in carrying out daily tasks and involves cognitive processes of interaction, such as thinking, speaking, and others [3]. Such concepts may be divided in two ways: experimental and reflexive. With regard to the first, it involves the action and reaction of the humans involved in a given activity; while the second involves the thought, the comparison and the decision-making, this one develops ideas giving way to creativity [4].

These cognitive models use some paradigms for functionalities such as attention, perception, comprehension and memorization. Attention is related to the alert level of the organism. Perception is the relationship of the individual to the cultural context.

The comprehension refers to the correspondence of the message meanings attributed by the source; and the memorization by selective retention of the message [5].

The role of IE is the application of specific techniques that provide a tight balance among man, his work and the environment. When applied, and managed correctly in the institutions, it enables the worker (or user) higher rates of health, comfort and safety perception [6].

2.2 Design Research in Brazil

The consequences of the design, as well as its inter and multidisciplinary approach, promoted the formalization of the Graduate Programs in Design, both at Masters level and doctorate in Brazil. Regarding the interdisciplinary of the design research, the varied backgrounds of the programs' professors promotes the development of research based on topics related to their areas of expertise, thus stimulating the research interdisciplinarity [7].

This permeability of information among areas of knowledge contributes to the generation of joint productions and to proposals for new born research fields and related interests. So, the specialties of the lines of research linked to the Design are established, such as the Graphic Design or specifically the Informational Ergonomics.

The concentration areas and lines of research, characterized by multi and interdisciplinarity, provide to the researcher the opportunity to reflect and discuss about challenging issues that result from economic, social and cultural needs of the reality in which they operate.

However, for the contributions acquired within the academies to be effective and validated, the research carried out should be available to access by interested parties, as those are configured as essential tools for reflection, discussion and democratization of scientific knowledge of the area. Scientific dissemination is characterized by its ability to transmit to the society the knowledge of new discoveries, new materials, new methodologies, and others [8].

In this sense, the scientific production of the Design area helps to consolidate it as a scientific field that is able to contribute to the development of society by promoting the construction of critical knowledge. The scientific conferences as well as journals, and books consist of one of the effective actions for the exchange of knowledge. Through those channels, the results of research are disseminated, shared and put to debate, collaborating with the learning process and the collaboration among the areas.

One of the main Brazilian design conferences is the P&D Design that takes place every two years, and contributes to the discussion and dissemination of research. The 1st P&D Design took place in São Paulo/SP in 1994 and expanded over time: 2nd P&D Design - Belo Horizonte/MG, 1996; 3rd P&D Design - Rio de Janeiro/RJ, 1998; 4th P&D Design - Novo Hamburgo/RS, 2000; 5th P&D Design - Brasília/DF, 2002; 6th P&D Design - São Paulo/SP, 2004; 7th P&D Design - Curitiba/PR, 2006; 8th P&D Design - São Paulo/SP, 2008; 9th P&D Design - São Paulo/SP, 2010; 10th P&D Design - São Luís/MA, 2012; and 11th P&D Design - Gramado/RS, 2014.

Other two important annual conferences to the area of Design are the ERGODE-SIGN and USIHC, which occur together and have the main focus in the areas of Ergonomics and Usability. Their first editions took place in Rio de Janeiro/RJ from 2001 to 2005, since then, other cities have hosted such events, as follows: 2006 in Bauru/SP; 2007 in Balneário Camboriú/SC; 2008 in São Luís/MA; 2009 in Curitiba/PR; 2010 in Rio de Janeiro/RJ; 2011 in Manaus/AM; 2012 in Natal/RN; 2013 in Juiz de Fora/MG; and 2014 in Joinville/SC.

Previous studies indicate that, in recent years, the Brazilian scenario has an improvement on the number of publications on the fields of this paper, such as Graphic Design, and especially the IE [13, 14]. Thus, an updated bibliometric research about the publications of those areas provides data to portray the evolution of scientific research and it can also identify their quantitative profile.

2.3   Bibliometrics

The bibliometrics is an area of studies of Information Sciences employing mathematical and statistical tools to investigate and quantify the processes of written communication, so it is a set of research methods, using quantitative data analysis, it can map certain scientific field, while acting as behavioral analysis tool of researchers in the decision-making for the construction of this knowledge [9].

The word 'bibliometrics' was first used in the work entitled *Traité de Documentation* in 1934 by Paul Otlet, defined as "the set of the bibliology that deals with the extent or amount applied to books" [12, p. 60]. However, it was in 1969 that Alan Pritchard popularized the term defining it as "all studies that seek to quantify the writing communication processes" [12, p. 60]. Pritchard suggested that the word 'bibliometrics' should replace the term previously used "statistical bibliography" first mentioned in 1922 by Edward Wyndham Hulme [9–12].

Currently, bibliometrics has three basic principles: the principle of Lotka, describing the productivity of authors; the principle of Zipf, which describes the use frequency of words in a given text; and the principle of Bradford, which describes the distribution of the periodical literature in a specific area. The Lotka's Law, also known as the Inverse Square Law, was formulated in 1926. This law follows the principle that many researchers publish little and few researchers publish a lot, so a great number of publications comes from a small number of efficient producers. In contrast, Zipf's Law, formulated in 1949, became known as the Minimum Effort Law. This law is based on the relation between words in a given text and the serial order of those words, so by the frequency which the words appear in various texts it is possible to generate an ordered list of a certain subject [9–11].

Finally, the Law of Bradford, also known as Dispersion Law, allows to estimate the relevance of journals in a given area of knowledge, in other words, the productivity of journals. As the initial articles are introduced in the publications in the media targeted to them, the discussion on the topics increases, attracting more articles about the subject discussed. In the course of scientific events, it takes a greater range and developments, resulting in centers of studies and research, making the subject deeper and broader, producing more knowledge about the area and, finally, spreading this new theme. In this context, bibliometrics is a useful tool to estimate development and growth of a focused area [10].

3 Methodology

According to the objectives of this study, the bibliometric analysis was focused on concepts related to Bradford's Law. However, the analysis was not limited to productivity in the journals, but to the production of institutions and to the topics published in conferences, in order to study possible links among subject areas and centers of study or research.

We reviewed and analyzed all the proceedings of ERGODESIGN/USIHC from 2010 to 2014; and also the annals of the P&D Design editions from 2010 to 2014. Data from previous editions of those events were obtained in studies published by [13, 14]. To collect data, each paper was read individually, and this procedure was standardized for all analyzes. Then, it was calculated the total number of articles in each issue of the Conferences, and it was tried to obtain the total number of items that encompassed the theme "Graphic Design" and the total number of articles dealing about "Informational Ergonomics".

It was considered as "Graphic Design" publications that dealt with any theme related to the display of imagery or visual information, but not the formal configuration (three-dimensional) of a product. In "Informational Ergonomics" it was considered the articles which dealt with analyzes and methods to display that information in order to improve the user interface, both in physical and digital media.

The productions related to "Graphic Design" were also subdivided by state of the federation, it was considered as origin only the state of the first author. In the case of absence of such information, we attempted to locate them at Lattes (Brazilian curricula database) of each author. Then, the general data was organized in a spreadsheet and graphics were generated for a better visualization of the results. Data analysis was based on descriptive statistics, grouping the data based on previously defined criteria.

4 Results

The collected data allowed to identify a significant increase in the number of papers published in ERGODESIGN/USIHC since their first edition. Between 2010 and 2011 the number of publications practically doubled, from 125 to 232 papers. In more recent editions, the number of published papers oscillated at approximately 200 papers. Because this event is unique to issues related to ergonomics, the articles related to graphic design are automatically related to IE. Figure 1 shows a graph of the evolution of the total number of papers and, among them, the number of papers related to Informational Ergonomics.

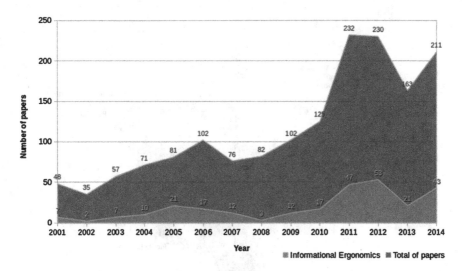

Fig. 1. Total number of articles per year and related to Informational Ergonomics published in ERGODESIGN/USIHC (Source: the authors).

In Fig. 1 it is possible to observe that the total number of papers related to IE almost tripled between 2010 and 2011, going from 17 to 47 papers. In percentage terms, it has increased from approximately 14 % to 20 % of the total of the event. In the edition of 2013 that percentage followed the fall in the number of publications, but it showed a new rise in the last edition, held in 2014. The historical percentage suggested by the data series obtained for EI articles in relation to the total for this event is 17 %.

When analyzing the geographical distribution of papers related to graphic design published in this event, it is noticed that there is a concentration of publications in the Southeast and South region, mainly in the states of Rio de Janeiro, Sao Paulo, Parana, Santa Catarina and Rio Grande do Sul. Figure 2 shows the map of Brazil and the quantitative distribution of papers in each State of the Federation. The omitted States have not added any publication in all editions of the event.

For the P&D Design, the biggest design conference in Brazil, it is also observed an increase in the number of publications. For this event, the multiplicity of themes first demand the identification of papers related to graphic design area. Thus, Fig. 3 shows the total number of papers per edition and, among them, the amount of publications related to graphic design accounted between 2010 and 2014 editions. The data are associated to those presented in [14].

It is noted that the total number of papers increased from 529 to 923 between 2010 and 2012 editions of that event. This growth was accompanied by the quantitative increase of papers related to graphic design (from 109 to 263). In percentage terms, the field increased from 21 % to 28 % of the total. In the edition of 2014 however, they opted for a more compact conference and the total of approved papers fell to 322, and 87 of those were related to graphic design. This reduction did not affect the relative participation of the area, which remained at 27 % of the published papers.

Fig. 2. Distribution of articles published in ERGODESIGN/USIHC by states in Brazil (Source: the authors).

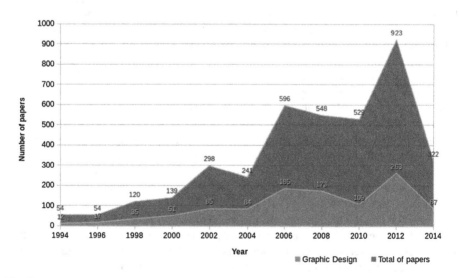

Fig. 3. Total number of articles per year related to Graphic Design published in P&D Design (Source: the authors).

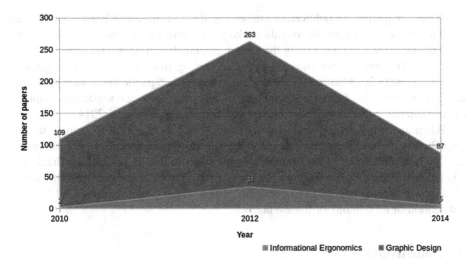

Fig. 4. Total number of articles per year related to Informational Ergonomics published in P&D Design (Source: the authors).

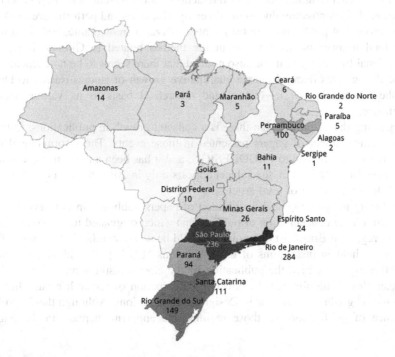

Fig. 5. Distribution of articles published in Graphic Design in the P&D Design conference by states of Brazil (Source: the authors).

When analyzing the publications related to the Informational Ergonomics (from 2010 to 2014), it was possible to realize a large quantum leap occurred in 2012. In the 2010 edition only 2 articles among the 109 of graphic design dealt with aspects related to IE. In 2012 this number changed to 34, increasing from 2 % to 14 % of graphic design papers. In 2014 that number fell again, where only 5 publications were related to IE, representing 6 % of graphic design articles. Figure 4 shows a comparative graph of the quantitative papers of graphic design and IE between 2010 and 2014.

When analyzing the geographical distribution of papers related to graphic design published in this event it can be noted, once again, a concentration of publications in the Southeast and South of Brazil, mainly in the states of Rio de Janeiro, Sao Paulo and Rio Grande do Sul. Figure 5 shows the map of Brazil and the quantitative distribution of papers in each State of the Federation. The omitted States have not added any publication in all editions of the event.

5 Conclusions

The results show that these conferences, throughout their editions, were organized by different research groups in Brazil. The recent expansion of graduate programs in design in the country promoted the scientific production in the area. However, the production in HCI (Human Computer Interaction) still represents a small portion of the production. This is possibly due to the diversity of themes and performance of Design.

The growth of publications in the events analyzed is remarkable, both with regard to the total number of articles and in the themes related to Graphic Design and Informational Ergonomics. It was also noticed that there seems to be no deepening in a specific theme. This demonstrates a quantitative growth of studies related to Design, from the construction of its history and theoretical basis to its various areas of performance.

Regarding the graphic design there is a constant growth in publications, following the increasing number of papers presented in those events. The Informational Ergonomics is strongly related to ERGODESIGN, and it has been a relevant topic since its first edition. In P&D Design, the subject appears only in 2012, but as a constant topic, which follows the trend of total articles.

Analyzing the geographical distribution of papers published in both events, it can be noticed a large concentration of publications which originated in the Southeast and Southern region of Brazil. At that point it should be noted that the first editions of both events were held in institutions of those locations [13, 14]. Considering the size of Brazil, that aspect favored the publication by the closest institutions.

It can also be highlighted the effective participation of research groups linked to *stricto sensu*[1] graduate programs in Design of those regions. Although there is still the prevalence of publications in those regions, the apparent increase in the national

---

[1] Graduate degrees in Brazil are divided in two types: *latu sensu* and *stricto sensu*. The *stricto sensu* graduate degree is generally for those who wish to pursue an academic career.

production was also promoted by concomitant progress of publications of research groups in other regions of the country.

This aspect also reflected in the location of the most recent editions of the analyzed events, hosted by institutions in different places, particularly some of the Northeast region of Brazil. It is also a result of the partnerships and the creation of Graduate Programs throughout the national territory. According to CAPES [15], only 18 Brazilian institutions have Graduate Programs in Design, and only seven of these Programs have lines of research directed linked to IE and Graphic Design. Those institutions are spread through the Southern (02), Southeast (02), Midwest (01), North (01) and Northeast (01) of Brazil.

It was also observed that the number of papers published in the different editions of those events, when compared, presents considerable quantitative difference, especially when analyzing the P&D Design proceedings. In such event, when comparing the numbers of approved and published articles between 2012 and 2014, it is observed that while in 2012 over 900 articles were approved, in 2014 that number was about 300. This fact is closely related to the size and ability of the institution in which the event is held.

Either way, the growth of total publications, accompanied by those relating to graphic design and Informational Ergonomics is consequence of the Design maturation in Brazil. Although there is still a small number of institutions which have *stricto sensu* graduate programs, that growth demonstrates the commitment of Brazilian researchers. The constant participation of the analyzed themes demonstrates the concern of the country with the issues related to the study and to the improvement of technological interfaces, particularly in information processing.

Acknowledgement. This study was supported by FAPESP (2013/11156-1), CAPES, CNPq (309290/2013-9).

References

1. Gomes Filho, J.: Design do objeto, bases conceituais. Escrituras Editora, São Paulo (2006)
2. Martins, L.B., Moraes, A.: Ergonomia Informacional: algumas considerações sobre o sistema humano-mensagem visual. In: Gestão da Informação na Competitividade das Organizações, vol. 1, pp. 165–181. Editora Universitaria da UFPE, Recife (2002)
3. Preece, J.: Design de Interação: Além da Interação Humano-Computador. Bookman, Porto Alegre (2005)
4. Norman, D.: Things that Make us Smart. Perseus Books, Cambridge (1993)
5. Moraes, A.: Design e Avaliação de Interface: ergodesign e interação humano computador/Organizadora: Anamaria de Moraes. iUsEr, Rio de Janeiro (2002)
6. Takeda, F., Xavier, A.A.P.: Ergonomia informacional: sistemas de informação e comunicação na gestão de riscos de acidentes numa planta de abate de frango. In: XV Simpep; Simpósio de engenharia de produção (2008)
7. Couto, R.M.S.: Pós-Graduação de Designers Brasileiros. In: Anais do Congresso Brasileiro de Pesquisa e Desenvolvimento em Design (2003), Brasília (2003)

8. Neves, E.P., Silva, D.N., Silva, J.C.P., Paschoarelli, L.C.: Panorama da pesquisa em Design no Brasil: a contribuição dos programas de pós-graduação em Design nas pesquisas científicas e no desenvolvimento da área. Arcos Design **8**(1), 78–95 (2014). http://www. e-publicacoes.uerj.br/index.php/arcosdesign

9. Vanti, N.A.P.: Da bibliometria à webometria: uma exploração conceitual dos mecanismos utilizados para medir o registro da informação e a difusão do conhecimento. Ciência da Informação **31**(2), 152–162 (2002)

10. Guedes, V.L.S., Borschiver, S.: Bibliometria: uma ferramenta estatística para a gestão da informação e do conhecimento, em sistemas de informação, de comunicação e de avaliação científica e tecnológica. In: 6 Encontro Nacional de Ciências da Informação, Salvador/BA (2005)

11. Araújo, C.A.: Bibliometria: evolução histórica e questões atuais. Em Questão **12**(1), 11–32 (2006)

12. Pinheiro, L.V.R.: Lei de Bradford: uma reformulação conceitual. Ciência da Informação **12** (2), 59–80 (1983)

13. Paschoarelli, L.C., Silva, J.C.P., Campos, L.F.A., Menin, M., Silva, J.C.R.P., Silva, D.C., Lanutti, J.N.L., Muniz, F.J.: A contribuição do design e artes gráficas na pesquisa e desenvolvimento em design no Brasil. In: Anais da 1 Conferência Internacional em Design e Artes Gráficas- ISEC- IPT, Lisboa (2010a)

14. Paschoarelli, L.C., Silva, J.C.P., Campos, L.F.A., Menin, M., Silva, J.C.R.P., Silva, D.C., Lanutti, J.N.L., Muniz, F.J.: Ergonomia informacional e a produção científica das áreas do design e artes gráficas. In: Anais da 1 Conferência Internacional em Design e Artes Gráficas-ISEC- IPT, Lisboa (2010b)

15. Coordenação de Aperfeiçoamento de Pessoal de Nível Superior. Avaliação da CAPES (2014). https://www.capes.gov.br/component/content/article/44-avaliacao/4662-ciencias-sociais-aplicadas-i

Beyond the Wall of Text: How Information Design Can Make Contracts User-Friendly

Stefania Passera[✉]

Department of Industrial Management and Engineering,
Aalto University School of Science, c/o Aalto Design Factory,
P.O. Box 17700, 00076 Aalto, Finland
stefania.passera@aalto.fi

Abstract. This study investigates the unique contribution of layout and visual cues to the comprehension of complex texts. Contracts are taken as a key example of cumbersome, complex texts that most laypeople do not like to read, and avoid reading altogether if possible. By means of information design, the meaning of contracts can be made more readily visible and understandable to their intended user-group. An experimental evaluation shows how it is not enough to simply reorganise the text in a more logical, user-friendly order, but real improvements in comprehension speed and accuracy can only be observed when enhancements to the textual structure of the contract are accompanied by an improved layout and other visual solutions.

Keywords: Document design · Information design · Contracts · Experimental evaluation · User experience · Usability · Complex information · Cognitive load theory

1 Introduction

Last year I attended a workshop led by a plain language expert, who provided several principles and examples on how to make contracts more understandable and user-friendly. The speaker guided the audience through an exercise where a very confusing leasing contract was re-ordered and given new, improved headings. Everyone in the room agreed that the restructured version of the contract was much better and appeared to better respond to the information needs of the intended readers. In his take-away message, the expert claimed that *'just by getting the structure and the headings right, we can probably solve 90 % of the contract's understandability issues'*. This statement sparked my researcher's curiosity and provided inspiration for the research questions behind this study: is good document structure the main solution to conveying complex information in a more logical and easier manner, or does visual display of information have a unique role in supporting comprehension? Is comprehension of meaning ultimately a verbal phenomenon, or can visual communication help people simply *see* meaning?

As an information designer, I do not doubt the effectiveness of structuring information as a way to make complex documents more transparent and accessible to their users. However, visually undifferentiated text alone does not provide salience or prominence to different bits of information, while, for easier reading, stronger attention

© Springer International Publishing Switzerland 2015
A. Marcus (Ed.): DUXU 2015, Part II, LNCS 9187, pp. 341–352, 2015.
DOI: 10.1007/978-3-319-20898-5_33

must be guided towards those parts that are more relevant to the user [1]. Visual cues can provide an 'attention hierarchy', making sure that what is most important is not overlooked. Additionally, people tend to find more usable what they find beautiful [2], and a wall of text simply looks scary, cumbersome and off-putting for most laypeople.

This study focusses on contracts, as they are a prototypical example of a common, completely textual, complex document. People usually do not like reading contracts, as they are dull, difficult and hard to understand for most. Everyone would agree that contracts are something important, but would gladly avoid reading a long text in legalese. For most, even after going through the effort of reading, contracts might still not be clear. Others are left with the doubt that they *might* have misunderstood something, and that will cause negative surprises in the future.

However, in the eyes of their creators – the lawyers – contracts try to accurately describe which rights, obligations, permissions and prohibitions apply to the signatories, and make them binding under the law [3]. The approach of legal scholars comes most typically from contract law and the law of the obligations [4], the body of principles and rules governing the rights and duties arising between individuals. The problem with this traditional view is that it focusses only on the essence and precision of the rules, but not at all on the needs and abilities of the individuals tasked with understanding and acting upon such rules. Rules matter to contract users only as long as they are instrumental in achieving their goals (e.g. how much, how and by when one should pay a bill in order to continue receiving electricity). It is then crucial to see contracts as a document genre similar to instructions and user guides: this is because not only do the rules need to be fair and consistent, but they also must be logically and clearly delivered if we want contract readers to apply them in practice and be compliant.

From a theoretical perspective, contracts constitute an interesting case, because they are purely textual documents, cognitively demanding and very close to zero in terms of eliciting positive experiences. This allows researchers to experimentally manipulate their structure and appearance in order to observe how information design solutions can affect comprehension and reader experience. From a practical perspective, several organisations could benefit from understanding how to make the meaning of contracts more visible and improve the overall contract-user experience. Companies can gain competitive advantage and improve their customer-centredness by developing and managing superior customer experiences [5]. In order to do that, they need to build meaningful customer touchpoints. In some industries – such as utilities, insurances, banking, online services and the rental market – contracts are a key customer touchpoint, as they 'officially' represent the service promise that the customer is signing up for. Transforming contracts into clear, engaging, transparent, visually pleasant instructions is an opportunity to build trust with consumers and deliver value.

This study seeks to determine which approaches are available for information designers and user-centric lawyers in order to make contracts more comprehensible and pleasant for their users. The need for both good information structure and visual information display are argued in the light of literature about cognitive load theory, user experience and usability. Both information structure and display can help in seeing intellectual performance, and their relative contributions were assessed and compared through an experiment on contract comprehension.

1.1 Cognitive Load Theory

Cognitive load theory (CLT) can help us understand why people struggle so much in reading and understanding contracts. Developed by Sweller, while initially studying problem solving [6], CLT postulates that learning happens best when information is presented in a way that takes into consideration human cognitive structures. Limited working memory capacity is one of the characteristic aspects of human cognition [7]: thus, comprehension and learning can be facilitated by presenting information in ways minimising working memory load.

In order to understand written texts people form mental models [8], mental representations based on the principles of causality, spatiality and temporality [9]. A chronological sequence of causally connected events is thus fairly easy to comprehend: this is because we mentally form a model integrating many details of the situation, with no need to store them all individually in our working memory. The mental model counts as a single element in the working memory, avoiding information overload. However, if working memory is overloaded in the first place we cannot form mental models, because information needs to be processed and integrated before being stored as knowledge in our long-term memory. In order to prevent overload, it is then useful to recognise different types of cognitive load [10]: *intrinsic load* is caused by the inherent difficulty and complexity of the subject matter, and it cannot be reduced; *extraneous load* is produced by the way in which content is presented, and can be reduced through design and instructional support; *germane load* is generated by information processing and integration into mental models, it can be affected by design and is not seen as a negative factor because schema formation supports learning. The task of designers is to create information structures and displays that reduce extraneous load and eventually increase germane load. Contracts contain lots of special terms, concepts and information (intrinsic load), and presenting this content as a wall of legalese text overloads readers without legal expertise (extrinsic load) and neither does it help them to develop mental models to make sense of the meaning (germane load).

In light of cognitive load theory, both information structure (how the content is ordered and organised) and information display (how it is visually presented) should play a key role in supporting comprehension and intellectual performance. A meaningful information structure helps readers to preserve continuity, allowing the formation of a useful and easy-to-process mental model. Visual information display further facilitates mental model creation by representing information structures and relationships more explicitly, so readers do not have to use cognitive resources to develop a mental model from scratch [11].

There are also further reasons why proper visual information display should enhance intellectual performance, and why a better but perceptually *invisible* information structure is probably not enough to reduce cognitive load. Firstly, the architecture of working memory is composed by specialised 'processors' devoted to process separately visuo-spatial information and speech/text, as well as components coordinating attention allocation and integrating visuo-spatial and phonological information with schematic long-term memory [12]. All processors have different and separate capacities, thus information processing should be more effective and sophisticated when both verbal and visual systems are activated. Secondly, people do not simply read texts in a linear fashion, but tend to skim and search for the most relevant bits of information. Visual cues (e.g. font size, boldface, bullet points, indentation, icons…) in the text assist readers in focussing on important items, better avoid distractors and process the text selectively when necessary [13], thus reducing the amount of information to be processed. Moreover, visual cues can simplify sense making by constraining possible interpretations. For instance, larger font size can be a cue for a heading, thus reducing possible ambiguities on the meaning and role of that bit of text, and thus reducing extraneous cognitive load. Thirdly, visible elements create an external persistent referent, enforcing consistency also in mental representations [14]. By 'externally storing' information working memory demands decrease, especially if we wish to explore relationships between different information, as 'statements that are distant in logical space can be brought beside each other in physical space' [14]. In this case, extraneous cognitive load is limited and more resources can be invested into mental model re-creation and manipulation [7].

In light of CLT, two hypotheses were formulated:

H1: Intellectual performance (comprehension and ease of comprehension) using a traditional text-only contract is worse than performance using a text-only contract where information has been better re-ordered and structured.

H2: Intellectual performance (comprehension and ease of comprehension) using either a text-only traditional contract or a restructured contract is worse than performance using a restructured contract where visual solutions are also employed.

1.2   User Experience

As already mentioned, people do not like to read contracts and in some cases avoid reading them altogether. It is not only a matter of cognitive effort, but also of negative emotions: we feel frustrated by lack of clarity and uncertainty and we do not feel in control. Assuming the predictions of CLT are correct, and design can indeed aid cognitive performance, the question on motivation remains open. How do we motivate people to engage with contracts, as their previous experiences of contracts have been consistently negative?

According to Hassenzahl and Tractinsky [15] UX research deals with emotions in two ways: either as consequences of use, or as antecedents of motivation to use and evaluative judgments. UX can be seen as expectations before use (*anticipated UX*), perceptions and judgements during and after a single use (*momentary UX* and *episodic UX*) and over repeated use in time (*cumulative UX*) [16], and it is easy to see how the loop closes and cumulative UX from previous experiences will affect future expectations. Cognitive load and perceived difficulty experienced in past interactions with contracts might prevent people from attempting to engage with contracts in the future, even if we decrease their complexity. For this reason, it is important for contracts designed with the intent of being user-friendlier to also look and feel different from other contracts. Research has shown that not only do people tend to find more usable what they find beautiful, but also that aesthetic perception overrules the degree of actual usability of an artifact when forming judgments on perceived usability [2]. Consequently, a visibly different design should have an edge over simple information restructuring in improving the overall experience of contract readers. A different appearance would immediately signal an intention to communicate more clearly with readers, and this in return might change their expectations, while a structural improvement cannot be easily discovered at a glance before use. However, the promise of simplicity needs to be kept during use. Research has shown how experiential judgments are affected by the satisfaction of two separate needs, the utilitarian (satisfaction of needs dictated by pragmatic, instrumental reasons) and the hedonic (the visceral need for affective gratification) [17, 18], and how those judgments can affect consumers' attitudes, preferences and decisions [19–22]. In the case of contracts, it can be argued that user experience will be positively affected by design solutions that not only functionally help in achieving comprehension goals, but also stimulate aesthetically and emotionally, before and during use. In terms of functionality, we can evaluate information restructuring versus information restructuring and visual redesign in terms of Norman's concepts of affordances and signifiers; in other words, what an artifact potentially allows users to do and what devices indicate when, how, where to use it [23]. Affordances without signifiers might not improve usability and user experience. A better contract structure can at best represent an affordance – as a logical structure *offers the functionality* of finding information smoothly – but visual design elements can be signifiers – as they also indicate *where* to search for a specific type of information and *how* to navigate the document. In terms of aesthetic stimulation and gratification, obviously a document with a good, clear, pleasant layout, typography and visual elements will trump an illegible wall of text. We can thus hypothesise the following:

H3: The experience of using a visually improved and logically restructured contract is more positive than the experiences elicited by using either a traditional text-only contract or a logically restructured contract.

2   Methods

2.1   Sample and Experimental Design

The study was carried out as an experiment in which participants had to answer 7 comprehension questions, using a contract text. After that, they also had to evaluate the experience of performing the comprehension tasks with the given contract through a self-administered questionnaire.

48 research participants, 24 female and 24 male master students, were recruited from at least 6 different European universities. The sample was widely diverse – 21 different nationalities and at least 6 different educational backgrounds (arts, law, business, engineering, sciences, other). In order to increase the validity of the experiment, the contract used in the experiment was the English version of the tenancy agreement for student apartments used in the Helsinki area: thus, students were the intended user group of this real document. This tenancy agreement was also chosen because its content was rather simple compared to other agreements: this arguably results in lower intrinsic cognitive load, with extraneous and germane cognitive loads (which can instead be affected by design solutions) remaining as the main components of overall cognitive load.

Fig. 1. Examples of one page of the three versions of the tenancy agreement: original agreement (left), restructured agreement (centre), visually redesigned and restructured agreement (right).

The experimental manipulation consisted of randomly assigning a differently designed version of the same contract text (Fig. 1) to the participants, divided in three groups:

- 'Textual/original' group (n = 16): the first group used the original, completely textual version of the tenancy agreement, an A4 document set in font size 6 pt, in a two-column layout;
- 'Textural/restructured' group (n = 17): the second group used a modified version of the original tenancy agreement. The document was still completely textual and presented in the same layout and font size as the original. However, the order of the clauses was modified so as to increase coherency, and more descriptive, plain language headings were added. Lastly, the original text was chunked down in bulleted lists;
- 'Visual/restructured' group (n = 15): the third group used another modified version of the agreement which, in addition to all the structural improvements of the second version, was also modified in terms of layout and design (bigger font size, icons suggestive of the topic of the clause, bigger headings, single column layout, wide white margins, ...). The content and the wording were unchanged.

2.2   Measures

Answering Speed. The first measure of intellectual performance considered the time taken by each participant to answer the 7 comprehension questions. The time taken to answer each question was measured individually and then summed to the others. This measure includes only the time taken to find the answer and write it down, but not the time taken to carefully read the question *before* starting the search for the correct answer. The participants were given 6.5 min for each question. The decision to limit the time available for each question was dictated by the fact that all questions dealt with very simple real-life questions of a tenant. If a tenant would take more than 6.5 min to find an answer to such a question from a one-page contract, it would mean that the contract is very badly designed for its scope and user group.

Answer Accuracy. The second measure of intellectual performance considered the correctness of each given answer. Answer accuracy was measured assigning one point for each correct answer, summing the scores over 7 questions. Partially correct answers were graded with 0.25, 0.5 and 0.75 points, depending on the magnitude of the mistakes and imprecisions, and thus the scores could vary between 0 (all wrong) and 7 (all correct).

Skipped Questions. The participants were given the possibility of skipping questions. They were told that skipping would equate saying '*I give up. This document is too badly designed, I think it is impossible to find the answer in the given time*'. Skipped questions were counted as a wrong answer (0 accuracy points) given in the maximum time allowed (6.5 min). Skipped questions were taken as a measure of the intrinsic difficulty of working with each version of the texts. If one version is more difficult to understand than the others, it will cause the participants to skip more questions overall.

User Experience. The HED/UT (Hedonic/Utilitarian) Scale [19] was chosen as a measure of UX, as it is a well-validated tool that allows taking into consideration both how useful/functional and gratifying/pleasurable the interaction with a product or service is. The analysis of HED/UT results is carried out graphically with the aid of a 2×2 matrix (Fig. 3), where the x-axis maps the hedonic score and the y-axis maps the utilitarian score. It is desirable to get a score of at least 4 points in each dimension, as 4 points is considered the threshold between low and high scores.

3   Results

3.1   Intellectual Performance

Answering Speed. The mean time taken to answer the 7 questions was longest in the textual/original group (896 s ± SD 333.65), and decreased in the textual/restructured group (827.11 s ± SD 464.15), with the visual/restructured group being the fastest (586.64 s ± SD 149.48) (Fig. 2). As the assumption of homogeneity of variances was violated (assessed through Levene's Test of Homogeneity of Variance, $p = 0.03$), the differences in score between the groups was investigated through a Welch ANOVA and resulted statistically significant ($F = 6.73$, $p = 0.004$). The significance of pairwise differences between groups was investigated through a post hoc Games-Howell test. The only statistically significant decrease in mean answering speed existed between the scores of the visual/restructured group and textual/original group (-309.37 s, $p = 0.008$). The results confirm Hypothesis 2, but fail to convincingly confirm Hypothesis 1. Simply restructuring the text is not enough to significantly improve the speed of searching and giving an answer, while employing visual elements in displaying information affects performance.

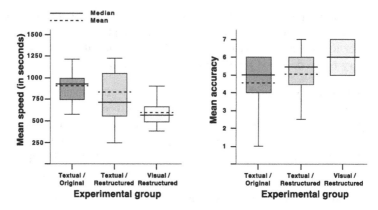

Fig. 2. Comparison of the performance scores in the 3 experimental groups: answering speed (left) and accuracy (right).

Answer Accuracy. Mean accuracy was lowest in the textual/original group (4.62 ± SD 1.54), increased in the textual/restructured group (5.09 ± SD 1.29) and was highest for the visual/restructured group (6 ± SD 0.87) (Fig. 2). Since there the data was not normally distributed and some genuine scores appeared nevertheless as outliers, the difference between group scores had to be assessed through the non-parametric Kruskal-Wallis H test. The difference among the 3 scores was overall significant ($\chi^2 = 7.53$, p = 0.023). Pairwise comparisons were performed using Dunn's procedure [24] with a Bonferroni correction for multiple comparisons. This post hoc analysis revealed a statistically significant difference only between the scores in the visual/restructured group and textual/original group (1.38 points, p = 0.022). This pattern mirrors what was already observed in regards to speed scores: accuracy some-what increases as the text is presented in a more logically structured way, but displaying information in a visual, user-friendly way increases comprehensibility even further (and significantly). Hypothesis 2 receives thus further support, while Hypothesis 1 is rejected.

Skipped Questions. Even though the difference in the amount of skipped questions in the three groups is not statistically significant, it is interesting to note that in the textual/original group three participants skipped questions (for a total of 6 missing answers) and two participants skipped questions in the textual/restructured group (for a total of 3 missing answers), while nobody in the visual/restructured group skipped any question. This matches the performance trends observed for speed and accuracy, with the visual/restructured contract seemingly better supporting comprehension and performance.

3.2   User Experience

HED/UT scores for the three experimental groups are displayed in Fig. 3, with the visual/restructured contract (HED = 4; UT = 6) scoring better than both textual/restructured contract (HED = 2; UT = 5) and textual/original contract (HED = 2;

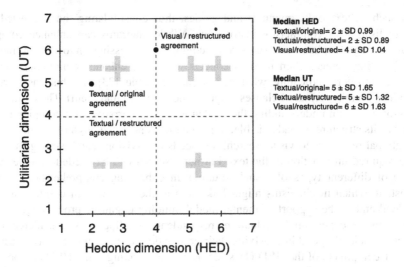

Fig. 3. HED/UT matrix showing the scores of the three experimental groups

UT = 5). The result of Mood's median test was statistically significant for both HED (χ^2 = 18.23, p < 0.001) and UT (χ^2 = 9.39, p = 0.009) dimensions. Logically restructuring the text seems to have no effect on user experience, while visibly discernible design improvements have a positive impact in terms of both instrumental and affective satisfaction. Not only does the contract feel more pleasant to use, but it also feels more useful and usable in completing the task. These results provide evidence in favour of Hypothesis 3.

4 Discussion

The results suggest that the visual display of information (visually perceptible information design solutions in terms of layout, typography and iconic language) is necessary, in addition to a logical structure of the text, in order to make the meaning of contract clauses clearer to readers. This is consistent with the results of previous studies about the effects of different types of visual representation on the comprehension of complex legal texts, across different user groups (e.g. civil servants [25], the general public [26, 27] and contract professionals [28]). Specifically, however, the results of this study should be better interpreted as supporting evidence for the need of making the structure and logic of the text visible: differently from the documents employed in the above mentioned studies – where explanatory diagrams such as timelines and flowcharts had a crucial role in demystifying the text and supporting comprehension – icons were the most visually noticeable element in the redesigned contract used in this experiment. Icons alone did not explain the details of the clauses or their logic, as a diagram would do, but were rather used to signal the topic discussed in the adjacent text. In Kong's words [29], icons played mostly an *identification* role in relation to the text. Identification is a key dynamic in multimodal texts, and especially in instructional genres such as textbooks, manuals and guides, thus consolidating the suggested re-conceptualisation of contracts-as-instructions. While diagrams can enhance comprehension through explanation, supporting cognitive processing involved in mental model building, icons (when used in concert with text) enhance comprehension by acting as signifiers indicating what actions are possible [23] (in this case, which instructions – in the format of clauses – apply, and where to find them). The extraneous load associated with understanding the hidden logic and narrative of a complex text is reduced as its structure is made visible: the reader does not need anymore to invest lots of attentional resources to visual search, nor needs to envision search strategies to dig out the required information of the text. Further research will be needed to understand the role of different types of visual solutions in enhancing comprehension, and to demonstrate which mechanisms might link them to the reduction of extraneous cognitive load and to the support of mental model building cognitive processing.

In terms of experiential evaluation, respondents in all groups considered their contracts sufficiently good in satisfying their pragmatic information needs, as measured by the UT component of the HED/UT scale. However, looking at the HED component, the two textual versions scored very poorly in terms of gratification, while the visual version obtained just a sufficient score in this respect, suggesting that legal documents are intrinsically unpleasant for laypeople. One reason could be that the rather stuffy language of the original agreement was used in all versions of the agreements. While the adoption of plain language is desirable in real life, it was undesirable in an experimental setting exclusively focussing on the contribution of information design solutions to comprehension. A manipulation of verbal language would introduce a confounding variable, and it would be difficult to correctly discern among effects due to plain language, logical structure and visual display. In order to analyse the effects of both verbal and visual language styles as predictors of both comprehension performance and experience, a new experiment with more participants and larger experimental groups would be necessary.

5   Conclusions

It is not enough to restructure texts in a meaningful, sensible way in order to make them more comprehensible. The visual presentation of legal texts strongly affects content comprehensibility and accessibility, making meaning more immediately available to readers. Logical structure and visual cues need to be planned and designed together in order to make documents clear, engaging, easily readable and skimmable. Suitable design solutions decrease extraneous cognitive load and support comprehension by supporting mental model formation. The look and feel of improved layouts, as well as the perceived ease of comprehension, also elicits more positive user experiences in interacting with legal texts – which is usually pretty poor. In many industries, contracts are important touchpoints with customers, but nowadays their potential is completely untapped: organisations seeking to be truly customer-centric should give information design serious consideration in order to transform contracts from necessary evils into clear, user-friendly interfaces.

Acknowledgments. This research was kindly funded by the FIMECC UXUS project (User Experience & Usability in Complex Systems) and Tekes – the Finnish Funding Agency for Technology and Innovation.

References

1. Albers, M.J.: Information salience and interpreting information. In: SIGDOC 2007, 25th Annual ACM International Conference on Design of Communication, pp. 80–86. ACM, New York (2007)
2. Tractinsky, N., Katz, A.S., Ikar, D.: What is beautiful is usable. Interact. Comput. **13**, 127–145 (2000)
3. Fryar, E.F.: Common-law due process rights in the law of contracts. Tex. Law Rev. **66**, 1021–1070 (1988)
4. Haapio, H.: Next generation contracts: a paradigm shift. Ph.D. thesis, Lexpert Ltd. (2013)
5. Zomerdijk, L.G., Voss, C.A.: Service design for experience-centric services. J. Serv. Res.-US **13**, 67–82 (2010)
6. Sweller, J.: Cognitive load during problem solving: effects on learning. Cogn. Sci. **12**(2), 257–285 (1988)
7. Sweller, J., van Merrienboer, J.J.G., Paas, F.G.W.C.: Cognitive architecture and instructional design. Ed. Psych. Rev. **10**(3), 251–296 (1998)
8. Johnson-Laird, P.N.: Mental Models: Towards a Cognitive Science of Language, Inference, and Consciousness. Cambridge University Press, Cambridge (1983)
9. Zwaan, R.A., Magliano, J.P., Graesser, A.C.: Dimensions of situation model construction in narrative comprehension. J. Exp. Psychol. Learn. **21**(2), 386–397 (1995)
10. Chandler, P., Sweller, J.: Cognitive load theory and the format of instruction. Cogn. Instr. **8**(4), 293–332 (1991)
11. Keller, T., Grimm, M.: The impact of dimensionality and color coding of information visualizations on knowledge acquisition. In: Tergan, S.-O., Keller, T. (eds.) Knowledge and Information Visualization. LNCS, vol. 3426, pp. 167–182. Springer, Heidelberg (2005)
12. Baddeley, A.D.: The episodic buffer: a new component of working memory? Trends Cogn. Sci. **4**(11), 417–423 (2000)
13. Gribbons, W.M.: Visual literacy in corporate communication: some implications for information design. IEEE T. Prof. Commun. **34**(1), 42–50 (1991)
14. Kirsh, D.: Thinking with external representations. AI Soc. **25**, 441–454 (2010)
15. Hassenzahl, M., Tractinsky, N.: User experience – a research agenda. Behav. Inf. Technol. **25**(2), 91–97 (2006)
16. Roto, V., Law, E., Vermeeren, A., Hoonhout, J.: User experience white paper: bringing clarity to the concept of user experience (2010). http://www.allaboutux.org/uxwhitepaper
17. Hassenzahl, M.: The interplay of beauty, goodness, and usability in interactive products. Hum.-Comput. Interact. **19**, 319–349 (2004)
18. Hassenzahl, M.: The effect of perceived hedonic quality on product appealingness. Int. J. Hum.-Comput. Int. **13**, 481–499 (2001)
19. Spangenberg, E.R., Voss, K.E., Crowley, A.E.: Measuring the hedonic and utilitarian dimensions of attitude: a generally applicable scale. Adv. Consum. Res. **24**, 235–241 (1997)
20. Voss, K.E., Spangenberg, E.R., Grohmann, B.: Measuring the hedonic and utilitarian dimensions of consumer attitude. J. Marketing Res. **40**(3), 310–320 (2003)
21. Batra, R., Ahtola, O.T.: Measuring the hedonic and utilitarian sources of consumer attitudes. Market. Lett. **2**(2), 159–170 (1991)

22. Holbrook, M.B., Hirschman, E.C.: The experiential aspects of consumption: consumer fantasies, feelings, and fun. J. Consum. Res. **9**, 132–140 (1982)
23. Norman, D.A.: The Design of Everyday Things: Revised and Expanded Edition. Basic Books, New York (2013)
24. Dunn, O.J.: Multiple comparisons using rank sums. Technometrics **6**, 241–252 (1964)
25. Passera, S., Pohjonen, S., Koskelainen, K., Anttila, S.: User-friendly contracting tools – a visual guide to facilitate public procurement contracting. In: Proceedings of the IACCM Academic Forum on Contract and Commercial Management 2013. IACCM, Ridgefield (2013)
26. GLPi, Schmolka, V.: Results of Usability Testing Research on Plain Language Draft Sections of the Employment Insurance Act. Justice Canada and Human Resources Development Canada (2000). http://www.davidberman.com/wp-content/uploads/glpi-english.pdf
27. Kay, M., Terry, M.: Textured agreements: re-envisioning electronic consent. In: Proceedings of the Sixth Symposium on Usable Privacy and Security. ACM, New York (2010)
28. Passera, S., Haapio, H.: The quest for clarity – how visualization improves the usability and user experience of contracts. In: Huang, W., Huang, M. (eds.) DVVA 2013: Innovative Approaches of Data Visualization and Visual Analytics, pp. 191–217. IGI Global, Hershey (2014)
29. Kong, K.: A taxonomy of the discourse relations between words and visuals. Inf. Design J. **14**(3), 207–230 (2006)

Digital Collections: Analysis of Collaborative Platforms

Camila Rodrigues[✉], Barbara Emanuel, and Marcos Martins

Escola Superior de Desenho Industrial – UERJ, Rio de Janeiro, Brazil
{falecomkamy,marc.a.martins}@gmail.com,
design@barbaraemanuel.com

Abstract. New information and communication technologies have changed the way people produce, remix and share data. The flow of ephemeral content, such as images, on social networks reveal the need to construct e analyze functional digital collections. The purpose of this work is to investigate the main standards established to build "good" digital collections and to apply the nine principles of NISO's report A Framework of Guidance for Building Good Digital Collection (2007) in the analyses of three collaborative platforms of digital collections: "Pinterest", "Arquigrafia" and "Street Art Rio".

Keywords: Collections · Collaboration · Memory · Interface design · Usability

1 Introduction

The rise of technological development and ubiquitous computing has increased production, reproduction and dissemination of content, making it increasingly accessible. Image flow is an important part of communication in today's digital environment, especially in social networks.

In this context, ephemerality is a relevant feature of images, as they get rapidly unavailable, except through search engines. It is relevant, then, to develop digital collections that preserve those images in order to keep their contribution to graphics memory.

The idea of an universal library with no limits of access has been envisioned since the library of Alexandria, in the Third Century BC. Nowadays, with internet's potential of quickly disseminating and accumulating information, this idea does not seem so utopian [1].

The power of collaborative production can increase the growth and strength of digital collections. Users, especially from younger generations, have integrated digital technologies so completely into their lives, that they have been assuming a role as creators and collaborators [2]. The internet transformed users from passive receptors to active agents, free to choose what content they want to consume, how they are going to interact with it, and the space-time where that relation is going to happen.

Collaborative production networks do not work based on exchange value of products, what makes people more interested in investing their time contributing with

A. Marcus (Ed.): DUXU 2015, Part II, LNCS 9187, pp. 353–362, 2015.
DOI: 10.1007/978-3-319-20898-5_34

the creation of content such as entries on *Wikipedia* and boards on *Pinterest*. Some users make that because it is fun; others, to give back knowledge to society; and others, in order to be recognized as part of a global initiative [3]. The creation of collaborative networks contributes to the establishment of new ethical, technical and management codes. This work aims to contribute to the study of digital collections management, particularly collaborative platforms, by summarizing standards to create those platforms, and by analyzing three collections with different scopes: international, national and local.

2   Digital Collections

Digital collections are groups of objects that are selected, managed— in visual, and textual terms —to simplify their discovery, access and meaning to the user [1]. The digital environment provides innovative ways of dealing with data and consequently new ways of producing, reproducing and disseminating knowledge and information.

The emerging community that works with digital collections is systematizing standards of good practices since the mid-1990s, when the need for developing national archives appeared. First, libraries have grown and, with them, the collection of digital images and born-digital content. Since the early 2000s, the area has been strengthened by museums that are engaged in preserving digital art: "These distinct domains have been coming together with the common objective of preserving digital content for use by current and future users". [1]

For this essay, the most suitable guideline for the analysis is A Framework of Guidance for Building Good Digital Collections (2007), because it is about practical principles of collection management, being better suited to an investigation about design, usability and interaction aspects. The principles of this framework will be presented as follows.

3   Methodology

For this research, the first step was to define criteria for the selection of digital collections that should be relevant to the analysis, which are: (1) being available on the internet with free access; (2) belonging to a collaborative platform; and (3) being from different structural realities to provide comparisons.

The second step was the selection of websites to be analyzed. The chosen platforms were (a) *Pinterest*, an international collection with very large content coverage; (b) *Arquigrafia*, an academic initiative operating within national scope (Brazil) with architecture-related content; and (c) *Street Art Rio*, an independent regional initiative (Rio de Janeiro) with specific content, covering only local urban art.

The parameters for the analysis of each website were determined based on the third version of A Framework of Guidance for Building Good Digital Collections that defines international principles for what would be a good digital collection. By good, the report means "useful and relevant collections that served the needs of one or more communities of users" in relation to "usability, accessibility and fitness for use". Besides the context of use, new issues became relevant in the matured digital environment, such as "reuse, repackage and repurpose" [2].

The guides are not definitive because "every digital collection-building initiative is unique, with its own users, goals and needs" [2]. But some standards work as analytical tools to assess the existing collections and to guide the development of new ones. The nine principles presented by NISO are as follows:

1. **Collection policy**
   The purpose of the organization behind the collection must be clear and explicit for the user. Even in cases where the users are stimulated to deposit their own intellectual properties, there are benefits from a clear, but fairly flexible, policy that will help to regulate the judgment of content relevance.

2. **Description by metadata**
   The detailed description of the collected object must be available, to register and to access. It helps the users to be aware of the context; to find the collection on the digital environment; to understand and reframe the content; and to search specific objects among others.

3. **Active content management**
   Collections must be curated and actively managed during its entire lifecycle, from the moment that the object is collected until its obsolescence. In collaborative platforms this area is particularly a challenge because the interface must persuade the user to register and update their own information in the most complete way.

4. **Accessibility**
   Contents of a digital collection must be available with as little as possible usability impediments. In this area, three attributes are important: availability (through the web using known technologies); usability (learning time and easy use of the available functionalities) and accessibility (work in different browsers, operating systems and screen resolutions; different languages; and adaptability for people with disabilities).

5. **Intellectual property rights**
   Collections must present the copyright policy over the rights of the original owner of source material, the permission to digitize and make the content available; and the permission of subsequent use of the materials. If the materials have no restrictions on use, such freedom must be clear and explicit in the website.

6. **Analytics data**
   Platforms must have mechanisms to measure its use. The criteria and evaluation method will differ according to the objectives of the collection and to the answers for the questions: "who is using what, how and why?"

7. **Interoperability**

Collections must be designed to support interoperability, which means that they must have the ability to adapt their metadata to work in different devices, systems and applications.

8. **Integration with user's workflow**

Websites must be constructed following the pattern of how users deal with that kind of information, making the interaction more natural, which makes it easier for them to contribute to the platform.

9. **Sustainability**

Digital collections must be sustainable over time which requires organizational, financial and technical perspective.

To conclude, the results were confronted to see the similarities and differences between the three different platforms.

4   Analysis

Pinterest

https://www.pinterest.com/

Pinterest is an online tool to make digital collections that help users organize, classify and share images they find on the internet with the index resource. In this case, the collection embraces a large number of subjects with boards personalized by the users. (Fig. 1).

Fig. 1. Pinterest homepage when user is logged in. (Source: pinterest.com)

Principle	Analysis
Collection policy	Homepage, if user is logged in: pins from users/boards/keywords followed by the user.
	Info about the company: accessed through the Help section or an "about link" hidden in the search menu; clear information, illustrated by images and videos.
	Privacy Policy page: describes what kind of information the website can collect and how it can be used.
Description by metadata	All content can be identified with metadata: name of the board, image description and source. When you search for a tag, the website suggests other tags related to that content in order to maximize the experience.
Active content management	The content registered on the website is constantly managed by other users that can re-pin it with different metadata, like it and share it.
Accessibility	The website is available in thirty different languages.
	To access the platform, users must create an account with their e-mail or log in with their Facebook account.
	The interface is responsive to different screen resolutions and operating systems.
Principle	Analysis
Intellectual property rights	Copyright policy in accordance with the *Digital Millennium Copyright Act* of 1998.
	"You grant Pinterest and its users a non-exclusive, royalty-free, transferable, sub licensable, worldwide license to use, store, display, reproduce, re-pin, modify, create derivative works, perform, and distribute your User Content on Pinterest solely for the purposes of operating, developing, providing, and using the Pinterest Products. Nothing in these Terms shall restrict other legal rights Pinterest may have to User Content, for example under other licenses. We reserve the right to remove or modify User Content for any reason; including User Content that we believe violates these Terms or our policies." [www.pinterest.com]
Analytics data	Analytics data about each pin: number of re-pins, number of "likes", username of its first "pinner".
	Data about users: number of pins, boards, likes, followers and following.
Interoperability	Adaptable for different devices: mobile, tablets, and other gadgets with *IOS* and *Android* system.
Integrate with user's workflow	Includes widgets that make the experience more fluid, such as a "pin it" button users can install on their browsers to facilitate pinning, and widget for developers to add a "Pin it" button to every image of a website (Fig. 2).
Sustainability	The company behind *Pinterest*, launched in 2008, has a big financial, administrative and executive structure.

Fig. 2. "Pin it button" added into the image from another website. (Source: urbanarts.com.br)

Arquigrafia

http://www.arquigrafia.org.br/

Arquigrafia is a digital collaborative platform, launched in 2009 by Universidade de São Paulo (USP), with the purpose of contributing with the memory of Brazilian architecture by registering constructions and their modifications over time. The database is formed by the users, who are responsible to feed it with photographies and their cataloging information. (Fig. 3).

Fig. 3. Landing page of Arquigrafia. (Source: arquigrafia.org.br)

Principle	Analysis
Collection policy	No explicit and defined policy available. Website described as being "perpetual beta", that is, in constant adaptation to the academic researches related to that.
	Information about who manages the platform and the copyright policy summarized in two sections: The project ("O projeto") and Help ("Ajuda").
Description by metadata	Images registered with metadata: name of the construction, description, image authorship, upload date, date the photo was taken, building authorship, date of construction, address, geolocation, evaluation and related tags.
	Information about users: name, profile photography, education data, and contact.
Active content management	Only users can edit their uploaded content, there is no constant management by other users or administrators.
Accessibility	Available in Portuguese only.
	Not adaptable to different operating systems or screen resolutions, neither to people with disabilities.
Intellectual property rights	Creative Commons 3.0 license: content can be shared and adapted, even for commercial use, provided that is given the "appropriate credit, used a link to the license and indicate the changes if were made". [4]
Analytics data	Data about each image: number of visualizations, evaluations and comments.
	An automatic counter shows the total number of images uploaded to the platform.
Interoperability	Not adaptable for mobile devices yet (there is a plan to integrate the platform to Android/Google system so users will be able to capture, upload and georeference in real time).
Integrate with user's workflow	Because of the lack of interoperability the website is not deeply integrated with the user's workflow. To upload new information, users must access the platform directly and log in; there are no resources to expedite the access.
Sustainability	*Arquigrafia* is based in a university and is funded by public initiatives that allow them to hire private companies, for services such as code development, design and communications.

Street Art Rio

http://streetartrio.com.br/

Street Art Rio is an independent initiative, launched in 2014, with the purpose of mapping the work of local urban artists through a collaborative action. It is a movement to identify authorship, and catalogue places of urban art manifestations in Rio de Janeiro. (Fig. 4).

Fig. 4. Homepage and a work internal page of Street Art Rio. (Source: streetartrio.com.br)

Principle	Analysis
Collection policy	Collection purpose and movement goals are explicit on the website. The collection is used as a commercial tool by urban artists to propagate their work, as a collection by urban arts admirers, and as a hiring tool by companies that want to hire artists work.
Description by metadata	Image upload through metadata: users post an image on *Instagram* with the hashtag #StreetArtRio and indicate the precise location of it, then the image is automatically traceable by the platform administrators and can be added to the collection if it is relevant.
	Data available of each image: username of the user who posted, date and time that the photography was captured and published, filter

(Continued)

(Continued)

Principle	Analysis
	used on that image, the artist and his related work, and a map with the geolocation.
Active content management	The content is constantly managed and curated (administrators must approve the information before it is published on the website).
Accessibility	Available in Portuguese only.
Intellectual property rights	There is no reference of intellectual property rights on the website.
Analytics data	Map with the number of tagged photos by location.
	Data for each image: number of views, likes and comments.
	Integration with analytics data from sharing on related social networks *Twitter, Facebook, Google + , StumbleUpon* and *Pinterest*.
Interoperability	The interface is responsive to different devices.
Integrate with user's workflow	The platform is very integrated with the user's workflow because the process of uploading an image is through *Instagram*, a mobile application that most of the users already have the habit to operate frequently.
Sustainability	Because this is an independent initiative, with no big company behind it, it is more difficult to guarantee the maintenance of the collection.

Comparing the three platforms, we can observe that *Pinterest* is the most developed one because it works with a big financial and organizational structure behind the collection. This support allows the website to be more adaptable to users' needs, to meet design principles and to provide a more complete experience integrated with different devices and systems. *Arquigrafia* has a very relevant content to the specific public of architecture because it is directly related to one of the most important Brazilian universities. Nevertheless, this platform is the most limited in terms of development, because of its dependence on different public initiatives, having to deal with bureaucracy, what considerably slows the process of applying any change to the website. *Street Art Rio* has functional features to meet users' needs, is integrated with daily use apps, and has an intuitive interface. As an independent initiative, the platform uses more simple development resources, but they are very adapted to its target audience.

5   Conclusion

In the digital environment, the reach of the content is massive, and, excluding the language and technological limitations, the capacity of producing and sharing information is growing exponentially. In this context, new dynamics of storage arise to preserve the digital data.

Observing the new dynamics through the three analyzed platforms, we conclude that the main obstacles to free development are the regulatory statements behind the companies that run the collections. Private platforms are usually concerned not only with quality of design, but also with adaptability to user needs. *Pinterest*, being managed by a big company, includes several features developed especially for its global target. On the other hand, *Street Art Rio*, being an independent initiative, uses more integrated standard resources, allowing a flexible and optimized expansion at a low cost. Public platforms, such as *Arquigrafia*, may have broad access to financial resources, but must deal with academic and noncommercial aspects, which make them slower and less flexible, especially on usability and visual elements.

Furthermore, on the three cases, for being digital platforms, the collections are influenced by the technological convergence that helps the reduction of communicational limits. This aspect makes the development of a common language possible, allowing groups to connect, regardless of if it is international, national or local. It is important to create mechanisms to collect, catalogue and preserve that shared information, especially the graphic materials, in order to build a collective memory of digital-born content. Standards related to digital collections can be the basis to establishing guidelines for the analysis of usability, interactivity and design aspects.

References

1. Managing Digital Collections: a collaborative initiative of the South African framework. South Africa: National Research Foundation (NRF) (2010)
2. NISO Framework Working Group, A Framework of Guidance for Building Good Digital Collections, 3rd (edn.) (2007)
3. Lima, Clóvis Ricardo Montenegro de. Produção colaborativa na sociedade da informação / Clóvis Ricardo Montenegro de Lima, Rose Marie Santini. - Rio de Janeiro: E-papers (2008)
4. Creative Commons – Atribuição 3.0 Não Adaptada (2014). http://creativecommons.org/licenses/by/3.0/deed.pt_BR

Interactive Multisensory Data Representation

Patricia Search[(✉)]

Rensselaer Polytechnic Institute, Troy, NY, USA
searcp@rpi.edu

Abstract. Large data sets require new forms of data representation that reduce the complexity of the information, and help users identify trends and communicate the meaning of the data to diverse audiences. With multisensory data design, it is possible to increase the number of variables and relationships that can be represented simultaneously. Sound, touch, gesture, and movement can enhance the perception of data relationships. Complex data sets also require new ways of organizing databases that encourage the development of new perspectives and facilitate collaboration. Audiovisual metadata is an alternative to text-based metadata that supports data exploration by providing a flexible format for database organization. With these new approaches to data representation, it is important to understand the semiotics of multisensory data design.

Keywords: Data visualization · Multisensory data representation · Data sonification · Audiovisual metadata

1 Introduction

The "big data revolution" presents challenges for the designers of new technologies that capture and analyze data. Researchers and businesses are also challenged to find the most effective ways to use the large amounts of data that are now available to them. According to IBM, 2.5 exabytes (2.5 billion gigabytes) of data were generated daily in 2012 [1], and that number is increasing each year. Harvard Professor Gary King [2] pointed out that the big data revolution is not the quantity of big data, but the fact that we now have the necessary software for statistical and computational analysis of the data, as well as tools for linking datasets and visualizing the information.

However, with the large amounts of data that are being generated each day, new forms of data representation are necessary, so users can represent multiple variables simultaneously, identify trends from different perspectives, and communicate the meaning of the data to diverse audiences. In addition, there is a need to create tools that work across disciplines for interdisciplinary research.

Multisensory data representation can enhance the user experience and make data analysis accessible to different audiences through intuitive tools that leverage our innate abilities to understand information with different sensory modalities [3]. Loftin [4] noted that there are limits to the number of variables we can process visually, but the brain is capable of processing information from multiple senses simultaneously. By using multiple senses, it is possible to increase the number of variables and relationships that can be represented in complex data sets.

© Springer International Publishing Switzerland 2015
A. Marcus (Ed.): DUXU 2015, Part II, LNCS 9187, pp. 363–373, 2015.
DOI: 10.1007/978-3-319-20898-5_35

When designing these tools, it is important to understand the semiotic structure of each design element because the tools must map the audiovisual semantic and syntactic relationships to the variables in the data. Users must also be able to use different media to expand and refine paths through the data and create visual hierarchies that highlight specific relationships, patterns, and outliers. The exploration of complex data sets also requires flexible ways to organize and store data. Audiovisual metadata supports data exploration by providing a fluid database structure that encourages new perspectives and facilitates collaboration between users from different research communities.

This paper includes an analysis of the semiotics of multisensory data representation and provides some design objectives for audiovisual metadata for data organization.

2 Multimedia Data Representation

In multisensory data design, the granularity of audiovisual design ranges from specific or localized representation, which is achieved with graphics, to infinite or non-localized space, which is achieved with sound [5]. Visual encoding and semantic relationships can represent data details, patterns or trends, and the integrated whole.

The Gestalt principles of perception play an important role in helping the user identify patterns and relationships. For example, by assigning specific colors, shapes, textures, and sounds to different variables in a data set, it is possible to quickly identify groups of information and patterns represented by similar variables. The design elements, such as colors, textures, shape, and lines, must be distinctly different to avoid confusion and promote quick recognition. It is often possible to use established cognitive and emotional associations with design elements to enhance the communication process. For example, weather maps use colors to represent temperature—blue for cold and red for hot. Spatial mappings of data can define time-based relationships that occur sequentially or simultaneously. These representations may be very specific and show actual times, or they may be relational mappings that show order or simultaneous events. Visuals can depict these spatial mappings through position, transparency, and animation.

Three-dimensional representations of data provide opportunities to use another axis for mapping relationships such as dynamic changes over time and space. The extra dimension enables researchers to view representations from diverse perspectives and detect relationships that might be hidden with a two-dimensional mapping. It is important that the user be able to rotate these three-dimensional models to show all the spatial relationships. Transparent layers and visual coding with different colors, textures, shapes, line widths, or movement can be used to differentiate the layers of information that appear within a three-dimensional model.

Marc Downie [6], an artist and member of OpenEndedGroup, a digital art collective, used the open-source Field programming environment, with accelerated graphics processing and projection, to explore a dark data set and uncover properties in the data relationships. The data was actually the simulation output of the Dragonfly network topology for high-performance computing systems. With the visualization, it was possible to rotate a three-dimensional model and view the complex data representation from diverse perspectives (a video showing this data visualization is available at http://vimeo.com/79674603). Downie conducted this data visualization research at the Curtis R. Priem Experimental Media and Performing Arts Center (EMPAC) at Rensselaer Polytechnic Institute in Troy, New York. The visualization was displayed on a large-scale video wall where, using color, position, and other visual elements, it was possible to identify subtle changes in the data that revealed patterns.

Large-scale displays can be a valuable tool for multisensory data representation. With large video walls, it possible to view data relationships that are difficult or impossible to see on small monitors. The Collaborative Research Augmented Immersive Virtual Environment Laboratory (CRAIVE-Lab) at Rensselaer Polytechnic Institute is a state-of-the-art research space where it is possible to use a large-scale display, sound projection, and physical interaction to represent data relationships. Several projectors, hybrid tracking, and multiple point-of-convergence rendering techniques provide optimal and undistorted views at various distances. A multi-channel audio system and haptic display provide opportunities for multisensory data representation and research in cross-modal perception.

D.L. McGuiness, a leading expert in knowledge presentation and semantic web research, noted that the CRAIVE-Lab helped her visualize extremely large, labeled graphs (Fig. 1) that would have been "essentially impossible to see in perspective without access to a large display. Some people refer to these large graphs as 'hairballs' or 'ratsnests' that are relatively impenetrable. With environments such as CRAIVE, we can start to explore what previously seemed impenetrable" (personal communication, January 13, 2014).

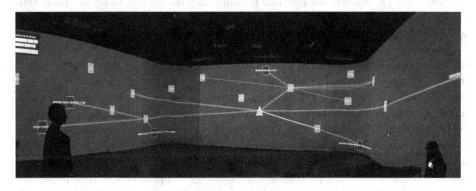

Fig. 1. Using the Collaborative Research Augmented Immersive Virtual Environment (CRAIVE) Laboratory at Rensselaer Polytechnic Institute to visualize very large networks of data (from research conducted by D.L. McGuinness) .

Stanford University has created the HANA Immersive Visualization Environment (HIVE) for collaborative data visualization. HIVE consists of a large video wall with 35 backlit monitors. The wall is 10 feet tall and 24 feet wide with 13440 x 5400 resolution [7]. Up to sixteen users can simultaneously connect to HIVE where they can explore multiple layers of data and zoom into details.

The Software Studies Initiative, led by Lev Manovich [8], used a display system with nearly 287 megapixels of screen resolution called HIPerSpace (Highly Interactive Parallelized Display Space), located at the California Institute for Telecommunications and Information Technology (Calit2) at the University of California, San Diego, to visualize data sets for cultural analytics. The research group developed software that enabled them to interactively display large numbers of paintings, magazine covers, comic book pages, and traversals through video games [9]. Using this state-of-the-art research environment, they were able to identify and analyze changes in artistic style as well as identify other relationships in the cultural data sets (images showing these visualizations are available at http://lab.softwarestudies.com/p/overview-slides-and-video-articles-why.html).

3   Multisensory Design

Despite all these advances in data visualization technology, the visual representation of data is limited by the number of visual characteristics that can be simultaneously assigned to the data without causing confusion or obscuring relationships [3]. By using multiple sensory modalities, it is possible to increase the number of data variables that can be represented in order to highlight trends, patterns, outliers, anomalies, and subtle details that might not be possible to identify with one form of sensory representation.

Different forms of sensory representation have unique semiotic structures which can also complement each other and call attention to relationships that might be missed. Tak and Toet [3] pointed out that multisensory data design can result in "data completion" which enables users to "fill in missing information from one sensory channel with cues from another sensory channel" (p. 559).

Various forms of data visualization have been in use for some time, but data sonification is an area of research that has yet to reach its full potential. Research has shown that the addition of audio cues can enhance the recognition of visual cues [10]. Sound can be both spatial and linear [11]. It can highlight individual elements in data relationships and represent dynamic changes over time. Tonality/atonality, audio progressions, modulation, rhythm, accent, synchronicity, and dissonance can define patterns, subtle changes, outliers, and anomalies. Sound penetrates space and can define relationships with the surrounding three-dimensional environment [11]. Stereo sound can add new dimensions to the perceptual experience by mapping data to multiple spatial parameters. Sound is not limited to the field of vision. It can augment what the viewer is seeing and not interfere with the visual representation of the data.

Rhythm is an important audiovisual design element in multisensory design. Rhythm in lines, forms, colors, and textures, can be used to organize data into visual patterns. Sound also adds strong rhythmic elements through tempo, beat, sound duration, silence, and repetition. In dynamic data sets, where the information changes in real time, rhythm is a unifying element throughout the interactive experience that can highlight changes in both the visual and audio information. Overlapping rhythms can create a counterpoint that also helps the user identify relationships between audiovisual variables.

Cross-modal perception can lead to unique perspectives from the integration of different forms of data representation. Sound and visuals encode information in different ways. The integration of cognitive and sensory information creates a meta-syntax that is transmodal [12]. The metasyntax creates a fluid semiosis by defining polysemiotic sensory and cognitive models that transcend the meaning of individual media or actions [13]. Semantic structures overlap and define a new audiovisual semiotics that integrates the syntax of the different media [13].

These fluid semantic structures can lead to new perceptual experiences that highlight relationships or patterns that are not evident in the individual audio or visual representations. In multimodal semiotics, the viewer must construct a system of relational codes to interpret the relationships. The different media create multiple levels of perceptual encoding, spatial and temporal relationships, and cognitive associations. Recursive patterns and layers of audiovisual data define multidimensional arrays that can represent simultaneous and sequential relationships and events [11, 14].

4 Semiotics of Action

With new technologies, the gestures and movements of the viewer also become part of the interactive experience and define a spatial grammar of interaction that integrates the virtual and physical spaces [15]. The sensory and rhythmic dimensions of interaction design enable users to engage in the interactive spatial representation of the data. This type of interaction design, called kinesthetic design, helps the viewer understand the visual and cognitive relationships in the spatial representation of information [5]. Berkeley [16] demonstrated that kinesthetic and tactile experiences shape our perception of space. Psychologists discovered that there is a relationship between physical movement and our visual and sensory interpretations of the space that begins to take shape during childhood [17, 18]. Piaget and Inhelder [17] noted that "spatial concepts are internalized actions, and not merely mental images of external things or events—or even images of the results of actions" (p. 455).

In immersive, interactive spaces such as the Cave Automatic Virtual Environment (CAVE), the orientation of the human body augments the perception of data relationships. Physical interaction is defined by the viewer's egocentric space, which refers to the orientation and location of the human body in the surrounding space. Rock [19] pointed out that humans use egocentric space to define objects and spatial relationships, such as up/down and near/far, in terms of the position of the body. Gaines [20] noted:

> The frontiers of space begin with the body of an individual subject. The physical limits of the body and its means of conscious perception, through sight, sound, smell, taste, touch and the reasoning mind, all engage in identifying the meanings of the things in the world of experience. (p. 174)

Just as a performance artist uses movement through space to define a message, gestures, movement, and physical interaction in multisensory data design can help the user understand the spatial and temporal relationships in data representation.

Physical interaction also adds rhythm, tempo, and direction to the syntax of the interaction design. The rhythm of movement and actions combines with the rhythm of images, sounds, and audiovisual transitions in the virtual space. Djajadiningrat, Matthews, and Stienstra [21] pointed out that the "semantics of motion" enables us to understand an interactive experience (pp. 10-11).

Interactivity may also include haptic interfaces that use inertia, force, torque, vibration, texture, and temperature to represent data variables and relationships. Haptic interfaces add another dimension to the semiotics of action by enabling users to interpret spatial relationships through the sense of touch. Palmerius [22] pointed out that "our sense of touch and kinesthetics is capable of supplying large amounts of intuitive information about the location, structure, stiffness and other material properties of objects" (p. 154). He went on to note that haptic feedback can reinforce visual information, provide complementary cues, and help the user find additional features.

5   Multimedia Metadata

5.1   Design Criteria

The multisensory user experience can also extend to database organization. Most interface designs and information architectures are based on sequential hierarchies that are derived from linguistic categories, deductive reasoning, and diachronic logic. Text-based metadata has been the standard for organizing data. Relationships are defined and organized by a priori ontological structures of metadata that make assumptions about data relationships instead of creating an open framework for exploring new networks and connections between ideas. This approach restricts and limits the possibilities for interpreting the information.

For complex databases, we need to develop alternative methods of organizing data that provide flexible ways to search and compare data by using audiovisual information, as well as text. With multimedia metadata, it is possible to define data as multidimensional, spatial, and temporal relationships. Flexible formats for organizing and accessing information support creative data exploration. Multisensory representations of metadata create dynamic semantic models and search methods that enable users to view data from diverse perspectives and identify new patterns and relationships.

Knowledge is also formed by collaborations and collective participation in defining data relationships. The process is fluid and dynamic, so users need access to information management and database systems that support this type of collaboration. The system should allow participants to use different media to define and revise relational models and connections between networks of information.

This collaborative system should be ontologically flat without predefined categories or metadata to avoid assumptions and preconceived ideas about the information and data relationships. Christie and Verran [23, 24] and Srinivasan and Huang [25] highlighted the importance of creating flexible systems that enable users to define relationships. This user-centered approach to data organization should allow users to do the following:

- employ search methods that use visuals, audio, text, and semantic mapping;
- create new metadata for groups of information or relationships;
- modify metadata to reflect new information or relationships;
- create links between data in different contexts;
- expand networks of information beyond the local database by including external links to additional data sets and data representations;

- search for temporal relationships in data; and
- collaborate with other researchers who can also modify the organization of the information and create new links to data.

Search methods that use diverse media and semantic mapping may lead to a new type of multimedia or cross-modal "meta-language" for searches. The meta-language would enable users to define relationships based on multiple meanings and audiovisual representations of the data. This cross-modal approach to defining searches can lead to new perspectives for defining data relationships for database organization and data analysis. Dunsire, Hillmann, Phipps, and Coyle [26] pointed out that "Without the necessity of defining an 'authoritative' or 'best' mapping, a metadata element can have more than one set of semantics at the same time; this means it should be a simple matter to move from different but compatible definitions as needed within an application" (pp. 32-33).

5.2 Multimedia Metadata Projects

There are several research projects using multimedia metadata tools that are laying the foundation for using these forms of metadata to organize complex data sets. In Australia, at the University of Queensland, Charles Darwin University, and the University of Melbourne, researchers have designed dynamic, multimedia metadata tools and interactive databases to archive indigenous knowledge traditions. Metadata that use diverse media (text, audio, images) and user-defined information structures are necessary to reflect the fluid relationships that characterize indigenous consciousness and cultural traditions.

Christie and Verran [23, 24] designed a database and file management system called TAMI (Text, Audio, Movies and Images) that is an audiovisual system designed to reflect and perpetuate indigenous knowledge traditions. Researchers in the School of Australian Indigenous Knowledge Systems at Charles Darwin University [27] pointed out that "The database is not a repository of knowledge. It is a digital context for knowledge production. It is work done together within the environment (digital and nondigital) which produces knowledge. The database is ontologically flat, it is the users who encode the relations between objects and the metadata which enriches them" (Description of the Problem, para. 1).

With this type of flexible database organization, researchers can change ontological relationships and discover new connections between ideas and database content. Srinivasan and Huang [25] also acknowledged the importance of using fluid ontologies for archiving indigenous data, and they demonstrated how this type of file management can be beneficial to digital museum archives and other online databases. Their concept of fluid ontologies included "flexible knowledge structures that evolve and adapt to communities' interest based on contextual information articulated by human contributors, curators, and viewers, as well as artificial bots that are able to track interaction histories and infer relationships among knowledge pieces and preferences of viewers" [25, p. 1]. They noted that knowledge structures should emerge from "the interaction with the very communities that are using the digital museum" and "be truly adaptive and reflective of the priorities and hierarchies of the participants (museum visitor, curator, or contributor)" [25, p. 4].

Srinivasan and Huang [25] developed a project called Eventspace for online exhibits. This project introduced the concept of "metaview." Users can create a metaview to show how they view the relationships in the database by rearranging the nodes representing the content. These metaviews lead to "snapshots" of the users' perspectives at specific times, and the different perspectives of the same data set result in the coexistence of "multiple, evolving ontologies" [25, p. 12]. This type of dynamic information architecture for data analysis can lead to new insights and interpretations of data relationships.

These types of interactive, semantic webs for metadata and multimedia databases are important design concepts for large, complex data sets that need to reflect the experiences and perspectives of diverse communities of researchers who collaborate on projects. If researchers are directly involved in the definition of knowledge structures and create interactive models that show where their piece of information fits into the larger context, they can gain new knowledge about data relationships [25]. In addition, a fluid ontology indicates how users interpret information and relationships over time, which adds another dimension to the knowledge structure. Srinivasan and Huang [25] pointed out that our perception of relationships often changes over time with new insights, knowledge, and experiences.

Jane Hunter, head of the ITEE (School of Information Technology and Electrical Engineering) eResearch Group at the University of Queensland in Brisbane, Australia, is assessing the value of semantic annotation systems in next-generation metadata tools. Hunter [28] pointed out the need to develop dynamic knowledge spaces for complex data representations where scholars can analyze and compare data, and attach annotations, citations, reviews, and links to other resources. She also noted that tools are necessary that can track the sources and context for this information and identify redundant, inconsistent, and incomplete information, in addition to indexing, searching, and archiving information [28].

These research projects in multimedia metadata for archiving cultural databases and data management are changing the way we think about data organization and exploration. Flexible, collaborative information management tools for collective data sharing and analysis are essential for data analysis across disciplines, as well as interdisciplinary research.

6 Future Directions

Multisensory data design can play an important role in the representation of relationships in large data sets. However, we need more research in order to develop design guidelines that specify which media are most effective for representing specific data relationships [4]. We also need research in cross-modal perception that helps us understand how we interpret the new syntax that results from the integration of the different semiotic structures in multimedia data representation. We can then determine the best ways to use this additional level of semiosis to represent complex data relationships.

Spatial representation of data presents new opportunities to explore data sets in large-scale, physical environments. However, multidimensional, virtual spaces for data exploration also offer new possibilities for data representation than can expand the way we perceive and process data relationships. Biocca [29] pointed out that "Spatial representation in advanced virtual environments is probably one of the most powerful systems for spatial representation and manipulation ever developed" because virtual reality environments "allow ways to represent, use, and manipulate space in manners that have no equivalent in physical space, and virtual environments represent space with only a subset of cues found in physical environments" (pp. 55-56). However, he also noted that "cyberspace as a design, communication, and cognitive environment remains largely unexplored" (p.56).

We also need more research on the most effective ways to use multimedia metadata to enhance data analysis and collaboration. Current projects that use multimedia metadata to archive cultural data provide the flexibility that is required for creative data exploration and collaborative research. However, we need to apply these tools to a wider range of disciplines and types of data to determine specific guidelines for using text, visuals, and sound to define metadata for different types of information in large data sets.

Finally, it is important to remember that big data is about narratives. The way data is organized and represented helps us understand those narratives. The senses provide an additional way for humans to connect emotionally and cognitively with those underlying stories and interpret their meaning, thus enabling data to take on social and cultural significance beyond their numerical representations.

The future holds many exciting challenges for researchers and interface designers who work with data analysis and representation. Data visualization and sonification will be augmented by the next generation of tools and innovative virtual environments for multisensory data design that channel our innate abilities to process different types of sensory data.

References

1. Wall, M.: Big Data: Are You Ready for the Blast-off? BBC NEWS Business, 3 March 2014. Retrieved from http://www.bbc.com/news/business-26383058
2. King, G.: Why Big Data is a Big Deal. Harvard Magazine, November-December 2014. Retrieved from http://harvardmagazine.com/2014/03/why-big-data-is-a-big-deal
3. Tak, S., Toet, L.: Towards interactive multisensory data representations. In: Proceedings of the International Conference on Computer Graphics Theory and Applications and International Conference Visualization Theory and Applications, pp. 558–561. SciTePress – Science and Technology Publications, Lisbon (2013)
4. Loftin, R.B.: Multisensory perception: beyond the visual in visualization. Comput. Sci. Eng. 5(4), 56–58 (2003)
5. Search, P.: The metastructural dynamics of interactive electronic design. Vis. Lang. Cult. Dimensions Vis. Commun. 37(2), 146–165 (2003)
6. Downie, M., Carothers, C., Goebel, J.: A New Paradigm for Interactive Exploration of Data with Live Coding (2013). Retrieved from http://vimeo.com/79674603

7. Stanford University: HANA Immersive Visualization Environment (HIVE) (2014). Retrieved from https://icme.stanford.edu/computer-resources/hive

8. Manovich, L.: Media Visualization: Visual Techniques for Exploring Large Media Collections (2012). Retrieved from http://manovich.net/content/04-projects/067-media-visualization-visual-techniques-for-exploring-large-media-collections/66-article-2011.pdf

9. Software Studies Initiative: Cultural Analytics 2014 (2014). Retrieved from http://lab.software studies.com/p/overview-slides-and-video-articles-why.html

10. Ngo, M.K., Spence, C.: Auditory, tactile, and multisensory cues facilitate search for dynamic visual stimuli. Attention, Percept. Psychophysics **72**(6), 1654–1664 (2010)

11. Search, P.: Kaleidoscope: the dynamic discourse of visual literacy in experience design. In: Avgerinou, M., Griffin, R., Giesen, J., Search, P., Spinillo. C. (eds.) Visual Literacy Beyond Frontiers: Information, Culture and Diversity, pp. 185–192. International Visual Literacy Association, Loretto (2008)

12. Macken-Horarik, M.: Interacting with the multimodal text: reflections on image and verbiage. Vis. Commun. **3**(1), 5–26 (2004)

13. Search, P.: Defining a sense of place in interactive multimedia design. In: Avgerinou, A., Search, P., Chandler, S. (eds.) Visual Literacy in the 21st Century: Trends, Demands, and Capacities, pp. 143–148. International Visual Literacy Association, Chicago (2011)

14. Search, P.: The dynamic aesthetics of experience design. In: Proceedings of the International Association of Empirical Aesthetics Congress, pp. 142–145. International Association of Empirical Aesthetics, Chicago (2008)

15. Search, P.: The spatial grammar of interaction design: weaving a tapestry of space and time in multimedia computing. In: Griffin, R., Cowden, B., Avgerinou, M. (eds.) Animating the Mind's Eye, pp. 185–190. International Visual Literacy Association, Loretto (2006)

16. Berkeley, G.: A New Theory of Vision and Other Writings. E. P. Dutton, New York (1922)

17. Piaget, J., Inhelder, B.: The Child's Concept of Space. Routledge and Kegan Paul, London (1956)

18. Gibson, J.: The Perception of the Visual World. Houghton Mifflin, Boston (1950)

19. Rock, I.: The perception of disoriented figures. In: Held, R. (ed.) Image, Object, and Illusion, pp. 71–78. W. H. Freeman and Company, San Francisco (1974)

20. Gaines, E.: Communication and the semiotics of space. J. Creative Commun. **1**(2), 173–181 (2006)

21. Djajadiningrat, J., Matthews, B., Stienstra, M.: Easy doesn't do it: skill and expression in tangible aesthetics. Pers. Ubiquit. Comput. **11**(8), 657–676 (2007)

22. Palmerius, K.L., Forsell, C.: The impact of feedback design in haptic volume visualization. In: Third Joint EuroHaptics Conference 2009 and Symposium on Haptic Interfaces for Virtual Environment and Teleoperator Systems, World Haptics 2009, pp. 154–159. IEEE Press, New York (2009)

23. Christie, M.: Aboriginal knowledge traditions in digital environments. J. Indigenous Educ. **34**, 61–66 (2005)

24. Verran, H., Christie, M.: Using/designing digital technologies of representation in aboriginal australian knowledge practices. Hum. Technol. **3**(2), 214–227 (2007)

25. Srinivasan, R., Huang, J.: Fluid ontologies for digital museums. Int. J. Digit. Libr. **5**(3), 193–204 (2005)

26. Dunsire, G., Hillmann, D., Phipps, J., Coyle, K.: A reconsideration of mapping in a semantic world. In: Proceedings of the International Conference on Dublin Core and Metadata Applications, pp. 26–36. Dublin Core Metadata Initiative (2011)

27. School of Australian Indigenous Knowledge Systems (Charles Darwin University): Indigenous Knowledge and Resource Management in Northern Australia (IKRMNA) (2005). Retrieved from http://www.cdu.edu.au/centres/ik/pdf/TAMI_soft_spec060105.pdf

28. Hunter, J.: Next generation metadata tools: supporting dynamic knowledge spaces. In: Kapitzke, C., Bruce, B.C. (eds.) Libr@ries: Changing Information Space and Practice, pp. 91–122. Lawrence Erlbaum Associates, Mahwah (2006)
29. Biocca, F.: The space of cognitive technology: the design medium and cognitive properties of virtual space. In: Beynon, M., Nehaniv, C.L., Dautenhahn, K. (eds.) CT 2001. LNCS (LNAI), vol. 2117, pp. 55–56. Springer, Heidelberg (2001)

An Interactive Guide to Design Animated Visual Instructions in Brazil

Carla G. Spinillo$^{(\boxtimes)}$ and Roberta Perozza

Department of Design, Federal University of Parana, Curitiba, Brazil
{cgspin,perozza.design}@gmail.com

Abstract. Animated visual instructions have been increasingly produced to support the industry of assembling products. Despite the growing demand for this type of instruction, in Brazil, little has been investigated on how animated instructions should be graphically presented to promote communication effectiveness. This paper discusses a research-based interactive guide to aid the design process of animated instructions in Brazil from user-centered design approach. First, to develop the guide, the graphic presentation of information of a sample of 23 animated instructions was assessed. Then, an experimental study on understanding and preference of narrative times (slow, spontaneous and accelerated) was investigated with 25 participants for an animation representative of the sample analyzed: the 3D puzzle assembly. Based on the results of the studies, guidelines were proposed to the interactive digital guide which usability was validated with 05 experts through checklist with heuristics, and with 10 potential users through post-interaction interviews. The results were generally positive about the content and graphic interface, but pointed to the need of improvements in navigation and menu hierarchy. Accordingly, adjustments were then made in the interactive guide in its final version.

Keywords: Animation · Visual instruction · Assembling · Interactive guide

1 Introduction

The production of animated visual instructions, referred to as Animated Procedural Pictorial Sequences (APPSs) has become a focus of several media companies in the design and supply of specialized services to their clients in the industry of assembling products. As a result, DIY digital manuals and animated instructions have been developed to provide necessary and accurate information to users of such products. Despite the growing demand for animated instructions, this is still an emerging topic in research, particularly from the perspective of information design/information ergonomics. In Brazil, little has been investigated on how animated instructions should be graphically presented to promote effectiveness in communicating assembling contents.

Nevertheless, the use of animation with educational purposes has been researched since the 1980s [1–5], indicating its beneficial influence on understanding of ideas and complex concepts as well as in facilitating the visualization of processes/procedures [6] Animation was also found to reduce the cognitive load [7], to aid in addressing specific cognitive demands of learning tasks [8], and to promote motivation in learning [2].

A. Marcus (Ed.): DUXU 2015, Part II, LNCS 9187, pp. 374–381, 2015.
DOI: 10.1007/978-3-319-20898-5_36

Regarding animation conveying task related contents, [6] found a higher efficiency of animation in procedural knowledge than in descriptive knowledge and problem-solving. This seems to indicate that animation is a valuable resource to represent tasks, since they involve performing sequences of steps [9].

The literature on the role of animation on learning has produced not only empirical evidence to support its use in educational/instructional contexts, but also principles and recommendations to the effective design of animation. In this regard, [10] proposed the following principles based upon studies on learning of scientific and mathematical explanations by students:

- Multimedia principle: content should be presented in animation and narration;
- Spatial contiguity principle: on screen text that refers to an animation should come close to it (e.g., caption, lable);
- Temporal contiguity principle: animation and narration must be presented simultaneously;
- Coherence principle: only relevant and coherent elements of an animation should be presented to avoid extraneous text, images and/or sounds;
- Modality principle: animation should be associated with narration rather than with text on screen;
- Redundancy principle: content should be presented in both animation and narration only. Thus, text on screen should not be employed, since it may jeopardize information processing (cognitive overload).
- Personalization principle: vebal content (on screen text/narration) should be presented in conversational manner to make the animation more friendly to users, aiding learning engagement.

Although those principles concern educational context, they also seem to be appropriate to animation in instructional/task related context, since both contexts regard learning. However, the principles proposed by Mayer and Moreno [10] seem to overlook an important aspect of learning from animation, that is interactivity that has been proved to promote comprehension [11]. Research on interactive animation has not only focused on the education field, but also on game design, looking at technical/technological aspects (e.g., software, tutorials), construction of narratives and characters, and task performance by players (e.g., [12–14]). Hence, there seems to be a lack of studies on interactive animation on the use, handling and/or assembling of products, despite its potential relevance to ease task comprehension and support performance. This was highlighted in a study conducted by Pottes [15] on interactive animated instruction, which presented positive results on participants' performance when interactive functions were provided.

Among the aspects of interactive animation representing procedures, the graphic presentation of information is worth highlighting. This is due to deficiencies in the ways content is visually presented may negatively affect comprehension of task related contents, whether in print or digital material [16, 17]. Regarding animated procedural pictorial sequences (APPSs), an analytical study carried out by Buba [18] found deficiencies in the graphic presentation of content in a software showing procedures for assembling, repairing and replacing mechanical components of the automotive industry. Poor legibility of text on screen, lack of visual emphasis, weak hierarchy of graphic components on the screen and misleading identification of elements on the menu were some of the drawbacks pointed out. Although her study did not investigate comprehension of the APPs examined, it is plausible to infer that those drawbacks would affect understanding of the procedures represented in the animations.

Thus, to design animated instructions not only multimedia aspects should be considered – as recommended in Moreno and Mayer's principles [10] – but also interactivity and graphic presentation of information. Accordingly, providing developers of animated instructions with guidance in this scope may support their decisions in the design process. An example of this is found in a research based digital guide to design medicine inserts in Brazil [19], which was validated with developers of the inserts. The results showed that the digital guide improved the design of inserts by aiding in the decision on the graphic presentation of information.

By considering this, together with the need for studies on Animated Procedural Pictorial Sequences (APPs) for assembling products, this paper presents a research-based interactive guide developed in Brazil to aid the design process of animated instructions from user-centered approach. The development of the guide was based upon related literature allied to outcomes of an analytical study on the graphic presentation of information in a sample of APPSs, and a study on comprehension of an APP representative of the sample. These are briefly explained next.

2   Contributions from the Analytical and Experimental Studies on APPSs to Develop the Interactive Guide

The analytical study examined a sample of 23 APPSs available in the internet and in manuals for assembling products. Their procedural (steps) and non-procedural (e.g., warnings, introductory information) contents were identified and their mode of presentation (audio/narration, text on screen and animation) as well as the graphic presentation of information regarding menus, animation style and framing, text-animation integration and the time related aspects (animation speed and time lapses). In general, the results showed a trend in representing assembling procedures through animation with text on screen. Photographic style (3D images) was generally employed in the animations. Regarding drawbacks in the APPs analyzed, they were found in the representation of warnings and actions in animated steps, high use of time lapses in sequences of steps, omission of the person performing the steps (i.e., ellipsis of the doer) and differences in animation speed. Among these outcomes, those on animation speed were considered for further investigation, since little has been researched on the influence of animation speed on understanding instructional content.

Thus, an APP on assembling a 3D puzzle was chosen to the experimental study as it was representative of the sample characteristics. The APP was adapted into three versions varying in speed of animation presentation: spontaneous (actual), accelerated and slow speed. Then, the APP versions were tested in comprehension and preference with 25 participants. The results indicated that the variation of presentation speed seemed not to affect the understanding of the animation content/task, but the participants' preference for the animation (which were for spontaneous, followed by accelerated and slow speeds). These results were related to participants' emotional reactions, in which spontaneous speed produced greater empathy, whereas slow speed higher rejection. Participants showed greater interest for the animation presented in accelerated speed however, it produced the lowest rate in comprehension.

The outcomes of the analytical and experimental studies supported the development of the content of the interactive guide to APPSs by providing evidence regarding deficiencies in the graphic presentation of information and the aspects that may affect their comprehension.

3 The Interactive Guide to Design APPs

The interactive guide to design APPs was developed based upon Garrett [20] five-planed model for user experience within websites, that has a bottom-up approach: (a) strategy plane: to identify the informational demands of potential users of interactive digital material, (b) scope plane: to define the content and functions of the interactive digital material, (c) structure plane: to organize the informational content, (d) skeleton plane: to define the location of the informational and functional elements on the screen to maintain consistency across levels and within each level, and (e) surface plane: to define the layout and graphic presentation of the material. Accordingly, a prototype version of the guide was developed for testing, as explained next.

In the strategy plane, the findings of empirical research on animation and the outcomes of the study on the APP comprehension and preference were considered. Perceptual cognitive aspects of animation and interaction that influence the communicative efficacy of digital artifacts mentioned in the literature were also taken into account. Then, the information needs of potential users of the Guide were determined, and the contents were compiled and organized according to the following requirements:

- Design the system as a practical guide, with easy and accessible contents.
- Produce text in clear/plain and objective language.
- Use examples and visual interactivity to support learning the guidelines.
- Use graphic elements to organized content into hierarchical topics.
- Structure the content as step-by-step navigation flow.
- Provide a printable version of the content to ease access in the workplace.
- Provide supporting documentation to strengthen the guidelines and to aid in the design process.

Next in the scope and structure planes, the menus and headings were defined considering the outcomes of the previous plane, as follows:

1. Presentation (what is the Guide for and how to use it).
2. APPs (definition and characteristics).
3. Problems regarding APPs.
4. The user centered design for APPs.
5. The guidelines and recommendations for content and graphic presentation.
6. How to evaluate APPs (suggestion of protocols and checklists).
7. Useful literature and links (abstracts/links).
8. The Guide map.
9. Contact us.

Then, the texts were produced for each heading, seeking a clear and objective language. The information architecture was designed based on criteria of proximity and pertinence of the content for the users.

Afterwards, the skeleton and surface planes were carried out in which the system/guide interface and navigation were designed for the Guide. A single grid showing fields for menus, main text and navigational elements was chosen for the interface. The system was structured to allow linear navigation of the contents in the main menu. A secondary menu presented icons related to general information and staff collaboration. Regarding clickable areas, two forms of interaction were made available: clicking on a link to access the examples illustrating the guidelines, and clicking on highlighted parts of the examples to see details of the image/animation.

Regarding graphic presentation of the interface, a color code and the typeface were defined. For the former, blue and gray were chosen as the main colors to follow the university institutional colors. Yellow and black were chosen as secondary colors to be employed for emphasis and for setting texts, respectively. The typeface Verdana was chosen for the texts due to its good legibility on screen. Figure 1 shows examples of screen shots of the Guide graphic interface. The prototype version of the interactive guide was then, validated in its usability as explained next.

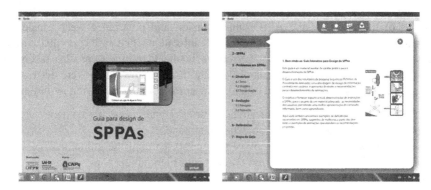

Fig. 1. Examples of the interface of Guide

4 Validating the Guide

The interactive guide was validated with five experts in graphic design/animation and with ten potential users. The expert validation made use of a protocol with heuristics and recommendations from the literature for the design of interactive digital artifacts and animation [10, 21]. Each expert was asked to freely navigate in the Guide and then complete the evaluation protocol individually and in an isolated manner. The validation with the ten users consisted of interviews post-interaction with open and closed questions. The interview protocol also presented statements about the Guide navigation and interface with scales varying from strongly agree to strongly disagree. Each participant (individually and in isolation) was asked to freely interact with the Guide and then perform the tasks for finding information in the Guide. Afterwards, the post-interaction interview was conducted about the tasks performed and participants' impressions. The results of the two validations were analyzed qualitatively to better identify participants' reactions and the aspects to be improved in the Guide for designing APPs.

The results of the validation with experts showed that in general, they considered the Guide to meet the heuristics provided on information design and usability, since 107 out of 155 responses were positive in this regard. All participants felt that the Guide was satisfactory in terms of content classification, location of menus, area for the map guide, icons consistency, clarity and intuitiveness of the interface graphic presentation. The main shortcoming pointed out by four of the five experts was a lack of visualization of the path taken during navigation. Moreover, weaknesses were identified regarding clarity of terms, amount of clickable areas to facilitate interaction, clarity of the system structure, and lack of cues for local and global orientation actions.

As for the validation with ten potential users, in general they considered finding information in the Guide easy, thus, succeeding in this task. However, they had difficulties in finding images illustrating the guidelines, since links were used to access those images, i.e., the images were not displayed near the guidelines. Although nine of the ten participants considered the content of the guide sufficient, they suggested the inclusion of more images showing details of the animated content. They also proposed adjustment in the informational hierarchy of the second level menu of the Guide. Regarding satisfaction, positive responses were given to a general assessment of the Guide, its content, information organization, navigation, and interactive resources. However, participants were not fully satisfied with certain navigation items and found animations lacking contents presented in the text.

By comparing the results of validation with experts and potential users, consistencies are found regarding positive overall assessment of the Guide and the negative evaluation of some items. Deficiencies identified by the experts in the heuristic evaluation were proven true during the participants' interaction with the Guide. On the other hand, the results showed that reactions of potential users differed from the experts' in aspects such as content to be animated and navigation features. This indicates that to assess effectiveness of interactive animated guides not only experts should be consulted and heuristic evaluation should be conducted, but also potential users should be listened and usability tests should be carried out. It is worth mentioning that the results of both validations were in alignment with literature findings on the role of animation in learning [7, 8, 10, 20].

Considering the results of the validation with experts and potential users, the following adjustments were made in Guide:

- Improvement of clarity of the text, avoiding technical terms.
- Inclusion of images as examples of contents and place them near theirs referring guidelines (avoiding links).
- Improvement in the navigation buttons.
- Inclusion of animations showing improvements with the use of the guidelines ('before' and 'after' situations).
- Inclusion of emphatic elements in text and pictures.

5   Final Considerations

Although the limited number of participants (experts and users) in the studies neither allows generalization nor takes effectiveness for grant, the results of the abovementioned studies indicate the potential of the interactive guide as a tool in the design process of animated procedural pictorial sequences. The contribution of the Guide for designing APPs can also regard its development process in which analytical and empirical research built the system/guide foundation. Deciding on the Guide content and interface was more than a technical choice in a design process: it was a user centered approach to it. Consulting APPs' developers (users of the Guide) and experts made conscientious design decisions possible.

Finally, we hope the interactive guide for APPs and its development process may contribute to improve the design of instructional digital material for users that are produced by the industry of assembling products in Brazil.

Acknowledgement. We would like to thank The National Council for Research and Development of Brazil (CNPq) for supporting this research, and the participants who volunteered to these studies.

References

1. Johnston, O., Thomas, F.: The Illusion of Life: Disney Animation, 576 p. Disney Editions, New York (1984, 1999)
2. Rieber, L.P.: Animation, incidental learning, and continuing motivation. J. Educ. Psychol. **83**, 318–328 (1991)
3. Chang, B.W., Ungar, D.: Animation: from cartoons to the user interface. In: 6th Annual ACM Symposium on User Interface Software and Technology, 45–55 pp. ACM, Atlanta, 3–5 November 1993
4. Lowe, R.K.: Extracting information from an animation during complex visual learning. Eur. J. Psychol. Educ. **14**, 225–244 (1999)
5. Fisher, S., Lowe, R.K., Schwan, S.: Effects of presentation speed of a dynamic visualization on the understanding of a mechanical system. In: Sun, R., Miyake, N. (eds.) Proceedings of the 28th Annual Conference of the Cognitive Science Society, pp. 1305–1310. Erlbaum, Mahwah (2006)
6. Hoffler, T.N., Leutner, D.: Instructional animation versus static pictures: a meta-analysis. Learn. Instruction **17**, 722–738 (2007)
7. Schnotz, W., Lowe, R.K.: A unified view of learning from animated and static graphics. In: Lowe, R.K., Schnotz, W. (eds.) Learning with Animation. Research Implications for Design, pp. 304–356. Cambridge University Press, New York (2008)
8. Tversky, B., Morrison, J.B.: Animation: can it facilitate? Int. J. Hum.-Comput. Stud. **57**(4), 247–262 (2002)
9. Weiss, R.E., Knowlton, D.S., Morrison, G.R.: Principles for using animation in computer-based instruction: theoretical heuristics for effective design. Comput. Hum. Behav. **18**, 465–477 (2002)
10. Mayer, R.E., Moreno, R.: Animation as an aid to multimedia learning. Educ. Psychol. Rev. **14**, 87–99 (2002)

11. Souza, J.M.B.: Towards the Optimization of Software Instructional Demonstrations, p. 227. Department of Typography and Graphic Communication, University of Reading, Reading (2008)
12. Santos, R.J., Battaiola, A.L., Dubiela, R.P.: Aspectos Fundamentais da Criação de Jogos em Shockwave 3D. In: SB Games, 2004, Curitiba. Anais do SB Games (2004)
13. Battaiola, A.L., Cowan, D.J., Pellano, A., Siruek, A.: Bridging sustainable engineering education through the use of interactive learning materials: An overview of an international project. In: Anais do GCETE'2005 - Global Congress on Engineering and Technology (2005)
14. Battaiola, A.L., Chagas, M.G., Domingues, D.G.: Jogos de Computador como uma Ferramenta de Ensino dos Cursos de Design. In: Anais do 7° P&D - Congresso de Pesquisa e Desenvolvimento em Design (2006)
15. Pottes, A.: Animação Multimídia de Instrução (AMI) visualizada em Dispositivo de Interação Móvel (DIM): Um estudo exploratório acerca da influência da flexibilidade de interação sobre a visualização da informação e a realização da tarefa. Dissertação de Mestrado, Departamento de Design. Universidade Federal do Paraná, UFPR (2012)
16. Spinillo, C.G., Azevedo, E.R., Benevides, D.: Visual instructions in health printed material an analytical study in PPS on how to use male and female condoms. In: Carla Galvão Spinillo; Solange Coutinho. (Org.). Selected Readings of the Information Design International Conference. Recife: SBDI, pp. 90–104 (2004)
17. Spinillo, C.G., Padovani, S., Miranda, F., Fujita, P.T.L.: Instruções visuais em bulas de medicamentos no Brasil: um estudo analítico sobre a representação pictórica da informação. In: Anais do 3° Congresso Internacional de Design da Informação, 2007, Curitiba. Curitiba: SBDI, 1CD-ROM (2007)
18. Buba, D.: Instruções visuais animadas para a indústria automotiva: uma abordagem analítica em design informacional. Monografia de Especialização em design informacional - Pontifícia Universidade Católica do Paraná (2008)
19. Spinillo, C.G., Souza, J.M.B., Barbosa, L.L.R.: Information system for health: a proposal of an animated instruction guide to design medicine inserts in Brazil. In: Proceedings of the 3rd International Conference on Applied Human Factors and Ergonomics (AHFE), vol. 1. USA Publishing, Louisville (2010)
20. Garrett, J.J.: The Elements of user Experience: User-Centered Design for the Web. AIGA | New Riders, New York (2003)
21. Ainsworth, S.: How do animations influence learning? In: Robinson, D., Schraw, G. (eds.) Current Perspectives on Cognition, Learning, and Instruction: Recent Innovations in Educational Technology that Facilitate Student Learning, pp. 37–67. Information Age Publishing, Charlotte (2008)

Lyricon (Lyrics + Earcons) Improves Identification of Auditory Cues

Yuanjing Sun[1] and Myounghoon Jeon[1,2(✉)]

[1] Mind Music Machine Lab, Cognitive & Learning Sciences,
Michigan Technological University, Houghton, MI, USA
{ysun4,mjeon}@mtu.edu
[2] Mind Music Machine Lab, Computer Science,
Michigan Technological University, Houghton, MI, USA

Abstract. Auditory researchers have developed various non-speech cues in designing auditory user interfaces. A preliminary study of "lyricons" (lyrics + earcons [1]) has provided a novel approach to devising auditory cues in electronic products, by combining the concurrent two layers of musical speech and earcons (short musical motives). An experiment on sound-function meaning mapping was conducted between earcons and lyricons. It demonstrated that lyricons significantly more enhanced the relevance between the sound and the meaning compared to earcons. Further analyses on error type and confusion matrix show that lyricons showed a higher identification rate and a shorter mapping time than earcons. Factors affecting auditory cue identification and application directions of lyricons are discussed.

Keywords: Auditory display · Auditory icons · Auditory user interface · Cognitive mapping · Earcons · Lyricons · Sonification

1 Introduction

Auditory researchers have developed various non-speech (e.g., auditory icons [2], earcons) and tweaked speech cues (e.g., spearcons [3], spindex [4]) in user interfaces. Auditory icons [1] use part of analogic sounds of the object or item. The sound can be thought of as the result from the interaction of real-world. Therefore, they are commonly used as feedback of an operation to enhance the realistic feeling of a virtual interface.

Earcons can represent more abstract operations or processes in user interfaces, by using well-structured musical motives. However, their indirect link to the referent has some limitations [e.g., 5] and requires users' learning. Stevens and her colleagues [5] claimed that users might not recognize up to 40 % of the earcons when there are more than seven earcons at the same time. However, with the application of some musical principles in designing earcons, people could recall up to 25 distinct and uninitiated earcons.

While speech is clearer than other auditory cues, speech might be more intrusive and less aesthetic. The most common application of speech, Telephone-based interface

© Springer International Publishing Switzerland 2015
A. Marcus (Ed.): DUXU 2015, Part II, LNCS 9187, pp. 382–389, 2015.
DOI: 10.1007/978-3-319-20898-5_37

(TBI) reveals three limits when speech is used alone. First, speech is not only slow and serial, but also makes users difficult to retrieve and scroll the target item in TBI. Also, it is hard for speech to concurrently represent both the content itself and the structure or the hierarchy of content (e.g., menu or function) [6]. Third, speech requires high quality of signal and an undistributed background as well. Researchers have also tried to tweak speech in designing auditory cues. Spearcons and spindex cues have shown successful cases in auditory menus, but each of them requires a specific context (e.g., spearcon: multi-dimensional menu, spindex: one-dimensional menu) [4] or optimal applications. Auditory cognition pathway [e.g., 7] illustrates speech interpretation procedure on a phonological level. Echoic memory is a type of the auditory short-term memory (STM), which functions when auditory stimuli are received by the ear until the lexical selection occurs. Spearcons and spindex cues can function as non-speech cues even before the lexical selection occurs.

From this background, "lyricons" (lyrics + earcons) [8] have provided a novel approach to combining the two layers of musical speech sounds (lyrics) and non-speech sounds (earcons) concurrently. This combination is expected to improve both semantics and aesthetics of auditory user interfaces. Such redundant displays might enhance user's recognition and interpretation of auditory cues, while improving the learnability for first-time users to operate auditory user interfaces.

The present study aims to: (1) briefly present the results of focus groups conducted to obtain users' attitude towards their awareness of auditory user interfaces and comments on the initial design of lyricons, (2) validate the effectiveness of lyricons compared to traditional earcons, and (3) introduce a framework to evaluate the recognition and identification of auditory cues.

2 Initial Design of Lyricons and Focus Group

2.1 Initial Design of Lyricons and Earcons

An experienced sound designer (> 15 years) created nine lyricons for nine basic functions of home appliances (Table 1). Earcon design follows literature and industry standards [9]. Lyrics came from previous research [8]. Ballas [10] once proposed four key factors affecting sound identification in the sensory transduction process, which include acoustic properties (e.g., intonation and stress), ecological frequency (how often the signal occurs in the environment), causal uncertainty (whether the signal is easily confusing with other signals), and sound typicality (how typical the signal is of a particular source). This framework lays the foundation of our design and evaluation method of lyricons. Based on that, the sound designer intended to instill a hierarchical implication in speech cues by systematically manipulating the sound variables. In this way, the number of musical notes, the range of frequency, and the total duration of the sound represent the ecological frequency [10] of the function, that is, "how often the function is used in daily life." For example, POWER-ON /OFF stays on the top level of the function hierarchy because it would only occur once at the very beginning or end of the use.

Table 1. Function names and denotation as well as corresponding musical lyrics components.

No.	Function name and denotation	Music notes	Lyric
20	Power On (boot up system)	C4G4E4G4C5	DaDiDaDiDang
16	Power Off (turn off system)	C5G4E4G4C4	DiDaDiDaDing
5	Function On (start laundry/wind)	C4D4E4	Func/Tion/On
2	Function Off (turn off or pause heat, wind)	E4D4C4	Func/Tion/Off
11	Magnitudeup (speed up, each step min to max)	G4A4	Up
12	Magnitude down (slow down, each step max to min)	A4G4	Down
1	Cancel (no, reject)	G5G5	Back
21	Touch (yes, entrance)	G5	Tink
22	Unavailable (Unavailable area, cannot work)	G1	Bang

In sum, the use of ecological frequency made the function hierarchy, with POWER-ON /OFF on top, FUNCTION ON/OFF below that, followed by MAGA-NITUDE CHANGE and CANCLE/TOUCH/UNAVAILABLE on the bottom. Such a combination is expected to enhance user's recognition and interpretation of auditory cues, while improving the learnability for first-time users to operate auditory interface.

2.2 Focus Group

To obtain users' comments on our initial lyricon designs, we conducted focus groups with twelve undergraduate students (mean age = 23, female = 5). They provided general comments on the issues of auditory user interfaces (e.g., annoyance, controllability, indexicability, emotional mapping, etc.) and recommendations about the next lyricon design (e.g., serial combination of speech and sound, using more than one instruments, etc.).

None of our participants has hearing impairments or professional music background. After a consent form procedure and introduction to the study, participants (3–5 in one session) discussed with a moderator their personal experience of the use of auditory user interfaces in electronic devices, and their advantages and disadvantages. Then, the moderator showed initial lyricon designs and participants provided comments on lyricons.

A majority of participants emphasized that auditory cues should convey a straightforward meaning, which is not necessarily the case in reality. They stated that they can easily fall into confusion when the meaning of the sound is uncertain, "Sometimes, I heard the sound but still don't know which part goes wrong, especially when I am driving. It's really annoying because neither can I stop the sound nor can I understand what the problem is." In addition to functional interpretation, some participants were likely to associate auditory cues with their memory or affect in their daily lives.

Sound could evoke emotions and the related context. Recall of memory could help to intuitively grasp the meaning of the designated function. For example, participant G mentioned, "I like the sound from vacuum when I just wake up. It links my memory with my mom." As long as the sound from products was used as a trigger of behavioral shift or attentional shift, participants allowed for an appropriate level of interference, "I like the prompt tone of SKYPE when someone is talking to me. I think it is OK for me if it's not too loud to be a noise." However, simultaneously, they wanted to have control over the auditory cue. Once they lost control of it, they tended to regard it as a noise. Some participants favored speech sounds, "I like natural voice to tell me what's wrong with my car," and "It will be even better if the oven can talk to me. I mean I like to pretend all equipment at home is a human," which supports the application of lyricons.

Participant L provided recommendations of the next lyricon designs, "To a new user, it will be better to have the speech part first and then, the sound, so he or she knows the specific function of the sound clearly. After a while, they can choose to skip the speech, but keep using the sound. If more instruments in different ranges were used, it would be easy to distinguish from each other."

3   Sound-Function Mapping Experiment

3.1   Method

We expect that lyricons outperform earcons, but a parallel combination of speech and earcons in lyricons might confuse users more [9]. Therefore, we conducted an empirical sound-function mapping experiment to compare the identification accuracy between lyricons and earcons.

Thirty-three undergraduate students (mean age = 21, 10 female) participated in the auditory cue-function mapping experiment. None of them has participated in the previous focus group session. They were randomly allocated to two groups: lyricon group or earcon group. After a consent form procedure, participants conducted a sound card sorting task [8]. Nine function-index cards were placed on the desk. Each card contained a definition and specific examples of the function. The sound stimuli consisted of nine lyricons and nine earcons (same as those used in lyricons). Participants listened to sound stimuli generated from a SONY sr16 computer using a Sennheiser HD380 pro headphone.

First, an experimenter explained the meaning of each function to participants. Then, participants paired each sound stimulus with the function that they believe the sound best represents. Participants were allowed to have as much time as they wanted to complete the sorting task.

3.2   Results

The results showed that the average of accuracy rate of the lyricon group (82.35 %) was almost double than that of the earcon group (46.53 %). An independent samples t-test showed a significant difference between the lyricon and the earcon groups, $t(30.4) = 3.60$, $p < 0.001$. Moreover, the sorting time of the lyricons ($M = 5.26$ min, $SD = 1.17$) was much shorter than that of the earcons ($M = 6.34$ min, $SD = 3.60$). We

Table 2. Confusion matrix of lyricon mapping results.

Intended answer	Power-on	Power-off	Function-on	Function-off	Magnitude up	Magnitude down	Cancel	Touch	Unavailable
Power-on	94.12%		5.88%						5.88%
Power-off		94.12%		5.88%	5.88%				
Function-on	5.88%		76.47%		5.88%	5.88%		17.65%	
Function-off		5.88%	11.76%	82.35%					
Magnitude up				11.76%	76.47%	5.88%			
Magnitude down						88.23%			11.76%
Cancel							88.23%	11.76%	
Touch			5.88%		11.76%		5.88%	58.82%	
Unavailable							5.88%	11.76%	82.35%

Table 3. Confusion matrix of earcon mapping results.

Intended answer	Power-on	Power-off	Function-on	Function-off	Magnitude up	Magnitude down	Cancel	Touch	Unavailable
Power-on	56.25%	12.50%	12.50%		18.75%				
Power-off	6.25%	50.00%		18.75%		18.75%	6.25%		
Function-on	31.25%	18.75%	25.00%		18.75%	6.25%			
Function-off		18.75%	6.25%	56.25%	6.25%	12.50%	6.25%		
Magnitude up	6.25%		25.00%	6.25%	31.25%	12.50%	12.50%		
Magnitude down			18.75%	12.50%	12.50%	25.00%	12.50%	6.25%	12.50%
Cancel			6.25%	6.25%	6.25%	12.50%	31.25%	31.25%	
Touch			6.25%		6.25%	6.25%	18.75%	62.50%	
Unavailable						6.25%	12.50%		81.26%

also plotted the confusion matrix to identify which functions confused the participants most (Tables 2 and 3).

3.3   Error Type Analysis

For further analysis, we divided mapping errors into three types: hierarchy error, tone polarity error, and random error. Hierarchy error means that participants can successfully recognize the pair, but mistakenly assign them in the wrong function hierarchy (e.g. Assigned MAGNITUDE UP/DOWN stimuli in FUNCTION ON/OFF labels). Tone polarity error means the right assignment to function hierarchy but put polarity upside down (Put MAGNITUDE UP in MAGNITUDE DOWN labels). The remaining errors are attributed to random error (see Fig. 1). In a diagram, the horizontal

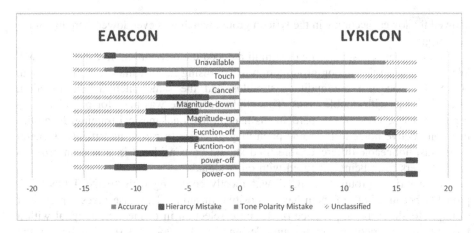

Fig. 1. Stacked bar of error type distribution diagram. Left side is the earcon group and right side is the lyricon group.

axis is the number of errors. The vertical axis represents nine functions. There are four patterns in legend to represent four conditions: blue is correct; thicker red is hierarchy error, green is tone polarity error and purple light diagonal pattern is random error. The diagram of error distribution reveals that the lyricon group made fewer hierarchy errors than the earcon group. Selective lyrics seemed to strengthen the signal-referent relationship, and eliminate the causal uncertainty in mapping.

4 Discussion

We also plotted the confusion matrix to identify which functions confused the participants most as showed in Table 2 and 3.

4.1 Confusion Matrix Analysis

When it comes to the phonological level process again, our participants in the earcon group seem to remember nine earcons only in the echoic memory before the lexical selection occurs. Lacking of direct connection with meaning might lead to low accuracy as well as longer time in the mapping task. Such processing might also require higher mental resources, and thereby, decreased the recognition performance. Without the help of lyrics, participants seem to have difficulty in identifying the relations between the sounds and the functions, and among nine earcons.

As mentioned, causal uncertainty refers to whether the signal is easily confusing with other signals [10]. It is an important calibration in measuring the confusion among a group of sound stimuli. In particular, "UNAVAILABLE" had the highest accuracy rates in both lyricon and earcon groups probably because its unique low pitch was distinctive from other stimuli. In contrast, the other single-tone function, "TOUCH" showed the lowest accuracy in the lyricon group, which was even lower than that of the earcon group.

Similarity in acoustic profile of stimuli reduced the recognition of a specific signal. We found that in the earcon group the most confusing factor came from the function, "CANCEL" because the auditory stimulus had the same pitch as the function, "TOUCH" but with double notes. This slight difference was hard for participants to capture because none of our participants had professional musical training. It implies that consecutive notes in the same pitch may give rise to causal uncertainty. General users' just-noticeable-difference threshold should be considered in design in order to prevent users from being confused with other signals.

In the lyricon group, "TOUCH" was mostly confusing with "FUNCTION-ON", probably because both of them have a positive meaning. This case gives a particular example to show the importance of the lyric selection in connecting a signal with a referent. In the lyricon group, a sound designer used a word, "BACK" as lyric in the lyricon, "CANCEL". It is an appropriate choice because "BACK" expresses a negative meaning, which is also popular in yes/no/cancel dialog boxes. It provides the context that successfully links the echoic memory with semantic meaning of the function. In contrast, the designer used "TINK" as lyric in the lyricon, "TOUCH" instead of other popular words in dialog boxes (for example: "Yes", "OK", "Enter", etc.) to express a positive meaning. The ambiguous word weakened the link in the lexical-semantic stage, and thus, misled participants to the other lexical candidate, "FUNCTION-ON".

5   Conclusion and Future Work

By designing lyricons, we attempted to integrate speech and non-speech cues to overcome existing problems in auditory user interface design. Our empirical experiment on sound-event mapping demonstrated that lyricons could enhance the relevance between the sound and the meaning compared to earcons. The lyricon group showed a higher identification rate and a shorter mapping time than the earcon group, which is promising in terms of lyricon applications in auditory user interfaces. Based on this experiment, we confirmed key factors [10] affecting sound cue identification – distinguishability, ecological frequency, lyric choice, etc. In lyricons, the lyric part can improve identification of the function, while the earcon part can imply the hierarchical structure of the functions.

In the current study, we used only the piano sound for the experimental purpose. More acoustic properties and musical parameters, such as timbre, register, tempo, rhythm, have already been included in auditory display design in industry to iteratively enhance lyricons' aesthetic quality. We plan to analyze phonetic patterns of each functional speech [e.g., speech-to-song illusion, 11] and to reflect them on the innate acoustic profiles of the earcon part in order to find an optimal combination of speech and musical clips. Such an endeavor may enhance participants' perception and interpretation of the message conveyed by lyricons. In a practical application, once users get familiar with lyricons, they could customize the earcon-only part without the lyric part. Based on this design and evaluation effort, researchers and practitioners could create more effective and efficient auditory interactions between a user and a system.

References

1. Blattner, M.M., Sumikawa, D.A., Greenberg, R.M.: Earcons and icons: their structure and common design principles. Hum. Comput. Interact. **4**, 11–44 (1989)
2. Gaver, W.W.: Auditory icons: using sound in computer interfaces. Hum. Comput. Interact. **2**, 167–177 (1986)
3. Walker, B.N., Lindsay, J., Nance, A., Nakano, Y., Palladino, D.K., Dingler, T., Jeon, M.: Spearcons (speech-based earcons) improve navigation performance in advanced auditory menus. Hum. Factors **55**(1), 157–182 (2012)
4. Jeon, M., Walker, B.N.: Spindex (speech index) improves auditory menu acceptance and navigation performance. ACM Trans. Accessible Comput. **3**(3), 10:11–26 (2011)
5. Stevens, C., Brennan, D., Parker, S.: Simultaneous manipulation of parameters of auditory icons to convey direction, size, and distance: effects on recognition and interpretation. In: Proceedings of the International Conference on Auditory Display (ICAD2004), Sydney, Australia (2014)
6. Brewster, S.A.: Using nonspeech sounds to provide navigation cues. ACM Trans. Comput. Hum. Interact. (TOCHI) **5**, 224–259 (1998)
7. Baldwin, C.L.: Auditory Cognition and Human Performance: Research and Applications. CRC Press, Boca Raton (2012)
8. Jeon, M.: Lyricons (lyrics + earcons): Designing a new auditory cue combining speech and sounds. In: Stephanidis, C. (ed.) HCII 2013, Part I. CCIS, vol. 373, pp. 342–346. Springer, Heidelberg (2013)
9. Jeon, M., Lee, J.-H.: The ecological AUI (auditory user interface) design and evaluation of user acceptance for various tasks on smartphones. In: Kurosu, M. (ed.) HCII/HCI 2013, Part IV. LNCS, vol. 8007, pp. 49–58. Springer, Heidelberg (2013)
10. Ballas, J.A.: Common factors in the identification of an assortment of brief everyday sounds. J. Exp. Psychol. Hum. Percept. Perform. **19**(2), 250–267 (1993)
11. Deutsch, D., Henthorn, T., Lapidis, R.: Illusory transformation from speech to song. J. Acoust. Soci. Am. **129**(4), 2245–2252 (2011)

Touch and Gesture DUXU

Evaluating Interaction Design in Brazilian Tablet Journalism: Gestural Interfaces and Affordance Communicability

Luiz Agner[1(✉)], Adriano Bernardo Renzi[2], Natanne Viegas[1], Priscila Buares[1], and Vitor Zanfagnini[1]

[1] Faculdades Integradas Helio Alonso/FACHA, Rio de Janeiro, Brazil
{luizagner,natanne.viegas,buarespriscila,
vitorzanfagnini13}@gmail.com
[2] Escola Superior de Desenho Industrial/UERJ, Rio de Janeiro, Brazil
adrianorenzi@gmail.com

Abstract. The present work aims to provide a contribution to the definition of new parameters to guide interface design and content publishing that will ensure the quality of gestural interaction in newspaper apps for tablets. Our case study is O Globo A Mais, a digital edition with unique content specially produced for iPad, launched by Rio de Janeiro's newspaper O Globo, one of the majors in Brazil. The research employed two techniques of qualitative emphasis: exploratory interviews and user observation focused on readers. We concluded that designers and journalists of O Globo A Mais should develop and refine their discourse to users through its gestural interfaces.

Keywords: Tablet · Journalism · Design · Affordance · Semiotics · Communicability

1 Introduction

In the last decade, the computer has become a fundamental mechanism of our culture. One can see that current gestural interfaces enable new reading practices which are mediated by portable devices such as e-book readers, smartphones or tablets - quickly absorbed by the editorial market.

The present work aims to evaluate the reception of journalistic content through a case study of O Globo A Mais, a digital edition with unique content specially produced for iPad and launched by Rio de Janeiro's newspaper O Globo, one of the largest distribution in Brazil, recently winning the Esso Journalism Award for Best Contribution to Brazilian Press, the most important contest in the country.

This research intended to provide parameters for the guidance of design, visual editing and content production, as well as the creation of interfaces, to ensure the quality of gestural interaction with news on tablets - respecting possibilities, limitations and cognitive requirements of the young generation readers, which are the targeted users of O Globo in their project.

© Springer International Publishing Switzerland 2015
A. Marcus (Ed.): DUXU 2015, Part II, LNCS 9187, pp. 393–402, 2015.
DOI: 10.1007/978-3-319-20898-5_38

2 Theoretical References

According to Palácios and Cunha [1], six fundamental properties characterize the spaces of journalistic information online nowadays: hypertextuality, interactivity, multimediality, personalization, continuous updating and memory.

Smartphones and tablets led to the emergence of a new element that is added to the above characteristics: tactility. In the point of view of the two referred authors, tactility is an important new characteristic of mobile communication devices and presentation of journalistic information that must be researched and tested.

This research intended to establish a dialogue with different theoretical views addressing the interaction between people and computers. The predominant and canonical theories of HCI are commonly knowledge based (Preece et al., 2002) [2]. Its roots came from cognitive psychology, cognitive sciences and artificial intelligence - disciplines that study cognition (the process by which one can acquire knowledge). They seek to understand the mental constraints of the users during their interaction with interfaces. On the other hand, there are also semiotic approaches to Human Computer Interaction - whose theoretical basis, Semiotics, is the discipline that studies signs, semiotic systems and communication. These were related to the work of semioticians like Charles Peirce, Jakobson and Umberto Eco.

In order to understand the applicability of systems, we decided to work with both the concept of usability (from the knowledge-based theories) as well as with the concept of communicability (by Semiotic Engineering).

Usability refers to the quality of system interactions with its users and includes several aspects such as ease of learning and use, user satisfaction and productivity, among others. On the other hand, communicability describes the property of a system to transmit to the user, in an appropriate manner, intentions and interaction principles that guided its design.

In the Semiotic Engineering (SE) point of view (De Souza et al., 1999) [3], the system interface is a message sent from the designer to the user. The designer is the author of this message transmitted to the user, and the Human-Computer Interaction reflects this meta process. Thus, interface design involves not only the intellectual conception of a system model, but also the communication of this model.

In semiotic approach, user interfaces can be viewed as one-shot, higher-order messages sent from designers to users. The content of such messages is a designer's conception of who the users are, what their needs and expectations are, and, more important, how the designer has chosen to meet these requirements through an inter-active artifact. The form of the messages is an interactive language. As Prates, De Souza and Barbosa [4] suggested:

> In parallel with software usability, we can then assess software communicability. Communi-cability is the property of software that efficiently and effectively conveys to users its underlying design intent and interactive principles [4].

It's important to add the work of Cavallo and Chartier [5] in our research: the historical foundation for understanding how tablet revolution can explain changes in reading practices. History of reading practices considers the "text world" as a world of objects, forms and rituals, with conventions and specific arrangements that lead the construction of meaning. Therefore, there is no text outside the support that provides the reading: authors do not write books, write texts that become written objects - manuscripts, engravings, printed or computerized -, handled differently by readers of flesh and blood.

Thus, Cavallo and Chartier stand against the representations of common sense in which the text exists in itself, apart from its materiality.

3   Tablets and Changes on the News' Market

In a seemingly perfect marriage to journalistic information, the tablet restitutes to readers the direct interaction that the mouse has denied them: readers now use their hands. By employing the fingers and gestures to directly manipulate information - swiping through pages of magazines or newspapers, activating images, links, buttons and videos - users rediscovered the naturalness of gesture-based interaction. The reader, with comfort and convenience, possibly leaning against a sofa, is invited to spend more time interacting with news. Research indicates that users spend an average of ten minutes reading news on a website (using desktop), 30 min reading a printed newspaper, and up to 40 min using a tablet such the iPad.

The graphical integrity of the visual hierarchy of information – an important feature of print journalism – returned to the forefront in tablets editions, resuming a prominent role in information architecture and rediscovering the power of visual communication from printed magazines: "The 'holy grail' of tablets is a pleasant reading experience that brings the advantages of the internet in a beautiful and pleasant graphical interface. This connects the print world and the digital" – as explained by Adriana Barsotti [6], chief editor of O Globo A Mais.

However, there are consistent complaints regarding news apps for tablets in Brazil. According to Primo [7], the Brazilian journals fail to achieve the full potential of these devices: simply converting printed pages to tablet format causes a setback that has long ago been surpassed by regular webdesign practices.

According to Telio Navega, designer of O Globo A Mais, part of the problem could be credited to the misunderstanding of the changes taking place in the habits of younger readers. Navega [8] considers that: "young readers are on the Internet, they do not buy or sign printed papers any more. This is the great difficulty of today's newspapers: journalists who work in newsrooms are older people who are far from new readers and can not understand what happens."

Journalistic tablet apps are already a failure, says Lund [9], following the end of the commercial experience of The Daily, discontinued after $ 30 million in annual losses. The magazines on tablet format are completely invisible to information flows that govern the Internet. When a publication is organized this way, stories can not be indexed by search engines.

Skeptic about the efforts of the news organizations, Stevens [10] observed that the current journalistic applications for tablets are mimicking the extremely heavy CD-Roms, which makes them less useful and less practical than the web itself. The web, with its open source technologies like HTML5 and CSS, is much more efficient and capable of reproducing the typical sophisticated graphic layouts of tablets.

This misconception, according to the author, will result in the definitive sentence of death of tablet journalism.

4 Tablet Usability and Perceived Affordances

When talking about tablet journalism interfaces, it's important to have a detailed approach at the notion of affordances. According to Nielsen and Budiu [11], affordance means "what you can do with something". On a touch screen, any single area may afford touching, tapping, sliding your finger, moving your finger in a zigzag pattern, or any other gesture.

Nielsen and Budiu explain that users also have to know that they can perform a specific action. Users can remember the gesture from past experiences, or they can infer the availability of the action from some visual indication on the screen. When people can see what they can do we are talking about "perceived affordances".

Norman [12] explains that the word affordance was coined to refer to the actionable properties between the world and an actor (a person or animal). The term "affordance" comes from the perceptual psychologist J. Gibson who developed an "ecological" alternative to cognitive approaches (*apud* Gaver, 1991).

Gibson (*apud* Gaver, 1991) [13] focuses almost exclusively on affordances which may be seen, but affordances per se are independent of perception. Separating affordances from the information available about them allows the distinction among correct rejections and perceived, hidden and false affordances:

> Common examples of affordances refer to perceptible affordances, in which there is perceptual information available for an existing affordance. If there is no information available for an existing affordance, it is hidden and must be inferred from other evidence. If information suggests a nonexistent affordance, a false affordance exists upon which people may mistakenly try to act. Finally, people will usually not think of a given action when there is no affordance for it nor any perceptual information suggesting it [13].

We ought not to confuse affordances with perceived affordances. Affordances reflect the possible relationships among actors and objects: they are properties of the world. Understanding correctly the concept of affordance and perceived affordances is essential to design apps with usability.

As Norman [12] stated:

> Affordances specify the range of possible activities, but affordances are of little use if they are not visible to the users. Hence, the art of the designer is to ensure that the desired, relevant actions are readily perceivable.

As affordances need to be perceived by users, we can conclude that there is a communicability issue [3, 4, 17]. Designers should clearly communicate to users the existence of affordances in the environment.

Perceived affordances are defended by Nielsen and Budiu [11] as a way to ensure good usability of iPad applications: to design better apps, it's important to add dimensionality and better define individual interactive areas to increase discoverability through perceived affordances. Also, it's better to loosen up the "etched-glass aesthetic" and create designs that go beyond the flatland of iPad's first-generation apps (this would emphasize affordances). Further recommendations are to include apps with Back buttons; broader use of Search; homepages; and direct access to articles by touching headlines on the front page; and support standard navigation.

5   Research Methods

The research employed in this study included two techniques of qualitative emphasis: (i) exploratory interviews with the editor and designers of O Globo A Mais, and (ii) user observation method based on cooperative evaluation method, focused on readers.

We called the user observation method "scenario and tasks based interviews" (Agner, Tavares and Ferreira, 2010) [14] and it was an informal kind of usability test.

A sample of undergraduate students of Communication participated of the proposed technique. We observed individually all their actions using O Globo A Mais and interviewed each one of them within their testing sessions, in order to evaluate the quality of gestural interfaces. The sample of participants was not probabilistic but guided to our research objectives. After application of a preliminary questionnaire, a group of six students was firstly selected. The number is due to the proximity of the guerrilla number indicated by Nielsen for the application of usability testing (*apud* Barnum et al., 2012) [15].

Each test participant completed a pre-test questionnaire to identify the details of his profile and experience with information technology. Then each selected student received a sheet of paper containing a scenario and eight written tasks to be performed to find published information in O Globo A Mais. During the user sessions - in which each participant sought to accomplish the proposed tasks – it was used think-aloud protocol while observing the interaction with an iPad.

6   Summary of Exploratory Interviews

As stated in previous section, one of our research qualitative techniques interviewed professionals involved with the production of journalistic content and news design: Adriana Barsotti, a journalist with master's degree in Communications and editor of O Globo A Mais; Telio Navega, blogger and news designer of O Globo A Mais; and Raquel Cordeiro, designer of O Globo A Mais, among others.

Editor Barsotti [6] pointed out that journalists, to date, never had to worry about interface usability problems, something new to the press professionals. Realizing that readers faced some difficulty navigating in the digital prototype, the team requested the inclusion of various metalinguistic signs as a navigational aid for its content. The editor showed preference of redundancy instead of risking more problems in navigation and content finding by users.

The news designer Telio Navega [8] commented that he enjoys so much the experience of working in such an innovative project as O Globo A Mais, which is a legitimate example of the "future of journalism". Moreover, he observed that young people have stopped to consume news through print journalism, giving their preference to online media. Navega [8] adds that the journalist of the newsroom is usually an older guy who has difficulty in keeping up and accepting the changes generated by the advent of online communication and social media. However, the company goal is to attract new audience and this would be done by launching the digital edition for the iPad. The goal has been achieved, since according to Navega, with the launch of iPad edition, O Globo newspaper nearly doubled its digital subscriber base.

According to Barsotti, the great advantage of tablet newspaper editions is catching the aesthetic print media model. Joining the two worlds (print and online), tablets deliver an enjoyable reading experience and a compelling and beautiful layout. In addition, journalists prefer tablets than websites as there would be in tablets more "glamour" and a satisfaction effect similar to that provided by print.

According to Navega [8], the "text journalist" loves the iPad because there is plenty of room for scrolling, so texts don't need to be cut off. And it may also be enriched with multimedia: video, photos and sounds.

Technically, the team of designers doesn't insert multimedia in Adobe software. Static pages are generated in JPG, then they are enriched using DigitalPages software, as informed by Cordeiro [16].

7 Some Test Results

We gathered data from empirical observations after reviewing and analysing 54 audio and video recordings. The usability issues found reflected problem categories similar to the ones identified by Nielsen and Norman [12] (Table 1).

As informed by Cordeiro [16], extra usability testing was held at O Globo and its results helped guide some changes when the team adopted a new Adobe InDesign template in late 2013. As an example of these changes, the cover had a problem in the upper headlines that were not perceived by the public, which was detected by these tests and fixed. Later on, O Globo A Mais edition was converted to support other formats: Android tablets, iOS and Android smartphones, including a Kindle Fire edition and e-readers. The team also produced a version for Web, through a private channel inside O Globo. Now a version for Windows Phone is being tested, said Cordeiro [16].

Other changes included were: (i) insertion of Index menu on the cover of the publication that is enabled from a tap on the logo; (ii) insertion of an Index page; (iii) icons are now associated with verbal labeling; (iv) sensitive areas became more clearly defined; (v) Return button has been fixed; (vi) a Social Media button has been inserted (however with a limited functionality). The Search function was again overlooked in the app reformulation, though identified as an important tool in usability tests.

As a result from our academic research, the magazine O Globo A Mais is experiencing a new round of usability tests, in order to validate changes undertaken and manage general conclusions for Brazilian journalism apps. We cannot deliver results of this second cycle of academic usability tests as they are still ongoing.

Table 1. Usability problems associated to categories.

Category	Usability issues
Affordance	Using the concept proposed by De Souza [17] there is a problem of *communicability* here. Several readers showed problems to perceive additional content. Besides, there are places where there is no explicit visual differentiation between sensitive and non-sensitive elements to tap
Feedback	Insufficient indications of the reader's location within the application: the reader sometimes does not know where he is. In the gallery, there is no feedback on how many photos there are and how many were already viewed
Consistencyinternal and/or external	The cover does not play the role of homepage. This contradicts the expectation of the reader of Y Generation who grew up browsing websites. There is also no Index Page in the publication. The app does not have a search tool for keywords as expected on standard use on the Web. There are contradictory ways to suggest the existence of more content in the same story: Graphically different symbols indicate the same functions. There are duplicated scrolls problems (scrolls within scrolls). Besides, there is an inconsistent use of verbal language
Reversibility	If the reader makes a wrong turn while navigating he can't revert to the previous position. That's because the Back button on the top of the screen makes the reader to close the application and go to Globo newsstand, but the user can't return to Cover screen
Detectability	The navigation bar disappears for much of the time during navigation. Besides, there is no textual labels on icons
Scalability	Although the publication is designed to portrait orientation, and minimizes this kind of problems, sometimes it may be difficult to display photos in landscape mode because the swipe area decreases; readers may also get confused with the swipe of videos
Reliability	Once you are in the Gallery and you want to swipe horizontally, you need to touch in a specific area, unlike the other pages. So, it seems to have a random response, which creates uncertainty

8 Partial Conclusions

Based on compiled and analyzed partial data, we prepared Table 2 with design requirements and provisory suggestions for tablet journalism editions in Brazil.

Remembering that there are predictions that point out that print newspapers would be extinct by 2030 in most of the world. In this context, studies in HCI have an important role when looking to make journalistic products be more effectively suited to the ergonomic needs and cognitive model of young readers.

Our studies and empirical observations led us to conclude that the set of seven categories of usability problems discovered by Norman and Nielsen [12] during their tests with tablets was also made present in the interaction of Brazilian readers with the

Table 2. Categories and design requirements for Brazilian tablet journalism.

Category	Design requirements	Goals
Affordance communicability	Visually differentiate the sensitive areas from the non-sensitive areas	Ensure the communicability of the interactive areas and affordances
	Since there is no mouse-over feature, visual language should be clear: use colors, visual effects and icons for indicate affordances	Ensure the reader access to additional content
	Use of verbal labeling systems associated with icons	
	Visual appearance should not be based only on the flatland print metaphor	
Feedback	Indicate sections clearly with appropriate tags like printed magazines do	Clearly signalize the existence of more content
	Create an Index page	Present information architecture of the app
	Use page numbering	
	Use numbering in photo gallery	
Consistency	Test solutions that break up with sedimented models	Ensure intuitive navigation within the content
	Respect widely known resources used on the web, like Back buttons and keyword Searches	
	Avoid icons with double or triple functionality	Avoid navigation errors
	Use verbal language consistently	Avoid disorientation of the reader
	Give the Cover page or Index page the role of a home page	Adapt publication for the mental model of the reader
	Respect interaction patterns proposed by the operating system	
Reversibility	Implement a simple way to Undo or Go Back	Ensure the fluidity of the reading
		Avoid destructive actions
	Implement a simple way to go to the Index page or Cover	Avoid that the reader be lost in the content
Detectability	Insert fixed navigation bar as the example of websites	Encourage exploratory navigation
	Ensure their permanent visibility	Make functions permanently accessible
	Employ verbal labeling system associated with iconic labeling system	
Scalability	Perform tests with readers with the two page orientations in order to	Ensure application performance in two

(*Continued*)

Table 2. (*Continued*)

Category	Design requirements	Goals
	view videos and photos in full screen	orientations (horizontal and vertical)
Reliability	Ensure that same gestures will result the same behavior	Increase security and the reader's confidence
	Avoid unusual responses for simple gestures like swipe and tap	Improve learnability
	Avoid surprises	

digital edition O Globo A Mais. The categories recorded problems included: (i) affordances (ii) feedback, (iii) consistency, (iv) reversibility, (v) detectability, (vi) scalability on different screens, and (vii) reliability in operations.

The observed problems were related to gestural interaction, the operating system iOS and the page design and content structure of O Globo A Mais. We also found communicability problems in the affordances as, on many occasions, these were not perceived by the users. Affordances need to be perceived by users. This may be considered an issue of communicability [3, 4, 17]. As they stated, the designer is the author of a message transmitted to the user and the Human Computer Interaction reflects a meta-communication process. Designers should clearly communicate to users the existence of affordances in the interface environment, as user interfaces can be viewed as higher-order messages sent from designers to users. So, we can say that designers and journalists of O Globo A Mais should develop and refine their discourse to users. Perceived affordances are also defended by Nielsen and Budiu [11] as a way to ensure usability of iPad applications. This means adopting a design that goes beyond the flat based model that reflects the paradigm of print magazines, and adopting standard navigation features such as keyword search and homepages. Some recent changes in O Globo A Mais has already begun to advance in this direction, after new usability tests.

One of the biggest problems of journalistic applications seems to be the paradigm which their interfaces are based on: while representing an hybrid metaphorical model between the print and online media, some applications are intentionally seeking to get away from web.

Thus, interfaces of journalistic apps are strongly based on the layout model of print magazines (which would provide more prestige and glamour than websites). The fact is reinforced by the technology available: the software used for production, Adobe InDesign, comes from the print publishing industry and reinforces these characteristics.

We have also concluded that, in Brazil, journalists and newsmakers have created content for tablet edition without due care with sedimented requirements and standards of Human-Computer Interaction. As we could observe in our case study, according to Cordeiro [16], there was no specific responsibility role for interaction design in the team of O Globo A Mais.

User centered and interaction design methods were not considered during the early development of the product O Globo A Mais. According to the publisher Adriana Barsotti [6], interaction design is a new theme for press professionals and is not part of the regular concerns of a team of journalists.

These problems may cause navigation difficulties or setbacks to the readers of Y generation, which are an important part of the target who the newspaper wants to retain in order to increase its digital subscribers and ensure the survival of its business model in a publishing market that goes through major changes in Brazil and around the world.

Acknowledgements. This research was made with the collaboration of undergraduate students of Social Communication (Department of Journalism/Advertising/PR) at Faculdades Integradas Helio Alonso (Facha) and post-graduate students of Interface Ergodesign, Usability and Information Architecture at the Pontifical Catholic University of Rio de Janeiro (PUC-Rio). This research is supported by FAPERJ - Fundação Carlos Chagas Filho de Amparo à Pesquisa do Estado do Rio de Janeiro (APQ1/2014).

References

1. Palácios, M., Cunha, R.: A Tactilidade em Dispositivos Móveis: Primeiras Reflexões e Ensaio de Tipologias. Contemporanea, comunicação e cultura **10**(03), 668–685 (2012)
2. Preece, J., Rogers, Y., Sharp, H.: Interaction Design: Beyond Human-Computer Interaction. Wiley, New York (2002)
3. De Souza, C., Leite, J., Prates, R.: BARBOSA, Simone. Projeto de Interfaces de Usuário - Perspectivas Cognitivas e Semióticas (1999)
4. Prates, R., De Souza, C., Barbosa, S.: A method for evaluating the communicability of user interfaces. Mag. Interact. ACM **7**(1), 31–38 (2000)
5. Cavallo, G., Chartier, R.: História da leitura no mundo ocidental. 2ª. Ed. São Paulo: Ática, 232 p. (1998)
6. Barsotti, A.: Author interview on 3 March 2012
7. Primo, A.: Núm3ro Primo: Jornalismo para iPad e Kindle. http://www.youtube.com. Accessed June 2011
8. Navega, T.: Author interview on 21 March 2012
9. Lund, J.: Why tablet magazines are a failure. http://gigaom.com/2013/10/06/tablet-magazines-failure/. Accessed October 2013
10. Stevens, C.: Designing for the iPad, 336 p. John Wiley & Sons, Chichester (2011)
11. Nielsen, J., Budiu, R.: Mobile Usability, 204 p. News Riders, Berkeley (2003)
12. Norman, D., Nielsen, J.: Gestural interfaces: A step backward in usability. Interactions **17** (5), 46–49 (2010)
13. Gaver, W.: Technology affordances. In: Proceeding CHI 1991 Proceedings of the SIGCHI Conference on Human Factors in Computing Systems, pp. 79–84. ACM, New York (1991)
14. Agner, L., Tavares, P., Ferreira, S.B.L.: Scenario and task based interview to evaluate usability of computer assisted data collection. In: Marcus, A. (ed.) HCII 2011 and DUXU 2011, Part II. LNCS, vol. 6770, pp. 349–358. Springer, Heidelberg (2011)
15. Barnum, et al.: The "Magic Number 5": Is It Enough for Web Testing?. CHI 2003, 5–10 April 2003, Ft. Lauderdale, Florida, USA. ACM 1-58113-630-7/03/0004. Panels CHI 2003: New Horizons CHI 2003, 5–10 April 2003, Ft. Lauderdale, Florida, USA. http://www.usna.edu/. Acessed 9 July 2012
16. Cordeiro, R.: Author interview on 23 December 2014
17. de Souza, C.S.: The Semiotic Engineering of Human-Computer Interaction. The MIT Press, Cambridge (2005)

Haptic Exploration Patterns in Virtual Line-Graph Comprehension

Özge Alaçam[1], Cengiz Acartürk[2(✉)], and Christopher Habel[1]

[1] Department of Informatics, University of Hamburg, Hamburg, Germany
{alacam,habel}@informatik.uni-hamburg.de
[2] Informatics Institute, Middle East Technical University, Ankara, Turkey
acarturk@metu.edu.tr

Abstract. Multi-modal interfaces that provide haptic access to statistical line graphs combined with verbal assistance are proposed as an effective tool to fulfill the needs of visually impaired people. Graphs do not only present data, they also provide and elicit the extraction of second order entities (such as *maxima* or *trends*), which are closely linked to shape properties of the graphs. In an experimental study, we investigated collaborative joint activities between haptic explorers of graphs and verbal assistants who helped haptic explorers to conceptualize local and non-local second-order concepts. The assistants have not only to decide *what to say* but in particular *when to say it*. Based on the empirical data of this experiment, we describe in the present paper the design of a feature set for describing patterns of haptic exploration, which is able to characterize the need for verbal assistance during the course of haptic exploration. We employed a (supervised) classification algorithm, namely the J48 decision tree. The constructed features within the range from *basic (low-level) user-action* features to *complex (high-level)* conceptual were categorized into four feature sets. All feature set combinations achieved high accuracy level. The best results in terms of sensitivity and specificity were achieved by adding the low-level graphical features.

Keywords: A classifier for haptic exploration patterns · Haptic graph comprehension · Verbal assistance

1 Designing Line Graphs for Accessibility

1.1 Accessibility for Visualizing Data: Haptic Line Graphs

Line graphs are means for data visualization, which aim at presenting or representing statistical data. By interpreting graphical constituents together with the graph-schema knowledge, users gain access to information about domain-specific events. For example, a line graph may represent population trends or change in monthly temperature in time-series. In the recent state of technology, graphs are frequently used tools that facilitate communication, thinking, reasoning. The immediate visual interpretation of the readers and easy design of line graphs by end-users result in their widespread use both in printed and digital communication settings.

A. Marcus (Ed.): DUXU 2015, Part II, LNCS 9187, pp. 403–414, 2015.
DOI: 10.1007/978-3-319-20898-5_39

Visually impaired users may explore graphs haptically, by hand-controlling a stylus of a force-feedback device, such as a Phantom Omni® (recently Geomagic® Touch-TM, see Fig. 1.a). The haptic exploration of a virtual graph using a stylus has to allow extracting information about geometrical properties of the graph lines. The user interprets the geometric forms as domain-specific events, in a similar way as users of visual graph displays do. However, in contrast to the ease of design as a visual representation, the design of haptic line graphs faces a set of challenges. These challenges are pertinent to the efficiency of haptic graphs in communication, thinking and reasoning. First and foremost, a drawback of haptic graphs (compared to visual graphs) is the restriction of the haptic sense in simultaneous perception of spatially distributed information [1]. In particular, the information extraction through haptic line graphs is based on specific explorations processes. For instance, line-tracing hand-movements aim at detecting shape properties during the course of haptic exploration. Moreover, the recognition of concavities and convexities, as well as the recognition of maxima and minima, are of major importance (see Fig. 1 for sample line graphs).

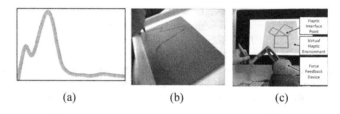

(a)   (b)   (c)

Fig. 1. (a) Sample haptic graph, (b) Exploration of a physical haptic map and (c) Phantom Omni® device and visualization in the domain of geometry.

The challenges for designing haptic line graphs apply to both simple line graphs that may be expected to be subject to straightforward user exploration, as well as to complex ones. For instance, the haptic exploration of a line graph with a single (global) maximum is only moderately difficult, whereas the haptic exploration of a line graph with several local extrema requires assistance in another modality. Those general observations about the user experience in haptic graphs suggest that multimodal exploration may facilitate graph comprehension by visually impaired individuals.

Multimodal exploration of haptic line graphs has been the topic of research since the past decade. The research has shown that providing additional information facilitates haptic-graph exploration. For instance, supplementing haptic exploration by aural assistance through the auditory channel (cf. Sonification) leads to better comprehension of haptic graphs [2]. In a series of prior studies, we have shown that appropriate spoken utterances (i.e. verbal assistance) facilitate haptic graph exploration [3–5]. For instance, verbal assistance improves detection and specification of local and global extrema in haptic graph lines. Therefore, as a novel, multimodal human-computer interaction method, a synchronous use of force-feedback exploration of haptic graphs and verbal assistance make statistical graphs accessible to visually impaired users.

In previous studies we have mainly focused on the *information content* of the verbal assistance that is to be delivered to the user of the haptic interface. In other words, this information has been about *"what to say"* to the user to improve his/her comprehension during the course of haptic exploration. The findings have shown that appropriate information content lead to a successful conceptualization of the events that are represented by graph lines. An equally important aspect in designing haptic graphs is to identify *"when to say"*, as well as *"what-to-say"*. In the present study, we aim at developing an automated mechanism, which is able to detect and predict whether the user needs verbal assistance, by analyzing his/her haptic exploration patterns.

1.2 Haptic Exploration as a Joint Activity: An Experimental Paradigm

The design of our model is based on the data collected by employing a specific experiment setting that was developed for studying the role of verbal assistance in haptic exploration [3–5]. The setting allowed us recording the information content of verbal assistances, as well as users' haptic exploration patterns before, during and after an explorer's help-request. In this experimental paradigm, verbally assisted haptic graph exploration is conceived as a task-oriented collaborative activity between two human partners, a (visually impaired) explorer (E) of a haptic graph and an observing assistant (A) providing verbal assistance (see Fig. 2).

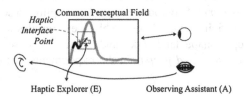

Fig. 2. Assisted haptic graph exploration as a joint activity

The alignment between the interlocutor's internal models (cf. Building common ground in [6]) and the availability of appropriate verbal assistance lead to a successful haptic comprehension of graphs. In this experimental paradigm, A observes E's exploration movements and provides appropriate verbal assistance upon requirements of E. During E's exploration, A analyzes the ongoing exploration event. In the long run, A has to take into account the history of exploration events, as well as the history of the verbal assistance, to be able to produce appropriate verbal assistance.

The experimental paradigm involved two human partners. An automatic verbal assistance system, which is able to predict when to produce an utterance for verbal assistance, should aim at modeling the alignment between the interlocutors and making communication between E and A efficient and effective. In the first prototype, called the OBSERVINGASSISTANT, we employed a rule-based approach. The system analyzes users' exploration patterns and triggers reactively canned text, as realized by the MARY text-to-speech system [7]. In the present study, we employ a machine-learning and classification perspective by means of analyzing the current position of exploration, the history of exploration movements, and the referring utterances (the referred locations and how these regions were referred). The following section provides the technical background for the model by introducing the shape concepts basic for graph-line descriptions.

1.3   Shape Concepts in Graph Line Descriptions

Qualitative approaches to shape representation usually focus on the shape of contours, e.g. [8, 9], and the curvature landmarks of contours [10]. These landmarks involve visually salient regions, such as *positive maxima* and *negative minima*, depending on the concepts of convexity and concavity of contours, and inflection points. A qualitative analysis of graph lines requires additional shape representations and shape cognition characteristics, which go beyond that of contours. This is because the interpretation of graphs lines requires graph-schema knowledge [11, 12]. The left-to-right orientation of graph lines, which usually relies on the writing direction, leads to conventionalized forms of interpretation. Graphs can also be interpreted with respect to orthogonal two-axes-systems. In haptic graphs, we also use a rectangular frame that induces an orthogonal system of axes. Accordingly, the functional characteristics of graph lines lead to the prominence of *value extrema* in graph lines, in contrast to *curvature extrema* of contours. Figure 3 exemplifies a set of basic geometric shape concepts for describing graph lines. Table 1 exemplifies some qualitative representations for selected shape landmarks and induced line segments (see [5] for details). Since we user *smoothed graphs* in the experiments, we classify extrema as *smooth points* (sp).

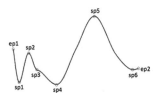

Fig. 3. Qualitative shape landmark ascription for a sample graph (augmented with orthogonal axes for making the reference frame in Table 1 explicit) ['ep' stands for *end point*].

In the previous studies, we focused on the qualitative ascriptions of each landmark and segment for the analysis of generation of referring expressions by an automated system. In the present study, our focus is to use this analysis together with exploration patterns to automatically predict when-to-say verbal assistance.

Table 1. Qualitatively described shape landmarks and shape segments

Landmarks	Local characteristics	Global properties
ep1	left end pt., local max.	Higher than sp1, sp2, sp3, sp4, sp5, ep2
sp1	smooth pt., local min.	Higher than sp4
⋮	⋮	⋮
sp5	smooth pt., local max.	Global max.
sp6	smooth pt., local min.	Higher than sp1, sp4, same height as sp3
Segments	**Shape characteristics**	**Vertical orientation**
ep1–sp1	curved	steeply downward
⋮	⋮	⋮
sp5–sp6	curved	steeply downward
sp6–ep2	curved /slightly straight	slightly upward

2 Data Collection: A Joint-Activity Experiment on Haptic Line Graph Exploration

In this section, we give a brief description of the experiment (participants, stimuli and procedure) that provides the data for haptic exploration patterns presented in Sect. 3 (see [5] for details of the experiment and the analysis of verbal utterances). Twenty-six participants (13 pairs of sighted and blindfolded university students) participated in the experiment. Each pair was composed of a haptic explorer (E) and a verbal assistant (A), as described in the previous section. The participants were located in separate rooms so that they communicated through speakers without visual contact. During the experiment session, E explored the graph haptically and A was able to display the graph and the current location of E's exploration, which was represented by an animated point marker on the visual graph presented at A's screen. However, haptic pointing was possible only for E. The haptic explorer E was instructed to explore the graph and ask for verbal assistance when needed, whereas the observer assistant A was instructed to provide verbal assistance shortly and plainly, when requested by E.

The participants were informed that the graphs represented populations of bird species in a lagoon and also about post-exploration tasks detailed below. The graphs employed in this study were taken from a publicly available consensus report [13]. Each graph had a different pattern in terms of the number and polarity of curvature landmarks, length and direction of line segments. In the experiment session, each participant was presented five haptic line graphs in random order. Haptic graph exploration was performed by moving the stylus of the haptic device, which can be moved in all three spatial dimensions (with six degree-of-freedom). The haptic graph proper (i.e., the line of the line graph) was represented by engraved concavities on a horizontal plane; therefore haptic explorers perceived the line as deeper than the other regions of the haptic surface. The numerical labels were not represented. The participants did not have time limitation. After the experiment session, both participants (E and A) were asked independently to present single-sentence verbal descriptions of the graphs to a hypothetical audience. Not all haptic exploration protocols had dialogue

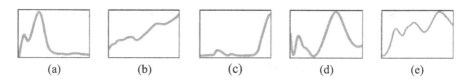

(a)   (b)   (c)   (d)   (e)

Fig. 4. Five different haptic graphs

or request for verbal assistance therefore 26 protocols from 7 pairs were chosen from the empirical data for the feature set construction mentioned in the next section.

3   Haptic Exploration Patterns

Our goal in the present study is to design a classifier for the exploration patterns, which is able to characterize the need for verbal assistance during the course of exploration. The raw data set consisted of the recorded locations of the stylus of the haptic device on the 2D horizontal plane (horizontal and vertical coordinates). In this section, feature construction and transformation from 2D raw data into a 14D feature set, cleansing and chunking procedures and classification of feature sets are presented.

3.1   Feature Construction and Transformation

As the first step in the model design the raw data points (i.e., the coordinates of the stylus) were segmented with respect to the landmarks of the graph lines (see Fig. 4). The segments were then labeled with their corresponding landmarks and line segments (Feature#3: Temporal Order in Table 2). For example the data point *(15,7)* was labeled *"SP3-SP4"* and the data point *(23,2)* was labeled *"SP4"* depending on the landmarks that the data points belonged to. After the labeling step, the features were identified within the range from *basic (low-level)* features to *complex (high-level)* features. The first feature set (*SET I*) in Table 2 contains a set of basic features that can be derived from haptic explorations. The second set (*SET II*) involves higher-level features, such as the direction change during the exploration of the same unit and the visit history (time sensitivity). Two low-level graphical features, namely the Graph ID and the size of the graphical unit, were added in the third set (*SET III*). The last set of features (*Set IV*) contains conceptual features.

Low-Level User Action Features. After the labeling of each data point, the Euclidean distance (Feature#4 in Table 2) between each consecutive data point was calculated. Time and speed were also fundamental features included in this data set. Afterwards, the direction of the action between each consecutive data point was labeled as shown in Fig. 5a. The Direction feature was not put directly into the final feature sets; instead it was used for calculating the number of direction changes in the same unit during the same action, as explained below. Data cleansing procedure was applied subsequently. As Grunwald et al. stated, "Human haptic perception is accompanied by movement pauses of the exploring fingers and hands in healthy humans" [14]. The raw data

Table 2. The list of features

SET I	Basic features	Type
	1. Participant ID	Numerical-unique ID
	2. Temporal order	Numerical
	3. Unit Label	Nominal
	Low-level user action features	
	4. Total distance	Numerical
	5. Speed	Numerical
	6. Duration	Numerical
SET II	*High-level user action features*	
	7. Direction change count	Numerical
	8. Visit count in last 10 segments (or Last 6)	Numerical
SET III	*Low-level graphical features (Perceptual)*	
	9. Graph ID	*Nominal- Unique ID*
	10. Unit size	Numerical
SET IV	*High-level graphical features (Conceptual)*	
	11. End point or Intermediate	*Nominal*
	12. Unit type	*Nominal*
	13. Qualitative ascriptions	*Nominal*
	Target feature	
	14. The availability of verbal assistance	*Nominal (VA+ /VA–)*

contained instances of "no-movement" between the continuous actions, as well, such as a *Left-Left-NoMovement-Left-Left-Left* pattern. Therefore the data points, which preceded and followed by an action in the same direction, were labeled with their temporal neighbors' direction.

High-Level User Action Features. The Direction change (Feature#7) between the two consecutive data points with different directions was also labeled with respect to the two axes. In other words, the action with a *Rightward-Increase*, when followed by

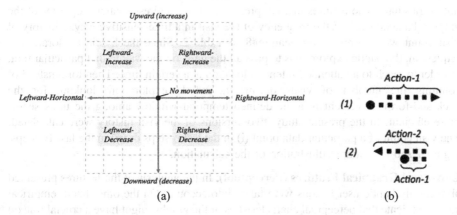

Fig. 5. (a) Labels for direction mapping and (b) simple user actions in 2-pixel-width haptic line

leftward actions or when followed by downward actions assumed to exhibit a direction change (see Fig. 5a). One should note that both the NoMovement instances and the actions with the change in the main direction need special attention. This is because the width of the haptic graph line is two-pixels in size. Therefore the data need to be corrected in order to eliminate the miscalculation of direction changes. Consider the following example to clarify the correction procedure: Let's assume that the dots in Fig. 5b correspond to pixels. When we look at just two consecutive actions, we can label the action presented in Fig. 5b.1 as *Right-Up-Right Right-Right*. However, the upward action in that case does not have a meaning in terms of the user's intended action, which is "*to move right*". Therefore the actions with main directions (*Left, Right, Up* and *Down*) were checked with respect to their previous and next directions. If the previous and next actions were in the same direction, then the value of this data point was updated. On the other hand, if they were different (Fig. 5b.2), then they were marked as a direction change (Feature#7).

It is a common practice to handle data *by chunking* with respect to the units (segments or landmarks). Therefore the next step in the analysis was to merge the data points that belonged to the same graph unit by taking their temporal order into account. Figure 6 illustrates a sample for the step-by-step chunking procedure. As a result of this procedure, the consecutive data points on the same region were merged, and their features (i.e. distance, time, direction count) were also merged.

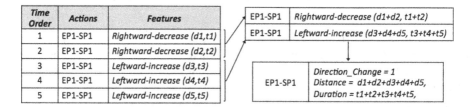

Fig. 6. Sample for the chunking procedure (d:distance, t = duration for each action)

Statistical line graphs are spatio-temporal representations when they represent time-series data. The features that are presented above address spatial properties of the graphs. To keep track of the frequency of the visit in a time-sensitive way, a history of visit count was addressed by Feature#8 in Table 2. Since the haptic exploration is sequential, the haptic explorer has to pass all the units on the way to that particular unit, in order to reach to an attended/intended location at a certain time. Therefore instead of counting the number of visits during the whole exploration, looking for the back-and-forth movement in a pre-defined temporal window among the units seems more efficient. In the present study, two versions of the visit history were calculated: The visit count of a particular data point (i) in the last 6-steps or (ii) in the last 10-steps. Figure 7 shows a simple illustration of the calculation.

Low-Level Graphical Features (Perceptual). In the analysis of the features presented above, only haptic user actions were taken into account. On the other hand, empirical studies indicate that perceptual characteristics of the graphs might have a crucial role on

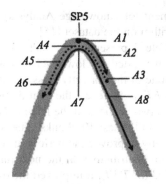

Chunks	Actions(A)	Last Visit Count
1	1. @SP5	Visit#=1
2	2. @SP5-SP6	Visit#=1
2	3. @SP5-SP6	Visit#=1
3	4. @SP5	Visit#=2
4	5. @SP4-SP5	Visit#=1
4	6. @SP4-SP5	Visit#=1
5	7. @SP5	Visit#=3
6	8. @SP5-SP6	Visit#=2

Fig. 7. A simple example for the calculation of the visit count

haptic exploration. Those characteristics were addressed in two features: The first feature (Feature#9) identifies the graph with a unique graph ID. The actual size of the graphical elements (the length of the units in pixels) comprised the second feature (Feature#10). The second feature highlights the perceptual saliency of the units (i.e., a long segment vs. a short segment).

High-Level Graphical Features (Conceptual). In the last feature set (*SET IV*), we used a set of conceptual features that were derived from the raw coordinate data. First, the units were split into two categories: intermediate units and end points (Feature#11). Empirical results indicated that the explorers might request assistance for descriptional instructions (i.e. the graph domain content) or navigational instructions about positioning (being at the start point, or being on the line, etc.). The navigational instructions were mostly asked for end points of the graph lines. Therefore the data points were also classified with respect to their location on the graph. After then, each data point was categorized into two, according to whether they belonged to a segment or they belonged to a landmark (Feature#12), e.g. "*SP1*": landmark, and "*SP1-SP2*": segment. The data points were the categorized with respect to their qualitative ascriptions, as described in Sect. 1.2 and Table 2 (i.e. "*Ep1-SP1*": steep, and "*SP5*": Global Max). Finally, the last feature represents a target feature, which is nominal, and it addresses the binary classification problem itself.

As a result of the feature construction and chunking procedures described above, 69,574 instances (data points with horizontal and vertical coordinates) were reduced to 8015 instances (units), which composed of the units without verbal assistance (6953 VA–) and the units with verbal assistance (1062 VA+).

3.2   Results

The goal of the present study has been to develop a feature set useful for detecting the need of assistance during haptic exploration and to test it, and not to make a comparative analysis of classification algorithms). The features were tested by using the J48 decision tree algorithm. This algorithm was selected, because it is fast, simple and it can be easily converted to a set of production rules. Also it does not have any priori assumptions about the nature of the data. Weka (Waikato Envirionment for Knowledge Analysis) environment was used to apply the classification algorithm on the dataset [15].

We employed 10-Folds Cross Validation. Table 3 presents the results for each combination of the feature sets. In the first trial, we tested the low-level user action feature set (*Set I*), the overall accuracy (*ACC*, the rate of the correctly classified items) was %91.79. Then, we added the features of the *SET II*. To reveal the contribution of the history window (Feature#8 in Table 2), we used two versions of the feature: (1) the visit count in the last 6 chunks, (2) the visit count in the last 10 chunks. The results showed that adding the high level user actions slightly improved the performance, and increasing the size of the history window was more contributive. In the next run, the low-level graphical features (perceptual) were added (*SET III*). It improved the overall accuracy of the model by approximately 2 %. As the last test, high-level graphical features (conceptual, *SET IV*) were added to the model, and this also slightly improved the overall accuracy.

Table 3. The results of J48 algorithm for the feature sets (VA: Verbal Assistance, TP: True Positive, FP: False Positive).

	Overall accuracy (ACC, %)	Kappa	VA	TP rate	FP rate	Precision	Recall
SET I (7)	91.79	.59	VA–	.97	.45	.93	.97
			VA+	.54	.02	.77	.54
SET I + II (v1) (9)	91.86	.59	VA–	.98	.46	.93	.98
			VA+	.54	.02	.78	.54
SET I + II (v2) (9)	92.50	.63	VA–	.98	.41	.94	.98
			VA+	.59	.02	.79	.59
SET I + II + III (11)	94.46	.73	VA–	.98	.32	.95	.98
			VA+	.68	.02	.87	.68
SET I + II + III + IV (13)	94.59	.75	VA–	.98	.29	.96	.98
			VA+	.70	.02	.86	.71

Although we obtained high accuracy results, even with *SET I* only, it should be noted that it is more important for the verbal assistance system to provide verbal assistance when it is needed, therefore correct classification of VA+ (*specificity*) cases have higher importance. As expected, the results are lower for VA+ cases than VA– cases due to the unbalanced distribution of the data set. Figure 8 illustrates the precision and recall values (presented in Table 3) for VA+ class. The results indicated that J48 performed better with the inclusion of graphical features, resulting improvement from 77 % to 86 % in the precision and from 54 % to 71 % in the recall rates for VA+ cases.

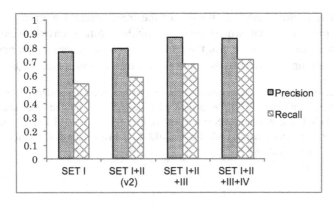

Fig. 8. Precision and recall values for VA+ Class

4   Conclusion

In this paper, we introduced a classifier that predicts whether verbal assistance is needed or not by analyzing haptic exploration patterns. The motivation of the study was that in addition to deciding *"what to say"* as a message carried by verbal assistance system, providing this content on the appropriate time (*"when to say"*) is also crucial in the implementation of automated verbal assistance system. The feature sets were derived from raw data (the coordinates of the stylus of the haptic device) obtained in an empirical study [5], which studied the production of referring expressions in a joint activity of a haptic explorer and a verbal assistant, namely the exploration of a haptic comprehension by a blind-folded person assisted verbally by an observer.

We employed a (supervised) classification algorithm, namely the J48 decision tree. All feature set combinations (starting from the low level user actions) achieved high accuracy level (> 91.5 %). The best results in terms of sensitivity (*true positive rate*) and specificity (*true negative rate*) were achieved by adding the low-level graphical features. On the other hand, adding the high-level graphical features slightly improved the classification. The results are in line with the experimental study [5], which showed that haptic explorers might have difficulty to grasp those conceptual features due to low bandwidth and sequentiality of the haptic exploration movement. Future work should address a detailed understanding the contribution of those conceptual features.

In the experimental study [5], the haptic explorers requested assistance when they needed, and as a response to the request, verbal assistance was provided by the assistant. Therefore both the content and the timing of the assistance were up to the haptic explorer. This resulted in an unbalanced distribution of data points in our data set: The instances without verbal assistance outnumbered the instances with verbal assistance. Therefore in our results, we focus more on the specificity over sensitivity.

Finally, the empirical data showed that 72.4 % of the verbal assistance was requested regarding start and end points. As a consequence, the majority of the data points, where verbal assistance was requested, belonged to a limited region. In future work, we plan to provide sonification to alert the haptic explorer about the start point and the end point of the graph line so that he/she may focus on communicating about the intermediate regions and the changes of the trend without worrying about navigational complexities. That would provide suitable testing environment, in more general, to assess the applicability of the feature set proposed here on the new data-set, and in more specific, to evaluate the contribution of the conceptual features.

Acknowledgment. The research reported in this paper has been supported by DFG (German Science Foundation) in ITRG 1247 'Cross-modal Interaction in Natural and Artificial Cognitive Systems', by Marie Curie Actions IRIS (ref. 610986, FP7-PEOPLE-2013-IAPP), and by METU Scientific Research Project scheme BAP–08-11-2012-121 'Investigation of Cognitive Processes in Multimodal Communication.'

References

1. Loomis, J.M., Klatzky, R.L., Lederman, S.J.: Similarity of tactual and visual picture recognition with limited field of view. Perception **20**, 167–177 (1991)
2. Yu, W., Brewster, S.A.: Evaluation of multimodal graphs for blind people. J. Univers. Access Inf. Soc. **2**, 105–124 (2003)
3. Alaçam, Ö., Habel, C., Acartürk, C.: Towards designing audio assistance for comprehending haptic graphs: a multimodal perspective. In: Stephanidis, C., Antona, M. (eds.) UAHCI 2013, Part I. LNCS, vol. 8009, pp. 409–418. Springer, Heidelberg (2013)
4. Acartürk, C., Alaçam, Ö., Habel, C.: Developing a verbal assistance system for line graph comprehension. In: Marcus, A. (ed.) DUXU 2014, Part II. LNCS, vol. 8518, pp. 373–382. Springer, Heidelberg (2014)
5. Alaçam, Ö., Acartürk, C., Habel, C.: Referring expressions in discourse about haptic line graphs . In: Rieser, V., Muller, P. (Eds.) Proceedings of the 18th Workshop on the Semantics and Pragmatics of Dialogue. SemDial 2014 – DialWatt, pp. 7–16 (2014)
6. Garrod, S., Pickering, M.J.: Why is conversation so easy? Trends Cogn. Sci. **8**, 8–11 (2004)
7. Kerzel, M., Alaçam, Ö., Habel, C., Acartürk, C.: Producing verbal descriptions for haptic line-graph explorations [Poster abstract]. In Rieser, V., Muller, P. (Eds.) Proceedings of the 18th Workshop on the Semantics and Pragmatics of Dialogue. SemDial 2014 – DialWatt, pp. 205–207 (2014)
8. Hoffman, D.D., Richards, W.A.: Parts of recognition. Cognition **8**, 65–96 (1984)
9. Eschenbach, C., Habel, C., Kulik, L., Leßmöllmann, A.: Shape nouns and shape concepts: a geometry for 'corner'. In: Freksa, C., Habel, C., Wender, K.F. (eds.) Spatial Cognition 1998. LNCS (LNAI), vol. 1404, pp. 177–201. Springer, Heidelberg (1998)
10. Cohen, E.H., Singh, M.: Geometric determinants of shape segmentation: tests using segment identification. Vis. Res. **47**(22), 2825–2840 (2007)
11. Kosslyn, S.M.: Understanding charts and graphs. Appl. Cogn. Psychol. **3**(3), 185–226 (1989)
12. Pinker, S.: A theory of graph comprehension. In: Freedle, R., (eds.) Artificial Intelligence and the Future of Testing, pp. 73–126. Erlbaum, Hillsdale (1998)
13. PRBO. Waterbird Census at Bolinas Lagoon, CA, Marin County. Public report by Wetlands Ecology Division, Point Reyes Bird Observatory (PRBO) Conservation Science (2012). http://www.prbo.org/cms/366. Retrieved on 29 January 2012
14. Grunwald, M., Muniyandi, M., Kim, H., Kim, J., Krause, F., Mueller, S., Srinivasan, M.A.: Human haptic perception is interrupted by explorative stops of milliseconds. Front. Psychol. **5**, 1–14 (2014)
15. Weka 3: data mining software in java. http://www.cs.waikato.ac.nz/ml/weka

Collaborative Tangible Interface (CoTI) for Complex Decision Support Systems

Salma Aldawood[1](✉), Faisal Aleissa[1], Almaha Almalki[1],
Tarfah Alrashed[1], Tariq Alhindi[1], Riyadh Alnasser[1],
Mohammad K. Hadhrawi[2], Anas Alfaris[1,2], and Areej Al-Wabi[1,3]

[1] Center for Complex Engineering Systems, King Abdulaziz City for Science
and Technology, Riyadh, Saudi Arabia
{s.aldawood,f.aleissa,a.almalki,t.alrashed,t.alhindi,
r.alnasser}@cces-kacst-mit.org
[2] Massachusetts Institute of Technology (MIT), Cambridge, MA, USA
{anas,mkh}@mit.edu
[3] Prince Sultan University, Riyadh, Saudi Arabia
awabil@pscw.psu.edu.sa

Abstract. In this paper, we present CoTI, a Collaborative Tangible Interface to support decision making in complex systems. We start by describing the system architecture and the tangible interaction interface with an overview of design considerations for information architecture, navigation layers on multi-touch surfaces, and interaction modalities. A case study showcasing the CoTI in the context of urban planning is presented and design implications for city planning and co-located collaborative decision making is discussed.

Keywords: TUI · Urban planning · Multi-touch · Fiducial · DSS · Complex systems

1 Introduction

In complex systems, multiple stakeholders from a variety of backgrounds need to interact collaboratively to make informative decisions. This collaboration is crucial especially in the context of urban planning where stakeholders use simulations for complex systems of city infrastructures that are interrelated, which generate a System of Systems (SoS). Simulating the behaviors of these systems and their interdependencies as well as assisting stakeholders in predicting future scenarios is challenging. Nevertheless, technologies have evolved through the years from web-based tools to tangible user interfaces (TUI) to support co-located collaborative decision making. Moreover, with the proliferation of multi-touch surfaces in decision support systems, a new form of TUIs has emerged to ease the decision making process by facilitating interactivity. Web-based decision support systems for infrastructure planning have been shown to be effective in supporting remote decision making [1]. However, web-based interaction inadequately supported joint scenarios/projections of interrelated decision dependencies. In recent years, TUIs such as multi-touch surfaces have been

© Springer International Publishing Switzerland 2015
A. Marcus (Ed.): DUXU 2015, Part II, LNCS 9187, pp. 415–424, 2015.
DOI: 10.1007/978-3-319-20898-5_40

shown to support collaborative decision-making by revealing interdependencies between the tangibles 'physical objects' and the interaction surface's users [5, 6].

In this paper we present (CoTI), a Collaborative Tangible Interface for complex systems that provides multi-touch interactive capabilities with analytical and visualization components to facilitate the decision making process. In CoTI, stakeholders can interact with the 3D objects that we called smart blocks (a more elaborate description in Sect. 3) and the multi-touch surface to get an immediate feedback for the impact of their decisions not only on the system under study but also on other related systems affected by those decisions. This adds another dimension to the thinking process, which enhances the users' experience and enable them to make more informed decisions by understanding the implication of their decisions on other systems. The objective of CoTI is to support the decision making in complex systems. Therefore, an integration with a simulation engine that performs real model analysis is essential. In our case study of urban planning for example, a simulation engine for analyzing the data of the urban, transportation, energy and water systems of the city has been integrated into the platform.

This paper is structured as follows. The following section describes related work in tangible user interfaces and urban planning tools. Following that, we present an overview of CoTI system architecture. Next, we present the CoTI tangible interaction surface configurations and the user interface design considerations. An in-depth description of CoTI decision support system is provided. We conclude with a case study showcasing the CoTI in the context of urban planning.

2 Background

In recent years, interactive technologies for supporting co-located and remote collaborative decision making have been designed to address the complexity and scalability of design challenges in complex system. Collaborative decision making was facilitated by direct manipulation tools such as 2D and 3D interfaces for information visualization and scenario projections [7, 12].

2.1 Tangible User Interfaces

Embedding digital information in tangible objects has led to the emergence of opportunities for designing intuitive interaction platforms in urban modeling. The context of urban planning in particular has experienced a trend in experimenting with different augmented reality and mixed reality tools in the past two decades [11, 13, 14]. More recently, tangible objects in dynamic models of urban areas have facilitated more flexibility in the design of hybrid physical and virtual interfaces.

2.2 Urban Design and Human-Computer Interaction (HCI)

Different TUIs have been developed to facilitate communication and collaboration for urban planners in decision making [9, 10]. One of the urban planning TUIs is the 'Mark IV' prototype developed by the Media lab, at Massachusetts Institute of Technology;

which is an interactive collaborative tangible interface for urban planners [8]. The model has a set of pre-defined user interactions; for example, urban planners can move tangible objects (buildings/amenities), and check the result of their interactions on a screen. The interface does not include a control panel for stakeholders to make changes to the model or the decision variables. One issue often cited as problematic with urban planning tools is the limited scope of application domains. For example, some of the TUIs tools focus either on energy or mobility. Comprehensive tools that examine the interdependencies are emerging for sustainable design and in the area of complex engineering. One example, 'UMI' is an urban modeling interface that integrates different models (walkability, energy, and daylight) in one tool to examine the interplay of decision variables on urban models [3]. Scalability and extendibility are important design consideration in systems engineering.

3 CoTI System's Architecture

CoTI is a collaborative tangible interactive tool that utilizes City Schema Decision Support System [2]. The system was designed in iterative design cycles with stakeholders and target users of the complex system involved as design informants. Stakeholders were engaged at different phases of the system's development process for eliciting feedback on high-fidelity prototypes. In earlier phases of the system development, we applied City Schema DSS on the Scout table [8], a simple TUI table for urban planning that allows for rapid prototyping with limited interactivity and limited number of simulations. We then applied the same DSS on the MARK IV [8]; an intuitive TUI table with more interactive capabilities but with constrained control over decision variables. CoTI is built to overcome the limitations of Scout and MARK IV tables and give the users more interactivity and control over the system. CoTI's architecture is comprised of three main layers: First, the tangible interaction surface which represent CoTI user interface and consists of user and user interface management components. While the user management component handles the authorization and conflicts between users, the user interface takes care of the projection of two main components: decision variables 'DVs' which are the inputs of the users to the simulation, and key performance indicators 'KPIs' which are the results that are produced by the simulation engine. Each one of these DVs and KPIs differ based on the user's location and expertise. Second, the CoTI decision support system which in turn consists of three main components: A detector of physical artifacts to detect any change that occurs in the physical surface (such as an object's position); a translator that maps and reflects detected changes on the physical surface with their digital representation, and a controller that connects both physical and digital artifacts together through an interactive interface for various simulation purposes. The third layer is the computational environment, which is a multi-modular simulation engine that provides various sophisticated simulations related to the study under which CoTI used such as operational energy, daylight and walkability. Figure 1 shows the high level architecture of CoTI.

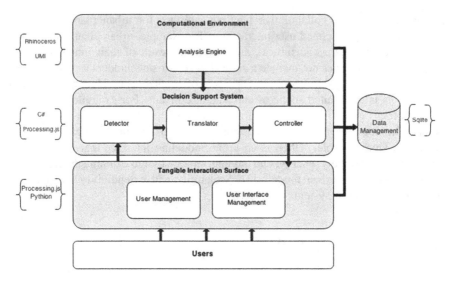

Fig. 1. The CoTI high level architecture

The framework was developed on the context of urban modeling; nevertheless, the workflow can be applied to different application domains. In the following sections, we describe in more detail the system design components, hardware and software.

3.1   Tangible Interaction Surface

The interaction surface includes three main components: A multi-touch table, tangible objects, and display and simulation.

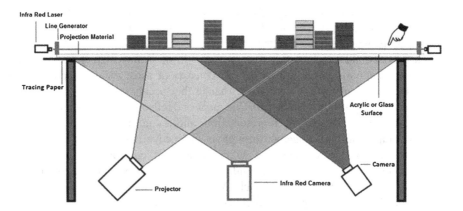

Fig. 2. CoTI multi-touch table configuration

i. The Multi-Touch Table In this section we describe CoTI's multi-touch table configuration with a description of hardware and software components. The system is shown in Fig. 2. The touch-surface is mounted horizontally as a table and it consists of a transparent acrylic glass (117 cm, 117 cm). We used 6 mm acrylic glass that is permeable to the infrared IR light. The outer perimeter of the surface is lined with tracing paper to allow rear projection onto the acrylic glass as well as to diffuse the direct projector lamp beam beneath the table. Eight lasers with a near IR range (850 nm) were mounted on the edges of the table. A line generator is attached at the end of each laser to distribute the beam covering an area with an angle of 120 degrees from the laser source. These lasers produce a plane of infrared light across the entire surface of the table. When a finger touches this plane of light, the light illuminates it. The sensing apparatus consists of a camera placed underneath the table. In our setup, a PS3 Eye camera is used. This camera is modified by attaching filter to it that only allows infrared light through. The camera sees the "blobs" of infrared light and tracks these points.

ii. Smart Blocks: Tangible Objects In order to detect tangible objects on the proposed multi-touch table, a unique fiducial is attached onto each smart block [4]. These fiducials help in identifying smart block's type (e.g. Tree, Building) and location on the interactive surface. A cross-platform computer vision framework reacTIVision [4] is used to allocate the x and y coordinates of the smart block with the use of Logitech HD Pro Webcam C920. ReacTIVision is an open source camera based two dimensional fiducial (marker) tracking system, which has the ability to track a large number of varied size fiducials with faster than real-time performance. ReacTIVision uses only cameras and projectors, which is usually required as part of the TUI implementation. In order to have a fast and accurate capturing of fiducials, the light source is placed next to the camera to enhance the camera's vision and therefore improve detection.

iii. Display/Simulation Due to the high complexity of CoTI, its user interface was carefully designed to ease the user-system interaction and decision making process. In order to design an interactive tangible user interface system that allows novice users to understand a concept as complex as urban planning in an engaging and informative way, we followed a multidisciplinary approach, combining human-computer interaction in tangible user interfaces, and psychology/human sciences. The CoTI TUI includes two main components: First, the interactive area where users are able to interact with the physical objects. And second, the decision variables where users are able to define and modify the physical objects' specifications. System results are presented in multiple ways to enhance the user experience and the level of understanding. Figure 3 shows the CoTI tangible interaction interface and its components.

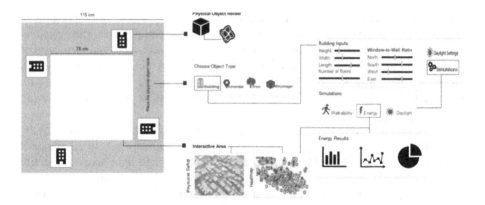

Fig. 3. The CoTI user interface

3.2   Decision Support System

In [1], we introduced a decision support system platform 'City Schema' that is designed to connect a tangible interface with a simulation engine to support collaborative city planning. This DSS connects the physical and the digital model together into one integrated system. The physical model is a tangible user interface with 3D representation of a city or neighborhood within the city that supports interactive and collaborative activities from multiple users. The simulation engine integrated into the platform is an urban modeling design tool that has several simulation modules such as operational energy, mobility, daylight, transportation and others [3]. City Schema DSS consists of: database management component, simulation modules management component, and an interactive user interface with dynamic visualization and decision scenario simulations. City Schema DSS is embedded in our CoTI platform with Fig. 4 highlighting the flow of events used to ensure the connectivity between the tangible interaction surface and the computational environment. The controller is to be considered the brain of CoTI as it receives commands from users, and coordinates the execution of each command among other components. After the controller scans and detects any physical modifications on the multi touch interaction surface, it projects the simulation results back to users as heat maps, statistics, and charts. The database management component can be used as a logical link to connect physical and digital artifacts together and it is responsible for the data storage and retrieval.

The workflow suggested in CoTI for the mapping between physical and digital model artifacts allows for direct manipulation on the interactive surface. CoTI utilizes reacTIVision framework to recognize and detect the physical artifacts by using fiducials to distinguish one object from another. Once the objects have been detected, a script in processing, an open source development environment used mainly for rapid vision-based prototypes, is used to keep track of each object's position, angle, and ID (fiducial ID). For each physical object, we distinguish between two types of attributes: user input such as name and type; and automatically detected attributes such as position and angle. All objects' attributes are saved within CoTI database for later analysis. In order to generate the graphical digital representations as a direct reflection of the

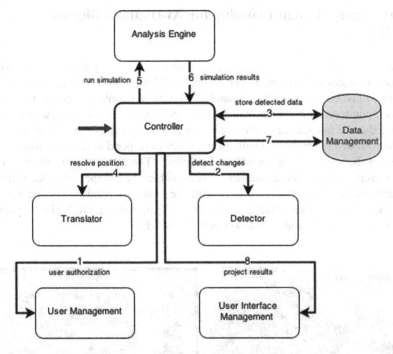

Fig. 4. The flow of events on CoTI DSS

physical artifacts in the TUI model, we utilized the CoTI database to create geometries that match an object's attributes. Finally, various simulations are to be run on the digital model that is generated, and reflected back on the physical model.

3.3 Computational Environment

The Computational Environment is a multi-modular simulation engine that gives stakeholders the ability to test the efficiency, sustainability and livability of cities and neighborhoods. It provides users with a choice to perform one of four possible simulations. The four available simulations supported by UMI are as follows: Operational Energy, Mobility, Daylight and Embodied Energy. First, the Operational Energy simulation, where users can create a detailed building template and assign them to different blocks. This simulation produces sophisticated analysis of the energy consumption for each building within the simulated area. Second, the Mobility simulation allows users to introduce amenities (e.g. banks, schools or restaurants) to the area under study and modify the road network. Two simulation results are computed for walkability and bike-ability which are calculated based on the accessibility and distance of each building to the different amenities available within the areas. Third, the Daylight simulation, which evaluates the design of buildings by calculating the solar radiation on the facades of buildings. Last, the Embodied Energy simulation, which calculates the consumption cost of the lifetime of each building within the area.

4 Case Study: Urban Planning for Al-Dhahira District in Riyadh

In the next few years and within the Riyadh center development plan, there will be significant changes and development in the Al-Dhahira district. For instance, new buildings will be built to meet the demand of the natural population growth in this area. Moreover, commercial buildings will be renovated, and a couple of new skyscrapers are planned to be introduced in this area. The different parts of the district have been designed with diverse building topologies in order to respond to different uses, as well as to reflect the specific location within the district. The central square of this district will be surrounded by three iconic skyscrapers with curved shapes and glazed façades which are protected by shading panels with the shape of palm leaves. Along King Fahad road side there is set of tall glazed buildings expected to serve business purposes. Figure 5 shows the old and new urban plan for the district.

Fig. 5. Al-Dhahira district old (right) and new (left) urban plans

We chose Al-Dhahira district as a case study because it is recognized as a high-intervention urban development zone, and it is in the early stages of the development. In modeling this urban area, we started by building the current state of Al-Dhahira district using LEGOs, and in which various computational simulations were executed. Results of these early computations were used as a benchmark for the new proposed plans. Every new session starts with the current state of Al-Dhahira district and allows the decision makers to propose their new plan by adding or removing buildings and/or changing buildings' attributes (e.g. number of floors, building type). With this setting, the decision makers can compare between different proposed plans and evaluate the performance of each one. All this is constructed around an interactive multi touch table that is intended to support collaboration, and reveal interdependencies between simulations' variables.

CoTI is tested in the context of urban planning in two sessions where the objective is to propose a new plan for Al-Dhahira district which provide a better performance than the existing plan. The decision variables included are related to accessibility (e.g. amenity' type and location) and energy efficiency (e.g. building's construction materials, cooling and lighting schedule,). The KPIs are heat-maps for walkability and energy efficiency projected for each building, an accumulative score (percentage) per simulation, and charts that inform users about their current performance per simulation compared to previous plans. In each session, users collaborate to generate different plans to assess how their decisions impact the future state of the district. The first session included two decision makers with urban planning background. The second session included four decision makers; the two urban planners from the first session with two energy planners. The two proposed plans achieved the objective of the session with different efficiency levels. While the first session showed a really good accessibility score (Walking\Biking), the second session showed a balance between accessibility and energy efficiency scores due to the better collaboration between decision makers from different background.

5 Conclusion

The CoTI described in this paper is a system that contributes to the urban planning domain with tangible collaborative tools designed for a wide spectrum of users. CoTI was designed with an emphasis on usability and enhancing the user experience of stakeholders involved in the decision making process. Insights from the design and development of CoTI have led to design implications for the context of urban and city planning systems. Design considerations for extending the interactivity to remote interaction and novel interaction modalities are areas for further research and development.

References

1. Hadhrawi, M.K., Nouh, M., Alfaris, A., Sanchez, A.: CoPI: a web-based collaborative planning interface platform. In: Yamamoto, S. (ed.) HCI 2013, Part III. LNCS, vol. 8018, pp. 287–296. Springer, Heidelberg (2013)
2. Aldawood, S., Aleissa, F., Alnasser, R., Alfaris, A., Al-Wabil, A.: Interaction design in a tangible collaborative decision support system: the city schema DSS. In: Stephanidis, C. (ed.) HCI 2014, Part II. CCIS, vol. 435, pp. 508–512. Springer, Heidelberg (2014). http://link.springer.com/chapter/10.1007/978-3-319-07854-0_88
3. Reinhart, C., Dogan, T., Jakubiec, J.A., Rakha, T., Sang, A.: Umi-an urban simulation environment for building energy use, daylighting and walkability. In: 13th Conference of International Building Performance Simulation Association, Chambery, France (2013)
4. Kaltenbrunner, M., Bencina, R.: reacTIVision: a computer-vision framework for table-based tangible interaction. In: Proceedings of the 1st International Conference on Tangible and Embedded Interaction, pp. 69–74. ACM, February 2007
5. Jingyan, Q., Yan, G., Huiwen, J.: TUI interactive product design. In: IEEE 10th International Conference on Computer-Aided Industrial Design and Conceptual Design, CAID and CD 2009, pp. 1455–1458. IEEE, November 2009
6. Ullmer, B.A. (1997). Models and mechanisms for tangible user interfaces (Doctoral dissertation, Massachusetts Institute of Technology)
7. Franke, I.S., Müller, M., Gründer, T., Groh, R.: FlexiWall: interaction in-between 2D and 3D interfaces. In: Stephanidis, C. (ed.) HCI 2014, Part I. CCIS, vol. 434, pp. 415–420. Springer, Heidelberg (2014)

8. Winder, I., Smuts, C., Hadhrawi, M., Sain, G., Fabian, J., Pefley, S., Mehendale, R. (2014). http://cp.media.mit.edu/city-simulation. Changing Places, MIT Media Lab. "CityScope: Augmented Reality City SImulation, MIT Prototype CityScope "Scout", "Mark IV"
9. Underkoffler, J., Ishii, H.: Urp: a luminous-tangible workbench for urban planning and design. In: Proceedings of the SIGCHI Conference on Human Factors in Computing Systems, pp. 386–393. ACM, May 1999
10. Ben-Joseph, E., Ishii, H., Underkoffler, J., Piper, B., Yeung, L.: Urban simulation and the luminous planning table bridging the gap between the digital and the tangible. J. Plan. Edu. Res. **21**(2), 196–203 (2001)
11. Ishii, H., Ben-Joseph, E., Underkoffler, J., Yeung, L., Chak, D., Kanji, Z., Piper, B.: Augmented urban planning workbench: overlaying drawings, physical models and digital simulation. In: Proceedings of the 1st International Symposium on Mixed and Augmented Reality, p. 203. IEEE Computer Society, September 2002
12. Wiza, W.: Interactive 3D visualization of search results. In: Cellary, W., Walczak, K. (eds.) Interactive 3D Multimedia Content, pp. 253–291. Springer, London (2012)
13. Corral-Soto, E.R., Tal, R., Wang, L., Persad, R., Chao, L., Solomon, C., Elder, J.H.: 3D town: the automatic urban awareness project. In: 2012 Ninth Conference on Computer and Robot Vision (CRV), pp. 433–440. IEEE, May 2012
14. Kang, J., Ryu, J.H.: Augmented reality window: digital reconstruction of a historical and cultural site for smart phones. In: 2010 IEEE International Symposium on Mixed and Augmented Reality-Arts, Media, and Humanities (ISMAR-AMH), pp. 67–68. IEEE, October 2010

User Study on 3D Multitouch Interaction (3DMi) and Gaze on Surface Computing

Eugene Ch'ng[1(✉)] and Neil Cooke[2]

[1] School of Computer Science, International Doctoral Innovation Centre,
University of Nottingham Ningbo China, 199 Taikang East Road,
Ningbo 315100, Zhejiang, China
eugene.chng@nottingham.edu.cn
[2] Department of Electronic Electrical and Computer Engineering,
University of Birmingham, Edgbaston B15 2TT, UK
n.j.cooke@bham.ac.uk

Abstract. On a multitouch table, user's interactions with 3D virtual representations of real objects should be influenced by task and their perceived physical characteristics. This article explores the development and user study of an interactive 3D application that allows users to explore virtual heritage objects on a surface device. To-date, most multitouch has focused on 2D or 2.5D systems. A user-study is reported where we analyse their multimodal behaviour – specifically how they interact on a surface device with objects that have similar properties to physical versions and the users' associated gaze patterns with touch. The study reveals that gaze characteristics are different according to their interaction intention in terms of position and duration of visual attention. We discovered that virtual objects afford the perception of haptic attributes ascribed to their equivalent physical objects, and that differences in the summary statistics of gaze showed consistent characteristics between people and differences between natural and task based activities. An awareness of user behaviours using natural gestures can inform the design of interactive 3D applications which complements the user's model of past experience with physical objects and with GUI interaction.

Keywords: Interactive 3D · Multitouch · Surface computing · Digital heritage · Gaze tracking

1 Introduction

Multitouch surface computing in public spaces dedicated to heritage such as museums provide the opportunity to enhance people's experience, affording social interaction with others around digitised knowledge sources and virtual artefacts. The broad goal of this research is to recreate virtual experience of heritage objects, with the purpose of drawing 3D digital heritage objects from the archives for public access. This paper addresses an important sub-goal – to understand how users would behave when given 3D objects to manipulate within the virtual environment, through multi-touch gestures on a surface computer in the social space of a museum. Specifically, how users would manipulate 3D objects that have simulated properties similar to their physical versions

© Springer International Publishing Switzerland 2015
A. Marcus (Ed.): DUXU 2015, Part II, LNCS 9187, pp. 425–433, 2015.
DOI: 10.1007/978-3-319-20898-5_41

(physics effects, collisions, weight, etc.) given simple tasks. In addition to capturing gestures, we measure the user's gaze direction with an eye tracker in order to better understand how a person's visual attention is allocated during multitouch gesture. Thus, we aim to show that on a multitouch table, users' interactions with 3D virtual representations of real objects should be influenced by task and their perceived physical characteristics.

The article begins with a background of this particular research and its interest. The motivation for access to heritage artefacts, particularly those from the archives is discussed. The next section reviews related topics. The article continues with the methodology, and the results and discussions section, which describe the subject and development of the multitouch application with observations from user-evaluation. The article ends with a conclusion and future direction.

2 The Virtual Within the Physical Space

Surface computing with simultaneous multitouch inputs adds a new dimension to the access of information. Initially, applications using surface computing were used for browsing images and videos. These were applications with very basic functionalities (see examples [5, 6]). However, the new paradigm needs new explorations in user interface design that incorporates collaborative features and user evaluation. As surface hardware, APIs and SDKs mature, more creative use will be expected.

One of the critical ways in which digital heritage objects can be made more accessible to a wider audience is the development of more intuitive user interfaces. The touch and gesture-based smartphones and tablet computers have, to date, 'taught' massive amounts of users the multitouch, gesture-based interaction model. It has revolutionised the way in which users access information. Larger touch-screens such as the iPad are allowing a wider set of gestures, e.g., the navigation between Apps of up to 4 fingers using the 'swipe' gesture as opposed to the PC-era 'Alt-TAB' key combinations on the keyboard. These developments are revolutionising both work and leisure. Computers are now intuitive for a broad range of potentially cyberphobic audiences that never knew the PC-era. Computers are for the first time useful and fun, as evident in news channels and magazines that interviewed the elderly of their experience of such devices.

The commercialisation of horizontally oriented tabletop computers such as Microsoft's Surface, PQLab, and Ideum's multitouch, multiuser (MTMU) tabletop computers for museum spaces are bringing general and research computing into another dimension. Large High Definition (HD) displays of up to 65" supporting up to 32 touches and 'pop-out' 3D stereographics already exists (the Digital Humanities Hub-commissioned Mechdyne MTMU tabletop computer at the Chowen Prototyping Hall, the University of Birmingham). The fusion of cutting-edge technological advancements on tabletops are ushering in functional capabilities that were not present in traditional computing environments. Traditional computing environments are sequential, with supposedly 'collaborative' tasks passed between workers either via email or via a single-display, single input terminal. Although concurrent versioning systems and computer supported collaborative work are available [8], there were issues

[7] associated with it, particularly via a single user terminal. Working together on location might be better as it resolves issues of psychological ownership and perceived document quality, as evident in a collaborative Google Doc study [1]. Multitouch and multiuser surface computing opens up possibilities where collaboration is transformed from sequential to simultaneous – all workers work on a task simultaneously. In this sense, learning and access of information becomes more natural.

Research have shown that direct-touch interfaces do evoke confusion for first time users using touch interaction, organisation of content, and occlusion in uncontrolled environments [11]. More recent research suggests that surface computing are providing scopes for interactions that are nearer in experience to physical interactions as compared to classical windowed interfaces [9]. Will users resort to physical interaction models on surface computing? The answer is no, on both past studies and our observations in the present research. Users are influenced by the desktop paradigm. Research on user-defined gestures in surface computing [12] suggests that the Windows desktop paradigm has a strong influence on users' mental models; that users rarely care about the number of fingers they employ; that one hand is preferred to two, and that on-screen widgets are needed. In our observation of user evaluation conducted in past open days and the present research, users are also influenced by the touch-based smartphones and tablet paradigms.

The behaviour of large crowds in uncontrolled environment suggests that users learn from each other. An observation [10] with 1199 participants reveals that users at a display attract other users, and a user's actions on the touch wall is learned by observers. An interesting result was "how these people were configured in groups of users and crowds of spectators rather than as individual users. They were able to use the display both in parallel and collectively by adopting different roles" – the use of the display was highly non-individualistic.

Whilst single and multiple user interactions have been studied to a certain extent, 3D Multitouch interaction (newly abbreviated here as 3DMi) is an entirely new area that is yet to be fully explored. 3D interaction in multitouch was briefly mentioned in 2008 by Bowman *et al.* [2], "The current trend towards multi-touch interfaces at least acknowledges that humans tend to act with more than one finger at a time, but still this is just scratching the surface of the immersive experience that virtual environments will offer in future computer applications. What about grasping, turning, pushing, throwing, and jumping when interacting with computer applications?" Indeed, intuitive 3DMi has a long way to go, but there needs to be a new initiative for research here considering that market trends have changed since 2008 with more demands for multitouch surface computing worldwide.

3   Methods

A surface computing 3DMi application was developed. The 3DMi incorporates 3D objects that simulate weight, friction and gravity. More details on the implementation can be acquired from two articles [3, 4].

To identify and distinguish gesture behaviours, 9 participants (A to I) were monitored while they interacted with 3DMi in distinct phases whilst wearing the Tobii Eye

Glasses for capturing monocular gaze position (point of view 56° horizontal and 40° vertical). 30 infrared markers were placed equidistant around the edges of the table. A separate video camera records the interactions. Gaze data for each mode and participant were analysed:

1. *Passive Gaze Observation*: participant listens and watches the Instructor.
2. *Active (Free Exploration)*: participant is free to explore and manipulate the objects on the table with no explicit aim.
3. *Active (Task-Specifics)*: the participant is given a specific task requiring the manipulation of the artefacts on the table to fulfil an educational objective.

The sections below present our findings.

3.1   Observations

Virtual objects do simulate the perceived haptic attributes of real objects (weight, surface textures). Due to the realistic physics simulation, observation of user interaction with objects suggests that their perception of the digital facsimiles correlated with that of physical objects:

- Dexterity is observed where quick learners (D) picked up gestures where tasks are accomplished quickly through taking advantage of the weight, size and the effects of gravity and velocity of the object – flicking objects to the intended location.
- The larger the virtual object, the less likely it will be pushed aside (A, C).
- Participants (E) pushed obstacles aside with the other hand whilst moving the task object to the destination.
- A correlation between the number of fingers used and the perceived weight of the objects (B, D).
- When there is friction (object resists movement), participants pressed down more heavily on the surface
- Double tap objects to select, a behaviour learned from mouse use. (D, F).
- Exploration of gesture limits. For example the extent of the zoom, the speed at which objects can be dragged (All).
- While moving virtual objects, users pass objects from one hand to another (All).

The following gaze behaviours were observed on all participants:

- Gaze follows an object when dragged; gaze is depended upon as there were no haptics on the touch screen.
- Head is oriented so that focus of touch is in the centre of vision (central bias).
- Gaze is rarely focused upon the hand but on the visible part of the underlying object.
- If both hands are dragging objects in the same direction, gaze will tend to fall on the object nearest to the target. If objects are dragged to different targets, then gaze will fall between them or onto their point of convergence (Fig. 1)
- Gaze is a reliable predictor of where the person will touch next (i.e. the next object to be grabbed) (Fig. 2)

Fig. 1. A participant's gaze patterns (in green) over a 0.5 window while conducting a multitouch gesture. Gaze moves between the two objects and their origin (the red square) (Color figure online).

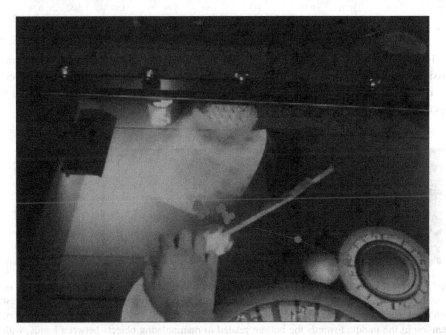

Fig. 2. Gaze tends to follow the object being dragged with fixations towards next object to be touched (in this example the large disc on the right).

3.2   Gaze Characteristics

Gaze characteristics are different in interaction modes for visual attention, position and duration (Table 1). Overall, passive interaction resulted in the shortest fixations (mean – 0.41 s, stdev = 0.35 s N = 640). Longer fixation durations are observed when the participants are actively using the table (mean = 0.64 s, stdev = 0.88 s, N = 715), with the imposition of a definitive task shortening the mean duration and its variance (mean = 0.52 s, stdev = 0.71 s, N = 820).

Table 1. Summary gaze statistics showing fixation duration distribution estimations per phase, per participant. All participants exhibited shorter fixation distributions with smaller standard deviation when actively engaged in the task, compared to when freely interacting with objects. The shortest fixation durations occur when users are not gesturing (passive mode). All times are in seconds.

Participant	Passive			Active - Free			Active - Task		
	Sample Count	Mean	Standard Deviation	Sample Count	Mean	Standard Deviation	Sample Count	Mean	Standard Deviation
A	140	0.38	0.31	166	0.67	0.84	168	0.45	0.34
B	77	0.39	0.22	58	1.1	1.91	94	0.84	1.46
C	–	–	–	86	0.66	0.63	94	0.44	0.32
D	89	0.49	0.4	90	0.54	0.81	126	0.46	0.39
E	121	0.41	0.34	104	0.4	0.34	131	0.52	0.69
G	91	0.48	0.54	118	0.76	0.88	93	0.66	0.9
I	122	0.34	0.24	93	0.48	0.37	114	0.38	0.28
All	640	0.41	0.35	715	0.64	0.88	820	0.52	0.71

Fixation positions also showed a difference (Fig. 3). For active interaction (free and passive), visual attention is focused on a position between the hands, particularly when the interaction is free. In passive mode, visual attention has a wider spread. Taken together, differences in gaze can be attributable to task.

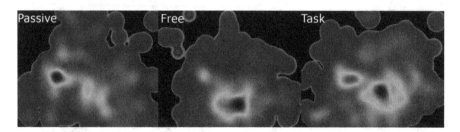

Fig. 3. Heat map visualisation of visual attention on touch table from all participants' point of view for the three different phases. Red shows the highest concentration of gaze, green the lowest with black showing no gaze. Active use of multitouch (Free and Task) show a concentration of attention in the middle towards the bottom related to manipulating objects between hands, with differences between Free and Task indicating a more dynamic exploration for Task, as the red is more dispersed. Passive (no multitouch) does not have a central concentration of fixations because users are not using their hands.

Differences in the summary statistics for gaze showed consistent characteristics between people and differences between natural and task based activities. This suggests that the natural state of interaction the application affords (free play state) and specific task based interaction states that can be inferred from gaze alone. These are preliminary results. Gaze characteristics can thus potentially be used in inference models to deduce the tasks undertaken by museum visitors and predict touch gestures allowing for applications to prime relevant information for access.

4 Conclusion

In this article, we presented our findings on the multimodal behaviour and gaze of users during 3D multitouch interaction, with a broad goal of recreating virtual experience of heritage objects, and a sub-goal of understanding user behaviour when given 3D objects to manipulate. The research has direct relevance to the access of heritage objects via digital means, which have important economic and social value. Heritage contributes directly and indirectly to the GDP of a country that hosts them and the public access and valorisation of heritage promotes the artistic, aesthetic, cognitive and recreation needs for individuals, households, and their national identity. Unrestricted access of heritage from the archives via digital interfaces allows the rediscovery of hidden source of information that may bridge relationship or chronological gaps amongst artefacts. The introduction of virtual information spaces hosting realistic laser-scanned 3D objects rendered in interactive real-time computer graphics, coupled with natural gestures in 3D multitouch screens are one of the important and accessible ways of interacting with heritage objects. These virtual environments occupy a little space (65" screens mounted vertically, or as table computers) and complement the limitations of space in museums, but the value that they are able to add to the learning, teaching, research, and access of heritage is significant.

In this article, we investigated how multitouch surface computing can contribute to the research and social interaction opportunities of accessing heritage objects to enhance users' experience around digitised knowledge sources and virtual artefacts. We explored the development and user study of a 3DMi application that allows users to explore virtual objects using natural gestures. Our study allows us to analyse their multimodal behaviour – specifically how they interact on a surface computer with objects that have similar properties to their physical versions, and the users' associated gaze patterns with touch.

We showed that on a multitouch table, users' interactions with 3D virtual representations of real objects are influenced by task and their perceived physical characteristics. Gaze characteristics are different according to interaction modes in terms of the allocation of visual attention. Virtual objects can afford haptic attributes of physical objects, although users may revert to old interaction modes from the Windows GUI era suggesting that the perception of affordance by system designers should not be assumed. Differences in the summary statistics for gaze demonstrate consistent characteristics between people, and differences between natural and task based activities. An awareness of how objects afford interaction in a natural state can inform design in order to encourage constructive activities.

Our study is an initial step of a broader goal to understanding user behaviour and multimodal interaction with 3D objects on surface computers. We believe the findings articulated in this research will contribute to better design of 3D multitouch applications using natural gestures.

Future studies will involve a redesign of the interactive 3D application to compensate for users' perception of virtual objects in relation to their understanding of the haptics and physics of real objects. We aim to also conduct studies on multiuser and multitouch collaborative tasks involving two, and up to four users in the evaluation to gain understanding of how users behave in a collaborative digital table, monitoring gaze patterns to assist in resolving gesture intent.

Acknowledgements. This work was supported by The International Doctoral Innovation Centre (IDIC) scholarship scheme at the University of Nottingham Ningbo China. We also greatly acknowledge the support from Ningbo Education Bureau, Ningbo Science and Technology Bureau, China's MoST and The University of Nottingham. The project is partially supported by NBSTB Project 2012B10055.

References

1. Blau, I., Caspi, A.: What type of collaboration helps? psychological ownership, perceived learning and outcome quality of collaboration. In: Proceedings of the Chais Conference on Instructional Technologies Research 2009: Learning in the Technological era (Raanana, 2009), pp. 48–55 (2009)
2. Bowman, D.A.: Interaction techniques for common tasks in immersive virtual environments. Citeseer (1999)
3. Ch'ng, E.: New ways of accessing information spaces using 3D multitouch tables. In: Proceedings of the Art, Design and Virtual Worlds Conference, Cyberworlds 2012, 25–27 September 2012, Darmstadt, Germany (2012)
4. Ch'ng, E.: The Mirror Between Two Worlds: 3D Surface Computing Interaction for Digital Objects and Environments Digital Media and Technologies for Virtual Artistic Spaces. IGI Global, USA (2013)
5. Ciocca, G., et al.: Browsing museum image collections on a multi-touch table. Inf. Syst. **37**(2), 169–182 (2012)
6. Correia, N., et al.: A multi-touch tabletop for robust multimedia interaction in museums. In: ACM International Conference on Interactive Tabletops and Surfaces. ACM (2010)
7. Dekeyser, S., Watson, R.: Extending Google Docs to Collaborate on Researchpapers. The University of Southern Queensland, Australia (2006)
8. Eseryel, D., et al.: Review of computer-supported collaborative work systems. Edu. Technol. Soc. **5**(2), 1–8 (2002)
9. North, C., Dwyer, T., Lee, B., Fisher, D., Isenberg, P., Robertson, G., Inkpen, K.: Understanding multi-touch manipulation for surface computing. In: Gross, T., Gulliksen, J., Kotzé, P., Oestreicher, L., Palanque, P., Prates, R.O., Winckler, M. (eds.) INTERACT 2009. LNCS, vol. 5727, pp. 236–249. Springer, Heidelberg (2009)
10. Peltonen, P., et al.: It's Mine, Don't Touch!: interactions at a large multi-touch display in a city centre. In: Proceedings of the Twenty-Sixth Annual SIGCHI Conference on Human Factors in Computing Systems. ACM (2008)

11. Ryall, K., et al.: Experiences with and observations of direct-touch tabletops. In: Proceedings of the First IEEE International Workshop on Horizontal Interactive Human-Computer Systems, TABLETOP 2006 (2006)
12. Wobbrock, J.O., et al.: User-defined gestures for surface computing. In: Proceedings of the 27th International Conference on Human Factors in Computing Systems. ACM (2009)

CubeMate: A New Communication Device as Non-verbal Interface in a Shared Space

Roberta Grimaldi[1,2], Valentina Cipelli[1(✉)],
and Carlo Maria Medaglia[1]

[1] Link Campus University, Via Nomentana 335, 00162 Rome, Italy
{robertagrim,valentina.cipelli}@gmail.com,
c.medaglia@unilink.it
[2] ISIA Roma Design, Piazza della Maddalena 53, 00196 Rome, Italy

Abstract. Communication is made of both verbal and non-verbal components. The latter often provide much more meaning than people realize. Nowadays communication is more often technology mediated, this occurrence is transforming rules and channels of human communication. In this paper we illustrate the design of a new communication device, CubeMate, which can be used as nonverbal mood interface in various contexts of shared space (house, office, shared flat). The design of CubeMate follows the Interaction Design process. Its design, embracing Weiser's Calm Computing, focus on the Calmness, using a non-verbal output that doesn't overburden users attention. During two Maker Faire we have collected unstructured feedbacks and qualitative evaluations through a prototype trial. On the basis of these considerations we could identify achievable improvements and define several and cross application fields.

Keywords: Non verbal communication · Calm computing · Interaction design process · Proactive computing · Emoticons

1 Introduction

Communication is a process of continuous exchanging of verbal and non-verbal messages. Pre-requisite of communication is a message. This message must be conveyed through some medium to the recipient. It is essential that the recipient must accurately understand this message. Thus, communication is incomplete without a feedback from the recipient to the sender on how well the message is understood by him. Feedback may be verbal (through words) or non-verbal (in form of facial expressions, sighs, etc.). Non-verbal elements of communication can give important clues to the recipient for the interpretation of verbal message. Non-verbal communication works in conjunction with the words that we utter in six ways: to repeat, to emphasize, to complement, to contradict, to substitute and to regulate. So nonverbal elements are an essential part of the total communication package, and sometimes could be the only one.

Traditional dimensions of non-verbal communication are eight: physical appearance [1], proxemics [2], facial expressions [3], gestures and posture [4], tactile communication [5], eye contact, paralanguage and chronemics.

A. Marcus (Ed.): DUXU 2015, Part II, LNCS 9187, pp. 434–443, 2015.
DOI: 10.1007/978-3-319-20898-5_42

Two of the five primary functions of non-verbal behavior [3] are expression of emotion and communication of interpersonal attitudes. Regarding the first, emotions are expressed mainly through the face, body, and voice. About the second, the establishment and maintenance of relationships if often done through nonverbal signals. Planning our project we have focused on the facial expression dimension because non-verbal cues can regulate or control face-to-face interaction, conveying information about relational matters such as liking, respect, and social control.

In the past, some studies try to numerically quantify the contribution of each component in the communication process. The research on non-verbal messages conducted by Albert Meharabian in 1967 was often misquoted [6, 7, 9], diffusing the idea that the total meaning in every message is 7 % verbal, 38 % vocal and 55 % facial.

Lapakko [8] criticized this reduction of the complex world of communication into a tidy and precise quantification, because he supported that it is not possible to quantify the relative importance of the non-verbal and verbal communication.

Mehrabian [6, 7] also noted that this equation is applicable only to the communications of feelings and attitudes. Indeed, we can understand more about another person's feelings on non-verbal cues and less on the words that are used.

The fast changes and the evolving technologies at our disposal, have strong repercussions in the daily lives of each of us: we live, we communicate, we move really and virtually in the knowledge society and the network society [10]. Always, developments in technology and communications have gone hand-in-hand, and the latest technological developments such as Internet, Social Networking and mobile devices have changed rules and channels of human communication. In the past, people used to speak face-to-face. This communication paradigm allow them to read and pay attention to the body language, the facial expressions, the voice intonations and to understand the real meaning of that communication. Nowadays when we interact with others using EMC (Electronically Mediated Communication) we can do so asynchronously. This phenomenon makes the communication less spontaneous and more impersonal than in the past. The use of technology can be a great help to people in communicating, reducing the time it takes, but it can have consequence of reducing face-to-face interaction. There are differing views on the consequences of using technology in the communication. If on one hand there is the strict belief that the technologies are destroying human communication [11], on the other hand there is the opinion that using them does not mean that face-to-face interaction suffer. Rather, it is an extension of them [12]. It is certain that the communication with the introduction of the new technologies has changed the style and the syntax.

Words and graphics become more important in EMC than in face-to-face interactions, because when communicating electronically, you must rely solely on words to carry non-verbal messages. There is no tone of voice in the written message and it can be possible to see the facial expressions, body gesture and position of interlocutor. Everything, and the absence of all other paralinguistic elements, makes difficult to express emotions. So people use emoticons to provide emotional punctuation. The term "emoticon" is a blend of emotion and icon and even if originally they started as simple "pictographs", little by little they have become "non-verbal surrogates, suggestive of facial expression, and a further addition paralinguistic component to a message" [13] to "indicate the writer's mood or feeling" [14]. Emoticons diffusion makes them a universal visual language.

Given this theoretical framework and according to the belief that technology can be an extension of the face-to face relationships, in this paper we illustrate the design of a new communication device, CubeMate, which can be used as nonverbal interface in various contexts of shared space (house, office, shared flat). In the Sect. 2 we describe the project and the Interaction Design methodology followed, through four steps. Firstly, we identified the user needs about the communication in the shared space and after we establish the requirements. Second, we develop alternative design, to suggest ideas that meet the requirements. The third step describes the building of the interactive versions, focusing on the design of the interaction and related concept of Calm Computing. Following section reports our experiences in two Maker Faire and the qualitative evaluation of CubeMate. Finally, Sect. 4 presents our conclusion and future work.

2   CubeMate Design Process

2.1   User Needs and Requirements

The design of CubeMate follows the four basic steps of traditional process of Interaction Design [15]: identify needs and establishing requirements, develop alternative designs, build interactive versions of the designs and evaluate designs.

According to this, the first step to design something to support people is to know who our target users are and what kind of support an interactive product could usefully provide (identify needs and establishing requirements).

Firstly we have decided to work on solutions for shared spaces. This choice is motivated by the personal experience in our lab, where eight/ten persons share the same room. Through an informal brainstorming session we have identified the main user's needs and some requirements to satisfy. The project idea starts from the strong consideration that is difficult to live together with acquaintances in shared spaces (home, office, shared flat) where some things, like moods or feelings, are very hard to express.

Thanks to our design users should let each other know how they feel, when they want to be alone or when they want to be approached. Thus, to improve living side by side avoiding misunderstanding and fostering respect of everyone's spaces.

During this stage we have established some requirements and features to keep in mind during the entire design process: a simple and minimalist design to suggest the right way to interact with the object itself; the introduction of engaging and interactive solutions to make the product interesting and the necessity to use of a universal visual language, as emoticons, to help colleagues, friends and flat-mates sharing feelings through a non-verbal understated language. On the basis of these observations we have designed *"CubeMate"*, which can improve communication process reinforcing empathy through nonverbal cues.

The name CubeMate is a fusion of the words "Cube" and "Mate". This blend has been chosen for two reasons: the first is to refer to the cube shape of the product, the second is to emphasize the main task of the object that is to be an actual "mate" to the owner, helping his social life.

CubeMate is a small cube consisting of interactive and lighten faces. It displays facial expressions, through four emoticons, that correspond to four basic moods: happy, calm, angry and sad. Top faces of every single CubeMate are made in different colors to allow each person to choose the shade that best represents their personality, so as to feel more 'connected' to it. It can be placed in a common space of the office or the house so everyone can share his/her own mood through his/her own little cube.

2.2   Developing Alternative Designs

Later we focused on the development of alternative designs, to suggest ideas that meet the requirements. We have simultaneously developed the conceptual design, to describe what the product should do, and the physical design considering the details of the product, including the colors chosen, the materials used and the form factor of the object. In this stage we have explored several shapes and details in order to realize a product designed accurately in each of its parts. To reach this aim we have built two different physical prototypes. In both versions we focused on the strict relationship that exists between shape and function and we reflected upon the important role that the Affordance, perceived as an "aspect of an object which suggests how the object should be used" [16], plays during the design process.

The first prototype (A) of CubeMate was an 8,5 × 8,5 cm transparent Plexiglass cube. On the frontal face, there was placed a display for the smile. User could choose his/her mood interacting with a knob, whose rotation, to the right or the left, makes vary smile from the happy to the sad face.

The second version (B) consisted in an Opaline Plexiglass cube, opaque, 10 × 10 cm dimensions. On the frontal face, there was placed a LED display for the smile. The Polyurethane Gel covered the top face, under that we inserted a button. In this prototype, user interacts with cube with a simply touch on the top face changing LED displayed face.

2.3   Building Interactive Prototype

During the third step of the design process of CubeMate we have built the two-designed interactive prototypes. This step is more important and fundamental for the whole of the project. The most sensible way to evaluate and choose the fitting design for the stated function is to interact with it. We use the single-board micro-controller Arduino UNO that make it possible to build the most quick and interactive version of CubeMate.

Both versions of CubeMate, embracing Calm Computing construct [17], are *designed for the Periphery*, focusing on the Calmness. After the Mainframe era and the PC era, now we are living the Ubiquitous Computing era. The characteristic of this era, distributed computing in every aspects of our daily living, imposes a complete rethinking of "the goals, context and technology of the computer and all the other technology" [17]. The essential challenge in a world where computer are everywhere is to design technology that calm and leave us "more time to be more fully human" [17]. The difference in the Calm technology is how it engages and manages user attention. Engaging both the center and the periphery of attention, user is always aware of what is happening by periphery processing, without overburden center attention.

Fig. 1. At left Prototype (A) and at right Prototype (B)

Between the two prototypes (Fig. 1), according to the related Calm Technology notion of Affordances [16], we have chosen the prototype (B). This version is characterized by the more natural and intuitive interaction. It is characterized by a self-explained interaction, in a way that people naturally go to touch the top face of the cube, appealing from the Polyurethane Gel. The choice of specific materials as Opaline Plexiglass for cube's faces and Polyurethane Gel for the top face, besides on the basis of their intrinsic qualities, was made just considering the effect that they have on interaction: "the feeling when holding the object, the physical engagement with it, and the appropriation engendered by possessing one" [18]. In addition, the minimalist design allows an easy identification as a familiar device, which makes the user to be at ease with the cube. While with a rough version of the prototype (A) we immediately understood that the interaction was complex. User had to commit his/her attention totally on the interaction with the knob to choose the most representative smiley.

Unlike what was claimed by Weiser, CubeMate must be consciously activated by people involved in the communication process. By this way, this project realizes a shift "from proactive computing to proactive people" [19]. According to the Rogers proposal for an alternative agenda of the UbiComp Technologies, the main goal of this project is enable people to do what they want in a best way. In fact CubeMate provides information, through emoticon, that reinforce empathy and allows user to live a more engaged and actively communication. These different ways to design the UbiComp technologies are based on a different view of the users and its relationship with the technologies. For the traditional Ubiquitous Computing [17], technologies are embedded in the environment to reduce the need for humans to think yourself about every-day stuff, and doing it for them. In this view, users have only to react to the technology input that told them what have to do. Instead of the Rogers proposal, where the UbiComp technologies are designed to create a collaborative ecologies of tools and resources that augment human intellect and "provoke us to learn, understand and reflect more upon our interactions with technologies and each other" [19]. In fact CubeMate project shares the Rogers idea of proactive users that knowingly choose and show his/her mood. So it may augment people ability to understand their own and the others feelings, to learn how to interact with them.

By this way, CubeMate cannot be defined as a typical device of the Ubiquitous Computing era. Actually it does not have any connectivity, neither to connect to other smart object nor at the Internet. CubeMate working is based only on the users input, it does not take any information from sensor or any network.

3 Evaluation from Maker Faire Experiences

The main goal of the interaction design is to develop interactive products that are usable. The last step of the Interaction Design process concerns precisely the evaluation of the designs. Evaluation generally concerns the easy to learn, the effective to use, and the ability to provide an enjoyable user experience.

On the occasion of the Maker Faire Rome, the European Edition (3–5 October 2014) we presented the first four high-fidelity prototypes of CubeMate. We also exposed CubeMate in Elephant & Castle Mini Maker Faire 2014 (15th November 2014). According to the Maker Faire Official Site definition "Maker Faire is the Greatest Show (and Tell) on Earth - a family-friendly festival of invention, creativity and resourcefulness, and a celebration of the Maker movement" [20].

The idea to expose CubeMate in these two Maker Faire was born when we chose the open source electronics Arduino for build the interactive versions of the product designed. Thanks to this platform and other related knowledge and abilities of the Maker Movement, everyone could actually build interactive things, and not only. In our case, this world of resources and tools gives to the CubeMate idea the possibility to become reality.

Capitalizing on these experiences, during the two fairs we made the last step of the design process, involving fair visitors through CubeMate prototype trial. Given the environmental characteristics of the fairs, we could collect unstructured feedbacks and qualitative evaluations through, first, the observation of the users and, second, talking with them. The advantage of exposing CubeMate in events like the Maker Faire was the possibility to have feedbacks from a very large and diverse sample of users, in terms of age, cultural background, education, skills and interests (Fig. 2).

In the first moments of the approach to the Cube, we left user free to interact with it without explain anything. During these moments we could observe if the interaction with CubeMate was clear and intuitive. We have seen that the majority of users approach CubeMate touching immediately its top face. Talking with these users, this first approach was explained by the attraction both for the general design of the object and texture and for the colors of the top face gel. Only few users did not touch the cube and, after a brief observation of the Cube, asked to us: "What is it?" or "How does it work?".

The first group of users, continuing to interact with the cube, discovered by yourself the four emoticons, recognizing for the mood each represents. After this, these users requested to us what were the goals of the cube. So if the interaction with CubeMate is natural and intuitive, the aims are difficult to understand. This difficulty can be explained considering CubeMate was out of context than its natural context of use.

Through the talk with the users, we have collected various observations. Many adult users acknowledge the usefulness of CubeMate as a non-verbal mood interface, especially for the negative moods, in a shared space with strangers and newcomers, like the office. By this way, CubeMate could allow an effective communication, free of some emotional influences that could alter its real meaning.

During both the Maker Fairs, especially in the Education Day of Maker Faire Rome, many children, young boys and girls (under 18 years old) have interacted with CubeMate. Very little children (0–5 years) have seen it mainly as a toy, even using it, if requested, as a means to show their parents how they felt. Many teenagers, coherently age period living, have reported they would use CubeMate for sharing your mood with your friends. If someone of them suggested photographing the smile chosen and sending it to the friends, many requested if there was the Internet connectivity to send it automatically.

On the other hand, teenagers parents have seen in CubeMate a simply tool to better understand mood of their own children, so as to decide how to interact with them.

In the next future, we are planning an evaluation phase carried out through a structured usability test. This kind of test allows us to study CubeMate in its designed contexts of use (house, office, shared flat), to identify the efficiency and the possible effects of social and psychological dynamics that subsist in these shared spaces.

Meanwhile, on the basis of Maker Fairs experiences we could identify some physical and technological improvements for the next versions of CubeMate. It is essential to work both on a stronger internal structure and form factor in order to guarantee the strut strength. Simultaneously a single-board microcontroller as Arduino does not ensure a reliability and efficiency required by an end-user product. In addition, we evaluate to implement the connectivity.

Finally, on the basis of the user considerations we could define another interesting application fields. CubeMate could be used as a user-friendly tool for collecting quickly evaluation, supporting the sentiment analysis in a customer satisfaction studies. Furthermore it could be used as a tool for the pain evaluation (through the Faces Pain Scale [21]), or as a communication aid for people with disabilities and linguistic impairments. Non-verbal people with autism have often difficulties to communicate using natural languages. They can, however, learn to communicate through specific symbols and images. Based on this fact, El-Seoud et al. [22] designed a mobile based application. CubeMate could be used similarly, helping autistic people to express and communicate their emotion. It will be indispensable, for each of these applications, suitable studies for the specific users, the different aims and features, identifying possible changes in CubeMate design.

Fig. 2. The four high-fidelity prototype of CubeMate during the Maker Fairs

4   Conclusions and Future Work

We illustrate the importance of non-verbal components in the communication process. Among eight different dimensions of non-verbal communication, the Facial Expressions are the most important non-verbal channel for expressing attitudes and emotions to other people. Nowadays communication is more often technology mediated, transforming rules and channels of human communication. The emoticons, a simple "pictographs", allow users to express their own moods and feelings through tech-mediated communication.

According to this theoretical framework, in this paper we illustrate the design of a new communication device, CubeMate, which can be used as nonverbal interface in various contexts of shared space (house, office, shared flat). Its aim is to help users sharing each other some basic feelings through the non-verbal communication. The design of CubeMate follows Interaction Design process: identify needs and establishing requirements, develop alternative designs, build interactive versions of the designs, and evaluate designs.

We firstly chose to focus on the difficulty of living together with acquaintances in shared spaces. After we have established some requirements: minimalist and simple design; interactive solution; the use of a visual language. So CubeMate is a small cube consisting of interactive and lighten faces. It displays facial expressions, through four emoticons. It can be placed in a common space, so everyone can share his/her own mood and see the others one, reinforcing empathy and avoiding misunderstanding.

The second step concerns the development of alternative designs, differing shapes, materials and details, prototype (A) and (B). In both versions we focused on the strict relationship existed between the design of the object and how it should be used (Affordance).

The third step describes the building of the interactive versions of the prototypes, thanks to Arduino UNO. CubeMate idea and physical design was inspired by the Weiser concept of Calm Computing. Indeed, CubeMate design focus on the Calmness, using a non-verbal output that doesn't overburden users' attention. On the other hand, the CubeMate idea was founded on the idea of proactive users, for a technology that enable people to do what they want in a best way. Between the two prototypes, we have chosen the prototype B, characterized by a self-explained interaction and the minimalist design.

On the occasion of the European Edition of Maker Faire Rome (October 2014) and the Elephant & Castle Mini Maker Faire 2014 (November 2014) we exposed the first four high-fidelity prototypes of CubeMate. During the fairs we have collected unstructured feedbacks and qualitative evaluations through a prototype trial. On the basis of these considerations we could identify some physical and technological improvements. Furthermore we could define several and cross application fields, from communication aid for autistic people and linguistic impairments, to sentiment analysis for customer satisfaction.

In the Interaction Design process applied, iteration through the four activities is inevitable and indispensable. So the CubeMate design process is to be understood still in progress. Thanks to the evaluation phase, it is possible to deduce many potentialities depending on the context of use and the application field. But first of all, it will be central to test usability in the designed contexts of use (house, office, shared flat) to ascertain our initial hypothesis that CubeMate could improves general communication reinforcing empathy through nonverbal cues.

References

1. Richmond, V.P., McCroskey, J.C.: Nonverbal Behavior in Interpersonal Relations. Allyn and Bacon/Pearson Education, Boston (2004)
2. Hall, E.T.: The Hidden Dimension. Garden City, New York (1966)
3. Argyle, M.: Bodily Communication, 2nd edn. Methuen, New York (2008)
4. Goldman, E.: As Others See Us. Routledge, New York (1994)
5. Harris, T.E.: Applied Organizational Communication: Principles and Pragmatics for Future Practice. Lawrence Erlbaum Association, Mahwah (2002)
6. Mehrabian, A., Wiener, M.: Decoding of inconsistent communications. J. Pers. Soc. Psychol. **6**, 109–114 (1967)

7. Mehrabian, A., Ferris, S.R.: Inference of attitudes from nonverbal communication in two channels. J. Consult. Psychol. **31**(3), 48–258 (1967)
8. Lapakko, D.: Three cheers for language: a closer examination of a widely cited study of non-verbal communication. Commun. Educ. **46**(1), 63–67 (2009)
9. Mehrabian, A.: Silent Messages: Implicit Communication of Emotions and Attitudes, 2nded. Wadsworth, Belmont (1981)
10. Castells, M.: The Internet Galaxy: Reflections on the Internet, Business, and Society. Oxford University Press, Inc., New York (2001)
11. Zorofi, M., Gargari, A.S., Geshlagi, M., Tahvilda, Z.: The impact of media usage on students' social skills. Res. J. Appl. Sci. Eng. Technol. **3**(8), 731–736 (2011)
12. Jung Sook, L.: Online communication and adolescent social ties: Who benefits more from Internet use? J. Comput. Mediated Commun. **14**, 509–531 (2009)
13. Derks, D., Bos, A.E.R., Grumbkow, J.V.: Emoticons and social interaction on the Internet: The importance of social context. Comput. Hum. Behav. **23**(1), 842–849 (2007)
14. Gajadhar, J., Green, J.S.: The importance of nonverbal elements in online chat. Educase Quartely **4**, 63–64 (2005)
15. Preece, J., Rogers, Y., Sharp, H.: Interaction Design. Wiley, New York (2002)
16. Norman, D.A.: The Design of Everyday Things. Doubleday, New York (1988)
17. Weiser, M., Brown, J.S.: The Coming Age of Calm Technology, Xerox PARC, 5 October 1996. This paper is a revised version of: Weiser, M., Brown, J.S.: Designing Calm Technology, Xerox PARC, December 1995
18. Petrelli, D., Dulake, N., Marshall, M., Willox, M., Caparrelli, F., Goldberg, R.: Prototyping tangibles: exploring form and interaction. In: Proceedings of the 8th International Conference on Tangible, Embedded and Embodied Interaction - TEI 2014, pp. 41–48 (2014)
19. Rogers, Y.: Moving on from weiser's vision of calm computing: engaging ubicomp experiences. In: Dourish, P., Friday, A. (eds.) UbiComp 2006. LNCS, vol. 4206, pp. 404–421. Springer, Heidelberg (2006)
20. Maker Faire official website. http://makerfaire.com/makerfairehistory
21. Bieri, D., Reeve, R.A.: David Champion, G., Addicoat, L., Ziegler, J.B.: The faces pain scale for the self-assessment of the severity of pain experienced by children: development, initial validation and preliminary investigation for ratio scale properties. Pain **41**(2), 139–150 (1990)
22. Abou El-Seoud, M.S., Karkar, A., Al Ja'am, J.M., Karam, O.H.: A pictorial mobile-based communication application for non-verbal people with autism. In: 2014 International Conference on Interactive Collaborative Learning (ICL), pp. 529–534 (2014)

Transparent Organ©: Designing Luminaire Art Deco with Kinetic Interaction

Scottie Chih-Chieh Huang[(✉)]

Biologically Inspired Objects Laboratory, Department of Industrial Design
College of Architecture and Design, Chung Hua University, 707 Sec.2 WuFu,
Hsinchu, Taiwan
scottie.c.c.huang@gmail.com

Abstract. This paper purposed a novel concept for futuristic interactive product design, combined the emerging techniques of the digital design and fabrication, interactive kinetic structural system, and ambient display to form a hybrid luminaire art deco. This installation - Transparent Organ developing a specific characteristic of sensitive kinetic interaction in a computer augmented physical kinetic object producing ambient atmosphere in a space. It used digital fabrication with parametric design tools for construct transparent shape plays as a light conduction. The interactive system combined of capacitive touch sensor, dimming control, and motor controller for kinetic sculpture with adaptive algorithm. Furthermore, this precedent has demonstrated alternative aesthetics with functional applications in further interactive product design.

Keywords: Computer-aided design (CAD) · Kinetic sculpture · Interactive design · New media art

1 Introduction

Computer graphics and interactive techniques have changes the morphology of beauty in broad scales of design. CAD/CAM (Computer-Aided Design/Computer Aided Manufacturing) tools enable designer to break traditional limitation in making form freely [1], combining materials characteristics in fabricating processes making form complexity [2]. HCI (Human-Computer Interaction) techniques bring the possibilities for creating things with intelligent, communication, interaction, flexibility, and adaptability [3–5], not only augmented object with advanced features but also changes the definition of physical object in design. The futuristic interactive product emerges as the functional aesthetics object, embedded with smart application and displaying as a deco art in our living space.

Biological systems can be characterized as entities that "compute" material organization according to external performance criteria [6]. Biologically inspired computing consists with natural mechanism, generating organic form and making adaptive behavior on interaction, creating novel value in aesthetics representation. This paper presents our vision of futuristic product, which using natural mechanism to build novel morphology of beauty in design. The present work "Transparent Organ" is an interactive luminaire utilized by CAD/CAM and HCI techniques. According to the most

© Springer International Publishing Switzerland 2015
A. Marcus (Ed.): DUXU 2015, Part II, LNCS 9187, pp. 444–451, 2015.
DOI: 10.1007/978-3-319-20898-5_43

natural "forms" growth by the basic rules of symmetry and recursion. It used self-reorganized and synergy as main mechanisms for producing the "behaviours" with adaptation. This project demonstrates a novel approach to merge techniques for fabricating artificial nature, through the algorithm studies and simulating in "forms" and "behaviours" (Fig. 1).

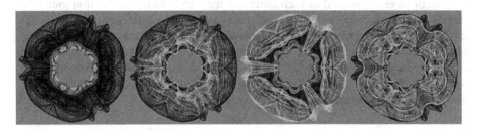

Fig. 1. Transparent Organ is inspired from the morphology of natural organism, and the visual representation from the Magnetic Resonance Imaging (MRI) sequences, shows the alternative aesthetics by diverse forms and functional organs.

2   Related Work

Emerging techniques bring novel design methods for create hybrid applications in design especially in architectural scale object. In terms of make forming, CAD/CAM tools provide designer to build alternative forms by inventing specific fabrication and design processes. Silk Pavilion [7] explores the relationship between digital and biological fibre-based fabrication on an architectural scale installation, discovering the silkworm's spinning behaviour, material and structural characterisation, computational simulation and fabrication strategy devised for the full-scale construction. Aerial robotic construction [8] offers a new approach to architecture using flying machines, investigates the design potential and material relationship between architecture and construction.

   In terms of making functional kinetic application with interactive techniques, Bubbles [9] demonstrated that interactive installation could be aware of a visitor coming and react with a spatially pneumatic form by deforming and performing dynamical behavior generated by real time calculations. The rolling bridge [10] presents a transformable structural design, which may opens smoothly, curling from a straight bridge into a circular sculpture, which uses a series of hydraulic cylinders integrated into its eight segments, causing its rolling character. The expanding video screen [11] demonstrates a giant screen that can change its size and shape, morph into a 7-story high cone-shaped structure, enveloping the band as it extends in the U2's concert. The actuated tensegrity structure [12] demonstrated a vision of building adaptability, which could change the shape of building's envelope in response to outside/inside sensors in the structure. These works bring a rich dynamic representation in both functional and aesthetics features.

Both kinetic function and dynamical forming merged together provide alternative applications in design. Hylozoic Soil [13] is an immersive, interactive environment made of tens of thousands of lightweight digitally-fabricated components fitted with meshed microprocessors and sensors. It contains infrared proximity sensors, micro-controllers, strands of titanium nickel memory wire, and custom circuit boards to perform mutual interactions between viewers and the kinetic object. The Muscle Tower [14] is an interactive & kinetic installation reacts to its environment, it consists of aluminium tubes, connected to each other and the FESTO-Muscles by iron joint. The FESTO-Muscles are controlled by a VirTools Script, which is connected to motion sensors. Outerspace [15] appears as a playful, curious creature exploring the surrounding space, looking for light, motion, and touch contact, and dynamical react with the posture changes in real-time adaptation. These works provide multiple approaches to utilize emerging techniques, discovering novel functional and aesthetics applications, to encourage recently boundary in design.

3   Digital Design and Fabrication

This work inspired from the morphology of natural organism, and the visual representation from the Magnetic Resonance Imaging (MRI) sequences, shows the alternative aesthetics by diverse forms and functional organs, emphasis novel design philosophy in functional aesthetics. In terms of design, we using generative algorithms Grasshopper, a graphical algorithm editor tightly integrated with Rhino's 3-D modeling tools to build form generators from the set of object relationship. The form is developing based on 3 rotational and reflection symmetry to generate, through the freely curve drawing and the setting with parametric adjusting and computing, the 3 rotational and reflection organic forms was build in virtual flexibility. In terms of manufacturing, in order to design the form as a light conduction for producing atmosphere in a space, this work used the layers of acrylic slice to fabricate the specific form with multiple sections in manufacturing apply. We used Grasshopper to setting up and generate the multiple sections drawing and then translating the files into laser cutting machine for manufacturing. Through the assembling of lots of numbered acrylic slices, the transparent form consists of layered light conduction patterns have been appearing (Figs. 2 and 3).

4   Interactive Kinetic Structural System

The interactive system designed on "Transparent Organ," used interactive techniques to developing kinetic sculpture with artificial behaviors as an embedded computing system. It used metaphor of "Phototropism" to build the algorithm for whisker-liked object, using actuators to control the wire's tension and compression for effecting physically transform on flexible structure design (see as in Fig. 4). Viewers may used touch evoke the light sources, immediately guide the bending directions facing to the light in a soothing way. The Phototropism metaphor is meant to simulate the natural phototropism of plants and create the kinetic structural system of the interaction between the kinetic art form and humans. The build biologic mechanism is aimed to

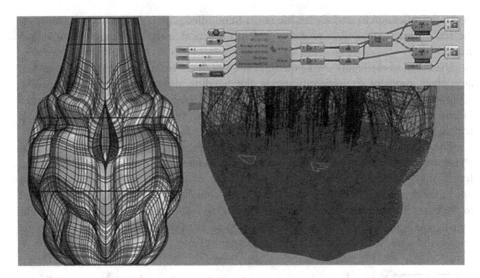

Fig. 2. This work using generative algorithms Grasshopper to build form generators from the set of object relationship, developing forms with three rotational and reflection symmetry.

Fig. 3. The work used script to generate the sections drawing into laser cutting machine for manufacturing, and then assembling of lots of numbered acrylic slices in to an organic form.

evoke the reflection to lead a wise life in the trend filled with high technologies and find the sentimental temperature probably lost in the recent smart application in mundane world.

Users can immediately evoke the light sources of different directions on the work at any given moment to indirectly guide the bending directions of the whisker-like sculptural objects to interact with. The interactive kinetic structural system merges kinetic sculpture and lighting control mechanism for new kind of luminaire art deco, which provides a kinetic interaction mode according to variable-lights.

The detail of kinetic structure, is made by a frame of whisker form is fixed on abase, majority of disk are interval fixed on the frame along one axis direction of the frame, majority of driver are arranged in the base, at least one wire is driven by each one of the driver so as to restrict the frame flexible, majority of light sensor are arranged in the base, the each one of light sensor is electrical connected to the driver, those light sensors can sensing the ambient light intensity, so as to command the drives to pull or release the wire, then enable to drive the frame flexible.

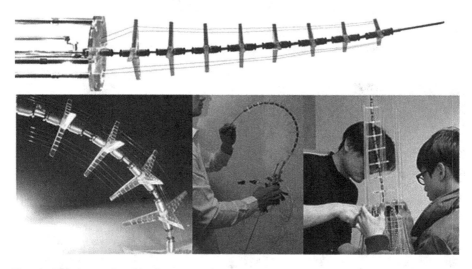

Fig. 4. The interactive kinetic structural system used metaphor of Phototropism building algorithm for whisker-liked object interact by using actuators to control the wire's tension and compression for effecting physically transform on flexible structure design.

5 Display as an Interactive Art

This work extends the technological installation art into the space issue, exploring the various features of the ambient display and transforming the kinetic interaction constitute with atmosphere display into a space. The presentation of this work is thus liberated, inviting user to experience the aesthetics into ambient space. Transparent Organ also integrates the kinetic architectural structure into "kinetic sculpture" development, and the service situation with alternative illumination function, encouraging user to interact with the luminaire. It thus creates an interactive relationship between the luminaire and users in the experimental performance.

In this project, the application of digital technology does not appeal to much practical function. Instead, it starts from the perspective of interactive art to search of possibilities to be attached to the furnishing elements, through which the form has been represented. It means that the application of interactive art bases on the expression of visual art and it further explores the functional interaction with participators in the space. The use of digital technology in "Transparent Organ" visualizes the phototropism metaphor mechanism to interact with users. There are three micro-sensors set up under the installation to detect users touch contact real-time. The micro-sensors stimulate the microprocessor's computing mechanism of the dynamic assemblies, calculated by the physical computing. The materiality of the digital information represents a biologic, which allows the real-time interaction with participators. In the work, the actuator element propels the material of the cable wire, changing the elasticity coefficient of the dynamic construction and stimulating the curves. In the end, it combines living beings' adaptive behaviors with kinetic motion and atmosphere in space to form the reaction (Fig. 5).

Fig. 5. Transparent Organ plays as a luminaire art deco, producing ambient atmosphere in a space.

6 Conclusion

In the project "Transparent Organ," digital technology plays an important role, which is not merely the tool to assist the artwork making process but an ambient display interface to create conversation and to connect the luminaire art deco and the users. Under the definition of computing mechanism, it starts a collaborated operation among the actuators, lighting, and sensors of the kinetic artifacts, revealing the effects of strategic kinetic interaction and the expansion of atmosphere. As for its cross-disciplinary integration, digital design and fabrication processes merged the virtual computation and physical properties together to form a workable framework for the interactive kinetic structural system, which combines the "adaptive interaction system" in the field of artificial intelligence and the "kinetic structural system" in the field of architecture technique to represent its phototropism metaphor behaviors. The adaptive interaction system augmented the luminaire with behavioral features. Through the kinetic structural system design, it demonstrates soft visual vocabulary, creating an intimate conversation with users.

Recently, the kinetic design has become an emerging trend. It adopts the developments of kinetic structures, actuators' components, robot technology, and kinetic transformative installation to create a luminaire art deco. Through the sensors, the installation can detect the behavioral changes of the participators in the environment in order to adjust its own behavior. These techniques allow the interactive installation to collective information from the environment, to changes its form as reaction, and to create a responsive space-situation art form. In the project "Transparent Organ," the computing mechanism and the bionic kinetic simulation create the artificial life metaphor through the substantial installation. It adopts techniques from the fields of electronics, electric machinery, and information process as well as the computing mechanisms of sensor's cyber system to produce a kinetic technological artwork with artificial perceptivity. The work is constituted by computing components, sensing components, and the components of the kinetic transformation mechanism within the systemic relationship of the interface. The bionic kinetic behaviors are created as the response to users' contact.

References

1. Mitchell, J.W., McCullough, M.: Digital Design Media. Wiley, New York (1994)
2. Baerlecken, D., Manegold, M., Reitz, J., Kuenstler, A.: Integrative parametric form-finding processes. In: Proceedings of the 15th International Conference on Computer Aided Architectural Design Research in Asia, pp. 303–312 (2010)
3. Huang, Y.C., Wu, K.Y., Liu, Y.T.: Future home design: an emotional communication channel approach to smart space. Pers. Ubiquit. Comput. 17(6), 1281–1293 (2013)
4. Coelho, M., Zigelbaum, Z.: Shape-changing interfaces. Pers. Ubiquit. Comput. J. 15(2), 161–173 (2011)
5. Schweikardt, E., Gross, M.D.: Experiments in design synthesis when behavior is determined by shape. Pers. Ubiquit. Comput. J. 15(2), 123–132 (2011)
6. Oxman, N., Laucks, J., Kayser, M., Duro-Royo, J., Gonzales-Uribe, C.: Silk pavilion: a case study in fiber-based digital fabrication. In: FABRICATE Conference Proceedings, pp. 248–255. Riverside Architectural Press, Ontario (2014)
7. Oxman, N.: Material-based design computation. Ph.D. Thesis, Department of Architecture, Massachusetts Institute of Technology (2010)
8. Mirjan, A., Gramazio, F., Kohler, M.: Building with flying robots. In: FABRICATE Conference Proceedings: Negotiating Design and Making, pp. 266–271. Riverside Architectural Press, Ontario (2014)

9. Fox, M., Kemp, M.: Interactive Architecture. Princeton Architectural Press, New York (2009)
10. Ahlquist, S., Fleischmann, M.: Computational spring systems: open design processes for complex structural systems. Archit. Design **79**(2), 130–133 (2009)
11. Hoberman, C.: Expanding video screen for U2 360°. Tour. Archit. Urban. **2010**(2), 119–121 (2010)
12. Sterk, T.D.: Using actuated tensegrity structures to produce a responsive architecture. In: 23th International Conference of the Association for Computer Aided Design in Architecture, pp. 24–27 (2003)
13. Beesley, P.: Hylozoic Ground. Riverside Architectural Press, Ontario (2010)
14. Oosterhuis, K., Biloria, N.: Interactions with proactive architectural spaces: the muscle projects. Commun. ACM **51**(6), 70–78 (2008)
15. Outerspace: reactive robotic creature. http://www.andrestubbe.com/outerspace/

Usability of Touchpad Based Game Controller Interfaces

Jonathon Kissinger and Tony Morelli[✉]

Department of Computer Science, Central Michigan University,
Mount Pleasant, USA
{kissilj,tony.morelli}@cmich.edu

Abstract. This paper examines the use of a new input device that is available on two video game systems released in the past year. The Ouya controller and the Dual Shock 4 controller for the Playstation 4 contain a touchpad located in the center of the control-ler. This type of input mechanism is also expected be a feature of the planned Steam Controller by Valve. Even though the touchpad is currently available to developers, few games take advantage of it. This paper analyzes the usability of touchpad based game interfaces for the Ouya Controller and the Dual Shock 4 controller in both a gaming environment and in a controlled user interface study. The results show that traditional thumbstick controls are preferred and perform significantly better than the touchpad interfaces for 2D driving games, and that hand posture can significantly affect the usability of game controller based touchpad interfaces.

Keywords: Video games · Console · Ouya · Android · iOS · Apple · Sony

1 Introduction

As new video game console hardware is released, game developers have access to new types of input mechanisms. In this paper the use of the touchpad integrated into the game controller is investigated. A touchpad on the game controller is available on the standard Ouya controller, Dual Shock 4 controller, and on the planned Steam Controller. With touchpads becoming a standard interface mechanism on game controllers, it is important that their usability is understood.

1.1 Game Consoles

Ouya [8] is a micro game console released in 2013. Ouya runs Android as its base operating system, which should allow for simple methods of porting mobile games, or may even allow some mobile games to run unmodified. The micro console is relatively inexpensive ($99) and comes with its own controller. Ouya's controller contains a directional pad, four action buttons, two analog sticks, two analog shoulder buttons, as well as a single touch touchpad centered on the top of the game controller. By default this touchpad is represented as a mouse on an Android device which allows games designed exclusively for touch to have some methods of interaction on the micro console without modifying the source code of the original game.

© Springer International Publishing Switzerland 2015
A. Marcus (Ed.): DUXU 2015, Part II, LNCS 9187, pp. 452–463, 2015.
DOI: 10.1007/978-3-319-20898-5_44

The Dual Shock 4 controller is the standard controller that ships with the Play-station 4 [9] game console. Like the Ouya controller, it contains a directional pad, four action buttons, two analog sticks, two analog shoulder buttons, as well as a single touch touchpad centered on the top of the game controller. The touchpad on the Dual Shock 4 controller has an expanded feature set when compared to Ouya's controller. The Dual Shock 4 is multi touch capable, and it also contains a physical delineation of the location of the touchpad and it is a movable surface. That is when the touchpad is *clicked*, it can physically move downward.

The Steam Controller [11] is a future product to be released by Valve for use on Steam Machine systems. Steam Machines will allow players to play PC based games through a more traditional console gaming experience. Valve has not committed to releasing a version of a Steam Machine, however they have committed to releasing a controller that can be used with their software running on Steam Machines created by third parties. The Steam Controller contains four action buttons and two shoulder buttons. The standard analog sticks have been replaced with two track pads (one for each thumb). Similar to the Oyua controller and the Dual Shock 4 controllers, the Steam Controller contains a touchpad centered and near the top of the controller.

1.2 Related Work

Not many games have made use of the touchpad feature of the new consoles [5]. This research seeks to discover uses for the touchpad or possibly uncover why its use is so rare. The research space handling fine motion controls is defined by Fitt's Law as shown in ISO 9421-9 [1]. This standard puts forth requirements for non-keyboard based input devices and also shows a user-based performance test. ISO 9421-9 has been used in analyzing different methods of video game input [7] and human computer interaction [6]. Natapov [7] looked into the performance differences of a Wii Remote, a standard gaming controller, and a computer mouse for a 2D target selection task. The Natapov study used mouse input as a baseline and then compared the two gaming control input options. Their study found that mouse based input performed better than controller or Wii Remote based input. This study will use the Natapov study as a baseline and draw parallels between Ouya's standard controller and the controller used in in that study before investigating new control mechanisms.

Throughput has also been shown to be an effective method of comparing pointing based interfaces as shown in [4]. Mouse down based selection tasks were shown to have higher performance than tasks based on mouse up events. As a result of this, the design involves touch down based selections. Throughput will be calculated for all fine motion selection tasks to ensure confidence in the experimental setup.

1.3 Contribution

This paper presents two different user studies investigating the use of the touchpad on game controllers. Section 2 compares different touchpad control methods with standard thumbstick controls by investigating their usage in a game environment. Section 3 compares 2D target acquisition using different game controller touchpad hand positions.

2 Use of Touchpad in Games

In order to test the use of the touchpad on a game controller, a game originally created for a mobile Android phone was ported to be used on the Ouya console. The original mobile game was written in CoronaSDK [3] and was chosen as it had features for testing the touchpad interface, as well as it could be easily ran on the Ouya console due to CoronaSDK supporting the console directly. The game was a top down driving game where the player was in control of a garbage truck. The truck would automatically move forward, and the controls for the player were to steer the truck left or right to pick up bags of garbage located on the right and left sides of the street. At the conclusion of the round, players could win bonus points by selecting green garbage bags from a grid shown on the screen. This game was chosen to test touchpad controls because it offers both gross motion controls (steering the truck) and fine motion controls (choosing a bonus garbage bag).

2.1 Interface Design

Three different input methods were identified (mouse like, thumbstick, and mobile like) to control the game play aspects and they will be described in detail below. A user study was performed to determine which input mechanism has the highest performance.

Looking at control options to handle the large motions required to steer the garbage truck, results were utilized from a study investigating different types of control mechanisms for different viewpoints of driving games [2]. This study showed thumbstick control of an overhead view (similar to this game) outperformed first person or third high perspective which makes thumbstick control a viable option for this style of game.

2.2 Mouse Like Interface

Easiest to implement, the mouse like interface was the result of simply rebuilding the game to run on Ouya. In this interface, players could control the truck by using Ouya's touchpad like a mouse on a laptop. Finger swipes would move a pointer on the screen, and when pressed a touch down event was triggered at the location of the pointer. A touch release event was triggered at the pointer's position on the screen when the player removed his finger from the touchpad after pressing down. Simply swiping the finger across the touchpad had no effect on the gameplay as it only moved the pointer across the screen. After pressing and holding on the touchpad, touch moved events were also registered.

When the round was over and the player was prompted to select trash bags in order to earn bonus points, the player would move the pointer to the desired target by swiping across the touchpad which moved the mouse pointer on the screen, then pressing down to select the target. This is much like using a touchpad on a laptop to select a target.

2.3   Thumbstick Interface

A more traditional console experience was available due to Ouya's controller. A thumbstick control mechanism was implemented where the truck's navigation was controlled by moving the left thumbstick left and right. Pressing the thumbstick left would move the truck to the left, and pressing right would move it to the right. The controls appeared intuitive and simple to use.

An issue arose at the completion of the round where the player had to select different trash bags to earn bonus points. In the original mobile version of the game, players could make their choice by simply tapping on the screen where their desired bag was located. In the mouse like interface, players would scroll the mouse pointer over to the location of the bag to select and then tap on the touchpad. In the thumbstick version, there was no method for the player to select a bag as there was no pointer. To make that portion of the game playable, a highlight method was implemented, where the selected bag was highlighted by a semi-transparent glow. The player could move through the different choices by moving the thumbstick to the left or to the right and the highlight would follow. When the player had the desired bag highlighted, he would press the O button on the controller to select the bag.

2.4   Mobile Like Interface

With all the control options available on Ouya, a new type of interface was utilized. In this method, the direction of the truck was determined by the direction of the touchpad swipes. That is, as the player moved his finger across the touchpad on the controller, the truck would follow. When the player stopped moving his finger, the truck would stop. This was all done by scrolling with the touchpad, there was no need to press, and then move as required by the default mouse actions. This allowed players a more standard mobile touch interface on Ouya. Several rail shooters exist where swiping will move the player to a different rail, and although the game did not have predefined rails, the truck would move in the direction the player swiped. One downside to this method was that the mouse pointer was still visible on the screen the entire time, although it had no effect on the gameplay. This could be distracting to players.

At the end of the round, it would be possible to use the mouse like interface in order to select a bag, however that may have been confusing to players. In the regular gameplay the pointer icon on the screen had no effect on the game, and then changing it to have some meaning in the bonus selection may be confusing. It was decided to not have the pointer have any effect on the controls. In the bonus selection round, the same highlight method described in the thumbstick section was used, except for the moving of the highlight was slightly different. Moving the highlight was done by swiping the finger across the touchpad, just as the steering the truck was done in this section. Once the player highlighted the desired bag, he would need to tap anywhere on the touchpad to make the selection.

2.5   User Study

In order to determine how different touchpad input mechanisms compare to thumbstick input on a 2D driving game, a user study was devised to play the three different modes of gameplay. The user study is to identify which methods of input work best on gross motion conversions (steering the truck) and which methods work best on fine motion conversions (choosing the bag at the end of the round). Players were randomly recruited for this study and all had no self-identified impairments or any kind of disability that would prevent the use of a mobile device or controlling Ouya through its controller. The subjects played the game in isolation with only the administrator of the study present.

For the user study, the game consisted of three 50 s rounds. Each round consisted of a different control mechanism, and contained the same number of bags, however the side of the street the bags were on was a random sequence. The game randomly chose the sequence of the three methods for each player. Prior to beginning each round, the game would display a message indicating which mode the player was about to play. The administrator also gave a quick demonstration of the method of play. When the player was confident the control mechanism was understood, he was given the controller and pressed the O button in order to initiate play. Each collected bag in the steering portion of the game was awarded points. Although the bags were presented at a consistent rate, players were awarded a score for each bag based on their ability to steer the truck to the correct side of the street. The quicker the truck was in the correct position to collect the bag, the more points the player received. This created an environment where the player had the desire to quickly use each method in order to obtain a high score.

The bonus bag selection portion of the game presented players with a 4 × 4 grid of garbage bags with five of them randomly colored green. The player would need to select all the green bags in order to complete the bag selection portion of the game. The quicker the player selected the bags, the more points he would be awarded. The game logged the location and time of the selections. The distance from the previous selection was also logged. All player interactions were logged with millisecond accuracy and were used in measuring the different interaction techniques.

The bags of garbage were presented to the player on either the right or left side of the screen in a random sequence. In order to have an element of unpredictability, it was possible for two or more sequential bags of trash to appear on the same side of the road. This could lead to an artificially lower reaction time as the player would not need to react to the situation. To account for this in the data analysis, the data for any bag that appeared on the same side of the screen without the player moving was not considered a qualifying bag and the data associated with that bag was not used in the calculations for this study.

The user study consisted of 15 graduate and undergraduate students playing through three levels. Each level provided the opportunity to collect 10 bags of trash in the steering portion of the game and requiring five bags to be selected in the bonus portion of the game. Players had five seconds to react to a bag coming down the street. If the bag was completely missed by the player, it was counted as a five second reaction time in the analysis. The horizontal rate of travel was consistent across all control mechanisms.

2.6   Technical Evaluation

The time required for a player to either successfully or unsuccessfully capture a qualifying bag was averaged for each player for each control mechanism. The results of these sets of data was averaged to determine the better control option. The average seek time for the controls are shown in Table 1. An analysis of variance (ANOVA) showed significant difference between the control methods for seek time $F(2,42) = 42.596$, $p < 0.01$. A post hoc Tukey test at the 95 % confidence level revealed that the Thumbstick controls were significantly better than either of the touchpad controls $(p < 0.01)$.

Table 1. Comparison of large motions

Control type	Avg seek time (ms)	Stdev
Thumbstick	2156.91	435.77
Mouse like	3930.62	641.15
Mobile like	3958.78	724.41

In addition to timing, how successful the player was in actually grabbing each bag was analyzed. The results are summarized in Table 2. An analysis of variance (ANOVA) for miss rates showed a significant difference, $F(2,42) = 25.21$, $p < 0.01$. A post hoc Tukey test at the 95 % confidence level showed the Thumbstick control significantly outperformed both methods of touchpad control $(p < 0.01)$. The ranking of all of the interaction techniques was consistent for the large motion steering portion of the game with thumbstick control being the most successful and mouse and mobile control trailing.

Table 2. Comparison of large motion miss rates

Control type	Avg miss rate	Stdev
Thumbstick	0.07	0.10
Mouse like	0.35	0.20
Mobile like	0.57	0.24

Small motion controls followed a similar trend with thumbstick control being the most successful followed by mouse and mobile controls. To evaluate small motions, players were to select five green highlighted bags on the screen from a grid of 16 total. In mouse like controls, players were able to directly move the mouse pointer on top of the desired bag. The other two controls featured a semi-transparent glow highlighting the bag to select. In the mouse like control mechanism it was possible for players to make a selection that was not on any target. In this case there was no penalty. Similarly, in the other two control mechanisms, players were always selecting a bag, however it was possible to select a bag that was not shown in green. In either case players were not penalized for making an incorrect selection.

The normalized time – taking into account distance - required to select each green bag was recorded and saved for later analysis. An analysis of variance (ANOVA) showed significant variation on this data $F(2,42) = 42.75$ $p < 0.01$. A post hoc Tukey test with a confidence level of 0.95 showed the Thumbstick control was significantly better than both of the touchpad control interfaces (p < 0.01).

The Natapov study [7], compared the performance of mouse based input, Wii Remote based input and standard gaming controller based input using throughput as a metric. Throughput was calculated for the three control mechanisms and summarized the findings in Table 3. The throughput values in bits per second were calculated according to the mean of means equation [10]. Comparing the throughput for the standard control mechanism, Ouya's thumbstick controls were found to have a throughput of 1.33 bits per second. The Natapov study found the standard gaming controller to have a throughput of 1.48 bps, compared to a mouse which was 3.78 bps. A different study [4] found throughput for mouse down selections to be 4.71 bps. The similar throughput for controller based interactions between this study and the Natapov study demonstrates the experimental setup is accurate.

Table 3. Throughput

Control type	Throughput (bps)
Thumbstick	1.33
Mouse like	0.65
Mobile like	0.38

The mouse like controls using Ouya's controller were found to have a throughput of 0.65 bps which is much lower than other studies found using a standard computer mouse. Although using the touchpad on Ouya as a mouse may be expected to have a similar throughput value, using the thumbs instead of the index finger may have had an influence on the results.

2.7   Game Interaction Recommendations

Although the game was quickly ported to run on Ouya, several issues were found when implementing different control mechanisms. In order to properly use the touchpad in a gaming environment, the following suggestions are made:

(1) *Hide the cursor unless it is useful* - Players in this study would focus on the visible mouse pointer even though it had no effect on certain control mechanisms.

(2) *Return actual press locations* - In order to better mimic touch based devices, the underlying drivers should always return the touch events including pressed, released, and moved in touchpad coordinates as opposed to screen mouse cursor coordinates.

(3) *Improve on fine movements* - Ouya's controller appears to have issues with small movements on the touchpad. If a touchpad is to be used for fine movements, it should be able to report small movements from the player to the game layer such that players can receive immediate feedback on their motions.

(4) *Add tactile feedback* - Ouya's controller may benefit from additional pieces of tactile information. A physical border around the active touch area may assist players in properly placing their thumbs on the touchpad.

3   ISO 9241-9 User Interface Study

To determine how hand position affected the usability of the DualShock 4 touchpad, a second user study was created where participants were asked to go through a series of 2 dimensional target selection tasks using four different hand positions. Hand positions have been investigated in different touch applications [12], however this study looks specifically at touchpad interfaces on game controllers. For this portion of the study, the Dual Shock 4 controller was used as it addresses some of the issues found in the previous game study using the Ouya console. The Dual Shock 4 contains tactile information about the bounds of the active touch area as well as a movable region that gives tactile acknowledgement of a successful click. In order to better represent how using a controller may work in a gaming environment, some of the exercises required players to also use the physical buttons as input.

The four hand positions were:

(1) *Finger Press* - Index Finger to move pointer and target selection by pressing the touchpad

(2) *Finger Button* - Index Finger to move pointer and target selection by pressing the X Button

(3) *Thumb Press* - Right Thumb to move pointer and target selection by pressing the touchpad

(4) *Thumb Button* - Right Thumb to move pointer and target selection by pressing the X Button

Users were presented with four different selection tasks for each of the hand positions as defined by the following:

(1)   15 Large targets around a large circle
(2)   7 Large targets around a small circle
(3)   13 Small targets around a small circle
(4)   23 Small targets around a large circle

The sequence of the selection tasks was always the same, however the sequence of hand positions was randomly chosen each time the game was run. At the conclusion of all four target selection tasks for all four hand positions, the user was presented with a score and a game over message. All participants in the study performed all 16 task combinations twice.

3.1   Target Selection Software

The user interface application software was created in Unity3D and handled the presentation of the targets, the random selection of input types, as well as a scoring mechanism. Although not directly relevant to the outcome of the user study, a score was given that represented how quickly the participant selected the targets. This was done to give motivation to the participants to select targets as quickly as possible. The score for each target selection began at 20,000 points, and one point was subtracted for each millisecond that it took for the participant to successfully acquire a target. If a target selection took longer than 20 s, the player was awarded 0 points for the selection of that target. Using this mechanism, a higher score was indicative of a better performing user. Players were notified of the highest score prior to beginning the first trial, and prior to beginning the second trial they were notified of the highest score as well as their previous score. Familiarity with the tasks and motivation to at the very least beat the player's own trial one score should increase the scores, or decrease the time required to select targets in the second round.

The application followed the patterns set forth within ISO 9241-9. Targets moved around circle with targets alternating roughly 180 degrees apart. For example, the first target was located at the 12 O'clock position, the second target would be located at the 6:30 position, the third target would be located at the 1 O'clock position, the fourth target would be located at the 7:30 position and so on. This pattern of target selection is suggested in ISO 9241-9. Players selected large targets in both a large diameter selection space and a small diameter selection space, and then selected small targets across the same two diameter selections spaces.

15 users (11 male), participated in the user study. 14 of the participants reported they were right handed and the average age was 29.67 years (SD = 6.71). Six of the participants preferred to use a touchpad over a mouse in regular everyday computer use. Participants performed the study in a quiet room with an administrator present, and completed both sessions of the 16 input combinations and target sizes in one sitting. At the conclusion of the user study, participants were given a brief written survey.

3.2   Results

The four different target selection tasks were analyzed separately, and each of the control types were compared. All players played through each of the selection tasks twice, and all data for their trials were used. A total of 5760 targets were selected throughout the user study and were used for the quantitative analysis.

In the large target around the large circle task, a analysis of variance (ANOVA) showed significant variation $F(3,116) = 4.02$, $p < 0.01$. A post hoc Tukey test at 9\% confidence level showed the only significant difference at $p < 0.05$ in this target selection task was that the Finger Press selection task was significantly faster than the Thumb Press selection task. All other comparisons yielded no significant difference. In the large target around the small circle task, a analysis of variance (ANOVA) showed no significant variation $F(3,116) = 2.52$, $p > 0.01$.

In the small target around the small circle task, a analysis of variance (ANOVA) showed significant variation $F(3,116) = 8.17$, $p < 0.01$. A post hoc Tukey test at 95 % confidence level showed the significant difference at $p < 0.05$ for three hand position combinations. Finger Press selection was significantly faster than both Thumb Press and Thumb Button selection. Finger Button was also significantly faster than Thumb and Tap selection. All other combinations yielded no significant difference.

In the small target around the large circle task, a analysis of variance (ANOVA) showed significant variation $F(3,116) = 11.78$, $p < 0.01$. A post hoc Tukey test at 95 % confidence level showed the significant difference at $p < 0.05$ for four hand position combinations. Finger Press selection was significantly faster than both Thumb Press and Thumb Button selection. Finger Button selection was also significantly faster than both Thumb Press and Thumb Button selection. All other combinations yielded no significant difference.

At the conclusion of their second trial, participants were asked to rank their preference of the four control options, with a value of 1 indicating the worst control mechanism, and a value of 4 indicating the most preferred control mechanism. Overall, participants preferred the control by using the index finger and making selections with the x button. A summary of the results is shown in Table 4. An ANOVA showed significant variation in these results $F(3,56) = 6.757$, $p < 0.01$. A post hoc Tukey test at 95 % confidence level showed that for $p < 0.01$, both Finger control mechanisms are significantly preferred to the Thumb Press control mechanism, and at the $p < 0.05$ level, the Finger Button control mechanism is significantly preferred over the Thumb Button control mechanism.

Table 4. User preference of control types (Higher is more preferred)

Control type	Avg rank	Stdev
Thumb Press	1.80	0.94
Thumb Button	2.07	1.10
Finger Press	3.00	1.13
Finger Button	3.13	0.74

Using Fitt's law, throughput was calculated for the 2D target acquisition test in the same manner as it was for the fine motor control section of the previously described game study. The results of the throughput test using the Playstation Dual Shock 4 controller show that the Finger Press interface combination produced the best throughput followed by Finger Button, Thumb Button, and the worst performing was the Thumb Press. The exact values are shown in Table 5.

Table 5. Dual Shock 4 Throughput (bps). Average is the average of all 4 target selection tasks. Large Circle/Small Target reports only on the last target selection task.

Control type	Avg	Large circle/small target
Thumb Press	0.45	0.49
Thumb Button	0.47	0.52
Finger Press	0.55	0.65
Finger Button	0.52	0.62

4 Discussion

The results shown in this user study present an issue for game developers wishing to use this new piece of game controller hardware. The touchpad performs worse than the standard thumbsticks, and worse than the results of previous studies that looked at the usability of a standard mouse. The first game developed for this user study pointed out the fact that the touch pad was worse than the thumbsticks. The follow up study showed index finger usage was significantly better than using the thumbs. The design of the controllers for both the Ouya controller and the Dual Shock 4 controller allow for natural access to the center touch area by the thumbs, however actually using this method yields poor performance. Using the index finger by itself yields the best performance for 2D target selection tasks which may indicate that the touchpad should only be used for menu access if it needs to be used. Using the touchpad for seldom used tasks such as browsing the internet through a gaming console may warrant the inclusion of this device on every controller, however if a console application such as a web browser is to be frequently used, console owners may prefer the convenience of a dedicated mouse interface.

5 Conclusion

This paper explored the use of a new feature which is becoming common on game controllers, the touchpad. An initial game showed that touchpad based control of a 2D driving game was significantly worse than using the standard thumbsticks. A more thorough investigation of the touchpad found interacting with the touchpad while using the index finger to be significantly better than using the touchpad with the thumbs. This indicates that the use of this type of interface may be best utilized when moving the hand position from the standard game controller grasp will not effect the overall game play experience such as navigating menus, or browsing the internet through a console.

References

1. 9421-9 Ergonomic requirements for office work with visual display terminals (vdts) - part 9: Requirements for non-keyboard input devices. International Organization for Standardization (2000)
2. Bateman, S., Doucette, A., Xiao, R., Gutwin, C., Mandryk, R.L., Cockburn, A.: Effects of view, input device, and track width on video game driving. In: Proceedings of Graphics Interface Conference 2011, pp. 207–214 (2011)
3. Corona Labs Inc. Cross platform mobile app development for ios and android, Nov 2013. http://www.coronalabs.com
4. Isokoski, P.: Variability of throughput in pointing device tests: Button up or button down? In: Proceedings of NirdiCHI 2006, pp. 68–77 (2006)
5. Kissinger, J., Morelli, T.: Ouya: The launch of anew video game paradigm. GSTF Int. J. Comput. 3(4), 48–54 (2014)
6. MacKenzie, I.S.: Fitts law as a research and design tool in human computer interaction. Hum.-Comput. Interact. 7, 91–139 (1992)
7. Natapov, D., Castellucci, S.J., MacKenzie, I.S: Iso9241-9 evaluation of video game controllers. In: Proceedings of Graphics Interface Conference 2009, pp. 223–230 (2009)
8. Ouya Inc. Ouya, Nov 2013. http://ouya.tv
9. Sony Computer Entertainment America LLC. Playstation 4, May 2014. http://us.playstation.com/ps4

10. Soukore, R.W., MacKenzie, I.S.: Towards a standard for pointing device evaluation, perspectives on 27 years of fitts law research in hci. Int. J. Hum.-Comput. Stud. **61**, 751–789 (2004)
11. Valve Corporation. Steam controller, May 2014. http://store.steampowered.com/livingroom/SteamController
12. Wobbrock, J.O., Myers, B.A., Aung, H.H.: The performance of hand postures in front and back-of-device interaction for mobile computing. Int. J. Hum.-Comput. Stud. **66**(12), 857–875 (2009)

Usability Evaluation of Kinect-Based System for Ballet Movements

Milka Trajkova$^{(\boxtimes)}$ and Mexhid Ferati

South East European University, Skopje, Macedonia
{mt19992,m.ferati}@seeu.edu.mk

Abstract. Since the 1800s, ballet education is influenced by the use of mirrors. The aim of this study is to evaluate a Kinect-based system called Super Mirror, to discover if it has an impact on the usability in ballet instruction. Ballet students were evaluated on eight ballet movements (plié, élevé, grand plié, battement tendu (front, side and back), passé and développé) to measure the Super Mirror's impact. The results show a potential usage in ballet education but improvements of Super Mirror are needed to comply with the standardized subject-matter expert's criteria.

Keywords: Usability · Kinect · Ballet · User evaluation

1 Introduction

Gray, a pioneer for dance technology once said, "Dance, the oldest art, is today but a young science" [6]. Ballet instruction roots in the studio and is composed of three components: barre, specialized flooring and mirrors. Today, its traditional approach is still in use; the learning environment of mirror use in ballet likely began sometime in the eighteenth century, although historically the genesis is not clearly documented [5]. Mirrors thus become central to a dancer's ballet education. The psychology of a dancer is built around it as it is taught around it. The mirror becomes the source for a dancer on how others view them and the portrayal of success of their technique [11]. A dancer's perception of themselves is partially bound to the existence of mirrors in traditional dance environments. It contributes a physical self-evaluation, behavior regulation, and competition in dancers [7]. Its traditional approach has been the subject of a new methodology suggested by Marquardt et al. titled, Super Mirror [9]. It is a system developed through the use of Kinect-based technology that "combines the functionality of studio mirrors and prescriptive images to provide the user with instructional feedback in real-time" [9].

While the Super Mirror and the similar YouMove system by Anderson et al. develop a comprehensive evaluative methodology [2], the focus was not on benchmarking the systems to the expertise of ballet teachers. A need remains for a method to evaluate the quality of feedback received from the Super Mirror, a reference system, to the expertise of a subject matter, a ballet teacher, a control. Testing the quality of feedback will indicate a level of effectiveness of the system and ensure potential efficiency as a learning tool for ballet. The purpose of this study focuses on the

© Springer International Publishing Switzerland 2015
A. Marcus (Ed.): DUXU 2015, Part II, LNCS 9187, pp. 464–472, 2015.
DOI: 10.1007/978-3-319-20898-5_45

effectiveness and efficiency of the feedback received from the Super Mirror on pre-professional ballet dancers. Can a system prove to be as accurate as a ballet teacher in assessing the quality of dancers' movements?

2 Related Work

Studying the effects of mirrors in dancers' perceptions of themselves with regard to their performance and as a guide to self-correction is not new. Studies by Radell et al. [12] have suggested that the use of a mirror in a ballet classroom may negatively affect the skill acquisition of the dancer and ultimately impact their performance, which has contradicted the results from Dearborn et al. [3]. The first study [12] has concluded that while 85.7 % of dancers remarked that the use of mirrors has influenced their understanding of the concepts taught, satisfaction with overall appearance decreased for high performing dancers in a mirrored class [11]. Green has expressed, in a critique of traditional dance instruction, "the constant focus on an externalized view of the body, as reflected in the mirror, objectifies the dancer's body and requires students to strive to achieve a specific 'look' while being 'corrected' so the students perform 'proper' dance technique" [7]. While the mirror provides immediate visual feedback in real-time, it also may result in a false perception of a dancer's weaknesses. The consciousness of thoughts contributed by the mirror may welcome detrimental effects in the overall well-being of the dancer and hinder the development of their technique.

In order to combat the given negative effects of mirror in ballet instruction, researchers have turned to technology to help aide teachers and students alike as a guide to self-correction. This study [2] compared the YouMove system to traditional video-based instruction methods and has discovered that learning increased using the system. Another study [4] reported the effects of real-time virtual reality (VR) feedback on motor skills and explored the ability to focus the learner to key features of a to-be learned action. Similarly, [16] has identified that video analyses support a basis for rank-specific supplemental training in ballet companies. Video analyses help, "teachers...tailor their classes to the appropriate intensity and can create combinations...that can replicate the demands of specific roles" [16]. Further studies [8] have revealed that students considered streaming video as effective for carrying out self-evaluation. Other studies have suggested computer animations benefit dancers with experience and are at least as effective for learners without dance experience in contrast to video [13].

3 Research Methodology

A controlled study was conducted using pre-professional ballet dancers to compare the Super Mirror's assessment of movements, an embedded reference system, to the evaluation of a ballet teacher, the control. A total of 5 ballet students from the State Ballet School, Ilija-Nikolovski Luj from Skopje, Macedonia were tested. The pre-professional students were between the ages of 16 to 18 with an average of 8.8 years of ballet education. Each student has class 5 times a week with each class lasting for an hour and 30 min, excluding rehearsals for performances. Eight movements provided by the Super Mirror: plié, élevé, grand plié, battement tendu (front, side and back), passé and développé were assessed. Each movement has an embedded reference model, a predefined movement template that measured the correct matches or "hits" as referred by the terminology reported in [9] by comparing the set of thresholds of the x, y and z rotational values of the left upper leg, right upper leg, left lower leg and right lower leg. The only interaction the Super Mirror had was motion-capture. This was "performed by joint skeleton tracking through a Kinect camera, and the transfer of input from the camera to the processor [was] mediated by the Synapse application [14]. The specific interfaces developed for [the] system use the Tryplex toolkit [15], a set of open source macro patches for Quartz Composer" [9].

Intentionally, each dancer began with alteration, either with or without the Super Mirror to nullify any possible effects of the dancer to accustom to the system. This will avoid the ability to receive a higher number of "hits" without achieving higher performance techniques. Additionally, to remove any influence caused by the Super Mirror, the teacher was positioned where she was unable to view the screen where the Super Mirror was projected. Differentiated from the YouMove design, the experiment added a control, a ballet teacher, for the purposed of testing the reference system, the Super Mirror.

3.1 Procedure

Testing the dancers involved setting up the Super Mirror and having the system displayed on a 37" LCD screen in a wide room to most closely resemble a ballet studio. A pre-test questionnaire was first distributed to all of the participants to capture certain demographics such as age, how long they have been dancing ballet for, how many hours per week do they dance, etc. The dancers were tested in an ascending order by grade in order to keep a clear and logical flow. One by one, the dancers were tested on the eight movements. Each movement was performed enface (to the front) according to a number of times predetermined from the ballet teacher. This number was due to the artistic nature of ballet. It was necessary and essential to mimic the number of times each movement was performed as in a typical ballet class to evoke as closely as possible its natural environment. All the movements, plié, grand plié, battement tendu (front, side and back), passé and développé except for élevé, were performed 4 times. Élevé was performed 8 times. Figure 1 explains the procedure of testing one participant.

Each test comprised of eight movements. Each movement was conducted in two sequences (S1 and S2). Each sequence comprised of two parts, P1 and P2 that included with and without (W/O) the Super Mirror. Between each sequence, a one-minute break was given to allow for rest. The teacher evaluated each part and assessed the student's performance on a scale of one to ten based on a set of criteria specific to each movement. During the test, when the part with the Super Mirror was included, the dancer's accuracy of performed movement was measured against the embedded reference model in the system. The dancers' successful performance was registered by the system as a number of matches or "hits" as offered by the terminology used in [9]. The roles of Kinect and the teacher were complementary. The teacher assessed the technique elements that were not tested by the system to determine its effectiveness. After all the students were tested, a System Usability Scale (SUS) was administered to both

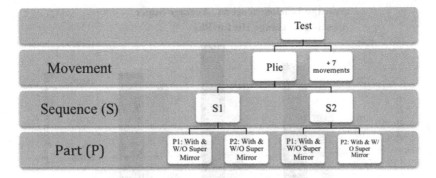

Fig. 1. Experiment procedure for a single participant

Fig. 2. Dancers performing a plié (left) and passé (right) using the Super Mirror

the students and the teacher, which also included open-ended questions. A short discussion was held to gather feedback about the system. Figure 2 shows the dancers using the Super Mirror during the experiment.

4 Results and Discussion

Data from previous studies involving the testing of the YouMove system [2] reveal the effectiveness of using such systems when compared to traditional video-based instruction methods. In our study, the focus was the comparison of such a system to the knowledge of a domain specific expert. The results concentrated on three specific

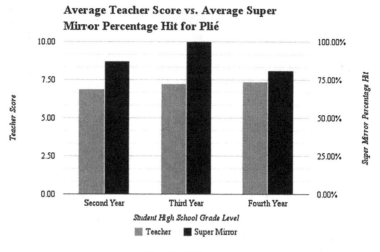

Fig. 3. Plié score

movements, plié, élevé and tendu front. The other five movements, grand plié, tendu side, tendu back, passé and développé to the side, were not included because the Super Mirror results were non-conclusive. This was most likely due to the inability to adapt the reference model of the movements to the height of the dancers.

Further investigation is needed to accurately calibrate the reference template to the specificity of each dancer. Adequately, the possibility for comparison between the Super Mirror and the teacher was impossible. The following figures represent aggregate results of the three movements. The aggregation of the scores of each movement was based on the grade level of the student (x-axis), the average teacher score (left y-axis) and the average Super Mirror hit (right y-axis). The teacher score was graded on a scale of 1-10, while the Super Mirror score was a ratio given as a percentage of the successful "hits" vs. the predetermined number of times a movement was performed. Figure 3 represents the assessment of the teacher score vs. the Super Mirror score in the movement of a plié. A plié is the bending of the knee or knees [1].

The teacher's score indicated a gradual level of increase with the experience level of the student. According to the subject-matter expert, the teacher scored the dancers on the following set of criteria for a plié: do heels lift from the floor, is weight distributed equally between both feet, are legs turned out from the hips, are shoulders back, is stomach in, is back straight, is torso strong, are ribs in, are hands soft, are arms synchronized with legs, and is bottom tucked in. As students move from year to year, their technique improves. Therefore the teacher's score was greater. However, the same trend is not seen with the Super Mirror. The results from the Super Mirror showed higher results compared to the teacher score. The Super Mirror "hits" compared only the angles of knee and hip joints with prerecorded angle widths [9]. This indicated that the Super Mirror score complexity is much lower than the teacher's. The Super Mirror did not carry the ability to view the dancer's technique as a whole therefore accounting for inaccurate results. Figure 4 represents the assessment of an élevé, a rise on demi-pointe [1]. According to the subject-matter expert, an élevé has the same complexity as a plié.

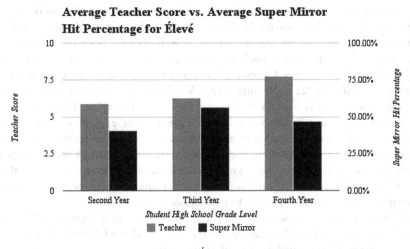

Fig. 4. Élevé score

The teacher assessed the dancers on the following set of criteria for an élevé: are legs turned out, is weight distributed between both feet, are knees straight, are shoulders back, is stomach in, is back straight, is torso aligned, are ribs in, and are heels turned out. The teacher's score also increased with the student's experience. The same explanation determined the score as a plié. As the students' advance, their technique improves; therefore the teacher's score increases. Contrary to a plié, the Super Mirror score is lower than the teacher's score. Our explanation was that the Super Mirror system does not detect the angles as well as the plié. Figure 5 represents the assessment of a tendu front. A battement tendu is an extension of the leg [1].

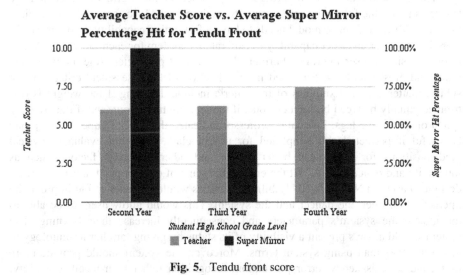

Fig. 5. Tendu front score

According to the subject-matter expert, a tendu is the most complex out of the three movements. The teacher assessed the dancers on the following set of criteria similar to the other two movements: are legs turned out, is weight of the body on the left foot, is tendu begun with a turned-out heel, are shoulders back, is stomach in, and is back straight. The teacher's scores follow the same pattern as the previous two movements i.e., increases with the level of complexity. We found a similar reaction where the Super Mirror system was not able to successfully detect the angles. The system scores show certain anomalies in the second year students. Our explanation was that the second year students were capable to negatively accustom to the faults of the system, although the teacher's scores were the lowest as expected. Most of the students recognized the system's inability to recognize a correct battement tendu. One student said, "I observed that I got a "hit" if I did some of the movements [battement tendu front] in a specific way that was inconsistent to ballet principles".

SUS presented a mean score of 57 for the students and a score of 42.5 for the teacher which indicated a below average result. A score above 68 would be considered as above average as presented by Usability.gov [17].

5 Conclusion

The Super Mirror is only capable to assess the partial complexity of the movements' i.e., the angle of joints to be within certain limits. The teacher score shows a pattern that is proportional to the level of the student's experience, while the Super Mirror shows opposite scoring compared to the teacher when the complexity of movement increases. Nevertheless, the Super Mirror shows a consistency of scores among the students for the same movement regardless of the opposition of the teacher that gives an opportunity to calibrate the system to match the teacher's scores.

With the know-how of our previous experience in the world of ballet and the teacher's input, the following improvements on the Super Mirror are envisioned. First, the Super Mirror reference model needs to have a fast tuning capability. In other words, there is a need for an easier capability to calibrate the system for each individual dancer through a simple user interface. Further, the measured parameters (the angles of the joints and hips) should be expanded in the direction of the assessment criteria of the subject-matter expert. Examples of the criteria include detecting if the weight is distributed equally between both feet or one, if the legs are turned out, and if the arms are synchronized to the legs. The ballet professor indicated that, "[The Super Mirror] may be useful if perfected and simplified for use in class. It cannot evaluate physical predispositions for a classical ballet dancer and other important factors, such as musicality and dance ability." At the end of this stage of development, a user interface designed based on Nielsen's 10 Usability Heuristics would be beneficial to improve the interaction between the dancer and the system. This would allow users to be able to manipulate the system's parameters and consequently increase their learning. The system should always present a visibility of its status by giving familiar terminology to the user rather than using system terms. Moreover, the system should provide more user control, consistency, error prevention, recognition rather than recall, flexibility, adequate error messages, and finally help and documentation [10].

Although initial testing of Super Mirror was not highly conclusive to test the effectiveness and efficiency of the feedback, these types of tools open the door to integrate a Kinect technology to ballet. Even more, it shows promise. With an adequate improvement of the system and a user-controlled capability to calibrate the parameters, a Kinect-based system has the potential to become a useful tool to students, teachers, and professionals. In a more advanced stage of development, the level of usability of the Super Mirror will further increase, if there is a measurement of the speed of movements, a correlation between the speed of movements and music, a correlation between the movement of head, arms, and feet, and the measurement of posture and balance. The most exciting part is the possibility of making a technical and even artistic assessment of the whole performance that could potentially benefit ballet competitions, and remove the bias of subject matter experts. The integration of video streaming, multiple networked Kinect sensors and cloud technology as a one system would move ballet from "Dance, the oldest art, is today but a young science" to the needs of 21st century ballet.

Acknowledgements. Authors would like to thank Joao Beira and Sebastian Kox for offering the Super Mirror system for testing and providing technical help. We thank Prof. Snezana Fili-povska, Ph.D. and Prof. Slagjana Spasenovska, M.A. for the insightful input regarding the fundamentals of ballet, through which many of the ideas in this paper were developed and shaped. We would also like to acknowledge the students from the State Ballet School, Ilija-Nikolovski Luj from Skopje, Macedonia who participated in the study.

References

1. American ballet theatre: american ballet theatre ballet dictionary. http://www.abt.org/education/dictionary/index.html
2. Anderson, F., Grossman, T., Matejka, J., Fitzmaurice, G.W.: YouMove: enhancing movement training with an augmented reality mirror. In: User Interface Software and Technology (UIST), pp. 311–320. ACM (2013)
3. Dearborn, K., Ross, R.: Dance learning and the mirror: comparison study of dance phrase learning with and without mirrors. J. Dance. Educ. **6**(4), 109–115 (2006)
4. Eaves, D.L., Breslin, G., van Schaik, P., Robinson, E., Spears, I.R.: The short-term effects of real-time virtual reality feedback on motor learning in dance. Presence: Teleoperators Virtual Environ. **20**(1), 62–77 (2011)
5. Foster, S.L., Desmond, J.: Dancing Bodies. New Cultural Studies of Dance, pp. 235–257. Duke University Press, Durham (1997)
6. Gray, J.A.: The dance teacher a computerized behavioral profile. J. Phys. Res. Edu. Dance **54**(9), 34–35 (1983)
7. Green, J.: Somatic authority and the myth of the ideal body in dance education. Dance Res. J. **31**(2), 80–100 (1999)
8. Leijen, Ä., Lam, I., Wildschut, L., Robert-Jan, S., Admiraal, W.: Streaming Video to enhance students' reflection in dance education. Comput. Edu. **52**(1), 169–176 (2009)
9. Marquardt, Z., Beira, J., Em, N., Paiva, I., Kox, S: Super mirror: a kinect interface for ballet dancers. In: CHI 2012 Extended Abstracts on Human Factors in Computing Systems, pp. 1619–1624. ACM (2012)

10. Nielsen norman group. http://www.nngroup.com/articles/ten-usability-heuristics/
11. Radell, S.A.: Mirrors in dance class: help or hindrance? In: International Association for Dance Medicine and Science (2013)
12. Radell, S.A., Adame, D.D., Cole, S.P.: Effect of teaching with mirrors on ballet dance performance: percept. Motor. Skill. **97**, 960–964 (2003)
13. Sukel, K.E., Catrambone, R., Essa, I., Brostow, G.: Presenting movement in a computer-based dance tutor. Int. J. Hum.-Comput. Int. **15**(3), 433–452 (2003)
14. Synapse - Synapse for kinect. http://synapsekinect.tumblr.com/post/6610177302/syn.apse
15. Tryplex - the toolkit for collaborative design innovation - Google project hosting. http://code.google.com/p/tryplex/
16. Twitchett, E., Angioi, M., Koutedakis, Y., Wyon, M.: Video analysis of classical ballet performance. J. Dance. Med. Sci. **13**(4), 124–128 (2009)
17. U.S. Department of Health and Human Services. The Research-Based Web Design and Usability Guidelines, Enlarged/Expanded edition. U.S. Government Printing Office, Washington (2006)

Integrating a Cognitive Modelling Framework into the Design Process of Touchscreen User Interfaces

Patrick K.A. Wollner$^{(\boxtimes)}$, Patrick M. Langdon, and P. John Clarkson

Department of Engineering, Engineering Design Centre, University of Cambridge,
Cambridge, UK
{pkaw2,pml24,pjc10}@cam.ac.uk

Abstract. Interface design is often constrained by the limited scope and resource-intensive nature of conventional user studies. We aim to unburden this process by introducing an automated user modelling framework that continuously injects design guidelines into the development process. We present a pipeline that converts a given user interface design into a widgetised data structure, executes a performance simulation based on the cognitive model of a user, and analyses its output to give design guidelines. We introduce the research methodology employed to create the model, implementation details of the model, and initial results from its validation. These include the dynamics of age-based modelling, the temporal integrity of the output of the cognitive model, and indications of the accuracy of the overall design guidelines produced.

Keywords: Inclusive design · Universal design · User interfaces · User experience · Usability testing · Cognitive modelling · Cognitive architectures

1 Introduction

The quality of user interface designs on touchscreen devices is often constrained by the lack of user testing on these interfaces during the developmental stage. This is the result of the incompatibility between the extremely short product cycles and the significantly greater time requirements for comprehensive and conclusive tests involving real users from a broad range of prior experiences.

In this paper, we introduce the overview of a user modelling pipeline which has the potential to be integrated into established user interface design processes without additional time affordances. Thereby, the pipeline allows access to new insights into the potential pitfalls of a given interface design proposal without creating additional friction in the process. In addition to the specifics of the pipeline and its usage, we outline how the Design Research Methodology (DRM) [3] was employed to realise the pipeline, including a brief overview of the results from its associated validation substage.

© Springer International Publishing Switzerland 2015
A. Marcus (Ed.): DUXU 2015, Part II, LNCS 9187, pp. 473–484, 2015.
DOI: 10.1007/978-3-319-20898-5_46

2   Methodology

The pipeline was designed employing an adapted version of the DRM [3], specifying the DRM Criteria to match the shortcomings of existing user modelling implementations, both in terms of their specificity to mobile touchscreen devices and the environments they are used in, as well as the quality of potential interpretations of their output. The integration of the DRM into the existing components is outlined in Fig. 1.

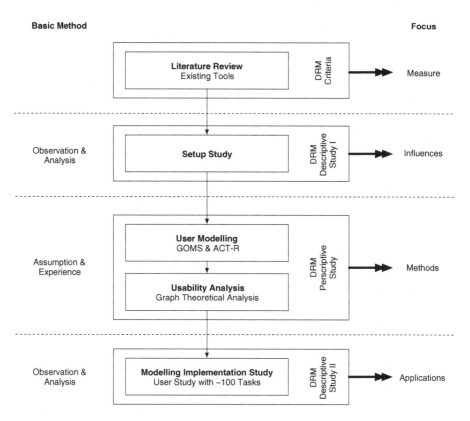

Fig. 1. Overview of the methodological approach

A comprehensive literature review was completed [12] to determine the DRM Criteria. In this case, the adaption of a pipeline, with the specific qualities applied to its potential for application in inclusive design, the overall applicability for touchscreen applications, and the specifics of mobile usage, signify the key research criteria.

The first Descriptive Study was completed as a pilot user study, using first-time-use tasks as an indicator of the factors that influence the aforementioned criteria. It was based on the observation and analysis of twelve users of first-time setup tasks and is outlined in Wollner et al. [10]. The focus of this work was to gather the necessary fundamental *influences* for all further work in this body of research.

Subsequently, the model was implemented utilising ACT-R [1] as the underlying cognitive architecture, combined with a GOMS-based widgetisation [5] of the elements on individual screens or screen states. According to the DRM, this was the Prescriptive Study associated with the body of the work. Based on a number of assumptions and the influences of existing work, the modelling was further extended and integrated with a usability analysis framework that employs graph theory and message passing – two interdependent approaches that integrate the density of user performance data with the sparse interconnectedness of the user interfaces tested. More specifically, the holistic analysis of the output was accomplished by employing a graph theoretical inference network, which is based on the network of the user interface states and the performance metrics generated by the cognitive model. This is outlined in Sect. 3.3.

Additionally, to impact the design process, the output of the inference network was transformed and thereby simplified to a topological representation of the screen states that could be interpreted directly by designers and developers alike, impacting the design process without generating additional friction in the process. This allowed the modelling implementation to be further refined, building the foundations of the pipeline introduced in this paper.

Finally, a validation study was completed, as outlined in Sect. 4. It is based on an analysis of the key determinants of the newly introduced methods and involved a sample of nearly 100 tasks performed by a sample of users with varying backgrounds, each performing four independent tasks on a mid-sized touchscreen device.

3 Pipeline and Usage

In contrast to existing tools and methods that aid the design of graphical user interface applications – particularly on touchscreen devices – we introduce an approach which consists of four distinct components. We translate the proposed design of a device into a machine-interpretable description, analyse it using a cognitive architecture (ACT-R, [1]), interpret the results by employing a graph theoretical approach, and, finally, inject the resulting insights into the design process. For each of the above steps, we have developed a comprehensive approach, which is outlined in a number of related previous publications (including [10–12]), is concatenated in the first author's thesis, and, more concisely, in this paper.

The pipeline was carefully constructed to meet the needs of modelling accuracy, design integration and design impact. As such, each of the above mentioned stages were developed on the basis of potential impact. Prior to going into more detail, the pipeline stages are outlined in the list below.

1. **Interface Representation.** The acquisition of a representation of an interface, containing the interconnectedness of all interface states as well as the widgetised visual design of the individual interface states.

2. **User Modelling.** The modelling stage in which a cognitive architecture is employed to simulate a range of user types on the interface representation.
3. **Usability Analysis.** A mathematical framework which exploits the information on the interconnectedness of the UI and the results from the User Modelling stage to approximate the anticipated interface progression of a real user.
4. **Design Injection.** An environment in which the output of the previous stages are visualised in a format that is of value to developers and designers, without the necessity of prior training and with the greatest possible impact on the design process.

3.1   Interface Representation

For modelling approaches to be implemented, it is necessary to translate a given design proposal into a machine-interpretable format. Utilising GOMS-variants [5] as the basis for this procedure, we read and analyse the widgets of any given design, categorise them into a predefined set of standard elements, and assign modelling classes accordingly. This descriptive process is performed in an XML format that is translated into so-called *chunks*, which, in turn, can be read by the modelling environment employed by the next step of the modelling framework.

In accomplishing this, we analysed existing GOMS implementations and extended them according to three key requirements: (i) an inclusive audience (i.e. older users or users with varying capabilities), (ii) touchscreen use and (iii) applicability in modelling mobile environments. There are a variety of GOMS implementations and extensions [4] that can be broken into four main categories and were analysed as such:

CMN-GOMS. A plain implementation of GOMS, written in pseudo-code first introduced by Card et al. [4].

KLM. Keystroke-Level modelling, as employed by GUI cognitive modelling software packages, such as CogTool [6] which acts as a simplified model/version of GOMS.

NGOMSL. Natural GOMS Language [8], which acts as a stricter version of GOMS, provides well-defined, structured natural language and estimates learning time.

CPM-GOMS. Cognitive perceptual motor analysis of activity path, this may also be described as a critical path method which is based on the parallel multi-processor stage of human information processing [7].

Within an inclusive context, it is especially important to outline the shortcomings of GOMS for highlighting the exclusion factors of the interfaces investigated with this method. Schrepp [9] outlines some of the challenges that GOMS-techniques face, with emphasis on the requirements of older users. The resulting work outlines how GOMS techniques could be "adapted to evaluate the efficiency of interface designs for [older and] disabled users" [9].

This included a particular focus on the factors of attention and repeated screen views, such as scrolling. More specifically, we defined a widgetised description of the impact of user attention in a range of scenarios on the widget in question, allowing the dependency of the part of the user interface to be defined by the impact it will suffer by limited user attention.

Likewise, a key component not covered by conventional GOMS implementations was the aspect of repeated views based on scrolling. Traditionally, elements of a user interface would only be seen once by the user, without the scope for scrolling the view. In reality – and mainly due to novel interaction techniques such as touchscreen user interfaces following the style guides of the major (mobile) operating systems such as iOS and Android – these elements have all become scrollable. As such, elements that would not be visible after an action on the interface now remain (partially) visible after the page (on which the widgets are contained) is scrolled. This is something that had to implemented in both the description of modelling and the interpretation of what GOMS segmentation of visual elements entails.

The result is a comprehensive approach in segmenting both the visual assets as well as the actions available on a user interface design into clearly defined, actionable and interpretable elements that are meaningful for the modelling procedure. We refer to sets of these elements as interface *states*.

3.2   User Modelling

With the interface segmentation defined as in Sect. 3.1, we are well prepared for a unified machine interpretation of a given design, thereby allowing for a full machine analysis of the described interface. This process has been initially developed by previous work [1]. Our contribution is predominantly in the area of interpreting the output of the previous stage and, more importantly, by introducing factors to the modelling procedure that allow for a representation of users with varying capabilities.

We accomplish this by utilising ACT-R [1], a Cognitive Architecture that has been in use (and actively developed) for decades and is particularly apt at giving insight to the simulated user behaviour of human-machine interfaces. The description to the modelling environment is accomplished by translating the XML-based descriptive factors into ACT-R-*interpretable* chunks that simulate both the input and output of a real user. Details of this process are outlined by previous work [11] and ample literature relating to ACT-R.

With the modelling process executed, the this stage of the framework outputs a fundamental dataset: the timings of each of the step of a user interface, given a specific route.

3.3   Usability Analysis

Routes and timings are particularly valuable in the process of assessing the usability of a given interface. Nonetheless, with these two sets of information segmented and hence assessed individually, their value is limited. The design specifications will provide all possible routes through the UI (the screen flow network). A user model will output, given a specific user interaction route, the timings associated with each step in the screen flow network. If this procedure is repeated many times, all possible routes a user may encounter given a specified interface, are covered by the model and hence a complete set of simulated user timings are captured.

This scenario of abundant, disjoint datasets raises the necessity for integrating the availability of scarce timings-data with the dense user journey data of the proposed interface design. More specifically, this means combining the timings captured from the modelling environment with the associated locations within a network of all available screens in the user interface. In previous work, we have called this process integrating the screen flow network with user data [12].

In the context of the framework introduced in this paper, we utilise an approach that is commonplace in mathematics and machine learning environments but not commonly used in the context of user interface development or usability analysis. By assigning a value to each stage (i.e. nodes) of the user interface that can be accessed by a user, a network is established. Next, all connections (i.e. vertices) between each of these states are analysed. This includes assigning a value that is based on the modelled user performance in the transition from each state to another. As defined in prior work [12], the analysis is performed in one of two modes: latitudinal progression or longitudinal progression. While the former represents the relative difficulty of a specific screen action for a specific user type, based on the overall results across multiple user types, the latter represents the probabilistic interpretation that a user will experience difficulties when transitioning from one screen to another.

With the network specified by the interconnectedness of the user interface and values to its vertices assigned by the two modes defined above, the values are propagated through the network utilising an adaptation of a message passing algorithm. This dynamically reassigns values for each of the nodes until the entire network of values converges (dependent on the quality of the modelled data). Once (and if) convergence is reached, the final node values represent a numerical classification of the likelihood that users will experience a bottleneck at each state of the user interface.

In summary, this generates one value associated with each screen or view (i.e. state) of the interface. This variable is representative of the relative complexity of that state compared to all other states (when assessed through longitudinal progression) or compared to a set of different user types (when assessed through latitudinal progression). We refer to sets of these descriptors as *complexity values*.

3.4   Design Injection

Complexity values can easily be made accessible through a dynamic, colour-coded or topological representation that indicates which screen requires the most attention at any point in the design process. While the focus of the development of the framework was not the design injection stage, we introduce a number of potential methods in which it can be integrated into the design process. This – in its conceptual design – is critical for the entire framework because it guides the overall flow of information and criteria for success of the associated research.

Two injection methods were analysed in the context of their feasibility and implementation potential: (i) a stand-alone representation on a dynamic, HTML5-based graph and (ii) the fully integrated approach, which is embedded in an integrated development environment (IDE) and dynamically outputs design recommendations as the interface is developed.

The stand-alone representation of the resultant, convergent values in a graph is useful if the analysis is performed once. The previous steps of the framework are entered manually by the designer or developer specifying the widgetised structure. The modelling and analysis phase are executed and a browser-based display shows a graphical network, based on the open source package Gephi. The visualisation contains nodes whose size are dependent on their interconnectedness, allowing the most frequently visited nodes to be analysed in the greatest depth. The colour of each node is dependent on the convergent complexity value (as defined in the previous Section). Here, it is important to highlight that the main intention of this approach is to provide an evidence-based visual summary of the components of a specified user interface design that are most difficult to reach, restricted by a set of assumptions set by the modelling environment. Both analysis modes, latitudinal progression or longitudinal progression can be displayed, allowing the analysis to favour either the progression according to an individual user's journey or the overall inclusivity of the design. Finally, based on user data, an age-corrective slider allows for the analysis to be adjusted for the anticipated age group of the modelled user.

The integrated, IDE-based integration of the framework serves a different purpose: it removes all friction from the modelling process, allowing the modelling to be executed frequently throughout the design process. The coded UI is extracted (in an automated fashion) from the development process and – once a property that solely connects screen actions with other screens – is established, translated into a simplified widgetised XML structure that can be interpreted by the modelling stage of the framework. Subsequently, the design is analysed and the results are displayed directly within the IDE. The representation of results is either in a list view that allows an ordering of screens based on their relative complexity values or in the same network representation that was introduced in the stand-alone variant described above. Additionally, a deep integration in established version control systems allows the tracking of UI design changes and the impact on complexity scores of individual screens. This allows for a design impact assessment throughout each iterative change of the design as well as a retrospective analysis thereof. Similarly to the stand-alone version of the design injection, an implementation of both usability analysis methods – latitudinal and longitudinal progression – can be modelled, as well as age-corrective measures for the intended age range of users.

4   Validation

The framework introduced in the previous section is partially validated through work relating to the individual stages and components of the framework. The approach of widgetising elements of a user interface through GOMS and various adaptions thereof is well established in literature. Similarly, the analysis of these widgetised structures has been implemented and validated in the context of follow-up work within the ACT-R modelling community, particularly through the implementation of the *device* module and its associated validation work [1]. Methods relating to message passing and, in particular, belief propagation, as implemented for the usability analysis of the work, are well established.

Because of the segmented nature of this prior validation work, a more complete validation of the pipeline was necessary in the context of the framework presented in this paper. In the context of the PhD Thesis on which this paper is based, a comprehensive user study was performed. Four distinct tasks on a mid-sized touchscreen device (1st Generation Apple iPad mini running iOS 7) were completed by a sample of users ($n = 28$) with a wide-ranging age distribution. This process had four distinct goals: (i) an analysis of the impact technology familiarity has on the performance of a task, (ii) an analysis of the impact age has on the performance of a task, (iii) the validation of the ACT-R modelling implementation introduced in this paper, and (iv) the validation of the usability analysis sub-stage introduced in this paper. While the specifics of this comprehensive study are beyond the scope of this paper, we present a summary of the methods used, as well as the key results.

4.1   Experimental Procedure

The participants were, following a brief outline of the work and written consent, asked to complete a technology familiarity questionnaire (TFQ), adapted from the version introduced by Blackler [2]. This was completed on a computer and included questions that related to the self-perceived competence as well as frequency of use of a number of devices and device classes, ranging from mobile phone to desktop computer. The results were scored using the same criteria as in previous work using this method of assessing technology familiarity [2].

Subsequently and in a randomised order to minimise ordering effects, each participant completed four tasks. Task one required the user to set an alarm using the built-in operating system's alarm functionality. Task two made use of the operating system's built-in reminders functionality and required the user to create three reminders and mark two as completed. Task three asked the user to find, order, and process an item in *Amazon*'s shopping application. The fourth and final task was split into three sub-tasks within the *Bloomberg* application. This involved looking up the value of a specific bond, reading the news headlines, and adding a stock to the built-in watch-list functionality of the app.

For each of the tasks, the user was observed using a wireless screen capture of the device, a video capture from above the device, and an audio recording. This allowed both the timings and route choices through each of the tasks to be captured and analysed. Finally, after the participant completed each of the tasks, a retrospective video analysis was performed. By presenting the user with a recording of his or her own interaction with each of the tasks (in the order the tasks were completed), the participant could comment on each of the steps previously undertaken. In addition to the quantitative data that resulted from the timings and route-choice analysis, this qualitative dataset allowed the precise location their usage bottleneck to be communicated, without the limitation of having to infer the location of greatest perceived complexity based on performance timings.

4.2 Results

While the learnings from the experimental work associated with the framework are wide-ranging, we focus on four key results: (i) the impact the TFQ had on the performance of each task, (ii) the impact the age of the participant had on the performance of each task, (iii) the validity of the timings that were generated by the model, based on the captured user timings and (iv) the validity of the complexity scores that were generated by the model, based on the captured user locations of perceived complexity through the retrospective video analysis stage of the experimental work.

Result 1: TFQ and User Performance Using the TFQ score of each participant and each participant's performance scores, based on the timing distribution of all steps of each completed task, we analysed the relationship between user performance and technological familiarity. The TFQ score was based on an adapted version of previous work by Blackler [2], as well as sub-scores thereof. We concluded that there is no significant effect of TFQ on user timings across all four tasks.

Result 2: Age and User Performance There was a significant difference in performance timings across three of four tasks based on three age levels ($p = 0.014$). More specifically, a correlative analysis thereof allowed us to specify a linear relationship between these two variables to some degree of certainty ($r^2 = 0.48$).

Result 3: ACT-R Model Validation Mean modelled performance timings from the ACT-R model correlated in trend with mean user performance timings of all users. Despite a comparably low correlative value ($r^2 = 0.61$), the ordering of empirical user performance and modelled user performance matched in three out of four tasks, across all participants.

Result 4: Usability Analysis Validation The most frequently self-defined locations of greatest complexity by participants for each task, matched three out of four tasks' usability analyses. More specifically, for two out of four tasks, the distribution of self-defined locations of greatest complexity was indicative of the modelled distribution of complexity values.

Other Results. Furthermore, insights on repeated actions within one task were acquired. These include that repeated tasks show increasing performance gains within one session, independent of whether the user had experience with the specific interface or screen network before. Further research is required to translate these validated hypotheses into concrete, validated numerical implementations of the model.

4.3   Discussion

The framework introduced in this paper is novel in its composition and application whilst being built utilising well-established methods. Hence, the holistic validation of the framework, as outlined in this Section is essential for its application. The clarity of Results 3 and 4 speak for themselves in terms of the applicability of the overall approach in the context of informing and improving user interface designs. It is clear that the timings – corrected for age – generated by the model are suitably indicative for the model to be utilised for the purpose defined in this paper. Similarly, the usability analysis performed in the latter stage of the framework produces a prioritisation of the four tasks (and their subtasks) that is suitable for locating potential performance bottlenecks once utilised by real users. It is important to note in this context that the results are constrained by the small sample size as well as by the specificity of the tasks chosen to test the framework on. Some of the tasks had been used by many of the participants before. Despite this, the overall trends across tasks remained constant, with one notable exception of task four. This is important because it underlines the independence of prior use on the model's validity, albeit only to the level of accuracy the model can provide.

The difference between the two modelling approaches – latitudinal and longitudinal progression – could not be established given the design of the experiment. While longitudinal progression focusses on a specific user type, latitudinal progression focusses on a specific subsection of the screen network. Given the sample size, these two factors could not be clearly segmented in the performance data and hence no conclusive findings could be made in relation to the two approaches. However, their combined validity was established. Further work is required to assess each individually.

Two additional insights generated by the validation stage included the impact of technological familiarity and age of the participants had on their performance on each of the tasks. It is clear that across all tasks, there was a monotonic relationship between age and performance timing. Additionally, we were able to define an indicative value of this relationship across three of four of the tasks for all users with a high correlative value, allowing an "age coefficient" to be defined. This means that the modelling output can be corrected for the age of the user through a linear transformation.

In contrast, no clear relationship between the TFQ and user performance was found. This may be a result of the method (the TFQ structure and/or scoring) or indicative of that technological familiarity has little to no impact on the performance of the tasks tested. To further this analysis, multiple scoring methods and sub-scores of the TFQ were tested in the context of performance data, resulting in the same result.

5   Conclusion

In this paper we introduce a framework that can be integrated into existing design processes of user interface designers and developers to improve the design of a given interface. We outline the DRM to be the underlying methodology and introduce the four stages of the model. Finally, we outline the process and key results of a validation study in this context.

We determine that while there is no clearly identifiable relationship between technological familiarity and task performance, there is a clear trend between the age of the user and the performance timings. Additionally, we identify that with these factors applied, a model of the user employing ACT-R can be utilised to indicate trends in timings of real users. By numerically combining the ACT-R model with a graphical representation of the modelled interface, the hotspots of the design can be indicatively identified. Finally, two potential methods of integrating the resultant performance values into the design process of interfaces are outlined, but remain to be fully implemented and validated.

Whilst the work, and in particular the validation work, introduced in this paper concentrates on the validation of the underlying processes (such as specific models and mathematical methods), further work will focus on a validation of the complete pipeline employed in design processes and hence provide the final necessary step to translate these findings into practice. Further work will also focus on extending the validation, such as increasing the number of data points (i.e. number of participants), introducing additional validation tasks with lower degrees of specificity and extending the validation procedure to the design impact of the entire framework.

References

1. Anderson, J.R., Bothell, D., Byrne, M.D., Douglass, S., Lebiere, C., Qin, Y.: An integrated theory of the mind. Psychol. Rev. **111**, 1036–1060 (2004)
2. Blackler, A.: Intuitive interaction with complex artefacts. Ph.D. thesis. Queensland University of Technology, Australia (2006)
3. Bracewell, R., Shea, K., Langdon, P., Blessing, L., Clarkson, P.: A methodology for computational design tool research. In: 13th International Conference on Engineering Design (ICED 2001), Glasgow, Scotland, UK, pp. 181–188 (2001)
4. Card, S.K., Moran, T.P., Newell, A.: The Psychology of Human-Computer Interaction. Erlbaum (1983). http://books.google.at/books?id=qU-DaL49R9EC
5. Card, S.K., Moran, T.P., Newell, A.: The keystroke-level model for user performance time with interactive systems. Commun. ACM **23**(7), 396–410 (1980). http://doi.acm.org/10.1145/358886.358895
6. John, B.E.: CogTool User Guide. Technical report (2009)

7. John, B.E., Gray, W.D.: CPM-GOMS: an analysis method for tasks with parallel activities. In: Conference Companion on Human Factors in Computing Systems. CHI 1995, pp. 393–394. ACM, New York (1995). http://doi.acm.org/10.1145/223355.223738

8. Kieras, D.: A guide to GOMS model usability evaluation using NGOMSL. In: Helander, M.G., Landauer, T.K., Pradhu, P.V. (eds.) Handbook of Human-Computer Interaction (2nd ed.), pp. 733–766. North-Holland, Amsterdam (1997)

9. Schrepp, M.: GOMS analysis as a tool to investigate the usability of web units for disabled users. Univ. Access Inf. Soc. 9(1), 77–86 (2009)

10. Wollner, P.K., Goldhaber, T., Mieczakowski, A., Langdon, P.M., Hosking, I.M., Clarkson, P.J., et al.: Evaluation of setup procedures on mobile devices based on users initial experience. In: The 9th NordDesign Conference on DS 71: Proceedings of NordDesign 2012, Aarlborg University, Denmark, 22–24.08.2012 (2012)

11. Wollner, P.K.A., Hosking, I., Langdon, P.M., Clarkson, P.J.: Improvements in interface design through implicit modeling. In: Stephanidis, C., Antona, M. (eds.) UAHCI/HCII 2013, Part I. LNCS, vol. 8009, pp. 127–136. Springer, Heidelberg (2013)

12. Wollner, P.K.A., Langdon, P.M., Clarkson, P.J.: A combinatory approach to assessing user performance of digital interfaces. In: Langdon, P.M., Lazar, J., Heylighen, A., Dong, H. (eds.) Inclusive Designing, Part II, pp. 39–48. Springer International Publishing, Switzerland (2014)

Mobile DUXU

Change News Reading Habit
in the Information Age
and Digital Mobile Devices

Juliana Nunes[✉] and Manuela Quaresma

LEUI | Laboratory of Ergodesign and Usability Interfaces, Pontifical Catholic
University of Rio de Janeiro (PUC-Rio), Rio de Janeiro, Brazil
jutricolor@gmail.com, mquaresma@puc-rio.br

Abstract. The news broadcasts are looking for their media formats as well as
users are choosing their news consumption preferences. Will be these companies
that produce and transmit news know who are these new users? Where the touch
points are and what kind of users are they interacting with? The purpose of this
paper is to present a study applied with users who consume print and online
newspaper and an analysis of two respectable newspapers: The New York
Times (USA daily news) and Estado de São Paulo (Brazilian daily news). The
questionnaire applied with users pointed behaviors and expectations about
current news consumption and the analysis of four smartphone apps evaluated
how these two newspapers are presenting its contents, and if these presentations
are in accordance with some data found in this study.

Keywords: Digital information · Mobile devices · Apps · News

1 Introduction

Apparently, traditional newspapers have been suffering to adapt its entire structure to
this actual news consumption habits. Habits that come from the ease to purchase
mobile devices and the wide access to wireless internet connection anytime and anywhere. And with the several channels available for this service, from traditional press
that still retains their printed versions, to the social networks. The age of digital
information and mobile devices, provides, thus, several news users' profile that consume in locations, platforms and various media. "It's not the first time that journalism
faces the evolution of the media in order to adapt. Throughout its history, the journalism presented different ways: from press to cinema, from radio to television, and
with the advent of internet, the modality of digital journalism" [1]. But, despite all these
changes, there has never been a phase that impact so negatively in the structure of the
century-old hegemony of the press companies as the current phase. Beyond all challenges mentioned above, there is also a change in the newspaper's relationship with its
reader. "The meeting of the digital ecosystem and the media ecosystem isn't unique to
mobile, but it should be noted that it is who allowed an unprecedented link between
device, consumption and identity of users" [2].

© Springer International Publishing Switzerland 2015
A. Marcus (Ed.): DUXU 2015, Part II, LNCS 9187, pp. 487–494, 2015.
DOI: 10.1007/978-3-319-20898-5_47

With the widespread use of mobile devices, the newspapers were driven to develop specific applications. "Think for a moment how difficult it is to build a meaningful experience for others. It is necessary first to understand your audience; what are their needs, abilities, interests, and expectations; and how to reach them" [3].

In order to attract and retain these 'mobile' readers, the press had to spread in various social networks, where there is a direct relation to news consumption among mobile device relationship and social network because "most of the social networks" traffic comes from smartphones. That's why our [the New York Times] competitors say the key to winning mobile is to win on social [4]. Quote corroborated by a study conducted in 2013 [5], which states that 64 % of American adults use Facebook and almost half of these public (30 %) consume news from this social network.

From the point of view of human computer interaction it's necessary to consider the macro and micro views of the system. The macro is the interconnection of systems, meaning, to recognize a structural unit that pervades the various mobile platforms and social networks that are strengthened every day in the news acquisition. The micro considers the individual aspects of each device taking advantage of its full potential to provide an interface and appropriate information architecture.

2 Problem

Much of what it's been seen in journalistic products texts and links are almost identical on the web and in app. "The transposition of content does not seem to take into account satisfactorily technological capabilities provided by the device characteristics and in this case it seems no difference on news of the structure when taken into account the digital media" [5].

The current scenario constitutes, thus, different profiles of users who consume news in different times, locations, platforms and media. It's perceived that many press companies create products and launch them on the market to see how users respond, on trial-and-error. At the other end, users get lost with so many variables and try to find themselves in the midst of so much information. So, for a successful project, designers should map and understand both the company's culture and the costumers' culture in order to fit the two poles, as shown in the Fig. 1.

Fig. 1. Design for a bi-cultural fit [6].

3   Methodology

Based on the analysis of some findings of a behavioral report [7] developed in a study for graduate discipline, this paper analyses two traditional newspapers in order to view some proposed solutions for digital platforms. Due to the credibility, tradition and innovation in its apps, the two selected newspapers were The New York Times (American daily news) and Estado de São Paulo (Brazilian daily news, known as Estadão). Four free apps of these newspapers (two for each) developed for iOS platform were analyzed in the iPhone device.

This report analysis brings up findings encountered in a research report develop with 95 users of printed and digital newspaper regarding habits consumption, connection with the world, usability and preferences and reliability.

4   Results

4.1   Study Report

The study investigated why there are still readers of print newspapers even with new possibilities and easy access to digital news, considering the transition moment of the newspaper industry. A questionnaire was used in order to map the behaviors of consumers regarding printed and online newspaper. The questionnaire was applied through personal contact and via internet. Data were analyzed with statistical methods, from the standpoint of the following perspectives: habit of consumption, connection with the world, usability and preferences and reliability.

Conclusions were formulated from the analysis based on these four perspectives. From this study, it can be seen that new technologies and greater internet access promoted a change in the habit of news consumers. It's noticed that the print newspaper users are more connected to entertainment and habitual behavior than to keep updated and informed.

In addition, the research detected an increase use of digital newspapers over the printed version in just a few future years. Since younger audience is more familiar with the handling of mobile devices while the older audience is transiting between the two media - print and digital.

Since the consume of digital newspapers is greater nowadays and with the aim to reach younger audience, traditional newspapers have to adapt their platforms to attend these new tendency. Below, the paper presents data of the behavioral report and analyses if the two newspapers are following the expectations.

4.2   Newspapers Analysis

Bet On Frequent News Update. The report research pointed a most of readers in the habit of newspapers users, where say it is important to be constantly updated with the day's top stories from different sources, as shown in Figs. 2 and 3.

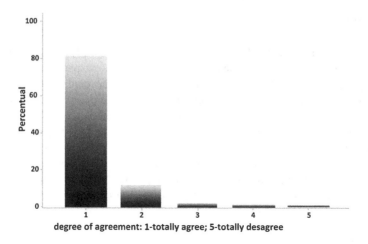

Fig. 2. Question on the chart: "I think important to be constantly updated with top stories of the day".

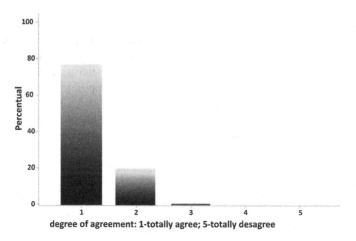

Fig. 3. Question on the chart: "I think it is important to have access to different opinions when reading news".

Both New York Times as Estado de São Paulo (Estadão) presented smartphone's solutions for frequently update the news. The first one quoted launched the NYT Now app, while the second bet on a radio version.

The NYT Now app presents easy accessible menu with three icons: news (presenting current news), picks (with the editors' picks from around the web today), and the favorites (news chosen by users).

With this type of configuration, the NYT Now app offers its users two of the demands indicated in the report. Updated news and news from other sources, as shown in Fig. 4.

Fig. 4. Menu from NYT Now app

At the end of each news post, the user knows how many hours ago the news are available in the app, with the possibility of sharing it through with the social networks and marking it favorites, as shown in Fig. 5.

Fig. 5. NYT Now app

News appear in blocks with the leading of the main news of the day (photo + text) and if user wants, by clicking on the block, he has the ability to read the whole news. It is perceived a clear consistency in the ordination of news. There is also concern with the user in show when ends the latest news and begin the oldest news, with a friendly message according to the Figure below (Fig. 6).

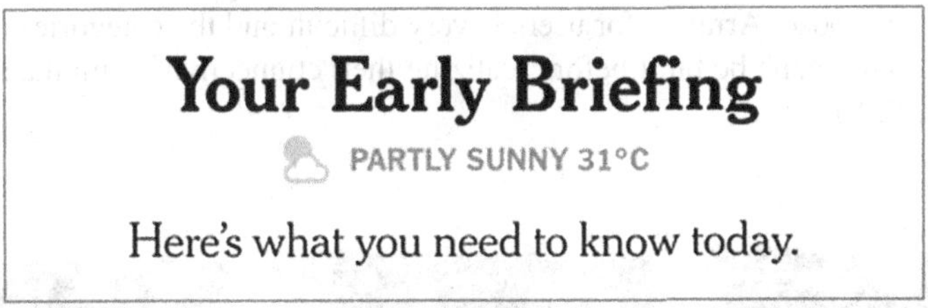

Your Early Briefing

🌥 PARTLY SUNNY 31°C

Here's what you need to know today.

Fig. 6. Message at the end of the most current news

The app from the newspaper Estado de São Paulo (Estadão) also has this ability to update its users through the radio, with the possibility of inserting audio, (something absent from the New York Times app). However, this is a clear example of non-use of device resources, which only has the function equal to the radio. When compared to a similar app, the CBN (Brazilian radio that plays news), with origins from a radio station, as opposed to a printed newspaper, it is observed a clear difference of use of the device features (Fig. 7).

Fig. 7. At left the home page and the only one from Estadão app and at right the podcast page from CBN app.

In the CBN app, (which includes live radio option), the menu also allows the visualization of the latest podcasts, with the possibility of downloading it to listen later. In addition, the user can also select the columnists of their interests to listen. In both options there is a possibility of sharing with social networks.

4.3   General News

In apps that have the role to encompass all news, and bring updates, it is perceived in the tray menu various topics of subjects. Although the New York Times allows customization of topics, which is the limit for topics and for news? One should really offer everything to the user? According to Morville [8], words helps users to find what they need and understand what they find. That's why the first step in taxonomy construction is defining its purpose. Arrange for users is very difficult and the categories are the root of this work, but it can't be built before realizing their connectivity with the system as a whole (Figs. 8, 9).

Fig. 8. Topics from Estadão tray menu app

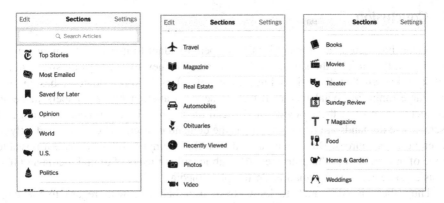

Fig. 9. Topics from New York Times list menu app

Who are the users of these apps? For the NYT, the icon clearly refers to the printed newspaper, which probably approach users that used to or still read printed newspaper. However, the public over 50 years believed to be easier to find news on the printed newspaper than the digital media (Figs. 10, 11).

Fig. 10. Thumb from NYT app

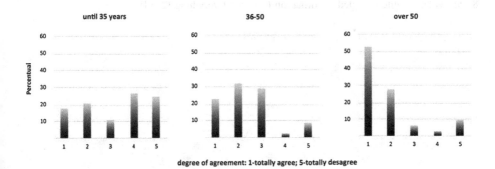

Fig. 11. Question on the chart "I think it's easier to find news on print newspaper to find news on digital one."

5   Conclusion

It is clear that there is an attempt by newspapers to adapt to its users' the new way of reading. In this article, the side view was the study of newspaper apps on smartphone, but it is known that there is a huge range of offers in other devices, besides the inevitable range of social media. It can be seen an attempt by newspapers in being connected in most of these devices and social media in order to broaden this range of users. Some demands are being known, as the demand of users to keep up constantly in different news sources. But it is notable that in the attempt to offer the widest possible range of information to the user, the older public still not users of digital media and find it easier to search for information on the print media.

Thus, there is still much to know from user behavior with regard to the consumption of news and companies that produce or broadcast news are still testing formulas to offer their services. I believe that the most coherent way in this time of uncertainty is design to fit a bi-culture, meaning, to know the culture of the company and to know new habits and behaviors of users of digital news.

References

1. Barbosa, S., Canavilhas, J. (org.): Notícias e Mobilidade: O jornalismo, na Era dos Dispositivos Móveis. LabCom, Covilhã (2013)
2. Conde, M.G., Canavilhas, J. (org.): Notícias e Mobilidade: O jornalismo, na Era dos Dispositivos Móveis. LabCom, Covilhã (2013)
3. Shedroff, N.: Information Interaction Design: A Unified Field Theory of Design (n.d.) (1994). http://www.nathan.com/thoughts/unified/unified.pdf. Accessed 5 July 2014
4. THE NEW YORK TIMES: Executive Sumary, New York, 97p., March 2014
5. PEW RESEARCH CENTER: News Use Across Social Media Platforms (2013). http://www.journalism.org/2013/11/14/news-use-across-social-media-platforms/. Accessed 1 December 2014
6. Morville, P.: Intertwingled: Information Changes Everything (2014)
7. Aquino, J.F.P., Barbosa, J.N., Paiva T.C.: Consumo de Notícias nas Plataformas Impressa e Online, 21p., November 2014
8. Morville, P.: Intertwingled: Information Changes Everything (2014)

Towards a Requirements Catalogue for Prototyping Tools of Mobile User Interfaces

Benjamin Bähr[✉]

Telekom Innovation Laboratories, Technische Universität Berlin,
Ernst-Reuter-Platz 7, 10587 Berlin, Germany
baehr@mailbox.tu-berlin.de

Abstract. User-Interface prototypes are important for testing software design ideas in early stages, where changes can still be considered. This is especially true for mobile app interfaces that have to take into account a number of specific challenges. Accordingly, prototyping tools are needed that consider the specific conditions under which mobile apps are usually developed. Research on the topic provides a fragmented picture of categories to rate the usefulness of development tools; a comprehensive taxonomy is missing. In this paper we address this gap in identifying a set of 16 requirements, which were derived from literature research and evaluated with experts. The categories were then applied by experts to judge a newly introduced prototyping platform, which can be used to develop mixed-fidelity app prototypes on the basis of paper sketches. Although we do not claim that the developed set of requirements is complete, the described work can already help builders of mobile app development and prototyping tools. It provides a guideline that displays the importance of different requirement criteria, dependent on different development conditions.

Keywords: App development · App design · Interface prototyping · Requirements metrics

1 Introduction

Helping the development process to become more targeted, prototypes are an important tool to gain feedback on ideas that are not yet fully implemented. Prototypes help to identify mistakes early enough to prevent cost extensive changes that can jeopardize the success of an entire development project. Software user-interface (UI) ideas are complex and hard to communicate. Therefore it is essential for their successful development, to conduct tests with prototypes. This is true for the UIs of mobile apps in particular, which have to take into account a number of specific challenges that derive from different mobile use-contexts and hardware limitations [32]. Compared to PC software, apps are typically smaller – but nonetheless well executed - products with limited scope and functionality. As a result, apps are usually created in comparably small, closely

© Springer International Publishing Switzerland 2015
A. Marcus (Ed.): DUXU 2015, Part II, LNCS 9187, pp. 495–507, 2015.
DOI: 10.1007/978-3-319-20898-5_48

collaborating teams. Hence, adaptations in software engineering concepts and new development tools are needed [12, 30].

This paper provides two main contributions: First, we present a new catalogue of requirements for mobile app development tools. The requirements were identified in a literature review and judged consecutively in expert reviews on their importance in different phases of the development. Insights from the expert survey provide general design guidelines for the conceptual design of app development tools in the future.

Our second contribution is the presentation of a new prototyping approach, which concept was first described in [2]. Our work is designed to support app development teams in their collaborative and creative work to create digital app prototypes. It offers tools that allow groups of designers to collaboratively work on user interface ideas on the basis of regular paper sheets. Designs created in this fashion can be converted into digital prototypes and then seamlessly tested, directly on a mobile device. This way, the tool facilitates the advantages for the design process of the classic paper-based prototyping approach, but overcomes its limitations for tests in the mobile context. At the same time it allows for native Android programming, to achieve advanced functionality within the prototype.

In a demo and tryout session we presented our prototyping system to a group of experts. A general discussion of the general suitability of the new approach was promoted to benefit typical app development processes. Furthermore, we asked the experts to rate the system with the newly identified requirements dimensions. This provided first insights on the usability and applicability of the developed requirement set. Additionally, a quantitative feedback on the strengths and weaknesses of our tool was gained.

2 Motivation and Related Work

2.1 Towards a Comprehensive Catalogue of Requirements

A comprehensive catalogue is needed, which displays the most important requirements developers and designers address at app prototyping tools. Such a catalogue can serve as a basis to design concepts for new prototyping techniques. Moreover, it can serve as a metric to compare different prototyping approaches with one another. However, related work only paints a fragmented picture of those requirements crucial to the assessment of prototyping tools. To help to sharpen this picture a literature review was conducted, in which last eight years publications in the field of HCI, mobile design, and software development were surveyed. This produced a set of 17 categories, for which aggregated examples and references can be found in the following paragraph.

Many authors stress the need for tools that allow a high freedom of design that leverages creativity to get quick prototypes of independent designs developed in parallel [5, 21, 24, 39]. This should preferably be done in group work sessions, collocated [14, 23, 24], or at different locations [4, 15, 16]. Different authors underline the importance for tools to support Expert Reviews [20, 28], yet others to support Design Reviews [5, 21]. Focusing on the prototype testing, different authors stress the importance of tests in the real use-context, an easy setup and distribution of user tests, and tests with a large number of users [14, 25, 27]. Authors that focus on high fidelity prototyping tools argue for development tools that support advanced prototype functionality, reusable prototypes and reusable programming code, simultaneous tests on different platforms, or ways for the definition of animations [7, 19, 20, 36]. Finally, different approaches [1, 29] concentrate on tools that allow for automated model-based evaluation.

3   Research Questions

After determining a set of 17 requirement categories from a literature review, we conducted expert interviews to get an answer to the following research questions. To provide an overall picture of the requirements' relevance and their completeness, we wanted to know 'Which of the suggested categories are generally most important, and which other requirements will experts name in addition?' (Q1). Furthermore, to get a better understanding on how to design tools that aim to support specific development stages, we asked the question 'Does the relevance of specific requirements alter in different development stages?' (Q2.1) and 'If so, which requirements are of special importance in early, medium, and late development stages' (Q2.2). To gain insight on the success of our approach and the suitability of its implementation, we aimed to generate feedback on 'How is the system judged in general and what are the biggest advantages and disadvantages'(Q3). Furthermore, we asked the experts to rate our system with respect to the suggested requirements categories. This generated data on 'How easy is it for experts to apply the suggested requirement dimensions in their ratings, and how is the prototyping system rated in respect to the suggested requirements categories' (Q4).

4   Description of the Surveyed Prototyping System

Our prototyping approach is based on previous concepts by [2] and aims at providing a helpful tool for heterogeneous teams of developers to work on app prototypes in earliest design stages. Accordingly, it conveys the idea of the PBP approach to a system, where prototypes that are designed on paper can be seamlessly converted into digital app prototypes that can be tested directly on the mobile device. It supplies tools that are used for the prototype design, the prototype creation, and the prototype testing.

The Design Workflow. The system uses a self-made overhead projected tabletop computing environment; built of a projector, a photo-, and a video camera. To not interfere with the group discussions and creative flow of the design group in the sketching process, our system is designed to be as unobtrusive as possible. At the beginning of the design process, a team will typically focus on exploring design ideas with paper sketches. Whenever the team feels like it, a paper sketch can quickly transformed into a digital image. For this, a high-resolution photo camera is integrated into the hardware setup, which images are cut and corrected from distortion effects. After a sheet is photographed, it is substituted with a blank paper with the same barcode-marker. Onto this paper, the system will now project the digital image version. Additional sketches can always be added into the projections. As the sheet is photographed the next time, this additional drawn content will be added to the digital version (compare Fig. 1a) A previous digital version can always be restored; therefore digitalization steps can be used to back up the evolving interface sketches.

Fig. 1.   (a) Merging sketches, (b) Storyboard View, (c) Running prototype

User-controls build the basis of the user-prototype interaction. The prototyping system currently supports buttons, checkboxes, text-boxes, picture-boxes, and video-boxes. With the help of a mobile device a control can be positioned on top of a digital sketch. For this purpose, the sketch is displayed on the device's screen whereupon simple swipe gestures are used to position and size controls. Depending on the controls' nature, specific attributes can be set. For example, buttons are defined with linking paths to other screens, or text-boxes can be set up with a text that will be displayed in the app. User-controls defined on the mobile device are immediately displayed as a projection on the related paper sheet, helping the group to keep track with the digital definitions.

The system supports two different sized paper variants for each screen: A 'normal version' that displays the screen in the typical size of a smartphone, and a 'zoom version' that is doubled in its size. With the double sized 'zoom version', sketches can be crafted in more detail and the photos taken of these sketches will produce a better image quality. The normal size marker on the other hand allows more paper sheets to be present on the table at once, and provides designers with a better impression of the actual device's proportions. If linking paths are defined for a button, the design tool displays these with connecting lines between the button and its targets. This way a storyboard view is displayed on the table surface, providing the design team with a good overview of the prototype's interaction path (Fig. 1b).

The Prototype Generation. After the design process is finished, the prototype generation is applied. This can be done either fully automatically, or with the editing of the prototype's programming code. The first option offers early and testable click-dummies with close to no effort; the second option lets the developers advance the prototype's functionality. Either way, the prototyping system generates Java classes as the basis for the prototype. In the automatized process, these classes are instantly compiled and packed with the prototype's images into the prototype source file.

If a development team however wants to advance the prototype's behavior, programming code can be added to these classes. Using the libraries of the android platform, developers can program into the classes with the same techniques they will use in the later product. This native prototype programming style offers two important advantages: First, the functionality of the prototype can be advanced to a high level. Second, the prototype code can be reused directly in the later product. This way the efforts of programming the prototype are not lost, when the prototype itself becomes discarded.

The prototype testing is done within a client-server system that supports developers with mechanisms for a flexible and comfortable evaluation of prototypes with usability experts or test users. The look and feel of the prototypes displayed on the mobile device is primarily determined by the paper sketch, which is loaded as the app's background. However, the prototype may use standard Android user-controls, which appear and function in a high fidelity version (see Fig. 1c). All interactions of a test user with a prototype are recorded. This logging data is uploaded to a server, where it can be easily used for statistical analysis, e.g. to calculate the average time it took a user to find a certain button.

5   Expert Interviews

We invited a total number of 15 experts (5 female, 10 male) to our labs. All experts were professionally involved in mobile app development projects for at least two years. Their role in the development varied between being software developer, designer, user researcher, and project manager. However, about half of the experts described themselves as holding several of these roles at the same time. The size of the projects the experts worked in varied from apps with 10 users to apps with 50 million users. The interview sessions were structured in three different phases, a pre-questionnaire, a demo/ trial and free discussion, and a post-questionnaire. We chose to administer our questionnaires with the online survey tool, which allowed us to implement dynamic questions and facilitated answering open-text items via keyboard input.

In a pre-questionnaire we gathered data on demographics and the personal experience in app development and design projects. Furthermore, we asked questions about the structure of usual development processes and about tools commonly applied. The experts were then asked to rate the importance of certain aspects of development tools for five different project stages, ranging from 'very early' to 'very late'. Experts rated the system on the 17 categories described in section motivation and related work. After that, we asked the participants to come up with additional evaluation dimensions that we might have missed, and to evaluate their importance in the five development stages. Upon completion of the questionnaire rating the requirement dimensions, the participants sat down with the experimenter at the prototyping tool. Following a prepared script, the experimenter now introduced the experts to the idea of the approach and gave them a step-by-step demo of the tools. The demo focused on the tabletop design tool, but included a showcase of our code generation and testing sessions as well. Experts were invited to ask questions free forward during the whole introductory process.

After the introduction the experts were asked to try the system themselves. Afterwards a free discussion about the approach was held. All sessions were recorded on video and audio to allow for post-analysis.

When the discussions came to an end, the experts were asked to answer further questions in a second online survey that now examined our system in particular. We asked for free text feedback about our tools, alongside with the rating of our system with respect to the requirement dimensions we ascertained earlier. Attributes added by participants to the 17 requirement dimensions were added dynamically as a rating dimension of our system as well.

5.1   Results

In order to answer the research questions, we used both sources of information: the data generated by the two surveys, and the feedback we recorded on video in the interview sessions. We therefore describe quantitative, as well as qualitative results from our study. Grouping of categories followed a visual inspection of the data.

Q1: Which of the suggested categories are generally most important, and which other requirements will experts name in addition? We specifically asked the experts about the importance of our suggested requirement dimensions in different design stages. The average rating of each category can be seen in the single charts that are compared in Fig. 2. In the charts, the confidence intervals for the means are displayed. The categories

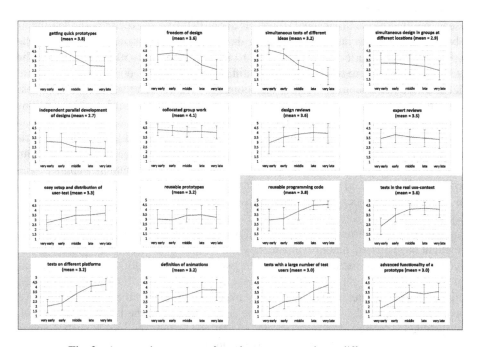

Fig. 2.   Average importance of requirement categories at different stages

are sorted in regard to their approximate gradient. Within these groups, the categories are sorted with respect to their average relevance over all development stages. The categories ranked highest over time are *collocated group work* (4.1), *getting quick prototypes* (3.8), and *reusable programming code* (3.8). The three lowest rated categories are *simultaneous design in groups at different locations* (2.9), *independent parallel development of designs* (2.7), and *automated model-based evaluations* (2.0). All but the last category are no more than 0.3 points below the middle ranking of 3. The category *automated model-based evaluations* was excluded from further analysis due to lack of importance to experts in any of the development stages (mean: 2.0).

New categories suggested by the experts were scarce. Just 3 of the 15 experts came up with suggestions, and not more than 5 attributes in total were proposed. The *'Usability of the tool itself'* was the only category named twice. All others, *'tutorials and help'*, *'fun to use'*, *'cross platform tool use'*, *'open source availability'*, and *'extend functionality'* were solely name once. Unfortunately, too little data could be generated to reasonably evaluate the newly suggested dimensions. The stage specific rating of the categories was in close to all cases neglected or set in unison to the highest value.

Fig. 3. Relevance of requirements at early, middle, and late design stages

Q2.1: Does the relevance of specific requirements alter in different development stages? As the grouping of the requirement graphs indicates, we found that the relevance of most dimensions vary in different development stages. The categories can be clearly grouped by their tendency to increase, remain equal, or drop in their importance during the course of the development. The difference between lowest and highest value is most prominent for the dimensions of the *simultaneous tests of different ideas* ($\Delta 2.8$), *tests with high numbers of users* ($\Delta 2.5$), and *tests on different platforms* ($\Delta 2.3$).

Q2.2: If so, which requirements are of special importance in early, medium, and late development stages? Figure 3 shows the aggregated ranking of each category in three different stages. To provide a clearer picture, we aggregated the two latest and two earliest phases in this presentation. The figures underline once more the changing relevance of the attributes. Here, especially remarkable cases are highlighted. The only category that was ranked in the top categories of all stages is *collocated group work*. *Design reviews* and *expert reviews* are ranked in the midfield of all stages. Especially high ranked for the early stages are categories like *getting quick prototypes, simultaneous tests of different ideas*, or *freedom of design*. Most favorably ranked in later stages are categories like *reusable programming code, tests on different platforms*, or *tests with a large number of users*. Some requirements change clearly in their ranking position at different development stages. Examples are marked with color in in the listings of Fig. 3 above.

Q3: How is the system judged in general and what are the biggest advantages and disadvantages? The general feedback of the invited experts was very positive. Our experts showed high interest in using the system and the discussions were vivid and long enduring. As part of the post-survey we asked to name the biggest advantages and disadvantages of the system in free text. Here, 13 of the 15 experts named the *'participatory work in groups'* and 10 the *'deployment and testing on the mobile device'* as a big advantage. Furthermore, 12 experts remarked 'the system's modularity and its adaptability to different purposes'. Nearly half of the experts addressed the system to be *'easy to use'* (7/15) and noted the *'work with paper'* (8/15) as important. Moreover, the system was described by 6 experts to be *'fast'*, 5 experts rated it to be *'well suited for interdisciplinary work'*, and 4 described that *'the system is fancy and produces a wow-effect when used with a customer'*.

Twice, experts stated that the system *'motivates to produce reusable code from day one'* and that its *'hardware setup is inexpensive and is based on components that exist in most offices'*. In contradiction to that, 6 experts regarded the system setup to be a disadvantage, stating that *'the setup is too complex'*. Comparing the system to existing desktop computer tools that provide visual programming functions, it was stated 3 times that the *'coding becomes necessary too early'*. Moreover, 2 experts criticized the use of mobile devices in the design process. They named *'no easy definition of widgets by just using pen and paper'* as a disadvantage.

Q4: How easy is it for experts to apply the suggested requirement dimensions in their ratings, and how is our system rated in respect to the suggested requirements categories? As part of the post-questionnaire, we asked the experts to rate our tools in the predefined requirement categories, along with those the users suggested. The rating was done on a 10-point scale, where 10 described the approach to be "really well suited" and 1 as "really badly suited" to meet the requirement. The experts used our requirement categories effortlessly. Questions about the dimensions meaning were solely asked about the requirement 'automated model based evaluation', which we discarded from our catalogue as explained above. Our system's abilities to support *'collaborative work'* and to 'get quick prototypes' were rated highest with 9.07, followed by 'tests with a large number of users' that was scored 8.14. The weakest ratings were given to the categories 'tests on different platforms' (5.77), 'advanced functionality of a prototype' (5.21), and the 'definition of animations' (3.15)-which was not yet implemented in the system. These judgments seem promising; comparative studies with other tools are necessary to evaluate such quantitative numbers.

6   Discussion and Outlook

We identified and evaluated a set of 16 requirements that experts judged to be important for development tools of mobile applications. Not many of the invited experts (5 out of 15) suggested attributes in addition to our catalogue. This does not prove that our catalogue is complete, but it still shows that we did not miss obvious requirements in our literature review. However, further research is necessary to investigate ways to quantify the identified categories with objective measures and questionnaires. This way, the suitability of tools to meet the needs of mobile development teams could be assessed and compared more easily in the future. Still, the created catalogue can already be used as a helpful design guideline for creating mobile development tools.

The results support the assumption that different requirements change in importance during the course of the development process. Therefore, tool designers should consider carefully which development phases their products address, and which specific requirements should be brought into focus. The shift of the requirements' relevance underlines the difficulty to provide tools, which are able to benefit the development process over a longer period of time. Isolated solutions that are limited in scope might be helpful in early development stages. Here, processes mostly follow a throw-away-prototyping style: the prototype is solely used to generate feedback on an idea, it itself however loses its value after the testing [39]. However, in later development stages, an evolutionary prototyping approach becomes more important. To sustain the reusability of prototypes, development tools have to support open exchange standards that allow for the transition of prototype results between one tool and another. Existing prototyping tools most often focus on their definition of interface functionality, usually on script languages, web technologies, or product specific pseudo-code. Our approach uses Java code, which is native to the Android platform, and can therefore be included easily in the programming without major adjustments. This way, our concept mixes a throwaway style design approach with an evolutionary coding style.

The received feedback on our prototyping system was generally positive. As pointed out above, the experts judged the design process to be well suited for collaborative teamwork and evaluated it to be easy and fast. Many experts emphasized their liking of paper as a simple and natural medium. Those with a programming background positively pointed out the uniqueness of native code editing and deployment to mobile devices. Experts across all backgrounds evaluated the design aspects of our tools equally positive. Contradicting statements were made about the complexity of our tabletop setup. However, experts that worked in bigger projects described the setup to be 'simple', where in contrast those from small ones called it 'too complex'.

Different experts criticized that programming code becomes necessary too early in our tools so far. They emphasized, that we should adapt some of the visual programming functions that tools like Axure or the appInventor provide. This way, within the prototype design process more complex behavior could be implemented. Additional native programming of prototype behavior could then be limited to more elaborated features. We will consider the integration of codeless programming techniques into the design tool in the future.

In the conception of our tools, we focused on providing open interfaces between the different system parts. This modularity allows users of our system to swap parts of the tools with other solution that might be more suitable for their purposes. Moreover, the easy swapping of system components provides researchers with a testing range to survey the whole app prototyping process. In the future, we will extend our system with additional modules and will support different export formats, which are specific to commonly used major development tools.

7   Conclusion

Developing mobile application prototypes is a complex process. Development teams usually face limited resources regarding time, money, and staff. At the same time, tests of apps with prototypes are essential to avoid pursuing nonviable ideas that can compromise the whole app project. We developed a system that allows development teams to easily create and test app prototypes in earliest design stages already. Our system focuses on supporting simultaneous teamwork in small groups to tackle creative tasks collaboratively. The approach merges classical paper prototyping with high-fidelity prototyping aspects in a tabletop computing environment that facilitates creative interdisciplinary teamwork.

Research on the nature of the development processes of mobile apps has produced a fragmented picture of different properties to rate the quality of development tools. However, no uniform picture is drawn and the relevance of categories in different development stages is rarely considered. We filled this gap in creating a requirements catalogue for app development tools. This was achieved by first identifying categories in a literature review, which were then evaluated with app industry experts. From these interviews we successfully identified a set of 16 requirement categories of development tools and gained an individual rating of the importance of these dimensions at different development stages. With the present paper, we want to emphasize the need for a standardized rating scheme for prototyping tools and give a first impulse for developing a taxonomy for this purpose.

We used the categories to evaluate our system with the invited experts. The feedback was generally positive and provided us with helpful insights for the further development of our tool. Results of the conducted expert survey show that the presented approach is well suited to promote the collaborative creative work on app prototypes in earliest design stages already.

Acknowledgments. This research was funded in the context of a BMBF *Softwarecampus* project and in the context of the interdisciplinary research project *Rethinking prototyping*, Einstein Foundation Berlin.

References

1. Amant, R.S., Horton, T.E., Ritter, F.E.: Model-based evaluation of expert cell phone menu interaction. ACM Trans. Comput.-Hum. Interact **14**, 1 (2007)
2. Bähr, B., Kratz, S., Rohs, M.: A tabletop system for supporting paper prototyping of mobile interfaces. ACM UBICOMP, WS PaperComp (2010)
3. Beyer, H., Holtzblatt, K.: Contextual Design: Defining Customer-Centered Systems (Interactive Technologies). Morgan Kaufmann, Brisbane (1997)
4. Borchers, J., Ringel, M., Tyler, J., Fox, A.: Stanford interactive workspaces: a framework for physical and graphical user interface prototyping. IEEE Wirel. Commun. **9**(6), 64–69 (2002)
5. Cherubini, M., Venolia, G., DeLine, R., Ko, A.J.: Let's go to the whiteboard: how and why software developers use drawings. In: Proceedings CHI 2007, pp. 557–566, ACM (2007)
6. Cook, D.J. Bailey, B.P.: Designers' use of paper and the implications for informal tools. In: Proceedings of the 17th Australia conference on Computer-Human Interaction: Citizens Online: Considerations for Today and the Future, CHISIG of Australia, pp. 1–10, (2005)
7. Dalmasso, I., Datta, S.K., Bonnet, C., Nikaein, N.: Survey, comparison and evaluation of cross platform mobile application development tools. IWCMC **2013**, 323–328 (2013)
8. Davis, R.C., Saponas, T.S., Shilman, M., Landay, J.A. Sketch, W.: Wizard of Oz prototyping of pen-based user interfaces. In: Proceedings of the 20th Annual ACM Symposium on User Interface Software and Technology, ACM, pp. 119–128 (2007)
9. Duh, H., Tan, G., Chen, V.: Usability evaluation for mobile device: a comparison of laboratory and field tests. In: Proceedings of the 8th Conference on Human-Computer Interaction with Mobile Devices and Services MobileHCI 2006, ACM Press, pp. 181–186 (2006)
10. Forlines, C., Wigdor, D., Shen, C., Balakrishnan, R.: Direct-touch vs. mouse input for tabletop displays. In: Proceedings of CHI 2007, ACM, pp. 647–656 (2007)
11. Goel, V.: Sketches of Thought (Bradford Books). The MIT Press, Cambridge (1995)
12. Hammershoj, A., Sapuppo, A., Tadayoni, R.: Challenges for mobile application development. In: ICIN pp. 1–8, (2010)
13. Hendry, D.G., Mackenzie, S., Kurth, A., Spielberg, F., Larkin, J.: Evaluating paper prototypes on the street. In: CHI 2005 Extended Abstracts on Human Factors in Computing Systems, ACM, pp. 1447–1450 (2005)
14. Holzmann, C., Vogler, M.: Building interactive prototypes of mobile user interfaces with a digital pen. In: Proceedings of the 10th Asia Pacific Conference on Computer Human Interaction, ACM, pp. 159–168 (2012)
15. Horst, W.: Supportive tools for collaborative prototyping. Nordes 4 (2011)
16. Hupfer, S., Cheng, L.-T., Ross, S., Patterson, J.: Introducing collaboration into an application development environment. In: Proceedings CSCW 2004, ACM, pp. 21–24 (2004)
17. Klemmer, S.R., Newman, M.W., Farrell, R., Bilezikjian, M., Landay, J.A.: The designers' outpost: a tangible interface for collaborative web site. In: Proceedings of the 14th Annual ACM Symposium on User Interface Software and Technology, ACM, pp. 1–10 (2001)
18. Klemmer, S.R., Sinha, A.K., Chen, J., Landay, J.A., Aboobaker, N., Wang, A.: Suede: A Wizard of Oz Prototyping Tool for Speech User Interfaces. In: Proceedings of the 13th Annual ACM Symposium on User Interface Software and Technology, ACM, pp. 1–10 (2000)

19. Koivisto, E.M.I., Suomela, R.: Using prototypes in early pervasive game development. In: Proceedings of the 2007 ACM SIGGRAPH Symposium on Video Games, ACM, pp. 149–156 (2007)
20. Korhonen, H., Paavilainen, J., Saarenpää, H.: Expert review method in game evaluations: comparison of two playability heuristic sets. In: Proceedings of the 13th International MindTrek Conference: Everyday Life in the Ubiquitous Era, ACM, pp. 74–81 (2009)
21. Landay, J.A. SILK: sketching interfaces like krazy. In: Proceedings of CHI 96, ACM, pp. 398–399 (1996)
22. Landay, J.A.: Interactive sketching for the early stages of user interface design (1996)
23. Leichtenstern, K., André, E.: MoPeDT: Features and evaluation of a user-centred prototyping tool. In: Proceedings of the 2nd ACM SIGCHI Symposium on Engineering Interactive Computing Systems, ACM, pp. 93–102 (2010)
24. Lin, J., Newman, M.W., Hong, J.I., Landay, J.A.: DENIM: Finding a tighter fit between tools and practice for web site design. In: Proceedings CHI 2000, ACM, pp. 510–517 (2000)
25. Lumsden, J., MacLean, R.: A comparison of pseudo-paper and paper prototyping methods for mobile evaluations. In: Meersman, R., Tari, Z., Herrero, P. (eds.) OTM-WS 2008. LNCS, vol. 5333, pp. 538–547. Springer, Heidelberg (2008)
26. Nagai, Y., Noguchi, H.: How designers transform keywords into visual images. In: Proceedings of the 4th Conference on Creativity and Cognition, ACM, pp. 118–125 (2002)
27. Nielsen, C.M., Overgaard, M., Pedersen, M.B., Stage, J., Stenild, S.: It's worth the hassle!: the added value of evaluating the usability of mobile systems in the field. In: NordiCHI'2006, ACM, pp. 272–280 (2006)
28. Nielsen, J., Molich, R.: Heuristic evaluation of user interfaces. In: Proceedings of the SIGCHI Conference on Human Factors in Computing Systems, ACM, pp. 249–256 (1990)
29. Paterno, F.: Model-Based Design and Evaluation of Interactive Applications. Springer, London (2000)
30. Rahimian, V., Ramsin, R.: Designing an agile methodology for mobile software development: a hybrid method engineering approach. In: Second International Conference on Research Challenges in Information Science, 2008. RCIS 2008, pp. 337–342 (2008)
31. De Sá, M., Carriço, L., Duarte, L., Reis, T.: A mixed-fidelity prototyping tool for mobile devices. In: Proceedings of the Working Conference on Advanced Visual Interfaces, ACM, pp. 25–232 (2008)
32. De Sá, M., Carriço, L., Lessons from early stages design of mobile applications. In: Proceedings of the 10th MobileHCI, ACM, pp. 127–136 (2008)
33. De Sá, M., Carriço, L.: Defining scenarios for mobile design and evaluation. In: CHI'2008 Extended Abstracts on Human Factors in Computing Systems, ACM, pp. 2847–2852 (2008)
34. Segura, V.C.V.B., Barbosa, S.D.J.: UISKEI++: multi-device wizard of oz prototyping. In: Proceedings of the 5th ACM SIGCHI Symposium on Engineering Interactive Computing Systems, ACM, pp. 171–174 (2013)
35. Seifert, J., Pfleging, B., del Carmen Valderrama Bahamóndez, E., Hermes, M., Rukzio, E., Schmidt, A.: Mobidev: a tool for creating apps on mobile phones. In: Proceedings of the 13th MobileHCI, ACM, pp. 109–112 (2011)
36. Smutny, P.: Mobile development tools and cross-platform solutions. In: Carpathian Control Conference (ICCC), 2012 13th International, pp. 653–656 (2012)
37. Snyder, C.: Paper Prototyping: The Fast and Easy Way to Design and Refine User Interfaces (The Morgan Kaufmann Series in Interactive Technologies). Morgan Kaufmann, Brisbane (2003)

38. Svanaes, D., Seland, G.: Putting the users center stage: role playing and low-fi prototyping enable end users to design mobile systems. In: Proceedings CHI 2004, ACM, pp. 479–486 (2004)

39. Szekely, P.: User interface prototyping: tools and techniques. In: ICSE Workshop on SE-HCI, pp. 76–92 (1994)

Approaching Users and Context of Use in the Design and Development of Mobile Systems

Eyal Eshet[1(✉)] and Harry Bouwman[2]

[1] Åbo Akademi University Turku, Turku, Finland
eeshet@abo.fi
[2] Delft University of Technology, Delft, The Netherlands
W.A.G.A.Bouwman@tudelft.nl

Abstract. Mobile systems are used by a large variety of users in heterogeneous and dynamic everyday life situations. Approaching users in these contexts poses a challenge for practitioners. To examine practitioners' effort in understanding users and contexts of use, we conducted 15 in-depth interviews with those involved in the design and development of mobile systems for media and finance. We observed that the efforts of design practitioners in subcontracting companies are commonly hindered by strict resource constraints from the client, which result in opportunistic and more obscured data on users. The findings draw attention to the role of the business environment on approaching users and context of use.

Keywords: Interaction design · Mobile computing · User studies · Context of use

1 Introduction

Understanding users and their context of use is a core principle of the User-Centered Design (UCD) philosophy, which has long been considered fundamental to the design of interactive systems [1]. More recently, the fields of User Experience (UX) [2] and Interaction Design [3] re-emphasize this principle. Until recent, computing devices were mainly stationary, resulting in usage in fairly homogeneous and stable contexts of use. In stationary settings, contextual considerations are limited and their influence on the system design fairly predictable [4].

In contrast, the context of use in mobile computing (hereafter, mobile context) is inherently dynamic and heterogeneous in nature with increased variability of systems, users and tasks [5]. Moreover, the context of use is subject to rapid and unpredictable changes [6] as the use of mobile computing is increasingly entwined with the continuous changing of context in people's everyday lives [7]. Consequently, understanding users in mobile contexts call for field-oriented user studies that span both spatial and temporal dimensions. Existing studies (e.g. [8]) observed that conducting user studies, particularly in naturalistic contexts of use, poses a major challenge for practitioners.

© Springer International Publishing Switzerland 2015
A. Marcus (Ed.): DUXU 2015, Part II, LNCS 9187, pp. 508–519, 2015.
DOI: 10.1007/978-3-319-20898-5_49

In order to support practitioners in this endeavor, a deep understanding of existing design practice and rationality is necessary [9]. However, empirical data on the professional practice in the industry, particularly with regard to field-oriented user studies, is limited. Hence, this paper aims to shed light on how users are approached in the design of mobile systems (e.g. the methods used, the types of users that inform the design), as well as the rationality for practitioners' course of action.

To answer these questions, we conducted in-depth interviews with 15 practitioners, mainly those in design roles, complemented by the views of software developers and project managers. All the practitioners are involved in the design and development of consumer mobile systems related to traditional media and finance. Overall, we examined six projects in media and seven in finance.

We contribute to the literature on design practice by emphasizing the business environment complexity and its influence on understanding users in context. Researchers with ambitions to support practice should consider the limitations caused by the business environment. Organizations, especially those that subcontract design services, should better support design practitioners in reaching the actual users.

2 Background and Related Work

Context is an important construct in design. According to Alexander [10], design is a problem-solving activity aimed at finding a fit between form, i.e. the solution to be created, and context, i.e. anything that places demands on the form and defines the problem. In Human-Computer Interaction (HCI), form is an interactive system, while context is anything that may affect system use. Hence, context is mostly referred as the context of use. The International Standardization Organization (ISO) in their standards for system usability (e.g. [11]), indicates that context of use is determined by characteristics of the users, their tasks, and the technical, physical, social and organizational environments in which a system is used. Successful implementation of interactive systems is believed to be dependent on practitioners' understanding of such contextual aspects [11].

Achieving this understanding requires the involvement of target users in their context of use throughout the project lifecycle. Gould, Boies and Ukelson [12] stress the 'early and continual focus on users' as a key principle for designing usable systems. Bevan and Macleod [13] argue that reliable evaluations should be conducted with "representative users performing representative work tasks in appropriate circumstances" [p. 55]. Last, follow-up evaluations should be conducted on actual system usage [11] to address the evolving nature of context [14].

Understanding of relevant contextual aspects becomes a more prominent challenge in mobile computing as the context of use is subject to rapid and unpredictable changes [6] with new classes of users and tasks [5]. Dix et al. [7] argue that the use of mobile devices is entwined in the contexts of everyday life. Indeed, the recent proliferation of touch-based carry-on devices (e.g. smartphone, tablet) highlights this embedded-ness of technology in all daily activities. Essentially, approaching such heterogeneous and dynamic contexts of use emphasizes ethnographic-oriented user studies [15] with active participation of target users [14]. The importance of longitudinal studies was emphasized in understanding the actual use of technologies [16] and to capture experiential outcomes (e.g. expectations and motivations) in relation to the situated context [2]. Bentley and Barrett [17] argue that integrating mobile experiences "into the contexts of daily life is often the hardest part to get right" [p. 34]. From a design and development perspective, conducting user studies in situ requires resources that are often in short supply.

Existing surveys on the UCD practice (e.g. [18, 19]) have not focused on the development of software for mobile computing, let alone from a mobile context lens. Nevertheless, the studies indicate on the commonly used methods, such as interview and usability testing. Time and budget constraints along with the lack of experienced personnel and lack of management support are underlined as the major factors that affect the UCD practice.

Monahan et al. [20] emphasized mobile computing by focusing on the utilization of contextual field methods, although respondents were not limited to those involved in mobile computing. Practitioners mostly used interview and user observation, while resource constraints was a major factor affecting the execution of user studies.

Aiming at understanding the design practice of mobile systems from a context of use perspective, Eshet and Bouwman [8] conducted a survey with practitioners in design, management, and development roles. The authors observed that the methods often used by practitioners are more suitable for addressing a stationary context rather than the mobile context. They argue that time and budget constraints as well as practitioners' experience and competence mainly affect the selection of UCD methods.

Dow et al. [21] conducted a qualitative study with 11 designers in various fields, aiming at improving the design of ubiquitous computing systems. While storytelling is highlighted as a key design activity to communicate the intended context of use, it is unclear how designers gain insights to create the stories. In another qualitative study with 11 designers, who work on context-aware systems, Bauer et al. [22] aimed at understanding designers' view and use of context. While the authors discuss the use of artifacts and other representations in conveying contextual information, the means of obtaining insights about users and their context of use is not mentioned. The authors emphasize designers' "difficulty in finding ways to explore the user's interaction with the system in context" [ibid, p. 434] and the role of designers' experience in alleviating such challenge.

The challenge to approach users in situations that are beyond a fixed space and limited time led to efforts by researchers to devise new approaches. For instance, to uncover relevant contextual aspects, self-reporting diary studies have been suggested (e.g. [23, 24]); and to make evaluations more lifelike, a usability lab augmented with situational elements is advocated [25] (for reviews of methods, see e.g. [16, 26, 27]).

However, Stolterman [9] points to the underutilization of scientifically devised methods by professional practitioners. The discrepancy between the design practice in academic and in industry settings results from the fundamentally different objectives and work circumstance. Consequently, Stolterman [9] calls for a deeper understanding of the existing practice and rationality of practitioners.

3 Methodology

3.1 Study Approach

To complement the largely 'snapshot' view provided by existing surveys, we used open-ended interviews that allows to 'go deep' on a specific topic [28], in this case approaching users and context in the design and development of mobile systems.

Acknowledging the distinct backgrounds and views of the internal and external stakeholders that are involved in projects [29], we approached practitioners in various roles: design-oriented, business/management and software development. The triangulation of perspectives by different informants increases the accuracy of findings [30]. Taking the substantial differences between scientific methods and the design practice in industry into account [9], we focused on practitioners in commercial companies.

Regarding mobile, we focused on carry-on devices [7], i.e. touch-based smartphone and tablet, given practitioners' engagement with both form factors. We define mobile system as a software program that runs on these devices, whether native platform application (i.e. mobile app), browser-based web application (e.g. HTML5) or a hybrid solution. As such systems abounds, we limit the scope to media (e.g. news, magazines, TV), and finance (e.g. banking, payment, investment). These categories represent everyday use of mobile, while differ in user base, e.g. anyone in media vs. customers in finance, and perceived contexts of use, e.g. heterogeneous and generic vs. more specifically defined. Last, we mainly considered consumer systems (B2C), as they demonstrate a greater spread of contexts of use in everyday life.

3.2 Sample

We conducted interviews with 15 practitioners (N_p) in Finland during October 2013 – March 2014. The participants were approached through an online search and by using a snowball sampling. Most participants ($N_p = 11$) work in design-related roles, while other participants have business/management roles ($N_p = 2$) and software development roles ($N_p = 2$). Participants' professional experience ranges between 1-15 years (avg. 10.5; med. 10; std. dev. 3.72), while professional experience with mobile computing varies between 1-15 years (avg. 8.7; med. 9; std. dev. 3.45). Six participants were involved with six different media system projects and nine participants with seven different finance system projects. A total of 14 interviews were conducted: 13 individual and an interview with two practitioners. Except for one remote interview online, all interviews took place in situ.

Participants work in 11 companies of different sizes: two companies are small with up to 50 employees, four are medium-sized with as far as 1000 employees, and five companies are large with over 1000 employees. Medium and large companies include big players in the market. Seven companies are subcontractors that provide IT solutions, while four companies design and develop in-house or use external services.

3.3 Interview Procedure

Following the open-ended type of interviews [31], we used the following high-level topics to guide the discussion: perception of mobile users and means of defining users; perception of the usage environment; methods, techniques and tools to gain user insights; means to interpret the data and generate design ideas; means to evaluate the design practice and project; organizational project settings; professional background and work responsibilities.

Interviews lasted between 36–94 min. (avg. 59 min.) and audio-recorded for transcription and further analysis. The main part of the interview focused on walking through a particular, preferably recent or current, project that fit the study scope.

3.4 Data Analysis

The analysis was largely organized in three phases. First, the interviews were transcribed following a rather denaturalized approach [32]. After that, transcripts were sent to participants for validation. Next, we read through the transcripts. Secondly, following a grounded theory approach [33], we coded the transcripts using Atlas.ti ([34], http://www.atlasti.com/). Last, we explored the findings by using a cross-case synthesis table [31], along with an experimental framework.

Following Miles and Huberman [35] recommendation for having initial list of codes, we coded instances in which practitioners employed relevant UCD methods and techniques, including less-formal ones. For eliciting the factors that affect practitioners in their efforts to understand users in context, we started by open coding followed by axial and selective coding. With axial coding, we aimed at finding dimensions and relationships between the initial factor categories, while the selective coding aimed at identifying the core factors. The coding scheme was complemented with code definitions.

The cross-case synthesis table was used to explore patterns in practitioners work. The synthesis matrix incorporates an array of attributes, including project meta-data (e.g. media/finance category, subcontractor/in-house position, target user definition), UCD methods and the phase in which they were used (requirements, evaluation, usage), type of users involved (e.g. project-internal, social peer groups, actual/representative), type of contexts studied (e.g. artificial, partly representational, naturalistic), length of studying users (ad hoc vs. longitudinal), the factors that affect practitioners' work and other indicators that can help to explain their work motives. Examining certain attributes can indicate on a specific pattern in practitioners' work.

The experimental tabular framework examines the core principles required in order to address the mobile context and the project phases in which the principles should be applied. Grounded in the UCD philosophy (as explained in the background section), the principles include the involvement of **target users**, who are studied in their **real-life contexts** over **time**. The phases include the **requirements** phase to understand user needs and inform the design; the **evaluation**, to test design proposals; and actual **usage**, to continually adapt systems to the evolving and changing nature of context and user needs. The framework emphasizes the method in which practitioners approached target users in actual context over time, to varied extent.

4 Findings

4.1 Approaching Target Users

Table 1 presents the methods that practitioners used in understanding target users and actual context. Out of the 13 examined projects, practitioners approached the intended user group, during one or more phases, in eight projects. Of these projects, studies that involve real-life contexts of use were conducted in six projects, in which five of them were also carried out to some temporal length. The number in brackets denotes the number of projects in which the method was employed.

To understand users, practitioners mainly relied on interviews in early requirements phase, while pilot and lab testing were used for evaluating solutions. Real-life context was studied in early phase by using contextual interview and ethnography. Evaluations in context were conducted with a pilot test. Fairly the same applies to conducting studies over time. Evidently, studying ordinary situations is a great challenge, resulting in only three projects in which practitioners made early efforts to approach users in their daily life. Diary study was not used, considered to be less cost-efficient, i.e. more time consuming and uncertain in producing valuable insights. Interestingly, an augmented usability lab to resemble in-shop payment experience was used in early phase rather than in evaluation, to uncover issues with various payment methods.

Also noticeable is the lack of user studies during the usage of systems. While practitioners often gain insights on the actual usage through various user feedback channels and usage analytics, we included in the framework only studies in which users are intentionally approached.

We observed that practitioners approached target users in four out of four in-house design projects against four out of nine projects in which the design service was subcontracted. Particularly, projects in the usage phase are all in-house. In addition, in six out of the eight projects in the framework practitioners highlighted that approaching users was managed by their own, or by the client, organization.

Table 1. Methods used in projects that approached target users

Requirements	Evaluation	Usage
Contextual interview (2)[a] [b]	Pilot test (4)[a] [b]	Phone interview (1)[b]
Interview (2)	Lab usability test (2)	Survey (1)
Survey (2)	Interviews (1)	
Ethnography (1)[a] [b]		
Augmented lab (1)		

[a] Study conducted in real-life context
[b] Study conducted over time

4.2   Approaching Other Types of Users

In the other five projects, practitioners did not approach actual or representative users. Table 2 presents the type of users and how they were involved throughout the project. Noticeably, practitioners gained user insights from those who are easily available, e.g. colleagues and client personnel (some are involved in the project) and their close social peers like friends and relatives.

Given the lack of target user insights, practitioners mainly use workshop settings to brainstorm and generate ideas, both internally and with the client. User needs are therefore based on the assumptions of those participating in the workshops. Evaluations are commonly informal by giving the system to colleagues and client personnel to use for some time. By this, practitioners gain some insights into relevant contextual aspects, although the usage by tech-savvy people and those familiar with the system may mislead design practitioners. The visible lack of efforts to understand the actual usage is likely the result of these five projects being in a subcontractor position, in which the work is often characterized by a short-term contract.

Besides that, clients play a more significant role on discouraging practitioners in their effort to approach users. First of all, given that users are often the client's customers, clients may be reluctant to share this asset. Secondly, clients strictly limit the project resources to the essential design and development, which leaves no room for conducting user studies. Consequently, practitioners often ground their understanding of users on external data sources that are provided by the client as well as by social peers. While time and budget constraints were mentioned by most practitioners in this study, Table 2 shows that practitioners in subcontracting firms are less likely to approach users in actual contexts of use than their counterparts who work in-house.

Table 2.   Approaching users other than the target group

Phase / Type of users	Requirements	Evaluation	Usage
Social peers	Concept ideation and validation with relatives (1)	Testing with friends, neighbors (1)	
Project internal	Workshop with client (4) Concept ideation and validation with colleagues (1)	Testing by colleagues (4) Testing by client (3) Pilot with client personnel (1)	
Random		Testing with random people on the street (1)	

5 Discussion

Mobile systems are nowadays an integral part of people's everyday life. Understanding users needs in these dynamic and heterogeneous contexts is a challenge faced by practitioners. We conducted in-depth interviews with various mobile practitioners in different companies, aiming at shedding light on their efforts to approach users in actual contexts. In this section we discuss our main finding, namely the reliance on traditional UCD methods and the influence of the business environment on practitioners efforts to understand users. Last, we discuss the limitations of the study.

Overall, approaching users is difficult, while conducting user study in naturalistic contexts occurs in very few exceptional cases. Prior studies (e.g. [8, 18, 20]) already observed the low utilization of field-oriented studies, urging scholars to explore alternative ways to study users in context. As discussed before in this paper, numerous methods have been conceived and practiced by researchers.

In contrast, practitioners mainly rely on traditional methods to understand users and context. The use of interviews (incl. contextual), surveys, usability lab and pilot test indicate on practitioners' inclination to use established methods. Most likely, practitioners are familiar with these methods from their formal education, training and/or professional work, since practitioners' experience is a major factor affecting the choice of methods [8]. Considering resource constraints, which are well known determinants of the design practice (e.g. [8, 18, 20]), practitioners incline to use methods that are perceived to produce relevant insights within time and budget limitations. Hence, practitioners may perceive other methods as less cost-effective or may not have experience using them.

Gaining experience with a new method, like diary study and rapid ethnography, requires first awareness of it and demonstration of its cost-justification. Such knowledge is acquired largely through formal education and training. Hence, cost-efficient user study approaches should be promoted in the education of professional designers, while new approaches should be distributed beyond the academia. In addition, researchers, who work on new approaches to solve the problems of practitioners, should be more thoughtful of the complexity, uncertainty and value conflicts in the problems faced by professional practitioners [36]. One such complexity is the business environment.

Users and context are more likely to be approached in in-house, rather than in subcontracted, projects. According to Barney [37], organizations can achieve a competitive advantage by investing in valuable, rare and hard to imitate resources and capabilities. Design competences, e.g. trained professionals and their work activities (incl. UCD methods), can be considered a part of the organizational resources and capabilities. Apparently, organizations that invest in in-house design competences understand its strategic value, which makes it more likely that practitioners would be supported in their efforts to understand users and context. Organizations that subcontract design competences from a third party may be more interested in the cost-efficient delivery of the outcome and less knowledgeable in the operational activities required in achieving a usable and useful outcome. Moreover, our findings suggest that users are more likely to be approached when the organization alleviates the burden of recruiting users, such as in providing access to its customer base.

The business relationship has a more significant effect on understanding users and context. With few resources available for conducting user studies, practitioners in a subcontracting type of relationship mainly rely on user data that is provided by the client. Such understanding of users adds another level of obscurity to the common second-order understanding as discussed by Krippendorf [38]. That is, practitioners understanding of users is embedded in the understanding of client's understanding of users' understanding of something. This recursive course of action significantly affects the understanding of user needs, especially in light of the business perspective of the client. Looking for workarounds to achieve a second-order understanding of users, practitioners default to gain insights from close social peers that may or may not represent their target users.

This practice is assumed to be common, since design practitioners are mostly employed by professional usability/UX consultants or software houses [8, 20]. Schön [36] warns on the negative effect from a practice that becomes repetitive, essentially "the practitioner may miss important opportunities to think about what he is doing … he is drawn into patterns of errors which he cannot correct" [p. 61]. Since practitioners are not experimenting with actual users, becoming accustomed to a third-order understanding of users may affect practitioners' knowledge about users as well as the development of competences to gain new knowledge, especially considering the shift to mobile computing with its notable impact on understanding people.

The business environment complexity in the work of design practitioners is often overlooked in HCI research. Obviously, simulating the business environment in research is difficult. One suggestion is to foster more collaboration between research and practice by means of action research type of studies that are conducted within actual settings of professional practice.

The limitations of the study include our sample, which is based on practitioners in a specific country. Based on the practitioners' professional experience and distribution in terms of company sizes and type (in-house, subcontractor), we assume that the sample reflects the business practice in Finland. Additionally, we conducted interviews in the Netherlands to further develop and validate our findings. Regarding systems, we acknowledge the fact that other categories may have more specific use cases (e.g. business, games) and encourage the examination of possible differences.

Second, we relied merely on practitioners' recollections of their activities. As such, the responses can be biased or may simply suffer from an inaccurate articulation of the events due to poor recall. We alleviated this shortcoming by focusing on experiences from a particular and recent project. An ethnographic-oriented study of the topic would be obviously valuable.

Third, the analysis of verbal text is inherently selective and interpretive [35]. The selection of data is based on the questions that guided the study and by looking for commonalities instead of unique statements. To address possible misinterpretations on words and statements, we asked participants to review their transcripts, read through the transcripts several times, and focused on the meaning in the context of statements rather than specific words.

Last, the findings are limited in the sense that they merely focus on the design practice, while the evaluation of the actual use of systems and the relations between this evaluation and the design practice was not tested. That is, does a better-informed design lead to better performing systems from a user perspective?

6 Conclusion

In this paper we examined the design practice of mobile systems, particularly regarding the approaching of users and contexts of use. We used interviews to collect data from mobile practitioners, mainly in design roles. Our main finding emphasizes the business environment complexity and offers a valuable contribution to interaction design theory, education and practice, particularly with the current transition to mobile systems and the significant effect of mobility on context.

Our findings show that practitioners mostly use traditional methods to understand users and context, such as interviews, surveys and lab testing. These methods are very limited with regard to gaining insights on users in context. As practitioners tend to use methods they are familiar with, this has implications on the education and training of design practitioners in approaches that are more suitable to understand users in dynamic and heterogeneous contexts.

Moreover, we emphasize the business environment complexity that practitioners face in their effort to understand users and context and that is often overlooked in HCI research. Essentially, we observed that in-house design practitioners are more likely to approach users and context of use than their counterparts in subcontracting organizations. In addition, design practitioners in subcontracting firms are often dependent on a third-order understanding of users through the client organization, which obscure their necessary understanding of target users in context. Hence, organizations that obtain external design competences and wish to address user needs should make more effort to support design practitioners in actualizing their expertise. We highlight the facilitation of access to users as an example of such support.

Researchers that aim at solving the problems of professional designers in their efforts to understand users and context should show careful consideration to the business environment complexity. This can be achieved by acting as a researcher-practitioner and gaining a first-order understanding of the rich and complex problems that professional practitioners face.

Acknowledgments. We are grateful to the participants for sharing their experiences with us. The study was supported by grants from Turku Centre for Computer Science, Åbo Akademi Foundation and the Foundation for Economic Education in Finland.

References

1. Gould, J.D., Lewis, C.: Designing for usability: key principles and what designers think. Commun. ACM **28**, 300–311 (1985)

2. Hassenzahl, M., Tractinsky, N.: User experience - a research agenda. Behav. Inf. Technol. **25**, 91–97 (2006)
3. Rogers, Y., Sharp, H., Preece, J.: Interaction design: beyond human-computer interaction. Wiley, New York (2007)
4. Hinman, R.: The Mobile Frontier. Rosenfeld Media, Brooklyn (2012)
5. Johnson, P.: Usability and mobility; interactions on the move. In: Proceedings of the First Workshop on Human-Computer Interaction with Mobile Devices (1998)
6. Forman, G.H., Zahorjan, J.: The challenges of mobile computing. Computer **27**, 38–47 (1994)
7. Dix, A., Rodden, T., Davies, N., Trevor, J., Friday, A., Palfreyman, K.: Exploiting space and location as a design framework for interactive mobile systems. ACM Trans. Comput.-Hum. Interact. **7**, 285–321 (2000)
8. Eshet, E., Bouwman, H.: Addressing the Context of Use in Mobile Computing: a Survey on the State of the Practice. Interact. Comput. iwu002 (2014)
9. Stolterman, E.: The nature of design practice and implications for interaction design research. Int. J. Des. **2**, 55–65 (2008)
10. Alexander, C.: Notes on the Synthesis of Form. Harvard University Press, Cambridge (1964)
11. ISO: ISO 9241-210:2010 Ergonomics of human-system interaction-Part 210: Human-centred design for interactive systems. International Organization for Standardization, Geneva (2010)
12. Gould, J.D., Boies, S.J., Ukelson, J.: How to design usable systems. Handbook of human-computer interaction. **2**, 231–254 (1988)
13. Bevan, N., Macleod, M.: Usability measurement in context. Behav. Inf. Technol. **13**, 132–145 (1994)
14. Dourish, P.: What we talk about when we talk about context. Pers. Ubiquitous Comput. **8**, 19–30 (2004)
15. Greenberg, S.: Context as a dynamic construct. Hum.-Comput. Interact. **16**, 257–268 (2001)
16. Hagen, P., Robertson, T., Kan, M., Sadler, K.: Emerging research methods for understanding mobile technology use. In: Proceedings of the 17th Australia conference on Computer-Human Interaction: Citizens Online: Considerations for Today and the Future, pp. 1–10 (2005)
17. Bentley, F., Barrett, E.: Building Mobile Experiences. MIT Press, Cambridge (2012)
18. Rosenbaum, S., Rohn, J.A., Humburg, J.: A toolkit for strategic usability. In: Proceedings of the SIGCHI conference on Human Factors in Computing Systems (CHI 2000), pp. 337–344. ACM Press (2000)
19. Bygstad, B., Ghinea, G., Brevik, E.: Software development methods and usability: Perspectives from a survey in the software industry in Norway. Interact. Comput. **20**, 375–385 (2008)
20. Monahan, K., Lahteenmaki, M., McDonald, S., Cockton, G.: An investigation into the use of field methods in the design and evaluation of interactive systems. In: Proceedings of the 22nd British HCI Group Annual Conference on People and Computers: Culture, Creativity, Interaction, vol. 1, pp. 99–108. British Computer Society, Swinton (2008)
21. Dow, S., Saponas, T.S., Li, Y., Landay, J.A.: External representations in ubiquitous computing design and the implications for design tools. In: Proceedings of the 6th Conference on Designing Interactive Systems, pp. 241–250. ACM, New York (2006)
22. Bauer, J.S., Newman, M.W., Kientz, J.A.: What designers talk about when they talk about context. Hum.-Comput. Interac. **29**, 420–450 (2014)
23. Consolvo, S., Walker, M.: Using the experience sampling method to evaluate ubicomp applications. IEEE Pervasive Comput. **2**, 24–31 (2003)

24. Brandt, J., Weiss, N., Klemmer, S.R.: txt 4 l8r: lowering the burden for diary studies under mobile conditions. In: CHI 2007 extended abstracts on Human Factors in Computing Systems, pp. 2303–2308. ACM, New York (2007)

25. Kjeldskov, J., Stage, J.: New techniques for usability evaluation of mobile systems. Int. J. Hum Comput Stud. **60**, 599–620 (2004)

26. Coursaris, C.K., Kim, D.J.: A Meta-Analytical Review of Empirical Mobile Usability Studies. J. Usability Stud. **6**, 11:117 (2011)

27. Eshet, E.: Human-centered design in mobile application development: emerging methods. IJMHCI **4**, 1–21 (2012)

28. Lazar, J., Feng, J.H., Hochheiser, H.: Research Methods in Human-computer Interaction. Wiley, New York (2010)

29. Suchman, L.: Located accountabilities in technology production. Scand. J. Inf. Syst. **14**, 91–105 (2002)

30. Patton, M.Q.: How to Use Qualitative Methods in Evaluation. SAGE Publications, Thousand Oaks (1987)

31. Yin, R.K.: Case study research: design and methods, 3rd edn. Sage Publications Inc., CA (2003)

32. Oliver, D.G., Serovich, J.M., Mason, T.L.: Constraints and opportunities with interview transcription: towards reflection in qualitative research. Soc. Forces **84**, 1273–1289 (2005)

33. Strauss, A., Corbin, J.M.: Basics of Qualitative Research: Grounded Theory Procedures and Techniques. Sage Publications Inc., Thousand Oaks (1990)

34. Muhr, T.: ATLAS/ti — A prototype for the support of text interpretation. Qual Sociol. **14**, 349–371 (1991)

35. Miles, M.B., Huberman, A.M.: Qualitative Data Analysis: An Expanded Sourcebook. SAGE Publications, Thousand Oaks (1994)

36. Schön, D.A.: The Reflective Practitioner: How Professionals Think In Action. Basic Books, New York (1984)

37. Barney, J.: Firm Resources and Sustained Competitive Advantage. J. Manag. **17**, 99–120 (1991)

38. Krippendorff, K.: The Semantic Turn: A New Foundation for Design. CRC Press, Boca Raton (2005)

The Importance of Metaphors for User Interaction with Mobile Devices

Chrysoula Gatsou[(⊠)]

Faculty of Fine Arts and Design, TEI of Athens, Athens, Greece
cgatsou@teiath.gr

Abstract. The use of metaphor is essential in user interface design, particularly for the mobile landscape, as the visual environment continues to be populated with more and more mobile electronic devices. A metaphor allows us to understand one concept in terms of another. Although considerable research has gone into the mobile technology, little attention has been paid to mobile interface metaphor, which is the key to user interaction. This paper explores the role of metaphor in interfaces in facilitating user interaction with mobile devices. It presents a classification of metaphors. It also proposes a framework with salient factors in relation to visual communication with metaphors. It also offers some thoughts on the use of new metaphors.

Keywords: Metaphors · Mobile devices · Visual communication · Mental models · User experience

1 Introduction

Mobile devices are now an essential part of our daily life. Recently there have been rapid developments in the direction of more intuitive and seamless interface designs. Areas of research that have emerged from this include ubiquitous computing, intelligent environments and tangible user interfaces. The use of metaphor is essential to user interface design, particularly in regard to the mobile device landscape, as increasing numbers of mobile electronic devices continue to populate the visual environment. Metaphors offer a rich domain within which to construct interactive mobile interfaces and to tackle problems that users often face when using mobile applications.

As devices get smaller and more ubiquitous, the metaphor of the desktop is becoming increasingly unwieldy when applied to handheld devices, mobile phones, and mobile environments [1]. Brewster et al., note the inadequacy of desktop metaphors when used in relation to information presentation in mobile computing [2].

Metaphors should suit both the functional needs they serve and their natural environment. A mobile-phone type interface on a computer with a large monitor is as illogical as a large monitor-style interface on a mobile phone. Metaphors are effective tools for facilitating mutual understanding in communications. They are the tools by means of which people give symbolic form to abstract concepts, so as to communicate them in a comprehensible manner.

This paper explores the role of metaphor in interfaces with the aim of facilitating user interaction with mobile devices. The paper opens with a literature review, which

© Springer International Publishing Switzerland 2015
A. Marcus (Ed.): DUXU 2015, Part II, LNCS 9187, pp. 520–529, 2015.
DOI: 10.1007/978-3-319-20898-5_50

establishes the theoretical background for the study. It then offers a classificatory schema of metaphors, suggests a framework with factors relevant to visual communication through metaphor. It offers some thoughts on the use of new metaphors before offering some conclusions.

2 Background

2.1 Metaphors

The word 'metaphor' derives from the Greek μεταφορά (metaphora), which means exactly 'transferring' or 'conveying'. Aristotle's definition of metaphor is still highly applicable today. He notes that a "metaphor consists in giving the thing a name that belongs to something else" [3].

The first modern theorist to introduce the idea that the use of metaphor is all-pervasive in language and that metaphor is a cognitive mechanism was Richards. According to Richards, metaphors consist of two parts: a vehicle and a tenor. The vehicle is the concept that we are familiar with and the tenor is the concept to which the metaphor is applied [4]. Lakoff and Johnson's conceptual view of metaphor has largely dominated the field since the 1980s. In their view, metaphors are systematic thought structures that link two conceptual domains. The 'source' domain is essential in structuring the 'target' domain through a metaphorical link, or 'conceptual metaphor' [5]. Erickson furthermore notes that metaphors *"function as natural models, allowing us to take our knowledge of familiar, concrete objects and experiences and use it to give structure to more abstract concepts"* [6].

Metaphor is not just a literary matter, however. It is fundamental to the way we think. In the development of interactive systems, we are constantly trying to describe to others a new domain, such as a new application, a different design or new interactive facilities. Thus we have to use metaphor to explain this new domain in terms of something that is more familiar. In Blackwell's view, within a few years the metaphorical use of a term becomes established in the language to such an extent that one forgets that was a metaphor before [7].

2.2 Mental Models

Marcus and Gould note that user interfaces consist of the following components: metaphors, mental models, navigation, interactions and appearances. Metaphor is the use of a familiar concept to explain a new one [8]. The term "mental model" has been used in many contexts and for many purposes. It was first mentioned by Craik in his 1943 book, *The Nature of Explanation* [9]. Leiser argues that a mental model of a user interface consists of a set of representations of the relationship between user actions and system responses [10]. This view rests on Johnson-Laird's view of mental models as a form of knowledge representation and their manipulation as a form of reasoning, in which a mental model is regarded as the set of possible representations of the available information [11]. Mental models have been used in human-computer interaction and have resulted in increasing usability. Staggers and Norcio propose definitions of users' mental models that base the users' models of a system on their experience of the system [12]. According to Cooper *et al.* the closer the represented model comes to the user's mental model, the easier it is to understand the programme [13]. Figure 1 shows the implementation or system model, the user's mental model and the represented (designer's) model. The designer is called in to bridge the gap between the two.

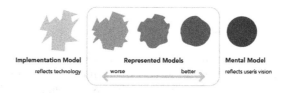

Fig. 1. The represented model (Cooper et al., 2007)

2.3   Why Metaphors are Important

Carroll *et al.* suggest that the metaphor approach *"seeks to increase the initial familiarity of actions, procedures and concepts by making them similar to actions, procedures and concepts that are already known"* [14]. Metaphor, far from being merely a literary device, is fundamental to the way we think. In the development of interactive systems the designer is constantly called on to describe to users a new domain, such as a new application, a different design or new interactive facilities. Thus one has to use metaphor to explain such new domains in terms familiar to the potential user.

When considering the idea of navigating an interactive system, many people immediately think that navigation consists of attempting to reach a specific destination, in the way in which internet users navigate or explore as they follow links from one place to another. The metaphor used in the iPad (iBooks) drives the user clearly to select a book (Fig. 2).

Fig. 2. Mobile interface metaphors

However, some metaphors used by the iPad are ambiguous. Few potential users, for example, know what the green button labelled "SkyGrid" means. On the other hand, the file sharing tool Dropbox makes use of a metaphor to explain their services to the potential user. In the Dropbox name and logo reference is made to a 'Dropbox', that is, a box into which one can drop things, everyone being familiar with the concept of a cardboard box to store things. Dropbox has adapted this concept and transferred it to an online tool that stores documents. The increase of mobile devices and multiple functions forces designers to develop new modes and modalities of physical interaction techniques [15].

3   Classification of Interface Metaphors

When considering research into interface metaphors, it is important to draw up categories in order to make the study of important material more comprehensible. The classification of common metaphors is part of an effort to facilitate the design of more efficient interfaces. In 1980, cognitive linguists Lakoff and Johnson established the conceptual metaphor theory, which they called 'cognitive metaphor theory' [5]. They argued that metaphors are both pervasive in language and are essential part to our conceptual system of thought and action. They introduced three categories of metaphors, ontological, orientational, or structural:

- Ontological metaphors rest on our physical experiences with physical objects. Ontological metaphors help us to represent an abstract thing in terms of something concrete such as an object, substance, container or person.
- Orientational metaphor is a metaphor in which concepts are spatially related to each other such as up-down, in-out, front-back, on-off, near-far, central-peripheral.
- Structural metaphors allow us to structure one concept in terms of another.

In Hutchins' view, "*metaphors reach the user community as ways of talking about the behavior of the system and provide the users with resources for thinking about what the machine is doing*". He suggested three types of metaphor illustrating different aspects of the human-computer interface [16].

- Activity metaphors refer to the user's high-level goals and structure expectations concerning to the outcome of the activity, for instance, writing a document.
- Mode of interaction metaphors concern the user's view of the computer, for example, whether they regard it as a conversation partner, or an archiving tool.
- Task domain metaphors offer a structure to help the user understand computer-based objects and operations.

Condon and Keuneke focused on interface metaphors and classified them on the basis of the underlying metaphor, rather than the medium in which the metaphor is presented [17]. Their classification involves three categories:

- Spatial metaphors define 2D or 3D spaces, in which interactions and activities take place,
- Activity-based metaphors, which define the actions that can be performed upon the information or people within the space,
- Interactional metaphors, which support specific forms of communication.

Carroll et al. [14] gives three theories underlining research on metaphors:

- Structural approaches interpret the metaphor process in terms of the mapping between the knowledge of target domains and the knowledge of source domains.

- Operational approaches attempt to prove the quantifiable effects of metaphors on user performance.
- Pragmatic approaches primarily focus on what types of objective or contextual concerns might limit the deductive functions of metaphors.

Of all these categories, structural and spatial metaphors have been used most broadly in interface design. The principle of the spatial metaphor is that locating information on the internet involves faculties similar to those employed when navigating in physical space. Furthermore, my own view is that structural metaphors are the most specific of all metaphor types and are also the most sensitive to cultural influences.

4   Factors Affecting Visual Communication Through Metaphors

Cognitive research on interface mobile metaphors has identified a number of significant factors that may fundamentally affect the comprehension of metaphors. On the basis of the literature review above and our own previous research into user visual communication with mobile interface metaphors [18, 19], we focus on three factors, namely culture, context and user experience.

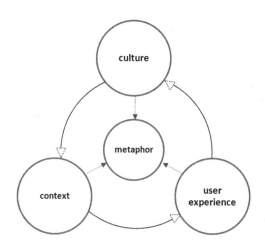

Fig. 3. Factors influencing metaphors' comprehension

4.1   Culture

Cultural differences may make basic metaphors used in a mobile interface design incomprehensible to users from other cultures [19]. Culture is a concept that is difficult to define and measure. In the view of Hofstede and Hofstede, culture is the collective programming of the mind that separates one group of people from another [20]. They argue that culture can be defined as *"the forms of things that people have in mind, their models for perceiving, relating or otherwise interpreting them"*.

Metaphors present particular problems because images that may be comprehensible in one culture may be unknown in another [21]. The cultural environment of the user consists of their ethnicity, their range of experience, which is related to their socio-economic background. However the author's previous empirical work has found that cultural differences may also is defined by age [18].

4.2 Context

The dynamics of cognitive processes involves the vast number of contexts in which the meanings are constructed. Therefore what something means to an individual depends very much on the context of the interaction. In regard to how users and designers perceive the meaning of products, Krippendorf suggested that *"objects are always seen in a context (of other things, situations and users, including the observing self)"* [22]. Context can influence user interaction at different levels. For example, it can contribute very strongly to whether an experience is positive or negative or to how far users accept the service in question. As Macdonald stresses, visual symbolism is not universal. Perception, recognition and acceptance of an object is determined by the context in which it is used and by the nature and cultural conditioning of the user [23]. Multiple contexts can interact with each other in ways that are not fixed. Preece *et al.* define context of use as *"the circumstances in which the interactive product is expected to operate"*, and include the social, technological, organisational and physical environment [24]. Buxton argues that technologies do not exist in a vacuum. In any meaningful sense, they only have meaning, or relevance, in a social and physical context [25].

4.3 User Experience

Stone *et al.* argue that use of metaphor is pointless, if the physical analogue to the metaphor is outside the user's experience [26]. Any connection with the real world can potentially be used as the vehicle for any metaphor. Users are individuals who have a great deal of real world experience to rely on when attempting to understand matters. Shedroff [27] gives a definition of user experience as follows:

> *"The overall experience, in general or specifics, a user, customer, or audience member has with a product, service or event. In the usability field, this experience is usually defined in terms of ease-of-use. However, the experience encompasses more than merely function and flow, but the understanding compiled through all of the senses."*

In order to compile a full list of potential vehicles, it is crucial to consider exactly who is going to use the application, so as to be able to choose the proper types of vehicles.

Erickson's approach to the overall design of metaphors is first to understand the functionality of the system, then to identify users' problem areas and finally to generate metaphors that might help, evaluating them according to the criteria just discussed [28].

In summary, all these three factors offer a structure that helps in drawing together the various complex aspects involved in the evolution of new metaphors designed to improve interaction with mobile devices.

5 From Mobile Metaphors to Cloud Metaphor

The revolution in mobility and ease of access has changed the user's mental model regarding ownership of files. It has also decreased the importance of where we now save our files. Many files are shared online on websites. For example, there is the *instagram* application, where users upload photos, *Pinterest* or *Google Docs*. (See Fig. 3). Our every day computing activities increasingly involve the use of a Web-based tool, sharing, e-mail, word processing or photo editing. Users may store their emails and other documents on the Web and they can also create links directly to those files to be shared with their friends, family, colleagues or classmates. These new contexts have changed our digital behavior significantly. It is possible that a number of people never open a desktop application. This situation is gradually leading to the design of new metaphors.

| Instagram | Pinterest | Google docs |

Fig. 4. Sharing mobile applications metaphors

As new ways of navigation, searching and organizing personal data appear, people become more mobile, enjoy large amounts of data storage and are able to perform complex tasks anywhere. This change means that users have to deal with the different representations of visual metaphors which have started appearing in mobile applications. Ubiquitous and mobile computing is the post-desktop model of human-computer interaction, in which the information computing and processing functionalities are interlaced within daily activities and objectives.

It is obvious that individuals will want to be able to use many different devices to access data and applications. A mobile cloud can be accessed through various devices. As cloud computing continues to offer an increasing number of services to the user, there is an increasing demand for new design metaphors, driven by the new requirements of cloud computing. This new landscape requires a careful response on the part of designers, so that metaphors will be understood and adopted by the users (Fig. 5).

| Siri, Apple | SkyDrive | SkyDrive folder |

Fig. 5. New mental models for cloud metaphors

Users are required to structure new mental models suitable for the new environment. For example users of the application Skydrive who search for documents files in yellow folders now confront icons consisting of small blue clouds, instead of previous icons (See Fig. 4). Another paradigm is Siri, a voice interaction search service on the latest iOS, which understands its user's intentions and offers him or her the best options.

Moran and Zhai in their article *Beyond the desktop metaphor in seven dimensions* propose seven principles to aid the development of the desktop information model into to a much powerful model that can be used to support user interaction with mobile applications. They propose the idea of a *personal information cloud* [29]. In their second principle *"From desktop to a diverse set of visual representations"* they illustrate the new landscape emphasizing the need for visual representations which represent mobile applications. They argue that *"in the future a variety of advanced visual representations may be adapted to specific problem domains and different device forms, complementing the basic conventional desktop metaphor"*.

In Marcus' [30] view, metaphor is not likely to disappear in the near future. However, its use will expand to designing agents that assist our computing tasks.

This new mobile era demands effective visual communication between new representations of metaphors and users, so as to make user interaction as smooth and easy as possible.

6 Conclusion

The use of metaphors in mobile devices allows potential users to understand possibly unfamiliar phenomena by making associations with familiar objects and feelings. This paper has presented how mobile metaphors can be applied to facilitate human-computer interaction and improve interface design for mobile applications.

The classifications of Lakoff and Johnson [5], Hutchins [16] Condon and Keuneke [17] and Carroll et al. [14] provide starting points for how metaphors can be selected during mobile interface design for user visual communication and interaction. Furthermore we have offered a framework involving salient factors such as culture, context and user experience in relation to a user's visual communication by means of metaphors. The paper also presents some thoughts on the use of new landscape of metaphors like cloud computing.

The outcomes of this study offer a foundation for future research in the area of mobile metaphors. Moreover, there is a clear need for research, given the rise of cloud computing, in order to produce effective representations based on culturally-dependent metaphors.

References

1. Saffer, D.: Designing for Interaction: Creating Innovative Applications and Devices, 2nd edn. New Riders Publishing, Thousand Oaks (2009)
2. Brewster, S., Leplâtre, G., Crease, G.: Using non-speech sounds in mobile computing devices. In: First Workshop on Human Computer Interaction with Mobile Devices, Glasgow, Scotland (1998)
3. Aristotle.: The Poetics. In: McKeon R. (Ed. and Trans). Introduction to Aristotle, 2nd edn. University of Chicago Press, Chicago (1973)
4. Richards, I.A.: The Philosophy of Rhetoric. Oxford University Press, Oxford (1936)
5. Lakoff, G., Johnson, M.: Metaphors We Live By. The University of Chicago Press, Chicago (1980)
6. Erickson, T.: Working with interface metaphors. In: Laurel, B. (ed.) The Art of Human-Computer Interface Design, pp. 65–73. Addison-Wesley Publishing Company, Reading (1990)
7. Blackwell, A.F.: The reification of metaphor as a design tool. ACM Transactions on Computer–HumanInteraction (TOCHI) 13(4), 490–530 (2006)
8. Marcus, A., Gould, E.W.: Crosscurrents: Cultural dimensions and global web user-interface design. ACM Interact. 7(4), 32–46 (2000)
9. Craik, K.J.W.: The nature of explanation. Cambridge University Press, Cambridge (1967)
10. Leiser, B.: The presence phenomenon and other problems of applying mental models to user interface design and evaluation. In: Rodgers, Y., Rutherford, A., et al. (eds.) Models in the Mind - Theory, Perspective, and Application. Academic Press, London (1992)
11. Johnson-Laird, P.N.: Mental Models. Harvard University Press, Cambridge (1983)
12. Staggers, N., Norcio, A.: Mental models: concepts for human-computer interaction research. Int. J. Man Mach. Stud. 38, 587–605 (1993)
13. Cooper, A., Reimann, R., Cronin, D.: About Face 3: The Essentials of User Interface Design. Wiley, New York (2007)
14. Carroll, J.M., Mack, R.L., Kellogg, W.A.: Interface metaphors and user interface design. In: Helander, M. (ed.) Handbook of Human– Computer Interaction, pp. 67–85. Elsevier Science Publishers, Amsterdam (1988)
15. Kaptelinin, V., Czerwinski, M.: Introduction: The desktop metaphor and new uses of technology. In: Kaptelinin, V., Czerwinski, M. (eds.) Beyond the Desktop Metaphor: Designing Integrated Digital Work Environments, pp. 335–354. MIT Press, Cambridge (2007)
16. Hutchins, E.: Metaphors for interface design. In: Taylor, M.M., Neel, F., Bouwhuis, D.G. (eds.) The Structure of Multimodal Dialogues, pp. 11–28. North-Holland, Amsterdam (1989)
17. Condon, C., Keuneke, S.: Metaphors and layers of signification: the consequences for advanced user service interfaces. In: Kugler, H.-J., Mullery, A., Niebert, N. (eds.) Towards a Pan-European Telecommunication Service Infrastructure — IS&N 1994. LNCS, vol. 851, pp. 75–87. Springer, Heidelberg (1994)

18. Gatsou, C., Politis, A., Zevgolis, D.: Text vs visual metaphor in mobile interfaces for novice user interaction. In: Proceedings of 16th International Conference on Electronic Publishing, pp. 271–279 (2012)

19. Gatsou, C., Politis, A., Zevgolis, D.: The importance of mobile interface icons on user interaction. IJCSA Int. J. Comput. Sci. Appl. **9**(3), 92–107 (2012)

20. Hofstede, G., Hofstede, J.G.: Cultures and Organizations. Software of the Mind. Intercultural Cooperation and its Importance for Survival. Mc Graw-Hill, New York (2005)

21. Hackos, J., Redish, J.: User and Task Analysis for Interface Design. Wiley, New York (1998)

22. Krippendorf, K.: On the essential contexts of artifacts or on the preposition that design is making sense (of things). In: Margolin, V., Buchanan, R. (eds.) The Idea of Design, pp. 156–184. The MIT Press, Cambridge (2000)

23. Macdonald, A.S.: Developing a qualitative sense. In: Stanton, N. (ed.) Human Factors in Consumer Product Design Design and Evaluation, pp. 175–191. Taylor and Francis, London (1998)

24. Preece, J., Rogers, Y., Sharp, H.: Interaction Design: Beyond HumanComputer Interaction. Wiley, NY (2007)

25. Buxton, B.: Sketching user experiences: getting the design right and the right design. Morgan Kaufmann, San Francisco (2007)

26. Stone, D., Jarrett, C., Woodroffe, M., Minocha, S.: User Interface Design and Evaluation. Morgan Kaufmann, San Francisco (2005)

27. Shedroff, N.: An Evolving Glossary of Experience Design (2008). Online glossary http://www.nathan.com/ed/glossary/. Accessed 19 May 2013

28. Erickson, T.D.: Working with interface metaphors. In: Laurel, B. (ed.) The Art of Human-Computer Interface Design, pp. 65–73. Addison-Wesley Publishing Company, Reading (1990)

29. Moran, T.P., Zhai, S.: Beyond the desktop metaphor in seven dimensions. In: Kaptelinin, V., Czerwinski, M. (eds.) Beyond the Desktop Metaphor: Designing Integrated Digital Work Environments, pp. 335–354. MIT Press, Cambridge (2007)

30. Marcus, A.: Metaphors and user interfaces in the 21st century. Interactions **9**, 7–10 (2002)

Keyword Input via Digits: Simplified Smartphone Interface for Information Retrieval

Masanobu Higashida[1(✉)] and Toru Ishida[2]

[1] NTT Software Corporation, Minatomirai, Nishi-ku, Yokohama, Japan
higashida.masanobu@po.ntts.co.jp
[2] Department of Social Informatics, Kyoto University,
Yoshida-honmachi, Kyoto, Japan
ishida@i.kyoto-u.ac.jp

Abstract. This paper reports an application for smartphones that allows users to use digits for simple keyword input and its usability evaluation. This input method, called "one touch character", helps users to enter keywords into a search engine entry field. Its easy-to-learn and easy-to-use characteristics make it highly effective in encouraging the elderly, who generally dislike IT systems, to search for information on the Internet. This smartphone application was tested by 30 subjects, ranging from young adults to the elderly, from the aspects of operation time and error rate. "One-touch-character" is also compared with other character input methods, such as "multi-touch-per-character" and "flick".

Keywords: Smartphone application · Character input method · One-touch-character · Flick · Multi-touch-per-character

1 Introduction

When using personal computers or computer terminals with keyboard, most Japanese had little problem with inputting Japanese characters through these terminals. They usually used the Roman character input method using QWERTY keyboards, just as westerners use them.

In the last decade, mobile phones with touch tone keys and displays were rapidly adopted in Japan. They are being used in addition as both telephone terminals and computer terminals, by connecting them to the Internet and accessing information they wanted to know about.

Two input methods have been developed to use touch tone keys, "one-touch-character (OTC)" and "multi-touch-per-character (MTPC)" in this time period. The seventy one Japanese hiragana characters (Japanese syllabary: 46 basic unvoiced sound and 25 voiced sound characters) were allocated to ten digit keys just as the 26 English alphabets were allocated to the digits 2 to digit 9 keys (Table 1). It is very complicated to do this, because the Japanese syllabary has almost three times as many characters as the English alphabet.

Basically, five characters sharing the same consonant are allocated to the same digit. Two basic ideas have been proposed to distribute voiced sound characters: one is

© Springer International Publishing Switzerland 2015
A. Marcus (Ed.): DUXU 2015, Part II, LNCS 9187, pp. 530–540, 2015.
DOI: 10.1007/978-3-319-20898-5_51

Table 1. Japanese syllabary including voiced sound characters and assignment to digits

あ （ A）	い （ I ）	う （ U）	え （ E）	お （ O）	Vowels→1
か （KA）	き （KI）	く （KU）	け （KE）	こ （KO）	K→digit 2
さ （SA）	し （SI）	す （SU）	せ （SE）	そ （SO）	S→digit 3
た （TA）	ち （TI）	つ （TU）	て （TE）	と （TO）	T→digit 4
な （NA）	に （NI）	ぬ （NU）	ね （NE）	の （NO）	N→digit 5
は （HA）	ひ （HI）	ふ （HU）	へ （HE）	ほ （HO）	H→digit 6
ま （MA）	み （MI）	む （MU）	め （ME）	も （MO）	M→digit 7
や （YA）		ゆ （YU）		よ （YO）	Y→digit 8
ら （RA）	り （RI ）	る （RU）	れ （RE）	ろ （RO）	R→digit 9
わ （WA）				を （WO）	W→digit 0
ん （ N）					N→digit 0
が （GA）	ぎ （GI）	ぐ （GU）	げ （GE）	ご （GO）	G→digit 2
ざ （ZA）	じ （ZI）	ず （ZU）	ぜ （ZE）	ぞ （ZO）	Z→digit 3
だ （DA）	ぢ （DI）	づ （DU）	で （DE）	ど （DO）	D→digit 4
ば （BA）	び （BI）	ぶ （BU）	べ （BE）	ぼ （BO）	B→digit 6
ぱ （PA）	ぴ （PI）	ぷ （PU）	ぺ （PE）	ぽ （PO）	P→digit 6

to allocate a voiced consonant row with similar hiragana image to the same digit (ex. "は(HA)", "ば(BA)", "ぱ(PA)" → digit 6), the other is to request users to additionally touch the "*" key to indicate that the first touched unvoiced sound character should be changed to a voiced sound character (ex. "さ(SA)"+"*" → "ざ (ZA)").

With the OTC method, users just touch the digit to which the desired character was allocated without indicating which one of the characters was intended (ex. Press digit "1" for "お (O)", and press digit "3" for "す (SU)"). With the MTPC method, users need to press the same digit multiple times until they get the intended character on the display (ex. Press digit "1" 5 times to get "お (O)", and press "3" 3 times to get "す (SU)").

Though OTC was once used in an automated directory assistance service in the 1990's [1], followed by research activities T9 [2] and "single-stroke-per-character" [3], MTPC has become the dominant input method because most mobile phone users preferred it for editing mail messages.

MTPC provided users with a convenient tool for communicating over the Internet even outside the home. This trend was greatly accelerated after smartphones were launched in 2008. Smartphones offer the innovative input method called "flick", which takes full advantage of the software touch tone keys displayed on the touch screen. This method can identify an intended character when the finger flicks in the direction of the intended character; several candidates are shown around the touched key (ex. Press "3" and flick "up" to get "す (SU)" and press "3" and flick "right" to get "せ (SE)") [4].

Though this "touch and flick" operation seemed very troublesome and time consuming to the middle and the elderly, students and young adults quickly mastered the "flick (Flick)" input method and they can now input characters much faster than with the MTPC method. This means they have an even more powerful tool for character input. Recently, scenes of young people enjoying the information they acquired by retrieval or writing/reading e-mails, can be observed everywhere in Japan in commuter trains, on sidewalks and at stations.

Thus, almost all of the young, most of the middle-aged and some of the elderly can take advantage of the search function to get target information, the holdouts became information-retrieval illiterates.

Based on the recognition that those who are not well trained in the quick input operation like "flick" should have as much opportunity to enjoy information from the Internet as the young, including dictionaries or encyclopedias, time tables, and highway traffic information, we decided to assist them and to ease their frustrations by introducing the OTC input method; it is designed to help users to effectively input Japanese characters to best utilize the smartphone environment.+

2   One-Touch-Character (OTC) Input Method for Smartphones

We had a precursory experience with the OTC input method, which was introduced in the commercial service of a fully automated directory assistance system in 1997 [1].

This service was developed assuming that touch tone telephones without displays at home represented the majority of terminals. Keywords for the directory service were address (city name, town name, etc.) and subscriber's name. Users input these keywords as digit sequences via the touch tone keys in response to the voice prompts from the system.

If the city name entered by a user with digits created an ambiguity (an input digit sequence has multiple hiragana city name candidates), the system asked for the input of additional address section names at a lower level (ex. town name or street name). The connection between the first digits of a city name and the second digits for the additional address name input should resolve the ambiguity and identify the target address.

If the target subscriber name was ambiguous (multiple hiragana names for an input digit sequence), the system asked for address input to solve the problem. In most cases, city-town address digits and subscriber name digits could simultaneously identify the search address area and target subscriber name in hiragana.

This OTC input method and natural disambiguation process was well accepted by the users and the total number of accesses to this service reached sixteen million in nine years until the service was terminated in 2007.

After our service commenced, research started on T9 [2] and "single-stroke-per-character" [3]; both apply prediction techniques to input digit sequences to retrieve and show candidates of hiragana or kanji expressions. Similar input methods with predicative dictionary-based disambiguation were investigated in other countries [5–7]. However, these proposals achieved a very small market share compared to MTPC or Flick input method. The main reason is that these proposals target the same market, editing Japanese sentences or mail messages, and used Japanese dictionaries with huge collections of proper nouns such as place names, landmarks, and personal names. OTC-like input methods usually present many more candidates for an entered digit sequence compared to other input methods which rely on the entry of hiragana sequences.

Thus, we take two lessons from our experience [1] and, in addition, from subsequent research activities such as T9 [2] and "single-stroke-per-character" [3].

One is that the OTC approach works pretty well in search tasks if the target database is smartly organized, but not in text/messaging activities because of the difficulty of downsizing the dictionary size so as to restrict the number of candidates for each entered digit. Databases intended for search query input should respond with just one, or a few candidates, at most, for each digit.

The other is that input keywords should be short to avoid human input errors and should be fully entered by users as digit sequences. In fact, the original directory assistance service divided long addresses into short section names like city names and town names, mostly less than ten characters each, for easier input.

3 An Application Developed Around OTC Input Method

3.1 Smartphone Applications that Suit OTC Input

Taking the lessons mentioned above into consideration, we decided to develop an information retrieval application in a restricted area, such as landmarks, sightseeing points, biographical dictionaries, movie/TV talents, and athletes. One more important factor is that the data for retrieval should be freely and automatically collected by accessing the Internet and should be transposed into a defined format.

We finally selected a Japanese Who's who as the target database. Dictionary entries were was extracted from the Japanese Wikipedia (open source) of 2013. Each entry consists of a personal name in Kanji (Chinese characters), its hiragana spelling, its ten keypad digits converted from hiragana spellings, and its URL to link to the original content.

The database contains about 130 thousand entries covering Japanese historical persons, statesmen, scholars in various areas, movie/TV talents, athletes in various sports, people in the spotlight. A check of the data showed that 65 % of personal names with different hiragana spelling were converted into different digit sequences. The remaining names collide: in one case, ten different personal names yielded the same digits. However, selecting one of those candidates is not a serious problem.

3.2 Application Development

A search application for this Who's who was developed to determine whether the proposed OTC input method was efficient at finding a person's name and retrieving full information from Wikipedia. A typical scene is a user watching a TV program who becomes curious about a person mentioned and wants more information about him/her. This application is named "Shirabetai (check a person in the spotlight)".

This application was installed on the smartphone Galaxy Note (SC-01F) running Android OS.

3.3   User Interface and Operation

Four panel shots of search process execution are shown in Fig. 1. In the first panel, the user learns how to input a keyword using the OTC input method, from a simple explanation "One touch for each character!" and press the "Start" key to start a search.

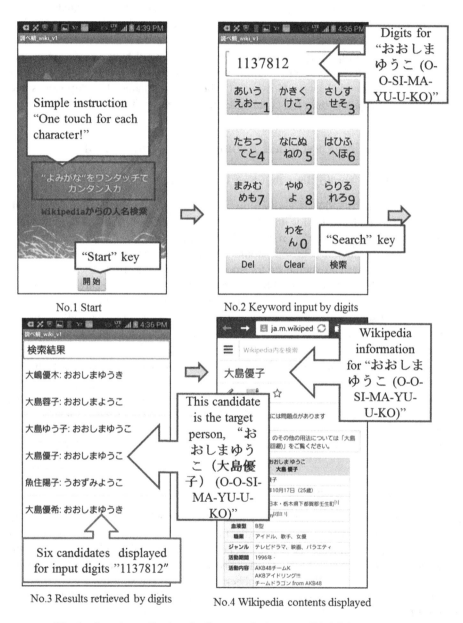

Fig. 1. Sample application for "one touch character (OTC)" input method

The example, a Japanese female talent in the spotlight "おおしまゆうこ (O-O-SI-MA-YU-U-KO) (大島優子)," is entered via OTC according to Table 1, see the second shot. The keyword slot shows the translation of the digits "1137812".

The third panel displays the retrieved result. In this case, six candidates are retrieved by digits "1137812". Two different surnames, "おおしま (O-O-SI-MA)", "うおずみ (U-O-ZU-MI)," and three different given names, "ゆうき (YU-U-KI)", "ようこ (YO-U-KO)", "ゆうこ (YU-U-KO)," are retrieved. The hiragana sequences of these names clearly share the same consonants with different vowels, except the vowel row. Five of the six surnames are "おおしま (O-O-SI-MA)", and other one is "うおずみ (U-O-ZU-MI)". Three of six given names are "ゆうこ (YU-U-KO)"'s, two are "ようこ (YO-U-KO)"'s and the last one is "ゆうき (YU-U-KI)". There are two "おおしまゆうこ (O-O-SI-MA-YU-U-KO)"'s and "おおしまゆうき (O-O-SI-MA-YU-U-KI)"'s with different Kanji readings. A user can use Kanji readings to select the intended one when multiple candidates appear with same hiragana sequences on the panel. As the fourth candidate "大島優子 おおしまゆうこ (O-O-SI-MA-YU-U-KO)" is the target name, the user touches it to get full information about the talent.

After this operation, the screen changes to the fourth screen to show the Wikipedia information accessed via the URL.

The above shows a typical instance of severe collision. However, as mentioned in Sect. 3.1, in most cases only a single candidate is returned. For example, the digits "163031" yields only "あべしんぞう(阿倍晋三)(A-BE-SI-N-ZO-U), prime minister of Japan" as the search result.

4 Usability Comparison Experiment

4.1 Experiment Purposes

This experiment has two purposes. One is to evaluate the popularity of this smartphone application. The other is to evaluate the usability of the proposed OTC input method, compared with MTPC and Flick input methods on smartphones.

A recent study [8] investigated the usability of text input methods for smartphone among the elderly, including MTPC (called "Mobile" in this paper) and two different Flick input methods. However they could not make it clear which input method is most suitable for the elderly, partly because they only focused to the elderly subjects who are not familiar with smartphones and the paucity of input methods at that time.

In our experiment, 30 subjects were selected with wide variety of ages, from twenties to eighties. We set three groups; Young (20–35), most are Flick experts and MTPC experienced. Middle (36–65), most are MTPC experts but novices for Flick, and Elderly (66–85) most are novices or novices for all three methods.

We intended to clarify the differences among the three age groups.

4.2 Experimental Conditions

A smartphone hosting the sample application and a name list used for character input were prepared as follows:

1. The application was installed on a smartphone (Galaxy Note SC-01F), and presented to each subject.
2. Forty personal names, famous and familiar to all subjects, were listed in hiragana characters.
3. Two extra input interfaces, MTPC and Flick, are prepared on the same smartphone.
4. Before the experiment, each subject was informed that they were to enter 40 personal names (261 hiragana characters) using the three different input methods. A detail explanation of each input method was provided if requested. Practice with unfamiliar methods was also allowed using personal names not on the test list.
5. The sequence of input methods was randomly determined for each subject.

Objective data (operation times and error rates) and subjective data (interviews and opinions) were collected and analyzed. Operation time to complete the character input operation was measured and the average operation time to input a hiragana character was calculated. Erroneous entries during the input operation (40 names) were counted by a watcher and averaged per personal name.

5   Results and Discussions

5.1   Application Popularity Evaluations

This application was assessed as positive by 70 % of subjects, mostly supported by Middle and Elderly, negative by 20 % and neutral by10 %. Those who answered negative were mostly Young, who can directly access Wikipedia without using an ambiguity-directed OTC input method. But they recognized that the Elderly would prefer the simple OTC input method, by acknowledging the difficulty the Elderly face in dealing with new interfaces. Middle shared the above Young opinion about the Elderly preference for OTC.

During interview collection, we had a chance to demonstrate this search application to a physically handicapped patient suffering ALS (amyotrophic lateral sclerosis). A supportive comment was obtained from him to promote this kind of application with OTC method to reduce character input labor as a welfare activity.

5.2   Operation Times and Error Rates

Remarkable trends were observed in terms of operation times and error rates as shown in Figs. 2 and 3 for OPTC and Fig. 4 for ERPW.

– Operation Time Per Character (OTPC) (Figs. 2, 3)

Comparison of average OTPCs for the three different input methods among the three age groups is shown in Fig. 2.

OPTC was shortest for Young, followed by Middle and Elderly, in every input method. OTPC ratios between Elderly and Young are 3.2 in OTC, 3.6 in Flick and 3.9 in MTPC. This suggests OTC is the most preferred method for the Elderly.

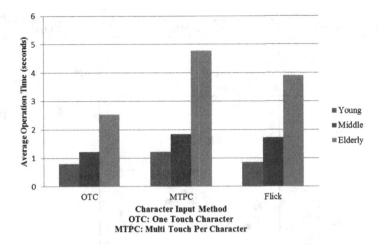

Fig. 2. Operation Time Per Character (OTPC)

OTPC comparisons among the three methods by age groups are shown as follows.

Young: OTC ≒ Flick < MTPC
Middle: OTC < Flick≒ MTPC
Elderly: OTC < Flick< MTPC

Considering that expected average operations are 1.0 for OTC, 1.8 for Flick and 3.0 for MTPC, the Young are seen as quick learners of the Flick method as the OTC method. This also means the Young are adaptable and flexible enough to adjust to any input method.

Middle operates the three input methods pretty well. Though Middle is quickest with the OTC method, the OTPC ratios of other two methods compared to OTC are less than 2.

Elderly recorded the longest OTPC, but again OTC yields the shortest OTPC, almost half of that of others. This implies that OTC suits the Elderly, though ERPW is comparatively high.

To discover individual subject behaviors and obtain trends from different age groups, a scatter diagram was made, see Fig. 3.

Young are not concerned about the differences among the three methods. Most of them can operate even Flick input with less ERPW just fast as or faster than OTC, though they learned the new input method in this experiment. In Flick, they can operate "touch and flick" operation (two finger motions) in a moment like one touch operation for other input operations. It is rational that they need more time for MTPC input because MTPC requires exact multi touching finger motions to get the correct character.

On the other hand, the Elderly demonstrated significant differences among the three methods. Every of them achieved fastest speed (OTPC) with OTC, middle speed with Flick and slow speed with MTPC. It can be clearly said that the OTC input method best suits the Elderly. They seemed to have been annoyed for a long time by being forced to use MTPC for Japanese character input.

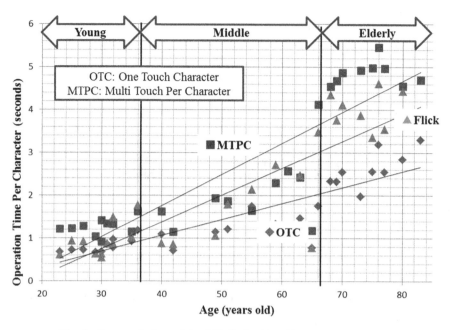

Fig. 3. Scattered plots of the OTPCs for 30 subjects grouped by age

Nothing particular can be observed from the Middle data. Middle's preferences for the input methods seem to mainly depend on the working environment and experience.

– Error Rate Per Word (ERPW) (Fig. 4)

ERPW heavily depends on the individual's mental attitude and willingness to experiment. Subjects who tried to break OTPC records tend to high ERPW. On the contrary,

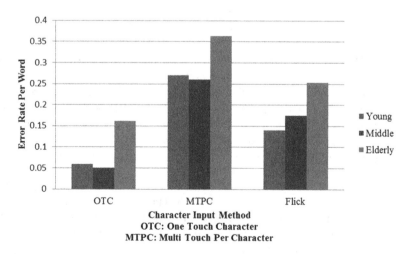

Fig. 4. Error Rate Per Word (personal name) (ERPW)

subjects who were very careful in inputting each hiragana character might have low OTPC but also low EPRW.

From average ERPW point of view, a remarkable trend can be observed in the collected data. In every input method, ERPW is the least with OTC, followed by Flick and MTPC. MTPC achieved the lowest performance regardless of age group for two reasons: average number of touches is the highest among the three input methods and entering consecutive hiragana characters in the same row (ex. "す(SU)" after "さ(SA)") needs extra operation to set the first input character (ex. "さ(SA)" in this case). Subjects sometimes messed up this extra operation.

ERPW of Flick is comparatively low because a subject can select the intended hiragana by selecting one from five hiragana candidates displayed immediately after the first key touch.

As OTC is free from the above mentioned problems, Young and Middle recorded very low ERPW rates. Elderly made some errors due to careless operation.

6 Conclusion

Our daily life has experienced extensive change with the adoption of mobile phones with Internet access. Though mobile phones can be recognized as handheld wireless telephony devices with Internet accesses which additionally provide e-mailing functions, the smartphones that emerged in 2008 are seen more as personal computers that can perform various tasks including telephony and e-mailing.

Every year, a variety of new models with lots of new features are put on the market.

Whether the Japanese like it or not, virtually all mobile devices now have the ability to wirelessly access the Internet, either as a tablet or a smartphone with a screen panel. As these types of device normally do not have a dedicated QWERTY keyboard or touch-tone keys, users must master at least one of the character input methods provided by the vendor, either a software keyboard or a set of touch-tone keys displayed on the panel.

Aiming to send e-mail or short messages to friends or parents, most Japanese kids and students usually begin to learn Japanese character input methods using mobile phones or smartphones before using QWERTY keyboards.

Thus most of the young subjects tested herein were well accustomed to inputting Japanese characters via software touch-tone keys. On the other hand, older subjects are novices at doing so, because they generally learned to use QWERTY keyboards in the office before trying to use touch-tone-keys for character input.

In this situation, we proposed an easy-to-learn and easy-to-operate Japanese character input method named "one-touch-character (OTC)", especially for those who have become holdouts as regards information retrieval and provided a sample retrieval application to show how this input method works.

Evaluations of this input method in comparison with MTPC and Flick method using the same touch-tone-key set on a smartphone display were executed.

As a result, the OTC input method is well accepted by Young and Middle, not to mention by the Elderly. Using OTC, the Elderly can input keywords in the shortest time with the lowest error rate. Striking to say, the Young do not mind the difference in operation of the three methods. Even with single keyword input operation, an expert can use the three methods in a mixed way, and so best utilize the advantages of each method. The results confirm that OTC method will be well received.

Regarding our sample application, the Elderly were mostly satisfied with the information provided, and appreciated its usefulness and convenience. The Young were not so impressed, because they can input keywords by hiragana characters directly into the Wikipedia site.

Further study will identify search applications that can better satisfy users' strong curiosity via simplified keyword input interfaces. At the same time, we have to establish the OTC presence and secure market popularity in Japanese character input operations.

References

1. Higashida, M.: A fully automated directory assistance service that accommodates degenerated keyword input via telephones. In: Proceedings of Pacific Telecommunications Conference 1997, pp. 167–174 (1997)
2. REDUCED KEYBOARD DISAMBIGUATING COMPUTER, US Patent, 5,818,437, October 6 1998
3. Tanaka-ishii, K., Inutuka, Y., Takeuchi, M.: Japanese text input system with digits. In: Proceedings of Human Language Technology Conference, pp.1–8 (2001)
4. Alternative Japanese iPhone Input Method in the Wild. http://www.japannewbie.com/2010/05/10/alternative-japanese-iphone-input-method-in-the-wild/
5. UzZaman, N., Kahn, M.: T12: an advancecd text input system with phonetic support for mobile devices. In: The Second International Conference on Mobile Technology, Applications and Systems, pp. 52–58 (2005)
6. Rajeshkannan, R., Nareshkumar, M., Ganesan, R., Balakrishnan, R.: Language localization for mobile phones. In: Mobile and Pervasive Computing 2008 (CoMPC-2008), pp. 52–55 (2008)
7. Li, F.C.Y., Guy, R.T., Yatani, K., Troung, K.N.: The 1 line keyboard: a QWERTY layout in a single line. In: Proceedings of the 24th Annual ACM Symposium on User Interface Software and Technology (UIST11), pp. 461–470 (2011)
8. Hamano, M., Nishiguchi, N.: Usability evaluation of text input methods for smartphone among the elderly. In: 2013 International Conference on Biometrics and Kansei Engineering, pp. 277–280 (2013)

Smartphone Application Usability Evaluation: The Applicability of Traditional Heuristics

Ger Joyce[(⊠)], Mariana Lilley, Trevor Barker, and Amanda Jefferies

School of Computer Science, University of Hertfordshire College Lane,
Hertfordshire, Hatfield AL10 9AB, UK
gerjoyce@outlook.com,
{m.lilley, t.l.barker, a.l.jefferies}@herts.ac.uk

Abstract. The Heuristic Evaluation method has been popular with HCI experts for over 20 years. Yet, we believe that the set of heuristics defined by Nielsen in 1994 needs to be modified prior to the usability evaluation of smartphone applications. In this paper, we investigate the applicability of each of Nielsen's traditional heuristics to the usability evaluation of smartphone applications following an analysis of 105 peer-reviewed papers. It is anticipated that this work might benefit HCI practitioners, educators and researchers as they attempt to define usability heuristics for smartphone applications. This set of heuristics, once defined, could enable the discovery of usability issues early in the smartphone application development life cycle, while continuing to be a discount usability engineering method as originally defined by Nielsen.

Keywords: Mobile · Usability · Heuristic evaluation · Smartphone application

1 Introduction

Within the field of Human-Computer Interaction (HCI), expert-based usability inspection methods are well established. The Heuristic Evaluation method, defined originally by Jakob Nielsen and Rolf Molich and later modified by Nielsen [1], in particular is widely known for being fast, relatively inexpensive and easy to learn.

In an interview with Jenny Preece [2], Nielsen stated "You can identify a lot of issues with a phone or other mobile user experience by using exactly the same heuristics as you would for any other platform". While we agree that a Heuristic Evaluation could work well in the mobile domain, we do not believe that the set of heuristics defined by Nielsen is the best set of heuristics to evaluate the usability of smartphone applications.

To this end, this paper reports on an investigation of Nielsen's statement by analysing 105 peer-reviewed papers in the field of usability evaluation, particularly an Heuristic Evaluation. The analysis informed the investigation into the applicability of each of Nielsen's heuristics when applied to the usability evaluation of smartphone applications. This approach helps to point out where some of Nielsen's heuristics might be deemed inapplicable to smartphone applications and where perceived gaps might occur during a usability evaluation.

© Springer International Publishing Switzerland 2015
A. Marcus (Ed.): DUXU 2015, Part II, LNCS 9187, pp. 541–550, 2015.
DOI: 10.1007/978-3-319-20898-5_52

Modifying this traditional set of heuristics to ensure as many usability issues as possible are discovered, as well as creating new heuristics to cover the perceived gaps, could prove effective in the usability evaluation of smartphone applications. Thus, it is hoped that this work will be most beneficial to HCI practitioners, educators and researchers as they seek to develop new and modified usability evaluation paradigms for smartphone applications. Ultimately this effort might lead to smartphone applications that are easier to use and easier to learn, resulting in less frustrated smartphone users.

2   Related Work

Other research teams have also investigated the applicability of Nielsen's traditional heuristics to other domains. Examples include Educational Media [3]; Groupware Based on the Mechanics of Collaboration [4]; Ambient Displays [5]; Adaptive Learning Environments [6]; Playability of Games [7]; Intensive Care Unit Infusion Pumps [8]; Intrusion Detection Systems [9]; Virtual Reality Applications [10]; Electronic Shopping [11]; and Child E-learning Applications [12].

As mobile devices became more popular, researchers recognized that usability methods, including Nielsen's traditional heuristics, did not work well within the mobile domain [13–15]. This led to research into a set of heuristics for the mobile domain, most notably from:

- Bertini et al. [16], which concentrated on the operating system, the loss of, and the ergonomics of the mobile device;
- Inostroza et al. [17], which concentrated on touchscreen devices, changing little from Nielsen's heuristics, in a study which led to statistically insignificant results.

While also concentrating on the mobile domain, this investigation differs from previous research by concentrating on how Nielsen's heuristics apply to smartphone applications. The resulting research can be used by HCI practitioners, educators and researchers in their quest to define a new set of heuristics dedicated to the usability evaluation of smartphone applications.

3   Investigation

The following investigation takes each of Nielsen's heuristics in turn, investigating their applicability to the usability evaluation of smartphone applications based on an analysis of 105 peer-reviewed papers in the field of usability evaluation, particularly Heuristic Evaluation.

Traditional Heuristic 1: Visibility of System Status – The system should always keep users informed about what is going on, through appropriate feedback within reasonable time.

Investigation. Keeping the user informed is vital on any system [18]. In addition to Nielsen's first heuristic, Tognazzini [19] also included "Latency Reduction" in his First

Principles of Interaction Design. However, within the mobile domain, this heuristic in itself might not be enough as smartphone application users tend to be even more impatient than desktop application users [20]. Therefore, 'a reasonable timeframe' might need to be much shorter for smartphone applications in order to avoid frustrating and confusing users. This, however, needs to be balanced as too many notifications will simply annoy users.

Traditional Heuristic 2: Match between System and the Real World – The system should speak the users' language, with words, phrases and concepts familiar to the user, rather than system-oriented terms. Follow real-world conventions, making information appear in a natural and logical order.

Investigation. This is an important heuristic for smartphone applications. Developers should use techniques such as scenarios [21, 22] and list key characteristics of users [23] when initially starting work on the creation of a smartphone application. This allows for the identification of the type of tasks and users that will use the application. From this knowledge, a style guide containing the words, phrases and concepts familiar to the user would be selected for use on the interface [24]. The style guide will also help to ensure words, phrases and concepts are used consistently and in a natural and logical order throughout the application [25, 26]. Platform and industry standards can also be used as guidelines to apply consistent mapping to user interactions, including touchscreen gesture motions, to ensure interactions occur as users expect.

Traditional Heuristic 3: User Control and Freedom – Users often choose system functions by mistake and will need a clearly marked "emergency exit" to leave the unwanted state without having to go through an extended dialogue. Support undo and redo.

Investigation. The title of this heuristic can be ambiguous. For instance, within the mobile domain it could be associated with the ability to customize a smartphone application. In fact, the heuristic is related to navigation and user errors, both of which need to be heuristics in themselves. Therefore, when defining a set of heuristics for smartphone applications, a better solution might be to specifically call out these two areas separately. As heuristics about errors will be covered below, a heuristic that considers navigation would be clearer for evaluators.

Traditional Heuristic 4: Consistency and Standards – Users should not have to wonder whether different words, situations, or actions mean the same thing. Follow platform conventions.

Investigation. As discussed in the second heuristic, consistency is important. This is where a style guide of terms to be used and look-and-feel can be beneficial. The guidelines set out by each mobile Operating System developer, including Apple and Google can be very helpful in creating smartphone applications that conform to expected standards.

While it is important to stay with known conventions, it is also important to experience to see what works well in the mobile domain. Therefore, this heuristic should not be seen as a barrier to the introduction to new ideas. A short FAQ or interactive help functionality might be used to introduce first time users to terms and gestures they may be unfamiliar with [27].

Traditional Heuristic 5: Error Prevention – Even better than good error messages is a careful design which prevents a problem from occurring in the first place. Either eliminate error-prone conditions or check for them and present users with a confirmation option before they commit to the action.

Investigation. Both of Nielsen's heuristics 5 and 9 concentrate on errors [1]. Bertini et al. [16] recognized this, deciding to combine both into a simpler heuristic titled "Realistic Error Management", which is also our recommendation.

Yet, while combining errors into one heuristic is a simpler approach, as Nielsen's alluded to, there are two important parts to errors; namely, preventing errors, and assisting users should an error occur in a way that is easily understood. Both need to be addressed within smartphone application heuristics.

In relation to error prevention, Hoekman [28] calls for smartphone application developers to practice poka-yoke. The term "Poka-yoke" roughly translates from Japanese as "mistake proofing". Hence, a poka-yoke user interface is designed to prevent a mistake from being made. Myszewski [29] further defines poka-yoke by stating that "A poka-yoke solution makes the issue of human error irrelevant regardless what are causes and effects of the error. Elimination of human error becomes a technical question. If there is no possibility to apply poka-yoke, then some less effective solutions have to be considered". Smartphone application developers can therefore create a more robust, user-friendly application by considering the errors users might make, including when they are using the smartphone in various contexts such as sitting or walking, then ensuring everything is done to eliminate the possibility of the error occurring.

If a situation exists where poka-yoke cannot be applied whereby potential errors cannot be prevented, such as a navigation error or an incorrectly typed word, users should be allowed to undo their mistake, go back to the previous screen or to exit the application easily if they wish to do so. Should the user try to attempt to proceed when it is not possible to do so, the application should display an error message that is understandable, letting the user know what the problem is, how to solve it and to quickly move on.

Traditional Heuristic 6: Recognition Rather than Recall – Minimize the user's memory load by making objects, actions, and options visible. The user should not have to remember information from one part of the dialogue to another. Instructions for use of the system should be visible or easily retrievable whenever appropriate.

Investigation. Mobile interfaces tend to be small (generally between 2" to 6"). Therefore, making objects, actions, and options visible, as this heuristic requests, might not be a good idea within a smartphone application. A better practise is to ensure that only the elements and information needed right away should be displayed at any one time. However, it is important to ensure that vital information needed by the user is part of the objects, actions, and options displayed, with any other elements that are not immediately required being removed. This is also touched upon in heuristic 8.

Traditional Heuristic 7: Flexibility and Efficiency of Use – Accelerators – unseen by the novice user – may often speed up the interaction for the expert user such that the system can cater to both inexperienced and experienced users. Allow users to tailor frequent actions.

Investigation. Accelerators are important to smartphone application users. Consider, for instance, the ability to install widgets on their device interfaces for easier access to important information. Smartphone application developers might also consider context along with customizability. Applications that fall into this category are for example those that change to a brighter screen in a dark room, or change interface elements to larger, easier to tap buttons when a user is driving or running.

However, this heuristic might be confused with heuristic 3: "User Control and Freedom", which would need to be considered when defining a set of heuristics for smartphone applications. Whereas, heuristic 3 concentrates on the ability to recover from errors with undo, as well as navigation issues, this heuristic concentrates on customisability. This should be made clearer in any newly defined smartphone heuristics.

Traditional Heuristic 8: Aesthetic and Minimalist Design – Dialogues should not contain information which is irrelevant or rarely needed. Every extra unit of information in a dialogue competes with the relevant units of information and diminishes their relative visibility.

Investigation. Aesthetic and minimalist design lends itself to a simple, easy-to-use interface, and is prominent in other design guidelines including those from Gerhardt-Powals [30] whereby one of the User Interface Design principles state "Include in the displays only that information needed by the user at a given time". This is more difficult to achieve in practice, but should be a goal for all designers.

Focusing on the mobile domain, this heuristic seems applicable in its current form. However, the heuristic does not quite capture exactly what we need in the design of a smartphone application, which creates gaps when considering a set of heuristics for this domain. Ideally, a set of heuristics for smartphone applications should consider that applications need to be:

- Simple – Hoekman [28] supports this by applying the Japanese system of the 5S's (described in detail by Ortiz [31]) to mobile interfaces to decide what is absolutely necessary and what can be disregarded, arguing that every element chosen causes cognitive load on users.
- Focused on one task – Though simple, the interface should have all the elements required to complete a singular task, be that to display the information a user needs, to show options or settings, to allow the user to interact with the application and so on. This allows single tasks, even if part of a larger application, to be completed quickly and easily, even by people on the move. Clark [27] reinforces this thought by reminding us that "The best [mobile] apps fold neatly into a busy schedule".
- Visually pleasing – While Clark [27] states that the beauty of an application is primarily in its functionality, Gong and Tarasewich [32] suggest that a mobile application "will stand out if it is attractive". In practical terms, both are correct. A mobile application needs to be functional and aesthetic. Marinacci [33] even suggests that if an application is visually pleasing, a user would be more inclined to wait longer as they wait for information to download, more so than a mobile application that does the same thing, but does not look as good.
- Learnable and Intuitive – Given the lack of in-depth help and documentation available for mobile devices, as well as the interruptions users face as they interact

with mobile applications, an intuitive, easy-to-learn interface is vital [34]. In fact, it has been suggested that even though the learnability of a software application has always been important, it is even more important in the mobile context [35].

- Glanceable by allowing main information to be taken in quickly – Chittaro [36] is an advocate of mobile application displays that can be viewed at a glance for people on the go. However, while Bertini et al. [16] also recognized the importance of glanceable mobile interfaces, the researchers decided to create one heuristic to cover very different problems in their heuristic "Ease of input, screen readability and glanceability". Similarly another heuristic was created named "Good ergonomics and minimalist design", whereby other aspects of the interface, as well as the design of the actual device itself, were discussed. Some of these issues are beyond the scope of a smartphone-deployed mobile application evaluation and the influence of application developers, as well as the fact that separate heuristics considered the mobile interface, it is proposed to create one heuristic that considers the items discussed in this section, while omitting items beyond the scope of a mobile application evaluation.

Traditional Heuristic 9: Help Users Recognize, Diagnose, and Recover from Errors – Error messages should be expressed in plain language (no codes), precisely indicate the problem, and constructively suggest a solution.

Investigation. This heuristic is vital for smartphone applications as much as it is for any type of interface. However, as Nielsen's heuristics 5 and 9 consider errors, we have covered this in our investigation of "Traditional Heuristic 5: Error prevention". We recommend that a single heuristic is defined for error prevention and assisting users should errors occur to simplify an eventual set of smartphone application heuristics.

Traditional Heuristic 10: Help and Documentation – Even though it is better if the system can be used without documentation, it may be necessary to provide help and documentation. Any such information should be easy to search, focused on the user's task, list concrete steps to be carried out, and not be too large.

Investigation. While it would seem unlikely that a usable smartphone application would require Help and Documentation, from his findings Bertini et al. [16] suggested that "people using mobile applications still expect such applications to provide help. Though they might prefer that the help be 'interactive', non-distractive, not be a separate task."

On a related note, Clark [27] observed that the use of an interactive welcome mat for first-timers showing an overlay pointing to the main features of the interface and how to interact with the application made the "apps first screen more inviting and helpful". As a welcome mat is interactive, non-distractive and not be a separate task, it ties in with the findings from Bertini et al. Once first-time users interact with the application and discover its main features, they can dismiss the welcome mat and later become familiar with the more intricate settings, should they wish to do so.

In addition, there are as yet no established gesture guidelines for smartphone applications [38, 40]. Therefore, Help and documentation and/or first time user tutorials may offer a way for new users to learn how to use a smartphone application [27]. This is echoed by research that has suggested that many first time users will avail of tutorials to some extent [39, 40].

4 Closing the Gaps

Having investigated Nielsen's traditional heuristics for their applicability in the usability evaluation of smartphone applications, we find that we are missing vital areas related both to the smartphone applications themselves, as well as their environment. To that end, HCI practitioners, researchers and educators interested in the development of usability heuristics for smartphone applications should also consider the following:

- Context of use – The importance of glanceability was already discussed, whereby the context of use could be a busy user possibly mobile themselves while walking, cycling or driving. Other types of context of use include where users have to contend with poor lighting conditions and high ambient noise [41]. It is improbable to cover all scenarios and environments where a smartphone application is likely to be used, yet a set of heuristics dedicated to this domain should include a form of context-of-use so it is at least considered by evaluators.
- Content Input – Smartphone applications are difficult to use from a content input perspective. Input tends to be more difficult and slower while on the move [42]. A set of heuristics for smartphone applications should consider this. For instance, to ensure users can input the content accurately, an application might have keyboard buttons that are as large as possible, and offer multimodal types of input entry [43].
- Use of microphone, camera and sensors – Smartphone applications contain a multitude of features and complex sensors, such as a microphone, camera, GPS, accelerometer, and gyroscope [41, 42]. These can be used in any number of situations and should therefore be considered when developing smartphone application heuristics. For instance, consider applications that use these features and sensors to:
  - assist in content input;
  - display more data in landscape mode;
  - adapt an interface while running or driving;
  - inform users when friends are close by;
  - move objects in a game.
  - Identifiable Icon – an icon for a smartphone application should be aesthetic and identifiable as it is the only item a user sees when searching a mobile device interface for the application they wish to launch [27].

5 Conclusion

An Heuristic Evaluation is a low cost, effective, relatively fast usability evaluation method that has been popular since the early 1990's. In this paper, we argue that without modification the method might not be as effective when evaluating the usability of smartphone applications. To back up our claim, we investigated Nielsen's traditional heuristics and their applicability to the usability of smartphone applications by considering the potential problems and gaps with the method based on a review of 105 peer-reviewed papers.

Defining a set of heuristics that prove effective in the usability evaluation of smartphone applications could allow evaluators to discover a substantial number of usability issues prior to more expensive usability methods being used during the latter stages of the development life cycle. Ideally the set of usability heuristics developed for smartphone applications would maintain the quick-to-use, easy-to-learn, and inexpensive-to-conduct benefits of Nielsen's traditional heuristics.

It is anticipated that this work might benefit HCI practitioners, educators and researchers in their quest to develop usability heuristics, and other usability evaluation paradigms, for smartphone applications. To take this work forward in developing a set of usability heuristics for smartphone applications, HCI experts might consider the information presented under each heuristic, subsequently modifying and removing heuristics, as well as covering gaps with the creation of new heuristics. A Heuristic Evaluation could be conducted to evaluate the effectiveness of the new set of heuristics against smartphone applications in sketch, prototype or final format.

Acknowledgements. The authors are grateful to the School of Computer Science, University of Hertfordshire and to Rapid7 for providing funding.

References

1. Nielsen, J.: Usability inspection methods. In: Conference Companion on Human Factors in Computing Systems, pp. 413–414 (1994)
2. Rogers, Y., Sharp, H., Preece, J.: Interaction Design: Beyond Human-Computer Interaction. Wiley, New York (2011)
3. Albion, P.R.: Heuristic evaluation of educational multimedia: from theory to practise. In: Proceedings ASCILITE 1999: 16th Annual Conference of the Australasian Society for Computers in Learning in Tertiary Education: Responding to Diversity, pp. 9–15. Australasian Society for Computers in Learning in Tertiary Education (ASCILITE) (1999)
4. Baker, K., Greenberg, S., Gutwin, C.: Heuristic evaluation of groupware based on the mechanics of collaboration. In: Nigay, L., Little, M. (eds.) EHCI 2001. LNCS, vol. 2254, pp. 123–139. Springer, Heidelberg (2001)
5. Mankoff, J., Dey, A.K.a. K., Hsieh, G., Kientz, J., Lederer, S., Ames, M.: Heuristic evaluation of ambient displays. In: Proceedings of SIGCHI Conference Human Factors Computing System, pp. 169–176 (2003)
6. Magoulas, G.D., Chen, S.Y., Papanikolaou, K.A.: Integrating layered and heuristic evaluation for adaptive learning environments. In: Proceedings of the Second Workshop on Empirical Evaluation of Adaptive Systems, held at the 9th International Conference on User Modeling UM 2003, Pittsburgh. pp. 5–14 (2003)
7. Desurvire, H., Caplan, M., Toth, J. a: Using heuristics to evaluate the playability of games. In: CHI 2004 Extended Abstracts on Human Factors in Computing Systems, pp. 1509–1512 (2004)
8. Graham, M.J., Kubose, T.K., Jordan, D., Zhang, J., Johnson, T.R., Patel, V.L.: Heuristic evaluation of infusion pumps: implications for patient safety in Intensive Care Units. Int. J. Med. Inform. **73**, 771–779 (2004)
9. Zhou, A.T., Blustein, J., Zincir-Heywood, N.: Improving intrusion detection systems through heuristic evaluation. In: Canadian Conference on Electrical and Computer Engineering, vol. 3, pp. 1641–1644 (2004)

10. Sutcliffe, A., Gault, B.: Heuristic evaluation of virtual reality applications. Interact. Comput. **16**, 831–849 (2004)
11. Chen, S.Y., Macredie, R.D.: The assessment of usability of electronic shopping: a heuristic evaluation. Int. J. Inf. Manage. **25**, 516–532 (2005)
12. Alsumait, A.A., Al-Osaimi, A.: Usability heuristics evaluation for child e-learning applications. J. Softw. **5**, 425–430 (2010)
13. Ketola, P., Röykkee, M.: The three facets of usability in mobile handsets. In: CHI 2001 Workshop: Mobile Communications: Understanding Users, Adoption and Design (2001)
14. Dunlop, M., Brewster, S.: The challenge of mobile devices for human computer interaction. Pers. Ubiquitous Comput. **6**(4), 235–236 (2002)
15. Po, S., Howard, S., Vetere, F., Skov, M.B.: Heuristic evaluation and mobile usability: bridging the realism gap. Mob. Hum.-Comput. Interact. **2004**(3160), 591–592 (2004)
16. Bertini, E., Gabrielli, S., Kimani, S.: Appropriating and assessing heuristics for mobile computing. In: Proceedings of the Working Conference on Advanced Visual Interfaces, pp. 119–126 (2006)
17. Inostroza, R., Rusu, C., Roncagliolo, S., Jimenez, C., Rusu, V.: Usability heuristics for touchscreen-based mobile devices. In: Proceedings of the Ninth International Conference on Information Technology: New Generations (ITNG), pp. 662–667. IEEE, Las Vegas (2012)
18. Neil, T.: Mobile Design Pattern Gallery. O'Reilly Media, USA (2012)
19. Tognazzini, B.: First principles of interaction design (2003). http://www.asktog.com/basics/firstPrinciples.html
20. Nilsson, E.G.: Design patterns for user interface for mobile applications. Adv. Eng. Softw. **40**, 1318–1328 (2009)
21. Nardi, B.a: The use of scenarios in design. ACM SIGCHI Bull. **24**, 13–14 (1992)
22. Elkoutbi, M., Khriss, I., Keller, R.K.: Generating user interface prototypes from scenarios. In: Proceedings. IEEE International Symposium on Requirements Engineering, pp. 150–158 (1999)
23. Jacko, J.A.: Human Computer Interaction Handbook: Fundamentals, Evolving Technologies, and Emerging Applications, 3rd edn. CRC Press, Boca Raton (2012)
24. Galitz, W.O.: The Essential Guide to User Interface Design: An Introduction to GUI Design Principles and Techniques. Wiley, New York (2007)
25. Nielsen, J.: Coordinating user interfaces for consistency. ACM SIGCHI Bull. **20**, 63–65 (1989)
26. Stone, D., Jarrett, C., Woodroffe, M., Minocha, S.: User Interface Design and Evaluation. Morgan Kaufmann, Los Altos (2005)
27. Clark, J.: Tapworthy: Designing Great iPhone Apps. O'Reilly Media, USA (2010)
28. Hoekman, R.: Designing the Obvious: A Common Sense Approach to Web and Mobile Application Design. Pearson Education, Berkley (2010)
29. Myszewski, J.M.: Management responsibility for human errors. TQM J. **24**, 326–337 (2012)
30. Gerhardt-Powals, J.: Cognitive engineering principles for enhancing human-computer performance. Int. J. Hum. Comput. Interact. **8**, 189–211 (1996)
31. Ortiz, C.A.: The Psychology of Lean Improvements: Why Organizations must Overcome Resistance and Change the Culture. CRC Press, Boca Raton (2012)
32. Gong, J., Tarasewich, P.: Guidelines for handheld mobile device interface design. In: Proceedings of DSI 2004 Annual Meeting, pp. 3751–3756 (2004)
33. Marinacci, J.: Building Mobile Applications with Java: Using the Google Web Toolkit and PhoneGap. O'Reilly Media, USA (2012)
34. Lee, V., Schneider, H., Schell, R.: Mobile Applications: Architecture, Design, and Development. Prentice Hall, Saddle River (2004)

35. Longoria, R.: Designing Software for the Mobile Context: A Practitioner's Guide. Springer, London (2004)
36. Chittaro, L.: Designing visual user interfaces for mobile applications. In: Proceedings of the 3rd ACM SIGCHI Symposium on Engineering Interactive Computing Systems - EICS 2011, pp. 331–332 (2011)
37. Norman, D.A., Nielsen, J.: Gestural interfaces: a step backward in usability. Interactions **17**, 46–49 (2010). doi:10.1145/1836216.1836228
38. Anderson, F., Bischof, W.F.: Learning and performance with gesture guides. In: Proceedings of CHI 2013, pp. 1109–1118. ACM (2013)
39. Inbar, O., Lavie, T., Meyer, J.: Acceptable intrusiveness of online help in mobile devices. In: Proceedings of the 11th International Conference on Human-Computer Interaction with Mobile Devices and Services, p. 26. ACM (2009)
40. Tokárová, L., Weideman, M.: Understanding the process of learning touch-screen mobile applications. In: Proceedings of the 31st ACM International Conference on Design of Communication - SIGDOC 2013, pp. 157–164. ACM Press, New York (2013)
41. Duh, H.B.-L., Tan, G.C.B., Chen, V.H.: Usability evaluation for mobile device: a comparison of laboratory and field tests. In: Proceedings of MobileHCI, pp. 181–186 (2006)
42. Arif, A., Iltisberger, B., Stuerzlinger, W.: Extending mobile user ambient awareness for nomadic text entry. In; Proceedings of the 23rd Australian Computer-Human Interaction Conference, pp. 21–30 (2011)
43. Tan, Z.-H., Lindberg, B.: Speech recognition on mobile devices. In: Jiang, X., Ma, M.Y., Chen, C.W. (eds.) Mobile Multimedia Processing. LNCS, vol. 5960, pp. 221–237. Springer, Heidelberg (2010)
44. Waqar, W., Chen, Y., Vardy, A.: Exploiting smartphone sensors for indoor positioning: a survey. In: Proceedings of the Newfoundland Conference on Electrical and Computer Engineering (2011)
45. Han, M., Vinh, L.T., Lee, Y.K., Lee, S.: Comprehensive context recognizer based on multimodal sensors in a smartphone. Sensors (Switzerland). **12**, 12588–12605 (2012)

Elements of Properties of User Experience in Cloud Computing Documentation Platform According to Smart Device Screen Size Changes: Focus on Google Docs and Naver Office

Min Kyung Kang[✉] and Sung Woo Kim

Interaction Design, Graduation School of Techno Design,
Kookmin University, Seoul, Korea
kaangbba@gmail.com, caerang@kookmin.ac.kr

Abstract. As the smart devices marketplace becomes increasingly more competitive, the usage accessibility of individuals has improved and services development is more active. Among these developments, use of the Cloud Office Platform as a collaboration tool for cooperation in Cloud Computing is on the rise. The N-Screen, with its limited function and amount of information displayed depending on screen size, also requires that a seamless user environment be provided. This paper analyzes user experience (UX) factors and characteristics using patterns and functions that should be taken into consideration for utilization of the Cloud Office Platform based on web browsers on PCs and Mobiles. This analysis is called the "Consistency of Character" analysis, and this paper proposes a research method in which it is incorporated.

Keywords: Mobile services · User experience (UX) · Consistency of character · Cloud computing · Online office · Document authoring tool

1 Introduction

With the development of information environments that interact with information technology (IT), new smart devices of varied screen sizes are released constantly in the market. Users provide smart devices developed with modified screen sizes with new roles and purpose. In recent times, new terms such as "Smart Work" and "Smart Office" have been created, and related services developed. These trends have also affected content usage behavior. Such change is caused by the importance of efficient collaboration and increased tasks in cloud computing environments, led by documentation platforms. Collaboration in cloud computing environments is currently in a phase of constantly creating an ecosystem around documentation platforms developed by portals.

To provide a cooperative tool in cloud computing, it is important to know usage behaviors for the same content on different devices with different screen sizes, as well as the experience and characteristics to be provided to users, in order to provide devices with distinct characteristics and corresponding services. However, related research still remains insufficient.

© Springer International Publishing Switzerland 2015
A. Marcus (Ed.): DUXU 2015, Part II, LNCS 9187, pp. 551–562, 2015.
DOI: 10.1007/978-3-319-20898-5_53

1.1   Research Objective

The development of Smart work and Smart devices has resulted in "collaboration" action being a key experience. The important task of "document work" exists not only in companies but also in any group that engages in collaboration with a fixed process. In this paper, the functions of a document authoring tool for transferring from PC to Mobile during document processing and the factors and characteristics of the user experience (UX) are analyzed based on the level of importance. This is used to improve the quality of cloud computing office document processing on N-Screen devices.

Therefore, this study aims to analyze the UX elements and properties that must be provided according to screen size in cloud computing, by focusing on documentation platforms. The UX elements and properties to be analyzed are those that establish a relationship between information displayed differently according to device screen size and user context, specified and referred to as Consistency of Character in this study.

1.2   Contents of Research

In this paper, the service context and UX of Clouding Computing based on N-Screen environments is investigated to propose UX factors and characteristics that providers should consider in order to reduce the service information and function based on the device standard. To this end, this study aims to present the UX elements and properties to be considered from the perspective of providers. Therefore, we provide guidelines for the elements and properties of UX-based service design to be considered for new services in cloud computing environments.

2   Theoretical Background

2.1   Cloud Computing and N-Screen

Due to the increased application function according to the evolution of Mobile devices such as smart phones and development of the broadband network, Ubiquitous Mobile service of based on cloud computing is also emerging as the life revolves around [1]. That is, the user is that the same device can be used through a variety of content and can use the contents in accordance with the characteristics of various devices [2]. By providing most of the content and information stored in the cloud and can be used consistently contents UX between devices, it's offering a convenient environment for users and can promote the content consumption. Cloud services will be the backbone N-Screen-to-3S (Sync, Shift, Share), on footing this player, etc. offers a variety of additional services and applications will be [3]. To the application service canvas for receiving in a number of configurations via the connection between the application, it was that the web contents fusion function can be the service is realized only by the user's own [4].

2.2 Consistency of UX in N-Screen Environment

Consistency in design is simply more than one element is not meant to "sound the same", this is a lot of complex issues to consider. In order to discuss the consistency because there are fundamentally many layers, levels and dimension to consider. That is a consistent design style of integrating into the inner surface than to match the same can be said to attain intuitively [5]. Nielsen [8] said, when the user about the consistency to transfer skills from one system to another, defined as improve user's Possibility to which time is easy usability and learnability on another system [6]. The workshop opened with the theme of CHI 2006 [9] explain to divide the consistency in user-level and interface-level in multi-platform environments, user-level means "The transfer of knowledge that as the user transfers the platform, you can take the seamless same task", 'Cognitive convenience' and 'User will feel as if they were in the house'. Consistency of Interface-level means that it would be possible for the same functions, such as the selection of the design, such as the widget is always the same action at the interface of the other platform [6].

The concept of 'consistency' to be covering in this study is called 'Consistency of Character' which UX elements and properties that to connect information Display each other according to the screen size of the smart device and the relationship between the use context, and it proceeds to deduct the research.

3 Theoretical Background

3.1 Preceding Research on Cloud Office Platform: Understanding the Document Authoring Tool

Classification of Document Authoring Tools. Cloud computing document authoring tools are classified as seen in Table 1 based on research method. For the subject of research relevant to the objective of the study to be selected, the cloud computing office tool (cloud office) that allows compatibility and provides standardized document forms during collaboration is examined.

Definition of the Cloud Office Platform. Before going into the actual research, preliminary research was conducted on document processing using online office tools based on cloud computing on an N-Screen. A document authoring tool developed domestically and abroad was also utilized.

Table 1. Classification of document authoring tools

Online document authoring tool (Based on N-Screen)	Cloud note		Compatible operating systems (Compatible or not)
	Online office (= Cloud office tool)	Based on web browser	
		Based on installation program	

Among the online office tools, the cloud computing office tool that matches with the above conditions to be studied is referred to as the "Cloud Office Platform" in this paper.

3.2   Preceding Research on Cloud Office Platform: Cloud Office Platform Case

Among the Cloud Office Platforms developed, Korean Naver Office and Polaris Office, and American Google Docs and MS Office 365 were used to conduct a case analysis and comparison, as shown in Table 2.

Table 2. Cloud Office Platform—domestic and foreign cases

Korea	Naver Office / Naver Corp.	Polaris Office / Infraware Inc.
Type	Web app based web browser	App based on installation program
Features	• Spreads the center of Korea portal: Naver's users • Possess the office business system 'Naver Works' eco-system based on enterprise cloud • Way to web-centric document distribution	• Office program into 60% of the smart phone (Samsung, LG and etc.) is installed in advance • Development of the PC version after mobile and tablet application development
Major-Ex	• High compatibility with various office documents: talking into account the specificity of the Korea office market share (HWP, ODF, PDF and etc.) • MS Office documents outside Korea share high domestic word processing 'HWP' editable • Utilization is possible of the data provided by the Naver	• Feature Support complex formatting or functionality written in MS Office • Shared document based on a mobile address book
Foreign	Google Docs / Google Inc.	MS Office 365 / Microsoft Corp.
Type	Web app based on web browser	App based on installation program
Features	• Possess the enterprise 'Apps for Business' eco-system through the Google Apps Marketplace • Syntagmatically available a variety of services through the Google Apps	• Change of MS Office according to Windows version update • Maintaining the existing system of installation MS Office of cloud services: be quick to user's adapt • Liaison between the installation MS Office and MS Office 365
Major-Ex	• To offer personalized service center of the 'sharing' and 'collaboration' • Auto save recorded: View document update record • Provide correct feedback on usage (ex: WYSIWYG, When collaborating input status, etc.)	• The provision of integrated apps through Office store with installation Office • Use the system that it's familiar with the existing approach to cloud • Construction of ecological social center (ex: Document access via the Drop box)

4 Research Method

4.1 Research Question

Of the various document authoring tools based on cloud computing, Google Docs and Naver Office met the standards below and were the ones primarily used in this research.

- Office tool developed at a representative portal site based on domestic and foreign standards.
- Cloud computing based web application office tool that can perform word processing in an internet browser and application (no installation-type offline document authoring tool is developed separately, only the online office tool is provided).
- N-screen office tool, facilitating word processing on both PC and Mobile.

In this study, we aimed to utilize the selected Cloud Office Platform to answer the following research questions in regard to information processing services provided in cloud computing:

- *Research Question 1:* How does the context used by users affect the use of the platform based on device changes?
- *Research Question 2:* How do the functions derived on the platform affect the use of the platform?

4.2 Research Procedure: Research Process and Research Analysis Method

Previous Research: For the Service typology from the perspective of Design Information Framework (2013) interaction and UX attributes, 11 different interaction attributes selected by Lim et al. [11] and 18 sub-elements of the UX factors selected by Park et al. [12] were used [7]. Florins et al. [10] argued that consistency needs to be maintained based on three levels: Perceptual continuity, Cognitive continuity, and Functional continuity based on Donald Norman's action theory [5]. These were taken into consideration, and, of the three, our focus was on functional continuity. Further, of the three categories in the sub-elements (Usability, Affect, and User Value), the Usability attribute with a high relationship with functional continuity was used for mapping.

User Research: This user research was carried contextual inquiry (CI) and user in-depth interview out that Targeting the twenties to thirties male and female respondents seen that using Naver Office and Google Docs user of the N-screen service to analyze usage patterns on PC and Mobile for the use context.

In the research investigation, the research subject's function and service range were restricted based on analysis results of preceding investigations:

a. Depending on the software company's market direction, the supplied operating system's compatibility and support for different web browsers and smart devices, and the possibility of a new function was excluded.

b. Company Cloud Office Platform is limited in the functions provided and application use of devices based on the pricing policy. Thus, of the company version users, only the Google Docs service is discussed.

4.3   Research Procedure: User Investigation

Cloud Computing Platform Use-Attitude and Use Functions for Each Device: The CI conducted during the user investigation was to observe the use environment for each device, and conduct in-depth user interviews aimed at observing the Cloud Office Platform function used on PC and Mobiles, depending on the use-attitude and context and also aimed to analyze the main experience users have based on the use functions. First, the comparison function needed to deduct users' use functions was extracted for each document form: Google Docs and Naver Office for PC and Mobile use. In addition, to equalize the levels of the functions to compare in each office document's form, of the functions shown on screen while running on the platform, functions existing at a depth of one were compared. Of the user's use function, more than 70 % had usability, and the same functions of a document form were said to be the main use functions. The operating system was set Windows and Android up.

When the number of functions for comparison is observed more closely, it can be seen that Google Docs doubled Naver Office in terms of the number of functions for the PC. Google Docs showed 3–4 times differences between the number of functions for PC and Mobile while Naver Office showed almost no function differences between the two devices. Thus, for Naver Office, UX based on the function difference between PC and Mobile use is provided identically, regardless of each function's use-frequency.

Looking at the main use functions in Table 3 below, for PC, simple editing functions are in the majority, whereas for Mobile, checking functions are in the majority. The distinctive point is that for PC, the document itself was newly made but for the Mobile the document was opened and only the name was changed. On the Mobile, the existing file was opened and reviewed but a new document was not made and edited. According to CI, for the N-Screen, working on Mobile consecutively after the PC became more inconvenient and vice versa. Further, working on a document on Mobile after creating it on a PC was much less frequent. The main reason for this is that a Mobile was used simply to check the document being worked on using the PC or to briefly modify texts and new documents were not made to edit. Another major reason is that concentration was reduced because of the smaller screen size. Because users did not have high expectations about multiple functions of Mobile, there was no reduction in use. Moreover, there was difficulty using the Mobile functions to input information by touching it. Unlike a Mobile, if a PC is not connected to a wired or a wireless network, internet data cannot be used, causing restrictions. Further, when the network is unstable and multiple users are editing the same document, errors occur, so users do not use the application in this situation. For these reasons, the reliability of automatic saving is guaranteed only for one-time or volatile documents. Mobile is used on the move because of easier mobility and the convenience of relatively free network use, but because of the screen size, the office platform is used less often and the quality of work falls.

Table 3. Google Docs and Naver Office use-behavior on PC and mobile

Device	PC		Mobile	
	Google Docs	Naver Office	Google Docs	Naver Office
Key usage functions	a. Text editing (Font, Font size, Weight, Italic, Underline, Color, Style, Alignment)		a. Document home	
	b. New		b. Changing the file name	
	c. Open		c. Open	
	d. Share		d. Share	
	e. Insert (Shapes, Lines, Tables, Images)		*How to share: Google Docs - files and folders, Naver Office - folders)	
	f. Modification (Copy, Paste)			
	g. Print			
N-Screen usage patterns	From PC to mobile		From mobile to PC	
	1. Screen size changes due to decrease the amount used of features		1. Distance to the entry that occurs due to the small screen size	
	- Simple text entry and editing			
	- The difficulty of finding documents		- No sophisticated editing	
	- UI is different from the PC: Confused about function location		- Operation error (ex: making type error, editing error, etc.)	
	2. Reduce usage: Provides functions that do not fit with the device input methods			
	- Difficult of usage of function due to feature a touch			
Unused-Key usage patterns	• When you're moving (if notebook)		• When the PC is available	
	• When a network connection is not stable		• When the elaborate operation required	
			• When the operating system version according to the office version does not match (updated or not)	
	• When necessary fonts and keyboard shortcuts are supported and not be compatible	• When collaboration is required		

UX Factor Deduction: According to the results of a user in-depth interview conducted, the main experience on the Cloud Office Platform is continuity. Continuity can be divided into two concepts: compatibility between software for document extension and consistency between PC and Mobile for simple document editing. For the latter, which is applicable to this research, for substituting experience with functions for the 11 types of interaction and UX interaction attributes and seven UX Sub-elements, usability mapping was implemented to classify the main use functions between PC and Mobile based on the main use attributes. The same use behaviors for Google Docs and Naver Office were selected as standards for the use behaviors.

The main use functions, based on usage on different devices, have differences in usage depending on the situation; however, when using the device, the same functions as in the platform were used. In addition, opening and sharing is applicable in all cases. This result shows the usage attribute for users who use the Cloud Office Platform as a collaboration tool, and this can be seen as a function of the Cloud Office Platform in close association with the users. When the use functions of each use attribute are observed, those with the same attributes are grouped and have been reclassified for interaction attributes and UX Sub-elements: usability (Table 4).

Table 4. Main use function mapping based on main use attribute

	PC				Mobile	
	Key usage patterns	Key usage functions			Key usage patterns	Key usage functions
A1	Document sharing is required situation	Open, Share		A2	Document sharing is required situation	Open, Share
B	Implementing sophisticated tasks	Text editing, Open, Share, Insert, Modification	New, Print	E	Check document enforcement	Document home, Changing the file name, Open, Share
	Sitting in state				Moving state	
C	Reliable network environment		New		Unavailable environment the PC	
D	Flexible work environment				Performed a simple text modifications	

4.4   Research Procedure: UX Attribute Analysis for Different Platform Uses on Cloud Computing Document Processing

On the basis of the mapping materials above, the same use functions of Google Docs and Naver Office were grouped together and reclassified into 11 different interaction attributes and seven UX Sub-elements: Usability. The UX attributes of the main use behaviors and main use functions were matched. They were classified into 22 attributes including two attributes that were different from the 11 types of interaction attributes.

For UX attribute matching, university students and employees working at UX businesses were selected to form two groups of five, and workshops were conducted twice for each group. Through these workshops, the same use attributes that were grouped according to the same use functions were matched. On the basis of the matched attributes, the attributes that were the same for both PC and Mobile were selected and a Cloud Office Platform Consistency of Character was created, as shown in Table 5.

Table 5. PC and Mobile Cloud Office Platform Consistency of Character based on the mapped use attributes and functions.

Google Docs/Naver Office							
		PC				Mobile	
Interaction attributes		A1	B	C	D	A2	E
Connectivity	Independent						
	Networked	O	O	O	O	O	O
Continuity	Discrete						
	Continuous	O	O	O	O	O	O
Directness	Indirect						
	Direct	O	O	O	O	O	O
Movement	Static	O	O	O	O	O	O
	Dynamic						
Orderliness	Random						
	Orderly	O	O	O	O	O	O
Proximity	Precise	O	O	O	O	O	O
	Proximate						
Pace	Slow						
	Fast	O	O	O	O	O	O
Resolution	Scarce					O	O
	Dense	O	O	O	O		
Speed	Delaying						
	Rapid	O	O	O	O	O	O
State	Fixed						
	Changing	O	O	O	O	O	O
Time-depth	Concurrent	O	O	O	O		
	Sequential					O	O
Elements of UX		A1	B	C	D	A2	E
Sub-elements of Usability	Simplicity	O				O	O
	Directness	O	O	O	O	O	O
	Efficiency	O	O	O			
	Informativeness, Flexibility, Learnability, User Support	O	O	O	O	O	O

5 Research Analysis Results and Conclusion

5.1 Research Results

A total of 15 attributes, Networked, Continuous, Direct, Static, Orderly, Precise, Fast, Rapid, Changing, Simplicity, Directness, Informativeness, Flexibility, Learnability, User support, fulfil A1 and A2, open and sharing functions derived from the same UX factor between PC and Mobile at the same time. Fourteen attributes, excluding simplicity, belong to all use behaviors. The relevant attributes were classified as shown in Table 6 on the basis of their use function. Contextuality is an experience attribute that must be formed when the function used must change owing to an external or internal situation, Accessibility is an experience attribute that must be formed when each function needs to be provided during use, Communicability is an experience attribute that must be formed when the function first provides a function to the user. These three experience attributes, Contextuality, Accessibility, Communicability, are consistency of characters derived depending on the PC and Mobile screen size, when using the Cloud Office Platform.

Table 6. Three types of experience attributes of Consistency of Character

Consistency of Character	Interaction attributes	Elements of UX (Usability)
Contextuality	Networked, Continuous, Fast, Changing	Flexibility
Accessibility	Precise	Simplicity, Directness, Learnability
Communicability	Direct, Static, Orderly, Rapid	Informativeness, User support

5.2 Research Result

This study focused on cloud computing word processing platforms and analyzed the UX factors and characteristics that should be provided based on screen size. The standard screen devices used for comparison were Windows PC and Android Mobiles. The Cloud Office Platforms observed were Google Docs and Naver Office. The use-behavior based on the user environment and the frequency of use for the functions were compared, and UX elements, the open and sharing function, were created. Subsequently, the classified main use functions based on the main use behaviors were mapped together and grouped according to similar function use behaviors. The grouped use behaviors were matched through 11 types of interaction attributes and seven UX Sub-elements based on usability. The matched experience attributes were grouped based on the function's use relationship in terms of Contextuality, Accessibility, and Communicability. In addition, these three experience attributes form the Cloud Office Platform's UX characteristics and Consistency of Character.

The answers to the research questions posed in this study are as follows:

In cloud computing, when information is reduced, services are provided.

- *Research Question 1:* How does the user's use context affect the platform used based on device changes?

  A PC is equipped with a large screen, keyboard, and mouse. Consequently, most elaborate and complicated work is done on the PC. Use behaviors change depending on the network situation. When the network is safe and the work environment is relatively fluid, PC was used, but even Notebooks will not be used if the network is unstable. On the other hand, because Mobiles have flexible networks, they can be used while on the move. However, because of their small screens, they are mostly used for viewing or to input simple texts. Mistakes and errors occurring because of the small screens make users wary. The fact that their input methods are different from those of a PC make Mobile use environment worse and reduce the scope of work that can be done on Mobiles.

- *Research Question 2:* How do the functions derived on the platform affect the platform used?

  When comparative analysis was conducted on the use behaviors and use functions of Google Docs and Naver Office, the frequency of use of each office platform's distinct characteristic was not mentioned compared to the frequency of use of editing function with simple document writing. Thus, depending on the device used, there were overlapped functions, mostly related to basic editing functions. There was an editing function on a Mobile but even from simple text edits, there were many errors arising because of the touch type input, hence, it was not used with high reliability. Thus, in the Cloud Office Platform, users suggested diversification of document basic templates and functions customized for viewers.

References

1. Lee, S.Y.: A Study on the Introduction of Desktop Virtualization by Implementing of Cloud Computing Technology, p. 1 (2012)
2. Lim, S.H., Lee, Y.J.: N-Screen service users' motivations for use and dissatisfying factors. J. Korea Contents Assoc. **13**(3), 100 (2003)
3. Choi, J.H.: N-screen content service implementation cases. Commun. Korean Inst. Inf. Sci. Eng. **29**(7), 55 (2011)
4. Jo, C.S.: Collaboration service technology through N-Screen utilization. In: 3rd N-Screen Service Workshop on Korea Institute of Communications and Information Sciences, pp. 49–52 (2011)
5. Eun, Y.: Design attributes for consistent user experience of multi device service. J. Korean Soc. Des. Sci. **25**(1), 139–140 (2011)
6. Shin, H.J., Jeong, S.M., Lee, J.Y., Song, H.C.: A study of family UI on multi-platform. In: HCIK 2009, vol. 2009, no. 2, p. 1031 (2009)
7. Choi, J.Y., Lee, H.J., Cho, Y.H., Oh, D.W.: Service typlology from the perspective of design information framework. In: HCIK 2013, vol. 2013, no. 1, p. 309 (2013)
8. Nielsen, J.: User Interfaces for Consistency. The Morgan Kaufmann Series in Interactive Technologies, Neuauflage 202 edn. Morgan Kaufmann Publishers, San Francisco (1989)

9. Richter, K., Nichols, J., Gajos, K., Seffah, A.: The many faces of consistency in cross-platform design. In: Proceedings of the CHI 2006 Workshop on the Many Face of Consistency in Cross-Platform Design (2006)

10. Florins, M., Trevisan, D.G., Vanderdonckt, J.: The continuity property in mixed reality and multiplatform systems: a comparative study. In: Proceedings of the CADUI, pp. 321–332 (2004)

11. Lim, Y.K., Stolterman, E., Jung, H.K., Donaldson, J.: Interaction gestalt and the design of aesthetic interactions. In: DPPI 2007 Proceedings of the 2007 Conference on Designing Pleasurable Products, pp. 248–249 (2007)

12. Park, J.H., Han, S.H., Kim, H.K., Cho, Y.S., Park, W.K.: Developing elements of user experience for mobile phones and services: survey, interview, and observation approaches. Hum. Factors Ergon. Manuf. Serv. Ind. 23(4), 288–289 (2011)

Virtual Touchpad for Cursor Control of Touchscreen Thumb Operation in the Mobile Context

Yu Ren Lai and T.K. Philip Hwang[✉]

National Taipei University of Technology, P.O. Box 2813 no.1, Sec. 3, E. Rd.,
Taipei 10608, Taiwan, R.O.C.
phwang@ntut.edu.tw

Abstract. This study formulated existing virtual pointing techniques for cursor control in the mobile context of touchscreen thumb operation. Three virtual pointing models were developed, including: **Virtual Touchpad**, **Virtual Joystick** and **Virtual Direction Key**. In order to verify their usability and feasibility, a user study was employed to evaluate the usability of three virtual pointing models, followed by the focus group interview to experienced usability designers, in which, constraints of touchscreen cursor control in mobile context were defined and rated against three virtual pointing models. Research findings: (1) Virtual Touchpad was significantly efficient than others, while Virtual Direction Key presented lower error rate, although insignificantly. (2) Constraints of touchscreen cursor control in mobile context include: stable and simple operation, Interruptible operation is better and avoids accurate pointing. Virtual Direction Key stood out as the most stable, simple and interruptible pointing control.

Keywords: Virtual touchpad · Cursor control · Thumb operation

1 Introduction

Before the popularity of smartphones, most people commonly used mobile phones with only one hand [1]. Interfaces that allow one-handed operation interaction can provide a significant advantage in which users can use the other hand for mobile tasks [2]. With the smart-phones enter people's lives. There are more and more applications let us to use that also mean we will get a lot of information on smartphone. In this way people need the bigger screen to display more information on screen. Therefore, more and more smartphone manufacturers have been launched large-screen smartphones. Apple also launch two new iPhones, the 4.7-inch iPhone 6 and the 5.5-inch iPhone 6 Plus. It seem like large-screen is the trend of smartphone in the future. However, there exist a comfort zone on the smartphone screen in thumb operation scenarios [3]. Hoober [4] shows that users prefer to use large-screen smartphones with only one hand in the majority of the time (Fig. 1). Unfortunately, according to the design guidelines of the smartphone. Apple and Android are all suggested that navigation and functionality buttons should be placed on the top of screen. The top bar in the screen facilitates the

A. Marcus (Ed.): DUXU 2015, Part II, LNCS 9187, pp. 563–574, 2015.
DOI: 10.1007/978-3-319-20898-5_54

discovery of functions, where the user's hands would never cover them. Since smartphone screens are getting larger, it is much difficult for thumbs to reach the upper area of the screen especially in one-handed operation scenarios. In order to build interfaces that explicitly accommodate thumb interaction by ensuring that all targets are thumb sized and within thumb reach, this paper proposes three virtual pointing techniques (touchpad, joystick and direction key) interfaces located in comfort zone of thumb operation. All models of Virtual Touchpad aimed to control the cursor for reaching every part of the screen.

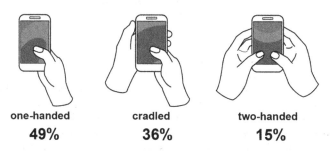

Fig. 1. User held their phones in three ways (source adapted from Hoober, 2013)

2 Related Work

2.1 Pointing Technique

Pointing to targets is a fundamental task in graphical user interfaces (GUI's) [5]. According whether the input and display space unified, the pointing technique can classify as direct interaction and indirect interaction [6].

Direct Pointing Technique. A direct pointing device has a unified input and display surface such as touch-screens, or display tablets operated with a pen. Direct touch has a lot of advantage: (1) it's a form of direct manipulation that is easy to learn. (2) It's a fastest pointing way. (2) It has easier hand-eye coordination than mouse or keyboards. (3) It doesn't need additional desk space [7]. But is also exists some dis-advantages like high error rate, lower accuracy and occluded problem by finger [8, 9].

Indirect Pointing Technique. An indirect pointing device isn't providing input in the same physical space as the output. For example, when users use a mouse that they must move the mouse on one surface (like a desk) to indicate a point on the screen. Typically they require more explicit feedback and representation of the pointing device (such as a cursor), the intended target on the screen (such as highlighting icons when the cursor hovers over them), and the current state of the device (such as whether a button is held or not). However, indirect pointing has an obviously advantage that indirect input is a better way to point large or far interaction surfaces, since it requires less body movement, and also allows interaction at a distance from the display [6].

The indirect pointing usually includes mouse, trackballs, touchpads, joysticks and arrow keys. For typical pointing tasks the mouse is the most common to use on a desktop computer, one can point with the mouse about as well as with the hand itself [6]. A trackball senses the relative motion of a partially exposed ball in two degrees of freedom. Trackballs require frequent clutching movements because users must lift and reposition their hand after rolling the ball a short distance [6]. A Touchpad is a small and touch-sensitive tablets often found on notebook. Touchpads usually use relative mode for cursor control because they are too small to map to an entire screen, they necessitates frequent clutching when user use it. Most touchpads also have an absolute mode to allow interactions such as character entry [6]. There are two kind of joystick: (1) an isometric joystick is a force-sensing joystick that returns to center when released. (2) Isotonic joysticks sense angle of deflection. In isometric joysticks, the rate of cursor movement is proportional to the force exerted on the stick; as a result, users must practice in order to achieve good cursor control. The arrow keys are buttons on a computer keyboard that is programmed or designated to move the cursor in a specified direction. Arrow keys are commonly used for selection around documents [10].

2.2   Existing Solutions in Remote Screen Operation

As the screen size of mobile phones is ever increasing, such screen area become difficult for thumbs to cover and reach on one-handed operation scenarios. It causes that some target in this area can't be touched by thumb because there exist a big distance between thumb and targets. The solutions must shorten the distant between the target and thumb. We classify these further into direct and indirect interaction methods.

Direct Interaction: The Target Closed to the Thumb. This method is like put the target into the comfort zone of thumb. ArchMenu and ThumbMenu [11] apply the stacked pie menu that makes items to surround the thumb (Fig. 2a and b). This way facilitates one-handed interaction on small touchscreen devices. Nudelman [12] presented a C-Swipe gesture that let user use C-Swipe to raise a semicircular pie menu on the screen of smartphone, which surround the thumb. This method allows the user to tap the options which originally in the top of the screen (Fig. 2c). However, those methods can only tap the functions, it can't tap into the content, such as a list. As Apps become more complex, this approach does not necessarily meet the all of needs.

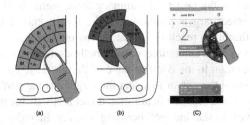

(a)   (b)   (c)

Fig. 2. (a) ArchMenu (b) ThumbMenu (c) using c-swipe to raise a semicircular pie menu (Source adapted from Hout et al. 2007 and Nudelman, 2013).

Faced with this problem there are plenty of manufacturers now that offer some interface features to facilitate the one-handed operation of today's big-screen phones (as shown in Fig. 3). When user open the one-handed mode that will resize the feature or entire screen and place it on the right or left of the screen. Apple also has one-handed mode and invented a name for the new feature, which called Reachability. It is activated by double tapping on the home key. It basically shrinks the interface, too, but in a manner that just slides it halfway down, so that you can reach whatever was unreachable at the top of the screen before. In summary those methods all move the distant target to the comfort zone of thumb then let the thumb can direct touch the target.

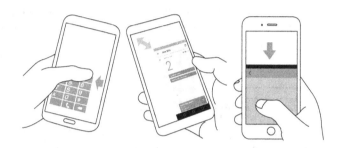

Fig. 3. Existing solution in large-screen smartphone

Indirect Interaction: Extending Thumb to Reach the Target. To solve this problem, we observe the operation scenarios of a touchpad TV remote control suitable for thumb use on one-handed operation scenarios. Choi et al. [13] show that a remote with small touchpad can control the cursor to pointing at the far target on large-screen TV (Fig. 4a). ThumbSpace [2], it's inspiration from the large screen devices and wall-sized displays both confront issues with out-of reach interface objects. ThumbSpace requires setup a proxy view that like an absolute touchpad (as show in Fig. 4b). When user's thumb touches a ThumbSpace area, the associated object on the screen is highlighted. Yu et al. [14] also introduced BezelSpace, a proxy region is the same as ThumbSpace, but the location of proxy region adaptively shifts according to any bezel swipe initial location on the screen (Fig. 4c). When use it, users need to continue to drag ones finger from the edge of screen and across the screen to control the mapped "magnetized" cursor and aim it towards the target. In summary those methods also utilized a cursor (pointing device) to select targets positioned at the farther end of the screen and it is like extending your thumb to reach the distant areas on screen.

The research shows that extendible cursor methods have the better performance than move the distant target to the comfort zone of thumb [15]. Yu showed that setting a virtual touchpad control the cursor to select the target has the perfect performance. It shows that the indirect methods may better than direct methods for resolving the thumb reach problem. However, the indirect pointing usually includes mouse, trackballs, joysticks, touchpads and arrow keys but which method has the better performance on pointing. The most common evaluation measures the efficiency of pointing devices are speed and accuracy. Cart et al. [16] measured mean pointing times and error rates for the mouse, rate-controlled isometric joystick, step keys, and text keys. They found the mouse to be the fastest and lower error rate of the devices. MacKenzie et al. [17] compares the efficiency of pointing devices for the mouse, trackballs, touchpads and joysticks. The publication showed the mouse to be the fastest pointing device but they're no significant different between each method. In those researches, they evaluate several pointing devices in real but we were interested in users' behavior and efficiency when we employ those pointing techniques on virtual scenario.

In this paper we focus on the evaluation of indirect pointing devices in precision cursor positioning tasks on smartphone. Considering the operation behavior of touchscreen, two methods include mouse and trackballs may not suitable for using on touchscreen. They require frequent clutching movements because users must lift and reposition their hand after rolling the mouse and ball a short distance. The other hand those methods aren't suitable for virtualization. Finally we chose the touchpad, joysticks and arrow keys to evaluate the efficiency of pointing on touchscreen of smartphone.

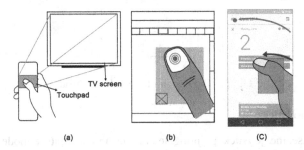

(a)   (b)   (C)

Fig. 4. (a) Using touchpad for TV remote control scenarios (b) ThumbSpace (c) BezelSpace (Source adapted from Choi et al. 2011, Kalson et al. 2007 and Yu et al. 2013).

3 Developing Interface of Virtual Pointing Control

We understand that the pointing technique can help us to point the target accurately by the cursor. However, there have not been any researches compare the efficiency of pointing techniques on large mobile touchscreen. We developed three mobile inter-action techniques using pointing technique: Virtual Touchpad, Virtual Joystick and Virtual Directing Key. Our method includes two steps: (1) firstly, user performs the triggering gesture to open the virtual pointing interface (2) Secondly, user employ their thumb to operate the virtual pointing interface to select a target. We use the bezel swipe gesture as the triggering gesture. The bezel swipe gesture has the advantages of enabling users' thumbs to easily access functionality by activating a thin button [18]. Yu et al. [14] show that swipe gesture can adaptively find individual users comfortable range of motion for the thumb.

3.1   Virtual Touchpad

In this method, we set a semitransparent rectangle proxy region which mapping to the whole touch-screen of smartphone and it like an absolute touchpad. Avoiding the cursor suddenly jumps to the new position, we set a red dot on the rectangle area which position is mapping to the cursor (Fig. 5). In this way user can employ their thumb to drag the red dot on the rectangle area to control the cursor toward the target and it also fit the Fitt's law. The Virtual Touchpad operation scenario as following: (1) when user bezel swipe from the edge of screen, the touchpad and mapping cursor appear. (2) A user tap the red dot and drag it to control the cursor to the target and the cursor can dynamic capture closest target as the bubble cursor [5]. (3) The target is selected when a user's thumb lifts from the screen.

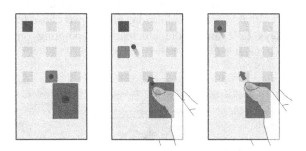

Fig. 5. The design of Virtual Touchpad

3.2   Virtual Joystick

This method use the joystick pointing technique and it control mode inspire from operation way of the game on the tablet. The red dot on the interface represents the stick of the joystick and the circular region represents the red dot can movable range (Fig. 6). When the cursor moves, it is based on the distance between red dot and the center of circular region, if the red dot farther form the center of circular region the cursor moves faster. The Virtual Joystick operation scenario as following: (1) when user bezel swipe from the edge of screen, the virtual joystick and cursor appear (Fig. 6b). (2) A user drag the red dot to control the cursor and it can dynamic capture closest target. (3) The target is selected when a user's thumb lifts from the screen.

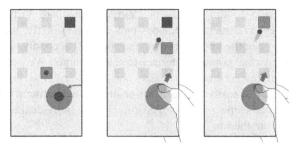

Fig. 6. The design of Virtual Joystick

3.3   Virtual Direction Key

This method use the arrow key pointing technique, it common use on computer keyboard and usually arranged in an inverted-T layout. Furthermore, this method is also common use to navigation or changes the function in feature phone by the number key. The keys can move the cursor to jump a target to another target in a specified direction (as object pointing). We refer to step key [19] and set the Virtual Direction key (Fig. 7). We propose that Virtual Direction Key works as follows: (1) object cursor appears when the bezel swipe occurs. (2) Users tap the direction key to control the object cursor and aim it towards the target. (3) The target is selected when a user's thumb tap the ok key.

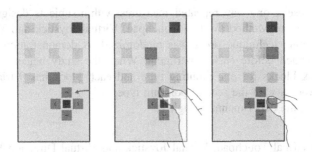

Fig. 7. The design of Virtual Direction Key

4   Usability Study and Feasibility Analysis

4.1   Usability Study

A usability study was designed to evaluate three kinds of cursor control interface: Virtual Touchpad, Virtual Joystick and Virtual Direction Key in terms of usability, efficiency and user satisfaction.

Devices and Participants. In this study, these interface techniques are implemented on the Android Platform, and the experiments ran on the Samsung Galaxy Note2 (80.5 × 151.1 × 9.4 mm, 5.5" display, 1280 × 720 screen resolution). Ten participants (7 Male, 3 Female), ranging in age from 21 to 38 years of age with an average age of 27 years of age, and all participants were right-handed and had experience with touchscreen based smartphones. The experiment required an hour per participant, and they were received NT$150 upon the completion of the experiment.

Tasks. Kalson show that most people are used to operate the phone with one hand while walking or standing. Thus, in this study each participant was asked to stand and hold the device with the dominant hand and manipulate it only with the thumb while the experiment performed. They were asked to conduct a series of target selection tasks. According to the minimal touch area command in current mobile UI design guide, we set 7 mm × 7 mm as the rectangular target size and the target color is grey in normal situation. Based on the arrangement of icon on the home screen in current smartphone, we divided the screen into a 5 × 6 grid and the target will be evenly distributed in the grid. To ensure the users utilize the cursor control technique in every selection tasks, we ask each target should appear outside the thumb comfort zone. Targets appeared 9 times in a random order for each block. When target appear on screen there is only one target was painted blues for each trial; other keep grey. When the target was focused or selected, the color changed to green. When a participant succeeded in correctly selecting a target, they received haptic feedback through a vibration motor and the next target was generated immediately. If a participant failed to use pointing technique to select a target, no feedback was provided to ensure that the participant would try again. The participants were instructed to select the blue targets as quickly and accurately as possible.

Methods. We use a one-way repeated measures within-subjects design. The independent variables are Method (Virtual Touchpad, Virtual Joystick and Virtual Direction Key). Pointing technique order was randomized. A demonstration and practice phase was provided before each experiment. When the study began, users need to complete 6 task blocks for one pointing type and each block has 9 trials, and then repeated the process with the second pointing type.

In summary, the experimental design is:

10 participants
× 3 Methods (Virtual Touchpad, Virtual Joystick and Virtual Direction Key)
× 6 Blocks
× 9 trials = 1,620 trials completed

After completing one method, participants were asked to complete the satisfaction questionnaire (a seven-point Likert scale) and interviewed for ten minutes. They were asked for any opinions about our interfaces, such as the reasons for their answers, frustrating experiences, and suggestions for each configuration.

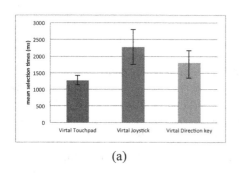
(a)

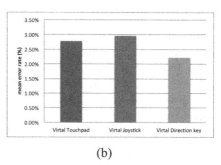
(b)

Fig. 8 (a) Mean selection times (b) Mean error rate

4.2   Data Analysis of User Study

Selection Time. Selection time was defined as the elapsed time between a target appearance and the target is selected successfully. Trials with selection errors were excluded from analysis. We analyzed results by one-way repeated-measure ANOVA and find a significant effect on selection time ($F_{2,27}$ = 29.649, p < .001 with Mauchly Spherical Test, p > .05). Post hoc pairwise comparisons show that all methods differ significantly from each other, especial the Virtual Touchpad to Virtual Joystick and Virtual Direction Key. Overall, Virtual Touchpad is significantly faster (M = 1271.01 ms, SD = 175.45 ms) than Virtual Joystick (M = 2272.179 ms, SD = 522.65 ms) and Virtual Direction Key (M = 1806.1 ms, SD = 374.4 ms) (Fig. 8a).

Error Rate. The error rate was defined as the number of erroneous selections during one block. It includes empty and wrong target selections. We analyzed results by one-way repeated-measure ANOVA but we find there is no significant effect on error rate ($F_{2,27}$ = 0.251, p > .05). Post hoc pairwise comparisons show that all methods no significant with each other. The object pointing and semantic pointing may explain this. Because in Virtual Touchpad and Virtual Joystick, the cursor can dynamic capture the closest target. In this approach, a user doesn't need to accurately move the cursor to target. Overall, Virtual Direction Key is more accuracy (M = 2.78 %, SD = 3.3 %)) than Virtual Joystick (M = 2.96 %, SD = 2.5 %) and Virtual Touchpad (M = 2.2 %, SD = 2.87 %) (Fig. 8b).

User Satisfaction. After experiments done we do a questionnaire to evaluate the user satisfaction. In this questionnaire Virtual Touchpad has a great performance across all categories on a 7-point Likert scale. We believe the shape of virtual touchpad mapping to the touch screen and the cursor can dynamic capture the nearest target (Semantic pointing) cause this result. Participants also report that they can move their thumb easily by the corresponding direction of target on virtual touchpad (Fig. 9).

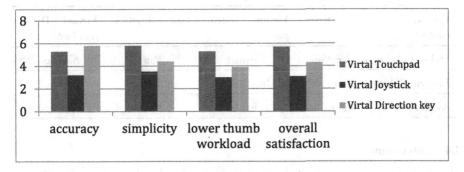

Fig. 9 User satisfaction score

4.3   Focus Group Interview and Evaluation

All models (design) in this study were developed to improve selection operation for targets that are out of thumb reach. While the usability study was carried out in a controlled environment, the real user's mobility context should take moving vehicle and surrounding crowds into consideration. Thus, the operation details of each model need to be carefully examined to ensure that they meet the challenge of mobile context.

A focus group interview to seven experienced usability designers was carried out. The **first stage** of the focus group interview was to define constraints of touchscreen cursor control in mobile context, followed by the **second stage**, in which every individual model was rated against constraints of cursor control in mobile context.

Findings of Focus Group Interview. Defined constraints of cursor in mobile context include:

1. Stable and simple operation are required. People may use mobile devices when they're standing, walking, riding a bus or train.
2. Interruptible operation is better. Any operation required continuous thumb tap and drag is not suitable in the mobile context, in which a user's operation might be disturbed by passersby, jolts on a vehicle or jerks of surrounding crowds.
3. Avoid accurate pointing. Selection targets in the virtual pointing control panel should not be smaller than 9.2 mm [20].

Evaluation of Experienced Usability Designers. The evaluation of cursor control models was done by the same group of experienced usability designers. The average rating is shown in Table 1. Virtual Direction Key stood out as the most stable, simple and Interruptible pointing control.

In addition, operation feedback should be taken into consideration, according to the interviewees.

Table 1. Evaluation of cursor control model against constraints of thumb operation in mobile context.

Constraints / virtual cursor control	Virtual Touch-pad	Virtual Joystick	Virtual Direction key
Stable and simple operation	Satisfied	Fair	Satisfied
Interruptible operation	Unsatisfied	Unsatisfied	Satisfied
Avoid accurate pointing	Fair	Fair	Satisfied

4.4   Discussion

The results in our experiment show that Virtual Touchpad performed a better efficiency than others did. Most users reported that they could smoothly control the cursor through Virtual Touchpad. This is because the shape and scale of virtual touchpad was designed for mapping to the touchscreen that make the cursor control predictable.

However, the results show that the Virtual Joystick has the worst performance in both efficiency and satisfaction. All participants reported that the movement of cursor is inconsistent with thumb operation. In our observation, when users intended to shift moving direction of the cursor, virtual joystick provided no feedback to the thumb, which confused the user. As a result, in the context of virtual pointing control, the more consistence between thumb and cursor, the better efficiency and satisfaction were reported.

Although Virtual Direction Key performed less efficient than Virtual Touchpad did, but most users remarked its accuracy. Meanwhile, users also reported that they sometimes feel impatient because this method requires frequent taping the direction key. However, experts regarded that Virtual Direction Key is a better means of touchscreen cursor control in mobile context.

5 Conclusion

This study formulated existing virtual pointing techniques for cursor control in the mobile context of touchscreen thumb operation. Three virtual pointing models were developed, including: Virtual Touchpad, Virtual Joystick and Virtual Direction Key.

The usability tests reveal: (1) Virtual Touchpad was significantly efficient than others, while Virtual Direction Key presented lower error rate, although insignificantly. (2) Virtual Touchpad has a favored performance across most categories (accuracy, simplicity, thumb workload, and overall satisfaction) in user satisfaction test.

The feasibility study remarks: (1) constraints of touchscreen cursor control in mobile context include: stable and simple operation, interruptible operation is better and avoid accurate pointing. (2) Virtual Direction Key stood out as the most stable, simple and interruptible pointing control. (3) All virtual pointing models require further improvement on operation feedback. As a result, taking usability and feasibility into consideration, the Virtual Direction Key is a better means of touchscreen cursor control in mobile context.

References

1. Karlson, A.K., Bederson, B.B., Contreras-Vidal, J.L.: Understanding single-handed mobile device interaction. In: Lumsden, J. (ed.) Handbook of Research on User Interface Design and Evaluation for Mobile Technology, pp. 86–101. National Research Council of Canada Institute for Information Technology, Hershey (2006)
2. Karlson, A.K., Bederson, B.B.: ThumbSpace: generalized one-handed input for touchscreen-based mobile devices. In: Baranauskas, C., Abascal, J., Barbosa, S.D.J. (eds.) INTERACT 2007. LNCS, vol. 4662, pp. 324–338. Springer, Heidelberg (2007)
3. Clark, J.: Tapworthy: Designing Great iPhone Apps. O'Reilly Media, Canada (2010)
4. Hoober, S.: How do users really hold mobile devices? UX- matters (2013). http://goo.gl/SbDQXA. Accessed 18 Sep 2014
5. Grossman, T, Balakrishnan, R.: The bubble cursor: enhancing target acquisition by dynamic resizing of the cursor activation area. In: Proceedings of CHI 2005, pp. 281–290 (2005)

6. Hinckley, K.: Input technologies and techniques. In: Jacko, J.A., Sears, A. (eds.) The Human-Computer Interaction Handbook: Fundamentals, Evolving Technologies, and Emerging Applications, pp. 151–168. Lawrence Erlbaum Associates, London (2002)
7. Shneiderman, B.: Touchscreens now offer compelling uses. IEEE Softw. **8**(2), 93–94 (1991)
8. Vogel, D., Baudisch, P.: Shift: a technique for operating pen-based interfaces using touch. In: Proceedings of CHI 2007, pp. 657– 666 (2007)
9. Forlines, C., Wigdor, D., Shen, C., Balakrishnan, R.: Direct-touch vs. mice input for tabletop displays. In: Proceedings of CHI 2007. ACM, pp. 647–656 (2007)
10. Rose, C., Hacker, B.: Inside Macintosh: More Macintosh Toolbox. Apple Computer, Inc., Addison-Wesley Pub. Co., Cupertino, Boston (1985)
11. Huot, S., Lecolinet, E.: ArchMenu et ThumbMenu: Contrôler son dispositif mobile "sur le pouce". In: Proceedings of ICPS IHM 2007, pp. 107–110 (2007)
12. Nudelman, G.: C-Swipe: An Ergonomic Solution To Navigation Fragmentation On Android. Smashing Magazine (2013). http://goo.gl/OG3o1k. Accessed 20 Sep 2014
13. Choi, S., Han, J., Lee, G., et al.: RemoteTouch: touch-screen-like interaction in the TV viewing environment. In: Proceedings of CHI 2011, pp. 393–402. ACM Press (2011)
14. Yu, N. H., Huang, D.Y., Hsu, J.J., Hung, Y.P.: Rapid selection of hard-to-access targets by thumb on mobile touch-screens. In: Proceedings of MobileHCI 2013, pp. 400– 403 (2013)
15. Kim, S., Yu, J., Lee, G.: Interaction techniques for unreachable objects on the touchscreen. In: Proceedings of OzCHI 2012, pp. 295–298 (2012)
16. Oulasvirta, A., Tamminen, S., Roto, V., Kuorelahti, J.: Interaction in 4-second bursts: the fragmented nature of attentional resources in mobile HCI. In: Proceedings of CHI 2005, pp. 919–928. ACM Press (2005)
17. Smith, T.F., Waterman, M.S.: Identification of common molecular subsequences. J. Mol. Biol. **147**, 195–197 (1981)
18. Card, S., English, W., Burr, B.: Evaluation of mouse, rate-controlled isometric joystick, step keys, and text keys for text selection on a CRT. Ergonomics **21**(8), 601–613 (1978)
19. MacKenzie, I.S., Kauppinen, T., Silfverberg, M.: Accuracy measures for evaluating computer pointing devices. Proceedings of ACM CHI 2001, pp. 9–16 (2001)
20. Parhi, P., Karlson, A.K., Bederson, B.B. Target size study for one-handed thumb use on small touchscreen devices. In: Proceedings of Mobile HCI 2006, pp. 203–210. ACM Press (2006)

The Interaction with Smartphones in the Brazilian Driving Context

Manuela Quaresma$^{(\boxtimes)}$, Rafael Cirino Gonçalves, Jhonnata Oliveira, and Marcela Rodrigues

LEUI | Laboratory of Ergodesign and Usability Interfaces, PUC-Rio University,
Rio de Janeiro, Brazil
mquaresma@puc-rio.br,
{rafaelcirinogoncalves,oliveira.jhonnata}@gmail.com,
marcelarodrigues-@hotmail.com

Abstract. This article presents a survey, constructed in an online platform, with the aim to analyze and understand the Brazilians' attitudes and strategies when interacting with smartphone in the driving context. The survey was composed of 30 questions with the purpose to gather information of the target group: Brazilians with 18 years old or more, with license to drive and with the habit of using the smartphone while driving. The results show that Brazilian drivers have non-safety behavior when interacting visually and manually with the smartphone inside the vehicle, which reflects an existing behavior in the context of Brazilian traffic.

Keywords: Driver behavior · Smartphone · In-vehicle devices · Interface design

1 Introduction

The usage of smartphones has been growing more and more and it's now part of the daily lives of many people, whether at home, at work or in commuting around town. According to report "The Mobile Economy in Latin America" [1], Brazil is the fifth-largest global smartphone market. In September 2014 the country had 89.5 million of smartphone connections, that means 32.4 % of smartphone adoption and the tendency is to grow until 72.2 % in 2020.

This higher demand for smartphones has provoked worldwide a raise in application sales in the biggest app stores (Apple App Store, Google Play e Windows Phone). With the GPS antenna on smartphones, many applications are now being developed to help users and drivers on their commutes. Nowadays, there are several smartphone apps designed to be used while driving a vehicle, whether to guide the driver along the way he should go, either to give information about the traffic and to warn about the events that are occurring in the traffic (such as accidents, road works, etc.), and many other services. This means that apps for drivers offer different possibilities, not limiting to information about traffic, which requires an intense manual and visual interaction with smartphones while driving.

© Springer International Publishing Switzerland 2015
A. Marcus (Ed.): DUXU 2015, Part II, LNCS 9187, pp. 575–586, 2015.
DOI: 10.1007/978-3-319-20898-5_55

However, the usage of smartphone apps into vehicles requires complete attention, because of the complexity of this context. Many researchers on road safety [2–4] affirm that the driving environment is very complex, so, the addition of any new service not directly related to the primary driving task (such as maintain the lateral vehicle control and share the route with other users) may impair the road safety.

The interference caused by the interaction with smartphones must be as minimal as possible during the driving task, in order to avoid driver distractions. Thus, it is necessary to understand the drivers' needs and attitudes when interacting with smartphones, in order to suggest better solutions, making the secondary tasks as natural as possible. According to Ramm et al. [5], the more natural the interaction with in-vehicle devices the less distractions may occur during the driving task.

The whole driving context does not include only the driver-smartphone interaction, but many others like different devices into the vehicle and external/internal interferences that may impair the good performance in the driving task [2]. Consequently, the context of use should be considered when designing mobile apps.

According to Wroblewsky [6] and Clark [7], smartphone apps cannot be dissociated to its context of use, so they must consider specific aspects of the environment it will be used. Each user has his way to do certain task, but knowing the user is not enough to understand how the tasks work. That's why many apps don't fit exactly with the user's needs. According to Schumman [8] apud Magnusson [9], every activity has social circumstances and different environments, so the focus must be in how the tasks are being done, what interferes and what changes its course. This will give the necessary background to develop products more suited to the real world.

2 Driving Context and the Interaction with in-Vehicle Devices

The traffic environment is a very big system, with too many variables involved, requiring much effort of the driver in many tasks. McKnight and Adams [3] proved that the driving task is composed by more than 1500 simultaneous mental activities, making the driver incapable to maintain the focus on the primary task, thus increasing the risk of accidents.

Alongside the complexity of the driving task, products for use into the vehicle are increasingly emerging in the market, but some of them are not focused on the driving task. Lee et al. [10] define the driving context as a constant struggle for attention between secondary tasks into the vehicle and the primary driving task. Each secondary task can severely impair the performance of the primary task, increasing the risk of accidents. Every time someone engages in a secondary task, our attention in the primary one lowers, so, in order to avoid risks, the demand of the secondary task must be alternated with the demand of the primary one. Every time there is a surge of demand of both tasks, the driver may not be able to handle both tasks effectively, which may cause risks [10].

When performing a secondary task in the driving context, many important points must be considered regarding the interaction with a given device, such as the driver's field of view, vehicle vibration, the reach of interface/controls, the information presentation and so on. All these points are constantly competing for the driver's attention that must be focused on looking at the road. According to the NHTSA guidelines [11], there are three types of distraction when interacting with in-vehicle information and communication system: visual, when the user takes the eye off the road to see another information; manual, when the user takes the hand off the steering wheel to manipulate a device; and cognitive, when the user takes your mind away from the driving task. Many factors such as interaction frequency and duration can interfere directly on the impact of distractions. Secondary tasks that remain during a long period, even if they are low level, can be very dangerous. Meschtscherjakov et al. [12] apud Ramm et al. [5] argue that "contemporary cars are often cluttered with buttons, knobs and touchscreens" that causes "a high level of mental workload and distraction". However, the in-vehicle devices are not the only ones that can cause distractions. Portable devices like smartphones could also impair the driving task.

3 Brazilian Context of Driving

The Brazilian driver has some characteristics that reflect the history of the country. According to Machado [13], the traffic is not above the society, but is a product of it. A society that is discriminatory, inhuman and disorganized will have traffic with the same characteristics. "The personality doesn't change when we sit against the steering wheel of the car. The change that may happen is that some characteristics are normally exalted in our coexistence with other, starting to manifest themselves more deeply: the desire of being the best, the braver, the need to show that we are capable to take risk without accidents, etc. Normally one can say that the man drives the way he lives" [14].

Damatta [15] declares that the traffic is regulated by public rules, that are applied to each people equally, but, due the fact that most vehicles are individual environments, people tent to feel "apart" and "beyond" these rules, which means that everyone tends to overestimate their personal abilities over both rules and other users of this public space. This phenomenon is enforced in Brazil; because of historical issues related to problems on traffic supervision and road infrastructure collaborates on an inconsequent behavior [13].

Considering the Brazilian drivers and their context of driving, some questions must be answered: How drivers have been using their smartphones while driving? What kind of information they access while driving? What is the frequency of use of apps while driving?

4 Methodology

This study aimed to analyze the most common attitudes and strategies of Brazilian drivers in interacting with smartphones while driving. This is part of a wider research that the main goal is to create usability guidelines to the design of smartphone applications for drivers based on a user centered design perspective.

In order to achieve the proposed objectives, the study used a direct user approach to understand the way drivers use their smartphones while driving, taking into account their opinion, constraints and use strategies. The method chosen was an online survey, due its wide range of distribution and accuracy of findings [16].

The full survey consisted of 27 closed-end questions and three open-ended questions divided into four sections, with some of them focused directly in identify the drivers' attitudes, strategies and behavior. Section 1 composed by 6 questions was used to screen out the target participants for this research: Brazilians with 18 years old or more, with license to drive that had the habit of using the smartphone while driving. All the respondents that did not fit in this profile were guided directly to the end of the survey. Section 2 was focused on gathering information about the interaction with the smartphone, not related to the software interaction, but to the physical environment and the hardware. Section 3, in opposition to the last one, was totally focused on the interaction with the apps. At last, Sect. 4 was composed by demographic questions, to better understand the sample of respondents.

With the purpose to eliminate any bias due to order effects, in all the questions of this survey in which the order of answers options was irrelevant (not a scale) the options were randomized. The reason behind this was to eliminate possible order effects when asking participants about their behavior using their smartphones while driving.

The Eval & GO system (www.evalandgo.com) was used to create the survey and promote online via Internet access. The survey was distributed by email and by direct link, which were followed by a recruiting message, calling for participants. The emails were sent to mailing lists; to the student corpus of PUC-Rio University and to volunteers, that accepted to distribute the survey to their own contacts network. The direct link was posted in many Brazilian blogs and forums related to smartphones or to vehicles (where it was believed to have people that may fit to the research profile) and in social networks (like Facebook, Twitter and LinkedIn).

Branching structures were used in the survey design to conduct the participant to certain pages according to his profile and skip logics were also used to avoid respondents to face questions that were not relevant, based on their previous responses. The average time spent to complete the survey was approximately fifteen minutes. The system was protected against the possibility of one same participant repeat the survey based on IP address. The survey was available online from October of 2014 to January of 2015 for a period of 3 months and a half.

5 Results

The survey gathered the total of 381 responses, being 244 corresponding to the target respondents' profile. Most respondents were in the ranges 18–29 years old and 30–39 years old, corresponding to 64 % of total respondents. Overall, the gender distribution of the sample was pretty similar, being 52 % male and 48 % female. All the sample of this study was composed by Brazilian people and can only be representative for this population, due to specific variables from Brazilian driving context. The findings of this study were divided in three main topics, each one with its own scope:

5.1 Smartphone Interaction

The data showed that smartphones have being largely used alongside the driving task. 79 % of the respondents said that they use their smartphone while driving, which is a substantial number, considering all the implications to the use of portable devices while driving. It is believed that due to the new dynamics of communication and the ubiquity of several technologies in our daily life, the use of smartphone while driving is now commonsense. Wroblewsky [6] affirms that because of its mobility, smartphones can be used in almost any context or situation, becoming one companion to almost any task, and driving is no exception.

Also, the data presented a straight relationship between the judgment of driving skills the respondent believes to have and the smartphone frequency of use while driving. The Fig. 1 shows that the major part of the respondents that believes to have very good driving skills uses smartphone apps every time they drive (54 %), while those that consider to have good driving skills have a more distributed smartphone apps frequency of use. On the other hand, most of the people (87 %) that consider to have an average driving skills use smartphones apps two times a week or less. So, it can be assumed that the more confidence someone has in his driving skills, the higher is the probability to use smartphone apps while driving.

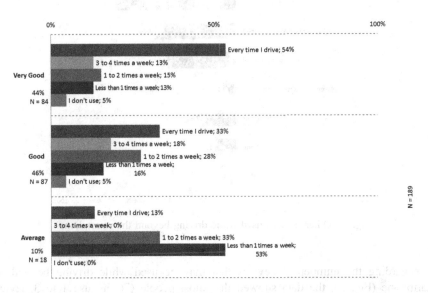

Fig. 1. Judgment of driving skills and the smartphone apps frequency of use

According to McKnight and Adams [3], it is believed that due to the complexity of the driving task, many people may struggle to keep a good performance on the primary task while performing a secondary one. However, as attested by Damatta [15], some drivers in their vehicles tend to feel more capable of performing tasks than the average of the population, assuming that they are fully capable of perform both activities without serious damage on their performance. As can be seen, the respondents present a risk behavior because most of them consider themselves to have very good (44 %) or good (46 %) driving skills, and no one considers to have skills below average. In addition, they consider themselves able to perform secondary tasks with frequency simultaneously to driving task without realizing the aggregate risks in this performance, despite the use of mobile phones inside the vehicle be prohibited in Brazil.

Considering other devices that may be used while driving beyond the smartphone (Fig. 2), the data showed that most people use the OEM audio system (70 %) alongside the smartphone, followed by OEM/portable GPS system (46 %), MP3 players/iPod connected to the vehicle (39 %), trip computers (17 %) and OEM/portable DVD player or TV (7 %). This behavior is entirely reasonable because, in general, smartphones have additional functionalities to OEM audio system, while the functionalities of other devices may be replaced by applications available for smartphones, such as GPS systems and MP3 players/iPod (which were formerly used before the advent of smartphones). Gradually the convergence of many technologies for smartphones is becoming a reality, that is, a tendency for a near future.

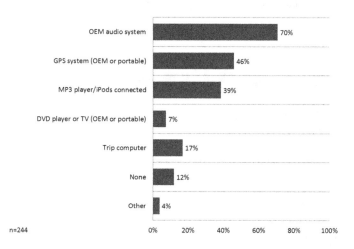

Fig. 2. Other devices used while driving beyond the smartphone

Regarding the number of devices that may be used while driving beyond the smartphone (Fig. 3), the data showed that most people (76 %) use 1 to 3 devices alongside the smartphone into the vehicle and the percentage decreases as the number of used devices increases. Despite this decline, many devices seem to be used concomitantly with smartphones, which is worrisome because the chances of the driver to engage in multiple secondary tasks are much higher. The greater the number of devices in the vehicle, the stronger is the possibility of driver distraction, the higher the risk of

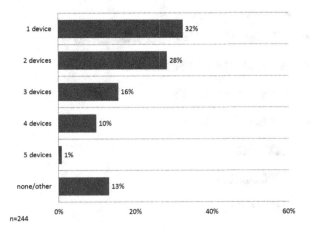

Fig. 3. Number of devices used while driving beyond the smartphone

accidents. The convergence of technologies and functionalities into a single device can be a solution, but it will only be successful and safe if the system interface is well designed, in a way that it does not interfere in the driving task.

5.2 Smartphone's Location and Access

With respect the question that focused on the place where the respondents locate their smartphone into the vehicle (Fig. 4), it was found that the most common places are near the gear shifter (45 %) and on the lap of the driver (35 %). Probably, these places are used to allow an easy arm/hand reach to grab and drop the smartphone, once text messaging is one of the most frequent tasks performed with mobile phones [17]. So, people tend favor closer places to locate their smartphones rather locate them on windshield mounts (15 %) or dashboard mounts (14 %), which are safer places considering the visual attention that the driver must to keep to look at the road. Locating the smartphone far below the driver's line of sight looking at the road can offer risks to him by both diverting his sight off the road to grab and interact with the smartphone and keeping his hand off the steering wheel to hold the device [11].

It is believed that this behavior is related to some factors that favor its occurrence. The first factor to be pointed out is the security of the driver when exposing the smartphone (very expensive in Brazil) for muggers through the vehicle's windows. Machado [13] says that Brazil has epidemic problems related to road security: "We feel constantly threatened, frightened, hoping that urban violence not catch us". Thus, using safer mounts on windshields or dashboard may expose the smartphone too much, making the driver a target for urban violence. This may be a reason why drivers "hide" the smartphones on their laps or near the gear shifter.

Another reason to be pointed out is the comfort in holding the smartphone by hand during the interaction. Since vehicles are in constant trepidation and the difficulty to touch small targets on touchscreens, the respondents may prefer to hold the device by

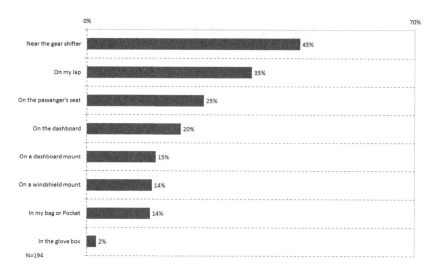

Fig. 4. Places where the smartphone are located into the vehicle

their hands to have more accuracy in typing. Moreover, they use apps that require to typing on small keyboards, like chats (see also Fig. 5).

The location where people place their smartphone into the vehicle influences some other decisions related to the interaction, such as the finger used to interact with the interface. The data shows that in most cases users prefer to use thumb (55 %) over index (42 %) and middle (7 %) fingers for interacting (minor and ring fingers were not selected as a option).

The only smartphone locations where the index achieved higher rates were for windshield mount and dashboard. It is believed that the location of the smartphone display right in front the driver's view may favor the reach of the index, but, even with this result, the rate of the thumb is still very high. As said before, the vehicle vibration may be a factor that favors the holding of smartphone by hand during the interaction. Another reason to be considered is that, outside the vehicle people usually interact with their smartphones with the thumb finger, and that may be a factor that favors the permanence of this behavior inside the vehicle.

5.3   Safety Aspects

Concerning the safety issues, the results showed that by many reasons, most of Brazilians do not have a safety oriented driving behavior. As seen before, most of people locate their smartphones in places that can lead to visual and manual distractions. Also, they are using multiples devices while driving that can compete to the control of the vehicle.

Another factor that presents a non-safety oriented behavior is the use of smartphone apps not related to the driving task, like chat apps, social networks, e-mail and SMS/MMS. Figure 5 shows that there is a high percentage of use of chats apps (51 %)

and SMS/MMS (23 %) while driving, most of them to be more available to family or friends according to other questions.

Many researchers are studying the effects of text messaging while driving and the risks to road safety. In a study conducted by Hosking et al. apud Hallet et al. [17], they found out that participants drivers spent up 400 % more time text messaging than performing other tasks. Not only the visual and manual distraction is a concern when analyzing the effects text messaging, but also the cognitive distraction should be taken into account when considering this behavior. Regan et al. [2] affirms that texting while driving is one of the topics of research in driver distraction, and is considered one of the main sources of distraction. Campaigns like the distraction.gov (http://www.distraction.gov/) promoted by NHTSA alert about the serious risks related to the texting while driving, but even so, people still present a high percentage of use of chat apps.

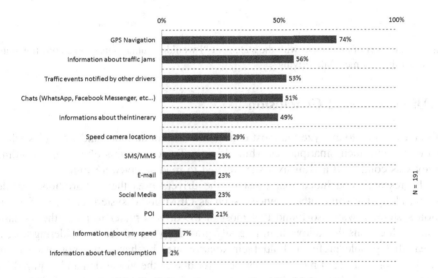

Fig. 5. Information accessed while driving

Even ignoring some safety issues, respondents seem to be concerned about their own safety. Figure 6 shows an analysis of the level of agreement with the statement "I wouldn't mind to use some apps functions that might distract me while driving", using a 7-point Likert scale. The data presented show a very disperse result with no answer above 40 % of agreement, which shows some divergent opinions, but with the bell curve tending to disagree with the statement. This means, according to the data, that respondents do mind to use apps that may cause distraction. There is a clear controversy in these data, showing that drivers with a non-safety oriented behavior are concerned about their safety. It is almost evident that there is no perception about the risk inherent in their attitudes, and they think they are not exposed to risks. It is also believed that this phenomenon is related to the fact that drivers inside their vehicles tend to feel above of any danger in the traffic, blaming the outside environment for all the risks [13, 15].

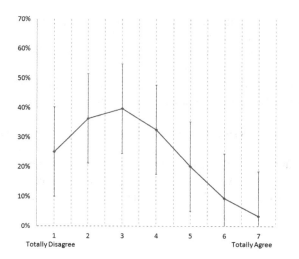

Fig. 6. The level of agreement with the statement "I wouldn't mind to use some apps functions that might distract me while driving".

6   Discussion and Conclusion

This study aimed to analyze the most common Brazilian attitudes and strategies when interacting with their smartphones while driving. To achieve this objective, an online survey was conducted and many issues related to road safety were found.

The research concluded that most of the drivers uses their smartphones while driving, alongside some other devices, such as OEM audio system and a GPS navigation system. It was also found that most of the drivers prefer to place their smartphones in locations that allow them to easily grab/drop the device. Considering this, it is clear that people prefer to hold their smartphones by hand, and not place it on windshield or dashboard mounts, where is safer due to the visual demand required by driving task. This behavior can be related to many factors, such as the use of chats apps while driving, the habit of using the smartphone holding by hand in other contexts or even the comfort to grab/drop the device easily at any time. Those facts also interfere in the way drivers connect their smartphones with the vehicle, in order to allow the free mobility of the device by hand (the most common connection is by Bluetooth).

It is believed that most of the decisions about the use of smartphone while driving are narrowly related to the driver's self-confidence and to social/cultural aspects that may affect the way drivers concern themselves to the safety aspects [14]. As said before, self-confident drivers may feel themselves above all the rules and immune to the dangers related to the traffic environment [13, 15], without even perceiving them, consequently favoring comfort aspects rather than safety ones (e.g. placing the smartphone on the lap).

Considering the influence that self confidence and the low/non consideration of safety aspects may have in the way people interact with their smartphones while driving, it can be concluded that those variables are crucial factors for the interaction process, defining attitudes, strategies and approaches. If those variables are so crucial for the interaction, they cannot be ignored in the design of applications for drivers. Designers must be aware of all those factors and how they affect the interaction, in order to adapt the product to the real context of use, mitigating the potential risks inherent to them.

Even knowing the sample of respondents of this research is restricted to Brazil, the findings of the study are similar to other researches about drivers' behavior in other countries, with a whole different environment for driving task. Studies conducted by Hallet et al. [17] in New Zealand, by Magnusson et al. [9] in Sweden and Heikkinen et al. [18] in Finland, also concluded that drivers tend to have a non-safety oriented behavior while driving. It is believed that this is a tendency directly related to the driving context, being so; this must be a top priority for studies related to the road safety. Some projects seem to indicate this awareness, such as the Open Mobile Alliance, led by Google Inc. and some automakers, in order to develop safe technology for vehicles based on the Android system. Apple Inc. also released in partnership with some automakers the CarPlay, a technology that connects the iPhone to the built-in display of the vehicle with the goal of a safer interaction. However, this technology is still restricted to few expensive vehicles.

This study is part of a wider research about usability of smartphone applications for drivers. For the next step, the research will conduct field studies to better understand the data found in this survey and validate some hypotheses, to transform them in guidelines for the design of applications for drivers.

Acknowledgements. To CNPq and FAPERJ for financing the PIBITI grants.

References

1. GSMA: The Mobile Economy Latin America 2014. GSMA Intelligence, London (2014)
2. Regan, M., Lee, J.D., Young, K.: Sources of driver distraction. In: Regan, M., Lee, J.D., Young, K. (eds.) Driver Distraction: Theory, Effects and Mitigation. CRC Press, Boca Raton (2009)
3. McKnight, A.J., Adams, B.B.: Driver Education Task Analysis: Volume II: Task Analysis Methods. NHTSA, Washington (1970)
4. Burns, P.: Strategies for reducing driver distraction from in-vehicle telematics devices: a discussion document - transport Canada (2003). http://www.tc.gc.ca/eng/roadsafety/tp-tp14133-menu-147.htm
5. Ramm, S., Giacomin, J., Robertson, D., Malizia, A.: A first approach to understanding and measuring naturalness in driver-car interaction. Paper presented at the Automotive UI, Seattle (2014)
6. Wroblewsky, L.: Mobile First. A Book Apart, New York (2011)
7. Clark, J.: Tapworthy: designing great iPhone apps. O'Reilly Media, Sebastopol (2010)
8. Suchman, L.: Human and Machine Reconfigurations: Plans and Situated Actions. Cambridge University Press, Cambridge (2006)

9. Magnusson, C., Larsson, A., Warell, A., Eftring, H., Hedvall, P.-O.: Bringing the mobile context into industrial design and development. Paper presented at the NordiCHI 2012, Copenhagen, Denmark (2012)
10. Lee, J.D., Regan, M., Young, K.L.: Defining driver distraction. In: Regan, M., Lee, J.D., Young, K.L. (eds.) Driver Distraction: Theory, Effects and Mitigation. CRC Press, Boca Raton (2009)
11. National Highway Traffic Safety Administration: Visual-manual NHTSA driver distraction guidelines for in-vehicle electronic devices. National Highway Traffic Safety Administration (2013)
12. Meschtscherjakov, A., Wilfinger, D., Gridling, N., Neureiter, K., Tscheligi, M.: Capture the car!: qualitative in-situ methods to grasp the automotive context. Paper presented at the 3rd International Conference on Automotive User Interfaces and Interactive Vehicular Applications (2011)
13. Machado, A.P.: Um Olhar da Psicologia Social Sobre o Trânsito. In: Hoffmann, M.H., et al. (eds.) Comportamento Humano no Trânsito, 2nd edn. Cosac Naif, Sao Paulo (2012)
14. Lemes, E.C.: Trânsito em Comunidade: Um Estudo Prospectivo na Busca Pela Redução de Acidentes. In: Hoffmann, M.H., et al. (eds.) Comportamento Humano no Trânsito, 2nd edn. Cosac Naif, Sao Paulo (2012)
15. Damatta, R.: Fé em Deus e pé na tábua, vol. 1. Rocco, Rio de Janeiro (2010)
16. Kircher, K.: Driver distraction: a review of the literature. VTI: Rapport 594A. Statens vag- och transportforskningsinstitut, Linköping (2007)
17. Hallett, C., Lambert, A., Regan, M.A.: Text messaging amongst New Zealand drivers: prevalence and risk perception. Transp. Res. Part F Traffic Psychol. Behav. 15(3), 261–271 (2012)
18. Heikkinen, J., Mäkinen, E., Lylykangas, J., Pakkanen, T., Väänänen-VainioMattila, K., Raisamo, R.: Mobile devices as infotainment user interfaces in the car: contextual study and design implications, Munich, Germany (2013)

Significance of Line Length
for Tablet PC Users

Waqas Ali Sahito[1(✉)], Hashim Iqbal Chunpir[3,4], Zahid Hussain[1],
Syed Raheel Hassan[2], and Frederik Schulte[4]

[1] Department of Information Technology,
Quaid-e-Awam University of Engineering, Science and Technology,
Nawabshah, Pakistan
{waqasali,zhussain}@quest.edu.pk
[2] Department of Computer Systems Engineering,
Quaid-e-Awam University of Engineering, Science and Technology,
Nawabshah, Pakistan
raheel.hassan@quest.edu.pk
[3] German Climate Computing Centre, Hamburg, Germany
chunpir@dkrz.de
[4] University of Hamburg, Hamburg, Germany
chunpir@dkrz.de, frederik.schulte@uni-hamburg.de

Abstract. This paper presents key findings about on-screen optimal line length for tablet personal computers (PCs). It examines the effects of four different line lengths on the reading speed and reading efficiency. Seventy participants ranging between the ages of 20 and 40 participated in this study. They read four different texts with an average length of 2000 characters. The texts contained substitution words, which were to be detected by the subjects to measure reading accuracy. Moreover, the subjects were asked to subjectively vote on their reading experience in the context of subjective measures like reading speed and accuracy. The results of the study revealed that 90 characters per line (CPL) were preferred by most of the participants. Nonetheless, some participants falling between the ages of 35 and 40 years preferred 60 CPL. The findings presented in this paper are quite worthwhile as the Tablet PC are extensively used for e-reading. In essence, this study suggests optimal line length for reading on screen using Tablet PC and eventually benefiting people who use Tablet PC for reading, hailing from every walk of life.

Keywords: Optimal line length · Reading efficiency · E-reading · Substitution of words

1 Introduction

Electronic devices like Tablet PCs and e-readers are widely used these days. According to the Pew Internet and American Project 34 % of the adults in USA are having Tablet PC [10]. This study has shown that people belonging to all walks of life and of every age use Tablet PC for accessing textbooks and other reading material. This paper

© Springer International Publishing Switzerland 2015
A. Marcus (Ed.): DUXU 2015, Part II, LNCS 9187, pp. 587–596, 2015.
DOI: 10.1007/978-3-319-20898-5_56

communicates the empirical findings about determining an *optimal line length* for reading using Tablet PC. The terms line length and optimal line length are defined in Sects. 1.1 and 1.2, respectively. Results were obtained via questionnaires and survey forms were filled by target participants. A readability test was conducted using a survey, to find the right amount of characters for reading on Tablet PC. The participants were asked to vote about their preferred line length using Tablet PC and their data was collected for analysis. Today, majority of the users prefer Tablet PC for reading books and other information online. Consequently, this research provides a contribution towards the field of e-reading. On one hand, publishers can benefit from the results of this research for publishing books and papers for portable devices like Tablet PC. On the other hand, users will also profit from this research as they will experience faster reading. The important terms used in this paper are defined as follows:

1.1 Line Length

Line length of a text is a measure i.e. the physical length of a line (e.g. by adjusting margins) or it can be measured by characters in a line. The line length display devices due to different screen sizes on different devices such as Laptop, Desktop, Tablet PC and others. It also depends on features such as single column or multi column documents, the amount of text containing number of words and the number of characters available in a single line.

1.2 Optimal Line Length

Optimal line length has a proper amount of text in a single line. Moreover, it makes a line easily readable by users, who read books, newspapers or any other reading material, using a Tablet PC's screen display. It can be obtained by having an appropriate amount of text present in a line which makes users comfortable to read, from the available reading material on a Tablet PC.

1.3 Importance of Optimal Line Length

It is an essential element to have an optimal line length for the readers in order to avoid reading errors. Most of the time readers make mistakes while reading text which is not clearly presented in magazines, books and onscreen using Tablet PC or e-readers [11]. Most of the books and newspapers have varying text styles which lead readers towards making mistakes [12]. Having the right amount of characters on each line is important for the "readability of text".

Figure 1 shows a sample of different line lengths available for the readers while reading from different sources like online reading material. First paragraph in the figure contains 85 characters per line while the second paragraph contains 120 characters per line and the third paragraph has 120 characters per line with small text size.

Line length can be measured by the physical length of the line or can refer to the number of characters per line. The number of characters per line will be determined by the physical length and type size. Keeping the same physical length will result in more characters per line with a smaller type size.

Line length can be measured by the physical length of the line or can refer to the number of characters per line. The number of characters per line will be determined by the physical length and type size. Keeping the same physical length will result in more characters per line with a smaller type size.

Line length can be measured by the physical length of the line or can refer to the number of characters per line. The number of characters per line will be determined by the physical length and type size. Keeping the same physical length will result in more characters per line with a smaller type size.

Fig. 1. Sample of different line lengths

Figure 1. The excerpt shows the sample of different line lengths available for the readers while reading from different sources. First paragraph in the figure contains 85 characters per line while the second paragraph contains 120 characters per line and the third paragraph has 120 characters per line with small text size.

2   Previous Studies

Los Angeles Unified District approved iPads for every child in the district's schools [10]. According to a survey, 34 % of the adults own a Tablet PC in USA [11]. In January 2012, 29 % of U.S. adults of 18 years of age and older are using Tablet PC devices for reading electronic text e.g. Kindle or Nook [12]. According to the data about the use of a Tablet PC, collected by Springer book publisher surveys, five educational institutions in Europe, US, and Asia had found that 73 % of readers used e-books, with most accessing e-books on a weekly or monthly basis. The line length of a text in online books is far different from newspapers. It has been seen that most of the newspapers use very narrow line length in their publications. However, wider line lengths are used for publication of books. On screen readability has variant line length because of multiple sizes of screens. Weber conducted a study on "Line length of newspapers and books" and found that in newspapers and books the line length need to be four inches and it should never exceed than six inches [2]. According to Tinker et al., the best line length for reading books and other information need to be between 3 and 3.5 inches [1]. Moreover, they found that if the line length exceeds 7.5 inches, it becomes very difficult for the reader to find the next line after finishing the first line. Ducknicky et al. were the first to find out the optimal line length for onscreen readability [3]. They went on saying that if the text is stretched to full screen it becomes easier to read than the text only filled one third of the screen. Dyson et al. shows that the reading efficiency of the readers increases by more number of letters per line [4]. Bernard et al. examined three different line lengths (3.3, 5.7 and 9.6 inches) with same size of text that was 12 points in times new roman [5]. The results of the experiments performed by Shaikh were similar with the study conducted on difference of reading speed for efficiency conducted by Shaikh [6]. The study investigated the line length for reading online newspapers and books vs. paper based reading. On the other front, in most of the studies it can be seen that longer line lengths lead towards faster and efficient reading while medium line lengths lead towards the average reading. In view of this the readers preferred line length between 90 CPL to 120 CPL. Previous studies did not focused on different environments where the people may read using a portable device. However, this study focused on indoor and outdoor environments for reading using Tablet PC.

As early as the 1980s, studies dealing with the comparison between screen and paper emerged in the scientific community, reacting to the basic change in methods of displaying information occasioned by the introduction of the Personal Computer (PC) across office sites [7].

As a result of this development, people often prefer to access information on computers because of the accessibility of the information, the ability to change text to the desired size, ease of archiving and organization, the avoidance of paper costs and reduction of paper use, and environmental benefits [8].

Researchers still lack information on "how readers actually engage with these different formats of digital text vs. printed text, their reasons for choosing one format over another [9]".

3   Problems Faced During on Screen Reading

Researchers working on readability for the last many decades highlighted various issues in readability which includes Font Size, Text Style, Number of words per line and Number of characters per line. This study focuses on characters per line (CPL) aspect while reading on-screen, using a Tablet PC. These issues are very common and faced by most of the users using Tablet PCs for e-reading. This study helps to overcome the issues by providing the optimal line length for e-reading. In this connection, this research covers many aspects of the on-screen readability by focusing on the different users in different environments such as indoor and outdoor usage of Tablet PC. Different age groups were considered for this research in order to obtain better results for this study and to overcome the problems of various readers in the domain of e-reading.

3.1   Critical Parameters for Efficient Online Reading for Tablet PC

The correct parameters for online reading are reading speed, reading efficiency and reading comprehension by finding the mistakes in the text. It is very common to have proof reading mistakes while reading any text online. Thus, to overcome these problems this study focused on the parameters mentioned earlier. The experiments were designed in a way so that the parameters of this research work can be obtained; Shaikh [6] used the same design pattern for the parameters mentioned above having slight difference. They have performed the tests using desktop computers. Such issues are faced while reading text in different conditions like traveling where reader is unable to focus on the text and in different environments. It becomes totally different to read on-screen while you are in your office or any other indoor place but when the Tablet PC is used in outdoor environments. Reading efficiency of the users is affected depending upon the place and environment. Tablet PC is a portable device so all these problems are always present while using Tablet PC, because it can be used anywhere like in office or travelling so these all points need to be taken in consideration.

4 Methodology

The readability tests of this study focused on subjective method of collecting the data from various participants. The subjective method was applied using questionnaires, interviews, surveys and feedback forms. Every participant filled one of each forms like questionnaire, survey and feedback. The questionnaires and feedback forms were designed by following famous online survey platforms like survey monkey. The participants used Tablet PC for reading on-screen. The subjective method was used so that the participants can express their opinion about their reading experience. In this method participants were provided with questionnaires, survey forms and feedback forms to gauge "on screen readability". The participants were asked to provide their prior information about the optimal line length in terms of character per line while reading on a Tablet PC. Selection of the participants was based upon different age groups, qualification, experience in terms of computer usage and different fields. The selection of the participants was done based upon different age groups and qualification level. Every participant was asked to read four different texts containing same amount of words, each text contained substitute words which were intentionally replaced and participants were asked to detect those words while reading the text from Tablet PC.

5 Results

The results were generated from the data collected through subjective method. These results contain only subjective data, the first part of the data was based on participants' demographic data which is based upon the participants information relating to their age groups, level of education and experience in using computers. On the other hand, the second part of the data was based on participants' preferences regarding the optimal line length for Tablet PC.

5.1 Demographic Data

Table 1 illustrates the number of male and female participants of the study. Table 2, on the hand, provides insights into the distribution age among the participating users. While Table 3, distinguishes participating user groups according to their educational background. The participants have been selected in this way to represent the major user groups on a regional level.

The information in the following Table 4 provides data about the participants having computer usage experience in terms of years.

Table 1. Number of Male and Female Participants

S no.	Gender	No: of Participants
1	Male	50
2	Female	25

Table 2. Age groups of the participants

S no.	Age groups in terms of years	Number of participants
01	20–25	22
02	25–30	19
03	30–35	16
04	35–40	13

Table 3. Qualification level of participants

S no.	Education level	No: of participants
1	Undergraduate	35
2	Post graduate	15
3	Others	20

Table 4. PC usage experience of the participants

S no.	PC experience in years	No: of participants
01	4 years	30
02	6 years	22
03	8 years	13
04	10 and above years	10

5.2   Subjective Data

The results of this study are visualized in the form of pie-charts in the figures from Figs. 2, 3, 4 and 5 based on the subjective data collected from the participants. The pie-charts, plotted in these figures as per various age groups from 20 to 25 years, from 25 to 30 years, from 30 to 35 years and from 35 to 40 years of age groups respectively. From the figures, the results show that the majority of the participants preferred 90 CPL over other line lengths, altogether. In Figs. 3 and 5 preferred line length is 60 CPL, while in Fig. 2 the participants selected 90 CPL while 120 CPL was the second preference.

As per the results portrayed in Fig. 3, 90 CPL is highly preferred by the participants whereas Fig. 4 clearly indicates that participants of the age group of 30 to 35 years like 60 CPL for on screen readability. However, according to Fig. 3 there is tendency of participants to like 60 CPL for reading as well. According to Fig. 5, the age group of 35 to 40 years prefers 30 CPL the most, for reading from Tablet PC screen.

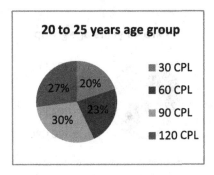

Fig. 2. Preference of 20 to 25 years of age group participants

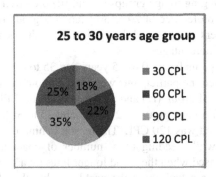

Fig. 3. Preference of 25 to 30 years of age group participants

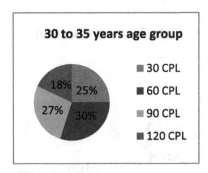

Fig. 4. Preference of 30 to 35 years of age group participants

6 Discussion

The subjective results show that most of the users preferred 90 CPL when they read any text on Tablet PC. The participants were divided into four age groups (i) 20 to 25 years (ii) 25 to 30 years (iii) 30 to 35 years and (iv) 35 to 40 yrs. A key factor that was

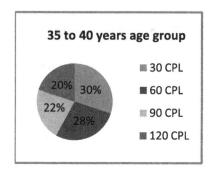

Fig. 5. Preference of 35 to 40 years of age group participants

noticed that people belonging to age groups (i) and (ii) preferred 90 and 120 CPL. The above figures show the preference of 20 to 30 years age group participants, horizontal line shows the characters per line while vertical line shows the preference of the participants in terms of percentage.

However, the participants from 30 to 35 years and 35 to 40 years preferred 60 CPL. During the feedback when the participants were asked about their preferred line length, it was found that people of group (iv) and above selected 60 CPL because of eye sight issues and participants from age group of 20 to 25 and 25 to 30 years preferred 90 CPL on first priority and second was 120 CPL. The reason behind their choice was that they felt more comfortable while reading more number of characters per line and their reading speed also increased when they read longer lines on a Tablet PC screen. During the tests participants were asked about the problems that they face. Moreover, color blindness test was also conducted of every participant participating in the readability surveys of this study (Figs. 6, 7).

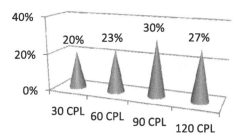

Fig. 6. Preference of participants of 20 to 25 yrs.

The readability tests were conducted in a university environment and that is the reason why the age groups of participants were from 20 to 40 years. The participants were mostly students and university teachers. The text used in the readability contained same font size of 12 pts and same font style Times new roman because of the consistency. All the participants were non-native English speakers. This applies to the

25 to 25 years age group

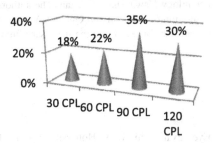

Fig. 7. Preference of participants of 25 to 30 yrs.

majority of the population in the world, which are non-native speakers. Moreover, this research focuses on the participants from Pakistan. Results might have been slightly different if the same research work would have been carried out in different countries with different languages. There is a need to have a similar type of research work with the participants belonging to different language groups as well as different cultures. Moreover, older age groups can be included in future to conduct further experiments.

7 Conclusion and Future Work

In this research work, it was found that majority of participants preferred 90 CPL over other variants of CPL. Participants of age group from 20 to 30 years liked longer lines while reading on a Tablet PC. Whereas, the participants of 30 to 40 years of age group preferred 60 CPL. Results indicate that as people grow older they find difficulties while reading on a Tablet PC screen. There are numerous reasons for such difficulties such as eye sight problems [1]. Many participants of older age found that it was hard reading longer lines on a Tablet PC. Furthermore, it is evident from this study that younger adults from age group of 20 to 30 years like longer line length 90 CPL to 120 CPL, however, people of older age prefer shorter lines (i.e. having lesser number of characters), while reading on a Tablet PC screen. The previous studies were mainly conducted on larger screens such as desktop computers and laptop screens. Desktops computers are mostly used indoor, for instance; in offices or homes. However, a Tablet PC is a portable device; therefore, there is a substantial difference in environments as well as mobility aspects. Reading on a screen in an office and reading while moving in a bus or any other outdoor mobile environment has totally different effects on readability. This work covers most of the aspects of the users using Tablet PC regularly, as already discussed above. Furthermore, this work recommends that 90 CPL is preferred for publishing books and papers for e-reading. In future, this study will be further extended by collecting additional data through more experiments by including more participants. Moreover, these results will be compared with subjective results to find out the difference between the participants' actual choice of line length while reading on Tablet PC and their subjective opinion. Besides, this work will be further continued for additional mobile devices having different screen sizes and also based on different operating systems.

Acknowledgment. This is Master's research work carried out at Quaid-e-Awam University of Engineering Science and Technology Nawabshah Pakistan. The authors are very much thankful to the Higher Education Commission of Pakistan and Quaid-e-Awam University of Engineering, Science and Technology, Nawabshah for providing the necessary funding and resources during the research.

References

1. Weber, A.: About Eye exams in Den Hoheren schools Darmstadt division for Gesunheitspflege. J. Appl. Psychol. **11**, 3–9 (1999)
2. Tinker, M.A., Paterson, D.G.: Studies of typographical factors influencing speed of reading: length of line. J. Appl. Psychol. **13**(3), 205–219 (1929)
3. Duchnicky, J.L., Kolers, P.A.: Readability of text scrolled on visual display terminals as a function of window size. Hum. Factors J. **25**(6), 683–692 (1983)
4. Dyson, M.C., Kipping, G.J.: The effects of line length and method of movement on patterns of reading from screen. Visible Lang. J. **32**(2), 150–181 (1998)
5. Bernard, M., Fernandez, M., Hull, S.: The effects of line length on children and adults' online reading performance. Usability News Web Newslett. **4**(2), (2002)
6. Shaikh, A.D.: The effects of line length on reading online news. Usability News Web Newslett. **7**(2), (2005)
7. Holzinger, A., Baernthaler, M. Pammer, W., Katz, H.: Investigating paper vs. screen in real-life hospital workflows: performance contradicts perceived superiority of paper in the user experience. Int. J. Hum. Comput. Stud. **69**(9), (2011)
8. Rho, Y.J., Gedeon, T.D.: Academic articles on the web: reading patterns and formats. Int. J. Hum. Comput. Interact. **12**, 219–240 (2000)
9. Spencer, C.: Research on learners preferences for reading from a printed text or from a computer screen. J. Distance Educ. **21**(1), 33–50 (2006)
10. Blume, H. L.A. school board OKs $30 million for Apple iPads. Los Angeles Times. Los Angeles. Retrieved from http://articles.latimes.com/2013/jun/18/local/la-me-ln-lausd-chooses-ipads-for-pilot-20130618 (2013, June 18)
11. Brenner, J., Pew internet: Mobile. Pew Internet and American Life Project. http://pewinternet.org/Commentary/2012/February/Pew-Internet-Mobile.aspx (2013)
12. Rainie, L., Zickuhr, K., Purcell, K., Madden, M., Brenner, J.: The rise of e-reading. Retrieved from http://libraries.pewinternet.org/2012/04/04/the-rise-of-e-reading/ (2012)

A Field Study on Basic Usage Patterns of Traditional Watch and Smart Phone for Designing Smart Watch

Zijian Zhu[1]([⊠]), Haidi Song[2], and Sung Woo Kim[1]

[1] Graduate School Techno Design, Kookmin University,
Seoul, Republic of Korea
zijian870928@gmail.com, caerang@kookmin.ac.kr
[2] Peking University, Beijing, People's Republic of China
heidisong1011@gmail.com

Abstract. This paper researches towards people who used traditional watches and smart phone at the same time for 8 participants by diary method. Smart watch look same with the traditional watch and the basic mechanism of interaction is same as Smartphone, not taking special characteristics of watch into account. In this research, we extracted basic design elements and framework for designing smart watches based on basic usage patterns derived from a series of systematic user studies.

Keywords: Design thinking · Diary study · User experience · User behavior

1 Introduction

The development of technology is always beyond people's imagination. With the development of IoT (Internet of Things), the wearable device serves as an important entrance and develops a lot in recent years. Although the conceptualized "Google glass" suffers criticism, it does not influence 2013 to be called "the first year of wearable". All kinds of wearable devices emerge like mushrooms after rain, and as the leader who strikes a pose on the stage frequently, the watch is likely to become the greatest technological revolution followed after smart phone [1], and it also turns into the hottest topic in 2014's smart device market. However, there are many reasons resulted in shortage of understanding towards smart watch by users. The smart watch is a wearable device, the experience and functions provided by which shall be blended in human's daily life naturally, the service provided by which shall be more superior to smart phone, and then its value could be reflected. How to design smart watch, and how to make more people to accept, use are the starting points of this paper. By possessing the attributes of watch and smartphone simultaneously, more than simple accessory to smart phone, the smart watch needs to have its specific Identity. Through analogy method, conclusion and extension of partial experience, we believe that by understanding the Basic Pattern of the traditional watch and smart phone daily used by users, valuable reference and basis could be provided for design of smart watch.

© Springer International Publishing Switzerland 2015
A. Marcus (Ed.): DUXU 2015, Part II, LNCS 9187, pp. 597–608, 2015.
DOI: 10.1007/978-3-319-20898-5_57

2 Related Work

Let's see traditional watch and mobile phone first. From the birth to today, watch has already developed its particular cultural characteristic. The smart phone is the technological product nowadays, and it has changed the world. The types that people use for gaining all sorts of information are no longer traditional and single. People use the screen with the size of palm to connect the world. In the meantime, wearable device will play a crucial role in big data along with the popularization. Next, we will elaborate the basic attribute of each device in each field.

2.1 Understanding the Smart Phone Attributes

In recent years, the mobile phone is no longer a simple communication tool. With the technical progress, mobile network and services like social contact have turned into the indispensable DNA [5] in mobile phone. The user could use mobile phone to get information and do network social contact anywhere, anytime, and the diverse applications (Apps) in it turn into the main entrance for searching information, doing social activities, recreation and study [6]. The smart phone with diversified functions provides services in different fields, impacting different users' usage habits all the time [7]. On account of the smart phone's characteristic "on-the-move", channels for users to get information become more diversified, and the Internet use becomes more fragmented [8]. "Always on" is also one of the most differences between smart phone and computer. The users install various cell phone applications, they are facilitated and their lives have been changed. Nonetheless, trouble of "text message noise" from all kinds of text messages may be caused to users. For instance, when one focuses on work, it comes news feed, then he might be disturbed. The smart phone develops quickly in recent years, with the sell of iphone6, the small screen mobile phone (with the size below 4 inch) died away gradually, and the big screen mobile phone enters into thousands of households. In 2015, the screen size for smart phone will over 5 inch. But like coin has two sides, when users use big screen mobile phone, all kinds of service experience will be further improved, and in the meantime, some troubles will be brought, such as inconvenient operation by one-hand, inconvenient for taking along, etc.

2.2 Understanding the Traditional Watch Attributes

Before the horologe came out, the main usage of desk clock was astronomical observation. After that the geographic transition facilitated invention of navigation clock, and the train departure at fixed time promoted portable pocket watch. The invention of watch derived from a visual concept, making clock with large size convenient to take along and people to know time. Actually behind the watch, in-depth culture and significance exist. With the widespread circumstance of "one person with many watches", the watch pursuing by people is no longer the single timing function, but expansion of functional scope and increase of art taste, via diversified watchcase types and watch plate designs, as well as a fashionable accessory which reflects individuality and identity. Timing, accessory, status symbol and other functions, making watch succeed its own significance. So what is the attribute to watch? For students in the examination room, it is a tool for timing; for successful people, it stands for carrier of identity and status; for fashionable figures, it is the embellishment of trend.

Designing smart watch and understanding the attributes of traditional watch appear important particularly.

2.3 The Status of Wearable Device

Since the appearance of the first wearable computer [9], up until walking into public views nowadays, the wearable device goes through countless iteration. Now with the big data, cloud computing, data mining and analysis, gradual maturing of internet of things, if pushing the wearable device to a mass market with more fields is needed, the present ecological chain to all kinds of platforms must be combined, thus more convenient and fast service experience could be provided for users.

For the past two years, the wearable device developed rapidly, and the main battlefield for products with public grade was on wrist. The wristband or smart watches released by manufacturers may be called all flowers bloom together. However, the vital point to the user had not been hit. The functions or services provided by them could be realized on mobile phone as well, resulting in reduction of dependence degree by users little by little. Besides defects on function, imperfect aspects showed on service. So the status of smart phone cannot be shook at present. We consider that the orientation to the smart watch of the new generation is not a device that exists solely, but shall act as the "second screen" to the smart phone. Meanwhile, ecological chain with multi-screen linkage shall be added, specific advantage shall be given play, more intimate and smart mobile service shall be provided for users.

3 Diary Study

This paper used diary method [4], which could reflect daily behavioral habit to a person accurately. Basic using forms to smart phones and watches could be known from all kinds of conditions where the participants are in. We need to know the temporal and location context that users use watches and mobile phones, how to use and what are their feelings.

3.1 Study Setup

We prepared experimental requirements and diary format (Fig. 1) by making use of Google docs and Google sheet. Recording the forms from using watches and mobile phones by participants were required. The formats of diary was classified in accordance of the using situations, which included service time, using place, using function and how to use, finally using feelings shall be described and evaluations shall be made. The

			Smart Watch		
DATE	TIME	LOCATION	FUNCTIONS	EVALUATION	GRADE
2014-12-23	8: 10	家	戴上手表	从充电器上拿下，电量100%，但是还有低担心。	4
	8: 20-9: 00	路上	反复看手表，确认时间	10次大概会有一次反应不灵敏，总体来说ok。	4
	11: 20	教室	收到消息	上课时候，不方便拿看手机，手表接到了消息	4
	12: 10	路上	看时间	在阳光下也可以很好显示。	5
	14: 00	教室	收到消息，在手机上面打开	没听到手机的振动，但是手表及时提醒了消息。5分	5
	14: 25	教室	收到警告	离开手机，超出手表接收范围，发出警告。3分	3
	15:25	路上	收到电话的提醒	周围环境复杂没有感觉到手表的振动，感觉到手机的振动	2
	18: 00	路上	低电量提醒	电池使用的太快	1
	18: 30	家	到家充电	放在电脑旁边，就是一个电子钟，但是放在充电座上就不能接收消息	2
Avg					3.333333333

Fig. 1. Diary sample (by Chinese)

aim was to know the influences from using motivation and functions from the users. We requested participants to record twice a day, one was at noon, recording from get up in the morning to noon; the other was before go to bed in the evening, recording the activities from afternoon to night. In addition, we checked the records every day, and reminded or guided the participants via text message or leaving a message. Due to human has sluggishness, for the sake of getting better data, we provided US$5 as the survey subsidy for each participant per day.

Device

- Carry mobile phone (provided for oneself) with the version above Android OS 4.3.
- Traditional watch (provided for oneself).
- The smart watch provided is Moto 360 (provided by us). Moto 360 has Android Wear. The reason why adding smart watch in the survey is to let participant try out directly, which is convenient for us to know their usage experience, provide data and reference for designing better smart watch.

Participants. The selected participants must wear traditional watch and use smart phone (Android OS 4.3) at the same time. We found 8 eligible persons, 4 men and 4 ladies with the age distribution 20–32 years old, average age 26.3 and SD 4.06. Their occupations are student, teacher, tour guide, company employee, etc. Because of different occupations and living habits, the using forms to devices like mobile phone and watch are distinct.

Process and Data Collection. The survey period for each participant is two weeks and divided into 2 phases (Fig. 2). The first phase is one week. Every day the participants needed to record their usage conditions towards traditional watches and mobile phones,

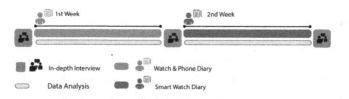

Fig. 2. The data collection process

as per the diary form provided by us. The second phase is one week, too. The volunteers would be requested to wear Moto360 smart watches and record their everyday usage conditions. Before the diary survey, we made an in-depth visit, which was for knowing the basic conditions from the surveyed objects on using watches and mobile phones. After the first week closes, we made a second in-depth interview, of which the content would be set in line with the record conditions from the participants in the first week. After the users recorded the usage conditions for one week, we made the third in-depth visit, of which the content was about smart watch. During using smart watch in the second week, except writing using feelings, the score evaluation shall be filled, which was, from 1–5 (1-totally dissatisfied, 2-not too satisfied, 3-general, 4-satisfied, 5-very satisfied). Because of the participants have not used smart watch before, and it is a new device, this research is used for knowing the subjective feelings from the participants.

4 Finding and Discussion

During the data collection process for eight weeks, we get 976 records in total, 122 records for each participants on average (Min: 61, Max: 172, SD: 36.4). During the whole process, users recorded their usage conditions on mobile phone and watch every day indeed. At the first interview, we found there were 6 persons use watch for more than 5 years, some of them used watch for more than 10 years, which held 75 %; there were 2 persons who started to use watch from last year. Every person used smart phone for more than 4 years.

4.1 A Traditional Watch Usage Pattern

Through first week's research, there are 264 usage diaries collected in total, 33 diaries per person on average. All the participants wore watches with round watch plate. During the 1st in-depth interview, all of them said that they started to look at watch from childhood. The people surrounded were wearing watches with round watch plates. So they felt they got used to look at watch of this type. Secondly, It is observed that the first demand to watch is decoration, that is, the watch should have nature of jewelry. During the in-depth interview, there were 5 persons put forward high demand on appearance. Meanwhile, they said that the styles of watches were various, and there were a lot of choices, so they would not buy at will, and they mainly focused on the appearance. There were 3 participants said that they had many watches, and they would select which to wear according to the occasions. All of 8 participants wore traditional watches with pointers. Compared with watches of digital display, they got used to look at pointers so that efficiency on obtaining time information would be higher. On the condition that the watch was not lost or not damaged, they would not consider changing watch. In the meantime, participants did not have requirements on whether to add functions to the watches they wore, such as alarm clock, second chronograph, etc. They felt that adding these functions appeared cumbersome, and would not be used. The watch was ok by just showing time. The participants' behaviors on wearing

Table 1. Distribution of diary entries

Location	Entries	% diary entries
Indoor	186 (at home 95)	69.4 %
Outdoor	78	30.6 %

watches were constant. When they were out, they would wear their watches naturally. If they forgot, they would feel slightly uncomfortable even they had mobile phones to look at time.

Among the records collected, we divide the situations of using watch into indoor and outdoor, see Table 1. For the indoor, it includes by walk, in transit, etc., which belong to situation under the unfixed surroundings. For the outdoor, it includes at home, classroom, café, etc. which belong to situation under the fixed surroundings. Among the 186 diaries, 95 diaries are made at home, which occupies 35 % of all the watch records. If using watch at home, the 100 % condition is taking off the watch, and then placing at a comparatively fixed place, for the sake of searching, and when going out, it could be found quickly and wore. 3 participants said that his watch was metal watchband, which could be erected on the table, and when at work or home, the watch could be used as clock. Because metal watchband will hinder work, especially when one uses laptop, the laptop or the watchband may be scratched. However, influence will not be brought to work for the participants who use leather watchband. There are 91 records not taken at home, for example, under the circumstances of working for a long time at café or library, the participants would take off watches as per condition. There are 7 such diaries, which occupies 2.6 % of the watch records.

To sum, users care more about the appearance and wearing feeling to watch. If a lady wears a cumbersome metal watch, she will be prominent in secular eyes. Therefore the watch shall be worn by right person in appropriate occasion. And due to wearing watch for one day, the comfortable sensation is extremely important, so don't let the wrist feel pressure.

4.2 Mobile Phone Usage Pattern

We've collected 427 usable data from smart phone diaries. Through the first time in-depth visit, we learn about that there are 42.3 Apps installed in mobile phone per capita, with the maximum of 146 and minimum 23 Apps. There are 7 APPs used per capita per day, and they would put the Apps of common use on the first page of the display screen. Heavy users of mobile phone exist among these participants. Some of them used more than 7 h and some of them used for no more than 1 h, with the per capita 2–3 per day. Combining with the in-depth interview, we classify the 8 participants into 5 user types. Except the inherent communicating functions to mobile phone, the diversified services constitute different roles the mobile phone played in their hands (Fig. 3).

Main Usage Patterns	"Assistant Manager"	"Lifestyle Hub"	"Society of Friends"	"Access Information"	"Entertainment Center"
Used primarily for	Chatting	Doing	Chatting	Browsing/Search	Doing
Most Frequent Task	Calling and Management Work	Using apps that support the uses lifestyle	Using Social apps to show lifestyle and connecting to people	Using news apps or browsing to pick up information	Using entertainment apps to have games or others
Level of Mobile Interdependency	Low	High	High	Medium	Medium
What Determined Mobile Concern	· Security · Battery life	· Network connection · Security	· Network connection · Security · Battery life	· Data plan · Network connection	· Function of device · Data plan · Battery
Description	Just for calling/SMS and Management Work	The smart phone supports the user's activities, with apps selected by the user to improve his life	Lots of society activities, keep track with friends with the device	This is the typical usage pattern to access information and study tool	A variation of the Entertainment usage pattern. to listen music and game

Fig. 3. A taxonomy of smart phone's basic usage pattern

This Figure shows the degrees of dependency from all kinds of users, common task and the fields they cared about. By comprehensive understanding towards them, it means favorable guidance for analyzing following diaries.

We used affinity diagram technique [12] and divided the original data into 10 categories, Call/SMS, social contact, personal management, obtaining information, entertainment, daily information, phone management, daily record, study and else (Table 2).

Most data belong to communication. As the inherent attribute to mobile phone, the communication holds 25.7 %, which is the top one. Secondly is the social behavior.

Table 2. Breakdown of smart phone needs by categories. Examples for each category are from real diary entries.

Category	Diary Example	#of Entries	%of Entries
Call/SMS	Walking on the road, a call came and answers it	110	25.7 %
Social contact	Waiting friends on café, open Facebook...	85	19.9 %
Personal management	Setup alarm for early wake up	56	13.1 %
Obtaining information	Research something on web	41	9.6 %
Entertainment	Break time, have mobile game	39	9.5 %
Daily information	Check weather before leaving home	37	8.6 %
Phone management	Apps need update	30	7.0 %
Daily record	Have funny time, take a picture	15	3.5 %
Study	Improve my English	12	2.8 %
Etc.	Transfer accounts to friends	3	0.7 %
SUM		427	100 %

Many social network sites break away from browser, develop their own service platforms of vertical type, providing convenient service for users. For all the activities of social contact, we divide into Social Connection and Social Avoidance as per the motivation [11]. "I am waiting my friend at café. I have nothing else to do, so I open wechat to check friend circle and chat with my friends." There are 59 such records, which occupies 69 % of the total social contact category. For unable or would not like to check the information push during work or have class, we call social avoidance, which prevails among the participants. Personal agenda management occupies 13.1 % of the total records. The participants expressed that they would plan and remind what they were going to do by using the schedule management tool on the mobile phone. So the speedy and accurate schedule reminding function appears particularly important. All of the 8 participants had their constant habits when use mobile phone, and they said that, "even though changing new mobile phone, function definitions will be set up as the previous mobile phone. For example, I will download the same apps, and then put the apps which are commonly used by me on the first page, arrange all the apps according to the using frequentness." Therefore, during using new devices, the interface and information architecture shall keep consistency with the original one, making users grasp quickly and reducing the learning cost.

All of the participants expressed that the smart phone was the crucial personal good, their important information were stored inside, and even the band cards were associated with. In case the mobile phone was lost, that would be more terrible than the wallet was lost, so they all set lot kinds of safeguard measure. Meanwhile, they worried about that the contents might be seen by others when they were using mobile phones. So the security and privacy were most concerned by them. Moreover, we found that these participants mentioned they preferred more about mobile phone with large screen, owning to this kind of mobile phone could provide better experience in terms of work, study, entertainment and others. However, it could be slightly demanding on operating, especially for the ladies with smaller hands. Under some special conditions, e.g. on the crowded bus, the restriction of space is inconvenient for operation with single hand. By this time if the important information or phone call comes, people will be in hurry-scurry. The participants expressed that under special conditions, it would be better there was more faster or convenient query method.

We divide the using situations into indoor and outdoor. Same as the results from our previous in-depth interview, there were 224 diaries show the participants would take out their mobile phones from bags and pockets indoors and put within their sights, for the convenience of checking information quickly and preventing omission. In the meantime, under the quiet situations indoors, they would set their mobile phones mute or vibrated. There were 49 diaries referred that omission happened even putting by their sides, which explained that more direct ways were needed for reminding, for the sake of omission. On the contrary, under the outdoor situations, the proportion of omission information occupies 81 %. The 8 participants got used to put the mobile phones into pockets and bags. Due to the outdoor environment is complex, the probability of missing picking up rises largely, the using place play vital role to receive information successfully. Sometimes when they received push, the act of "catching a glimpse" holds 47 %, that is to say, if it was not significant information, they would delay their response. It is observed that more efficient information receiving way could enhance the usage experience.

Finally, the occasion had direct influence to the using behaviors for participants. They hoped there would be more convenient and faster information obtaining way, for the sake of enhancing work and learning efficiency. Secondly, the security for the mobile phone was what they concerned, for ensuring the privacy not disclosed.

4.3 Smart Watch Usage Pattern

Within the first week by using smart watch, we've collected 285 diaries in total (Table 3), with 40 diaries per capita. According to the subjective feelings to evaluate, the average score is 3.5 points with the highest 4.1 points and lowest 3.0 points. The entire using feeling is a little more than "general" grade, which is 3.5 points. During this week, we did not deploy task to participants on intention because we wanted to get natural data. Among the diaries, they worried about the electric quantity most during the first two days, but decrease was shown in the subsequent days. In the using survey towards watch previously, we mentioned that "watch will be taken off naturally when go back home, and put in a place easy to find". While the charger of smart watch happens to be a nice solution, because as long as it is put on the table, it will do quick charge, and show time as an electronic clock. Meanwhile by putting on the table, it has decorative effect. After go back home, about the matter of "take off watch, put somewhere" needs to get solution.

From the diaries, we found that the participants could play smart watches easily, no difficulties were found during using process. So we think easy to play and low learning costs are important. Among the diaries, we find that the main dissatisfaction to wearing watch comes from appearance, the style cannot be chosen, and female participants have thin wrists, so the watches appear prominent. Meanwhile, watch possesses strong feelings of modeling, science and technology, but weak decoration.

"Check time" holds 27.3 % of the diaries. All of the records show that by over-turning wrist, the screen will be lightened automatic, so it is natural there is no heterogeneous sense. From the records after using, all people expressed that the times of taking out mobile phones from pockets were obviously cut down, there was no need to

Table 3. A taxonomy of smart watches' basic usage pattern

Category	#of entries	%of entries
Notification	97	25.7 %
Check time	78	19.9 %
Battery management	54	13.1 %
Wear	34	9.6 %
Sync with other device	13	9.5 %
Movement tracking	6	8.6 %
Etc.	4	7.0 %
SUM	285	100 %

worry about miss notification, and information could be viewed even the mobile phones were out of range of visibility. This is because the watch is worn on wrist, which is more efficient than mobile phone reminds. In case of information is pushed to watch, just a glance is needed, and if timely response is not needed, one could ignore it for the moment, the watch saves both time and labor. The smart watch is restricted by the size of the screen, and the voice is the main input pattern. Among the diaries, there were 8 diaries related to voice input (2.8 %), and they expressed that it was inconvenient to speak towards a watch, and people surrounded would feel strange. Moreover, they would feel their privacy was disclosed if the speaking voice was heard by anyone else, so the condition of replying text message by voice was almost indoor behavior. The mobile phone cannot be next to the skin completely, the service provided by the watch could come down to the places where mobile phone could not reach, such as detection of physical condition during doing exercise. The demand of synchronization with mobile phone is not manifested extraordinarily, which accounts for only 4.5 % of the overall records. It was mainly used as "remote control" to mobile phone, controlling music, removing information push, etc. The participants wished more abundant sync to promote the feasibility to the watch.

4.4 Study Limitations

Firstly, due to restrictions from some conditions, when we collected volunteers, we had not considered users of middle age (above 40 years old). Secondly, However as to the smart watch, it is a new thing. The participants had not formed fixed cognition. In addition, the using process of only 1 week is exploration stage, recording the subjective using feeling. With the increase of using time, the product will generate new experience [10]. The research data at this stage could provide a reference for this pattern of smart watch during using in preliminary stage.

5 Results and Discussion

From the above chapters, we get much enlightenment from the 8 participants, whose daily using behaviors were collected. In this chapter we will elaborate our conclusion.

5.1 Designing Smart Watch

Based on the characteristic to each device, there are differences on the interactive ways and information accesses provided. With the development of mobile network, the information obtained from pc belongs to "*slow interaction*". From the device size and operational experience, the user could browse information with big space and operate the dimensionality. While the mobile phone has strong mobility, and its service time is fragmented, so it belongs to "*quick interaction*" as well as suits quick receiving and sending information. By the wearable attribute and tiny screen, the "*simple interaction*" to smart watch can reflect its characteristic better. We will design from two layers: experience and function. For the experience layer, the major center lies in person. And for the function layer, the major layer lies in device (Fig. 4).

Experiential Level (People)	Functional Level (Device)	Both (People/Device)
Wearability Sociality Fit to Contextual Visibility High Mobility Continuity	Compatibility Continuity Security	Continuity

Fig. 4.

5.2   Experiential and Functional Level

We will elaborate the experience layer by taking user-centered design as starting point. Firstly is the *wearability*, that is, the watch weight, material and wearing comfort level. Because of the vivo environment needs good physical support, that is to say the carry type shall be according with human engineering and more natural, and then the distance between watch and wearer could be reduced. Secondly is the *sociality* shall conform to present era, viewpoint and culture. The modeling shall not be excessively scientific, or beyond user's scope of cognition. It shall be accepted by social system (for instance, it should not cause many disputes as Google Glass). Its appearance shall be accepted by the public, so that the viewers and users could feel comfortable and not consider it is heterogeneous. In general, that's "make device blend in us, rather than we blend in device". *High mobility* refers to not separating with one's body under any occasion and fitting with body's height, as well as possessing more mobility compared with other mobile devices. Thirdly is the *continuity*. Due to the date is generated from human behaviors, whether the collected data is continuous and accurate will impact the users. Fourthly is *security*. In data era, one device includes all privacy to a user, so enhancing the security could promote using confidence to user. Fifthly, *fit to contextual*, this includes using appropriate functions in appropriate occasion, such as reminding weather, traffic condition when going out, pushing news when on a bus, schedule reminding during work, quick viewing information, etc. The better the combination between function and occasion, the better will the experience. Finally is *visibility*. The favorable visual experience could impact user to use the device, especially with minimum screen, the reasonable information architecture and visual metaphor could boost information reception efficiency.

The good hardware support is the basis to promote functionality, so the smart watch shall have *compatibility* with other devices, for the convenience of quick synchronization between user and device. Not only the hardware compatibility is important, but also the software compatibility is important, and it becomes an entrance for interactive service. The *continuity* is the different from experience layer. Whether the received data is complete or not, the network is unable to connect or hardware factors like insufficient power could have impact on data reception. When it comes down to money or information with high privacy, the *security* will become crucial. So the services related to security functions shall be more perfect, such as fingerprint encryption and others.

6 Conclusion

We did diary survey towards 8 participants when they used smart phone and traditional watch for two weeks in this paper. Through in-depth visit and diary record, we know the using patterns towards smart phone and traditional watch from these participants. By applying analogy and analyzing via thought of concluding and expanding partial experience, finally we get human experience and device functions, which are *wearability, sociality, high mobility, continuity, security, fit to contextual, visibility and compatibility.* We hope this conclusion could provide reference for designing smart watch, meanwhile could provide design thought for other products. Through this survey, we get the guidance frame for designing smart watch. In the subsequent study, we will discuss the interactive mode for smart watch. It is predicted that in 2015, with the apple watch appearing on the market, the smart watch will come with force and enter into our life. In the meantime, it will join in ecological system of smart phone, tablet PC and computer, providing more convenient life for us.

References

1. Hashmi, A., Berry, H., Temam, O., Lipasti, M.: Automatic abstraction and fault tolerance in cortical microarchitectures. In: Proceedings of the 38th Annual International Symposium on Computer Architecture, New York (2011)
2. Alben, L.: Quality of experience: defining the criteria for effective interaction design. Interactions **3**(3), 11–15 (1996)
3. Desmet, P., Hekkert, P.: Framework for product experience. Int. J. Des. **1**(1), 57–66 (2007)
4. Singh, A., Malhorta, S.: A researcher's guide to running diary studies. In: APCHI 2013, pp. 296–300 (2013)
5. Cisco virtual networking index: Global mobile data traffic forecast update (2010–2015). http://www.cisco.com/en/US/solutions/collateral/ns341/ns525/ns537/ns705/ns827/whitepaperc11-520862.html. Accessed 21 Mar 2011
6. Satyanarayanan, M.: Swiss Army Knife or Wallet? IEEE Pervasive Comput. **4**(2), 2–3 (2005)
7. Demumieux, R., Losquin, P.: Gather customer's real usage on mobile phones. In: Proceedings of the 7th International Conference on Human Computer Interaction with Mobile Devices & Services, pp. 267–270. ACM (2005)
8. Nylander, S., Lundquist, T., Brännström, A.: At home and with computer access: why and where people use cell phones to access the internet. In: Proceedings of CHI 2009, pp. 1639–1642. ACM (2009)
9. Thorp, E.: The invention of the first wearable computer. In: Proceedings of ISWC 1998, pp. 4–8 (1998)
10. Karapanos, E., Zimmerman, J., Forlizzi, J., Martens, J.-B.: User experience over time: an initial framework. In: CHI 2009, pp. 729–738 (2009)
11. Taylor, C.A., Samuels, N., Ramey, J.A.: Always on: a framework for understanding personal mobile web motivations, behaviors, and contexts of use. Int. J. Mob. Hum. Comput. Interact. **1**(4), 24–41 (2009)
12. Hackos, J., Redish, J.: User and Task Analysis for Interface Design. Wiley, New York (1998)

Wearable DUXU

Adapting Smart Textiles to Develop Soft Interactive Tool Kits for Applying in Sewing Projects

Aqua Chuan-Yu Chen[✉]

Department of Product Design, Ming Chuan University, Taipei, Taiwan
aquachen@mail.mcu.edu.tw

Abstract. Characteristics of Smart Textiles are not only have the tactile, somatosensory, temperature, etc., but also provides the effects of light, temperature regulation, power storage, water, and other functions, and mean while preserving the fabric originally unique soft feature which can be braided, stitching, folding, extended class organic qualities, to replace environment unfriendly plastic products, more affinity exists in life. The research starts with the textiles that can achieve the electronic functions. And base on the setting function of sensors and receivers to design many customized modules. We make textiles as electronic circuits to provide proper interactions modes that are corresponding to the situational reaction as well as input and output context design for the desirable behaviors. The establishment of an integrated modeling original design draft, electronic circuits, and smart textile design flow of customized products provide niche related industry to establish a smart fabric in the integrity of the program of customized products designed to integrate the use of soft wearable models. The development of soft too kits by smart textiles is according to the investigations of interaction concept from electronics, then design and develop the interaction IC boards by adapting textiles that can conduct or with optic and heating functions. For the interaction, we need to decide the interactive scenarios corresponding to the behaviors, design electronic circuits and control program. Overall, a well-designed process integration soft tool kits will be introduced. The use of digital printing and embroidery to accurately reproduce the original creative spirit. The establishment of this design research of customized textile goods providing benefit to establish a niche model in the relevant industry. Based on this, the purpose of the study is as follows:

(1) The establishment of the custom product design process of smart textile in order to be understood and used by their customers and designers coordination between each issues.
(2) Analysis of smart textiles to develop interaction modes of soft tool kits.
(3) Dissemble performance of smart textiles and apply textiles made soft tool kits on design projects for hand crafts.

Keywords: Product design · E-fabric · Smart textiles · Interactive · Toolkits

© Springer International Publishing Switzerland 2015
A. Marcus (Ed.): DUXU 2015, Part II, LNCS 9187, pp. 611–621, 2015.
DOI: 10.1007/978-3-319-20898-5_58

1 Introduction

The Maker Movement is prevailing and gradually gathered more and more market prototypes with their own operating, in the meanwhile, developing new products and services. Clever makers combined innovative technologies, such as Arduino micro-controllers and personal 3D printers, contributed to innovation of manufacturing, engineering, industrial design, hardware technology, and education. Many Makers are amateurs, fanatics or student (non-professional), but they are a source of creativity in the community in which providing fascinating ideas and giving value of the product. Even some Maker finally become entrepreneurs, but also founded his own company's business. In terms of textiles industry which lots of woman interested in, the question of how to participate in this time remarkable activity has become an urgent issue. For a long time, the usage of textiles are either traditional hand crafts or making cloth in fashion industry. However, in relation with the ubiquitous computing and intelligent technology, textiles failed to provide a new form to intervene in the innovative product development, nor can provide a "self-made" and understandable tool kits for people who related to wearable technology. In this study, the main objective of the research echoes the possibility of making smart textiles applications popular for the public especially for woman. According to preliminary research results, we further promote a more convenient smart textiles interactive tool kits, and suggest many types of combinations which are not by welding, but by sewing or engaging. Providing advantage of soft flexible characteristics for making applications of its texture to health care, warmth design projects and so on.

Smart Textiles not only with the physical characteristics of the tactile senses, apparent temperature, etc., which can provide light, temperature regulation, electricity storage, water, odor and other functions which similar to electronic products and at the same time retain the original unique soft fabric, closeness, wearable, stitching, folding, flexibility and other organic qualities, is more suitable to replace chilled, environmentally unfriendly plastic products, the possibility of a more intimate wear that close to everyday life [1]. Though there are many Lego related blocks for interactive (e.g., littleBits) [2], but so far with textile-oriented development of soft switch, control board, or the input/output tool kits for education has not yet been found on the market.

The smart textiles' characteristics for transmitting electronics' are different from the ordinary textiles. Besides, their warmness and softness are different from plastic products. Specific smart textiles can replace hard circuit, presented light and temperature feedback. In this study, a website system was designed to test the user experiences and usability in order to find out the appropriate design process management to complete design ideas, and the use of real performance of commodities and demand patterns of behavior.

This study was funded by the Ministry of Science and Technology of Taiwan (grant number: 102-2221-E-130-023 -). A services website (http://www.e-textiles.tw/) was constructed for custom design firm or makers. The data survey from the smart textiles related to sewing projects, electronics and digital technology. The research subjects are correlation with whom engage in customized merchandise studio or individuals. Some soft fabric interactive tools were designed for the application of entrepreneurs and its user experiences and usability were revealed through a constructed website system to explore a well-designed process integration management models in which entrepreneurs, consumers and material providers [3].

We want to let girls, children, adults, or designers with no electronics background can use approachable soft tool kits to add their own creativity and make their own "product". And in the meantime, understand how electronic equipment originally supposed to work in the surrounding they live every day.

2 Literature Research

Smart textiles have often reminiscent those can deliver exceptional performance with light, sound, electricity, input and feedback. They also commonly were defined as detection of physiological signals or mood changes, and feedback information to the controller to determine what is the reaction on the textiles. Sensatex in Atlanta, U.S [4] launched smart shirt that can be used for medical care in 2006. This shirt can be used for accurate remote monitoring of health indicators of the body's functions, such as heart rate, breathing rate and body temperature, and the data is transmitted from the personal monitors to the monitoring center for doctor to analysis and processing [5]. Once, there are unusual circumstances, it can remind the doctor by itself through networking immediately. Experts in Philips Co. have developed two experimental magical clothing which color can vary and shown by skirt and the garment according to a wearer's mood changes or emotional perception [6].

2.1 Smart Textiles, E-Textiles

Textiles that are able to sense stimuli from the environment, to react to them and adapt to them by integration of functionalities in the textile structure. The stimulus as well as the response can have an electrical, thermal, chemical, magnetic or other origin.

Advanced materials, such as breathing, fire-resistant or ultrastrong fabrics, are according to this definition not considered as intelligent, no matter how high-technological they might be.

The extent of intelligence can be divided in three subgroups:

- passive smart textiles can only sense the environment, they are sensors;
- active smart textiles can sense the stimuli from the environment and also react to them, besides the sensor function, they also have an actuator function;
- Finally, very smart textiles take a step further, having the gift to adapt their behavior to the circumstances.

Basically, 5 functions can be distinguished in smart textiles: Sensors, Data processing, Actuators, Storage, and Communication [7]. From the analysis of the Taiwan Textile Research Institute (TTRI) [8], as well as throughout the relevant research results, relationships between human-computer interaction and smart textiles are listed as Table 1:

Table 1. Related Smart textiles technologies [3] [8]

Energy	Input/Sensor	Processing	Output/Feedback
Development of mobile energy textile technology	Physiology monitoring textiles development (health indicators: heart rate, respiratory rate and body temperature)	Application of conductive materials processing technology	Monitor(Mobile phone, Nursery station)
		Development of conductive nano silver ink	LED embedded and photonic textiles technology
			Development of electro-thermal textile

2.2 Soft Interactive Kits

The so-called electronic interactive kit must initiate interactive response, perceived ability to response; simple manipulation. Advanced applications even need to change the way to make manipulation fun and with learning ability. Joanna Berzowska has shown her work in may field which include Biofeedback and wearable health monitoring, surveillance and privacy, consumer products, universal connectivity, lifestyle products experiments in reactive fashion [9, 10]. In this study, through the analysis of existing interactive kit, we summarized with the feasibility of interactive programs, try to use smart fabric to replace the existing tool kits.

- Initiate interactive response: interactive voice, video infrared.
- Summary judgment: perceived ability to cope with human cognition.
- Change and learning ability: combine with cloud network information e.g. music and so on.

Classification of Smart Textiles Interactive Toolkit: Currently interactive kits associated with textiles on electronic retails such as Sparkfun [11] or many other wearable devices shopping website are subdivided into five categories. However, for inventors who did not have the basic programming knowledge to understand the combination and application of these kits are really a difficult job to do. Moreover place these hard shell kits on a soft cloth applications should affect very much the appearance of the works. (Table 2).

2.3 Educational Interactive Block

Currently most of the electronic interactive elements are in the form of building blocks for easier to use and more intuitive to present concepts. For example, robot Lego Mindstorms EV3 for robot, Concept of education building block like littleBits [2] to apply to everyday life, as well as the company produced Chicco GIGO Arduino materials. (Table 3).

Table 2. Types of the electronic for textiles

Power	Input	Controller	Output	Materials
Battery	Sound	LilyPad	ELastoLite kit	Conductive fabric
Activator	Motion	Aniomagic	LED display	Heating pad
Switch	Image			Conductive thread

Table 3. Related interaction kits

Interaction Learning Kits	
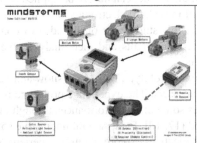	1. LEGO MINDSTORMS EV3 set to create and command robots that walk, talk, think and do anything you can imagine and bring them to life with an easy, intuitive and icon-based programming interface. Grab the enclosed remote control and take on challenging ready-made missions or download the free app and command your robot using your smart device. [12]
	2. LittleBits Electronic littleBits is the easiest and most extensive way to learn and prototype with electronics. We are making hardware limitless with our award-winning, ever-growing library of electronic modules, ranging from the very simple (power, sensors, LED) to the very complex (wireless, programmable). [2] ∘
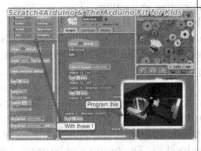	3. S4A (Scratch for Arduino) Chicco company combined three building blocks of the creative blocks, Arduino electronic building blocks, and S4A interactive software, designed an interesting learning materials : GIGO Arduino. It allows users to adjust and vary changes in Scratch program and read back to Arduino. Besides to interact with the role on screen, it can also control motor movement and external sensors, so that players can create their own interactive human-machine effect [13].

For interaction tools kit, there are three modules of it design patterns:

1. Programming: Free interactive learning software (e.g., Scratch for Arduino (S4A) and compatible learning hardware or blocks).
2. Electronic, Mechanism: Open architecture Arduino control circuit board or electronic control blocks.
3. Resource: Open learning courses in order to support users.

Integration of the three areas not only is the sum of the three specialized fields, but multiplied them by very combination of changes. It makes learning with high affinity and minimum threshold.

3 Research Methods

Currently interaction tool kits made of plastic on the market can hardly be applied on to textiles and wearable devices. The appearances of these hard electronics tool kit on soft fabric is quite unexpected and weird. Therefore, this study base on the idea of combined the characteristics of the fabric and electronic circuits and then analyzed their usage to apply on different soft material projects.

First, the study adapt research tool of experience prototype [14–16] to show and test the solution through an active participation of the users. The experience prototype is a simulation of the service experience that foresees some of its performances through the use of the specific physical touch points involved [17, 18]. First, several interactive soft toolkits were designed and used in the sewing projects to explore the user experiences. Second, a website was built where smart textiles are offered and encourage more people to use these soft tool kits in their sewing projects to collect more ideas of how to apply these soft interaction toolkits in works. The data were sorting out through the systematic way in order to find out an appropriate set of soft interactive DIY kit applications in the design process for designers, artists, etc. For those who usually do not have programming background can still apply in the design innovation stage, we answer the questions of what are the essential equipment for the soft interaction kits? How can this kits to be simple in manipulation? Safe design are necessary. According to the soft tool kits' development and we look forward that they can be accepted by female who are interested both fashion and interactive technology. They are tools to help creativeness not limited under the technology. (Table 4).

The experience prototypes are used to analyze what may be composed by dismantling the different types of sensing and feedback with soft fabrics corresponding plastic electronic product features while doing the sewing projects and find out the interactive operation setting of choice. Besides, define how we can use smart textile to replace the hard plastic interactive kit, so as to set up a soft sensing, control and feedback tool kits. The social networking website is to collect projects from different users to explore the application of distributed species of smart textile and to promote and enrich the usage of the application from the toolkits. The results can be applied to the fashion industry and wearable technology sectors. The process of the research are as following:

Table 4. Smart textiles interaction DIY kits research structure:

First: experience prototypes phase	Research	Idea Development	Modeling
	Textiles sewing works	Human interaction connection	Function prototypes: textiles connecting parts
	Electronic interaction tool kits	Input/output connection	
Second: application development phase	Website networking	User experience feedback	Develop more ideas of Soft tool kits applications

1. Analysis of human-computer interaction based on the use of interactive situational demands, the dismantling of different sensing, control and feedback types.
2. Data collection and analysis of smart textiles.
3. From deconstruction to application of smart textiles, a complete set of soft sensing, control and feedback tool kits was structured that provides the easy access toolkit in creative process for designers or makers.

4   Result

Wearable technology has become a keen issue today, however, if only electronic or programming experts are able to be competent to use the applications, it will slow the limitations of creativity and innovation possibilities. The concept of this study is to make non-engineers - especially young girls - to get interest in science and technology.

There are two group of specialties involved in this research. Designers developed various concepts starting from understanding and implementing the smart textiles, and engineers try to show functional operation. Moreover, through meetings with users to review each case of the proposed projects, many prototype concept mapping were finally completed. Developed smart textiles interactive prototypes for soft toolkits can be used as an important sources of reference in textiles and IT wearable technology industry, or content-related design development process. (Table 5).

Construction of the Smart Textiles Interaction Soft Tool Kit Prototypes. "Button" is almost the first thing to start an electronic. Each project is also relying on input to generate feedback. In order to adapt to the fabric softness, we designed soft button. The button is set to trigger the behavior (e.g., the lights shine, controllers, heat pad or cloth, sound, motor functioning, and even cloud network). See the website of the relevant operation below: (Fig. 1).

Smart textiles were composed as many electronic components, and by adapting the fabric's unique connecting ways of fastening, stitching, etc., a set of simple electronic wire components were developed and can be freely combined interactive DIY kits. To

Table 5. Relevant videos of Soft interactive kit [20].

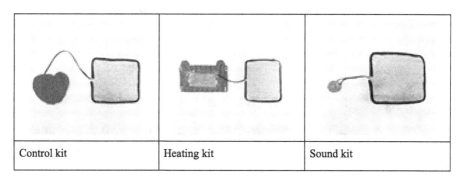

Control kit	Heating kit	Sound kit

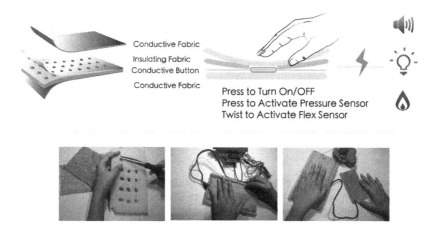

Conductive Fabric
Insulating Fabric
Conductive Button
Conductive Fabric

Press to Turn On/OFF
Press to Activate Pressure Sensor
Twist to Activate Flex Sensor

Fig. 1. Smart textiles ON/OFF switch

allow users to assemble circuit in creative activities, as simple as much to replace different smart fabric electronic modules is important. Each package represents a particular function are pre-designed (i.e., lighting, sound, motor, or sensor) and following the original fabric connected logic and details were designed not assembled the wrong way i.e., distinguish between output power, input, wire to make larger circuits. If interactive kit connected to each other, you can create a heating pillow; a cloth knob can be placed in the middle to create a minor dimmer; or a hat with tracer; all possibilities as much as possible to use the smart textiles to achieve softness and affinity products. (Fig. 2).

Construction of the Internet Community. This phase focuses on non-engineering backgrounds for interactive applications and with the aim of investigation the feasibility of smart textiles Soft tool kits provided for real life application for reference.

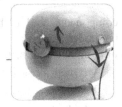

Button for Control   **Zipper for Storage**   **Button for Connect**

Fig. 2. Parts connected different smart textiles kits

Table 6. Social networking websites

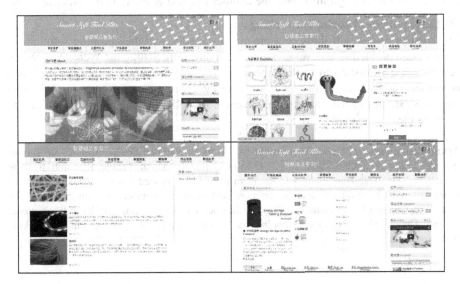

The prototypes start the discussions of the user experiences. Furthermore, establish a social networking website provide the chance to communicate and resolve the incomplete or uncertain messages. Through the power of social networking sites, the accumulation of various applications of the smart textiles tool kits is getting more. And by revealing the innovation process, a clear and convenient user reference library is established gradually where ideas can be found in order to stimulate the possibility of innovation. (Table 6).

5   Conclusion

Using smart textiles to create interactive toolkit and adapt in process is effective for enhancing the strength of the creativities. An overview of the results can be divided into four oriented as following:

(1) Applicable smart textiles selected

Collected smart textiles to meet the services of electronic components, and to be relatively echoes intelligent electronic function. Behaviors and attitudes sensed by the input soft toolkits and output by soft interaction toolkits become another interactive types of products.

(2) Behavior and sensor feedback for textiles

Textiles compare to electronic products used in a manner closer to the body. The way textiles can be combined together are also different from interactive blocks. Research focus at this stage divided into three types: Function, Appearance, Operation feeling, as well as the effect of use. Conversion material will result in changing the design concepts because of different input and feedback task and limit, so the use of the prototype to construct and test design ideas become another fast and effective communication tool.

(3) Development of social networking

The creative maker will think of a preliminary model, and then propose solutions to solve design problems, or develop other design direction. Setting the Website of certain activities and workshop to explore the smart textiles interaction toolkits applied as a commodity development cases, in order to get the appropriate usage patterns. Whereby some case studies of the smart textiles interaction toolkit to show as video, in order to be more clear and simple way to use it.

Acknowledgments. The researcher would like to thank National Science Council of Taiwan sponsored this research (NSC102-2221-E-130-023-) and Taiwan Textile Research Institute (TTRI) and Dr. Nian-Hao Wang and his team provided advanced functional textiles and the experts from TTRI to offer treasurable opinions and technical suggestions. I am grateful to the Prof. Wen-Chang Chen, Institute of Polymer Science and Engineering (IPSE) at the National Taiwan University (NTU) for providing invaluable support in making reliable working prototypes.

References

1. Chen, A.C.: Designing for the daily-life applications with functional textiles. In: IASDAR Proceeding 2012, Tokyo (2012)
2. Bdeir, A.: Electronics as material: littleBits. In: TEI 2009 Proceedings of the 3rd International Conference on Tangible and Embedded Interaction (2009)
3. Chen, A.C.: Using smart textiles in customized product design children's drawings as example. In: Stephanidis, C. (ed.) HCI 2014, Part I. CCIS, vol. 434, pp. 79–84. Springer, Heidelberg (2014)
4. SYSTEX.: Definition of Smart Textiles. http://www.systex.org/content/definition-smart-textiles. Accessed 16 Mar 2013
5. Philips Design, SKIN probe project (2006). http://www.design.philips.com/philips/sites/philipsdesign/about/design/designportfolio/design_futures/dresses.page
6. Kholiya, R., Jahan, S.: Electronic textiles innovations & diversified. Colourage **57**(12), 45–54 (2010)
7. Van Langenhove, L., Hertleer, C.: Smart clothing: a new life. Int. J. Clothing Sci. Technol. **16**(1/2), 63–72 (2004)

8. TTRI, 2011 Annual report_substainable innovation: dream com true, Taiwan Textile Research Institute, Taipei (2011)
9. Berzowska, J.: Electronic textiles: wearable computers, reactive fashion, and soft computation. Textile **3**(1), 2–19 (2005)
10. Berzowska, J.: http://www.xslabs.net/
11. Sparkfun electronic (2015). https://www.sparkfun.com/
12. Ball, C., Moller, F., Pau, R.: The mindstorm effect: a gender analysis on the influence of LEGO mindstorms in computer science education. In: WiPSCE 2012 Proceedings of the 7th Workshop in Primary and Secondary Computing Education. pp. 141–142, ACM (2012)
13. About S4A, Citilab. http://s4a.cat/. Accessed 2015
14. Buchenau, M., Suri, J.F.: Experience Prototyping. In: Consolvo, S., (ed.) Proceeding of Designing Interactive Systems (DIS), pp. 424–433. ACM (2007)
15. Dow, S.P., Glassco, A.: Paralled prototyping leads to better design results, more divergence, and increased self-efficacy, ACM Trans. Comput. Hum. Interact. 17(4) (2010) doi: 10.1145/1879831.1879836
16. Buchenau, M., Suri, J.F.: Experience Prototyping. In: Symposium on Designing Interactive Systems (2000)
17. Park, S., Jayaraman, S.: Smart textiles: wearable electronic systems. MRS Bull. **28**(08), 585–591 (2003)
18. Davis, F.: Perceived usefulness, perceived ease of use and user acceptance of information technology. MIS Q. **13**(3), 319–340 (1989)
19. Bonato, P.: Advances in wearable technology for rehabilitation. Stud. Health Technol. Inform. **145**, 145–159 (2009)
20. Chen, A.C.-Y.: ET@CSLAB (e-textiles at Creative Service Lab). http://www.etextiles.tw/etm12.asp. Accessed 2015

Evolutionary Wearables

Patricia Flanagan$^{(\boxtimes)}$

Hong Kong Baptist University, Kowloon Tong, Hong Kong, Republic of China
tricia@triciaflanagan.com, flanagan@hkbu.edu.hk

Abstract. Early development of Wearables emerged through professional silos of computer science and fashion design and resulted in two distinct branches typified by an aesthetic approach from fashion and by a function and ocular-centric approach from science. Attempts at collaboration between these silos tended to bring the two methodologies into conflict and often produced awkward results. Computer science is a field traditionally dominated by men and fashion design by women, so what is the future for wearable's evolution as professions are becoming less gendered? In 2009 the author established the Wearables Lab in Hong Kong. In 2012 and 2014 the Wearables Lab hosted research initiatives specifically focused on haptic interfaces where wearables are viewed as an interface between the body and the world. This article maps key themes of this research leading to speculative designs for evolutionary wearables.

Keywords: Wearables · Haptic interface Sunaptic sculpture Cyborganic Cybernetics Systems thinking Neganthropocene Gender equality

1 Introduction

The early development in Wearables emerged through professional silos of both computer science and fashion design and resulted in two distinct branches typified by an aesthetic approach from fashion often using light in garments, and by a function-led approach from science with most research spent on ocular centric devises – the wearable head mounted computers by Steve Mann for example. The methodology of the scientist is based on truth, finding the most eloquent solutions and proving their validity, where as the designer/artist finds a solution successful if it opens questions, or dialogue rather than definitive answers. Hence attempts at collaboration between these silos tended to bring the two methodologies into conflict and often produced awkward results. Computer science is a field traditionally dominated by men and fashion design by women, so what is the future for Wearable's evolution as professions are becoming less gendered?

Influencing Wearable's evolution has been its miniaturization and lower costs for higher performance widgets, effectively moving design from corporate and university research into the hands of makers. The rise in a community commons approach to knowledge has led to incredible innovation in wearable design. Since 2009 the Wearables Lab at the Academy of Visual Arts in Hong Kong has been dedicated to exploring and developing Wearables. The success of the Wearables Lab is in part due to the fact that it has not grown from a fashion or computer science department but the

A. Marcus (Ed.): DUXU 2015, Part II, LNCS 9187, pp. 622–630, 2015.
DOI: 10.1007/978-3-319-20898-5_59

creative space of an art school resulting in critical rather than affirmative design solutions [1]. In 2012 and 2014 the Wearables Lab hosted research initiatives focused on haptic interfaces [2]. This article maps key themes of the author's research into Wearables leading to a speculative design future of evolutionary Wearables.

2 Women in Design, User Experience and Usability

An invitation to contribute to a session on Women in Design, User Experience and Usability at HCI 2015 is a privileged opportunity to share research, at the same time it was with some trepidation that the author approached the gendered title, preferring not to illuminate gender and focus on research. Having said this, it is within research itself, embedded in the language of our recorded history, that gender inequality is firmly entrenched. The pay gap between men and women is still evident although it has been lessening for decades. A recent study from Harvard University [3] looked at the gap and found that it gets larger for women toward the middle of their careers. Women are more likely to take time off to raise a family than men, and the gap shrinks again after the child-rearing years. Different industries are less flexible than others. In corporate, law and financial sectors the gap is much greater in mid-career than in the information technology (IT) industry, health and science where more flexibility has been embraced and therefore it is easier to work part-time or from home to accommodate raising a family. "Information and communication technology (ICT) and the science, engineering and technology (SET) sectors remain dominated by men in almost all European states" [4]. In the game industry "Women are underrepresented in core creation and development roles, such as coders, designers and artists. []...It would appear that occupational segregation still persists in this relatively new, male dominated industry" [5].

In the UK the Equal Opportunities Commission (EOC) found that occupational segregation was one of the strongest influences on youth when choosing their career path and that they focused on areas where their gender is represented [6]. Stereotypes prevail – considering that the visual arts and fashion industries are areas that are predominantly populated by women in tertiary education, there is a clear disparity in the fact that the big names in these industries are still predominantly male. On a more positive note many countries have seen an increase in woman participating in the workforce. One of the best examples is in the Netherlands where women's participation in the workforce grew from 31 % in 1975 to 69 % in 2006 [7]. Women are becoming more integrated in the workforce but are still behind in terms of full time employment and wage levels. Every culture and country has different attitudes and laws, and although ICT may offer greater flexibility that can help accommodate the schedules of parenting, we can not claim the issue of gender inequality does not still exist. In India where the IT service industry is enormous the wage discrepancy between men and women is 60 %. Women are viewed as second-class citizens. Men still hold the balance of power.

Karl Marx's belief was that only if the family unit was made redundant, so that women and families were not dependent on men as care givers, could there be equality between the sexes where men and women come together truly of free will without need.

Childcare should be a community concern. The individualization fostered under the prevailing globally dominant neo-liberal capitalism makes equality impossible in this sense. Kant's view is that we are in a state of constant oscillation between our desire for self-sufficiency and the need for others. Social groups form from the tension between competition for self-gain and the solidarity of the group advantage [7]. The current generation is one of the first in history who can survive individually and afford to live independently. This is a product of wealthy societies and the technological age we live in [8]. Many people choose to live alone, but perhaps rather than blind individualism, we would gain more by imagining societies that value reciprocity and empathy as it is through community that the body politic speaks. We need to embrace equality between the sexes but also find equality between all living beings; humanities egocentrism has led to the current environmental crisis. Communism and capitalism are presented as the only two variables and yet neither seems to be working. We need to search for an alternative – a third space – and this is where critical thinking, imagination and creativity are vital. Human Computer Interaction (HCI) is part of our natural techno-genesis and it opens new ways to perceive one's self and the world around us that can help us in this endeavor.

Creativity requires diversity and imagination; equality does not imply androgyny and it follows that we should embrace our differences as it provides greater diversity. In 1973 Schein outlined feminine traits including kindness, warmth, sympathy and selflessness, and masculine ones such as rationality, aggression, competitiveness, forcefulness, decisiveness, strength, independence and self-confidence. Are these traits socially constructed, stereotypes or genetic? Physiologically the left and right hemispheres of the brain compliment each other as thoughts move back and forth between them. The left hemisphere is analytical and logical and the right is more holistic and artistic [9]. The left is more dominant, but they work together keeping each other in check to help us make the right decisions. The corpus callosum is a shaft of nerves connecting the two halves. The female callosum is frequently larger than in men [10]. Specifically the posterior portion of the corpus callosum, called the splenium is larger than in males. "This finding could be related to possible gender differences in the degree of lateralization for visuospatial functions." [11]. This could explain the widely held belief that women are better at multi-tasking than men. Do women view the world differently? The neuroscientist David Eagleman [12] found that 15 % of women possess a fourth type of color photoreceptor that enables them to discriminate between colors that look identical to the rest of us who have only three.

The historical development of (HCI) has focused on ocular-centric, screen-based interaction. This is in line with the Cartesian approach across western theory, which since the enlightenment has attempted to separate fact from mysticism and led to the belief that the mind is equated with knowledge and intelligence and the body with nature. The result is that current wearable technology design practices represent a reductionist view of human capacity. The democratization of technology in recent years has opened the field of HCI to other methodologies and knowledge fields such as the arts and humanities, for example social science, anthropology and ethnography. HCI is an inherently interdisciplinary field. Discourse around design is changing, away from purely functional attributes and technical capacities toward a multisensory materiality [13] to develop a connoisseurship of somasethetic qualities [14].

3   Systems Thinking

Systems-thinking is the logic that defines the information age. We live in the era of cybernetics and the systemic organization of information enable collective forms of intelligence, these cybernetic methods of collective intelligence are transforming the way we think and will be key in defining our future. The interface itself is an aesthetic form to be crafted, not just used as a tool for production. The interface as an aesthetic form provides us with a way to redefine and view our contemporary reality [15]. Technology, conditions the way we think as individuals and as collectives.

For Marx value is expressed as labor power, for Joseph Beuys value comes from 'creativity'. The focus of "Joseph Beuys aesthetic is embedded in the idea of alignment, perpetuation, and addition. Rather than advocating intervention, he believed it was the artist's task to discover connections and expand upon them" [16]. Beuys promulgated the term 'social sculpture' which identifies his belief in the social value of creativity. Future Wearables will engage creativity to combine aesthetic and kinesthetic with interface and experience design, as Wearables evolve into more than worn objects of desire but extensions of the body and tools of interactivity. Wearables will embody technical systems that will undeniably condition individual and collective thinking, as have technologies of the past [17]. Beuys work signified a turn in attitude away from objects as the locus of meaning of an artwork, to thinking about what operates between them. Bourriaud's notion of relational aesthetics grew in popularity in the 2000's using metaphors of 'post-production' and 'the artist as Deejay' to further define the role of the artist as a modeler of activity, directing and distributing flows of information [18]. Susan Elizabeth Ryan's definition of Wearables is useful here. She describes, "dress acts" as "hybrid acts of communication in which the behavior of wearing is bound up with the materiality of garments and devices—and focuses on the use of digital technology as part of such systems of meaning" [19].

3.1   Sunaptic Sculpture

The term Sunaptic Sculpture [20] emerged in the authors work in 2003, a neologism to distinguish it from its predecessors predominantly though not exclusively 'social sculpture' and 'relational aesthetics'. At this time her research concerned arts status as an object and established arts practice based in communication and relationships. In line with Søren Pold's appeal to consider the interface as an aesthetic form, Sunaptic sculpture describes artwork that is inclusive of social systems in the Beuysian sense but may equally operate at the level of micro or macro systems (inside or outside the body). The term acknowledges interconnectedness, it accommodates both digital and analogue and promulgates the affordances of haptic interfaces as spaces for creativity. Sunaptic sculpture describes a contemporary interface where "Aesthetics can offer a critical reflection on the issue of representation: on how the representation is related to the material through which it is carried out, and to how it is related to the cultural context in which it functions" [21]. This is design that encourages creativity, inspires intelligence and promotes curiosity and enquiry.

A trans-disciplinary approach in an interconnected world is the natural form for interaction design. To further investigate the future possibilities for Wearables the author has led two intensive trans-disciplinary, intercultural research workshops. Haptic InterFace (HIF) 2012 and 2014 exploring the themes of 'praxis' (2012) and 'designing experience' (2014). Twenty professionals and creative thinkers from many backgrounds and cultures come together for ten-days of hands-on experimentation. HIF participants 2014 were Sara Adhitya urban design, Meiyi Cheung fashion design, Emma Cooper architecture, Beck Davis product design, Jared Donovan interaction design, Raune Frankjaer inter-media design, Daniel Gilgen spatial communication and physical computing, Rafael Gomez industrial design, Dave Hrymkiw robotics, Erina Kashihara light Wearables, Tobias Klein architecture and art, Zoe Mahony fashion design, Kit Messham-Muir art theory, Ann Morrison interaction design and installation art, Roger Ng mathematics, patternmaking and philosophy, Jake Oliver-Fishman art, Elizabeth Shaw jewelry. Participants collaborated on prototypes such as a gauntlet to analyze the tremor of Parkinson's disease and a tremor inspired series of jewelry; biodress; contiguous living systems; a gesture recognition aid for interactive teaching; version two of the sensate vest; self lighting umbrellas that leverage small network communication fields to generate visual sequencing patterns across crowd environments; and a theatrical collar that communicates by fanning out in reaction to movement. HIF participants collaborate on prototypes and the results are exhibited internationally. The 2014 prototypes were exhibited in Hong Kong and the final projects are destined for exhibition in Brisbane in 2015.

4   Evolutionary Wearables

4.1   Cyborganic

The first generation cyberneticists Norbert Wiener, Julian Bigelow, Arturo Rosenblueth, Gregory Bateson, Margaret Mead and Warren McCulloch described their core theme of interest as – circular, causal and feedback mechanisms in biological and social systems. Javier Livas describes Cybernetics as a prodigious super-science of interconnectedness that will save the planet from reductionist, authoritarian, corrupt, anti-democratic, or just plain stupid governance. More than a decade after Wiener published his book *Cybernetics: Or Control and Communication in the Animal and the Machine* (1950) [22] Manfred Clynes and Nathan S. Kline started using the term Cyborg (1960) [23]. The dystopian images that science fiction movies have propagated about the cyborg promulgate fear of the mechanic and are bias toward it being evil. Today anything with 'cyber' in the title is treated as synonymous with 'computer'. Although cybernetics is the science of the information age (and the tools of that age are computers), cybernetics itself is a much broader topic. To distinguish a more positive approach and regain an equal focus on the organic aspect of cybernetic research in this area, the author and her collaborators at the Wearables Lab use another variation: cyborganic.

Bio-dress (Fig. 1) seeks to foster empathetic relationships between plants and humans by mirroring state changes in a specific plant on the body through a wearable

Fig. 1. Biodress, Sara Adhitya, Beck Davis, Raune Frankjaer, Zoe Mahony and Tricia Flanagan. Photo: Beck Davis.

tech garment. Thermo-chromic paints combined with memory wire, create movement and color-change in the leaf inspired textile surface of the garment in reaction to EEG output from the plant. Steam pleated organza on the shoulder areas appear to breathe in reaction to the air quality reading.

4.2   Egocentric to Eco-Centric

We live in the anthropocene, a term yet to be sanctified by the Statigraphy Commission of the Geological Society, but none-the-less a powerful recognition of an epoch where human activity (as pervasive as natural forces) has driven global ecological change. The typical worldview of the anthropocene is that it is an ecological issue. Its main opposition is from the perspective of an economic worldview that predicts financial crisis hinged on the impact of most of the suggestions made by ecologists. What is called for is a shift in our perception from egocentric (where we see ourselves as something other than nature), to an eco-centric perception where we are intrinsically interconnected. Trans-disciplinary approaches must be adopted. "…trans-disciplinary is impelled by external conditions but also by the conviction that disciplines do not have proprietary rights over their domains. […] Ecological thought is changing the ways in which our practices might operate in the future" [24]. Acknowledging the anthropocene shifts our thinking about Wearables away from standalone products to ones that are intrinsically connected to the processes and actions that surround them, to imagine objects in terms of ecologies and lifecycles. To think about interconnectedness in this way makes matter a dynamic, transformative proposition and this is where approaches like Synaptic Sculpture are useful as they aim to sculpt matter in connection with thought and data.

Post-colonial theory, has long been discussing the Other taken to mean any minority to the majority, and it acknowledges that history has been written predominantly from one perspective (white western male). Acknowledging other perspectives has involved a process of rewriting history, first from a feminist perspective and then gradually incorporating ethnic and religious groups. This is an on-going process, with the latest iteration including non-human life. This reinterpretation of our culture is not on the grounds of a moral imperative to be inclusive, rather an acknowledgement of the networks that sustain us and the implications of maintaining a culturally limited perspective, one that was "fuelled by the accelerated use of carbon-based energy to prioritize human life at the expense of other forms of life treated as 'natural resources'" [25].

4.3   Ecosystems and Evolutionary Wearables

Future cities will be configurations of intelligent ambient spaces, where physical infrastructure as well as what we wear, is embedded with sensing and computational technology as invisible as electricity is today [26].

An interesting way that we can challenge our human-centric view of the world is to subvert our methodologies and imagine the body as a floating wetland system and our cities as bodies [27]. The future of wearable technology lies at the intersection of biotechnology, nanotechnology and materials science [28]. These fields are opening up new worlds of discovery, such as dissolving technology that can be used in biomedical applications that do their job and then disappear, and electronic wetware [29] or green consumer electronics that can safely cycle through the ecosystem.

Robots are replacing jobs heralding mass unemployment, new economic climates need to be imagined that are not based on old work models but new kinds of systems of value. "In this regard the early Marx's emphasis on the radical and revolutionary function of Bildung (communities of collective self-learning) comes to define non-statist and autonomous forms of productive, intellectual and creative community" [30]. Our ability to imagine the future enables us to design for the future. "For the first few hundred million years after their initial appearance on the planet, our brains were stuck in the permanent present, and most brains still are today. But not yours and mine, because two or three million years ago our ancestors began a great escape from the here and now" [31]. Theoretical quantum physics proposes that the great escape from our liminal perception may have only just begun. Our relationship with the world is evolving from one in which historically we were hunter gatherers 'using' the products of the world; then we learnt to harness the energy in production of materials, 'controlling the natural world' around us through industrialization; and now there is a need for us to imagine the future, to 'design and craft our own world' [32]. Our task is to redefine value in terms of our economy, we have to reimagine the Internet as a generous interface rather than a space of capital colonization and hyper-marketing and at the interface between the body and the world we must create evolutionary Wearables for the Neganthropocene.

Acknowledgments. Haptic InterFace was possible through kind support from Seeed Studios Shenzhen and the Woolmark Company Australia.

Patricia Flanagan Orcid.org/0000-0003-2605-7630

References

1. Dunne, A., Raby, F.: Design Noir: The Secret Life of Electronic Objects. August Media and Birkhèauser, London Basel and Switzerland (2001)
2. Flanagan, P.: Haptic interface (2014) http://hapticinterface.hkbu.edu.hk. Accessed 21 March 2014
3. Goldin, C.: A grand gender convergence: its last chapter. Am. Econ. Rev. **104**(4), 1091–1119 (2014)
4. Thewlis, M., Miller, L., Neathey, F.: Advancing Women in the Workplace: Statistical Analysis. EOC Working Paper Series, vol. 12. Equal Opportunities Commission, Manchester (2004)
5. Prescott, J., Bogg, J.: Segregation in a male-dominated industry: women working in the computer games industry. Int. J. Gend. Sci. Technol. **3**(1), 205–227 (2011)
6. Miller, L., Neathey, F., Pollard, E., Hill, D.: Occupational Segregation, Gender Gaps and Skill Gaps. Equal Opportunities Commission Working paper series, vol. 15. Equal Opportunities Commission, Manchester (2004)
7. van Vuuren, E.K.: The trend in female labour force participation: what can be expected for the future? Empir. Econ. **40**(3), 729–753 (2011)
8. Sandra, T.L.: Does living alone drive you mad?, 29 January 2015. New York Magazine, New York Media LLC (2015) http://nymag.com/thecut/2015/01/does-living-alone-drive-you-mad.html?mid=nymag_press. Accessed 25 March 2015
9. Kaku, M.: The Future of the Mind, p. 37. Doubleday, New York (2014)
10. Holloway, R., Anderson, P., Defendini, R., Harper, C.: Sexual dimorphism of the human corpus callosum from three independent samples: relative size of the corpus callosum. Am. J. Phys. Anthropol. **92**, 481–498 (1993)
11. DeLacoste-Utamsing, C., Holloway, R.L.: Sexual dimorphism in the human corpus callosum. Science **216**(4553), 1431–1432 (1982)
12. Eagleman, D.: Incognito: The Secret Lives of the Brain. Pantheon Books, New York (2011)
13. Howes, D.: Aestheticization takes comman. In: Howes, D. (ed.) Empire of the Senses: The Sensual Culture Reader Sensory Formations Series, pp. 245–250. Berg, Oxford and New York (2003)
14. Schiphorst, T.: Self-evidence: applying somatic connoisseurship to experience design, pp. 145–160. doi:10.1145/1979742.1979640
15. Pold, S.: Interface realisms: the interface as Aesthetic. Postmod. Cult. **15**(2), 9 (2005)
16. Kort, P.: Beuys: the profile of a successor. In: Rey, G. (ed.) Joseph Beuys: Mapping the Legacy, p. 23. D.A.P, New York (2001)
17. Stiegler, B.: Technics and Time. Stanford University Press, Calif (1998)
18. Bourriaud, N.: Postproduction - Culture as a Screenplay: How Art Reprograms the World (J. Herman Trans.), 2nd edn. Lukas and Sternberg, New York (2005)
19. Ryan, S. E., EBSCO Publishing (Firm): Garments of Paradise: Wearable Discourse in the Digital Age. The MIT Press, Cambridge (2014)
20. Flanagan, P.: The ethics of collaboration. J. Contem. Art, no. 14, 37–50 (February 2011)
21. Pold, S.: Interface realisms: the interface as aesthetic form. Postmod. Cult. **15**(2), 109 (2005)
22. Wiener, N.: The Human use of Human Beings: Cybernetics and Society. Free Association, London (1989). (Original Publication 1950)
23. Clynes, M.E., Kline, N.S.: Cyborgs and space. Astronautics, pp. 26–76 (September 1960)
24. Bennett, J.: Living in the Anthropocene. In: The Book of Books, Documenta (Exhibition) Kassel, G. 2. Documenta 13, pp. 345–357. Hatje Cantz, Ostfildern (2012)

25. Bennett, J.: Living in the Anthropocene, In: The Book of Books, Documenta (Exhibition) Kassel, G. 2. Documenta 13, p. 9. Hatje Cantz, Ostfildern (2012)
26. Greenfield, A.: Everyware: The Dawning Age of Ubiquitous Computing. New Riders, Berkeley (2006)
27. Kelley, L.: Digesting Wetlands, Paper presented at 3rd International Conference on Transdisciplinary Imaging at the Intersection of Art, Science and Culture – Cloud and Molecular Aesthetic, Pera Museum, Istanbul, Turkey (2014). Available at ocradst.org/cloudandmolecularaesthetics/digesting-wetlands/. Abstract accessed 30 August 2014
28. Milburn, C.: Nano/Splatter: disintegrating the postbiological body. In: New Literary History. Essays Probing the Boundaries of the Human in Science (Spring), vol. 36, no. 2, pp. 283–311. John Hopkins University Press (2005). Available at http://www.jstor.org/stable/20057893. Accessed 28 February 2015
29. Doyle, R.: Wetwares: Experiments in Postvital Living, vol. 24. University of Minnesota Press, Minneapolis (2003)
30. Roberts, J.: Art, 'Enclave Theory' and the communist imaginary. Third Text, Special Issue: Art, Praxis Commun. Come **23**(4), 353–367 (2009). doi:10.1080/09528820903116494
31. Gilbert, D.: Stumbling on Happiness, p. 15. Alfred A. Knopf, New York (2006)
32. Flanagan, P., Voss, M.H.: Intimacy and extimacy – the ethics, power and potential of wearable technologies. In: Barfield, W., Caudell, T. (eds.) Fundamentals of Wearable Computing and Augmented Reality, 2nd edn, p. 45. Taylor and Francis, New York (2016)

Transcending Disciplinary, Cultural and National Boundaries: Emergent Technologies, New Education Landscape and the Cloud Workshop Project

Rafael Gomez[1(✉)], Patricia Flanagan[2], and Rebekah Davis[3]

[1] Queensland University of Technology, Brisbane, Australia
r.gomez@qut.edu.au
[2] Hong Kong Baptist University, Hong Kong, China
tricia@triciaflanagan.com
[3] Griffith University, Nathan, Australia
beck.davis@griffith.edu.au

Abstract. As technology continues to become more accessible, miniaturised and diffused into the environment, the potential of wearable technology to impact our lives in significant ways becomes increasingly viable. Wearables afford unique interaction, communication and functional capabilities between users, their environment as well as access to information and digital data. Wearables also demand an inter-disciplinary approach and, depending on the purpose, can be fashioned to transcend cultural, national and spatial boundaries. This paper presents the Cloud Workshop project based on the theme of 'Wearables and Wellbeing; Enriching connections between citizens in the Asia-Pacific region', initiated through a cooperative partnership between Queensland University of Technology (QUT), Hong Kong Baptist University (HKBU) and Griffith University (GU). The project was unique due to its inter-disciplinary, inter-cultural and inter-national scope that occurred simultaneously between Australia and Hong Kong.

1 Introduction

Developing innovative methods for teaching design and creative practice within higher education is critical. The development of 21st century skills is essential in ensuring students become critically informed creative leaders capable of understanding the broader implications of technological changes of the future and respond in a creative, ethical and responsible manner. The project augments, extends and constructs learning as a result of wearable technology's affordances. To achieve this the project involved teams comprising students from visual arts, industrial design, product design, fashion design and interaction design who cooperated throughout a two-week period in an attempt to develop innovative concepts that blended art, design and technology in response to the project theme. Students were presented with a challenge to design wearables that transcend various boundaries including cultures, nations and space. In total five groups worked together across disciplines, with different cultural backgrounds

© Springer International Publishing Switzerland 2015
A. Marcus (Ed.): DUXU 2015, Part II, LNCS 9187, pp. 631–642, 2015.
DOI: 10.1007/978-3-319-20898-5_60

in two countries to explore the potential of technology from a human-computer interaction perspective. An unpacking of the workshop structure, pedagogy and final student outcomes are discussed revealing distinct benefits as well as certain learning and technological challenges. The future potential for the project within the context of human-computer interaction is outlined.

2 Technological Shifts

As technology continues to become more accessible, miniaturised and diffused into the environment, the potential of wearable devices to impact our lives in significant ways becomes increasingly viable [1, 2]. Wearables afford unique interaction, communication and functional capabilities between users, their environment as well as access to information and digital data that was previously not possible [3, 4].

Part-product, part-fashion and part-technological creations, wearables demand an inter-disciplinary approach and, depending on the purpose, can be fashioned to transcend cultural, national and spatial boundaries. It is this specific criterion that was the focus of exploration with the Cloud Workshop project developed as an inter-national, inter-cultural and inter-disciplinary collaboration.

This paper presents Cloud Workshop based on the theme of 'Wearables and Wellbeing; Enriching connections between citizens in the Asia-Pacific region' initiated by the authors as a cooperative partnership between Queensland University of Technology (QUT), Hong Kong Baptist University (HKBU) and Griffith University (GU). Through this project we explore the ways in which wearables can transcend disciplinary, cultural and distance boundaries often imposed by other types of interactive devices. We found the project permitted students to bridge distance and cultural gaps while also permitting students from various disciplines to come together to envision creative human-computer interactive art and design outcomes.

3 Classroom of the Future: Transcending Boundaries

Students were presented with a challenge to design wearables that transcended cultures, nations and space. Being in two locations separated by large distances, interdisciplinary teams were asked to create wearable concepts that functioned across, and linked through, this distance. The final solutions could not function as separate entities but rather exist as a bridge to connect the design that shared data and information through the cloud in some way.

Teams comprising various creative disciplines such as visual arts, industrial design, product design, fashion design and interaction design cooperated throughout an intensive two-week workshop. Utilising digital technologies to overcome physical distances and cultural divides, the program challenged students to envision future ideas for wearable technologies that enriched connections between citizens in the Asia-Pacific region.

Using emergent technologies as a channel for information exchange in a multitude of ways, rather than a trickle down approach to knowledge dissemination, Cloud

Workshop was based on active engagement in knowledge generation through practice based experimentation and ongoing problem solving. Hence, the focus was on sharing knowledge between participants. The educator's role, rather than hierarchical oracle, was facilitator of learning experiences. This involved creating a framework for activities to happen, as well as anticipating and responding to deficits in information or emerging roadblocks to thinking by changing pace, drawing focus or exposing participants to specialist knowledge.

From the onset of the project students gained exposure to different perspectives to the research theme from the vantage of the three facilitators' varied professional disciplines and research interests. Connecting via live digital video streaming enabled the project participants to access a wealth of shared knowledge, extending across the professors research fields as well as the participants interests and skills. Everyone's perspectives were equally valid and learning was acknowledged as a two way process. The project became coherent through a shared mindset – to move things forward.

The acceptance of difference is an inherent factor that the students first observed as the facilitators shared their views and quickly adopted themselves as they began to work in inter-disciplinary, inter-cultural, inter-national project teams. Knowledge generation became a shared activity. This is a cornerstone, coherent with a perspective that predicates "postmodern knowledge is not simply a tool of the authorities; it refines our sensitivity to difference and reinforces our ability to tolerate the incommensurable. Its principle is not the expert's homology, but the inventor's paralogy..." [5].

The ecology of working with emergent technologies, that is a feature of both the theme of the workshop (wearables) and the context of the work environment (cloud computing), is that it is defined by change. Pedagogy within the digital technology sphere is 'messy'. It is both protean – as software screens are unstable and can change rapidly; and opaque – as you can't see from the outside how it works inside. Survival in this environment involves flexibility and creativity. Teacher's primary role becomes that of change agent, activator, or accelerator. They are the designer of the context around pedagogy, content and technology. Shuman's model of Pedagogy, Content, Knowledge (PCK) is well known to educationalists, where pedagogy and content need to be brought together to enable learning [6]. The evolution in educational theory posited here contextualise Shulmans work in the contemporary paradigm, technologies deliver access to information so the teacher is no longer the sole provider of knowledge, instead they guide learners in how best to navigate the relationships between Technological Pedagogical Content Knowledge. (TPACK) is the revised acronym posited by Mishra and Koehler [7].

The Cloud Workshop project is an example of pedagogy that transcends disciplinary, cultural and national boundaries. There are other reasons to validate this approach:

1. New media and emergent technological environments are the predominant workspace where design of the future will take place.
2. Knowledge acquisition is a whole body experience, not an activity of the mind alone. Learning is an individual organic process, so contrary to the current predominant approach in education to standardise learning and to prioritise the mind

over the body, learning environments need diversity to engage the whole body physically and cognitively for creativity to thrive.

The workshop leverages the portability of online digital technology and the affordances of mobility to enable participants to engage in collective design processes where and when they choose. Within this space of learning it is never clear where the end is as information is ongoing. There are no right and wrong answers and no absolute judgements, everything is relative. Every solution leads to new problems, or opens new possibilities. It is as if the workshop door is never closed. Learning is ongoing. In the 21st century emergent technologies are constantly transforming the way we access data. Higher education and teaching is transitioning slowly compared to the adoption of these tools by society. People expect to be able to access and perform tasks, whether for work, study or play, all the time and everywhere.

The architecture of the Cloud Workshop included connecting two physical workshops, the Wearables Lab at HKBU and The Edge at the State Library of Queensland, via live video streaming. These spaces became the physical hubs for activity, facilitating live-streamed lectures, group presentations, feedback sessions and prototyping. The Cloud Workshop website (www.hifcloudworkshop.com) stored programme information, schedules, links to resources and documented the resulting projects. The Cloud Workshop Facebook page connected the workshop activities into to participant's social lives and provided a space for ongoing blogging and discussion (www.facebook.com/groups/187119418091614/). In addition the five group projects established social media platforms as workspace for their individual project and utilised shared domains in the cloud, such as Google docs, Google drive, Dropbox and the like, to facilitate exchange and work on shared drawings, documents and images.

Fig. 1. Virtual doorway set-up for pop-up exhibition (left, HK; right, AU)

The configuration of a pop-up exhibition took place in two connected galleries linked via a virtual doorway (live-stream video projection) (Fig. 1). The exhibition housed the resulting wearable design prototypes generated in the preceding two-week intensive workshop. From either gallery visitors could look into the other space through the (virtual) doorway. To launch the exhibition, group participants presented their prototypes to the audience simultaneously across the two countries. Half of each group were on either side of the virtual doorway, physical components of each project could be viewed in both galleries, and a video documentary bridged the divide by providing a complete picture of each project.

Victor Hugo predicted that "the dominant idea of each generation would, in future, be embedded in a new material…" [8]. The media of communication, the technology, is bound to the way in which we think. The cognitive process for Palaeolithic man, whose advanced technological tool was the stone axe, differs from that of Shamanic societies whose tools are objects that connect physical to spiritual worlds. Societies think differently in alphabetic systems than those who adopted ideographic writing systems. Different cognitive processes evolved once we developed handwriting, which restructured consciousness in that it produced a form of retention. This dramatically shifted again with the widespread use of the printing press. In the digital era retention and dissemination are altered again. In each case accessibility to knowledge creates different forms of politically coherent communities. "Thinking is conditioned but not determined by technical conditions" [9].

The Cloud Workshop project augments, extends and constructs learning as a result of wearable technology's affordances. Many of the boundaries that define the limitations of conventional classroom-based teaching are overcome. Restrictions to learning are based largely on educational foundations that were designed for 20th century industrialisation where the aim was to standardise learning and produce workers for different levels of society. The focus on producing uniformity is at odds with societies need to stimulate creative minds to continue the organic evolution and intelligence of our species. "Implicit in electronic culture is the idea of multilevel participation in the creative process" [10]. In the 21st century the roles of work and life are evolving. Factories are becoming automated and robots will do much of the work of the future. In fact, the word 'robot' comes from the Czech word for 'worker' (appearing in the title of a 1920's play by Karel Capek) [11]. We live in a globalised world and students in the creative fields need to engage in learning in global and connected contexts so as to meet the demands of the 21st century economy.

4   IoT, Emergent Technologies and Future Practice

As objects and artifacts become increasingly interconnected and the Internet of Things (IoT) takes hold, new markets are emerging and new modes of teaching and learning are also being developed. The potential implications of ubiquitous technological interactions via tangible and ambient media have never been more real or more accessible [12]. Within this frame, wearable technology is an "emerging interdisciplinary field, bringing together concepts and expertise from a variety of disciplines, ranging from materials science, through computer engineering to textile design" [13]. Wearables that live on, near or in our bodies give rise to a previously unimaginable level of data about people and environments not previously available. By enabling the connection of divergent data sets, wearables provide life-augmenting levels of interactivity [12].

Providing an opportunity for students to engage with the emergent technologies is critical given Hughes' assertion that "artifacts are socially malleable when industries are young, but resistant to social influence once they have matured" [14]. Given the techno-social implications of wearable technology, the workshop made an attempt to introduce students to critical theory of technology [15] and understandings surrounding technology and the lifeworld [16]. To do this, as outlined in Sect. 2, a learning context that explored the implications of connectivity, interactivity and cross-cultural collaboration was established through a physical yet temporal 'cloud' based teaching environment. Within this experimental classroom, students from the three universities were brought together, organised into multi-disciplinary teams and issued with a project brief. By attending Cloud Workshop, students were encouraged to engage both physically (design through making) and virtually (design through collaboration). This physical/virtual collaborative 'space' provided a unique opportunity for students to learn about wearable technology, associate technologies, future practice and interdisciplinary collaboration. Academically, it was anticipated that problematising 'connections through wearable technology' would provide a platform for rich exploration and investigation into the realm of future technology and associate potential scenarios.

Table 1. Group divisions and theme

Group	Project description	Students	Outcome
Techlace (n = 6)	Displays the wearer's emotions to assist communication between strangers or across different cultures	1 × QUT 2 × GU 3 × HKBU	Prototype - accessory and garment
Illumine (n = 5)	An attempt at sustainable wearable costume that explores connections between people to enhance large scale events (e.g. music festivals) and create digital surfaces made up of hundreds of people, each becoming as a pixel on a screen	1 × QUT 2 × GU 2 × HKBU	Prototype - Origami folded paper - worn garment (various combinations)
Sine Language (n = 6)	A sophisticated glove and neck garment used to break down language barriers between cultures through the use of persistence of vision	2 × QUT 2 × GU 2 × HKBU	Prototype - dress in combination with glove (predominantly an accessory)
Ignite (n = 5)	A dance garment that enhanced the dancers' movements and actions and transmitted this information across countries	2 × QUT 1 × GU 2 × HKBU	Prototype - dance costume, worn garment
Gutan (n = 5)	An exploratory fashion garment and bracelet that evokes ideas of celebration and friendship. It transmitted various messages from bracelet to wearable garment to connect people across the globe	1 × QUT 2 × GU 2 × HKBU	Prototype - 3D printed bracelet, accessory

Simultaneous connections between Australia and Hong Kong were achieved by organising the students into five groups, consisting of students from each university (QUT, GU and HKBU). A breakdown of each group, theme, distribution per institution and outcome is provided in Table 1. As illustrated in this table, each group maintained a unique approached to the set task. For the purpose of this paper, three projects; (i) Techlace, (ii) Sine Language, and (iii) Illumine, are explored as exemplars of concepts that attempt to confront ideas of cultural, national and spatial boundaries.

Techlace. The mantra underpinning the concept direction of Techlace is "feelings are beautiful, why hide them?". To serve this purpose, Techlace was created as a necklace and dress combination prototype to convey emotions through visual non-verbal cues using the process of illumination (Figs. 2 and 3). By centring the design on non-verbal approaches to conveying emotion, the team were able to transcend cultural boundaries as the point of 'communication' exists between the necklace of one wearer and the dress worn by another. This concept aimed to help people understand one another and to understand if they are being offensive in another country (they are not familiar with) and/or enable shy people to easily express emotion (refer Fig. 3). The necklace component was designed in Brisbane and the dress component in Hong Kong.

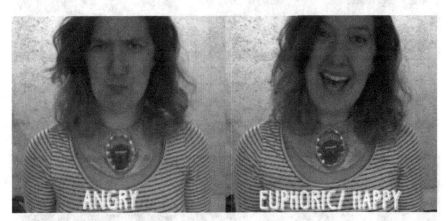

Fig. 2. Techlace expressing emotions 'angry' and 'euphoric/happy' (Australia)

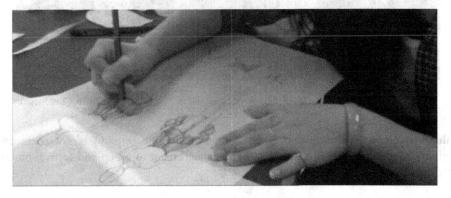

Fig. 3. Techlace dress design (Hong Kong)

Sine Language. Sine language centred on breaking down language barriers between cultures by developing a sophisticated glove and headpiece as a method of interacting in order to facilitate non-verbal communication between people. Through persistence of vision technology, the glove was designed to send a message (Fig. 4). As a wearer's hand moves, a visual representation of a word is created (in a nominated language), and the headpiece subsequently receives the message and transmits a reaction/response (Fig. 5). The glove is designed so it can be programmed and configured to represent different languages, depending on the context, as illustrated in Fig. 5.

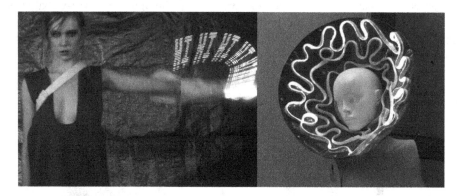

Fig. 4. Sine Language transmission in English "Hi" (left, AU) and headpiece receiving (right, HK)

Fig. 5. Visual representation of the glove capabilities "Nei Hou" (Hello in Cantonese)

Illumine. Unlike Techlace and Sine Language, Illumine (Fig. 6) is not so much person-to-person communication, rather the enhancement of group and festival-based experience.

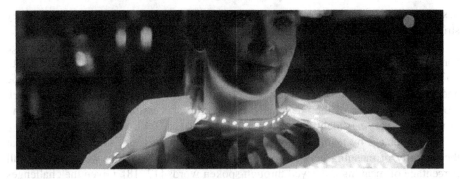

Fig. 6. Illumine, worn item is equivalent to one pixel (refer Fig. 7)

Fig. 7. Illumine, example of collective visual display

Illumine is designed to enhance interactions between people at public events. Using this product, each person at the event becomes a co-contributor to the immersive nature of the space. The garment worn individually acts as a collective visual display as people gather and coalesce to experience the festival or concert, with each person effectively becoming a 'pixel' in a larger display at the event (Fig. 7). As illustrated in Fig. 6, Illumine when worn, rests across the users' shoulders. This proposed design is made of paper and is recyclable to enhance sustainability of the 'one off' festival event item.

5   Observations and Discussion

In each instance, the student teams identified future opportunities for wearables that promote and assist non-verbal modes of communicating. The focus of each prototype to enrich connections 'visually', are mostly likely, due to the workshop framework centred on working in cross-cultural interdisplinary teams. The creative outcomes produced also attempted to transcend the distance boundaries by sharing and transferring data and information across the two locations. This particular aspect of the design however, appeared to pose significant challenges for the groups, as they struggled to successfully blend ideas that were culturally sensitive or meaningful.

Working in mixed teams was challenging given the different time zones, language barriers and varying levels of skill and capabilities. In most cases groups had limited to no knowledge of coding, sensors, arduinos or programming, resulting in limited scope and understanding of how to 'apply' the preferred technology at a sophisticated level. However, regardless of the challenges, each group successfully produced a working prototype of varying fidelity.

The emphasis by teams on non-verbal communication is not surprising given that the majority of meaning between people is conveyed non-verbally with only a small percentage of meaning conveyed through spoken words [17, 18]. Given the challenges faced by teams during Skype meetings, it is logical to assume this inspired the non-verbal focus of the proposed wearable prototypes. Moreover, it can be argued that each prototype pertained "telepresence" as the resultant of each team was a form of mediation of experiences of geographically dispersed agents. Teams achieved this by ameliorating their physical and/or psychological proximity through particular communication technologies [17, 19, 20].

Finally, it is believed that the workshop success was co-dependent on an effective integration of pedagogical and technological objectives. Embedding technology within a block delivery program run parallel in differing countries – was both intense and highly productive. Communicative and technological struggles aside (i.e., lack of programming knowledge, and or understanding of sensors), students commented during and post-event about their productivity, their pride in the outcomes as well as their surprise at what was achieved in the short timeframe. The inclusion of technology and non-technology related items as part of the collaborative learning process links well with current research that cites a need to increase the use of IT for educational purposes [21]. While this observation is positive, it is clear that establishing richer links between the use of technology and desired educational outcomes [21] are needed.

6 Conclusion and Future Work

Wearables afford unique interaction, communication and functional capabilities between users and their environment with the capacity to drastically impact people's lives. This paper outlined Cloud Workshop, which focused on utilising wearables as a source of creative inspiration for art and design students to explore the transcendence of disciplinary, cultural and national boundaries.

Developing innovative methods for teaching creative practice is critical in the 21st century that will ensure students become more critically informed creative leaders capable of understanding the broader implications of emerging technologies. The ecology of working with new media, that is a feature of both the theme of the workshop (wearables) and the context of the work environment (cloud computing), is that it is defined by change. As a result the workshop was based on active engagement in knowledge generation through practice based experimentation and ongoing problem solving.

In all, five groups presented projects varying in scope and approach. The paper highlights three projects including Techlace, Sine Language and Illumine, as exemplars of wearable creations that offer novel ways of interaction. In each instance, the student teams identified future opportunities for wearables that promote and assist non-verbal modes of communicating.

Cloud workshop was largely successful but further developments are needed. Any success is co-dependent on an effective integration of pedagogical and technological objectives. Students commented during and post-event about their productivity, their pride in the outcomes as well as their surprise at what was achieved in the short timeframe. Nevertheless, there were distinct communicative and technological struggles. It was also clear that establishing richer links between the use of technology and desired educational outcomes [21] are needed. Future versions of the workshop are already planned. Three main elements considered for change in the next round include preparing more thoroughly for the cultural exchange between students, providing more structure around project themes, and supporting students with expert knowledge around coding. It is hoped these changes will improve the pedagogical and learning outcomes and result in improved and more sophisticated wearable prototypes. Technology and creativity are the drivers of the Cloud Workshop, and as [22] highlighted "new technologies have had an immense impact on the how we live, work and communicate… " and it is for this reason that "teaching and learning in this emerging world needs to emphasize these twin issues—technology and creativity" [22].

References

1. Swan, M.: Sensor mania! The internet of things, wearable computing, objective metrics, and the quantified self 2.0. J. Sens. Actuator Netw. **1**(3), 217–253 (2012)
2. Wei, J.: How wearables intersect with the cloud and the internet of things: considerations for the developers of wearables. Consum. Electron. Mag. IEEE **3**(3), 53–56 (2014)
3. Chen, C.Y., Tsai, W.L.: The key success factors of wearable computing devices: An user-centricity perspective. In: WHICEB Proceedings Paper 50 (2014)
4. Wallace, J.E.: Exploring the design potential of wearable technology and functional fashion. Doctoral dissertation, University of Cincinnati (2014)
5. Lyotard, J.F.: The Postmodern Condition: A Report on Knowledge. Manchester University Press, Manchester (1984)
6. Shulman, L.S.: Those who understand: Knowledge growth in teaching. Educ. Res. **15**(2), 4–14 (1986)
7. Mishra, P., & Koehler, M.J.: Introducing technological pedagogical content knowledge. Paper presented the Annual Meeting of the American Educational Research Association, New York, March 24–28 (2008)
8. Hugo, V.: Notre Dame de Paris. Vol. XII. Harvard Classics Shelf of Fiction. P.F. Collier & Son, New York, Accessed Feb 15, 2015 (1917) www.Bartleby.com/br/312.html
9. Steigler, B.: Hermeneutics, heuristics and paideia in the digital episteme. In: Presentation at *Creating Minds*, Conference on Reading and Writing in the Digital World, University of California, Berkeley, 23 Oct Accessed 14 Feb 2015 (2013) https://www.youtube.com/watch?v=FjIsiHzOS1g

10. Gould, G.: Strauss and the Electronic Future. The Saturday Review, New York, pp. 58–59 (1964)
11. Kaku, M.: The Future of The Mind: The Scientific Quest to Understand, Enhance, and Empower the Mind. Doubleday, New York (2014)
12. Davis, B., Gomez, R.: Wearable technology: the next frontier? Design online, Accessed 6 March 2015 (2014) http://designonline.org.au/content/wearable-technology-the-next-frontier/
13. Smith, D.: Smart clothes and wearable technology. Artif. Intell. Soc. **22**, 1–3 (2007)
14. Cavanagh, T.: Diverse designing: sorting out function and intention in artifacts. In: Vermaas, P.E., Kroes, P., Light, A., Moore, S.A. (eds.) Philosophy and Design: from Engineering to Architecture. Springer, Netherlands (2008)
15. Feenberg, A.: Transforming Technology: A Critical Theory Revisited. Oxford University Press, Oxford (2002)
16. Idhe, D.: Technology and the Lifeworld: From Garden to Earth. Bloomington, Indiana (1990)
17. Heiss, L.: Enabled apparel: the role of digitally enhanced apparel in promoting remote empathic connection. Artif. Intell. Soc. **22**, 15–24 (2007)
18. Charlesworth, J.: Wearables as "relationship tools". Artif. Intell. Soc. **22**, 63–84 (2007)
19. Milne, E.: Email and Epistolary Technologies: Presence, Intimacy. Disembodiment, Fibreculture J. (2003). 2
20. Steuer, J.: Defining virtual reality: dimensions determinin telepresence. J. Commun. **42**, 73–93 (1992)
21. Laird, T.F.N., Kuh, G.D.: Student experiences with information technology and their relationship to other aspects of student engagment. Res. High. Educ. **46**, 211–233 (2005)
22. Mishra, P., The Deep-Play Research Group: Rethinking technology & creativity in the 21st century: Crayons are the future. TechTrends **56**(5), 13–16 (2012)

Digital Craftsmanship
The Making of Incunabula, a Fully 3D Printed Wearable Dress

Tobias Klein[(⊠)]

School of Creative Media, City University of Hong Kong, Kowloon, Hong Kong
office@kleintobias.com

Abstract. The paper discusses the possibilities for 3D printing to help over-come the historic schism between manual labour/craftsmanship versus tech-nology, specifically its potential to enable digital craftsmanship. Firstly, It contextualizes digital craftsmanship and introduces debates relating to tooling, application and design strategies, in particular in the field of architecture. Sec-ondly, the paper articulates digital craftsmanship's properties and associated strategies by discussing three examples of the author's work. Lastly, it draws attention to the confluence of these properties and agencies through an analysis of the design and 3D printing of a fully wearable dress, titled Incunabula.

Keywords: 3D printing · Digital craftsmanship

1 Digital Craftsmanship – Context

Since the beginning of modernism and the associated industrial revolution, the growing separation of form-making from material condition has been seen as opposed to craft production. Sennet's definition of a process in which the practitioner is deeply invested in the outcome and takes care to do excellent work was superseded [1]. A continuous development led to modernism's tenets such as form following function and concurrently concept associated with ancient craft, such as integrating material properties with construction methods were lost.

Accelerated by the digital revolution, this widening gap between form and matter eventually resulted in the failure of digital form [2]. At the same time, the questioning of form led to alternative design approaches that prioritized material-based design computation and to a re-thinking of craftsmanship in digital environments [3, 4].

Arguably, 3D printing technology has created and facilitated a new, material-based approach to design. It has become one of the core technologies in the burgeoning maker culture [5]. This marks an important change in how we articulate design and making and is widely seen as counter-acting an industry-led decline of craftsmanship by enabling the democratising process of individual making. Both ease of use and availability of soft- and hardware for 3D print, coupled with a marked decline in associated costs of such printing in recent years, has led to significant changes in the creative and design industries. Virtually all areas of design have been affected, from the sole-trader and domestic settings up to much larger scale like Academia or industry

© Springer International Publishing Switzerland 2015
A. Marcus (Ed.): DUXU 2015, Part II, LNCS 9187, pp. 643–654, 2015.
DOI: 10.1007/978-3-319-20898-5_61

level. Not surprisingly, therefore, 3D printing has been called a disruptive technology and a 'game changer' by one of the most significant economic reports in the industry [6], making it evident that additive manufacturing will optimize existing manufacturing industries because of its flexibility. One such example is that 25 % of current Boeing airplane parts are being 3D printed, saving significant costs in material, time and weight. The technology facilitates alternative models of production and organization and also alternative models for start-ups that can have lower initial set-up costs and be able to rapidly produce high quality product that rival existing cost-intensive design to manufacturing methods. This phenomenon is creating a wealth of creativity in all sectors and across scales and is unarguably a catalyst for new developments and the optimization of existing processes.

However, within this digital revolution of designing and creating, making and manufacturing, it is important to acknowledge that the optimization of existing designs is still prevalent, as opposed to the design of completely new objects. This is exemplified by the number of 3D prints that are digital replicas of existing objects, uploaded onto democratized maker websites such as Thingyverse or Google warehouse [7]. This suggests that the current state of 3D printing favors a model of replication and the automation of previously criticized modernism, in contrast to any realization of 3D print's potential to reactivate values and qualities of a craftsmanship.

In the fields of architecture and architectural research, the global discourse about digital craftsmanship is characterized by diametrically opposed views, but at the same time is applicable to other design disciplines. On the one hand, there is the thesis that digital craftsmanship translates as digital construction in architecture today, which continues an architectural tradition [8]. This leads to more sophisticated CAD/CAM procedures involving robotic arms and even UAVs, commonly referred to as drones, erecting brick walls in a new process of construction. This view favors a mechanistic approach and tool-based debate about craftsmanship that sees it as a coherent and planned method of constructing and managing digital production.

The opposite view, which highlights the level skillfulness needed to use 3D modeling tools is also referred to as digital craftsmanship and values what some may term digital bravado [9]. Remarkably, both views seem to only marginally take into account ideas of craftsmanship as a cultural heritage that has extensive relationships between art and technology.

The following examples illustrate the current polarized discussion surrounding digital craftsmanship and the properties associated with this craftmanship. In their work, Subdivided column, Dillenburger and Hansmeyer achieve a synthesis of formal and material properties through advanced use of altered subdivision algorithms, using 2D laser cutting technology to craft and assemble a series of large-scale columns made of cardboard. The result is a mesmerizing start of a much larger work of art in which the genesis of its immersive quality lies within its formal and material properties.

A further example that attests to digital craftsmanship is their more recent work, Digital Grotesque, currently exhibited in the FRAAC, Orleans (2014). It presents the first fully 3D printed human scale environment using Voxeljet's sand based 3D printing [10]. While it lacks detail and material sophistication compared to other 3D printed works, its scale and inclusive character are a milestone for the development of 3D printing as a form of craftsmanship in Architecture [11]. As the makers' state,

A unique language of form is developed that transcends rationality and celebrates spatial expression: a digital exuberance [12].

The term digital exuberance is a fitting term to describe the qualities of digital craftsmanship that they explore, specifically, the culturally articulated symmetrical arrangement, reminiscent of the baroque period allows speculation into a new craftsmanship led design in architecture to come.

While Dillenburger and Hansmeyer work at fully immersive scale and, through the use of algorithms, develop a homogenous quality of a total work of art, the works of Marjan Colletti, close the gap between optimization, technology and art. He advocates research by design into the digital grotesque and convoluted, as he describes it, and articulates craftsmanship within 3D print by addressing cultural values [13]. It is his culturally embedded understanding that differentiates his architectural approach to craftsmanship from making that depends upon a functionally oriented input-output objectivity. Colletti is not hindered by a simple input-output mechanistic approach but advocates the masterful use of all tools without restrictions to their genesis. He does this within a cultural framework of operation, for example allowing style periods from the baroque and Rococo to influence and characterize his works.

2 Digital Craftsmanship – Qualities

Three projects made by the author are now described in order to demonstrate procedures, references, techniques and strategies unique to digital craftsmanship. All of the following are governed by bringing together contemporary CAD techniques and CAD/CAM technologies with sensitivities to site and with culturally-specific design narratives, intuitive non-linear design processes, and historical architectural references. Here, the creator-craftsman takes on a multiplicity of roles, including architect, designer and cultural agitator and by so doing finally has the chance to overcome the fifteenth- and sixteenth-century separation between intellectual and manual labour. This model for being a digital craftsman also bridges the nineteenth-century gulf between automatic mechanization and poetic creation.

2.1 The Integration and Transition Between Actual Objects and Materiality and Digital Models in the form of 3D Scanning and the Implementation in a 3D Print Workflow

In 2006, we created and 3D printed a series of works titled, *Synthetic Syncretism*. The work argues for what, in theological research, is commonly referred to as the merging or synthesis of two entirely different cultural and religious frameworks into a hybrid belief system, known as a syncretic religion (examples of such include the Santeria in Cuba, a merging of Catholicism and Yoruba based religion, and many more). In the context of a digital craftsmanship, the syncretism between the craft and the digital is at the center of this work. The dichotomy between the direct physicality of manual craft and objects and the virtual nature of digital based work is epitomized in the work by using 3D scanning and the incorporation of physical, biological artefacts into the working process.

This body of work subsequently became the foundation for a series of explorations into the use of 3D printing as a new tool in the expression what we term today, digital craftsmanship. *Synthetic Syncretism* is a speculative architectural project that articulates, through the creation of a series of 3D printed objects, ranging in scale from model to prototype, a culturally embedded understanding of digital craftsmanship.

The project establishes a relationship between a culturally based craftsmanship and local narratives, rituals, biological remains and 3D printing. The starting point is a local burial culture in Havana, Cuba and hybrid religion, Santeria. Initial studies of this syncretic religion showed rituals centered on the dual worshipping of catholic Saints as deities in the Sanitarian religion. Visits to the local cemetery, the Necropolis de Cristobal Colon, revealed rituals including animal sacrifices with the physical bone remains of these found scattered in the graveyard. The fragments and traces of these rituals were collected by the author and brought back to London. The procedure of scanning the remains into a digital format compatible with 3D software did not exist at the time but is fairly standard today. The time intensive 3D scanning included the processing from point-cloud data into precise data mesh models with 0.1 mm tolerance. The resulting mesh data was operational using commonly available digital software platforms such as 3D Studio Max or equal mesh modelling software used in the animation industries (see. Fig. 1).

In the technical framework of the project *Synthetic Syncretism* and the debate around digital craftsmanship, the translation from actual biological fragments to a digital data set, is comparable with the creation of a mold for casting in sculpture or taking measurements during the design of a garment. The very fabric of the project stems from the rituals of its cultural background and the translation from the mortal physical remains to the scale-less, ephemeral digital is a significant step. The artwork expresses site specific narratives and simultaneously creates a cultural framework for 'reading' craftsmanship.

As one can see from the right side of the illustration (Fig. 1), in the next step the digital skeletal form is used as a starting point for digital mimicry and sculpting.

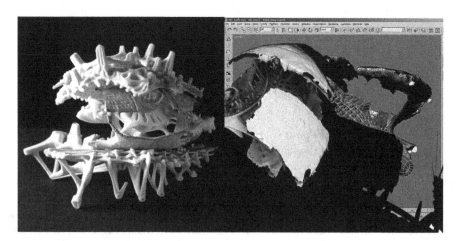

Fig. 1. 3D Scan of found tortoise shell and 3D Print using artificial sandstone by Z-corp within the bone structure of the tortoise shell.

Through a process similar to the physical building up of a clay model, yet relating to the existing digital scan, the added sculpture is 3D modeled along the digital bone structures to form vessels, embedded within the virtual data of the skeletal remains. In the case of the tortoise shell (Fig. 1), the process also included the de-construction of the individual bone segments to fit newly 3D printed organs and vessels back into the naturally grown shell and its later re-construction.

2.2 The Changed Relationship Between Materials and Tooling and Resulting Collaborative Designs that Would not be Able to be Produced Using Processes Other Than 3D Printing

In the framework of a competition, organized by the Sir John Soane Museum in London, we collaborated with a recent jewelry graduate from the Royal College of Art, Silvia Weidenbach, to create the work GLOW (Fig. 2). The work is a new translation of the traditional relationship between hand and intellect as a feedback mechanism in craft, and shows the advantages such a digital translation might yield. The work was entirely conceived using Computer Aided Design (CAD) packages and no model was built and no physicality was tested before the final 3D print. This complete transition from physical to digital form might be seen as a controversial form of digital craftsmanship. As Richard Sennett puts it:

> "Every good Craftsman conducts a Dialogue between concrete practices and thinking, this Dialogue evolves into sustaining habits, and these habits establish a rhythm between problem solving and problem finding [1]".

Thus the continuous dialogue between material properties, the manual and intellectual feedback, defines craft and seemingly stands in opposition to the lack of materiality within such digital crafting. When articulating craft, the interface or tool is a

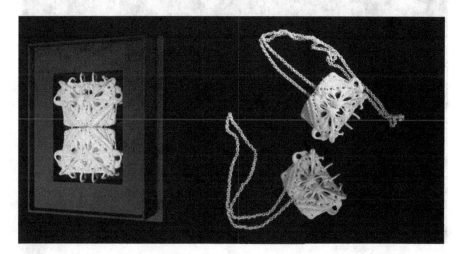

Fig. 2. 'GLOW' commissioned by the Sir John Soane Museum and in collaboration with Silvia Weidenbach.

vital part of craftsmanship and was the main problem in the translation, is that the traditional craft of Ms. Weidenbach was incompatible with standard interface tools and computer peripherals such as the mouse and keyboard. To address this, using the facilities of the Royal College of Art, we replaced the 2D mouse interface with a haptic device by Geomagics [14]. This interface tool facilitates fully 3D free movement and feedback via a controlled robotic arm. Through registering the resistance of the digital material which is shown on the screen in front of Ms Weidenbach, and through allowing full 3D movement, we translated the haptic feedback inherent to the traditional material approach and translated her experience of the craft of traditional jewelry as part of our collaboration. Through these changes to interface and tool, we extended traditional techniques like symmetry to expand the traditional craft.

GLOW is a symmetrical mirrored object that, by breaking the object in half at the designed break points becomes 2 necklaces. The object can only be produced using 3D printing as the action of breaking the object releases complete 3D printed chains for both necklaces that are stored in the interior of the previously closed object (Fig. 2).

2.3 The Ability to Articulate and Craft Non-related Data Sets Within a Set Cultural Referential Framework, Resulting in a Hybrid Non-scalar, yet Referential Construct

Through the work, Contoured Embodiment (Fig. 3), we explore the potential of digital craftsmanship to transcend the scale and origin of scanned objects and its ability to translate and graft different data-sets within a specific cultural framework.

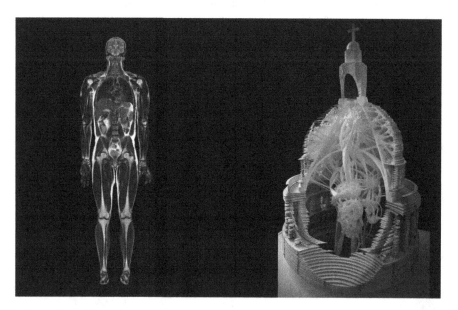

Fig. 3. Author's Magnetic Resonance Image Scan and the work Contoured embodiment using the Author's MRI Scanned data in a model of St Paul's Cathedral in London.

By contrast to the previous that introduced procedures to scan the surface of an object and translate it into a shell like 3D model, Contoured Embodiment uses Magnetic Resonance Image Scans of the author's own body. These scans have the advantage of creating volumetric data sets in the sense that they are creating not a surface driven model, but one using Voxels to articulate spatial and material density [15].

The work uses the author's heart in the cultural framework of the iconography of the Catholic Sacred Heart of Jesus, it places the biologically-derived artefact into the cultural context of the ecclesial architecture of Sir Christopher Wren's baroque masterpiece, St Paul's Cathedral. The resulting gradient voxel data of the author's own body becomes a digital embodiment that bridges between iconography, structure, scale and biology. This work transfers the volumetric medical data of the human body, re-articulating scale and properties. Through imitation and the crafting of ventricular connections it fits the biological artefact with surgical precision into the architectural model of St. Paul's Cathedral. The architecture of the ecclesial space, often compared to the corpus Christi, becomes the garment of a translated embodied data set.

3   Incunabula - A Dress Using Digital Craftsmanship

The London College of Fashion's invitation to respond, from the perspective of fashion, to Rem Koolhaas's brief, Absorbing Modernity: 1914 – 2014, offered an ideal opportunity to test some of the ideas and methods that are referred to as properties of digital craftsmanship and the amalgamation of craft as a technique and digital manufacturing. In particular, the questioning of Modernity as a dominant force in design today was a key element in the design of the dress, which was designed as an evolution and translation from the traditional hand-craftsmanship of Irish crochet techniques into 3D printed technologies. It required the transfer from an intricate textile design, based on a single thread, into a volumetric manufacturing technique without the loss of historic context. At the same time the work had to be achieved without the replication of a technique and design to make a different material, as criticized by the author in the first part of the paper. Koolhaas's oppositional argument to modernity resulted in the building of a false suspended office ceiling beneath a Venetian dome. It resolutely visualises the contradiction between art and engineering and the dilemma of a craftsmanship in modernity. Against the background of that debate, the hybrid design of Incunabula poses the question about the relationship between art and technology in the framework of digital craftsmanship.

Incunabula differs tremendously to other 3D printed fashion designs, in its materiality as well as in the techniques and craftsmanship used to produce the dress. Currently, wearable design that is 3D printed is commonly designed in two ways. One, seen in some of the works of Iris van Herpen and Daniel Widrig, uses a shell like print that allows very little flexibility but a great detail [16]. The second type of design differs to the first in that it is able to be flexible, via a subdivided approach. When looking at existing 3D printed fashion, particularly in regard to the recent published work, Kinematic Dress, by Nervous System, supported by Shapeways [17], one can see that the designs rely on mechanical connections such as hinges or chainmail-like

Fig. 4. Stills of the film made by SHOWstudio from the dress Incunabula http://showstudio. com/project/1914_now.

arrangements. Both approaches are based on the fact that, to date, very little 3D printable substrates or filaments exist that combine the material properties of fibers, specifically to be flexible yet strong enough not to rip apart under stress.

When approached to design the dress and to collaborate with Joris Debo, Creative Director of Materialise, we faced the challenge of completely re-inventing this tried and tested typology, as the material we would use is a flexible thermo-polymer that combine the above mentioned properties of flexibility and strength. The result is a multi-layered main fabric, with the addition of a large interlocked bib, referencing the common use of Irish Crochet to be implemented into wedding gowns at the time, as well as the addition of articulated arms that would eventually be used to connect the 3D printed fabric to a pleated organza (Fig. 4).

3.1 Geometric Design of the Pattern and Relation to the Bending in Two Directions

To design a fabric using a flexible material meant that, instead of an arrangement of static elements that are interwoven as described, Incunabula uses a balance between the material's own flexibility and a multilayered textile design to generate flexibility in two directions. It uses two interlocking and articulated layers of material, imitating the base structure of a crochet and the interwoven details and floral patterns.

The first layer of the fabric uses the idea of a multidirectional base grid of cells that are elongated hexagons. The individual grid cells start at the top of the garment, arranged at a 45 degree angle and change with every row till they are orthogonal. The idea behind the dress is to express verticality in the fabric by rotating each individual cell row by row by 5 degrees. (Figure 6 right side) The cell size also changes in a

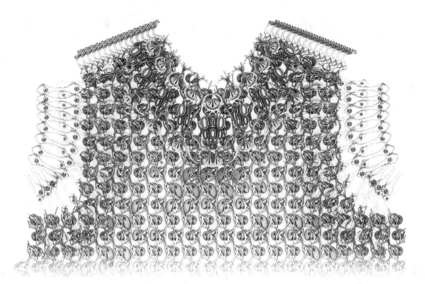

Fig. 5. Complete upper part of the overlaid 3D printed fabric layers including the bib and arms

continuous gradient, cells are vertically connected, yet only in the last third of the dress are they also partially horizontally connected (Fig. 5). We will refer to this first layer of the garment as the matrix (a). This matrix is able to achieve visually the same continuity as we can see in the crochet techniques of the time, yet it also allows a high degree of flexibility that shapes the dress according to the human body. The arrangement of connections vertically, yet not horizontally, allows the smallest curves of the body to be described, while also allowing the design to stretch and alter the visibility through the crochet-like material.

The second layer, matrix (b), is constructed as a series of 3 different sized, interconnected volumetric dots. The dots are designed to have a main body that is changing in size, a hook to connect to matrix (a), similar to Velcro-tape, and a connecting stem leading to a secondary grid. While the material is a flexible 3D print, it contains enough flexibility, yet toughness for these hooks to be interlocked with the hexagonal grid of matrix (a). The difference in sizes of the elements expresses the idea of creating transparency and opacity through variation of the sizes and thus allows the fabric to be more porous where the size of the hook is smaller and appear more opaque at locations and areas with the larger hooks. Additionally, the dots are similar to the described cells of matrix (a), rotating clock and anti-clockwise, row by row, imitating the gradual shift common to crochet techniques. Furthermore, the grid connecting the dots also rotates from a 45 degree oriented grid, connecting the dots, to a parallel grid at the end of the dress as shown in Fig. 6 sample A, B and C. In conclusion, we articulated variety and diversity through the introduction of rotating and mirroring elements and additionally created ornamental diversity, through the different sizing of the dots. We extended the possibility of articulating these even further by connecting the dots with a layered sub-matrix (Fig. 6).

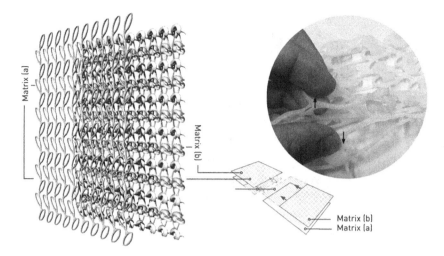

Fig. 6. Construction of the multi-layered 3D printed fabric using vertical and lateral connectivity to achieve flexibility and diversity.

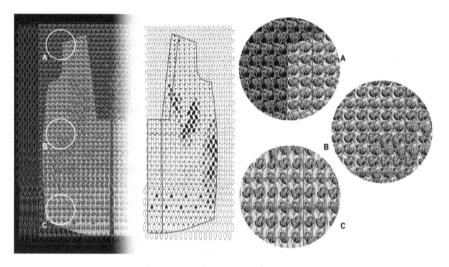

Fig. 7. Combined illustration of Alexandra Verschueren's sketch and translations into the grid matrix (a) and (b), excerpts of the rotating grid cells and dot articulation.

3.2 Production and Assembly

A further reason for this multi-layered approach in the design of a 3D printed fabric that translates the values and properties of Irish Crochet techniques, lies within the machining and associated building box sizes. At the current level of technology, it is not yet feasible to produce large-scale versions of 3D printers for a high definition print. The maximum build envelope in the machine we used, the EOS FORMIGA P110, is 200 mm × 250 mm with a maximum building height of 330 mm. In order not to have to stich the various pieces together using a thread, we developed a system of overlaying pieces of separated matrix (a) and (b) (Fig. 5). This allowed us, through the horizontal disconnection of matrix (a) and the ability to reconnect using the hooks within matrix (b), to create a fabric that behaves assembled as if being 3D printed in one go. It furthermore helped to work economically as well as ecologically (through the minimization of off-cut material). The pieces were 3D printed and assembled using a precise catalogue overlapping elements (Fig. 6, left side) (Fig. 7).

3.3   Conclusion

In conclusion, the dress is an experiment in translating the traditional and highly intricate craftsmanship of specific textile construction to the precision and material properties of a 3D printed craft. While acknowledging the qualities of the craft of Irish crochet, the author does not attempt to imitate or create a replica as seen often in 3D printing, yet attempts to design according to the material and digital constraints in as much as described by Sennet's work on the idea and construction of craftsmanship and thus constitutes a work in the field of digital craftsmanship.

Acknowledgments. We would like to thank the project team of Incunabula, consisting of fashion curator Kaat Debo, ModeMuseum Antwerp, fashion designer Alexandra Verschueren, 3D-printing manufacturer Materialise, under the supervision of Creative Director Joris Debo, Prof. Kurt Vanhoutte, University of Antwerp and the film director Marie Schuller for SHOWstudio. The dress was made into a film, shot by SHOWstudio, directed by Marie Schuller, and was shown at the Venice Biennale 2014 and can be seen at: http://showstudio.com/project/1914_now.

References

1. Sennett, R.: The Craftsman. Yale University Press, New Haven (2008)
2. Aureli, P.V.: Architecture and Content: Who's Afraid of the Form-Object? Log, 29–36 (2004)
3. Oxman, N.: Digital craft: Fabrication-based design in the age of digital production. In: Workshop Proceedings for Ubicomp 2007: International Conference on Ubiquitous Computing, pp. 534–538 (2007)
4. Oxman, N.: Material-based design computation. Massachusetts Institute of Technology (2010)
5. Tanenbaum, J.G., et al.: Democratizing technology: pleasure, utility and expressiveness in DIY and maker practice. In: Proceedings of the SIGCHI Conference on Human Factors in Computing Systems, pp. 2603–2612 (2013)
6. Wohlers, T., Caffrey, T.: Additive Manufacturing and 3D Printing State of the Industry Annual Worldwide Progress Report. Wohlers Associates, Fort Collins (2013)
7. Killi, S., Morrison, A.: Models for product design and development in Additive Manufacturing. In: High Value Manufacturing: Advanced Research in Virtual and Rapid Prototyping: Proceedings of the 6th International Conference on Advanced Research in Virtual and Rapid Prototyping, Leiria, Portugal, p. 405, 1–5 October, 2013
8. Gramazio, F., Kohler, M.: Digital Materiality in Architecture. Lars Muller, Baden (2008)

9. Alonso, H.D.: "Close Up." Architectural Design 84.4, pp. 62–67. John Wiley & Sons (2014)
10. Voxeljet, company website. http://www.voxeljet.de/en/case-studies/case-studies/entirely-3d-printed-room/
11. Garcia, M. (ed.): Future Details of Architecture. Wiley, Chichester (2014)
12. Dillenburger, B., Hansmeyer, M.: The resolution of architecture in the digital age. In: Zhang, J., Sun, C. (eds.) CAAD Futures 2013. CCIS, vol. 369, pp. 347–357. Springer, Heidelberg (2013)
13. Colletti, M.: Exuberance and digital virtuosity. Architectural Des. **80**(2), 8–15 (2010)
14. Geomagics, company website. http://geomagic.com/en/products-landing-pages/haptic
15. Caon, M.: Voxel-based computational models of real human anatomy: a review. Radiat. Environmental Biophys. **42**(4), 229–235 (2004)
16. Su, N., Pirani, N.: Emergence of 3D Printed Fashion: Navigating the Ambiguity of Materiality Through Collective Design (2013)
17. Nervous System corporate website. http://n-e-r-v-o-u-s.com/projects/sets/kinematics-dress/

Designing a Vibrotactile Language
for a Wearable Vest

Ann Morrison[1]([✉]), Hendrik Knoche[1], and Cristina Manresa-Yee[2]

[1] Department of Architecture, Design and Media Technology,
Aalborg University, Rendsburggade 14, 9000 Aalborg, Denmark
morrison@create.aau.dk
[2] Department of Mathematics and Computer Science, University of Balearic
Islands, Crta.Valldemossa km 7.5, 07122 Palma, Spain

Abstract. We designed a wearable vest that houses a set of actuators to be placed at specific points on the body. We developed vibrotactile patterns to induce five sensation types: (1) Calming, (2 patterns, Up and Down back) (2) Feel Good (4 patterns in different directions around the waist), (3) Activating (2 patterns, Tarzan and Shiver, on top front of body and then down the back as well for Shiver), (4) Navigation (2 patterns, Turn Left and Turn Right, prompting on back then opposite side front waist) for full body turning and (5) Warning, (1 pattern on solar plexus) to slow down or stop the wearers. We made an overlap between the pulses, which were of longer durations than the short burst saltation pulses designed to induce muscle movement. Our participants responded well to the Calming and Feel Good patterns, but reported mixed responses to Activation, Navigation and Warning patterns.

Keywords: Wearable technology · Vibrotactile patterns · Calming effects

1 Introduction

In this paper, we investigate responses to a series of vibrotactile patterns designed for a wearable vest. The patterns are designed to provide sensations at a specific series of points on the body in order to energise, calm, feel-good, warn and/or assist with whole body navigation (turning the body) for the wearers.

We examine novel placement and patterns for vibrotactile actuators on the body housed in the wearable vest. In collaborating with a kinesiologist studying neurophysiology to design the intended affects, the placement and patterns were informed by, but unusual to much work in the area. We designed flowing style motions on the body with the vibrotactile pulses to emulate sensations such as stroking up or down the back to relax a person— 'there, there, it's okay'—and patterns of activation—emulating thumping the chest to bring the energy levels up, or vibrating with a series of fast over-laying patterns at the solar plexus to warn or stop the person if they are in danger. We work with activation, calming, feel good and warning patterns at sympathetic meridian points and junctions in the body. We also work with turning and guiding the whole body. The vibrotactile sensations emulate the types of touch patterns a kinesiologist-neurophysiologist uses to slow down or activate areas in the body.

© Springer International Publishing Switzerland 2015
A. Marcus (Ed.): DUXU 2015, Part II, LNCS 9187, pp. 655–666, 2015.
DOI: 10.1007/978-3-319-20898-5_62

Fig. 1. Participants 'playing' with the sensations at the wall, a swipe on the wall is felt in the same direction on the body, up, down or sideways left to right, or right to left.

In order to have an interactive environment for the vest wearer, we built an interactive vibrotactile work named The Humming Wall: a 12 m long by 3.5 m wide and 2.7 m high wall for interacting with the vest and general public use. While this aspect of the interaction is not the focus of this paper and will be reported elsewhere, it is important to note that the wall sends and receives vibrotactile and physiological interactions with and to the vibrotactile wearable vest. This means vest wearers can see, hear and feel their own heartbeat and breath in the vibroacoustics of the wall. In addition, participants can swipe and knock on The Humming Wall and the vest wearer is effectively swiped and knocked upon (triggering the patterns we designed for in the vest). Stroking up or down the wall produces stroking up and down the vest. Swiping sideways produces sensations around the waist in the same direction as the swipe (see Fig. 1 for an example).

2   Related Background

Smart wearables and fitness gadgets are big right now. The fitness market place is rife with small wearable technologies that track and respond to physiological data. Core to these advances is the bringing together of interdisciplinary teams from diverse technology fields of software design, electronic design and manufacture and healthcare. Wearable technologies adding stress level readings and integrated fall detection and alarm function which automatically alert designated contacts that the user is in need of assistance are also coming onto the market, expanding the market beyond fitness to include assistive technologies.

Research on vibrotactile interfaces for disabled users has largely focused on visually-impaired users to assist interaction with others and the environment: to enhance navigation [1], to interact with nearby objects [2], to present graphical information non-visually [6], to enrich interpersonal communication [8], to play videogames [20] or to teach choreographed dance [3]. Other research addresses problems with hearing impairments, using vibrotactile interfaces to translate sounds (music, speech or environmental noises) into physical vibrations [4, 5]. For example, the Music-touch Shoes, embedded with a vibrotactile interface, were used by dancers with hearing impairments to feel the rhythm and tempo of music through variable stimulation signals in the soles of the shoes [5].

Vibrotactile information can act as a supportive function to motivate users' actions. Spelmezan et al. [6] demonstrated that 10 patterns developed as a tactile language could assist athletes to improve their motor skills in snowboarding. Further, work by Rosenthal et al. uses a Vibrotactile Belt for teaching choreographed dance through vibrotactile cues [3]. Nummenmaa et al. asked people to draw-map where they thought emotions such as anger, fear, joy, happiness, sadness etc. resided in the body [7]. Similarly, Arafsha et al., asked participants to draw where love, joy, surprise, anger, sorrow, fear resided and included 3 types of haptic feedback with vibration, rhythm and warmth as enhancers [8], building on a long history of 'hugging' jackets and toys—enhancing feel good and comforter variations.

There are many factors to be considered with designing for the body, for long term wear, for comfort, for accuracy, to support movement, for a variety of body shapes and sizes etc. Placement location, number and types of tactors, arrangement, frequency, spacing, tempo, sequencing, connection methods and duration are all important factors when designing a wearable vibrotactile 'outfit' [9, 10]. Karuei et al. identified the wrists and spine as consistently most sensitive sites and found movement to be an impacting factor in decreasing detection rate [10] where Morrison et al. found doing other activities reduced detection performance of vibrotactile stimuli [11]. Much vibrotactile research works with ensuring each tactor can be individually felt and ensuring distance between vibrators and pauses between vibrations are correct to ensure this (see for example [12–14]), in particular to elicit the effect of movement. While these and other works motivated and informed the work we do here, our priority is also to calm people, to work with and adjust their emotional and physical states, to activate-motivate them to action and to gently guide the participants' navigation.

3 System: The Vest and the Patterns

The Vest. The vest is made of two layers—the inner layer comprises an adjustable harness and the outer a padded stretchable vest. The inner adjustable harness, is a 'one-size-fits all' that holds 32 actuators, moveable in order to ensure they are located on the correct location points for each different shaped body (Fig. 2a, b). The outer snuggly-fitting vest is a padded layered stretchable vest, made in 3 adjustable sizes and designed to keep the eccentric rotating mass actuators tightly placed against the bowed-curved areas of the body, such as the lower back and chest, to ensure the vibrations are evenly felt in all areas. The lower harness fits around the legs, ensuring that the harness will stay pulled down holding the actuators in place as the participants move about.

We integrated Zephyr's BioHarness 3 [15] into the harness and vest system to read the heartbeat and breath rate of the wearer in real-time. Two custom-made electronic boards drive the wearable system. One board acts for communication and the other powers and controls the actuators.

The outer shell–made in 3 adjustable sizes—is a padded layered stretchable vest designed to keep the actuators tightly placed against the bowed-curved areas of the body, such as the lower back and chest, to ensure the vibrations are evenly felt in all

Fig. 2. a. Inner Layer Adjustable Harness Front. b. Inner Layer Harness Back. Blue dots indicate actuator positions for up and down patterns. c. Outer padded stretchable vest and skirt

areas. We offered an adjustable skirt-apron for the sake of modesty and/or aesthetics, particularly for those wearing dresses (Fig. 2c).

The Vibrotactile Patterns. We collaborated on positioning of the actuators, rhythms of pulses and patterns and the combinations with an experienced Kinesiologist training in Neurophysiology and working with responsive points and zones of the body. We combined the different pulses, overlaps, rhythms and patterns to emulate the hands on work that a Kinesiologist does in activating or calming down inactive or overactive sequential points of the body. Kinesiology works with an understanding of the body as a set of rhizome like structures stemming from functioning communication tracks between the larger organs—the meridian system. The touch can be calming but is more often probing, even jabbing in a sequence of jiggle, pause, jiggle series (similar to saltation effect) but set up in a longer series of rhythms, with the body then given time to process and assimilate before the next points are accessed to be activated and/or calmed. The patterns we developed fall into five categories: (1) Calming and/or Feel Good (Back and Waist); (2) Feel Good (Waist); (3) Activating (Front and Back); (4) Navigation (whole body) and (5) Warning (Mid front). The actuators operate in overlapping patterns in order to provide various haptic synesthesia sensations such as sense of movement up down or around the body, a body shiver, states of activation and/or calming as well as providing navigational whole body-turning cues. For example, actions such as (1) calming-comforting; stroking the back to calm or comfort a person, (see Fig. 2b), (2) guidance-navigation; placing hands on nape of back and shoulder and turning at the hip as if to support and guide an elder and/or (3) warning; stopping the body with pulses to the solar plexus—acting as if a warning. Activation patterns found mostly on the front of the body include Shiver and Tarzan sequences with for example, pulses in the top two actuators under the collarbones in rapid succession, then for a longer duration (appearing stronger) pulses to the midpoint actuator emulating 'The Tarzan Effect'—Tarzan thumps his chest to raise his energy levels before action. Shiver includes shorter version of these same front patterns followed by patterns up and down the back (a whole body shiver-shudder, akin to what we might experience while saying 'somebody walked over my grave'.

See Fig. 3 for positioning of actuators on the body and indication of the naming scheme for each actuator and Table 1 for information on a selection of the patterns. Table 1 includes the sensation category, location on the body, the pattern structure, total duration of the overall pattern, individual activation length (act.), overlap of

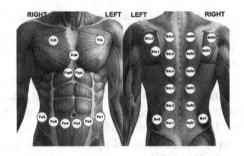

Fig. 3. Actuator naming scheme, e.g. actuators at front waist: Fw1 FrontWaistActuator1[st], (actuators numbered 1-6, from left to right); then continues to back waist: Bw7, position BackWaistActuator 7th at right side. Other codes include: FcR: FrontChestRight (&Left&Middle), BsL1: BackSpineLeft1st (1-6), FspR: FrontSolarplexusRight (&Left), BhR1: BackHand-Right1st (of 2&Left repeat).

Table 1. Pattern structure details

	Up	Down	Shiver	Tarzan	Turn Left	Stop
sensat.	calming	calming	activating	activating	navigation	alert
location	back	back	front, back	front	back, waist	front
len.	1225	1225	1200	2300	2500	900
act.	350	350	500	500	500	900
overl.	175	175	400	200	0	0
ampl.	3500	3500	4000	4000	4000	4000
step 0	BsL1, BsR1	BsL6, BsR6	FcM	FcL, FcR	Bw7	FspL, FspR
1	BsL2, BsR2	BsL5, BsR5	FcL, FcR	FcL, FcR	BhR1, BhR2	
2	BsL3, BsR3	BsL4, BsR4	BhL2, BhR2	FcL, FcR	Fw3, Fw2	
3	BsL4, BsR4	BsL3, BsR3	BsL5, BsR5	FcL, FcR	Fw2, Fw1	
4	BsL5, BsR5	BsL2, BsR2	BsL4, BsR4		Fw1, BW8	
5	BsL6, BsR6	BsL1, BsR1	BsL3, BsR3	FcM		
6			BsL2, BsR2			
7			FcM	Fw6, Bw7		Fw5, Fw2
8				Fw5,Fw4		Fw4, Fw3
9			FcM			

consecutive activations (overl.), amplitude of activation (ampl.), and the activators as they were activated with each step in sequence. In this first trial, the duration and amplitude were replicated throughout the whole pattern.

In the patterns we deliberately overlap transitions between 0–400 ms (with most between 200–350 ms) and vary duration from 175–500 ms to enable a smooth flowing sensation between pulses, rather than working with the short bursts of 100 ms followed by repetitions of 50 ms that are used to produce saltation effects. Saltation, works as a perceptual illusion, where rapid vibrotactile pulses delivered first to one location and then to another on the skin produces the sensation of a virtual vibration between the two vibrators [12]. Saltation is used to motivate particular movements: flexion, extension, abduction, adduction and rotation. For example, to flex and extend the elbow [16], three vibration motors were placed on an arm band between 6.4 to 7.6 cm apart [12] on the bicep muscle above the elbow joint near the muscle/joint/body part involved in the fundamental movement [13]. In that instant, the pattern of vibration using the saltation illusion, pulsed three motors located in line to render directional information on the skin. The standard burst duration of 100 ms was used with 50 ms inter-burst interval for repetitions, considered optimal to elicit saltation [12] and subsequently used successfully [13, 14]. For the pattern each vibration cue is repeated in sequence as recommended [13] for improved user perception.

For this particular case study, identification of actual location and/or flexion, extension, abduction, adduction and rotation of muscles is not the aim of the work. Rather, emulating natural-enough touch is the effect we are working towards. To do this we have overlaps between the vibrators, so e.g. BackSideLeft6 vibrator is still operating when BackSideLeft5 actuator kicks in. As the pulsations move up both sides of the spine this is repeated at the same time on the right side of the spine at Back-SideRight6 (BsR6) and BsR65. The overlap where both vibrators are operating at the same time is 175 ms. This continues throughout the pattern with a 175 ms overlap between BackSideLeft4 (&BsR4), BackSideLeft3 (&BsR3), BackSideLeft2 (&BsR3) and BackSideLeft1 (&BsR1). The duration of the individual activation length (act.), overlap of consecutive activations (overl.) and amplitude of activation (ampl.) are then played the same for all steps on the back Up and Down patterns. We developed this range of vibrotactile patterns in the vest to induce five sensation types in situ: (1) Calming, (2 patterns, Up and Down back) (2) Feel Good (4 patterns in different combinations and directions around waist), (3) Activating (2 patterns, Shiver and Tarzan), (4) Navigation prompts (2 patterns, Turn Left and Turn Right on back and opposite front waist) for full body turning and (5) Information-Warning, (1 pattern on solar plexus) to slow down or stop. In addition, the vibroacoustic *Humming Wall* reacts to human touch—knock, swipe etc.—and conveys these both at the wall and to the vest and responds to and displays the heartbeat and breath rate of the vest wearer.

4 The Trial: Procedure

We ran trials for 5 weeks at Utzon Park, Aalborg. From our preliminary tests, we found it worked better to have pairs experience the wall-vest interactions, so we asked participants to invite a friend, colleague, family-member or loved one rather than pair with an unknown researcher. The duration of the trials varied from between 1.5 to 4 h per pair, averaging 2.5 h. We ran the trials in four phases: (1) *Fitting*, 15-35 min; (2) *Training with vest*, participants walked up and down in the park (1 researcher guided and 1 videoed) while being introduced to the ten vibration patterns for 3 times for each pattern (median length of 10 s for all three together). Participants were asked to *talk aloud* their responses to the sensations. After this, participants and researchers stopped and participants articulated their responses to a repeat of each individual pattern, walking slowly while experiencing and discussing the ones related to motion,

10–15 min; (3) *Interaction*: We sectioned the wall into zones of discrete either (1) calming or (2) energising activities. Participants and their pair interacted with 5 zones at *The Humming Wall,* with a repeat visit to each of the two physiology zones (calming)—one displaying heartbeat, the other breath rate, making 7 stops in all. The other three zones responded to gestures (energising). The participants were instructed on what to do in each zone (e.g., knock on these 3 panels; swipe these 3 panels; sit & breathe). All knocks and swipes on the wall were relayed to and felt in the vest, 20–90 min; (4) *Evaluation,* 15–40 min.

The Participants. We enlisted 39 volunteers with ages ranging from 12 to 65 years (average age 39), 20 females and 19 males. 19 people participated in mixed gender groups, 11 in female/female and 9 in male/male groups (uneven numbers are due to only one participant from one of the pairs wearing a vest). Most people paired with close or good friends (11), their partners (10), colleagues (10), family members (5), or social friends or acquaintances (3). 22 self-reported basic or average IT skills with 17 advanced or above, with 28 spending on average more than 20 h on a computer each week and 12 enjoyed playing a musical instrument regularly. 31 had tertiary level qualifications and 14 were knowledgeable about wearable technology.

Data Collection. We gathered data using quantitative and qualitative methods. Before the trial, the participants filled in informed consent forms and a demographic questionnaire asking about fitness levels; experience levels with IT, vibrotactile technology, embodied interaction, large public displays and playing musical instruments. Activity was logged for each participant from the haptics in the vest; the BioHarness: capturing heartbeat and breath; and actions on the wall: knocking and swiping, frequency, segment and direction. Each pair of participants was accompanied throughout the trial by two researchers, one guiding and one videoing. On return from the field, participants completed shortened adapted versions of questions from MEC Spatial Presence Questionnaire (MEC-SPQ) [17], Flow State Scale (FSS) [18] and Intrinsic Motivation Inventory (IMI) [19] to gauge reactions to the sensations in the vest and the interaction with *The Humming Wall.* The questionnaires comprised 21 X 5-level Likert-type items (from completely disagree to completely agree) to analyse and cross-check users' perceptions. The overall experience was measured through 10 semantic differential scale items with 5 levels (see Fig. 4). Lastly, each participant described their experience, highlighting aspects in semi-structured recorded interviews.

Fig. 4. Semantic differential values on overall experience (left), Word counts from debrief interviews by categories with terms mentioned in parentheses (right).

Data Processing and Analysis. Data post-processing tasks included transcribing user interviews and translating them into English for further analysis. We transcribed the talk aloud responses of the participants to each vibration and coded them numerically. From the English translations of the transcribed Danish debrief interviews we obtained word frequencies and included descriptive adjectives and nouns that received more than 10 mentions and grouped them into topics summarised in Fig. 4, right. We analysed all data sources across the demographic variables to ensure we tested for impact from gender, age, fitness levels and/or prior experience with IT, vibrotactile technology, embodied interaction, large public displays and playing musical instruments, etc. We also analysed logging of activity at the wall, reported elsewhere.

5 Results

In this section we report on findings from Questionnaires, System logging, Video footage and Semi-structured interviews. We concentrate on responses to patterns in the vest. Wall, physiological data and other interactions will be reported elsewhere.

The participants joined in the spirit of the trials and were generally interested in uncovering what the vest patterns might mean. Questionnaire results revealed users found it pleasant to complete the different activities, they concentrated, understood requirements, were active and most felt that they lost track of time during the trial.

Participants were asked how they experienced the vest (and the wall) during the experiment (see Fig. 4, left). They reported to be relaxed, even though they reported to be active as well. Further, users felt that it to be a personal, sensitive, open, warm and colourful experience. Participants exercising 2 or more times per week, found doing the tasks more pleasant, and reported warmer and more relaxed experiences than those exercising less. Those less knowledgeable with vibrotactile technology enjoyed learning how to do the tasks suggested by the sensation more, had a more personal but less active experience than the tech-savvy ones.

The semi-structured interviews used terms from the training phase and included questions such as *'How did you find: the sensations in the vest?' 'Did you prefer some patterns to others?'* in order to get participants expanding on their specific experiences. The most common words offered by participants in these interviews are depicted in Fig. 4, right. We received a variety of comments with many participants describing the interactions as fun, pleasurable, unusual or new and different. The most common expressed terms on enjoyment were: Fun, Like, Want, Pleasant-pleasure and Enjoy. People referred often to *feeling* and identified parts of the body: Back, Waist Front, Chest and Body per se as well as to Heart or heartbeat and Breath. They also referred often to movement, and/or Different-Confusing-New–Surprise and/or Calm-Relaxing-Natural (see Fig. 4, right).

When responding to the vest related questions, participants felt it was possible to be active in the surroundings, important to do well and did not feel much discomfort associated with the vibrations in the vest. In general users stated that they were concentrating on the sensations in the vest, and interpreted some sensations to hold greater meaning than others.

Many immediately found the experience enjoyable: '*Funny - different –a new experience*'. Others took time to adjust: '*In the beginning it was a new feeling, and it was stressful ... because it was a new experience in my life. Later I got used to it*'.

We used the numerically coded (1, 0, -1) talk aloud responses to the 10 patterns in a non-parametric Friedman test, which yielded a significant difference between patterns (see Fig. 5 for an overview of the averages). Post hoc comparisons showed that Up, Down, WaistLeftToRight and WaistRightToLeft all were significantly more positively evaluated than all other patterns (with the exception of WaistLeftToRight not being significantly different from TurnLeft and MidFrontToBack). Tarzan and Stop were evaluated more negatively—significantly worse than all other patterns apart from non-significant differences between Stop and both TurnRight and Shiver.

We asked '*Do the patterns suggest anything to you?*' Responses included sensations such as tickling, butterflies, hunger or goose bumps, for example_ '*some feeling was like butterflies in the stomach.*' And '*The tickling on the side... gave me goose bumps from the outside—like you didn't have the sensation but got the goose bumps anyway*' or—'*Solar plexus, not so bad once got used to it—at first didn't like it*'... '*it could be a warning of don't do that*'.

For some, the vibrations on the front of the body (the activating *Tarzan* and *Shiver* or Warning *Stop* patterns) were the most testing: '*Front—it was not uncomfortable but not as pleasant—the ones on the back are more natural so the front are not as natural*'. For others: '*The feeling in the chest was best, feel it better also at lower back—very nice*', while many more said similar about e.g. the back and waist. '*Up and down the back I liked the most. It is hard to tell, none were unpleasant.*'

Others differentiated between the up and down spine, finding up more activating '*swipe down on spine more calming, upwards more alert, enjoyable—stood me up*' and '*was like lifting me up with the up swipe, down swipe was just pleasant*'.

Sensations occurring in more than just one area of the body at the same time often confused people.

Some participants likened the sensation to a real touch: '*Putting up the same emotion as touch—bringing out the same sense of well-being or happiness as when somebody touches or pats or hugs you... the hug [Shiver] was very surprising*'. Many were more comfortable with familiar sensations: '*I like the one on my spine the most... it resembles what people do with the people they know, when they stroke them on the back or something. So I think it was the most comfortable one.*'

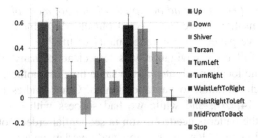

Fig. 5. Means of coded responses to the vibration patterns with error bars (std. error of mean)

6 Findings and Discussion

In this section we discuss findings from testing the different vibrotactile patterns. Some sensations made more sense than others, and this was confirmed in the video logging and in semi-structured interviews. We found people responded more positively to Up, Down, on the waist right to left and for waist left to right patterns, (calming patterns) than to e.g. Shiver, Tarzan (activating) or Turn Left and Stop (guiding). Still the reactions were mixed—some requested more activating (the chest—Tarzan or Shiver), while most preferred the calming sensations (waist and back). These were considered more comfortable, similar to what it feels like to be stroked by another. Vibrotactile technology experts had more active yet more relaxed experiences, while those less familiar had a more personal experience. While many were uncertain how to 'name the patterns or the experience', for most this was an activating-relaxing enjoyable experience. We would not expect that the activation and warning patterns would be considered as enjoyable as the calming and feel-good ones. They are designed to act to energise or force attention and while some participants reported enjoying these, we need to refine and investigate further to clarify impacting factors.

Language. In the training and interview discussions, many had difficulty when attempting to describe an unfamiliar new pattern. We found most struggled to find words to describe the sensations and convey their impressions: '*haven't felt before, yes single vibrations from mobile, but not all over body and flowing, so not sure how to describe what it does... is new*'. The terminology is not at hand for people to be able to easily describe their experiences [21]. For this study, we referred to the sensations as patterns but did not identify each one to the participants in order to avoid influencing their perception-experience. An existing language set is the H-E-Vocabulary, which uses terms such as 'Prickly' for 16 Hz sensations and 'Tingling' for 250 Hz [20], which could act as foundational work to expand upon with input from our own participants' responses.

Therapeutic. Several participants found the vest to be therapeutic or nurturing vibrating on previously sore parts of their body. '*I had an operation top of my waist, so at first it was 'ooh!' I am not used to being touched there any more. Then I got used to it and after a while it felt very safe and good to be touched there again. It was really helpful*'. For others their responsiveness increased: '*Surprised how sensitive I became, this increased during trial. More body got used to listening to the sensation, better it picked up on them.*' '*Start to feel, afterwards, become part of you—sensation quickly become natural, and it kept my mind occupied, when I got more physical*'. Such strong responses to the sensations were unexpected but clearly point to potential for rehabilitation and assistive patterns to improve quality of life.

Activating and full body navigation was less clear to many of our participants. Where more than one location vibrated at the same time as another, participants found difficulty with which vibration to pay attention to. Other studies have found similar outcomes [10, 13, 14, 20], and while we had success with several patterns using multiple locations, the patterns needed to run in sequential order, not at the same time. Interspersing saltation with longer duration and overlap patterns might assist with instigating full body turning for navigation patterns. It remains high priority, to be gentle to bodies (avoiding probing sensations, except for the warning pattern) given the potentially diverse audience—fit and fragile—that this work could be useful for.

7   Conclusion and Future Work

Our participants responded significantly more positively the Calming and Feel Good patterns, but reported mixed responses to Activation, Navigation and Warning patterns. Overall the participants were immersed and very positive: that the patterns felt good, were likened to real touch and the experience was fun and personal is reassuring for this first pass at emulating natural touch sensations with vibrotactile patterns. A key element missing in exploring tactile experience is an expansive vocabulary to adequately describe the nuances between the vibrotactile sensations and the patterns themselves. To address this in future versions, the training phase would familiarise participants with revised pattern names and include a set of terms and elements for consideration. We will add sensate terms identified by participants —hungry, ants, goosebumps, butterflies, tickling, and/or crawling as well as specifying location on parts of body, types of movement and mood-determiners (relaxed, activated, calm, overwhelmed, agitated etc.) as initial steps. For the activation, navigation and confusing or less comfortable patterns, we will investigate longer repeating pattern sequences, interspersing saltation and working with one body location at a time. We have a modified version of the revised patterns and vest ready to begin comparative impact factor testing. We contribute with evidence on the effectiveness of Calming and Feel Good patterns replicating natural touch and outline future work required for activating, navigation and warning patterns while contributing to building an expansive vocabulary for articulating vibrotactile sensations and patterns.

Acknowledgments. We thank the volunteers for the field trials, our Kinesiologist Bettina Eriksen and Aalborg Kommune for support. This work is supported by the EU funded project CultAR (FP7-ICT-2011-9 601139).

References

1. Ghiani, G., Leporini, B., Paternò, F.: Vibrotactile feedback to aid blind users of mobile guides. J. Vis. Lang. Comput. **20**, 305–317 (2009)
2. Bahram, S., Chakraborty, A., Ravindran, S., Amant, R.S.: Intelligent Interaction in Accessible Applications. A Multimodal End-2-End Approach to Accessible Computing, pp. 93–117. Springer, London (2013)
3. Rosenthal, J., Edwards, N., Villanueva, D., Krishna, S., McDaniel, T., Panchanathan, S.: Design, implementation, and case study of a pragmatic vibrotactile belt. IEEE Trans. Instrum. Meas. **60**, 114–125 (2011)
4. Nanayakkara, S., Taylor, E., Wyse, L., Ong, S.H.: An enhanced musical experience for the deaf: design and evaluation of a music display and a haptic chair. In: Proceedings of the CHI 2009, pp. 337–346. ACM (2009)

5. Yao, L., Shi, Y., Chi, H., Ji, X., Ying, F.: Music-touch shoes: vibrotactile interface for hearing impaired dancers. In: Proceedings of the TEI 2010, pp. 275–276. ACM (2010)
6. Spelmezan, D.: A language of tactile motion instructions. Ph.D. thesis (2011)
7. Nummenmaa, L., Glerean, E., Hari, R., Hietanen, J.K.: Bodily maps of emotions. Proc. Natl. Acad. Sci. **111**, 646–651 (2014)
8. Arafsha, F., Alam, K.M., El Saddik, A.: EmoJacket: Consumer centric wearable affective jacket to enhance emotional immersion. In: Proceedings of the IIT 2012, pp. 350–355 (2012)
9. Gemperle, F., Hirsch, T., Goode, A., Pearce, J., Siewiorek, D., Smailigic, A.: Wearable Vibro-tactile Display. Carnegie Mellon University, CMU Wearable Group (2003)
10. Karuei, I., MacLean, K.E., Foley-Fisher, Z., MacKenzie, R., Koch, S., El-Zohairy, M.: Detecting vibrations across the body in mobile contexts. In: Proceedings of the CHI 2011, pp. 3267–3276. ACM (2011)
11. Morrison, A., Knudsen, L., Andersen, H.J.: Urban vibrations: Sensitivities in the field with a broad demographic. In: Proceedings of the ISWC 2012, pp. 76–79. IEEE (2012)
12. Geldard, F.A., Sherrick, C.E.: The cutaneous" rabbit": a perceptual illusion. Science **178**, 178–179 (1972)
13. McDaniel, T., Villanueva, D., Krishna, S., Panchanathan, S.: MOVeMENT: A framework for systematically mapping vibrotactile stimulations to fundamental body movements. In: Proceedings of the HAVE 2010, pp. 1–6. IEEE (2010)
14. Spelmezan, D., Jacobs, M., Hilgers, A., Borchers, J.: Tactile motion instructions for physical activities. In: Proceedings of the CHI 2009, pp. 2243–2252. ACM (2009)
15. Zephyr. http://www.zephyr.com
16. Manresa-Yee, C., Morrison, A., Larsen, J.V., Varona, J.: A vibrotactile interface to motivate movement for children with severe to profound disabilities. In: INTERACCION 2014. ACM (2014)
17. Vorderer, P., Wirth, W., Gouveia, F.R., Biocca, F., Saari, T., Jäncke, F., Böcking, S., Schramm, H., Gysbers, A., Hartmann, T., others: MEC spatial presence questionnaire (MEC-SPQ): Short documentation and instructions for application. Rep. Eur. Community Proj. Presence MEC IST-2001-37661. 3 (2004)
18. Jackson, S.A., Marsh, H.W.: Others: Development and validation of a scale to measure optimal experience: The flow state scale. J. Sport Exerc. Psychol. **18**, 17–35 (1996)
19. Deci, E.L., Ryan, R.M.: The" what" and" why" of goal pursuits: Human needs and the self-determination of behavior. Psychol. Inq. **11**, 227–268 (2000)
20. Obrist, M., Seah, S.A., Subramanian, S.: Talking about tactile experiences. In: Proceedings of the CHI 2013, pp. 1659–1668. ACM (2013)
21. Moussette, C.: Simple haptics: Sketching perspectives for the design of haptic interactions (2012). http://www.diva-portal.org/smash/record.jsf?pid=diva2:558987

TattooAR: Augmented Reality Interactive Tattoos

Gabriela Schirmer Mauricio, João de Sá Bonelli[✉],
and Maria das Graças Chagas

Pontifical Catholic University of Rio de Janeiro (PUC-Rio),
Rio de Janeiro, Brazil
gabismauricio@gmail.com,
{joao-bonelli, chagas}@puc-rio.br

Abstract. This paper describes the design process of TattooAR mobile app, an experimental project that explores the use of tattoos as an artistic, interactive and dynamic wearable ornament. Tattoos have been used as different forms of expression throughout history, and in contemporary society people have been increasingly using tattoos as a form of art and a way to express themselves. TattooAR explores the frontiers between Art, Design and Technology by using Augmented Reality (AR) technologies in order to allow a basic skin tattoo to receive layers of image that transform it into different virtual tattoos that can be viewed on the screen of a mobile device and can also be shared in social networks.

Keywords: Interaction design · Education · Augmented reality · Tattoos

1 Introduction

Tattoos have been used as varied forms of expression throughout history and cultures. In contemporary society people have been increasingly using tattoos as a form of art and a way to express themselves into the world, generating individuality and exposing what they think, how they see life and society.

People's interpretation of the world changes as they live and interact with other people. The main objective of TattooAR Project is to explore the human body as a platform to express these mutant interpretations of the world through interactive and dynamic tattoos. The work explores the frontiers between Art, Design and Technology by using Augmented Reality (AR) technologies in order to allow a basic skin tattoo form to receive layers of image that transform it into different virtual tattoos that can be viewed on the screen of the mobile device and can also be shared in social networks.

This paper describes the design process of TattooAR mobile app, an experimental project that investigates the human body as a platform for self-expression and communication. It explores the use of tattoos as an artistic, interactive and dynamic wearable ornament.

© Springer International Publishing Switzerland 2015
A. Marcus (Ed.): DUXU 2015, Part II, LNCS 9187, pp. 667–674, 2015.
DOI: 10.1007/978-3-319-20898-5_63

2 Background: The Interaction Design Research Environment at PUC-Rio

TattooAR was developed as a final Project at the B.A. Course in Design for Digital Media at the Pontifical Catholic University of Rio de Janeiro (PUC-Rio). The Course is a pioneer Interaction Design teaching program in Brazil. The work was conducted by student Gabriela Schirmer Mauricio, under the academic supervision of Professors João Bonelli and Maria das Graças Chagas. During the Design process, reflective practice and experimentation were highly encouraged in the search for innovative and creative solutions. The experiments were built at the course's Physical Computing Lab (LIFE - Laboratório de Interfaces Físicas Experimentais), where the student was provided with the adequate environment to conduct creative experiments with Interaction Design techniques.

In the Design-Digital Media curriculum at PUC-Rio, Interaction Design is a significant field of study. Five individual classes cover specific aspects of Interaction Design: *Design e Expansão dos Sentidos* (Design and Expansion of the Senses); *Hipermídia* (Hypermedia); *Conceitos de Informática* (Introduction to computer programming); *Interfaces Físicas e Lógicas* (Physical Computing); and *Design de Objetos Inteligentes* (Design of Smart Objects). In the *Design and Expansion of the Senses* class the students are introduced to theoretic aspects of Interactive Media. In the *Hypermedia* class the students explore topics related to Information Architecture and Navigation. In the *Introduction to Computer Programming* class, the students acquire basic programming knowledge in the HTML and JavaScript programming languages. Subsequently, in the *Physical Computing* class, the students further their knowledge in programming and electronics while building experimental Physical Computing projects. Finally, in the *Smart Objects* class students develop innovative projects that make use of computational intelligence. These classes are responsible for providing the students with a vast array of theoretic and technical knowledge, which will become the student's toolkit to be used when developing their individual Interaction Design projects.[1]

Furthermore, in the curricular structure of the program, students are required to enroll in eight *Design Project* classes – that have a 10-hours-per-week schedule – before they can graduate. In the *Project* classes, the students are introduced to methodological aspects of design, while developing their individual Design projects that are presented on the end of the academic semester to an examination board of professors.

Also the Lab LIFE[2] is an initiative of PUC-Rio's Arts and Design Department that aims to provide an appropriate environment for the practical development of Physical Computing projects. The lab, established in 2009, currently has 36 sq. meters of floor space equipped with computers, open source software, electronic components, Arduino boards and a small library. The lab is planned to be a space dedicated to the creative experimentation in interaction design. The goal is to provide computational and

---

[1] Further information about the Design-Digital Media Undergraduate Program at PUC-Rio can be accessed at: http://www.puc-rio.br/ensinopesq/ccg/design_midiadigital.html.

[2] Further information about the LIFE Lab can be accessed at: http://www.life.dad.puc-rio.br.

electronic resources, in order to support the development of innovative Physical Computing projects.

In the context of this teaching environment described above, the TattooAR project was developed by student Gabriela Schirmer Mauricio extensively in the LIFE Lab, and presented as her final undergraduate project for the conclusion of the B.A. Design-Digital Media at PUC-Rio.

3 Motivation and Related Work

The TattooAR project was born from a desire to explore the body as a means of self-expression and creativity. A motivational starting point was the perception of the skin as being the surface of expression that is closest to the human being: our own body. The initial proposition of the project was to use the body as a surface for graphic information, in order to introduce interaction between people and making them change their perception.

In this context of the *Body as Surface*, the tattoo is a major form of expression that has been used through history in social contexts such as rites of passage and prisoner's marks. In contemporary society, tattoos have been widely used as a way to individualize and express ideas. Even though tattoos have been used for thousands of years as a tool for expression, they have the limitation of being static and permanent. The TattooAR project was born from the question: "how can Digital Design enhance the interactive experience of the tattoo?".

Being the student herself an illustrator and tattoo enthusiast, the project's goal became to explore the body as a surface for artistic expression by transforming something once permanent as a tattoo into a mutable form of art through the use of emerging digital and interactive technologies.

In searching for theoretic references, this research considers relevant the vision by Marshall McLuhan present in his seminal book 'Understanding Media: the extensions of man'. [1] In the chapter entitled 'The Medium is the Message' the author proposes a vision of Media as extensions of the human body. Also in the article 'Pequena Digressão Sobre a Natureza e Conceito do Design', [2] Rita Couto from PUC-Rio proposes a vision of Design as a multidisciplinary field of knowledge that has relation with the major areas of Science and Art.

In the Interaction Design research field, the design concept project 'SKIN: Tattoo' by Phillips [3], explores tattoos as a mutable form of expression and is a main reference for this research. Also 'Sixthsense' [4] by MIT's Pranav Mistry – a wearable interface that augments the real world with digital information – was inspirational in terms of establishing possible relations between virtual information and the human body. The projects 'Firewall' – an interactive installation by Mike Allison [8] – and 'Apparition' – a dance performance by Klaus Obermaier [9] – explore interactivity in an artistic approach while using projection as an extension of the human body.

The works by Katia Vega – namely the 'Beauty Technology', 'Blinkifier' and 'Twinkle Nails' projects [5–7] – explore new ways of interaction through the human body and are a main reference in the field of wearable technology.

In the tattoo field, relevant references are the works by Karl Marc [10] – who tattooed a QRCode marker in his own skin, establishing a link between the body and virtual information – and Shelley Jackson [11], who composed a narrative in several different tattoos, each word tattooed in a different person.

4   Design Process

The project's methodology was divided in steps that went from theoretic research – explicit in the previous topic – followed by a series of practical experiments. In a reflective practice approach, every single experiment led to testing and reflection upon its results. This reflection generated conclusions that inspired the conduction of the next experiment, and so forth, in a cyclical process. As a first step, the student started by experimenting with projection mapping technologies in order to have digital images projected onto the skin. The first software experiment was developed in the Processing environment [12], and used a color marker as a tracking reference for positioning a projected image on the user's skin (Fig. 1).

Even though these results seemed viable, the student considered an important technical requisite for the project that it should be portable, so that it could be used in the urban environment just like the real tattoo does. In searching for a mobile solution for her project, the student encountered the technology of Augmented Reality (AR) and used it in her next experiments. The AR opportunity was considered more viable, because it did not depend on a video projector to form the virtual image on the skin, and the mobile platform allowed for the desired portability and embodiment. Therefore the next effort became to try to develop an augmented reality application that would run on a smartphone – which she could achieve in the Processing development

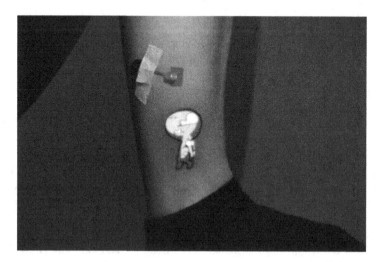

Fig. 1. Experiment in projection mapping: software developed in the Processing environment is used to track the position of a red led and use it as a reference to place a projected image precisely on the skin.

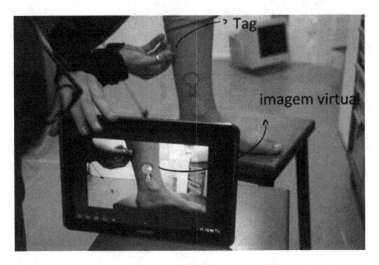

Fig. 2. Experiment in Augmented Reality. A color tag is used as a tracking reference for positioning a virtual image on the screen of the Android mobile device.

environment, using the Ketai Sensor Library [13] for the Google Android mobile platform [14] (Fig. 2).

Even though the student succeeded in the task of positioning a virtual image over a real image, the experiment still had a technical requisite: having to use a color tag to serve as a positioning reference for the virtual image. At this point the student made a shift to using the more complex Java programming language [15] used in the Android Development Toolkit (ADK) [16], becoming able to work with the Metaio Augmented Reality Software Library [17] in order to experiment her project's concept of AR Tattoo. The student was already proficient in the Processing programming language – which she learned in the *Physical Computing* class. Since Processing is based in the Java programming language, the Design student was able to easily move to the more complex Java development environment. Therefore the next software experiment was capable of tracking a shape – that was drawn on the skin – and precisely positioning a virtual image on the smartphone's display.

For the development of the tracking component – the part that is drawn on the user's skin – the young designer experimented with different graphic techniques such as rubber stamp, cutout, adhesive label and removable tattoo. In the graphic experimentation process, the student used the resources provided by PUC-Rio's LPG-Laboratório de Processos Gráficos (Lab for Graphic Processes), also revealing the important interdisciplinary approach present in this Design Program (Fig. 3).

After intensive testing, the removable tattoo format was chosen because it allowed for a more precise image tracking. The temporary tattoo is then applied in the user's skin in order to work as an Augmented Reality tag – and also as an outline for the virtual drawings. The graphic form of the temporary stamp was designed to fit artistic and functional purposes of the visualization. The drawings were based on the student's own tattoo, used in the first experimentations. The outline shape of a character is used

Fig. 3. A virtual image is positioned precisely over a drawing on the person's skin. In this experiment, a pen drawing over tracing paper was positioned on the user's arm and used as a tracking reference.

as a frame to explore new drawings. At this stage, several shapes were created and tested as tracking tags for the virtual drawing that would complete these outlines (Fig. 4).

For the final presentation of the project, the student demonstrated her Android mobile application that allows users to visualize and choose from previously stored tattoo art that can be seen on the skin without the permanence of real tattoo ink. The software also allows users to take pictures that can be saved on the device's gallery and also shared in social networks (Fig. 5).

Fig. 4. Testing different tag shapes

Fig. 5. A virtual tattoo created with the TattooAR app using augmented reality

5   Conclusions

Considering the development process of the TattooAR project, it becomes notable the relation between theory and practice. Theory background was accessed to inspire the project, while the reflective practical methodology fostered the development of a series of experiments that resulted in an innovative and creative solution to the design question posed in the beginning of the process: "how can Digital Design enhance the interactive experience of the tattoo?"

In addition, the project reveals an interesting interdisciplinary approach between the areas of Design and Computer Sciences. The student was able to test and experiment her proposed interaction concepts because she worked in a real-life context, in a design methodological process that was supported by the interdisciplinary knowledge of computer programming acquired in the Design-Digital Media Program at PUC-Rio. The knowledge of computer programming was determinant in this project's design process because it empowered the designer to test, experiment and experience her Design decisions.

The results achieved with this work contribute to the use of digital technology as a mean for human expression. The TattooAR mobile app explores one of the many ways to use Augmented Reality technology and proposes a new way to interact with tattoos. It allows for a shared interactive experience, where spectators are transformed into users and new interactive experiences are created as the users interact with their bodies. TattooAR adds an interesting contribution to the fields of Electronic Art, Design for Interactive Media, Augmented Reality and those related to Wearable Technology.

As further possibilities of the project, options like allowing the users to generate their own tattoos based on their individual drawings, and also animated motion tattoos are being considered, and should be produced in the near future.

References

1. Mc Luhan, M.: Undestanding Media: the Extensions of Man. MIT Press, Cambridge (1997)
2. Couto, R.: Pequena digressão sobre a natureza do design. Estudos em Design V, v.IV, n.2 (1996)
3. Philips SKIN: Tattoo. http://www.design.philips.com/about/design/designportfolio/design_futures/tattoo.page
4. Mistry, P., Maes, P.: SixthSense - A wearable gestural interface. In: Proceedings of SIGGRAPH Asia 2009, Emerging Technologies (2009)
5. Beauty Technology. http://groupware.secondlab.inf.puc-rio.br/beautytech
6. Flanagan, P.J.: Vega, K.; Fuks, H.: Blinklifier: The power of feedback loops for amplifying expressions through bodily worn objects. In: Proceedings of APCHI 2012, The 10th Asia Pacific Conference on Computer Human Interaction, vol 2, pp. 641-642 (2012)
7. Vega, K.: Exploring the power of feedback loops in wearables computers. In: Proceedings of 7th International Conference on Tangible, Embedded and Embodied Interaction, pp. 371-372 (2013)
8. Firewall. http://aaron-sherwood.com/blog/?p=558
9. Apparition. http://www.exile.at/apparition/project.html
10. Karl Marc. http://karlmarc.com
11. Skin: Project. http://ineradicablestain.com/skindex.html
12. Processing. https://processing.org
13. Ketai. https://code.google.com/p/ketai/
14. Processing for Android. https://github.com/processing/processing-android/wiki
15. Java. https://www.Java.com
16. Google Android. http://developer.android.com
17. Metaio. http://www.metaio.com

Flexible and Wearable Sensors

Kuniharu Takei[(✉)], Shingo Harada, Wataru Honda, Yuki Yamamoto,
Kenichiro Kanao, Takayuki Arie, and Seiji Akita

Department of Physics and Electronics, Osaka Prefecture University,
Osaka, Japan
takei@pe.osakafu-u.ac.jp

Abstract. Wearable devices using solid device components have recently been
released to purchase for different kinds of applications. However, ideal "wearable" devices should be like a cloth, so that they can be attached on a human
skin or cloth without awareness. To realize flexible and wearable electronics, a
challenge is how to form mechanically flexible electrical materials on a flexible
substrate. To address this requirement, we here propose and develop nanoma-
terial film formations on a macroscale flexible substrate using printing methods.
As examples, we present an artificial electronic skin (e-skin) for robotic/
prosthesis and a wearable device. By considering strain engineering, composition of materials into the film, and surface interaction to form uniform printing
films, a variety of flexible devices can be readily fabricated without using an
expensive tool such as a vacuum system.

Keywords: Flexible sensor · Wearable sensor · Printed electronics · Artificial
skin

1 Introduction

A variety of watch-type and glasses-type wearable devices have been widely available
to purchase for activity monitorings. However, every commercially available wearable
device is based on solid devices for circuits, sensors, and some other components. Ideal
wearable devices should be like a cloth or a bandage, so that they can be attached on a
human skin or cloth and interacted with humans without awareness during the use of
devices. To realize future flexible and wearable electronics, a bottleneck and a challenge are to form mechanically flexible electrical materials uniformly on a macroscale
flexible substrate without sacrificing the material performances. Since the flexible
wearable devices are probably torn readily and need to keep sanitary clean environments if the devices are attached directly on a human skin, the devices should be
disposal, so that the cost is another factor to achieve the flexible devices.

To address these requirements, we have developed macroscale printing methods of
inorganic nanomaterials and/or organic materials to form the uniform films for active
device components such as sensors and transistors economically on a variety of flexible
substrates [e.g. polyethylene (PE), polyethylene terephthalate (PET), silicone rubber,
and polyimide (PI)] [1–10]. Inorganic materials are usually mechanically rigid because
these are used as a bulk substrate. However, by shrinking to nano-scale size, they are

© Springer International Publishing Switzerland 2015
A. Marcus (Ed.): DUXU 2015, Part II, LNCS 9187, pp. 675–684, 2015.
DOI: 10.1007/978-3-319-20898-5_64

also mechanically flexible [11] at a bending radius at least 1 mm, which is good enough for flexible wearable devices.

In this report, we present some examples about not only wearable devices for human, but also sensor tape for other targets such as a robot and prosthesis. In particular, a fully-printed e-skin, which enables to detect tactile force, friction force, and temperature distributions, is demonstrated by considering a strain engineering [10]. Another application is a flexible and wearable device for a health monitoring, which is like a bandage to attach it on a human skin [7].

2   Multi-functional E-Skin

2.1   Three-Axis Force Sensor

To form a strain sensor using a screen printer, first, silver (Ag) (Asahi Chem., Japan) interconnection was screen-printed on a PET film. Ag film was cured at 130°C, followed by a strain sensor printing. For the strain sensor, a mixture of carbon nanotube (CNT) ink (SWeNT, USA) and Ag nanoparticle (NP) ink (PARU, Korea) was used as a screen print ink with the composition weight ratio of 5:3 as shown in Fig. 1. After printing the ink on a PE film with the alignment of Ag interconnections, the film was cured at 70°C.

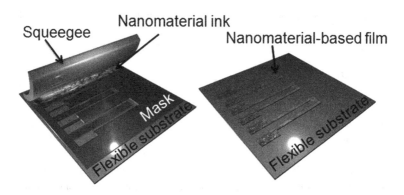

Fig. 1. Schematic of a screen print process for nanomaterial-based flexible sensor film

To create stress difference for tactile force and friction force, a three-dimensional prong with 2 mm height and 1 mm diameter was fabricated as we called "fingerprint-like structure". The fingerprint-like structure was formed by a soft-lithography technique using an acrylic plate mold and polydimethylsiloxane (PDMS) solution. After detaching PDMS-based fingerprint-like structure from the mold, it is laminated to a strain sensor sheet using an adhesive tape. Finally, to allow the strain sensor sheet to have stress distribution freely at tactile and friction forces, polyester film with 5 mm-diameter hole was laminated under the strain sensor sheet as described in Fig. 2.

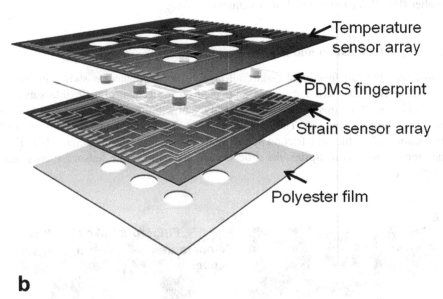

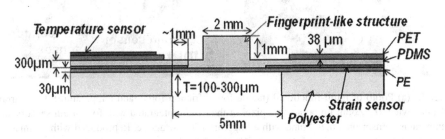

Fig. 2. (a) Schematic of each sensor layer and structure. e-skin device consists of 4 layers of a temperature sensor sheet, a fingerprint-like structure sheet, a strain sensor sheet, and a polyester sheet from top to bottom. (b) Schematic of the detail cross-sectional device of a pixel with device dimensions. Reproduced with permission from ref. [10] (Copyright 2014 American Chemical Society).

2.2 Temperature Sensor

Temperature sensor was printed on a PET film using a shadow printing method via a polyester hard mask. The ink for temperature sensor was prepared by mixing CNT ink (SWeNT, USA) and a conductive Poly(3,4-ethylenedioxythiophene)polystyrene sulfonate (PEDOT:PSS) (Sigma Aldrich, USA) with weight ratio of 1:3. The curing temperature of printed mixed ink was 70°C for more than 1 h. Subsequently, 6 mm diameter holes in PET film were formed by a laser cutter tool to laminate the strain sensor sheet and fingerprint-like structure. Due to good adhesion between PDMS for fingerprint-like structure and PET film, any adhesive tape was not used to laminate together (Fig. 2 for more detail of structures).

2.3   Layer Lamination and 3 × 3 Array E-Skin

To assemble the full functional e-skin, all layers were laminated as shown in Fig. 2. Since all sensors and structures were fabricated on a mechanically flexible substrate such as PE and PET films, e-skin can be readily bent without delamination or cracks of sensors as shown in Fig. 3a. The device has a 3 × 3 array to detect two-dimensional distributions of tactile and friction forces and temperature like a human skin. Four strain sensors with a fingerprint-like structure and one temperature sensor are integrated in a pixel (Fig. 3b).

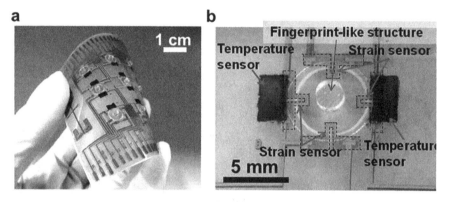

Fig. 3. (a) Photo of multi-functional (tactile force, friction force, and temperature) 3 × 3 array e-skin device. (b) Zoom-up photo of a pixel of the e-skin integrated with four strain sensors and temperature sensor on a membrane with a fingerprint-like structure. Reproduced with permission from ref. [10] (Copyright 2014 American Chemical Society).

2.4   Mechanism to Distinguish Friction Force from Tactile Force

Strain distribution is key information to observe tactile and friction forces in this device structure. Finite element method (FEM) simulation was conducted as shown in Fig. 4. When a tactile force is applied on top of a fingerprint-like structure, all membrane is depressed, resulting in that the strain/stress distribution is identical (Fig. 4b). On the other hand, when a friction force is applied, strain/stress distribution shows asymmetry around a fingerprint-like structure (Fig. 4c). By utilizing this distribution difference, tactile and friction force can be measured by integrating four strain sensors as shown in Figs. 4b and c. When a tactile pressure is applied, all strain sensors indicate the same stress. However, when a friction force is applied, strain sensor #2 indicates a higher stress than that of #4 in Fig. 4c whereas sensors #1 and #3 indicate the same stress.

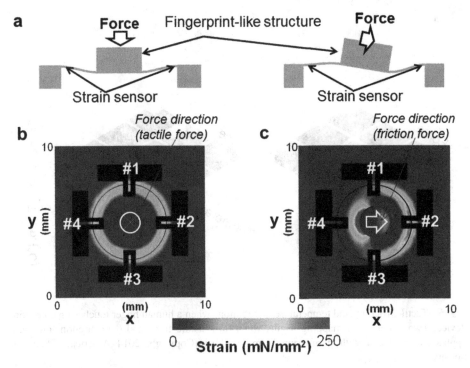

Fig. 4. Finite element method simulation. (a) Cross-sectional structural deformation when tactile force (left) and friction force (right) are applied on a fingerprint-like structure. Strain (stress) distribution in the integrated four strain sensor when (b) tactile force and (c) friction force are applied. Reproduced with permission from ref. [10] (Copyright 2014 American Chemical Society).

2.5   E-Skin Demonstration

As the first proof-of-concept of multi-functional e-skin, 3 × 3 array e-skin was demonstrated by touching the device to apply a tactile force and a friction force. Due to temperature difference between the room ($\sim$ 23°C), where the device was measured, and a human skin ($\sim$ 30°C), the temperature sensor also shows touch information. Figure 5 exhibits two-dimensional strain/stress and temperature distributions, and they clearly show that the multi-functional e-skin can successfully detect tactile, friction, and temperature distribution from economically fabricated fully printed sensor sheet (e-skin). Due to the high sensitivity of temperature sensor ($\sim$ 0.8 %/°C), radiation heat can be also detected, so that the pixel under a finger without touching the device physically indicates a temperature difference as shown in Figs. 5a and b. This suggests that the device is very similar function to one of human skin.

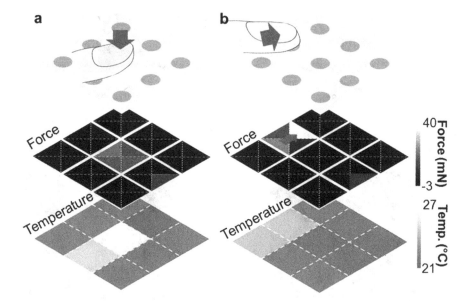

Fig. 5. Tactile, friction, and temperature distributions when a human finger touches on an e-skin device. Two-dimensional mapping results when (a) a tactile force and (b) a friction force are applied. Reproduced with permission from ref. [10] (Copyright 2014 American Chemical Society).

3   Wearable Smart Bandage

Next, a flexible and wearable device is introduced to show a variety of possibilities for macroscale and low-cost electronics. Especially, a flexible health monitoring device should open a next class of electronics that can be attached onto a human skin without awareness of human for a comfortable, convenient, and secure human life. As an example, smart bandage that can monitor temperature and deliver drug is demonstrated in this report.

3.1   Fabrication and Device Structure

The screen printing technique was mainly used to pattern Ag electrodes as explained in Fig. 1. First, Ag interconnection was printed on a Kapton substrate to form a wireless coil, a capacitive touch sensor, and electrodes for temperature sensor. After curing the Ag film at 130°C for 30 min, a temperature sensor with the same condition as explained above for e-skin was printed with the alignment of Ag electrodes. For a drug delivery pump, soft lithography technique was used to make a semi-sphere structure and microchannel using PDMS. After making an ejection hole of drug in the Kapton substrate, PDMS drug delivery pump was bonded on the Kapton substrate. Figure 6a exhibits

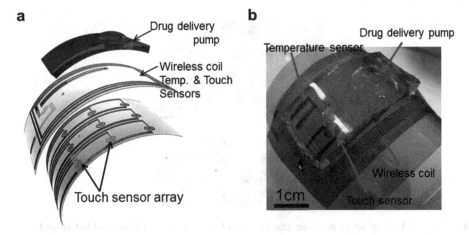

Fig. 6. (a) Schematic of the first proof-of-concept smart bandage integrated with a drug delivery pump, a wireless coil, a touch sensor, and a temperature sensor. (b) Photo of a fully printed smart bandage device on a Kapton substrate. Reproduced with permission from ref. [7] (Copyright 2014, John Wiley and Sons).

more detail of the smart bandage structure. Since all devices were fabricated on a flexible Kapton substrate and studied strain distribution, the device is mechanically flexible without any delamination of devices and cracks, it can be attached on a human body or any other surfaces as shown in Fig. 6b.

3.2 Drug Delivery Pump

Flexible PDMS-based drug delivery pump using a soft-lithography technique was bonded on a Kapton substrate integrated with a temperature sensor, a touch sensor, and a wireless coil as explained in Fig. 6. Due to a permanent bonding between PDMS and Kapton substrate, the drug delivery pump can be flexible and wearabe without any delamination (Fig. 7a). By applying a pressure onto the pump structure, dyed-water can be readily ejected through the ejection hole as shown in Fig. 7b. The threshold pressure to eject the liquid from the pump and ejection rate are $\sim$ 3.3 kPa and $\sim$ 35 nL/kPa, respective. That threshold pressure is like a gentle touch of a human, so that child and old-aged person can also operate this easily.

Due to wearable and flexible devices, the device should be non-invasive devices to prevent the controversy about medical ethic for the use of this device. To realize non-invasive drug delivery into a human, a diffusion type drug without using any needle should be appropriate for this application. However, the diffusion type drug is still limited to use for medical application. It is required to improve and develop the techniques and drugs for the future practical uses.

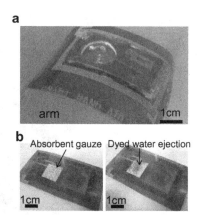

Fig. 7. (a) Photo of smart bandage attached on a human wrist. (b) Photos of before and after drug delivery (red-dyed water) from a pump to an absorbent gause. Reproduced with permission from ref. [7] (Copyright 2014, John Wiley and Sons)

3.3   Temperature and Wireless Touch Sensors

As a demonstration of printed flexible sensor, real-time measurements of integrated temperature sensor and wireless touch sensor were conducted by touching the device with a human finger. Figure 8 shows the results of human sensing. For the wireless detection, 42 MHz and 3 V transmission signal was used. The wireless coil shows the attenuation of transmission signal with ∼ 1.2 mV/mm (3.3 %/mm) at 2 V and 42 MHz as a function of coil distance. As the first demonstration of real-time monitoring, the

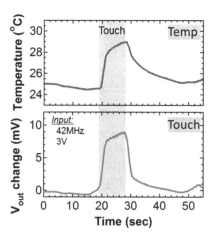

Fig. 8. Real-time temperature and wireless touch detections. Reproduced with permission from ref. [7] (Copyright 2014, John Wiley and Sons).

coil distance was only ~ 0.5 mm to observe clear sensing results. Figure 8 depicts that the integrated sensor with wireless coil can clearly measure information of human touch, suggesting that the device can be applied to human active monitoring.

3.4 Real-Time Human Skin Temperature Monitoring

Finally, real-time human skin temperature monitoring under some activities were demonstrated as the first proof-of-concept of a wearable device. To record the temperature information, a portable data logger was connected to the temperature sensor, and 5 V battery was used. The device was attached to an arm. Figure 9 exhibits the skin temperature during having a lunch with a spicy food and a short-time exercise. Since the normal human skin temperature is ~ 29-31°C, lunch with spicy food makes human skin temperature higher while a short-time exercise doesn't make a skin temperature change. Based on these results, we confirmed that the wearable temperature sensor can observe the skin temperature based on human activity with ~ 0.1°C resolutions.

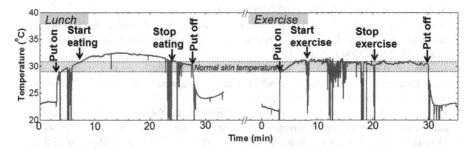

Fig. 9. Real-time human skin temperature monitoring during lunch with a spicy soup and a short-time exercise. The smart bandage was attached on an arm. Reproduced with permission from ref. [7] (Copyright 2014, John Wiley and Sons).

4 Summary

To realize future wearable electronics and sensor sheets for a variety of applications, flexible devices such as multi-functional e-skin and a smart bandage were introduced in this report. Those demonstrated devices are fabricated by a fully printing method, which allows us to realize macroscale flexible devices economically. The demonstrations described here are only a few examples. Currently, tremendous efforts are conducted to achieve high performance, multi-function, and low-cost wearable and flexible devices [1–15]. These contributions should open a next class of electronics.

Acknowledgements. This work was partially supported by JSPS KAKEN grants (#26630164 & 26709026), the Mazda Foundation, the Foundation Advanced Technology Institute, Tateichi Science and Technology Foundation, and Japan Prize Foundation.

References

1. Takei, K., Takahashi, T., Ho, J.C., Ko, H., Gillies, A.G., Leu, P.W., Fearing, R.S., Javey, A.: Nanowire active matrix circuitry for low-voltage macro-scale artificial skin. Nat. Mater. **9**, 821–826 (2010)
2. Takahashi, T., Takei, K., Adabi, E., Fan, Z., Niknejad, A., Javey, A.: Parallel array InAs nanowire transistors for mechanically bendable, ultra high frequency electronics. ACS Nano **4**, 5855–5860 (2010)
3. Takahashi, T., Takei, K., Gillies, A.G., Fearing, R.S., Javey, A.: Carbon nanotube active-matrix backplanes for conformal electronics and sensors. Nano Lett. **11**, 5408–5413 (2011)
4. Wang, C., Hwang, D., Yu, Z., Takei, K., Park, J., Chen, T., Ma, B., Javey, A.: User-interactive electronic-skin for instantaneous pressure visualization. Nat. Mater. **12**, 899–904 (2013)
5. Fan, Z., Ho, J.C., Takahashi, T., Yerushalmi, R., Takei, K., Ford, A.C., Chueh, Y.-L., Javey, A.: Toward the development of printable nanowire electronics and sensors. Adv. Mater. **21**, 3730–3743 (2009)
6. Takei, K., Yu, Z., Zheng, M., Ota, H., Takahashi, T., Javey, A.: Highly sensitive electronic whiskers based on patterned carbon nanotube and silver nanoparticle composite films. Proc. Natl. Acad. Sci. (PNAS) **111**, 1703–1707 (2014)
7. Honda, W., Harada, S., Arie, T., Akita, S., Takei, K.: Wearable human-interactive health-monitoring wireless devices fabricated by macroscale printing techniques. Adv. Func. Mater. **24**, 3299–3304 (2014)
8. Harada, S., Honda, W., Arie, T., Akita, S., Takei, K.: Fully printed, highly sensitive multi-functional artificial electronic whisker arrays integrated with strain and temperature sensors. ACS Nano **8**, 3921–3927 (2014)
9. Honda, W., Arie, T., Akita, S., Takei, K.: Printable and foldable electrodes based on a carbon nanotube-polymer composition. Phys. Status Solidi A **11**, 2631–2634 (2014)
10. Harada, S., Kanao, K., Yamamoto, Y., Arie, T., Akita, S., Takei, K.: Fully printed flexible fingerprint-like three-axis tactile and slip force and temperature sensors for artificial skin. ACS Nano **8**, 12851–12857 (2014)
11. Rogers, J.A., Lagally, M.G., Nuzzo, R.G.: Synthesis, assembly and applications of semiconductor nanomembranes. Nature **477**, 45–53 (2011)
12. Webb, R.C., et al.: Ultrathin conformal devices for precise and continuous thermal characterization of human skin. Nat. Mater. **12**, 938–944 (2013)
13. Kaltenbrunner, M., et al.: An ultra-lightweight design for imperceptible plastic electronics. Nature **498**, 458–463 (2013)
14. Someya, T., Kato, Y., Sekitani, T., Iba, S., Noguchi, Y., Murase, Y., Kawaguchi, H., Sakurai, T.: Conformable, flexible, large-area networks of pressure and thermal sensors with organic transistor active matrixes. Proc. Natl. Acad. Sci. (PNAS) **102**, 12321–12325 (2005)
15. Mannsfeld, S.C.B., Tee, B.C.-K., Stoltenberg, R.M., Chen, C.V.H.-H., Barman, S., Muir, B.V.O., Sokolov, A.N., Reese, C., Bao, Z.: Highly sensitive flexible pressure sensors with microstructured rubber dielectric layers. Nat. Mater. **9**, 859–864 (2010)

Tattoo Antenna Temporary Transfers Operating On-Skin (TATTOOS)

James Tribe[1], Dumtoochukwu Oyeka[2], John Batchelor[2],
Navjot Kaur[1], Diana Segura-Velandia[1], Andrew West[1], Robert Kay[1],
Katia Vega[3], and Will Whittow[1(✉)]

[1] Loughborough University, Loughborough, UK
{j.tribe,w.g.whittow}@lboro.ac.uk
[2] University of Kent, Canterbury, UK
J.C.Batchelor@kent.ac.uk
[3] Pontifical Catholic University of Rio de Janeiro, Rio de Janeiro, Brazil

Abstract. This paper discusses the development of RFID logo antennas based on the logos of Loughborough University and the University of Kent which can be tattooed directly onto the skin's surface. Hence, this paper uses aesthetic principles to create functional wearable technology. Simulations of possible designs for the tattoo tags have been carried out to optimize their performance. Prototypes of the tag designs were fabricated and read range measurements with the transfer tattoos on a volunteers arm were carried out to test the performance. Measured read ranges of approximately 0.5 m have been achieved with the tag only 10 μm from the body.

Keywords: Aesthetic design · Body centric communication · Conducting ink · RFID

1 Introduction

RFID technology is used for tracking a variety of items. There are numerous applications where tracking of people would be beneficial which include elderly people with dementia; athletes; military; firefighters and ticketing for music or sports events. Using a tattoo tag that can be mounted directly onto the skin has many advantages over more traditional RFID tags. These include the added security and convenience to the user as the tag cannot be stolen or lost. One of the most desirable attributes of an RFID tag tattooed on the skin is an attractive shape for example a star; a smiley face or the logo of a sports team or organisation.

This paper uses the logos of Loughborough University and University of Kent in the design of the RFID tags. The antenna designs are based on the nested slot line antenna used in [1] which has a slot as the main radiating element so there is a degree of flexibility in the shape. The size of the slot was adjusted to match the antenna to the RFID chip at the desired frequency of 868 MHz. Electromagnetic simulations of the antenna designs on a human body model were used to determine the efficiency and gain of the tattoo RFID tags.

© Springer International Publishing Switzerland 2015
A. Marcus (Ed.): DUXU 2015, Part II, LNCS 9187, pp. 685–695, 2015.
DOI: 10.1007/978-3-319-20898-5_65

The antenna designs were printed onto temporary transfer tattoo inkjet paper using electrically conductive paint. The antenna was on a thin layer of plastic (~ 10 μm) so it can be placed on the human body and read range measurements were carried out. The read range measurements were then compared to the simulated gain of the antennas.

2 Wearable Antennas

Wearable technology is a popular topic in multiple disciplines which include medicine, engineering, architecture and fashion [2]. In today's world the use of wireless connectivity is important which requires the development of wearable antennas. One of the difficulties with wearable antennas is attaining high levels of electromagnetic performance when in the presence of a human [3].

For the fabrication of wearable antennas a number of techniques have previously been used which have been reviewed in [4, 5]. The use of a conductive thread embroidered into clothing to create an antenna was used in [3, 6, 7]. These antennas have the advantage of flexibility and comfort for the user and do not need to be held in the hand. The efficiencies of these antennas are often reduced compared to their copper equivalents due to the embroidery process and the conductive threads used. An inkjet printed textile antenna was created in [8] which showed efficiencies of greater than 60 % with only a single layer of conducting ink. Another method for body mounted tags is to use printed circuit board substrate which regularly has a metal ground plan between the body and radiating tag. This can then be mounted on clothing or some object like a wrist band rather than directly on the skin [9, 10]. The interaction of passive metallic objects near, on and in the body has been previously examined in [11–17].

2.1 Logo Antennas

With the rapid advancement of wearable technology it is becoming commercially important that the antennas used are both functional and aesthetically pleasing so the user will be more accepting of the technology. This has led to research into logo antennas as in [18] which designed a patch antenna based on the Loughborough University shield. This work showed that the logo designs could be scaled to the required frequency and based on the geometry an optimal feed point can be chosen. With diverse designs there comes varying difficulties that have to be addressed such as concave sections, angular sections and disconnected sections.

In [19] a wearable logo textile antenna was designed based on the authors University name. It was shown that bending of the antenna affected the impedance matching but did not affect the radiation efficiency. The radiation pattern of the antenna was Omni-directional and was deformed at higher frequencies but showed good performance overall. The City University of Hong Kong's logo was designed as a patch antenna in [20]. The frequency band of the patch antenna was broadened by carefully designing slots. The wideband performance was created by effectively having two antennas with low Q so there was little reactance cancellation between them.

2.2 Transfer Tattoo Tags

In this paper the idea is to use a tag that is mounted directly on the skin, with a vanishingly thin insulating layer between the body and the tag antenna [21]. Tags such as these mean they can be used for sensing functions as they are more intimately interfaced with the skin. Additionally as these tags cannot be taken from one individual and passed onto another there is a physical security. Note, previous work demonstrates these tags last approximately 24 h without washing the skin surface and are temporary.

A possible process for creating the tags uses inkjet printing to deposit a layer of conducting ink on a transfer paper which is used for creating transfer tattoos. Once the tag design is printed onto the transfer surface of the tattoo paper, the ink is sintered to render the printed shape conducting. The sintering process usually involves heat but other techniques at lower temperatures such as plasma, chemical or photonic treatments can be used which save energy and reduce damage to transfer material. It is then required to mount an RFID transponder chip to the antenna structure which can be done using a conducting epoxy resin. The next step is to apply a thin adhesive polymer layer over the conducting surface which is used to attach the transfer to the skin. Once the transfer is applied water is used to remove the paper backing from the transfer.

The end result is a conductive RFID tag in between two polymer layers. This means that the ink is not in direct contact with the skin and fixes the fragile antenna structure. During the sintering stage there is optimization required between obtaining a high enough conductivity value in the ink without burning the paper or making the ink too frail. If the conductivity is not high enough the ink surface will degrade and break the circuit, whereas if the ink is too frail it will have an increased chance of failure while mounted on the flexible skin surface [22]. The use of this technique will result in the fabrication of logo tattoo antennas being a cheap and convenient process [23].

3 Antenna Design

The antenna designs were based on nested slot line antennas [24] which radiate at the RFID UHF band through surface currents being produced on a conductive patch. The schematic of the nested slot line can be seen in Fig. 1 and shows the parameters; l for slot length, w for slot width, L for antenna length, W for antenna width, t the distance the slot is from the edge, and G the gap width at the input for the antenna. The RFID chip is connected between the two coplanar lines at the gap G. The chip has a negative reactance so an inductance is required from the antenna to cancel it out for maximum power transmission. An inductance is produced by an electric field being induced inside the slot and a current loop caused to flow around the outside of it. The effective aperture size of the antenna is large enough to provide improved efficiency through the current being free to spread out over the patch, and the width of the slot being small compared to wavelength [25].

The antenna designs are based on the logos of Loughborough University and the University of Kent. For the University of Kent logo an image of the logo was subtracted from a patch antenna and the K of the logo was used as the slot for the antenna, see Fig. 2a. For the antenna based on the logo for Loughborough University an image

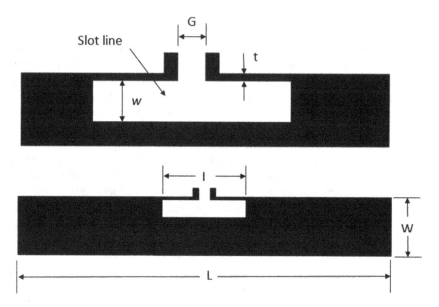

Fig. 1. Nested slot line antenna schematic

of the Loughborough University shield was converted to a CAD file so that it could be designed with a slot on the side of it, see Fig. 2b. Please note permission was requested to use the university logos for this paper and the institutions retain all copyright and trademark rights.

Fig. 2. Tattoo antenna designs: a) University of Kent logo, and b) Loughborough University shield.

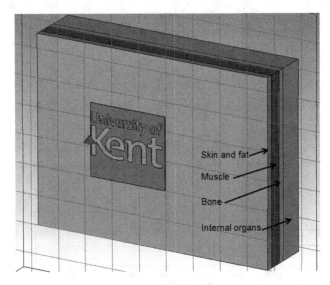

Fig. 3. RFID tag on human body model

4 Antenna Simulations

The tags were simulated using CST on a multilayer model of human tissue being used to represent the human body, see Fig. 3. The parameters used in the simulation for the model of the human body can be seen in Table 1 [26]. To represent the RFID chip an impedance of 23.3-j145 Ω for the port at the input to the antenna. The metal used for the antennas was copper at a thickness of 200 µm. The parameters of each tag were adjusted to get the tag to resonate at the required frequency of 868 MHz while optimizing the gain and efficiency. Both of the antennas had a gap width of 2 mm for the chip and had the slot 0.5 mm from the edge. The University of Kent antenna had a length of 50 mm, a width of 60 mm, a slot length of 20 mm and a slot width of 3 mm. The Loughborough University antenna had a length of 63 mm, a width 53 mm, a slot length of 24.5 mm and a slot width of 2 mm. The simulated s11 values for the University of Kent logo and the Loughborough University logo can be seen in Figs. 4 and 5 respectively. The gain values for the University of Kent logo antenna and the Loughborough University shield were -17.1 dBi and -19.9 dBi respectively. Note, these values are less than conventional antennas as there is only a 10 µm separation between the tag and the skin.

Table 1. Human model: electrical parameters at 900 MHz [26]

Layer	ε_r	σ (S/m)	Layer thickness (mm)
Skin and fat	14.5	0.25	5
Muscle	55	0.94	10
Bone	12.6	3.85	5
Internal organs	52	0.91	20

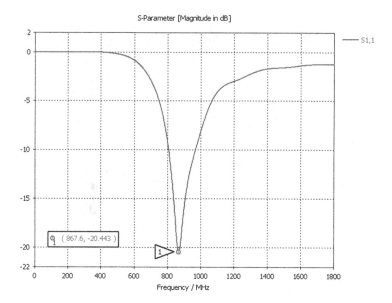

Fig. 4. Simulated s11 for University of Kent tag

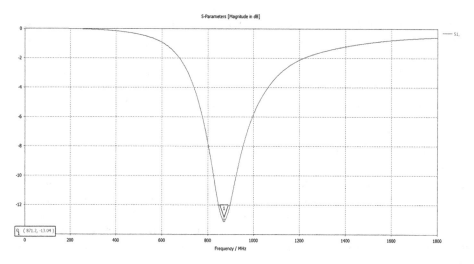

Fig. 5. Simulated s11 for Loughborough University tag

5   Fabrication and Read Range Measurements

The tags were fabricated by first etching the antenna structure pattern as a negative in a thin metal stencil; an example can be seen in Fig. 6 which was used for the Loughborough University logo antenna. An electrically conductive silver paint was then

Fig. 6. Loughborough University shield antenna stencil

Fig. 7. Loughborough University shield transfer tattoo tag on the arm of a volunteer

deposited on temporary transfer tattoo inkjet paper using the stencils as a profile to form the metalized layer. The RFID IC is then attached to the input ports of the tattoo tag antennas. The transfer tattoo tags can then be placed on a volunteer's arm. There is a thin layer of plastic between the skin of the volunteer and the antenna Fig. 7.

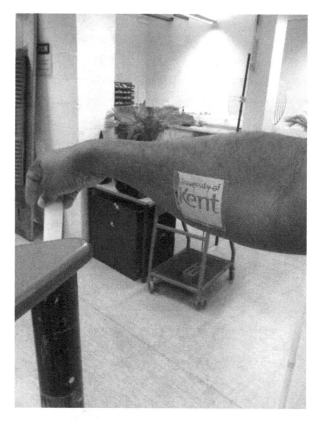

Fig. 8. Read range measurement of Kent logo tag

Read range measurements where then carried out using the Tagformance lite measurement device in Fig. 8. The read range measurements for the University of Kent logo tag can be seen in Fig. 9 which shows that the read range at the EU UHF RFID band (868 MHz) was 44 cm and at the US UHF RFID band (924 MHz) was 47 cm. The Loughborough University logo tag had a read range of 37 cm in the EU band and 49 cm in the US band which can be seen in Fig. 10. The Kent logo having a larger read range at the EU band is consistent with the simulations as it had a higher gain and radiation efficiency at that frequency.

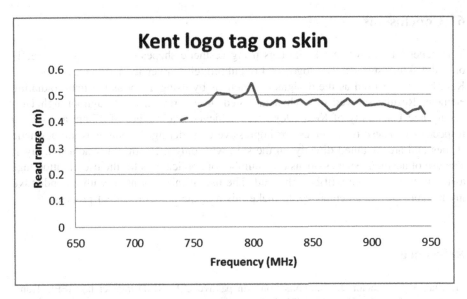

Fig. 9. University of Kent logo tag on skin read range measured results

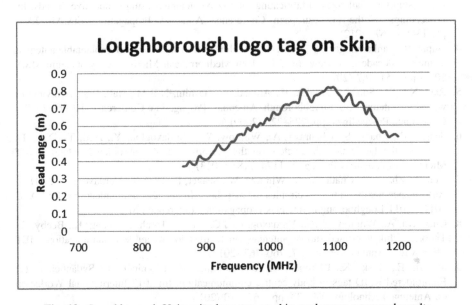

Fig. 10. Loughborough University logo tag on skin read range measured results

6 Conclusions

This paper has shown that RFID tags using aesthetic shapes can be tattooed directly onto the skin's surface. The logos of Loughborough University and the University of Kent have been used as the designs of antennas by using a slot as the main radiating element. Results showed that when mounted on a forearm, the Loughborough University and University of Kent's logo tags achieved read ranges of 37 cm and 44 cm respectively. These read ranges are impressive considering the antennas are aesthetic shapes and are mounted directly on the skin with only a 10 μm thick adhesive layer. The use of aesthetic shapes opens up a number of applications for the use of tattoo tags as the user experience will be enhanced. The use of inkjet printing with a conductive ink to fabricate the antennas could make this a cheap and convenient process.

References

1. Ziai, M., Batchelor, J.: Temporary on-skin passive UHF RFID transfer tag. IEEE Trans. Antennas Propag. **59**, 3565–3571 (2011)
2. Cranny-Francis, A., Hawkins, C.: Wearable technology. Vis. Commun. **7**, 267–270 (2008)
3. Chauraya, A., Zhang, S., Whittow, W., Acti, T., Seager, R., Dias, T., Vardaxoglou, Y.C.: Addressing the challenges of fabricating microwave antennas using conductive threads. In: Proceedings of the 6th European Conference Antennas Propagation, EuCAP 2012. pp. 1365–1367 (2012)
4. Gupta, B., Sankaralingam, S., Dhar, S.: Development of wearable and implantable antennas in the last decade: A review. In: 2010 10th Mediterranean Microwave Symposium MMS 2010, pp. 251–267 (2010)
5. Rais, N.H.M., Soh, P.J., Malek, F., Ahmad, S., Hashim, N.B.M., Hall, P.S.: A review of wearable antenna. In: Loughborough Antennas Propagation Conference LAPC 2009 - Conference Proceedings, pp. 225–228 (2009)
6. Seager, R., Zhang, S., Chauraya, A., Whittow, W., Vardaxoglou, Y., Acti, T., Dias, T.: Effect of the fabrication parameters on the performance of embroidered antennas. IET Microwaves Antennas Propag. **7**, 1174–1181 (2013)
7. Acti, T., Zhang, S., Chauraya, A., Whittow, W., Seager, R., Dias, T., Vardaxoglou, Y.: High performance flexible fabric electronics for megahertz frequency communications. In: LAPC 2011 - 2011 Loughborough Antennas Propagation Conference (2011)
8. Chauraya, A., Whittow, W.G., Vardaxoglou, J.C., Li, Y., Torah, R., Yang, K., Beeby, S., Tudor, J.: Inkjet printed dipole antennas on textiles for wearable communications. IET Microwaves Antennas Propag. **7**, 760–767 (2013)
9. Moradi, E., Koski, K., Ukkonen, L., Rahmat-Samii, Y., Björninen, T., Sydänheimo, L.: Embroidered RFID tags in body-centric communication. In: 2013 International Workshop on Antenna Technology (iWAT), pp. 367–370 (2013)
10. Manzari, S., Occhiuzzi, C., Marrocco, G.: Feasibility of body-centric systems using passive textile RFID tags. IEEE Antennas Propag. Mag. **54**, 49–62 (2012)
11. Panagamuwa, C.J., Whittow, W., Edwards, R., Vardaxoglou, J.C., McEvoy, P.: A study of the validation of RF energy specific absorption rates for simulations of anatomically correct head FDTD simulations and truncated DASY4 standard equipment measurements. In: European Conference on Antennas and Propagation, pp. 1–5 (2006)

12. Panagamuwa, C.J., Whittow, W.G., Edwards, R.M., Vardaxoglou, J.C.: Experimental verification of a modified Specific Anthropomorphic Mannequin (SAM) head used for SAR measurements. 2007 Loughborough Antennas Propagation Conference, LAPC 2007 Conference Proceedings, pp. 261–264 (2007)

13. Stergiou, K., Panagamuwa, C., Whittow, W., Edwards, R.: Effects of metallic semi-rimmed spectacles on SAR in the head from a 900 MHz frontal dipole source. In: Loughborough Antennas Propagation Conference, LAPC 2009 - Conference Proceedings, pp. 721–724 (2009)

14. Whittow, W.G., Panagamuwa, C.J., Edwards, R.M., Vardaxoglou, J.C.: On the effects of straight metallic jewellery on the specific absorption rates resulting from face-illuminating radio communication devices at popular cellular frequencies. Phys. Med. Biol. **53**, 1167–1182 (2008)

15. Whittow, W., Panagamuwa, C.J., Edwards, R., Vardaxoglou, J.C.: Specific absorption rates in the human head due to circular metallic earrings at 1800 MHz. In: 2007 Loughborough Antennas Propagation Conference, LAPC 2007 Conference Proceedings, pp. 277–280 (2007)

16. Whittow, W.G., Edwards, R.M., Panagamuwa, C.J., Vardaxoglou, J.C.: Effect of tongue jewellery and orthodontist metallic braces on the sar due to mobile phones in different anatomical human head models including children. In: 2008 Loughborough Antennas Propagation Conference, LAPC, pp. 293–296 (2008)

17. Panagamuwa, C.J., Whittow, W.G., Edwards, R.M., Vardaxoglou, J.C.: A study of the effects of metallic pins on SAR using a specific anthropomorphic mannequin (SAM) head phantom. In: European Conference on Antennas and Propogation, pp. 1–6 (2007)

18. Whittow, W.: Antenna emblems reshaped as icons and aesthetic logos (Aerial). Microw. Opt. Technol. Lett. **55**, 1711–1714 (2013)

19. Mahmud, M.S., Dey, S.: Design, performance and implementation of UWB wearable logo textile antenna. In: 2012 15 International Symposium Antenna Technology Application Electromagnetic, pp. 1–4 (2012)

20. Chow, Y., Fung, C.: The city university logo patch antenna. In: Asia Pacific Microwave Conference, pp. 4–7 (1997)

21. Ziai, M., Batchelor, J.: RFID TAGs as transfer tattoos. In: 2011 Loughborough Antennas and Propagation Conference (LAPC), pp. 1–4 (2011)

22. Sanchez-Romaguera, V., Ziai, M.A., Oyeka, D., Barbosa, S., Wheeler, J.S.R., Batchelor, J.C., Parker, E.A., Yeates, S.G.: Towards inkjet-printed low cost passive UHF RFID skin mounted tattoo paper tags based on silver nanoparticle inks. J. Mater. Chem. C. **1**, 6395 (2013)

23. Batchelor, J., Parker, E.: Inkjet printing of frequency selective surfaces. Electron. Lett. **45**, 1–2 (2009)

24. Marrocco, G.: RFID antennas for the UHF remote monitoring of human subjects. IEEE Trans. Antennas Propag. **55**, 1862–1870 (2007)

25. Kraus, J., Marhefka, R.: Antennas. McGraw-Hill, New York (1988)

26. Gabriel, C., Gabriel, S., Corthout, E.: The dielectric properties of biological tissues: I. Literature survey. Phys. Med. Biol. **41**, 2231–2249 (1996)

Hairware: Designing Conductive Hair Extensions for Seamless Interfaces

Katia Vega[1]([⊠]), Ricardo Aucelio[2], and Hugo Fuks[1]

[1] Department of Informatics, Pontifical Catholic University of Rio de Janeiro,
Rio de Janeiro, Brazil
{kvega,hugo}@inf.puc-rio.br
[2] Department of Chemistry, Pontifical Catholic University of Rio de Janeiro,
Rio de Janeiro, Brazil
aucelior@puc-rio.br

Abstract. Due to increasing advances in electronics, devices are getting even more small and powerful, making it possible the widespread of wearable computing. However, most wearable devices have the electronics very distinguished and placed on clothes and accessories. Our proposal is Beauty Technology, a wearable computing subfield that uses the body's surface as an interactive platform by integrating technology into beauty products applied directly to one's skin, fingernails, and hair. This paper presents Hairware, a Beauty Technology that fosters a seamlessly looking approach to wearables. It is artificial hair extensions that are chemically metalized to maintain a natural coloration and when connected to a microcontroller could be used as both, input and output devices. This paper describes the design process in creating these conductive hair extensions and discuses lessons learned in the development of them.

Keywords: Hairware · Conductive hair extensions · Beauty technology · Wearable computing

1 Introduction

The fact that big software companies such as Google, Motorola, Apple and Microsoft are creating wearable tech, and also the fashion industry icons like Nike and Adidas are making significant investments in this area is an indicator that wearables will become mainstream devices in the forthcoming years [1]. Google Glass [2] could be one of the clearest examples of wearable devices that have garnered great attention in recent years. These glasses embed a display coupled with a location awareness sensor, illustrating the potential of wearable computing technologies to tap into apps and enable the user to access information. Start-ups are also investing in wearables technologies. For example, Pebble [3] created a wristwatch designed to interact with an iPhone and in a short period of time it has broken records on the crowdfunding platform Kickstarter. However, currently most of these gadgets are designed for men and are supposed to be worn as clothing and accessories, where the technology is visible and the gestures needed for interacting with these devices are noticeable.

© Springer International Publishing Switzerland 2015
A. Marcus (Ed.): DUXU 2015, Part II, LNCS 9187, pp. 696–704, 2015.
DOI: 10.1007/978-3-319-20898-5_66

Given today's wearables revolution, the human body will become a new design standpoint. Thus, the next logical step in wearable computing seems to be the use of the body's roughly two square meters of skin as a canvas for applying sensors and attaching other computing devices in ways that enhance human experience. The body surface, i.e., the skin, nails and hair, plays crucial roles as a protective barrier, sensory monitor, heat and moisture regulator, and an integral part of the body's immune system. Nevertheless, humanity, since its inception, has used beauty products to adorn the body for a variety of reasons. Nowadays, beauty products have become quite sophisticated with advances in chemistry but have still remain an aesthetically functionality. Even more, the billionaire beauty business is constantly growing and most of women use these products in their daily basis, beauty products have not yet been thoroughly explored in relation to their use as wearable computing. Our goal is to disrupt this frontier by adding new functionality to beauty products using technology in a personal, seamless and fashionable way. Our proposal is Beauty Technology, a Wearable Computing subfield that uses the body's surface as an interactive platform by integrating technology into beauty products applied directly to one's skin, fingernails, and hair.

This paper makes use of (modified) hair extensions to design interfaces that, when applied to the body's surface, foster novel interaction possibilities. We propose Hairware, a Beauty Technology based on conductive hair extensions that are attached to a microcontroller in order to be used both as an input and an output device. Hairware acts as an input device by detecting a variety of strokes for triggering different devices. It also acts as an output device by controlling actuators like LEDs and vibration motors attached directly to the conductive hair extensions.

Section 2 identifies previous work on conductive materials for wearable computing and on body technologies. Section 3 presents our process for chemically metalizing hair extensions, to create a conductive material that when attached to a microcontroller could detect hair touch gestures for triggering devices and turn on actuators attached to this hair. Section 4 reviews the lessons learned from prototyping and using Hairware. Conclusion and future work are shown in the last section.

2   Related Work

Developments in novel materials are improving the ease of embedding technologies into fabrics as well as the use of implantable devices and biosensors [1]. Nanotechnology, biotechnology, information technology and cognitive technology are converging - making it possible to foresee wearables with their own power generation, flexible displays and electric-responsive materials [4]. Even more, the miniaturization and availability of electronic components has made possible the widespread adoption of wearable computing, moving from the realm of science fiction to the marketplace in areas such as fashion, health, and wellness for the aging and the disabled. Fibrous materials, such as textile and paper, are flexible, foldable, easily cut and attached to flexible substrates. Once they get electrical conductivity and good mechanical endurance against external deformation, they become attractive for flexible and wearable electronics [5]. Conductive fabrics that are created for wearable technologies are already at the marketplace. Conductive yarn, plated fabric, printing on fabric, and sewing on fabric are some approaches to create e-textiles that are used to embed electronics into textiles [6].

Wearables are already causing a rethinking of the boundaries of the body. Lucy McRae [7] envisions future possibilities of merging technology and the human body. Through artistic showcases, she redefines the body by mimicking its musculature, thus, changing the perception of our own body to create futuristic human shapes. Along these lines, LED eyelashes [8] expose the desire of many Asian women to show more of their eyes by lighting the eyelashes that follow pupil and head movements.

In previous works, Beauty Technologies presented Conductive Makeup [9–11] (Fig. 1) that is an aesthetic interface for detecting voluntary blinking, thus triggering devices according to programmed events. Conductive Makeup includes conductive eyeliner and black fake eyelashes that act as blinking switches. While conductive eyeliners connect sensors and actuators by using conductive materials that stick to the skin, replacing conventional eyeliners, conductive fake eyelashes sense the voluntary blinking. In order to prove the feasibility of the prototype as a conductive component, some applications were developed. Blinklifier [9] uses blinking for switching LEDs on and off on an artistic head dress. Arcana [10] uses blinking for changing music tracks and images visualizations. Superhero [11] (Fig. 1b) is another artistic application that makes use of Conductive Makeup for triggering a remote control to levitate an object.

Wigs could be used as to enhance someone's appearance and also to follow cultural and religious traditions. SmartWig [12] is a wearable device that uses the base of a wig for hiding electronics that communicates wirelessly with other external devices. SmartWig suggests applications that could fulfill a number of functions, from acting as a health care device that monitors users' vital signs to helping blind people navigate roads, or changes slides in a presentation by tapping their sideburns, under which buttons are hidden. A further potential improvement of the wig may use ultrasound

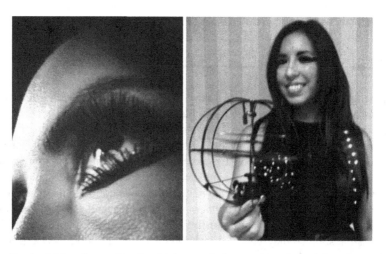

Fig. 1. Conductive makeup. (a) Conductive eyelashes and eyeliner in natural coloration. (b) Superhero project that levitates a drone by blinking.

waves to detect objects around a user. Hair accessories that vary from clips to corsages could be used for creating discreet and fashionable gadgets attached to the hair. First Sign Hair Clip [13] is a hair clip with electronics inside that communicates with a mobile application to automatically call for help and collect evidence when the user is in danger. The clip detects head impacts associated with a violent crime by using an accelerometer and gyroscope, which automatically triggers the alarm, while evidence is collected with a microphone.

3 Designing Hairware

The hair is public as everyone could see it, personal as it is a body part, and malleable as it suits cultural and personal preferences [14]. This work proposes the use of (modified) artificial hair extensions as a novel electronic device to be used in wearable computing. We used a chemical platting technique that makes the l hair extensions to be conductive but, at the same time, looks like human hair. Then, they could be connected to a microcontroller to be used as sensors or actuators. We use hair clips for attaching the circuit to the hair extensions in order to be easily removable and replaceable. Also this makes it possible to put the circuit in different accessory such as a hairclip, headband, brooch and the top of the hair extensions.

This section describes the materials and the prototyping process used. It also shows the feasibility of this technology as an input and output device.

3.1 Chemical Process for Creating Hairware

Artificial hair extensions are chemically metalized for acquiring electrical conductivity and also keeping a natural coloration. We used 6 strands of hair extensions of approximate 1.5 by 25 cm each. Before passing by the chemical process, they are cleaned and weighted. Tests are performed at DC voltages of 5 V, with a multimeter and a balance.

The chemical process is carried out in two phases: Activation and Electrolysis. During the first phase, artificial hair extensions, being plastic non-conducting surfaces, require some kind of activation to enable them to be submitted to an electrochemical process. For the first activation, hydrogen and tin (II) chloride are used. Then, a silver nitrate solution is added for the second activation, where the extensions are set up to catalyze electron transfer reactions, making them ready for metalizing. Next, electrolysis is used for platting them. Copper is electrochemically deposited for making them electrically conductive while "black nickel" gives the natural black effect. A copper plaque is needed for the electrolysis process. Table 1 shows the formulations and times needed for creating Hairware.

After the chemical process, the hair extensions are weighted. Table 2 shows each of the hair extensions initial weight, the final one and the percentage of weight variation. The hair extensions got an average of 21 % more of their original weight. Also electrical resistances of each hairpiece were measured with a multimeter. It is highly conductive with a surface resistivity of less than 5 ohm/sq.

Table 1. Hairware electrochemical process

	Formulation		Temp (° C)	Time (Min)
Activation 1	1 L	Final solution	21	7
	10 g	$SnCl_2$ ($2H_2O$)		
	40 mL	HCl ($\gg$37 %?)		
Activation 2	1 L	Final solution	21	7
	2 g	$AgNO_3$		
	10 mL	NH_3		
Copper electrolysis	1 L	Final solution	40	10
	14 g	$CuSO_4 \cdot 5H_2O$		
	30 g	Potassium sodium tartrate ($KNaC_4H_4O_6 \cdot 4H_2O$)		
	10 g	NaOH		
	40 mL	Formaldehyde (CH2O)		
Copper acid	1 L	Final solution	21	10
	220 g	$CuSO_4 \cdot 5H_2O$		
	34 mL	H_2SO_4		
	10 mL	Cupracid solution		
	0.5 mL	Cupracid brightener 210 Part A		
	0.5 mL	Cupracid brightener 210 Part B		
	0.12 g	NaCl		
Black nickel electrolysis	1 L	Final solution	21	10
	120 g	$NiSO_4$		
	40 g	$NiCl_2$		

Table 2. Hairware features

	Initial weight g	Final weight g	Δ Weight g %	Resistance Ω
Hairware 1	1.35	1.74	22.41	3.8
Hairware 2	1.08	1.16	6.90	4.2
Hairware 3	1.55	1.85	16.22	4.7
Hairware 4	1.34	1.55	13.55	4.8
Hairware 5	0.79	1.17	32.48	4.9
Hairware 6	0.85	1.29	34.11	4.4
1.16	**1.46**	**20.94**	**4.47**

3.2 Hairware as an Output Device

Figure 2 shows our first application for showing the feasibility of Hairware as an output device. Different kinds of actuators such as buzzers and LEDs could be attached to the conductive hair extensions to be triggered by a microcontroller. We connected 2 Hairware strands to LEDs using hairclips. Its positive pin connected to the sender pin in

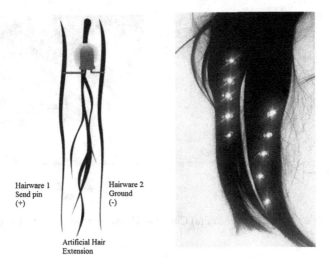

Hairware 1
Send pin
(+)

Hairware 2
Ground
(-)

Artificial Hair
Extension

Fig. 2. Hairware as an actuator. (a) Placing an LED on the conductive hair extensions. (b) Lighting Hairware.

the Arduino and the negative one connected to ground. Artificial hair extensions with no conductivity are placed between the conductive hair extensions for isolating them. This wearable turns on the LEDs attached to the hair and changes their intensity and the lighting effects could also repeat the rhythm of music. Other actuators such as buzzers and vibration motors could replace LEDs.

3.3 Hairware as an Input Device

In order to show the feasibility of using Hairware as an input device, we used it as a capacitance sensor that detects the touch on the extensions. We used an Arduino microcontroller, LEDs, resistors and 2 Hairware strands. Each of the Hairware strands is connected to a send and receive pin of the microcontroller and 2 LEDs are also connected. Figure 3 shows Hairware's capacitance sensors functionality. When the receive pin's state change by making a low touch on a strand, the corresponding LED is turned on. Thus, each LED is ON when this sensor detects when someone touches Hairware. This circuit creates a delay in the pulse that is the time the capacitor takes to charge and discharge. In this way, Hairware is used as a conductive surface that detects when another conductive surface approximates to it. Therefore, as the human body is conductive, the average internal resistance of a human trunk is $\sim 100\,\Omega$ [15], touching Hairware will affect capacitance and result in a different charging time.

Other approach of the use of Hairware as an input device is to use hair extensions as layers on the conductive hair extension. Three layers of non- conductive hair extensions are added for isolating the hair from the skin. Also, these layers improved the capacitor sensor values. Each time the user touch the top, middle or tip, the capacitor sensor differentiates these values. The circuit compares an output that transmits the pulse and an input, which receives the pulse. When a finger touches Hairware, it creates

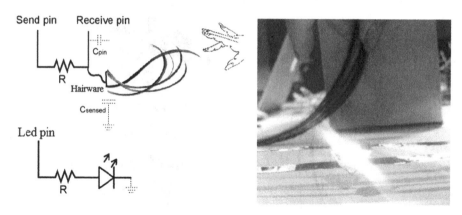

Fig. 3. Hairware as a capacitive sensor. (a) Circuit of Hairware as an input device. (b) Touching Hairware to trigger LEDs.

a delay in the pulse, and this delay is recalculated by the Arduino microcontroller. The circuit diagram is also composed with four 1 MΩ resistors and one 100pF capacitor. The resistors selects the sensitivity, bigger the resistor, the farther away it detects a human. With 4 MΩ resistors between the output and input pins the circuit is tuned to start to respond one inch away, just the sufficient to overcome the non-conductive hair layer. The small capacitor (100 pF) placed from sensor pin to ground improves stability and repeatability. Some LEDs were added to the system to give feedback to the user whenever a touch is detected.

4   Lessons Learned

Due to the proximity with the body, the term cyborg is commonly associated with wearable computing, and science fiction has foretold the merging of man and machine for many years, but it is usually presented as a human with electronics emerging from his skin. We will no doubt recognize that today's wearable technologies are nevertheless very 'distinguishable'. In this project, we propose interfaces "becoming" cyborgs but without having their stereotypical visual aesthetics. Our approach for using Hairware as an input device that senses human gestures with hair proposes that not only a technology is seamless, but also the gestures that trigger devices are unnoticed by an external observer. In this way, depending on the way Hairware is used, there are some concerns related to privacy that could be controversial.

Our first attempts in creating Hairware as an input device were measuring deformation of the object when it is squeeze. Thus, we enrolled the Skweezee workshop at TEI 2014 [16] that measured squeeze on deformable objects fulfilled with conductive wool. They measured the resistance difference when squeezed, thus the conductive filling lowering the resistance between any pair of electrodes. This approached didn't fit this project because almost doesn't change its resistance when it is twisted.

We observed that after the Copper electrolysis step, the extensions got a golden color. Our aim was to get a darker color thus we applied the "black nickel" electrolysis.

But, the metalizing process could be stopped there for a golden color of the hair extensions and also our chemical formulations could be modified with other materials in order to obtain different hair colors.

Due to the skin resistance, Hairware must be placed on any non-conductive material for isolating it from the skin like a shirt. Also other conductive materials like jewelry could affect the way it operates. Future works will include a new step in our chemical process that isolates all conductive hair extensions but preserving its capacitance sensitivity. Also part of it will be totally isolated to work as switches in different lengths of the hair, thus, gestures could be recognized.

The hair extensions after the chemical process gained almost 21 % of weight. Even that, we observed that is not a noticeable weight for a slight device. Even that most of the hair threads were totally conductive, a higher resistance was presented at some hair threads (about 120 ohms) and from the very beginning of the hair to the end.

5   Conclusion

Our aim is to develop wearable technologies that transform the body surface in an interactive platform in a way that a simple gesture could be an input for other devices and actuators could be placed on it. In this way we transform the body into a circuit's board. Beauty Technology that extends the concept of beauty products from altering and highlighting someone's appearance to giving her the power of digitally connect with herself and her environment. It hides technology on beauty products and places them on the body surface such as the hair, skin, and nails. Previous work showed Conductive Makeup, Tech Nails and FX e-makeup as the first beauty technologies. This work presented Hairware, conductive hair extensions with embedded hardware that can be used as both, an input and output for several devices but also looking as regular hair extensions. Our approach modified artificial hair extensions into a conductive material using a chemical process. Other materials such as conductive ink and gel hair could present conductivity but it is easily dried or taken away when the user touches it. Our chemical process could be modified with other reagents in order to get a different coloration of the hair. Braids and different hairstyles could be combined in order to keep the hair in a specific position.

The circuit that is connected to a microcontroller could be placed at the base of the hair extension, in an earring, in a necklace and at a hairclip. Due to the proximity of the hair and the sensitivity of the head, vibration motors could be include in order to make vibrating feedback noticeable for the user. Future works will add an isolator material at the end of the process so users won't need to have a direct contact with the conductive material. When it will be used as an output device, other actuators could replace the LEDs such as vibration motors and buzzers. When it will be used as an input device, it could be combined with other wearable devices such as glasses, brain waves and conductive makeup. Other materials such as beards and mustaches could be transformed into conductive materials and other techniques could be explored like the use of conductive polymers.

The gestures recognition in gadgets and the communication between them and smartphones is not new for wearable technologies. Our approach will recognize voluntary gestures on a part of the body. The big challenge for our gesture recognition system will be to differentiate the voluntary gestures of the user and her natural gestures with her hair in a way that do not interfere with her everyday activities. Future evaluations for comparing noticeable and seamless interfaces will be conducted.

Acknowledgments. Hugo Fuks (Project 302230/2008-4) is a recipient of a grant awarded by the National Research Council (CNPq). This work was partially financed by Research Support Foundation of the State of Rio de Janeiro-FAPERJ/INCT (E-26/170028/2008) and CNPq/INCT (557.128/2009-9). Katia Vega is a postdoctoral fellow with grant funding from PNPD/CAPES Portaria 086/2013. Ricardo Aucelio acknowledges FAPERJ (E-26/201.406/2014) and CNPq (302888/20132-6) scholarships. We also thanks to Hugo Rojas from EAQ Labs for his first insights in the chemical process used on Hairware and Paulo José dos Santos from the Department of Chemistry (PUC-Rio) for his support during the chemistry process.

References

1. Ranck, J.: The wearable computing market: a global analysis. (2012)
2. Google: Google Glass. http://www.google.com.br/glass/start/
3. Peeble: Pebble: E-Paper Watch for iPhone and Android. https://getpebble.com
4. Pearson, I.: The future of fashion. J. Commun. Netw. **4**, 68–72 (2005)
5. Lee, H.M., Choi, S.-Y., Jung, A., Ko, S.H.: Highly conductive aluminum textile and paper for flexible and wearable electronics. Angew. Chemie. **125**, 7872–7877 (2013)
6. Locher, I., Kirstein, T., Tröster, G.: Routing methods adapted to e-textiles. In: Proceedings of 37th International Symposium on Microelectronics (IMAPS), Long Beach (2004)
7. McRae, L., Hess, B.: LucyandBart. http://www.lucymcrae.net
8. Park, S.: LED Eyelashes. (2009)
9. Vega, K.F.C., Fuks, H.: Empowering electronic divas through beauty technology. In: Marcus, Aaron (ed.) DUXU 2013, Part III. LNCS, vol. 8014, pp. 237–245. Springer, Heidelberg (2013)
10. Vega, K., Fuks, H.: Beauty technology: body surface computing. Computer.(Long. Beach. Calif) **47**, 71–75 (2014)
11. Vega, K., Fuks, H.: Beauty technology as an interactive computing platform. In: Proceedings of the 2013 ACM International Conference on Interactive Tabletops and Surfaces, pp. 357–360. ACM, New York (2013)
12. Tobita, H., Kuzi, T.: SmartWig: wig-based wearable computing device for communication and entertainment. In: Proceedings of the International Working Conference on Advanced Visual Interfaces, pp. 299–302 (2012)
13. Sign, F.: Products - First Sign. http://www.firstsign.us/products/
14. Hallpike, C.R.: Social hair. Man. **4**, 256–264 (1969)
15. Webster, J.G.: Medical instrumentation: Application and Design. Houghton Mifflin Company, Boston (1973). 197& g
16. Tangible, E.: E.I.: Design Challenge. In: Seventh International Conference on TEI 2013. http://www.tei-conf.org/13/dc

Commiticator: Enhancing Non-verbal Communication by Means of Magnetic Vision

Anne Wiedau[1]([✉]), Daniel Gilgen[1], Raune Frankjær[1],
Tristan Goerlich[2], and Michael Wiedau[3]

[1] Department of Intermedia Design, Trier University of Applied Sciences,
54290 Trier, Germany
anne@wiedau.com, gilgen@hochschule-trier.de,
raune@frankjaer.de
[2] Department of Philosophy, University Trier, 54290 Trier, Germany
goerlichtristan@yahoo.de
[3] Department of Process Systems Engineering, RWTH Aachen University,
52056 Aachen, Germany
michael.wiedau@rwth-aachen.de

Abstract. Commitment is a key element in social behavior, especially when it comes to communication between two individuals in close relation to each other. Between people who have known each other for a longer period of time, communication often revolves around recent events and the act of sending a life sign takes precedence to the actual content of the information itself. Furthermore the constant accessibility through mobile media devices is increasingly creating the expectation of permanent communication between couples. The ongoing spread of wearable devices allows a permanent communication across physical distance but it sometimes also supports a leakage of situat awareness among their users.

The main concern of the Commiticator project lies within the development of a wearable device that can support the expression of commitment as an act of social interaction between two wearers. To study the acceptance of such a device, the already culturally established character of jewelry is used to create a jewelry set consisting of a ring and a locket.

To make an intuitive form of communication possible, the wearer's tactile sense is enhanced by the jewelry giving them a sense for a magnetic field that is enabled by the locket if it is activated by the partner. This creates a ping-pong like interaction between the wearers.

Keywords: Jewellery · Jewelry · Locket · Wearable · NUI · Smart object · Smart accessory · Magnetic vision · Communication · Commitment · Commiticator

1 Introduction

This research is part of a larger project which studies the area of conflict between ›jewelry culture‹ and ›digital culture‹. It is pursuing the idea of an exchange taking place in the transition between these medias.

© Springer International Publishing Switzerland 2015
A. Marcus (Ed.): DUXU 2015, Part II, LNCS 9187, pp. 705–714, 2015.
DOI: 10.1007/978-3-319-20898-5_67

The ongoing transformation to a digital culture does not spare the culture of wearing jewelry. Like other branches, the jewelry manufacturing finds itself in a mergence with the digital market. Jewelry, in a tradition going back millenniums, is changing in concern to its production (e.g. as a 3D-File), in its economical distribution structure (Industry 4.0, digitalization), as well as in its characteristics as a medium, especially as a medium of communication.

To enable a merge of the traditional and culturally settled inherent character of jewelry together with the decreasing size of intelligent acting digital hardware (like embedded systems), jewelry has the capability to transform into a kind of body worn computer. The idea of a suitable function enhancement of jewelry is a key element in this research paper. This includes the aim to answer the implied question how a jewelry point of view or ›form language‹ may be established in the area of body worn objects, that allows a traditional but in the same time modern view. If this merge is successful, jewelry itself can become a part of the debate about contemporary issues of digitalization.

1.1   Enhancement of Jewelry

Modern technology changes our daily life just by our use of it. Also the characteristics of jewelry are influenced if merged with recent technology.

Researchers such as Paul Watzlawick show how deep the presence of technology influences our lives and which importance it has in our daily communication and interaction [1]. The field of interaction and communication seems especially interesting if it comes to wearable technology as it breeds a close relation between the wearer and its technological device.

In actual forms of communication people benefit from the positive aspects of keeping in touch without the boundaries of physical distance. Nevertheless there are side effects of communication technology and their "excrescences" in the form of noisy gadget toys that have become annoying interrupters in our everyday life.

In most cases these interruptions are done purposely and are widely appreciated. Yet there is a point where they start to culminate and they add up to a nuisance, which is not only overwhelming but also becomes a disturbance for the surrounding people.

There appears to be a permanent crave for attention that manifests itself in an attention economy [2]. Consumers have to choose what and when they want to consume. The brain has to become sensitized for filtering information, to decide whether they are relevant or not.

In phases of pressure it is easy to become distracted by disturbances of any kind. There is always the risk of losing the balance and forgetting important social interaction while drifting away into the lure of virtuality.

Digital consumers are flooded with information wherever they may go, which carries the risk of getting lost in a massive amount of data. This results in an establishment of rules to find what is looked out for and the building of systems, which help sort out information of interest. These systems are applied in web stores like *Amazon* or in selective searches on *Google*. Even when it comes to social interaction, systems being allowed to decide in the user's presumable interest. In social networks like

Facebook, posts are preselected before relevant news is displayed. There are advantages and disadvantages in this preselection, especially if algorithms take over the user's natural task of reducing information in daily life [3]. This reduction draws the attention of a whole generation of media consumers [4] and is influencing how we, personally, filter the important from the less important. Becoming experts in selective communication although means accepting the loss of presumably less important information. Problems arise when the communication with people in the social environment becomes unbalanced.

The selection process in the media is assisted by the invention of technological structures. The spread of mobile technology especially in the form of wearable devices requires a transfer of those solutions into the sphere of physical products, especially if they fuse with the human body and make use of the human senses.

2 Observing Signs of Commitment Between Couples

To start the transfer of the previously described solution to a physical representation, the concentration has to be focused on one essential component in the first instance. This component was found by observing the behavior of a selected group of people for the Commiticator project.

The usage of mobile devices and the resulting constant accessibility lead to an observation when used by people in a close relationship: Their use of mobile text message systems in daily life shows the emergence of a specialized form of interaction. Between people who have known each other for a period of time, communication often splits into two main groups, one of which revolving around recent events. This happens for example on a practical level, when explicit information is shared with the other person like ›We don't have milk‹.

Another form is focused on commitment, for example ›Thinking of you‹ or ›How are you‹, although the sharing of media contents of any kind can be seen as a committing part of conversation.

Within the Commiticator project, a core group survey about the ›signs of commitment‹ was started and it revealed that about 50–80 % of the conversation was sent for reasons of commitment in one or the other form. When asked, the participants declared their actions as a subconscious act in the first hand. Nevertheless, nearly all agreed that they wanted to share a part of their own experiences to stay in contact with the other.

This behavior has been studied in several projects like the ones of Streyker [5] and Bennett [3]. They show that the information itself is not important in these kind of messages, which offer commitment in form of a "proof of life".

Furthermore commitment can be identified as a key element in social behavior, especially when it comes to communication between two people in close relation to each other.

The constant availability through mobile media devices overcomes the limitations of physical distance and is increasingly creating the expectation of permanent communication that especially follows a growing emotional connection. Yet often this is not possible due to external circumstances, and less an expression of unwillingness.

The aspects of commitment in communication between related people seems reason enough to explore it more explicitly and to make it the object of our investigation in the field of jewelry.

2.1 Jewelry as a Tool for Communication in Form of Commitment

As the Commiticator project is all about the development of a device that acts in the described space of communication between people in a close relation to each other, the character of jewelry can take the role as a key to assure the acceptance of such a tool. Following the typical characteristics of jewelry, especially in its function as a body worn medium, it allows a particular perspective on behavior among couples.

The characteristics of jewelry can be described in recognition of its anthropological roots, its mythological connotations and its contemporary expressions.

Jewelry is one of the oldest representational object humans have used to communicate. Archaeologists have dated excavated strung shells back to around 75 thousand years ago [6]. Regardless of what exactly inspired early humans to put shells on a string and wear them on their body, it can be assumed that, from the moment where the human brain was able to understand metaphors, humans must have seen what others were wearing and must have started to read this information. It is not hard to conclude that seeing the teeth of a predator hanging around the neck of a hunter is a form of acknowledging him as a successful hunter [7]. The high-end technical goods for example in the form of smart watches, which are often produced of rare or high valued materials, are a similar sign for success in the present day [8].

To wear a ring intentionally as a symbol is not as old as wearing shells, but especially the wedding ring is known all over the world as a sign of partnership [9]. Even if one would not know the meaning of a wedding ring, the human could interpret the materiality of gold as an archaic representation of sun and its eternal power. If there are two people wearing a similar object, it is easily understandable that they, sharing the same symbol, must be linked to each other in some way. Communication with objects worn on the body is still present in its traditional form and these messages are still as significant as millennia ago.

Furthermore there are aspects of jewelry as a commemorative object. People are obliviously turning their wedding ring or grabbing the locket as an object that is loaded with memories of a person. This is an expression of an intuitive and intimate relation to a person embodied by an object. This one-way-communication is often happening in a natural, non-disruptive and intuitive way. The person who is doing so is sending subconscious messages, being only able to imagine how a partner might be turning his or her ring at the same time. Commemorative objects fill the void that the impossibility of face-to-face interaction leaves in certain situation. This may be caused by death of the recipient, which also means the freeze of communication with that person, or it is just caused by distance that does not allow communication, for example if partners do not live in the same city or they are at work during the day. When studying a communication phenomenon facilitated by a piece of jewelry, it is helpful to be aware of the interaction happening within this void that occurs in communication.

As elaborated, the use of jewelry as a communication device cannot be viewed separately from its anthropological and historical context. It has been developed into an almost intuitive and universally understandable form of expression. Jewelry here is considered as an instrument that serves as a tool for researching the individual's reaction as a bearer of jewelry, along with ongoing events in the personal use of media and technology. Therefore, jewelry can although become a part of the debate about contemporary issues of digitalization.

2.2   Wearables

There have been several jewelry objects, that already made use of the characteristics of jewelry and are combining those with technology.

The term ›wearable‹ was affected by *MIT* professor Neil Gershenfeld who spoke about the wearable computer as a pervasive machine. In his idea about smart objects, wearables should serve as media prosthesis and enhance human abilities [10].

Smart jewelry objects are only one group of wearables. Best known are complex accessories like smart watches (*Apple Watch, Pebble*) and fitness bands (*Fitbit, Fuel Band, Jawbone Up*) but there also is smart jewelry in the form of pendants and lockets as well. The products on the market can be divided into five groups:

- gadgets (e.g. usb locked by *Swarovski*) and toys (e.g. digital diary, *iheartlocked*)
- medical helpers (e.g. pendant that manipulates electromagnetic fields, like *Q-Link*)
- sensors (e.g. weather sensor, like *CliMate*)
- input devices (e.g. gesture control, like *Logbar*)
- communication assistants (e.g. telephone assistant bracelet, like *MICA*)

Furthermore there are products that support the ideas of the Commiticator project. The *Shine* by *Misfit,* positions itself against current wearables as ›gadgety devices‹ by deploying aesthetics normally associated with jewelry. Another approach is the *Cuff* which can be integrated into existing wearable objects such as bracelets or pendants and functions as an enhancement of the mobile phone.

"*The Locket*", a smart pendant allows users to receive messages and see images from selected loved ones in a traditional locket form, is related to the Commiticator in its approach to allow more intimate modes of communication, expressed in a mini-malistic traditional form. Another similar emotional approach is the transfer of heart-beat through technical devices which can be seen in Projects like the *Hearter* by Alejandro Delgado Charra.

3   An Experimental Jewelry Device

As described before there is a potential for further research within the communication between two people if it comes to the exchange of signs of commitment. For that purpose, a wearable jewelry device has been developed. The device should meet the characteristics of jewelry, and also fulfill the criteria as a wearable (Fig. 1).

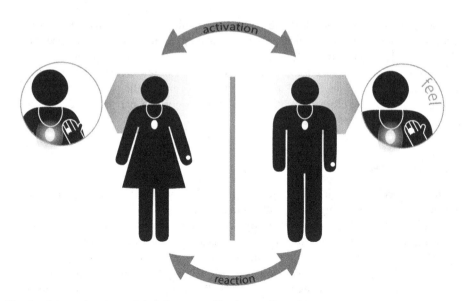

Fig. 1. Schematic view of the ping-pong like interaction with the help of the Commiticator locket

3.1 Components and Function

On the current market of wearables there are mostly watches and bracelets available such as the *Apple Watch* or the *Jawbone Up*, as well as flexible systems that can be worn on several positions on the body such as *Climate*, *Shine* and *Cuff*.

The Commiticator Project intends to underline the importance of relation between couples. To support this idea a ring and a locket for each one of the couple became the components of choice. As previously described, the ring is the eternal symbol for partnership and works as the initiator of the communication between the wearers.

To make use of the locket it requires a magnet on the finger ring. This can be done in an encapsulated fashion as displayed in the prototype ring but it is also possible to add a magnet to an already existing ring.

The locket is the second intimate jewelry object, as it holds traditionally commemorative objects. In the past it had a religious connotation and the lockets held personal relics or hair of a beloved person. Usually the locket held religious paintings and portraits inside the lockets. Nowadays they often hold photographs of beloved persons. As lockets are worn close to the heart, their position on the body correspond to emotional bindings and feelings of love and remembrance.

To make the Commiticator fit better in daily use, it is possible to wear the locket on a keychain or as a pocket watch but these are only further suggestions for its individualistic realization potentials.

3.2   Materiality

Due to its cheap price plastic is used in several wearable devices on the marked (e.g. *iheartlocket, Pebble, Cuff*). For the first prototypes of the Project plastic is used as a rapid prototyping material. For the long-term study a metal version is intended, as it allows the daily use without major deteriorations. It supports the aesthetic and haptics of a jewelry piece. This aesthetic match allows a higher acceptance as a body worn product for daily use for the average consumer.

3.3   Design

Its appearance is reduced and modern but is not thought as a standalone statement. Instead it refers to the lockets cultural history. The surface still shows the lines of the production process, which is done by a low detailed 3D-printing process. The generated 3D-print pattern underlines the contemporary approach and refers to its technological genesis.

Due to the metal casting process and the smiths works afterwards, the printed lines appear as an almost natural pattern, referring to the growth of wood. It although has a similarity with the ancient goldsmith technique, where castings are made in engraved cuttlefish bones that leads to individual layered patterns.

At the same time this pattern is a reminder of decorative engravings in the surface of traditional lockets. The surface can be read as an individual fingerprint and stands equally for the uniqueness every intimate relation has. So it fits to the implications of the ring component in the device.

3.4   Requirements for a Wearable Device

As seen in the previous examples, wearable pendants and lockets communicate with the wearer in different ways. They make use of the senses to signal the recipient, for example by the use of light (*Qlink*), vibration (*MICA*) or by warming up (*Remember Ring*). The warming up of a device worn on the neck did not find a high acceptance in the preceding inquiry for the Commiticator project. The participants sometimes did not feel the temperature or they expected it could become too hot.

The shown solutions did not fully support the idea of intimate communication, thus the Commiticator project makes use of the haptic sense.

Referring to the idea of Neil Gershenfeld [10], who saw the main purpose of wearable devices as an enhancement of human abilities, the concept of a ›magnetic vision‹ came into focus as it could enable an invisible and therefore intimate form of sense.

The term ›magnetic vision‹ was established in the body mod scene and is used to describe the sensation of a magnetic field, which can be located with the help of an implanted magnet under the skin. Often these implants are located on the back or the side of the hand but mostly on the side of the fingertip of the ring finger. These kind of implants are popular in subcultural scenes like the cyborg-scene, where members try to enhance their bodies by mechanical and technological devices, often inspired by science fiction models [11]. Furthermore, there is a rather established scientific approach to magnetic vision. Birds like doves orient themselves in the magnetic field to the earth and are able to navigate precisely due to their magnetic sense established by a field sensible part in their head [12]. The early state experiments revealed that it is not necessary to pass the border of the skin to enable the sensory experience of a magnetic field. It is also possible if a magnet is simply attached close to the hand.

Following that observation magnetic vision is established by enhancing the ring with a magnet. As the locket contains a magnet, close proximity between ring and pendant allows the wearer to sense the established magnetic field, whenever the partner sends the activating signal. The enhanced tactile sensation allows us to feel when the partner has recently been thinking of us and subsequently sends a signal back to the partner. This creates a ping-pong like interaction as the set of jewelry is worn.

3.5   Technological Solutions

The Commiticator is a set of jewelry, which consists of one ring and one pendant for each partner. The pendants of the two partners are wirelessly connected with each other. The prototype is built using an *Arduino* based microcontroller platform. The microcontroller is connected wirelessly to a cloud service (e.g. *Sparkcloud*) that enables the connection between the lockets. The locket includes a neodymium magnet that is pivot-mounted. A motor unlocks the magnet to turn in the right position when the input signal is received from the other locket and holds the position for a period of time. An included hall-sensor detects the magnetic field of the ring and sends out the activation signal, whenever the wearer is touching the locket with the ring. The device is powered by a polymer-lithium-ion battery.

3.6   Use Case Study

In the first stage of the project couples were asked about their usage of mobile communication devices especially as a tool to send signs of commitment to the partner.

Due to that experiment five groups could be identified as participants for the prototype study:

- normal couple (students, not living together)
- couple in a far distance relationship
- married couple (one partner working, one partner at home - live together)
- mother and child
- best friends.

The prototype was given to the selected core-group for two weeks to collect impressions and to be able to make further improvements on the device.

As the Commiticator investigates how private signs of commitment are facilitated by technology and its capability of changing behavior, the prototype-group had to answer several questions before and after the test period.

4 Result

Analyzing modern technological communication systems and how they function between couples and other peer to peer groups recover great potentials in the development of a device which is especially designed to express commitment discretely. First experiences with a prototype-group indicated, that such a device is in general welcomed by the participants. Especially the technical affine participants could imagine using such a device on a regular base. One criterion was to invent a convincing concept that works with the special characteristics of jewelry and benefits from its cultural implications. Because of its appearance as a locket, most of the participants would appreciate to see the device in a higher valued material. Nevertheless some sorted the device in the product category of gadgets as well as in jewelry. The participants also proposed several technical improvements such as a longer battery life and the integration of a battery low signal. They would prefer a smaller size of the locket as well as a more silent motor. Furthermore they wished a better connectivity through mobile services.

For the interval in which the magnet establishes a magnetic field, an average of 15 min could be determined as a useful middle, but this value is customizable in the code. The participants welcomed their enhanced ability to feel magnetic fields and discovered an aspect of playfulness in it.

A conclusion how far commitment is influenced by the use of the commiticator in the long run, could not be evaluated in the undertaken short-studies. As some of the participants started to use the device intuitively, they agreed that the device is supporting intuitive gestures and unconscious communication. As assumed earlier, the Commiticator could enable commitment across physical distance, without losing situated awareness. In doing so, the device could work as counter draft to the sometimes disturbing communication which accompanies people in everyday life.

4.1 Discussion

Due to its state as an early-prototype, several technical issues need to be solved. In the prototype experiment the groups had to deal with connection interruptions caused by the lag of network connectivity. Further there are concerns that the mechanical parts may not be stable enough, even though there have been no cases of material weakness in the preceding study. As those mechanical difficulties are solved in mechanical watches, these concerns can be avoided in later versions. The integration of those suggestions from the first trial experiments in the Commiticator may influence the result of the experiment. As the experiment supports a change of behavior by sending signs of commitment with the help of a technical device, there remaining concerns, if a behavior change is socially helpful and desirable. In a larger scale study, these questions will be scrutinized.

4.2 Outlook

The ideas and changes drawn from the prototype stage will be included in the final prototype. With the final prototype, there will be an accompanying long-term study to clarify how private signs of commitment, facilitated by technology, may be capable of changing human behavior. It will be interesting to see how the device is providing a private and intimate communication possibility for two people and if this is influencing couple structures. Further technical developments in the field of a ›true‹ magnetic vision could also mean a transgression onto the human body. Structurally the device could be enhanced and opened up for group-interactions. Technically it would be interesting to charge the locket wirelessly by induction. Further it would be interesting to follow the idea of an individual fingerprint on the locket with the help of 3D-printed structure variations, there has to be experiments with the plating of 3D-prints with gold or how 3D-printed forms could be used as stencils for the stamping process for gold sheets.

A larger scaled study would naturally be depending on the availability of a larger number of testing devices. The project is currently privately funded, so at the moment the capability of producing further prototypes is rather limited. It would be interesting to see how improved financial means and therefore enlarged production capabilities could provide the basic prerequisite for the realization of a larger scaled study. This could lay the foundation for an industrial sized production in the upcoming future.

References

1. Watzlawick, P., Bavelas, J.B., Jackson, D.D.: Pragmatics of Human Communication: A Study of Interactional Patterns, Pathologies and Paradoxes. WW Norton and Company, New York (2011)
2. Anderson, C.: The Long Tail: Why the Future of Business is Selling Less of More. Hachette Digital Inc., New York (2006)
3. Bennett, A., Kahn-Harris, K. (eds.): After subculture: Critical studies in contemporary youth culture. Basingstoke: Palgrave Macmillan (2004). See also: http://blog.sgws.org/eu-screen-time-policies-and-recommendations/. Last checked 18 February 2015
4. Rodriguez, M.G., Gumandi, K., Schoelkopf, B.: Quantifying Information Overload in Social Media and its Impact on Social Contagions (2014) CoRR, http://arxiv.org/abs/1403.683
5. Stryker, S., Serpe, R.T.: Commitment, identity salience, and role behavior: Theory and research example. In: Ickes, W., Knowles, E. (eds.) Personality, Roles, and Social Behavior, pp. 199–218. Springer, New York (1982)
6. Henshilwood, C., d' Errico, F., Vanhaeren, M., Van Niekerk, K., Jacobs, Z.: Middle stone age shell beads from South Africa. Science **304**(5669), 404 (2004)
7. Gebser, J.: Ursprung und Gegenwart: Die Fundamente der aperspektivischen Welt. Novalis-Verlag, Beitrag zu einer Geschichte der Bewußtwerdung (1986)
8. Altrichter, V.: Das Magische Objekt in der Moderne. Thinking jewelry, pp. 135–152. Arnoldsche Art Publishers (2011)
9. Billari, F.C., Prskawetz, A., Diaz, B.A., Fent, T.: The "Wedding-Ring": An agent- based marriage model based on social interaction. Demographic Res. **17**(17), 59 (2008)
10. Gershenfeld, N.: FAB: The Coming Revolution on Your Desktop. Basic Books, Cambridge (2005)
11. Terranova, T.: Posthuman unbounded: artificial evolution and high-tech subcultures. In: Robertson, G., Mash, M., Tucker, L., Bird, J., Curtis, B., Putnam, T. (eds.) FutureNatural: Nature, Science, Culture, pp. 146–164. Routledge, London (1996)
12. Baker, R.: Goal orientation by blindfolded humans after long-distance displacement: Possible involvement of a magnetic sense. Science **210**(4469), 555–557 (1980). American Association for the Advancement of Science

Author Index

Abbas, Aneela   II-243
Abyarjoo, Fatemeh   III-543
Acartürk, Cengiz   II-403
Agner, Luiz   I-339, II-393
Agra, Jarbas   III-292
Ahmad, Wan Fatimah Wan   I-138
Ahmed, Sumayyah   I-395
Aker, Çakır   III-3
Akita, Seiji   II-675
Alaçam, Özge   II-403
Albers, Michael J.   II-267
Aldawood, Salma   II-415
Aleissa, Faisal   II-415
Alencar, Renato   III-283
Alfaris, Anas   II-415
Al-Fayez, Amani   III-380
Alhindi, Tariq   II-415
Alhonsuo, Mira   I-470
Aljohani, Maha   III-119
Al-Kharji, Sarah   III-380
Almalki, Almaha   II-415
Almeida, Dicksson   III-303
Al-Mohammadi, Hanan   III-380
Al-Mutairi, Mona   III-380
Alnasser, Riyadh   II-415
Alomran, Hamad Ibrahim   III-131
Alrashed, Tarfah   II-415
Altmüller, Tobias   III-517
Al-Tuwaim, Anfal   III-380
Alves, Isadora N.   I-356
Al-Wabi, Areej   II-415
Amaral, Marília Abrahão   II-141
Amin, Rahul   I-481
Apablaza, Juan   I-237
Aquino Junior, Plinio Thomaz   II-118
Araújo, Cristiano C.   I-356
Araújo, Maria Gabriela   III-425
Araujo-Soares, Vera   I-548
Arie, Takayuki   II-675
Arnott, Bronia   I-548
Arredondo, Maria Teresa   II-153
Asthana, Siddhartha   I-101

Aucelio, Ricardo   II-696
Ayanoğlu, Hande   II-3
Azeem, Muhammad Waqas   I-113

Bähr, Benjamin   II-495
Baker, Jessie   III-368
Banerjee, Banny   I-436
Baradit, Stacey   II-107
Barattin, Daniela   I-179
Barker, Trevor   II-541
Barreto, Armando   III-543
Barros, Manuella Q.   I-224
Barros, Rafaela Q.   I-224
Batchelor, John   II-685
Belfort, Rui   I-130
Bellotti, Andréa   I-579
Beltrán, María Eugenia   II-153
Bendanna, Kristen   III-368
Bendoukha, Hayat   II-277
Bendoukha, Sofiane   II-277
Bengler, Klaus   III-517
Bentim, Claudia G.   II-131
Berger, Arne   II-196
Bevilacqua, Roberta   III-553
Bianchi, Silvia   III-13
Bim, Sílvia Amélia   II-141
Bittencourt, Sayonara   III-208
Biz, Pedro   I-579
Blustein, James   III-119
Bonfim, Gabriel   II-330
Boonbrahm, Poonpong   II-162
Boonbrahm, Salin   II-162
Borgeson, Sam   III-337
Borum, Nanna   III-142
Boscarioli, Clodis   II-141
Both, Andreas   I-256
Bøthun, Silje   III-587
Boto, Rita   II-3
Bouwman, Harry   II-508
Brahnam, Sheryl   II-172
Brejcha, Jan   I-3, I-122
Brennan, Erin   III-575

Brooks, Anthony Lewis   III-142
Buares, Priscila   II-393
Burris, Andrea   I-548
Butt, Muhammad Aadil   I-113
Bystřický, Jiří   I-3

Cabrera-Umpierrez, Maria Fernanda   II-153
Cai, Wenyi   III-562
Campos, Fábio   I-130
Candello, Heloisa   III-13
Cantoni, Lorenzo   I-149
Carvalho, Breno   III-251, III-292, III-283
Carvalho, Luiz Roberto   II-289
Cassa, Leandro   III-13
Cavallo, Filippo   III-553
Çay, Damla   III-357
Celi, Ernesto   III-153
Ch'ng, Eugene   II-425
Chammas, Adriana   I-339, II-23
Chang, Chia-Nien   III-496
Chasanidou, Dimitra   I-12
Chen, Aqua Chuan-Yu   II-611
Chen, Fang   III-450
Chen, Hon-Kai   I-559
Chen, Sheng-Chih   II-301
Chen, Xiao Jiao   I-24
Cheng, Ning Chun   II-206
Chiu, Ming-Hsin Phoebe   III-166
Chiu, Philip W.Y.   III-693
Chuan, Ngip Khean   I-138
Chunpir, Hashim Iqbal   II-587, III-25
Cipelli, Valentina   II-434
Clarkson, P. John   II-473
Clua, Esteban   III-315
Colley, Ashley   I-470
Colley, Bruno   III-283
Conrad, Isabel   III-553
Cook, Kristina   III-575
Cooke, Neil   II-425
Cooper, Peter   III-412
Correia, Walter   I-130
Cristo, Caio   III-425
Crosby, Martha E.   II-184
Cybis Pereira, Alice T.   II-289
Cypriano, Lucas   I-157

da Fonseca, Iguatemi E.   I-63
Dagge, Ricardo   II-34
Dahl, Yngve   III-587
Dario, Paolo   III-553

das Graças Chagas, Maria   II-667
Das, Anita   III-587
David, Salomão   I-149
Davis, Nora   III-368
Davis, Rebekah   II-631
de Azevedo, Bruno Alvares   III-662, III-672
de Freitas, Sydney Fernandes   I-644
de Lera, Eva   I-406
de los Rios, Silvia   II-153
de Lucena, Carlos Alberto Pereira   III-672
de Lucena, Carlos José Pereira   III-606,
    III-651, III-662
de Macedo Guimarães, Lia Buarque   II-14
de Pinho, André Luís Santos   III-197
de Sá Bonelli, João   II-667
DeMers, Kathleen   III-240
Desouzart, Gustavo   III-596
Dias, Miguel Sales   I-167
Ding, Li   II-45
Dong, Zhan Xun   III-36
dos Santos, Fátima Aparecida   II-252
dos Santos, Jorge R. Lopes   III-662
Du, Hao   II-45
Duarte, Emília   II-3, III-638
Dunbar, Jerone   III-439

El Mesbahi, Myriam   I-590
Elias, Herlander   III-251
Eloy, Sara   I-167
Emanuel, Barbara   I-417, II-353
Endara, Ariel Escobar   III-606
Eshet, Eyal   II-508
Esposito, Raffaele   III-553
Eugene, Wanda   III-439

Fabri, Marc   I-32
Fabri, Stefano   III-682
Falco, Marcelo   I-599
Fan, Yingjie   I-283
Faria, Paula C.L.A.   II-252
Farkas, Pavel   III-346
Feijó Filho, Jackson   I-428
Felici, Elisa   III-553
Ferati, Mexhid   II-464
Fernandes, Chrystinne Oliveira   III-651
Fernandes, Walkir   I-130
Filgueiras, Ernesto   II-34, III-185, III-596,
    III-251
Filippi, Stefano   I-179
Fiorini, Soeli T.   III-662

Fischer, Patrick   II-75
Flanagan, Patricia   II-622, II-631
Flora, June A.   I-436, III-337
Forlizzi, Jodi   I-490
Frajhof, Leonardo   III-662
Franchinni, Ana Elisa   II-131
Frankjær, Raune   I-447, II-705
Fu, Yunhui   I-481
Fuks, Hugo   II-696

Gaedke, Martin   I-256
Galabo, Rosendy Jess   I-191
Gasparini, Andrea Alessandro   I-12, III-173
Gasselseder, Hans-Peter   I-458
Gatsou, Chrysoula   II-520
Genç, Özge   III-357
Gilbert, Juan E.   I-481, III-439
Gilgen, Daniel   II-705
Gkouskos, Dimitrios   III-450
Glende, Sebastian   III-553
Goerlich, Tristan   II-705
Gomes, Andreia   III-185
Gomez, Rafael   II-631
Gonçalves, Rafael Cirino   III-462, II-575
Gray, Colleen   III-575
Greenshpan, Jacob   I-339
Grimaldi, Roberta   II-434
Grost, Timothy   III-529
Gu, Zhenyu   III-36
Guo, Lei   I-502

Habel, Christopher   II-403
Hadhrawi, Mohammad K.   II-415
Haid, Charlotte   I-609
Häkkilä, Jonna   I-470
Halbey, Julian   III-473
Han, Ting   III-562
Harada, Shingo   II-675
Harkke, Ville   I-269
Hassan, Syed Raheel   II-587
Heidt, Michael   I-44, II-196
Heilig, Leonard   I-283
Held, Theo   II-75
Hendrix, Renesha L.   III-439
Hertlein, Franziska   I-295
Hess, Steffen   II-95
Higashida, Masanobu   II-530
Hinterleitner, Bastian   I-295
Hirako, Hajime   II-307
Holdsworth, Kristen   III-368
Honda, Wataru   II-675

Hsieh, Hsiu Ching Laura   II-206
Huang, Scottie Chih-Chieh   II-444
Huang, Yu-Chun   III-263
Hussain, Zahid   II-587
Hwang, Chiung-Hui   II-301
Hwang, Hee Jae   II-214

Inget, Virve   I-470
Ingrosso, Andrea   III-682
Inoue, Satoru   II-307
Ishida, Toru   II-530
Islam, A.K.M. Najmul   III-46
Islam, Muhammad Nazrul   III-46
Iwamoto, Miyuki   III-616

Jackson, France   I-481
Jefferies, Amanda   II-541
Jeon, Myounghoon   II-382
Jiang, Changhua   II-45
Jin, Lu   I-53
Joyce, Ger   II-541
Ju, Da Young   II-214
Júnior, Iran   III-283

Kaewrat, Charlee   II-162
Kaltenthaler, Daniel   II-317
Kanao, Kenichiro   II-675
Kanellopoulos, Kalja   I-44, II-196
Kang, Min Kyung   II-551
Kaplan, Benjamin   III-517
Karbay, Edibe Betül   III-628
Karlin, Beth   III-368
Karlsson, MariAnne   III-450
Katelertprasert, Patiwat   II-162
Kaur, Navjot   II-685
Kautonen, Heli   III-104
Kay, Robert   II-685
Kennard, Teha   III-575
Khashman, Nouf   III-54
Kim, Min Ji   II-66
Kim, Sung Woo   II-66, II-551, II-597, III-485
Kirkby, David   III-368
Kissinger, Jonathon   II-452
Klein, Tobias   II-643
Klemcke, Susann   III-553
Knoche, Hendrik   II-655
Koshiyama, Débora   III-197
Kowalewski, Sylvia   III-473
Kremer, Simon   I-306
Kröger, Peer   II-317

Kronbauer, Artur H.   II-54
Kurdi, Heba   III-380
Kuru, Armağan   I-490
Kuwahara, Noriaki   III-616
Kwac, Jungsuk   III-337

Lageiro, Amélia   III-638
Lai, Yu Ren   II-563
Langdon, Patrick M.   II-473
Lanutti, Jamille   II-131
Lapaš, Tihana   III-271
Lau, Ka Chun   III-693
Lavin, Luís   III-185
Lee, Eunji   I-12
Lee, Heewon   III-485
Lee, Jin Ho   II-66
Lee, Jongsung   III-485
Lee, Jung Min   II-214
Lei, Tian   I-567
Lessa, Jefferson   III-315
Lessa, Washington Dias   I-579
Leung, Billy H.K.   III-693
Leung, Esther Y.Y.   III-693
Lewis, James R.   I-204
Li, Bin   I-567
Li, Hui   I-122
Li, Juan   I-567
Li, Yiqi   II-75
Liang, Qiwei   I-315
Liffick, Blaise W.   I-328
Lilley, Mariana   II-541
Lim, Linda   II-224
Lin, Jerry   II-87
Lin, Tingyi S.   III-496
Lindemann, Udo   I-306, I-609
Lins, Anthony   III-292
Lisboa, Catarina   III-638
Liu, Jun   III-562
Liu, Qiang   III-562
Liu, Zhengjie   I-122
Lo, Cheng-Hung   II-87
Lohrer, Johannes-Y.   II-317
Luan, Huanbo   I-502
Ludwig, Thomas   III-25
Luk, Chung-Hay   III-263

Machado, Díferson   II-54
Maciel, Cristiano   II-141
Magin, Dominik Pascal   II-95
Maguire, Martin   I-535

Maher, Deborah E.   I-204
Maier, Andreas   II-95
Manresa-Yee, Cristina   II-655
Marcellini, Fiorella   III-553
Marcus, Aaron   I-513, II-107
Marczal, Denise   II-118
Martin, James   I-481
Martins, Edgard Thomas   I-524
Martins, Isnard Thomas   I-524
Martins, Marcos   I-417, II-353
Martins, Valeska   III-292
May, Andrew   I-535
Medaglia, Carlo Maria   II-434, III-682
Medeiros, Anna C.S.   I-63
Medola, Fausto O.   II-131, II-330
Miao, Huitian   I-122
Michailidou, Ioanna   I-609
Miettinen, Satu   I-86
Mitchell, Val   I-535
Moldenhauer, Judith A.   III-390
Moldt, Daniel   II-277
Mont'Alvão, Cláudia Renata   II-23, III-94, III-672
Montenegro, Anselmo   III-315
Moorhead, Kathleen   III-240
Mora Fernández, Jorge I.   I-621
Morelli, Tony   II-452
Morimoto, Kazunari   III-616
Morrison, Ann   II-655

Nakajima, Tatsuo   I-654
Naskova, Julija   III-63
Nawrot, Ilona   II-232
Neto, Edvar   I-130, III-303
Neves, André   III-292
Neves, Erica   II-330
Niu, Yafeng   I-24
Nolan, Alison   III-439
Nunes, Juliana   II-487

Obermaier, Henriette   II-317
Oikonomou, George   III-412
O-Larnnithipong, Nonnarit   III-543
Oliveira, Eduardo   III-208
Oliveira, Jhonnata   II-575
Oliveira, Luis   I-535, I-548
Opromolla, Antonio   III-682
Orehovački, Tihomir   III-271
Ortega, Francisco   III-543
Ovesleová, Hana   III-218

Oyeka, Dumtoochukwu   II-685
Öztürk, Özgürol   III-3

Paelke, Volker   I-75
Pan, Jing   III-400
Paschoarelli, Luis C.   II-131, II-330
Passalacqua, Delia   III-682
Passera, Stefania   II-341
Pauzie, Annie   III-505
Paz, Freddy Asrael   I-212
Paz, Freddy   I-212
Pelegrino, Mateus   III-315
Peng, Liangrui   III-327
Penna, Leonardo   III-74
Penzenstadler, Birgit   I-634
Perozza, Roberta   II-374
Petersson Brooks, Eva   III-142
Petri, Anja   II-153
Pettersson, Ingrid   III-450
Pfeiffer, Linda   I-44
Philip Hwang, T.K.   II-563
Pinheiro, Mauro   I-157
Pinto, Fernando Miguel   I-167
Pontes, Gabriel   III-283
Poon, Carmen C.Y.   III-693
Posetti, Ben   III-82
Pow-Sang, José Antonio   I-212
Prata, Wilson   I-428

Quaresma, Manuela   II-23, II-575, II-487,
    III-74, III-462

Raffaele, Rennan   III-283
Rajagopal, Ram   III-337
Ramos, Tiago   III-208
Rantakari, Juho   I-470
Raposo, Alberto   III-662
Rapuano, Claudia   III-682
Rebelo, Francisco   II-34
Reijonen, Pekka   I-269
Reitan, Jarl   III-587
Renzi, Adriano Bernardo   I-339, I-644,
    II-393
Ribeiro, Carlos Eduardo   III-94
Ribeiro, Caroline   I-224
Rızvanoğlu, Kerem   III-628
Robier, Johannes   I-348
Röcker, Carsten   I-75

Rodrigues, Camila   I-417, II-353
Rodrigues, Marcela   II-575
Roncagliolo, Silvana   I-237
Rosenthal, Paul   I-44, II-196
Ross, Tracy   I-548
Rusu, Cristian   I-237
Rusu, Virginia Zaraza   I-237
Rusu, Virginica   I-237
Rytilahti, Piia   I-86

Sahito, Waqas Ali   II-587
Sakamoto, Mizuki   I-654
Saldanha, Nuno   I-167
Sanguinetti, Angela   I-395, III-368
Santa Rosa, José Guilherme   III-197
Santos, Celso A.S.   II-54
Santos, Gabriele   I-224
Santos, Lucas   III-425
Sardella, Adrieli   II-131
Sasaki, Toshiya   II-307
Schindler, Christian   II-153
Schirmer Mauricio, Gabriela   II-667
Schneider, Carlos Sergio   II-14
Schneidermeier, Tim   I-247, I-295
Schulte, Frederik   II-587
Schwartz, Molly   III-104
Search, Patricia   II-363
Segura-Velandia, Diana   II-685
Sener, Orhan   III-228
Sewata, Lanjakorn   II-162
Shahid, Hafiza Maimoona   I-113
Shao, Jiang   I-24
Sheikh, Farzan Javed   I-113
Sheikh, Javed Anjum   II-243
Shen, Yipei   I-502
Silva, Danilo   II-330
Silva, João   II-330
Silva, Paula Alexandra   I-179
Singh, Pushpendra   I-101
Sivaji, Ashok   I-138
Slany, Wolfgang   II-153
Soares Neto, Carlos   I-191
Soares, Marcelo M.   I-224, I-524, III-208,
    III-283, III-292
Sobral, Elzani   III-208
Song, Haidi   II-597
Sousa, Filipe   I-167
Speicher, Maximilian   I-256

Spieler, Bernadette   II-153
Spinillo, Carla G.   II-374
Stokols, Daniel   III-368
Sun, Yuanjing   II-382
Suzuki, Larissa   III-412

Takei, Kuniharu   II-675
Tan, Chin-Woo   III-337
Tangnimitchok, Sudarat   III-543
Tariq, Arslan   I-113
Tariq, Iqra   I-113
Tarkkanen, Kimmo   I-269
Tavares, Tatiana A.   I-63
Teichrieb, Veronica   III-303
Teixeira, Carla   III-292
Teixeira, João Marcelo   III-303
Teles, Júlia   II-3
Tiradentes Souto, Virginia   II-252, III-425
Torok, Leonardo   III-315
Torres, Rebeca   I-224
Trajkova, Milka   II-464
Trevisan, Daniela Gorski   III-315
Tribe, James   II-685
Tryfonas, Theo   III-412

Ugras, Tuba   III-228
Ursa, Yolanda   II-153
Utesch, Brian S.   I-204

Valle, Thiago   I-428
van der Meijden, Christiaan H.   II-317
Vasconcelos, Ana   I-167
Vasconcelos, Cristina N.   III-315
Vasconcelos, Erick   III-208
Vega, Katia   II-685, II-696
Viegas, Natanne   II-393
Vilar, Elisângela   I-167
Voit, Matthias   I-295
Volpi, Valentina   III-682
Voß, Stefan   I-283
Vuontisjärvi, Hanna-Riina   I-86

Walter, Nadine   III-517
Wang, Haiyan   I-24

Wang, Li   I-122, II-45
Wang, Peggy   III-529
Wang, Shengjin   III-327
Wang, Yuanqiong (Kathy)   II-224
Weaver, Margaret   II-172
Werner, Heron   III-662
West, Andrew   II-685
Wettemann, Carmen   III-517
Whittow, Will   II-685
Wiedau, Anne   II-705
Wiedau, Michael   II-705
Williams, Dean N.   III-25
Winter, Ute   III-529
Wolff, Christian   I-295
Wollner, Patrick K.A.   II-473
Wu, Lei   I-567
Wu, Tyan-Yu   I-559
Wu, Zhanwei   III-36

Ximenes, Bianca H.   I-356
Xu, Menghan   I-122
Xu, Qing   I-122
Xu, Yulin   II-45
Xue, Chengqi   I-24

Yam, Yeung   III-693
Yamamoto, Yuki   II-675
Yamazaki, Kazuhiko   II-307
Yang, Huahai   III-240
Yang, Shiqiang   I-502
Yang, Yi   III-327
Yantaç, Asım Evren   III-357
Yin, Zhengsheng   III-400
Yu, Jia Ming   III-36
Yuan, Xiaojun   III-240

Zanfagnini, Vitor   II-393
Zapata, Claudia   I-368
Zhang, Jing   I-24
Zhang, Liqun   I-379
Zheng, Yali L.   III-693
Zhu, Zijian   II-597
Ziefle, Martina   III-473
Zuanon, Rachel   I-599

Printed in the United States
By Bookmasters